HANDBOOK
OF
RELIGION

HANDBOOK OF RELIGION

A Christian Engagement
with Traditions,
Teachings, and Practices

TERRY C. MUCK,
HAROLD A. NETLAND, AND
GERALD R. McDERMOTT

EDITORS

Baker Academic
a division of Baker Publishing Group
Grand Rapids, Michigan

© 2014 by Baker Publishing Group

Published by Baker Academic
a division of Baker Publishing Group
P.O. Box 6287, Grand Rapids, MI 49516-6287
www.bakeracademic.com

Paperback edition published 2022
ISBN 978-1-5409-6624-7

All rights reserved. No part of this publication may be reproduced, stored in a retrieval system, or transmitted in any form or by any means—for example, electronic, photocopy, recording—without the prior written permission of the publisher. The only exception is brief quotations in printed reviews.

Hardcover Library of Congress Cataloging-in-Publication Control Number: 2014018019

Unless otherwise indicated, Scripture quotations are from the Holy Bible, New International Version®. NIV®. Copyright © 1973, 1978, 1984, 2011 by Biblica, Inc.™ Used by permission of Zondervan. All rights reserved worldwide. www.zondervan.com

Baker Publishing Group publications use paper produced from sustainable forestry practices and post-consumer waste whenever possible.

Contents

Preface xi

Part 1 Introduction 1

1. The Christian Study of World Religion 3
   Terry C. Muck

2. The Study of Religion 11
   Terry C. Muck

3. A Christian Theology of Religions 19
   Harold A. Netland

4. Christian Interaction with Other Religions 27
   Paul Louis Metzger

Part 2 World Religions 41

5. World Religions Introduction 43
   Terry C. Muck

6. Hinduism: History, Beliefs, Practices 49
   Richard Fox Young

7. Hinduism: Christian Contacts 56
   Richard Fox Young

8. Hinduism: Theological Exchanges 63
   Richard Fox Young

9. Hinduism: Current Issues 69
   Richard Fox Young

10. Hinduism: Adherent Essay 76
    Arvind Sharma

11. Buddhism: History, Beliefs, Practices 81
    Terry C. Muck

12. Buddhism: Christian Contacts 87
    Terry C. Muck

13. Buddhism: Theological Exchanges 96
    Terry C. Muck

14. Buddhism: Current Issues 104
    Terry C. Muck

15. Buddhism: Adherent Essay 111
    Rita M. Gross

16. Judaism: History, Beliefs, Practices 115
    Richard Robinson

17. Judaism: Christian Contacts 123
    Richard Robinson

18. Judaism: Theological Exchanges 130
    Richard Robinson

19. Judaism: Current Issues 137
    Richard Robinson

v

20. Judaism: Adherent Essay 144
    Yaakov Ariel
21. Islam: History, Beliefs, Practices 151
    Larry Poston
22. Islam: Christian Contacts 157
    Larry Poston
23. Islam: Theological Exchanges 165
    Larry Poston
24. Islam: Current Issues 171
    Larry Poston
25. Islam: Adherent Essay 177
    Sarmad Qutub and Musa Qutub

Part 3 Indigenous Religions 181

26. Indigenous Religions Introduction 183
    Terry C. Muck
27. India: History, Beliefs, Practices 187
    Eloise Hiebert Meneses
28. India: Christian Contacts 194
    Eloise Hiebert Meneses
29. India: Theological Exchanges 202
    Eloise Hiebert Meneses
30. India: Current Issues 209
    Eloise Hiebert Meneses
31. China: History, Beliefs, Practices 216
    Jonathan Seitz
32. China: Christian Contacts 222
    Jonathan Seitz
33. China: Theological Exchanges 228
    Jonathan Seitz
34. China: Current Issues 235
    Jonathan Seitz
35. Southeast Asia: History, Beliefs, Practices 240
    Russell H. Bowers
36. Southeast Asia: Christian Contacts 248
    Russell H. Bowers
37. Southeast Asia: Theological Exchanges 255
    Russell H. Bowers
38. Southeast Asia: Current Issues 262
    Russell H. Bowers
39. North Asia: History, Beliefs, Practices 269
    Sebastian Kim
40. North Asia: Christian Contacts 276
    Sebastian Kim
41. North Asia: Theological Exchanges 282
    Sebastian Kim
42. North Asia: Current Issues 289
    Sebastian Kim
43. Europe: History, Beliefs, Practices 295
    Richard Shaw
44. Europe: Christian Contacts 301
    Richard Shaw
45. Europe: Theological Exchanges 307
    Richard Shaw
46. Europe: Current Issues 313
    Richard Shaw
47. Middle East: History, Beliefs, Practices 320
    J. Andrew Dearman
48. Middle East: Christian Contacts 327
    J. Andrew Dearman
49. Middle East: Theological Exchanges 332
    J. Andrew Dearman
50. Middle East: Current Issues 338
    J. Andrew Dearman
51. Africa: History, Beliefs, Practices 343
    Irving Hexham

52. Africa: Christian Contacts 352
    Irving Hexham

53. Africa: Theological Exchanges 359
    Irving Hexham

54. Africa: Current Issues 367
    Irving Hexham

55. Oceania: History, Beliefs, Practices 374
    Charles Farhadian

56. Oceania: Christian Contacts 382
    Charles Farhadian

57. Oceania: Theological Exchanges 389
    Charles Farhadian

58. Oceania: Current Issues 395
    Charles Farhadian

59. North America: History, Beliefs, Practices 401
    Christopher Vecsey

60. North America: Christian Contacts 408
    Christopher Vecsey

61. North America: Theological Exchanges 414
    Christopher Vecsey

62. North America: Current Issues 420
    Christopher Vecsey

63. Meso- and South America: History, Beliefs, Practices 426
    William Svelmoe

64. Meso- and South America: Christian Contacts 434
    William Svelmoe

65. Meso- and South America: Theological Exchanges 441
    William Svelmoe

66. Meso- and South America: Current Issues 448
    William Svelmoe

Part 4 New Religious Movements 455

67. New Religious Movements (NRM) Introduction 457
    Terry C. Muck

68. NRM: Christian Derivatives Introduction 461
    Terry C. Muck

69. Church of Jesus Christ of Latter-Day Saints: History, Beliefs, Practices 463
    Craig Blomberg

70. Church of Jesus Christ of Latter-Day Saints: Theological Exchanges, Current Issues 468
    Craig Blomberg

71. Church of Jesus Christ of Latter-Day Saints: Adherent Essay 472
    Robert L. Millet

72. Jehovah's Witnesses: History, Beliefs, Practices 476
    George Chryssides

73. Jehovah's Witnesses: Theological Exchanges, Current Issues 481
    George Chryssides

74. Jehovah's Witnesses: Adherent Essay 485
    Rolf Furulli

75. Church of Christ, Scientist: History, Beliefs, Practices 489
    John K. Simmons

76. Church of Christ, Scientist: Adherent Essay 494
    Shirley Paulson

77. NRM: World Religion Derivatives Introduction 498
    Terry C. Muck

78. Nation of Islam: History, Beliefs, Practices 500
    Steven Tsoukalas

79. Nation of Islam: Theological Exchanges, Current Issues 505
    Steven Tsoukalas

80. Transcendental Meditation: History, Beliefs, Practices 510
Geoff Gilpin

81. Transcendental Meditation: Theological Exchanges, Current Issues 515
Geoff Gilpin

82. Soka Gakkai: History, Beliefs, Practices 520
Guy McCloskey

83. Soka Gakkai: Theological Exchanges, Current Issues 525
William Aiken

84. Soka Gakkai: Adherent Essay 529
Virginia Benson

85. NRM: Nature Religions Introduction 533
Terry C. Muck

86. Paganism and Neopaganism: History, Beliefs, Practices 535
John Morehead

87. Paganism and Neopaganism: Theological Exchanges, Current Issues 539
John Morehead

88. Paganism and Neopaganism: Adherent Essay 543
Gus diZerega

89. Gnosticism: History, Beliefs, Practices 547
Carl Raschke

90. Gnosticism: Theological Exchanges, Current Issues 552
Carl Raschke

91. Environmentalism: History, Beliefs, Practices 557
Calvin DeWitt

92. Environmentalism: Adherent Essay 562
Roger S. Gottlieb

93. NRM: A-Religions Introduction 566
Terry C. Muck

94. Cults: History, Beliefs, Practices 568
Suzanne Newcombe

95. Cults: Theological Exchanges, Current Issues 573
Sarah Harvey

96. Satanism: History, Beliefs, Practices 578
Kennet Granholm

97. Satanism: Theological Exchanges, Current Issues 583
Kennet Granholm

98. Satanism: Adherent Essay 588
Don Webb

99. Atheism: History, Beliefs, Practices 592
James A. Beverley

100. Atheism: Theological Exchanges, Current Issues 597
James A. Beverley

101. Atheism: Adherent Essay 602
Ed Buckner

102. NRM: Psychological Religions Introduction 606
Terry C. Muck

103. Scientology: History, Beliefs, Practices 608
Douglas Cowan

104. Scientology: Theological Exchanges, Current Issues 615
Douglas Cowan

105. Transpersonal Psychology: History, Beliefs, Practices 620
Frances S. Adeney

106. Transpersonal Psychology: Theological Exchanges, Current Issues 625
Frances S. Adeney

107. New Age: History, Beliefs, Practices 629
J. Gordon Melton

108. New Age: Theological Exchanges, Current Issues 635
J. Gordon Melton

109. NRM: Political and Economic Religions Introduction 641
Terry C. Muck

110. Civil Religion: History, Beliefs, Practices 643
Arthur Remillard

111. Civil Religion: Theological Exchanges, Current Issues 648
Arthur Remillard

112. Christian Identity: History, Beliefs, Practices 653
Michael Barkun

113. Christian Identity: Theological Exchanges, Current Issues 658
Michael Barkun

114. Marxism: History, Beliefs, Practices 663
James Thobaben

115. Marxism: Theological Exchanges, Current Issues 669
James Thobaben

116. Marxism: Adherent Essay 675
Roger S. Gottlieb

117. NRM: Social Religions Introduction 679
Terry C. Muck

118. Unification Church: History, Beliefs, Practices 681
James A. Beverley

119. Unification Church: Theological Exchanges, Current Issues 686
James A. Beverley

120. Freemasonry: History, Beliefs, Practices 690
Steven Tsoukalas

121. Freemasonry: Theological Exchanges, Current Issues 694
Steven Tsoukalas

122. The Family International: History, Beliefs, Practices 699
James Chancellor

123. The Family International: Theological Exchanges, Current Issues 705
James Chancellor

124. The Family International: Adherent Essay 710
Claire Borowik

125. Baha'i: History, Beliefs, Practices 714
Christopher Buck

126. Baha'i: Theological Exchanges, Current Issues 720
Christopher Buck

Part 5 Essays 725

127. Essays Introduction 727
Terry C. Muck

128. Religion and Science 729
S. Mark Heim

129. Religion and Gender 736
Ursula King

130. Religion and the Environment 746
Sandra L. Richter

131. Religion and Politics 756
Richard V. Pierard

132. Religion and Violence 764
Sallie B. King

133. Religion and Human Rights 774
Frances S. Adeney

134. Religion and the Family 781
Desiree L. Segura-April

List of Contributors 791
Index 795

Preface

The volume you have in your hands is an edited book. That means it is the product of many people, including an editor, two associate editors, and 55 contributors who together wrote the 134 essays and the 239 study aids scattered throughout the book. Because the topics of the essays are global in nature and the backgrounds of the essayists are diverse, the "voice" of the book is complicated. Perhaps as a starting place to explaining that complicated voice, it might be a good idea to introduce the editors and the essayists and the essays they wrote.

Editors

All three of the editors, Terry Muck, Harold Netland, and Gerald McDermott, are evangelical theologians and historians of religion. Terry Muck is the executive director of the Louisville Institute, Gerald McDermott is professor of religion at Roanoke (Virginia) College, and Harold Netland is professor of philosophy of religion at Trinity Evangelical Divinity School, Deerfield, Illinois. We all study the religions of the world in such a way as is consistent with the tenets of evangelical theology.

Yet this is not a book on the theology of religions. The essays in part 1 are explicitly theological in focus and are written by evangelicals with evangelical concerns in view. But the essays that follow are not intended to be exercises in theology of religions but rather descriptive in nature, introducing other religious traditions and their relation to Christianity. My (Terry Muck's) essays on Buddhism in part 2, for example, although written by an evangelical Christian, are primarily descriptive in introducing historical and current realities concerning Buddhism and its relation to Christianity. While consistent with my Christian commitments, these chapters reflect the widely accepted methodology of religious studies and could appear in a general text on Buddhism. Our purpose in the handbook is to provide an introduction to religious traditions in the world today and an overview of current issues in the encounter between these religions and Christianity. Thus, apart from the chapters in part 1, explicitly theological treatment of issues is minimal.

Essayists

Further, not all of the essayists in the book are orthodox Christians, and some do not even identify themselves as Christian. Most are Christians. But the adherent essays are obviously written by those committed to other religious traditions, and a few of the other chapters are written by distinguished scholars who do not claim to be Christian. One of our subgoals in selecting essayists was to choose as many scholars as possible who are both (1) orthodox Christians in their faith commitments and (2) expert scholars of religion, simply to show that being the first does not preclude being the second (and vice versa). Yet an equally important goal was to pick highly competent scholars in each religion area, and that meant sometimes going outside the Christian scholarly world.

The nature of our core assignment directive—*write essays that give answers to the questions Christians most commonly ask about non-Christian religions*—does not make it a requirement that the essayists be committed to orthodox Christian understandings of theology. In fact, such an assignment does not even require that the essayists be Christian, although it does demand that they have a good understanding of Christianity and Christian concerns. We believe that almost all of the essays reflect this understanding.

One example of this is our use of the word "Christian" in the subtitle of the book—*A Christian Engagement with Traditions, Teachings, and Practice*. This usage is meant to reflect the focus and perspective of the questions the essays are intended to answer rather than the orthodox bona fides of the authors.

Essays

Thus, the essays sometimes reflect positions that not all orthodox theologians would agree with. Key issues in religious studies, especially as they concern the relation of Christianity and other religious traditions, bristle with controversy. Disagreements among orthodox scholars on some of these matters are not unusual. The three editors of this handbook do not agree on all questions addressed in the chapters that follow. This is simply the nature of a scholarly edited book that deals with a subject such as religious studies. Scholars understand the value of a variety of perspectives on an issue, and we feel it is important for the contributors to give their perspectives even when we might disagree with what is being said. So as editors we offer an important disclaimer: we don't all agree with all the positions taken by authors of essays in this handbook.

Religion/Not a Religion

To perhaps further complicate the "voice" of this book, let me refer to an interesting question that surfaced in several contexts. The question has to do with what qualifies as a religion. There are two ways to determine the answer to this question: the scholarly and the experiential. Typically, scholars, when faced with such a situation, would begin by postulating a definition of religion and then compare with that definition social and psychological phenomena they run across in the field. When this is done, many such definitions would not include traditions such as Marxism and environmentalism as religious. Yet other definitions would include those as religious.

The experiential method, however, determines what is religious by how the adherents of that social phenomenon judge their movement. Few Marxists, for example, would consider their worldview to be religious. Some groups we deal with in this book as religions, such as Freemasonry, resist mightily the implication that they are religious movements. We include essays on these movements in this book, knowing that the very people we are talking about don't always see their group as a religion.

This may be a good place to point out the obvious fact that our coverage of religions in this handbook is selective, not comprehensive. Gordon Melton, for example, says that there are over fifteen hundred new religious movements in the United States alone, but we cover only a small fraction of them in part 4.

Study Aids

Finally, a word about the charts, graphs, maps, and other illustrations found throughout the book, which we call, collectively, "study aids." Many of these study aids make reference to religious statistics. These statistics come from four primary resources: Johnson and Ross, *Atlas of Global Christianity*; Barrett and Johnson, *World Christian Trends*; Moreau, *Evangelical Dictionary of World Missions*; and the website of the Central Intelligence Agency (https://www.cia.gov/index.html). Not all of these sources and not all contributors to this volume agree when it comes to dates and statistics. Hence, knowing both the temporariness and weaknesses of most religious statistics, we urge the reader to see them, first of all, as estimates, and, second, as having the most value not as absolute numbers but as comparative numbers, best used as relative comparisons with other religions.

Terry C. Muck
Woodhill, Summer 2013

Part 1

Introduction

1

The Christian Study of World Religion

Terry C. Muck

This handbook is for Christians interested in non-Christian religions. The essays answer questions Christians ask about religions that are not their own. Christians ask questions about other world religions, indigenous religions, and new religious movements. For that audience—Christians interested in non-Christian religions—the following essays meet four needs.

The Need for Information

First, the essays provide Christian students with basic information about world religions. They answer questions about those religions that Christians might ask precisely because they are Christians. For the most part these essays do not look at the other religions theologically, at least in the traditional way Christian theology is conceived, but neither do they attempt to answer all questions for all people. They take a scholarly look at the non-Christian religions but from a Christian scholar's point of view. What do I want or need to know about Hinduism? Or religion in China?

This approach makes this book unique among religious studies texts. In general, information about the world of religion that one finds in textbooks used by Christian students takes one of two approaches. The first is the *religious studies approach*, typified by the textbook I have used in my Introduction to World Religions class, which I have taught for twenty-five years: John and David Noss's *A History of the World's Religions*. This textbook and others like it attempt to present the teachings of the major world religions as narratives of the history, beliefs, and practices of those religions. Each of the chapters on Hinduism, Buddhism, Islam, and the others are presented without critique or favor. The focus is on "just the facts" with as little commentary as possible.

The second approach is the *theological approach*, illustrated by textbooks that describe not only what the other religions teach but also what is right and wrong with those religions from a Christian theological point of view. At their best, these textbooks discern God's creative activity and intent in the whole world of religion, although it is an attempt that begins with the normative standards of classical Christian orthodoxy. Traditionally, we have considered this kind of study of religion "partisan," while the Noss type of study has been considered "objective."

In the past, "objective" has been considered "neutral." More recently, however, postmodern philosophy has joined historic orthodox Christianity in affirming that when it comes to ultimate questions, there is no such thing as neutrality. In that sense, every account of religion, whether Christian or not, is "partisan." To the extent that each account attempts to be fair to other religions, it is also "objective." In this way of looking at things, "partisan" and "objective" are not mutually exclusive.

One is tempted to say that the essays in the book you hold in your hands are *neither* partisan *nor* objective, but it would be more accurate to say that they are *both* partisan *and* objective. They are partisan to the extent that they focus on questions Christians ask about other religions; they are objective in the sense that they present the best scholarly understandings of what the other religions teach. Indeed, we would hope that adherents of the religions covered can see themselves in the essays and agree with the way their teachings are presented. For many of the religions covered in this book, we have included what we call an "adherent essay," an essay written by a scholarly member of the religion being discussed. We believe this is what all serious writing and thinking about religion in the coming decades must be—a combination of objective religious studies and partisan theology (or buddhology or vedology or whatever).

Seeing the Big Picture

Second, the essays in this handbook provide a realistic portrait of religion in our twenty-first-century, postmodern world. The picture they paint is of a religious world where world religions such as Christianity and Islam and Buddhism do not exist in their pure, theoretical forms but always in admixtures with older, indigenous forms of religion, and always tempered, influenced, and sometimes even combined with new religious movements. The world religions may span the globe and have the capacity to penetrate all cultures, but the forms they take are in turn heavily influenced by those cultures and the religions that already exist in them.

The anthropologist nonpareil Clifford Geertz brought this to our attention years ago when he studied Islam in the context of both Indonesia (*Religions of Java*) and the northern African country of Morocco (*Islam Observed*). He discovered Islam in both countries. Many if not most Muslims acknowledged the orthodoxy of both forms of Islam in that they adhered to the Qur'an, the Five Pillars, and the traditional orthodoxies of all Islamic expressions. But Geertz also discovered different "Islams." The character and nature of Islamic expressions in each of these cultures produced an Islam that was easily distinguishable from its counterpart in the other country, sometimes to the extent that not all Muslims agreed to one another's so-called orthodoxy.

When Christians ask questions about religions, they do well to start with the basics—the history, beliefs, and practices that typify each religion. The history of Buddhism is the same, up to a certain point, for Buddhists everywhere. A core set of beliefs characterize almost all Buddhists. And certain practices tend to run across Buddhist traditions and Buddhist cultures. But at a certain point historical backgrounds diverge, beliefs take on unique nuance depending on cultural setting, and practices can vary widely.

Study Aid #1
Doing a Religious Audit

Answer the following questions:

1. What is the religious history of this place, with particular focus on the "original," indigenous religion?
2. What is the present-day, dominant world religion, and how did it come to dominate?
3. What new religious movements are present in this society? How prevalent are they? How many are there? Which are the strongest and most influential?
4. How do indigenous religious values still express themselves? Are their influences implicit or explicit?
5. Do the relationships between the dominant world religion and the new religious movements tend toward conflict, peaceful coexistence, or cooperation?

Use the following types of books:

1. A history of religion in this place. For example, James Huntley Grayson, *Korea: A Religious History* (Routledge, 2002).
2. A history of the coming of the dominant world religion to this country, area, and culture. For example, Ian Charles Harris, *Cambodian Buddhism: History and Practice* (University of Hawaii Press, 2008).
3. The story of new religious movements in this country, area, and culture. For example, Helen Hardacre, *Kurozumikyo and the New Religions of Japan* (Princeton University Press, 1986).
4. The continuing influence of indigenous religions. For example, Jack Weatherford, *Native Roots: How the Indians Enriched America* (Ballantine, 1992).

As an example, for a religious audit of religion in Morocco, read the following books and use them to answer the five questions above:

Clifford Geertz. *Islam Observed.* University of Chicago Press, 1971.
David McMurray. *In and Out of Morocco.* University of Minnesota Press, 2001.
Henri Tervasse. *History of Morocco.* Atlantides, 1952.
Malika Zeghal. *Islamism in Morocco.* Markus Weiner, 2008.

This handbook is based on the idea that for a scholar to understand any religious expression in a given geographical locale, he or she must understand at least the indigenous religion on which the culture was (and is) based, the world religion that has come to (usually) dominate, and the new religious movements that have (almost always) come to express the effects of modernity and postmodernity clashing with premodernity in that culture. We call this "doing a religious audit" of a particular culture. To understand Moroccan religion today, using this handbook, one would start by reading the essays on "Islam," then the essays written on the "Religions of Africa," and finally add studies of whatever African-initiated religions are growing in the Moroccan area. It is at the intersections of these three religious forces that most local expressions of religion are found today.

Radical Differentiation

Third, this handbook takes account of the radical differentiation of religion and religious practices in today's world. Religion in the twenty-first century rarely exists in its premodern form, as part of an undifferentiated tribal culture, where beliefs and practices seem to be part of a seamless and largely unreflected-upon whole. But religion in the twenty-first century has also moved beyond the compartmentalized, often privatized, differentiated phenomena observed by modern sociologists such as Talcott Parsons and sociologists of religion such as Robert Bellah. Religion today is neither undifferentiated nor differentiated, if by differentiated we mean religion has its own little compartment alongside the political compartment, the economic compartment, the culture compartment, and so forth. Instead, religion today is *radically* differentiated. What do we mean by *radically differentiated religion*?

In the 1960s, University of Chicago sociologist Talcott Parsons wrote a book (*The Evolution of Societies*) in which he described a theory of social action that characterized modern Western societies. He suggested that four systems dominate: the political, economic, social, and cultural. He called such societies differentiated because social functions that before had been generalized across social groupings in the premodern age had become specializations in the modern age. In Parson's theory of social action, he suggested that religion had become a specialty located within the cultural system. One of Parson's students, Robert Bellah, focused his

Study Aid #2
Religious Differentiation

In premodern times, societies tended to be undifferentiated religiously—religion and other social functions tended to blend together. In modern times, societies became increasingly differentiated religiously, with institutions and religious leaders separated and clearly defined over against each other. As we move into postmodernity, societies and cultural systems are becoming radically differentiated. In current cultures, especially in urban areas, one can find manifestations of all three of these types of religion.

Undifferentiated (Premodern)

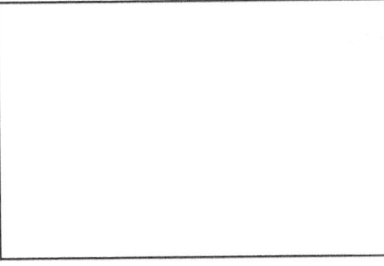

Differentiated (Modern)

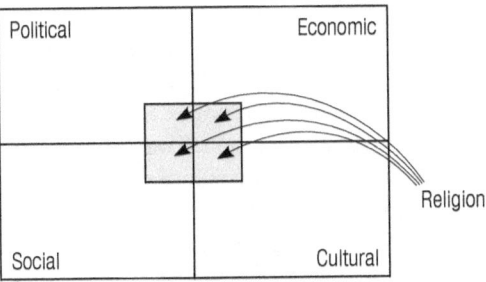

Radically Differentiated (Postmodern)

Sources: Talcott Parsons, *The Evolution of Societies*
Robert Bellah, *Beyond Belief*

work on the religion dimension, writing the well-known essay "Religious Evolution" (1991 [1970]), in which he described in historical detail the increasing complexity, and accompanying differentiation, that characterized modern religion. More recently Bellah turned the basic ideas in his seminal essay into his magnum opus, *Religion in Human Evolution: From the Paleolithic to the Axial Age* (2011).

What we see happening in the years since Parsons did his seminal work is an increasing differentiation within each of his major social spheres—the political, economic, social, and cultural. Most interesting to us, however, is that the presence of religion, in the form of new religious movements, is evident in all these spheres, not just the cultural. We have political religious expressions (Hindutva, Christian Identity), economic religious expressions (Marxism, the prosperity gospel), and social religious expressions (Amish religion, the Moonies), as well as cultural expressions. Religion is everywhere and expresses itself in all the societal forms we can imagine. We call this ubiquitous presence of religion in all social forms "radical differentiation."

Radical differentiation is seen most clearly in the section of the handbook devoted to new religious movements—we will say more about this phenomenon in that section.

Religious Identity

Fourth, this handbook by its structure and approach acknowledges the dynamic nature of religious identities in our complex, fluid world. Individual religious identities change and change often. A recent study by the Pew Forum on Religion and Public Life found that 44 percent of Americans had made a major religious change at some point in their life. Individuals in much of the world today are faced with unprecedented levels of freedom when it comes to religion. And even in cultures where such freedom does not yet exist (some of the Islamic world, for example), internet access provides what we might call virtual freedom of religion—that is, online exposure to the varieties of religious belief that span the globe.

Canadian social philosopher Charles Taylor makes note of this phenomenon in his book *A Secular Age* (2007), where he defines "secular" not as the absence of religion in a culture (its usual definition) but as the absence of compelling social forces mandating a specific choice of religion. The "secular" age we live in, according to Taylor, is one in which an almost bewildering variety of religious choices are available to us—including the choice of "no religion." The lack of social constraints on religious choice has an overall effect, perhaps, of devaluing religion overall. But its more compelling implication is what it does to individual religious identity, a topic written about in some detail by British sociologist of religion Zygmunt Bauman.

Bauman (2000) writes about what he calls "liquid modernity," a term that means in part that individual identity formation is no longer the once-for-all, hard-and-fast creation of personal identity (religion included) but a situation where identity formation (religion included) is a dynamic, fluid endeavor that may last a lifetime. Everything about our lives changes regularly—residence, occupation, family situation, and more—and successfully navigating such cultures requires one to be flexible and multiskilled. In fact, says Bauman, flexibility has replaced solidity as the most desired characteristic of successful identity formation. Recent surveys of Americans and their religious identities have upheld the tenets of Bauman's thesis—they note the overwhelming presence of religious change in people's lives when viewed over time.

Taking into account these trends in religious patterns of adherence around the world, this book is designed to be useful as a textbook for the Introduction to the World's Religions course that needs to be widely taught to Christian students in the future. Such a course differs from those being taught now in several ways.

First, such a course needs to be less oriented along the lines of a course on world religions, or another course on indigenous religions, or another course on new religious movements, and more toward a course that considers all three expressions of religion in a single setting. Given the constraints of time in such a course, this will mean that fewer facts about individual religions can be communicated (although the basic ones are still indispensable) and more about how the three expressions can be identified and how they interact with one another in specific cultures. That is, fewer facts and more methodological training will become de rigueur.

Second, religion as a generic category of human existence needs more emphasis. As religious combinations become an increasingly common feature of freely choosing human beings, we need to have students dig deeper into the roots of religion in the human being. It is one thing to make the historical observation that all cultures and peoples at all times have been religious in one sense or another; it is quite another to stimulate students to ask the questions as to why that is so—and how that looks in each discrete social setting. For Christian students, this will inevitably bring in theological discussions, but as we said above, that is unavoidable in the religion courses of the future.

Finally, religion must be increasingly seen as a dynamic quality of the human experience: people and cultures change the way they embrace and express their religions. To use a mathematical analogy, this means the introductory course in religion will need to become more of a calculus capable of observing constantly changing dynamics than either an arithmetic (just the facts, please) or an algebra (religion as symbol systems).

This handbook models what we believe is perhaps the single most important feature of twenty-first-century religious study: an attitude of respect toward religions of the peoples and cultures of the world—especially religions and cultures different from the ones we embrace. It is neither too trite nor too hyperbolic to say that the future of humanity in this nuclear age rests on Christians actualizing the Great Commandment to love our neighbors as ourselves.

I spent some of the summer of 2013 reading the inspiring writings of John Muir, the wilderness explorer and environmentalist of early America. His explorations of the inland mountains of the California and Nevada ranges reveal a person motivated not by a fear of the unknown but by an almost unparalleled excitement over what he might find in lands rarely trod by human foot. His work has value today precisely because of that excitement. John Muir expected to find great things in the wilderness, and when he did he was pleased almost beyond measure.

As we study and master the basics of religion in our world today, we will help our quest if we model it after John Muir's attitude. In Christian terms it means that as we explore religious vistas we have never seen before, we will be better served by looking for evidences of God's presence in the world God created eons ago, redeemed through Jesus Christ, and unfailingly sustains today by the Holy Spirit. The graces and gifts of that creation are still there. It is up to us to find them and identify them as such for all.

Before we begin the study of specific religions, we will say more about the two approaches to the study of religion: the religious studies approach and the theological approach. We use both in this book. An accurate and faithful understanding of religion for the Christian requires both, and one approach should not be put forward without reference to the other. For the purposes of discussing their complementary methodology, however, two separate essays detailing each are appropriate. And the fourth and final essay of this introductory section will discuss the various ways Christians interact with people of other religions.

2

The Study of Religion

Terry C. Muck

The modern scholarly study of religion might be defined this way: the comprehensive study of religions as phenomena by using both historical and systematic methodologies, as far as possible without dogmatic presuppositions, comparing and contrasting both universal and particular features of those religions.

The History of Religious Studies

The study of religion as a Western academic subject is a relatively new discipline. Prior to the mid-nineteenth century, when one studied "religion," the subject matter was one's own religion with occasional thoughts on how other religions compared with one's own religion. The study of religion, in other words, was almost synonymous with theology. In the mid-nineteenth century, several trends gave those occasional and dogmatic thoughts about other religions a new, distinctive character. One trend, ironically, was the Christian mission movement, which was reaching the peak of several centuries of development and whose practitioners were supplying Western scholars with a wealth of material on non-Christian religions. Second, at this same time, anthropologists and archaeologists were studying non-Western cultures and sending back an avalanche of data on cultural and religious practices from Asia, Africa, and Micronesia. Third was the full flowering of a way of looking at such data in a way that emphasized human rationality as opposed to divine agency. This Enlightenment viewpoint was tailor-made for attempts to make some sense of this body of religious information.

This early science of religion produced scholarly works of two types. One is typified by the work of a man often called the father of religious studies, Max Müller (1823–1900). Müller, using data obtained through his linguistic studies, traced the history of religious systems and then wrote comparative studies that made "religion" the underlying category of study rather than a specific religion. The second is typified by the work of James George Frazer (1854–1941), who took the catalog approach to making sense of this deluge of religious information. His twelve-volume *Golden Bough* is organized according to cross-religious categories, such as magic, taboo, and totemism, with religious data from different religious traditions filed under the appropriate heading.

> **Study Aid #3**
>
> **The Religious Studies Family Tree**
>
> The scholarly study of religion follows a different periodization than some other scholarly disciplines. The elements of the periodization are common (premodern, modern, postmodern), but religious studies has a very long "premodern" period and a very short "postmodern" period. Like most such disciplinary histories, all three periods continue to have influence in today's study of religion.
>
> **Premodern (up until 1850).** Because for premoderns religion was/is little differentiated from the rest of life, its "study" was coterminous with tribal history, including politics, economics, and cultural life. Most studies of religion during this period were merely the study of one's own "tribal" religion, what we would today call theology.
>
> When premodern manifestations of religion are studied today, the best methodologies are those of the archaeologists (since some of these religions are ancient) and anthropologists (since one goal of anthropology is to consider social groups in their entirety).
>
> **Transitions.** The transition to the modern period can be helpfully illustrated by three global meetings:
>
> > Parliament of World Religions (Chicago, 1893): This meeting is sometimes considered the first gathering of religious leaders from around the world. It is often pointed to as the event that initiated formal religious dialogue as a way for Christians to relate to people of other faiths.
> >
> > International Association for the History of Religion (Paris, 1900): This was the first of twenty such gatherings, held roughly every five years. Some scholars refer to this meeting as the first to focus on the academic study of religion.
> >
> > World Missionary Conference (Edinburgh, 1910): This conference is seen by some as the culmination of the nineteenth-century Protestant mission movement and by others as the beginning of the twentieth-century ecumenical movement. It is best seen as both—after this meeting, Christian mission changed.
>
> **Modern (1850–2000).** The so-called modern scholars of religion saw the need for descriptions of religion that were somehow distinguished from theological descriptions that served in-house communities of faith well but did little to consider religion as a generic category of human existence.
>
> > The founders of religious studies: Max Müller and James Frazer
> > The disciplines that contribute to religious studies:
> > Psychology: William James, Sigmund Freud, Carl Gustav Jung

Social sciences: Sociology (Émile Durkheim, Max Weber); Anthropology (E. B. Tylor, Wilhelm Schmidt)
Biblical studies: Julius Wellhausen, William Robertson Smith
Philosophy: Pierre Teilhard de Chardin, Rudolf Otto
Religious studies proper: Nathan Söderblom, Gerardus van der Leeuw, Joachim Wach

Postmodern (2000–present). The postmodern period represents the dawning awareness on religious studies scholars of the situatedness of all knowledge, depending on time (history) and place (context).

Based on Jacques Waardenburg, *Classical Approaches to the Study of Religion*, vol. 3.

One can see in this early work the influence of a positivistic approach to data—in short, the scientific model. The task of the scientist of religion was to gather as much data as possible, and then do theory construction that attempted to explain the data in wider and wider circles of inclusivity, with the goal not of discovering metaphysical truth but of describing accurately and meaningfully the religious phenomena of the world in which we live. Given this reliance on the scientific model (in an attempt to distinguish this study from theology), it is not surprising to find that when the prevailing scientific theory of the nineteenth century changed, the study of comparative religion began to change.

In some ways, Charles Darwin's theory of evolution was a godsend for comparative religionists. One effect of Darwin's explanatory thesis was to remove the need for constant, or even periodic, divine intervention in human affairs in order to explain why things happen as they do. Divine intervention, of course, was a staple of most premodern explanatory theses of religion. By making it scientifically respectable to offer secular explanations for human phenomena, evolutionism opened up a whole new arena of activity for the fledgling science of religion. Sociologists, psychologists, and philosophers quickly filled this new arena with huge explanatory theses that attempted globally to describe the origins and development of all religion in comprehensive schemata.

This was the age of the great sociologists of religion Émile Durkheim (1858–1917) and Max Weber (1864–1920). A uniquely American contribution to the discipline was offered by the psychologists of religion, headed by William James (1842–1910) and his *Varieties of Religious Experience*. Perhaps more than any other, the philosophers of religion began to produce systematic philosophies of the development of religious consciousness, such as that produced by Pierre Teilhard de Chardin (1881–1955).

This ferment of scholarly activity in kindred disciplines encouraged the carving out of methodologies designed specifically for the study of religion. Objective histories of specific religious traditions began to appear from the studies of scholars like Nathan Söderblom (1866–1931) and William Brede Kristensen (1867–1953). Other scholars, in the cataloging tradition of Frazer, adapted a methodology loosely related to Edmund Husserl's philosophical phenomenology and began to develop cross-religious categories in order to better compare and contrast religious traditions. Gerardus van der Leeuw (1890–1950) and Rudolf Otto (1869–1937) published works in what came to be called the phenomenology of religion tradition, which relied on a method that advocated a temporary suspension of one's own beliefs (*epochē*), in order to clearly identify the unique character of religious phenomena (*sui generis*), with the goal of understanding only (*Verstehen*). These two approaches to the collection of the data of religious studies—the longitudinal, historical study and the cross-sectional, phenomenological study—have been dominant methodologies in comparative religion.

In other ways, Darwin's theory of evolution sent the discipline of religious studies down a dead-end road. The search for a common origin of and developmental pattern for all religion became a remarkably contentious and ultimately frustrating enterprise. The data of religions from around the world proved to be elastic in the extreme when it came to theory shaping. Some of the developmental schemes posited all religions coming from animistic roots where all being is invested with spiritual power, moving toward a more well-defined polytheism, and finally to the great monotheistic religious traditions. Others of the developmental schemes took roughly the same material and posited theories that taught exactly the opposite: that the original conceptions of God were of high gods, monotheisms that over time devolved into polytheistic and then spiritist religions, with more and more layers of gods between humans and the high gods. And as more and more of the world's religious systems were studied, they proved as a group to be less and less amenable to universal, step-by-step developmental patterns.

In most academic circles, the recognition that these essentially Western-based universal categories and developmental patterns do not necessarily fit other cultures led to a move toward cultural relativism, which argued that no generalizations from culture to culture are possible. Each must be studied totally on its own terms. This move matched some of the insights of phenomenologists regarding the subjectivity of the religious scholar himself or herself, but went beyond those insights by suggesting that suspension of one's own point of view might be a chimera, that relativity extended not only to cultures but also to cultural observers. Many scholars began to see in cultural relativism a dead end as pronounced as the one faced by evolutionists—in this case, a dead end leading to an inability to have any kind of cross-cultural (and cross-religious) communication at all. This gave rise to two middle methodological roads between the metaphysical universalism of evolutionism and the radical particularism of phenomenology. The first came to be called functionalism, a view that did not find the core of religion in truth-claims of the gods or the gods' representatives, or in the unconnected, conditioned realities of discrete cultures, but in the function religion performed in addressing personal and societal needs. The needs that functionalists identified as "religious" varied. But for all functionalists, "religion is as religion does." Functionalist theories of religion are among the most widely used in religious studies today, and in one sense may be seen as extensions of Émile Durkheim's pioneering work. It is a methodology particularly useful to sociologists of religion, such as Joachim Wach (1898–1955) and Robert Bellah (1927–2013), and to anthropologists, such as Mary Douglas (1921–2007) and Clifford Geertz (1926–2006).

A second middle road between universalism and particularism is structuralism. With roots in the work of linguist Ferdinand de Saussure (1857–1913), and given methodological form by social anthropologist Claude Lévi-Strauss (1908–2009), structuralists see the use of language and language systems as the mediator between universals and particulars. Religions and cultures came to be viewed as analogous to languages. Each language (or religion) is different, with its own vocabulary and grammatical rules. Each language (or religion), however, also has structural features in common that seem to run across all languages or religions. Structuralists say these features allow people of one religious tradition to recognize themselves in another person's religious tradition, but to preserve the otherness of that tradition because those features' full meaning resides more in the holistic pattern of that religious tradition than in the content of a particular belief. The recognition of these common structural features allows empathy that may lead to accurate knowledge of the other, but not to understanding itself. Structuralism is on the cutting edge of approaches to religion being explored by scholars today. History-of-religions and phenomenological methodologies still provide much of the on-the-ground content and data of religious studies, but those data are increasingly filtered through the lens of structuralist forms.

How might this brief history of religious studies relate to Christians and their interests, especially Christians interested in maintaining their historical theological commitments? The short answer is that Christians can make good use of these different approaches to the study of religion so long as they see them as useful tools in gathering and handling data of a very specific nature and not as normative methodologies over against theological and revelatory ones. They become problematic for Christians when these theories begin to claim for themselves absolute status, replacing propositional and ethical absolutes with methodological ones.

But that short answer may not be enough. What kind of positive statement about a Christian approach to the study of religion can be made?

A Christian Approach to the Study of Religion

Is there a Christian approach to the study of religion? Should there be? If so, what is it?

These will seem like odd questions to most Western scholars of religion. Many, if not most, of them would answer something like this: the scholarly study of religion had its genesis and continues its existence precisely to create an objective alternative to the so-called Christian approach to the study of religion. That is, most scholars of religion see themselves engaged in an enterprise that either brackets theological commitments of any sort or eschews them altogether.

We would like to challenge that view. I remember having a conversation a number of years ago with such a scholar of religion about this very topic. At one point in our conversation he said, "What really scares me about evangelical Christians is that they bring a theology to the study of religion." My response was this: "What really scares me are scholars who study religion and think that they don't bring a 'theology' to their study of religion."

My point was that everyone brings ultimate value commitments of one sort or another to this scholarly endeavor. It is just that some are explicit and some are implicit. That is, some scholars are conscious of their commitments, and others don't realize what their commitments are. And I also believe strongly in a corollary to this position: since we all have regulating commitments of one sort or another (universals that we expect everyone participating in our scholarly field to acknowledge), those commitments necessarily need to be brought to consciousness and articulated so that we can more accurately engage and evaluate one another's work.

So let me try to articulate what I see as the theological commitments a Christian scholar brings to his or her work as a scholar of religion. Let me begin with what I have found to be a helpful analogy.

When the quintessential American theologian Jonathan Edwards asked a similar question about the religious affections—to paraphrase, is there such a thing as distinctively Christian religious affections?—his answer was something like this: Christian love looks something like non-Christian human love. Christian love does many of the same things as love expressed by non-Christians. Yet it is distinctive, because for the Christian, one loves others in obedience to God's commands and in imitation, as much as possible, of the way we believe God loves. And most important, the Christian is animated by the spirit of Christ, who changes the character of the Christian's affections.

Something similar applies to a Christian engaged in religious studies. Christians engaged in religious studies do many of the same things that non-Christian, even nonreligious, scholars do when they study religion. They are slaves to the facts. They strive for fairness and objectivity in their descriptions of other religions. They do not prematurely judge the observations they make about other religions' beliefs and practices. In short, they look very much like other members of their scholarly guild.

Yet there is such a thing as a Christian religious studies, distinctive from a Buddhist religious studies, a Hindu religious studies, an agnostic religious studies, a humanist religious studies. And its distinctiveness lies in three main areas: (1) a Christian brings a distinctive outlook to his or her study, an imagination that supplies a distinct motivation for studying other religions; (2) a Christian, because he or she is a Christian, will ask and focus on certain kinds of questions about other religions that others may or may not ask; and (3) a Christian seeks a distinctive payoff for his or her study of religion, which is to say that a Christian has a distinctive goal for the study of religion. Let's treat each of these in turn.

> **Study Aid #4**
>
> **Christian Religious Studies**
>
> A Christian religious studies looks very similar to the religious studies practiced by other religious studies scholars, and it wholeheartedly embraces the values shared by the religious studies guild:
>
> Accuracy Fairness Objectivity Respect
>
> Yet at three distinct points Christians go above and beyond the tenets required by the guild:
>
> 1. The Christian religious studies imagination
> 2. The Christian framework of questions
> 3. The Christian goal

The Christian Imagination

When Christians study the religions, they do so within this context: Christians believe that God is the ultimate creative power in the universe. God created everything, and God created the world good. By giving part of this creation—human beings—dominion over the rest, and by giving human beings a distinctive gift—the gift of free choice of relationship with God—different ways of approaching God (or not approaching God at all) are possible, and indeed have become actualized. The religions, Christians believe, are in part the result of this diversity of choice. Thus, when Christians study religions, their theological assumptions include the understanding that religions have developed as a result of God's created order, that each of the religions is more or less good and bad (good creation flawed by human sin), and that people who are members of other religions are created by God, in God's image. The Christian scholar of religions is open to the possibility that the religions have a spiritual dimension—they are not only human creations but also in some cases spiritual phenomena caused in part by spiritual forces. What we are studying when we study religions are phenomena resulting in large part from the universal, God-given human desire to know and relate to God, with both good and bad success.

Working within this motivational context, Christian scholars of religion do many of the same things that non-Christian scholars of religion do, but because of this context they may be doing those things for different reasons. The Christian motivation is to learn more about God's created order and the way that different peoples of the world have, knowingly or unknowingly, tried to realize their true nature by reaching out for a Creator they may know partially (through general revelation coming through nature and consciousness) or be only dimly aware of.

Christian Questions

For people who are self-consciously Christian, the comparative exercise—recognizing both similarities and differences—is a normal one. Christians have chosen the Christian way of reaching out to God. They have chosen it for many reasons, but one of them is usually that they think it is the best way of reaching out to God, the only way that will bring ultimate salvation. They know from observation that in the world of religion there are bad ways of reaching out to God—Satanism, for example. They also, however, see the good ways that people in other religions reach out to what Christians believe is God. Therefore Christians are comfortable asking questions that are comparative in nature. To be sure, like all religion scholars, their initial questions seek answers of fact. But observation inevitably leads to evaluation, perhaps first of the psychological and sociological effects of different religious traditions, but soon of the moral and theological ones as well. For Christian scholars of religion, these questions need not diminish the objectivity of their study; indeed, a loss of objectivity to unacknowledged partisanship would be just as damaging to the Christian scholar of religion as to the humanist scholar of religion or the Buddhist scholar of religion, and so on.

Christian Goals

Finally, the Christian scholar of religion admits that his or her final goal in any of life's endeavors, including the study of religion, is to be a better follower of the Creator God and the Creator God's Son. Faithfully followed, this goal, we believe, helps make Christians better scholars of religion than if they were following some more temporal goal.

3

A Christian Theology of Religions

Harold A. Netland

As the essays in this volume demonstrate, our world includes a bewildering diversity in religious belief and practice. That diversity raises questions for Christians: How should Christians think about the many different ways in which people understand and live out their religious commitments? How should we live among and relate to religious others? The theology of religions attempts to answer these and related questions.

Although Christian reflection upon other religious traditions has a long history, the theology of religions emerged as an academic discipline only in the late twentieth century. Veli-Matti Kärkkäinen defines the theology of religions as "that discipline of theological studies which attempts to account theologically for the meaning and value of other religions. Christian theology of religions attempts to think theologically about what it means for Christians to live with people of other faiths and about the relationship of Christianity to other religions" (Kärkkäinen 2003, 20).

The theology of religions is an attempt to understand and explain the broad range of religious phenomena in terms of Christian categories and assumptions, which are derived from God's revelation and the church's reflection upon this revelation through the ages. It seeks to explain theologically both why human beings are religious and the diverse ways that human religiosity is expressed (specific beliefs and practices). But the theology of religions also includes thinking theologically about how Christians ought to live among people of other faiths. What are our obligations as followers of Jesus Christ with respect to Hindus, Buddhists, Muslims, Mormons, Wiccans, and Baha'is—many of whom are now our neighbors?

During the past half century an astonishing variety of theologies of religion have been proposed (Kärkkäinen 2003; Knitter 2002). Clearly not all are equally acceptable. Minimally, an adequate Christian theology of religions should be (1) faithful to and shaped by the teachings, values, and assumptions of the Bible; (2) informed by the central confessions of the church throughout the centuries; and (3) phenomenologically accurate in how it depicts the beliefs, institutions, and practices of other religious traditions. As such, the theology of religions draws upon academic disciplines such as biblical studies, historical and systematic theology, anthropology and sociology of religions, history of religions, comparative religions, and the philosophy of religion.

Perspectives on Other Religions

Until the twentieth century, it was largely taken for granted by Christians that Christianity is the one true religion for all humankind. Christians believe that God revealed himself in a special manner to the Old Testament patriarchs and prophets, with God's self-revelation finding its culmination in the incarnation in Jesus Christ (Heb. 1:1–4). The Bible—not the sacred writings of other religions—is the divinely inspired written revelation of God and thus is fully authoritative. Salvation is a gift of God's grace and is possible only because of the unique person and work of Jesus Christ on the cross. Sinful human beings are saved by God's grace through repentance of sin and faith.

On this view, there is an inescapable particularity concerning Jesus Christ. Although God's love and mercy extend to all (John 3:16; 1 Tim. 2:3–4), salvation is limited to those who repent and accept by faith God's provision in Jesus Christ (John 3:36; 14:6; Acts 4:12). The particularity of the gospel has always been a stumbling block to many. It was widely accepted in the ancient Mediterranean world that the same deity could take on various forms and be called by different names in different cultures. Robert Wilken states, "The oldest and most enduring criticism of Christianity is an appeal to religious pluralism. . . . All the ancient critics of Christianity were united in affirming that there is no one way to the divine" (Wilken 1995, 27, 42). Significantly, it is within this context of religious syncretism and relativism that we find the New Testament putting forward Jesus Christ as the one Savior for all people.

After the seventeenth century, the broad consensus among Christians concerning Christianity as the one true religion began to fragment, although it was not until the late twentieth century that the full effects of this became evident. As Europeans learned about other cultures and religions, Christians began to grapple with the theological implications of religious diversity. Questions about other religious traditions were extensively debated among the nineteenth-century Protestant missionaries (Cracknell 1995). But it was during the twentieth century that such issues became especially prominent (Knitter 1985; Yates 1995).

It has become customary in recent literature to use three categories to depict Christian perspectives on other religions: exclusivism, inclusivism, and pluralism. Exclusivism is said to be the view that religious truth and salvation are restricted primarily, if not exclusively, to Christianity. Although some exclusivists allow that some truth may be found outside Christianity, all exclusivists believe salvation comes only through faith in Jesus Christ and identification with the Christian church. Something like exclusivism is said to be the traditional position of Christians until the modern era (Netland 2001, 23–54).

Inclusivism maintains the following two principles: (1) There is a sense in which Jesus Christ is superior to other religious figures, and in some sense it is through Christ that salvation is made available; and (2) God's grace and salvation, which are somehow based upon Jesus Christ, are also available and efficacious through other religions. The views of the Roman Catholic Church after Vatican II (1962–65) are often identified as inclusivistic (Knitter 1985, chap. 7; Dupuis 1997, chaps. 5–6).

Religious pluralism, by contrast, claims that the major religions are all more or less equally effective and legitimate alternative ways of responding to the one divine reality. All religions are in their own ways historically complex and culturally conditioned human responses to the one divine reality.

Although this taxonomy can be helpful, it tends to be simplistic and reductionistic (Netland 2008). For example, the three categories are usually defined in terms of the question of salvation (must one be an explicit Christian in order to be saved?). But the many issues and positions involved in this debate are sufficiently complex that they cannot be reduced to just three categories. Moreover, there are many other questions apart from the issue of salvation that need to be addressed in a theology of religions. When these other questions are considered, it becomes impossible to sort the various perspectives into three neat categories. It is more helpful to think in terms of a broad continuum of perspectives on other religions,

---

Study Aid #5

Outline of a Theology of Religions

Definition
Thematic boundaries
   Priority of scripture
   Description of religious phenomena
   Tension between universality and particularity
Theological themes
   Creation
   General revelation
   Common grace
   Sin
   Demonic influence

with very negative perspectives at one end and very positive perspectives on the other. Where one actually is placed within the continuum will depend in part upon the particular issue being addressed and the religious tradition one is considering.

Themes in a Christian Theology of Religions

Some core themes emerge as necessary parts of a historically orthodox theology of religions. Following is a description of the more prominent ones.

The Priority of Scripture

For some today, theology of religions is essentially an exercise in comparative religions or the philosophy of religion. John Hick, for example, along with other religious pluralists, engages in a kind of inductive global theologizing, drawing upon the resources and experiences of all the major religions, yet denying any single tradition definitive authority. The collective religious experiences of humankind form the basis for Hick's model of religious pluralism (see Hick 1995, 2004).

The historic Christian tradition, by contrast, insists that God has revealed himself in an authoritative manner in the incarnation and the Old and New Testaments. Thus a genuinely Christian theology of religions cannot be reduced to comparative religion, but must be shaped and disciplined by the inspired scriptures, which provide the authoritative framework from within which particular questions are to be addressed.

Describing Religious Phenomena Accurately

Since theology of religions includes providing a theological explanation of religious phenomena, it is essential that the wide range of phenomena associated with the lived realities of religious communities be portrayed accurately. In doing so we must give proper attention to both commonalities and differences across religious traditions. Evangelicals generally emphasize the differences between Christian faith and other religions but are often less willing to recognize commonalities. Pluralistic theologies of religion, on the other hand, focus upon similarities but ignore the striking incompatibilities between religions. But a responsible theology of religions will acknowledge both similarities and differences between the Christian faith and other religions, treating the religions as complex systems embodying elements of goodness and truth as well as evil and falsehood.

Universality and Particularity

If we are to be faithful to the witness of scripture, we must keep in proper tension the biblical emphases upon universality and particularity. God, the Creator of all people who has revealed himself to all humankind, loves all and "wants all people to be saved and to come to a knowledge of the truth" (1 Tim. 2:4). At the same time, the apex of God's self-revelation is in the incarnation in Jesus of Nazareth, and it is through this highly particular event in the first century CE that salvation is made available to those who come to God in repentance and faith (Heb. 1:1–4; John 3:16; 14:6; Acts 4:12). The theology of religions is formulated within the polarities of the biblical themes of universality and particularity.

Themes for Explaining Religion

Five broad theological themes—creation, general revelation, common grace, sin, and satanic/demonic influence—provide a helpful framework for understanding the religions. For example, the basic human capacity for religious awareness and expression, as well as the commonalities between Christian faith and other religions, can be explained largely in terms of the themes of creation, general revelation, and common grace. Scripture teaches that all human beings are created in God's image (Gen. 1:26–27; 5:1–3), that God has revealed something of himself and our obligation to him to all humankind through the created order (Acts 14:15–17; 17:22–28; Rom. 1:18–32; 2:14–15), and that there is a sense in which God's gracious provision extends to all humankind (Matt. 5:45). In light of this it is hardly surprising that we should find among humankind an acknowledgment of the spiritual dimension and some similarities between the Christian faith and other religious traditions.

But the religions (Christianity included) also include much that is false, idolatrous, and a perversion of God's creation and revelation. The biblical emphasis upon human sin and rebellion against God (Gen. 3; Rom. 1:18–32) accounts for the fact that we find in the religions not only goodness and some truth but also much that is profoundly evil and false. Sin operates on both the individual and social levels, where it becomes institutionalized within religious traditions. Moreover, a biblically faithful theology of religions must acknowledge the reality of the demonic realm and its influence in the religious domain (1 Cor. 10:20; 2 Cor. 4:4). Wherever there is falsehood and evil, there is the influence of the Adversary (John 8:44). But this influence should not be exaggerated. While it would be simplistic to deny the demonic element in the religions, it would also be misleading simply to explain the religions as nothing more than products of satanic deception and influence. Chris Wright articulates well the dialectic within the religions: "The fallen duplicity of man is that he simultaneously seeks after God his Maker and flees from God his Judge. Man's religions, therefore, simultaneously manifest both these human tendencies. This is what makes a simplistic verdict on other religions—whether blandly positive or wholly negative—so unsatisfactory and indeed unbiblical" (Wright 1984, 5).

The Manila Declaration, produced in 1992 by eighty-five evangelical theologians from twenty-eight countries who came together in Manila under the auspices of the World Evangelical Fellowship to address the theme "The Unique Christ in Our Pluralistic World," captures nicely the major contours of an evangelical theology of religions.

> The term "religion" refers to a complex phenomenon, and it is important to distinguish between its various aspects. In many societies, religion forms an important part of their identity. As such, a diversity of religions—or, more accurately, a diversity of certain aspects of the religions—may be affirmed as part of the richness of God's good creation, although it must be immediately added that people have often sinfully used these religions, including Christianity, to create a false ultimacy and superiority for their own cultures and religious groups.
>
> Religions may also be understood as expressions of the longing for communion with God, which is an essential human characteristic since we are created in the image of God for the purpose of service to him, fellowship with him, and praise for him. Here also, while always corrupted by sin in practice, we may affirm in principle the goodness of a diversity of some aspects of the religions.
>
> We are not able, however, to affirm the diversity of religions without qualification because religions teach a path to salvation, or a concept of salvation, that is not consistent with God's saving action in Jesus Christ as recorded in the Bible. To the extent that a religion points away from Jesus Christ, we deny the validity of that religion. We would also deny the validity of the Christian religion should it fail to proclaim Jesus as the Christ, the Lord of all creation, and the sole savior of the world. (Nicholls 1994, 15–16)

The Trinity and the Religions

The doctrine of the Trinity also has implications for theology of religions (D'Costa 2000; Kärkkäinen 2004; Vanhoozer 1997; Johnson 2011; McDermott and Netland 2014). God is present and active throughout the world as Father, Son, and Holy Spirit, and God's influence extends beyond the church. The Manila Declaration states, "Thus the true aspects of the world's religions stem from God's creative power or from the work of the Holy Spirit as he prepares individuals, people groups, and even whole cultures to hear about Jesus Christ" (Nicholls 1994, 16). At the same time, scripture provides little support for attempts to disconnect the eternal Logos or the Holy Spirit from the particularity of God's revelation and salvific activity in Jesus Christ. "Moreover, this same Trinitarian basis undergirds the decisive, normative, and unique work and person of the historical Jesus Christ" (ibid.).

Salvation and Religious Others

The scriptures insist that Jesus Christ is the only Savior for all humankind. But this naturally raises questions about the extent of salvation, especially as this relates to adherents of other religions. We will briefly summarize evangelical perspectives.

The biblical witness is clear on the following points: (1) All people are sinners and face God's just condemnation for sin. (2) Salvation is available only on the basis of the sinless person and atoning work of Jesus Christ. (3) No one is saved merely by doing good works or being religiously devout. (4) Salvation is always only by God's grace and must be personally accepted through faith. (5) Ultimately, not everyone will be saved. (6) God is entirely righteous, just, and fair in his dealings with humankind.

But is it nevertheless possible for those who have never heard the gospel to be saved? Contemporary evangelical responses fall into three broad categories. First, many evangelicals hold that only those who hear the gospel and explicitly respond in faith to Jesus Christ in this life can be saved. Explicit knowledge of the gospel of Jesus Christ is thus necessary for salvation (Nash 1994; Morgan and Peterson 2008). Many regard this as the traditional evangelical position, and it has been prominent in conservative evangelical theologies of mission.

The "wider hope" perspective, by contrast, maintains that on the basis of scripture we can expect that large numbers of those who never hear the gospel nevertheless will be saved (Pinnock 1992; Sanders 1992; Tiessen 2004). Although Jesus Christ is the one Savior for all people and salvation is possible only because of Christ's atoning work on the cross, this position holds that many might be saved apart from explicitly hearing the gospel.

Many evangelicals, however, find themselves somewhere between these two positions, convinced that each goes beyond what the biblical data affirm. Those in this group are willing to admit in principle that God might save those who have never explicitly heard the gospel, but they add that we simply do not know whether this occurs or, if so, how many might be saved in this manner (Erickson 1975; Stott 1985; Packer 1990; Wright 1990). The clear pattern in the New Testament is that people first hear the gospel and then, through the work of the Holy Spirit, respond in faith to the proclamation of the Word and are saved.

Study Aid #6

Similarities and Differences

Religions, including Christianity, can be considered in terms of beliefs or teachings, basic values or ethical ideals, rituals or practices, and institutions. When Christianity is compared with other religions such as Hinduism, Buddhism, Islam, Shinto, Sikhism, and Daoism, it becomes clear that there are similarities to aspects of some religions as well as differences. Each religious tradition needs to be considered on its own in relation to Christianity, and both similarities and differences need to be acknowledged. We should think of a continuum, with strong similarities on one end and strong differences on the other.

Similarities ──────────────────────────────── Differences
   Teachings   Values   Rituals   Institutions

A religion such as Islam will have greater similarities to Christianity in teachings than, for example, Buddhism, although Buddhism will have similarities to Christianity in values and ethical ideals.

Christian Mission and Religious Others

According to scripture, Jesus Christ is the only Lord and Savior for all humankind, including devout adherents of other religions. In obedience to our Lord and out of compassion for the lost, we are to "make disciples" of all people (Matt. 28:18–20). Thus, Christian mission, including evangelism, must be part of a theology of religions.

But the world in which we are to make disciples of Jesus Christ is one marked by religious strife and deep suspicion. We live in a postcolonialist world that is acutely aware of the injustices of four centuries of Western imperialism and that believes—rightly or wrongly—that Christianity bears much of the blame for such injustice. Deeply rooted ethnic, nationalistic, and religious tensions erupt into violence, causing many to wonder whether religiously diverse communities can indeed live together peacefully. Religious conversion is increasingly seen as an obstacle to peaceful coexistence. The issues here are complex and require the Christian to properly navigate two sets of obligations—our responsibilities as disciples of Jesus Christ and as good citizens, both locally and globally. In carrying out the Great Commission we are to follow the Great Commandment (Matt. 22:35–40). As Christ's disciples, we are to love God with our entire being and to love our neighbor—including religious others—as we love ourselves.

Christians must approach mission in today's world with an attitude of humility and repentance for the ways in which Christians have sometimes treated religious others in the past. New models of evangelism and disciple making must be developed that are appropriate for a world increasingly hostile to evangelism (Muck and Adeney 2009). So even as we embrace Buddhists and Muslims as fellow human beings created in God's image, we must also urge them to be reconciled to God through Jesus Christ.

4

Christian Interaction with Other Religions

PAUL LOUIS METZGER

The purpose of this chapter is to answer the following question: what are various ways that Christians interact with people of other religions? Themes that will be discussed include evangelism and proclamation, dialogue and neighborliness, and conversion and transformation. In keeping with the challenge raised at the close of the last chapter, Christians must demonstrate to a cynical world that our allegiance in word and deed to Jesus Christ as the one Lord and Savior over every tribe, tongue, and nation includes an unswerving commitment to the common good and appropriate affirmation of various forms of diversity among all peoples. This chapter will frame the discussion in view of this challenge.

Evangelism and Proclamation

The word "evangelism" comes from "evangel," which means "gospel" or "good news." More specifically, in the Christian context, "evangel" is often taken to refer to the good news of God's grace revealed in Jesus Christ to bring forgiveness of sins, peace to the nations, and restoration of the cosmos to God through Jesus's person and kingdom mission. The church is called to proclaim in word and deed the kingdom reign of God in Jesus Christ in the world (for a good source on various aspects of evangelism, see Chilcote and Warner 2008).

In its historical context, this rendition of "gospel" (*euangelion*), or good news, stood in marked contrast to the good news of Caesar and the deliverance and salvation he offered to his loyal subjects through his military campaigns and conquests. Against this Roman backdrop, it must have sounded very striking to those listening that the apostolic community proclaimed victory for those who became citizens of God's kingdom through faith in Jesus. The means of entrance into God's kingdom was striking: one did not need to be a Roman citizen to become a citizen of God's kingdom; faith alone was sufficient, and this regardless of one's status as highborn or lowborn, slave or free. Moreover, the source of entrance into God's kingdom was striking: victory for God's loyal subjects came not through Caesar's military conquests but through the just life of Jesus, whose unjust execution by Roman crucifixion and his resurrection to new life turned the tables on this world's system of retribution involving oppression. The *Pax Romana* ("peace of Rome") gave way to the *Pax Christi* ("peace of Christ"), which involved adherence to his code of grace, mercy, and enemy love (see, for example, Moltmann's 1993 theological analysis of the "crucified God," where he speaks of Christ's confrontation of the Roman system of retribution; see also Caird's 1956 [2003] treatment of Paul's doctrine of the principalities and powers, where he argues that "evil is defeated only if the injured person absorbs the evil and refuses to allow it to go any further"). While many found such a teaching scandalous, foolish, and weak in the Roman Empire, for those who believed, it was the wise and powerful good news of God's righteous deliverance for a world held in bondage to sin and despair and the inhumane treatment of one's fellows (see 1 Cor. 1:18–31).

No wonder the apostle Paul declared to the church in Rome that he was not ashamed of the gospel. As a servant of Christ Jesus set apart as an ambassador, a messenger of this gospel, or good news (Rom. 1:1), Paul was eager to proclaim this message to the nations so that people everywhere could become citizens of God's kingdom involving grace and peace by belonging to the risen Jesus through the obedience that comes by faith (Rom. 1:1–7). As a result of his own calling and belonging to Christ through the obedience by faith, Paul writes, "I am obligated both to Greeks and non-Greeks, both to the wise and the foolish. . . . For I am not ashamed of the gospel, because it is the power of God that brings salvation to everyone who believes: first to the Jew, then to the Gentile. For in the gospel the righteousness of God is revealed—a righteousness that is by faith from first to last, just as it is written: 'The righteous will live by faith'" (Rom. 1:14, 16–17).

The *Pax Romana* was forced on its subjects, whereas Jesus's peace, the *Pax Christi*, is formed in us by faith in his love, as we are identified with him. We often seek to bring peace and order to the chaos and violence of our world like Rome did—through greater violence. Christ brought about peace and order through the chaos of his own cross, as he suffered violence at the hands of Rome. Rome conquered by retribution, but Jesus by way of redemptive love.

No doubt this is one reason why the Romans under Nero and the like tried to stamp out Christianity. The *Pax Christi*'s growth and development would spell the death of Rome, as it elevated the weak and foolish by Greek and Roman standards and humbled the powerful and sophisticated—a point not lost on Paul (1 Cor.

1:18–31), the Romans, or Nietzsche (1968), but often lost on us. The Roman system could account for a plethora of religious traditions as long as their adherents allowed for the Romans to assimilate them within the Roman pantheon of the gods and with it Caesar worship. However, given their strict monotheism involving revelation of the named God of the universe, Judaism and Christianity refused to make such accommodations and see themselves as tribal religions whose deities could be mixed and matched with the gods of Rome. As a result, many Jews and Christians suffered greatly.

By no means did the Jews and Christians oppress the Romans; to the contrary, they were persecuted for their beliefs. It is ironic that people would view the adherents of the Jewish and Christian religions as worthy of suspicion, believing that they would not safeguard concern for the common good. As R. Kendall Soulen has argued, a nameless deity and a nameless people can be commodified, but not a named deity or people. Religious pluralism, old and new, for all its virtues in promoting tolerance and affirming human identity and safeguarding against oppression, does not safeguard adequately against the erosion of cultures and people groups, given that it maintains that God is ultimately beyond naming (Soulen 2005). While Christianity has often been guilty of oppression in its evangelistic proclamation throughout the world, such oppression and erosion of cultures does not arise from the heart of the gospel but runs counter to it. It is critically important that we regain this sense of what the good news of Jesus signifies and entails: namely, the preservation of people groups and cultures from the onslaught of commodification in view of the named God who became incarnate in the person of Jesus. As the good news of the incarnate Word is translated into the languages of various cultures, their own cultural distinctiveness and particularity are affirmed and preserved, not assimilated and eroded (see Vinoth Ramachandra's reflection on West African scholar Lamin Sanneh's discussion of Protestant mission strategies involving Bible translation and how that affirms the indigenous cultures to which the church bears witness; Ramachandra 2008).

Moving on, the above-mentioned hostility toward evangelism today is often bound up with views of the gospel and connotations with proclamation that are coercive, manipulative, and framed in terms of power politics. With that in mind, evangelistic proclamation today must entail concern for dialogue and neighborliness, and this regardless of whether someone comes to Christ. People who do not yet know Christ personally by faith are often increasingly cynical of evangelistically minded Christians' attempts to be cordial and friendly, viewing these efforts as a ruse for converting them to their position. Building on a point made in one of the preceding essays, we Christians must remind ourselves that the Great Commission (to make disciples of all the nations; Matt. 28:19) flows from the Great Commandments (to love God with all our being and love our neighbors as ourselves; Mark 12:30–31). Our approach to discipleship and evangelism must also be framed relationally, so much so that we never look at people as a means to an end of a certain state of transformation, whether it be Christian perfection or conversion, but rather that we love the people we engage regardless of whether they ever realize what we hope for them. If we approach our disciples in a utilitarian manner, we will likely do the same with those of other faiths and worldviews whom we seek to reach with the good news of God's love in Jesus.

Study Aid #7

Questionnaire on God, Religion, and Spirituality

Consider using some or all of the following questions when in conversation with people following a different spiritual path:

1. What comes to your mind when you think of God, religion, or spirituality?
2. What do you make of Christianity and the church?
3. John Lennon of the Beatles longed for a world without religion because he thought religion causes so much harm in the world. On a scale from one to ten (with ten being positive), where would you place religion in terms of causing good in the world? Why did you choose the number you did?
4. What specifically does spirituality have to do with truth, goodness, and beauty, respectively?
5. What is the greatest spiritual classic you have read (for example, the Qur'an, the Bible, the Book of Mormon, the Lotus Sutra, the Vedas, Friedrich Nietzsche's *Thus Spake Zarathustra*, Stephen Hawking's *A Brief History of Time*)? What stood out to you in your reading and why?
6. What do you think of Jesus?
7. How would you relate Jesus to other significant spiritual figures such as Moses, Buddha, Muhammad, Mahatma Gandhi, Mother Teresa, and the Dalai Lama?
8. What is the relation of tolerance to love? What does love look like to you?
9. How important is it to you to know if there is a God and if God has a purpose for your life? Why or why not?
10. If these things matter to you, how would you know God or God's will for you?
11. If there is a heaven, what would you envision it to be like? What about hell?
12. What happens to us when we die?
13. Where does evil come from? If it relates to human freedom, what would you do to remove evil from the world?
14. If there was a God who could hear and respond to you, what would you ask God for? Why?
15. Would you like to continue this conversation? I am open to your questions, too, on this subject. Anything is fair game.

Dialogue and Neighborliness

A utilitarian way of engaging people inside and outside the church does not account for how vitally we are connected to them. We do not have our existence outside those who are "other"; rather, we are who we are in relation to them, as those who are created in the image of the Triune God, who is relational at the core of God's being. The image of God, as articulated here, is framed relationally, as "man" is conceived as male and female in relation (Gen. 1:26–27; for further study of this view of the image of God as relational, see, for example, Barth 1958; see also Gunton 1992). The three persons of the Triune God are the divine being and constitute one another as persons in relation. As those created in the image of this God, humans are constituted as human subjects in relation to one another.

It follows from this relational creaturely constitution that the chief commandments given by God to humanity are to love God with all our hearts and to love our neighbors as ourselves (Mark 12:30–31). The "other" is one's neighbor regardless of difference in social status, actions, or religious affiliation. Attention to neighbor moves us beyond objectifying the religious other as stranger and leads us to enter into dialogical relation with them.

This is nowhere more clearly demonstrated in scripture than in the Word becoming flesh (John 1:14). The incarnate Word does not simply proclaim God's will but also lives it and enters into dialogical engagement with others in his midst. In view of the incarnation, evangelism and proclamation must involve dialogue at their core. Dialogue entails approaching the other not as an object but as a human subject. Jesus, who exists for others, gives rise to a church that is a community for others, and, as relational, is also shaped by the other's existence in dialogical encounter. (See Bonhoeffer's depiction of Christ as the man for others and his church as the community for others in *Letters and Papers from Prison*, 1967 [1953]; it is interesting to note that Bonhoeffer penned these words at a time when the orthodox confessing church was seen as losing its influence in an increasingly secular Europe.) Our uncommon God, revealed in the person of Jesus, makes space for the human other, including the diverse religious other, as neighbor, thereby promoting the common good. As the church's mission includes proclamation of just dealings flowing from Jesus's kingdom vision, it promotes thoughtful dialogue that affirms the particular identity and well-being of its diverse religious neighbor.

Further to what was stated above, seeing the other as a human subject who is dynamically related to us is bound up with the biblical notion of neighbor. If we love our neighbor as ourselves, we will treat them not as statistics but as persons in relation. Here we find an attitude of care and respect and honor, not simply for those with whom we have affinities but also for those who are outside our own cultural and religious traditions.

Contrary to much popular opinion, Jesus did not disparage those of other faith traditions but rather challenged the haughtiness of certain religious leaders in his own tradition. (Paul also affirmed those of other faith traditions in his engagement of the Athenians at Mars Hill in Acts 17; while he grieved over the Athenians' idolatry, he also affirmed their poets and various forms of religious expressions and sought to build bridges with them through proclamation involving dialogue.) Jesus's engagement of those of diverse religious paths is strikingly refreshing when set against the backdrop of how conservative Christians today often approach those of other faith traditions in polarizing terms. (See the analysis of Jesus's engagement of those of diverse religious perspectives in Robinson 2012.) For Jesus, evangelistic proclamation makes space for dialogue that affirms the religious other as beloved neighbor. (Please note: while dialogue in this context is not to be seen solely as a form of evangelism and is necessary for affirming the common good by way of religious diplomacy bound up with loving our diverse religious neighbors as ourselves, dialogue can function evangelistically; for a helpful statement of the complementary relation of dialogue and evangelism, see Mouw 2010 [1992], 114; for multifaceted treatments of interreligious dialogue, including the variety of ways that interreligious dialogue functions, from evangelical scholars in this field, see Muck 1993, 1997, and 2011; Netland 1991.)

Terry Muck discusses the often-neglected category of the affections in studies of interreligious dialogue. For Muck, such dialogue involves among other things "an emotion or attitude toward people of other religious traditions" (Muck 1997). Muck quotes Stanley J. Samartha in his expansion of this argument: "Dialogue is a mood, a spirit, an attitude of love and respect towards neighbors of other faiths. It regards partners as persons, not statistics" (Samartha 1981). For Muck, the evangelical community has not accounted for this affective dimension of interreligious dialogue (Muck 1997).

The need for consideration of the affections in engaging the religious other finds biblical support in Luke 10:25–37. The account of the Samaritan of exceptional mercy does not address interreligious dialogue directly, but it bears on our subject since it pertains to the affections in at least two ways. First, Jesus uses a Samaritan, rather than a Jew of high standing, to teach the Jewish religious leader who asks him what neighborliness looks like. Here, I believe, Jesus challenges the religious leader's affections of pride and presumption as well as indifference, as he makes use of a representative of a "mixed race of Israelite and non-Israelite" blooded people "despised by many pure-blooded Israelites because they believed that the Samaritans compromised the faith" (Bock 1996, 969; see also Geldenhuys 1950 for a brief discussion of the extremely hostile division between the Jews and Samaritans). The outsider or stranger in this passage (the Samaritan) is the one who cares for the Jewish other in need. Rather than being viewed as the person requiring help, the Samaritan is in the position of offering life-saving aid to the Jew. At best a guest on most accounts, it is the Samaritan who functions as host. Here it is worth noting how some forms of Christian tradition came to see this text: "Later Christian tradition sees the parable as an allegory of salvation, identifying the Samaritan—the radical religious other of first-century Judaism who plays the role of host for the 'half dead' son of Israel—as Christ" (Alexander and

Boys 2012, 53–57; see also their discussion of the scriptures' attentiveness to the dialectic of host and guest, including this text).

Jesus is not only the Samaritan host. He is also the Lord in need. In Matthew 25:31–46, we find that the Lord Jesus, who is the ultimate host, comes to the earth to provide salvation and judges the nations based on how they care for him by how they approach those most in need. One of the values to take away from the story is that if the Lord functions as host and guest, we should be humble enough to see ourselves as guests in need of help and be caring enough to see ourselves as hosts who attend to those in need. Furthermore, one should never view oneself as having power over the other of whatever demographic, including diverse religious traditions, regardless of the depth of benevolence or charity. How can it be otherwise, since the person in need to whom one gives aid represents in some manner the Lord, who is the ultimate guest and the host who cares for the needy, including us? The affection of humility and openness to mutuality of giving and receiving is central to the discussion of neighborliness and hospitality (evangelical treatments of hospitality include the following: Mouw 2010 [1992]; Pohl 1999; Yong 2008) and, by extension, interfaith dialogue. We will return to this subject when we discuss conversion and transformation. For even there, conversion and transformation are dynamic processes that continue to shape both the Christian and those the church seeks to reach through sharing the good news of God's grace in Jesus Christ.

Returning to the story of the Samaritan of extraordinary mercy in Luke 10, we find a second way that the account bears upon the subject of interreligious dialogue from the standpoint of the affections. The Samaritan in the story cares for the man in need at great risk and cost rather than objectifying this Jewish stranger as an otherwise oppressive Jewish figure whom he can justly ignore (assuming the person in need is a Je,w based on the context and audience); the Samaritan sees this stranger as his neighbor, whose need implicates him to the core of his existence and resources. The Samaritan in Jesus's story in Luke 10 does not simply love his beaten and near-dead neighbor with merciful thoughts. Nor does he perform stoic deeds of compassion. Rather, he takes pity on the Jewish man (Luke 10:33). As in the account of Jesus being moved to act compassionately in Matthew 9:35–38, compassion no doubt flows from the heart and shapes the thoughts and deeds of this Samaritan stranger, who functions as merciful host to the Jewish man in need, who is the guest. Mercy flows from his innermost being and leads him to risk his own safety and sacrifice his time and money.

Building on the last point, we must be attentive to a holistic engagement involving orthodoxy (head), orthopraxy (hands), and orthopathy (heart) in our engagement of the religious other. Each dimension is very important. However, the affections, under the guidance of the Spirit of the Word, serve as the ground of properly functioning thought and action.

> Acquiring cognitive knowledge and skills is certainly needful in their pastoral engagement with the people of other faiths. As critical as those skills might be, however,

they are still secondary to a more elemental aspect of affective formation through which the heart learns the grammars of neighborliness and hospitality resident in the heart of God. It is only with the heart being rightly cultivated in this way that knowledge and practice are given a right direction and governance to bear faithful witness to God. (Han, Metzger, and Muck 2012)

When such affective formation occurs, the church comes to engage the religious other in a way that makes space for the latter's own self-understanding. Rather than impose Christian categories on the religious other, it accounts for the various traditions' forms of self-expression, including its sacred stories, symbols, and communal rituals and experiences, even while holding firmly to ultimate Christian truth claims bound up with biblical revelation. (My work on how to discuss Jesus in a world of diverse paths is an example of a Christian apologetic that accounts for this particular dialogical approach to engaging the adherents of other religious traditions; see Metzger 2012.) Only when we honor the diverse religious others' persons, as well as their spiritual heritages, can we expect to build bridges of trust that affirm the common good and that bear witness to our uncommon God revealed in the person of Jesus, whether or not these neighbors and friends ever convert to the Christian faith by believing in him.

Study Aid #8

An Interreligious Examen

Following are questions you can ask yourself in order to gain insight to the way you view people of other religions.

1. When I look at the religious other, what do I consider first? Someone created in the image of God, someone with very different beliefs and practices, someone whose eternal destiny is unclear, or something else?
2. Do I ask open questions or leading questions of the religious other?
3. Do I listen to their answers for the sake of understanding, or am I thinking simply of my next response?
4. Am I interested in what they have to say about their views and mine as well?
5. Do I start out thinking of points of similarity or points of dissimilarity between those of other faiths and myself?
6. Do I think they have anything of value to share?
7. Do I view their faith and tradition primarily or perhaps exclusively from the standpoint of doctrine/truth claims, religious symbolism and rituals, sacred literature, or experiences? How do I view doctrine in relation to these other items?
8. Would I seek to be friends with a person of a different faith persuasion if I knew they would never become a Christian?
9. Would I invite them over for meals? Would I be willing to be a guest in their homes?
10. Would I be willing to go to hell if by doing so I could swap places with those people from other faith traditions that I hold most dear (Rom. 9:1–5)?

11. Would I be willing to do anything that is in my power and pleasing to God to foster their positive response to God's invitation to experience eternal life through Jesus?
12. How central is God's holy love revealed in Jesus to me (explicitly and/or implicitly) in terms of my conversation with them?
13. Am I willing to be patient toward those of other faiths if they have misunderstandings of Christianity? How important to me is being empathic and long-suffering toward the religious other who expresses grievances and even hostilities toward Christianity?

Conversion and Transformation

Biblically speaking, conversion does not equal coercion or involve forcing people to believe; still, there have been numerous accounts throughout history where the church, in alliance with a given state, forced people to convert or else enticed people by manufacturing beneficial social conditions for those who would convert to Christianity. Such instances do not equal conversion. Such conversions are at best skin deep and merely words. Forced confessions do not penetrate to the heart. Real conversion occurs when the Word is proclaimed and it creates faith in the heart concerning the person and finished work of Christ on their behalf (see Rom. 10:5–21). The Word that creates faith appeals to (not forces) the person's heart and mind, and the Spirit generates an internal transformation. (Karl Barth also speaks of how the Word does not compel but appeals; Barth 1954.) We do not convert others, and they do not convert themselves. It is the gracious work of God in their lives, whereby they are made new creations in Christ (2 Cor. 5:17; see also Eph. 2:4–9 and Titus 3:5–6).

In addition to the charge of coercion, another allegation often leveled at evangelistically minded Christians is that the call to conversion leads to intolerance. While evangelistically oriented Christians make the appeal to believe on Jesus as Lord for salvation (Rom. 10:9), since he is in their view the only way, truth, and life that leads to the Father (John 14:6–7), fair-minded Christian evangelists make space for other views and do not seek to remove them from the public square of dialogue and debate.

It is important to note that tolerance and its opposite function as properties of behaviors, not beliefs. If tolerance entails acceptance of another person's belief system, then anyone who rejects another's system of belief would be intolerant. When this equation occurs, the result is the death of reasonable discourse and dialogue that allows for differences and disagreements between devotees of various religions and spiritual paths (see Harold Netland's discussion of this topic; Netland 2008).

Going further, Christians are not the only ones engaged in evangelism. While many critics will refer to Christianity (and Islam) as an evangelistic religion and claim that most other religions are not, I would reason that any time we are arguing for a particular view (not simply a religious view) as having greater merit than another tradition, we are evangelizing. Evangelism is simply an attempt to persuade someone of a particular belief, attitude, or way of life. Everyone is an evangelist, even if they are simply asking someone to stop sharing their faith. They are seeking to persuade the other party to begin a new practice or discontinue an old one.

What does the preceding discussion have to do with conversion? Everyone is seeking to convert others when they call for a certain action such as "Believe in Jesus" or "Quit telling people they need to believe on Jesus to be saved." The call to conversion is bound up with the art of persuasion and is essential to any form of constructive engagement in the public square concerning the cultivation and preservation of the common good.

Now there are many forms of conversion, and not simply the kind that entails moving from one religious tradition or worldview to another. For example, dialogue that is aimed at cultivating understanding and tolerance is one attempt at conversion. Many evangelicals need to be converted from misperceptions and distortions of other traditions' claims and practices by way of gaining greater understanding of those traditions. Moreover, there is a need for conversion that takes us deeper into our own traditions. Interreligious dialogue must go beyond mere tolerance and mutual understanding to the deepening of various traditions' respective convictions through meaningful interaction with diverse religious others (Metzger 2011). Not only do people then convert to Christianity, but also Christians continue to be converted to Christ through their engagement of diverse religious practitioners. We undergo transformation continually, if we are alive and well. If we as the church and as Christians are not undergoing continual transformation on the path of salvation in Christ, we are on our way to death. (See Darrell L. Guder's [2000] treatment of the church's own need to undergo an ongoing transformation; also, the papal encyclical *Evangelii Nuntiandi* [1975] speaks of evangelism as going to the heart of the church's mission in the world and addresses the need for the church to be re-evangelized for a renewal of its proclamation in life and deed.) Christians engaged in interreligious discourse will often claim that God uses those of other faith traditions to deepen and solidify their own faith in Christ rather than harm it.

Last, where conversion to Christianity from another tradition occurs, it should never lead to intolerance of the other tradition but rather charity toward it. So often, Christians who are antagonistic to other traditions are not secure in their own positions and faith. As the Spirit of God pours the gift of God's love into our hearts and lives of faith and hope (Rom. 5:5; see also 1 Cor. 13), we are able to create more space for others, not less. When transformation of our lives in the Spirit occurs, our hearts and lives are expanded. As a result, we can listen to diverse religious others; look upon them with the eyes of Christ and his love; affirm their inherent dignity and worth as God's good creation; be humble and learn from them, including from their religious and spiritual perspectives; be long-suffering and empathic toward them in the midst of their grievances toward the church; and seek ways to resolve tensions. Such transformation in the Spirit occurs by and for our uncommon God revealed in Jesus, who leads us to pursue the common good.

> **Study Aid #9**
>
> **Conflict Resolution and Christian Witness**
>
> What do you do when engaging those who are hostile toward your Christian faith?
>
> 1. Ask them to share their perceptions and experiences. Make sure that your questions are open (not generally yes and no questions) and seek to clarify points and confirm through reiteration that you have grasped the key points.
> 2. Be empathic. Don't discount their perceptions and experiences. Don't say that real Christians don't operate that way. It is a cop-out, not a point of connection.
> 3. If they are open to engagement and entering into an open discussion, set forth what it is that is the heart of the Christian faith as you see it.
> 4. Welcome their feedback and their sharing of their own convictions on religion and spirituality. Be inquisitive, not inquisitional, in your questions and comments. If we want people to listen to us and understand us, including why we personally and passionately believe the way we do, we need to do the same toward them.
> 5. Avoid being reactive. Stay proactive. Stay on message concerning what you are about and what you believe is the essence of the Christian faith. Indicate that you are open to wrestling through the issues with them.
> 6. Account for key differences rather than sweep them aside, but try to problem solve on where you can find common ground.
> 7. Draw attention to those with whom you collaborate who represent that person's spiritual tradition or perspective at large. Ask them to join in the collaborative effort to build a connection with the person with whom you have the interreligious conflict.
> 8. Keep the door open to further engagement. Keep the conversation going. Seek to win and cultivate a personal friendship, not make an enemy. As Floyd McClung and Joe Aldrich said, "People don't care how much we know until they know how much we care" (Floyd McClung, quoted in Aldrich 1993, 35).

Sources for Part 1

Joseph C. Aldrich. *Lifestyle Evangelism*. Multnomah, 1993.

Scott C. Alexander and Mary C. Boys. "Christian Hospitality and Pastoral Practices from a Roman Catholic Perspective." *Theological Education* 47, no. 1 (Fall 2012): 47–73.

Karl Barth. *Against the Stream: Shorter Post-War Writings, 1946–1952*. SCM, 1954.

———. *Church Dogmatics* III/1: *The Doctrine of Creation*. Edited by G. W. Bromiley and T. F. Torrance. T&T Clark, 1958.

Zigmunt Bauman. *Liquid Modernity*. Polity, 2000.

Robert Bellah. *Religion in Human Evolution: From the Paleolithic to the Axial Age.* Belknap Press of Harvard University Press, 2011.

———. "Religious Evolution." In *Beyond Belief*, 20–50. University of California Press, 1991 (1970).

Darrell L. Bock. *Luke.* Vol. 2, *9:51–24:53.* Baker Exegetical Commentary on the New Testament. Baker, 1996.

Dietrich Bonhoeffer. *Letters and Papers from Prison.* Macmillan, 1967 (1953).

G. B. Caird. *Principalities and Powers: A Study in Pauline Theology.* Wipf & Stock, 2003 (1956).

Paul W. Chilcote and Laceye C. Warner, eds. *The Study of Evangelism: Exploring a Missional Practice of the Church.* Eerdmans, 2008.

Kenneth Cracknell. *Justice, Courtesy and Love: Theologians and Missionaries Encountering World Religions, 1846–1914.* Epworth, 1995.

Charles Darwin. *The Origin of the Species.* Penguin, 2003 (1853).

Gavin D'Costa. *The Meeting of the Religions and the Trinity.* Orbis Books, 2000.

Mary Douglas. *Purity and Danger: Pollution and Taboo.* Routledge, 2002 (1966).

Jacques Dupuis. *Toward a Christian Theology of Religious Pluralism.* Orbis Books, 1997.

Émile Durkheim. *Elementary Forms of Religious Life.* Oxford University Press, 2008 (1912).

Jonathan Edwards. *Religious Affections.* Vol. 2 of *Works.* Yale University Press, 2009.

Millard Erickson. "Hope for Those Who Haven't Heard? Yes, But . . ." *Evangelical Missions Quarterly* 11 (April 1975): 122–26.

James George Frazer. *The Golden Bough.* Oxford University Press, 2009 (1890).

Clifford Geertz. *Islam Observed.* University of Chicago Press, 1971.

———. *Religions of Java.* University of Chicago Press, 1976.

Norval Geldenhuys. *The Gospel of Luke.* The New International Commentary on the New Testament. Eerdmans, 1950.

Darrell L. Guder. *The Continuing Conversion of the Church.* Eerdmans, 2000.

Colin E. Gunton. "Trinity, Ontology and Anthropology: Towards a Renewal of the Doctrine of the *Imago Dei.*" In *Persons, Divine and Human*, edited by Christoph Schwöbel and Colin E. Gunton, 47–61. T&T Clark, 1992.

Sang-Ehil Han, Paul Louis Metzger, and Terry Muck. "Christian Hospitality and Pastoral Practices from an Evangelical Perspective." *Theological Education* 47, no. 1 (Fall 2012): 11–31.

John Hick. *A Christian Theology of Religions: The Rainbow of Faiths.* Westminster John Knox, 1995.

———. *An Interpretation of Religion: Human Responses to the Transcendent.* 2nd ed. Yale University Press, 2004.

Edmund Husserl. *Cartesian Meditations: An Introduction to Phenomenology.* Martinus Nijhoff, 1977 (1931).

William James. *Varieties of Religious Experience.* Library of America, 2009 (1902).

Keith Johnson. *Rethinking the Trinity and Religious Pluralism: An Augustinian Assessment.* InterVarsity, 2011.

Veli-Matti Kärkkäinen. *An Introduction to the Theology of Religions.* InterVarsity, 2003.

———. *Trinity and Religious Pluralism: The Doctrine of the Trinity in Christian Theology of Religions*. Ashgate, 2004.

Paul F. Knitter. *Introducing Theologies of Religions*. Orbis Books, 2002.

———. *No Other Name? A Critical Survey of Christian Attitudes toward the World Religions*. Orbis Books, 1985.

William Brede Kristensen. *The Meaning of Religion*. Martinus Nijhoff, 1960.

Gerardus van der Leeuw. *Religion in Essence and Manifestation*. Princeton University Press, 1986 (1933).

Claude Lévi-Strauss. *Myth and Meaning: Cracking the Code of Culture*. Schocken, 1995.

Gerald McDermott. *Can Evangelicals Learn from World Religions?* IVP Academic, 2000.

———. *God's Rivals: Why God Allows Different Religions—Insights from the Bible and the Early Church*. IVP Academic, 2007.

Gerald McDermott and Herold Netland. *A Trinitarian Theology of Religions: An Evangelical Proposal*. Oxford University Press, 2014.

Paul Louis Metzger. "Beyond the Culture Wars: Contours of Authentic Dialogue." In *A World for All? Global Civil Society in Political Theory and Trinitarian Theology*, edited by William F. Storrar, Peter J. Casarella, and Paul Louis Metzger, 294–95. Eerdmans, 2011.

———. *Connecting Christ: How to Discuss Jesus in a World of Diverse Paths*. Nelson, 2012.

Jürgen Moltmann. *The Crucified God: The Cross of Christ as the Foundation and Criticism of Christian Theology*. Fortress, 1993.

Christopher W. Morgan and Robert A. Peterson. *Faith Comes by Hearing: A Response to Inclusivism*. InterVarsity, 2008.

Richard J. Mouw. *Uncommon Decency: Christian Civility in an Uncivil World*. InterVarsity, 2010 (1992).

Terry C. Muck. "Evangelicals and Interreligious Dialogue." *Journal of the Evangelical Theological Society* 36, no. 4 (December 1993): 517–29.

———. "Interreligious Dialogue and Evangelism." *Buddhist-Christian Studies* 17 (1997): 139–51.

———. "Interreligious Dialogue: Conversations That Enable Christian Witness." *International Bulletin of Missionary Research* 35, no. 4 (October 2011): 187–92.

Terry C. Muck and Frances S. Adeney. *Christianity Encountering World Religions: The Practice of Mission in the Twenty-first Century*. Baker Academic, 2009.

John Muir. *John Muir: Nature Writings*. Library of America, 1997.

Max Müller. *Lectures on the Origin and Growth of Religion*. Forgotten Books, 2012 (1878).

Ronald Nash. *Is Jesus the Only Savior?* Zondervan, 1994.

Harold A. Netland. *Dissonant Voices: Religious Pluralism and the Question of Truth*. Eerdmans, 1991.

———. *Encountering Religious Pluralism: The Challenge to Christian Faith and Mission*. InterVarsity, 2001.

———. "Religious Exclusivism." In *Philosophy of Religion: Classic and Contemporary Issues*, edited by Paul Copan and Chad Meister, 67–80. Blackwell, 2008.

Bruce J. Nicholls, ed. *The Unique Christ in Our Pluralistic World.* Baker, 1994.

Friedrich Nietzsche. *The Antichrist.* In *The Portable Nietzsche*, edited by Walter Kaufmann, 633–44. Viking, 1968.

John Noss and David Noss. *A History of the World Religions.* 9th ed. Prentice Hall, 1994.

Rudolf Otto. *The Idea of the Holy.* Oxford University Press, 1958.

J. I. Packer. "Evangelicals and the Way of Salvation." In *Evangelical Affirmations*, edited by Kenneth S. Kantzer and Carl F. H. Henry, 107–36. Zondervan, 1990.

Talcott Parsons. *The Evolution of Societies.* Prentice Hall, 1997.

Clark Pinnock. *A Wideness in God's Mercy: The Finality of Jesus Christ in a World of Religions.* Zondervan, 1992.

Christine Pohl. *Making Room: Recovering Hospitality as a Christian Tradition.* Eerdmans, 1999.

Vinoth Ramachandra. *Subverting Global Myths: Theology and the Public Issues Shaping Our World.* IVP Academic, 2008.

Bob Robinson. *Jesus and the Religions: Retrieving a Neglected Example for a Multicultural World.* Wipf & Stock, 2012.

Stanley J. Samartha. *Courage for Dialogue: Ecumenical Issues in Interreligious Relationships.* WCC, 1981.

John Sanders. *No Other Name? An Investigation into the Destiny of the Unevangelized.* Eerdmans, 1992.

Ferdinand de Saussure. *Course in General Linguistics.* Oxford University Press, 2006 (1916).

R. Kendall Soulen. "Go Tell Pharaoh, or, Why Empires Prefer a Nameless God." *Cultural Encounters: A Journal for the Theology of Culture* 1, no. 2 (Summer 2005): 49–59.

John Stott. *The Authentic Jesus.* Marshall, Morgan & Scott, 1985.

Charles Taylor. *A Secular Age.* Belknap Press of Harvard University Press, 2007.

Pierre Teilhard de Chardin. *The Divine Milieu.* Harper Perennial Modern Classics, 2001 (1957).

Terrance Tiessen. *Who Can Be Saved?* InterVarsity, 2004.

Kevin Vanhoozer, ed. *The Trinity in a Pluralistic Age.* Eerdmans, 1997.

Joachim Wach. *The Comparative Study of Religion.* Columbia University Press, 1969 (1958).

Robert Louis Wilken. *Remembering the Christian Past.* Eerdmans, 1995.

Christopher J. H. Wright. "The Christian and Other Religions? The Biblical Evidence." *Themelios* 9, no. 2 (1984): 4–15.

———. *What's So Unique about Jesus?* Monarch, 1990.

Timothy Yates. *Christian Mission in the Twentieth Century.* Cambridge, 1995.

Amos Yong. *Hospitality and the Other: Pentecost, Christian Practices, and the Neighbor.* Orbis Books, 2008.

Part 2

World Religions

5

World Religions Introduction

Terry C. Muck

For some reason, in about 500 BCE, the world experienced a remarkable shift in its collective approach to religion. Prior to this time human religious experience had been largely local, monistic, unreflective, and world affirming. Beginning in 500 BCE that began to change. Religious expressions emerged that claimed universality for themselves and backed up that claim by teaching a transcendent realm to which we could all aspire, mainly by rejecting ultimate allegiances to the mundane world of our everyday experience.

The historical philosopher Karl Jaspers named this era the Axial Age. Sociologist Robert Bellah called the religions that emerged from this period historic religions. Max Müller said the age occurred because of worldwide social unrest and the resulting mass migrations from central Asia to the south. The prophet Isaiah chronicled the shift within the Judeo-Christian tradition from henotheism to monotheism by lamenting about his own spiritual condition: "Woe to me! . . . I am ruined! For I am a man of unclean lips" (6:5). The age of personal religion, focused largely on the individual human self, had begun.

Study Aid #10
World Religions (Adherents, 2010)

Christianity	2.3 billion
Islam	1.5 billion
Hinduism	1 billion
Buddhism	500 million
Judaism	14.5 million

Study Aid #11
World Map of Religious Distribution

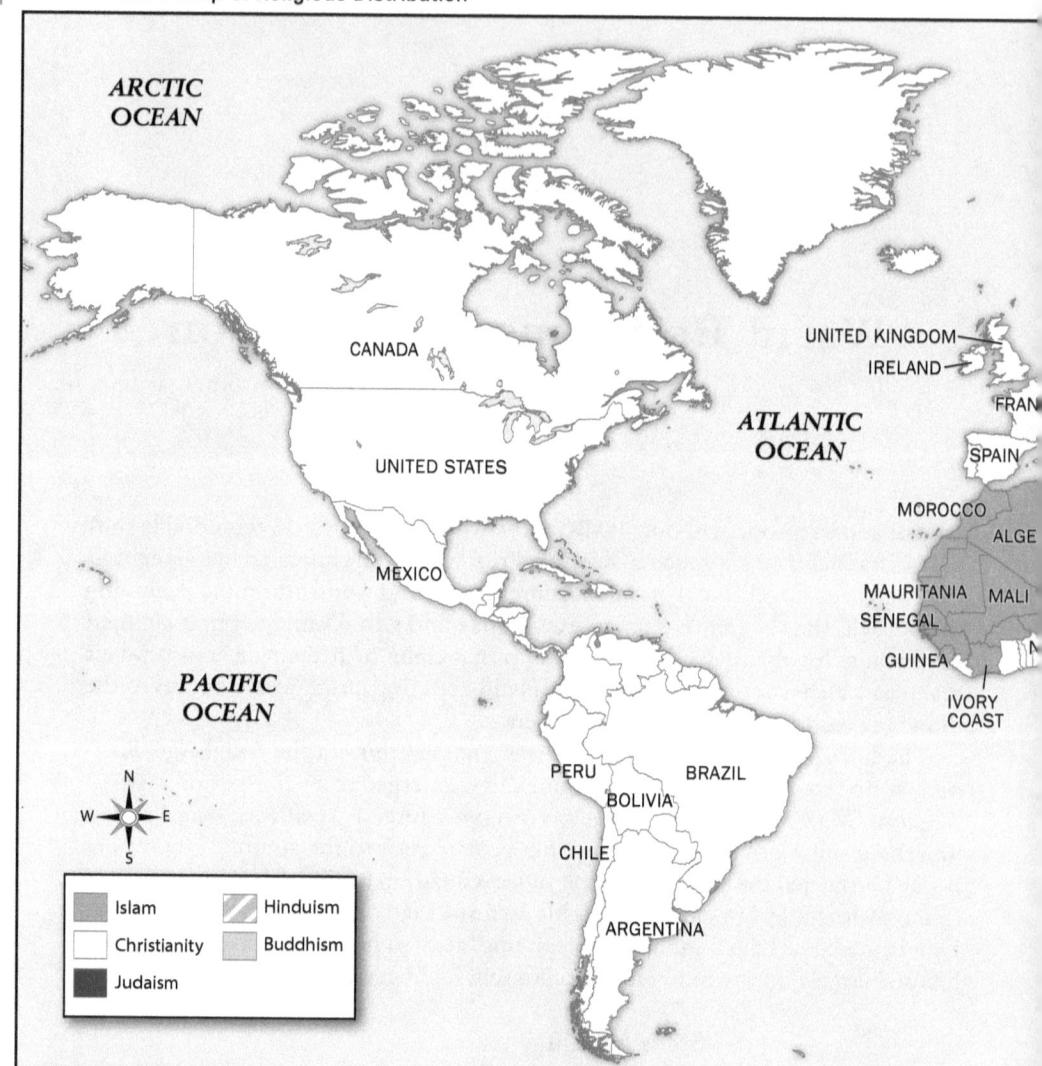

Today we commonly call the religions that emerged from the Axial Age world religions. World religions have three distinguishing characteristics. They are old, large, and cross-cultural.

The "old" characteristic is more descriptive than essential. Hinduism, Buddhism, Judaism, Christianity, and Islam have endured. They have been socially meaningful; that is, they have survived because they have satisfied human spiritual needs.

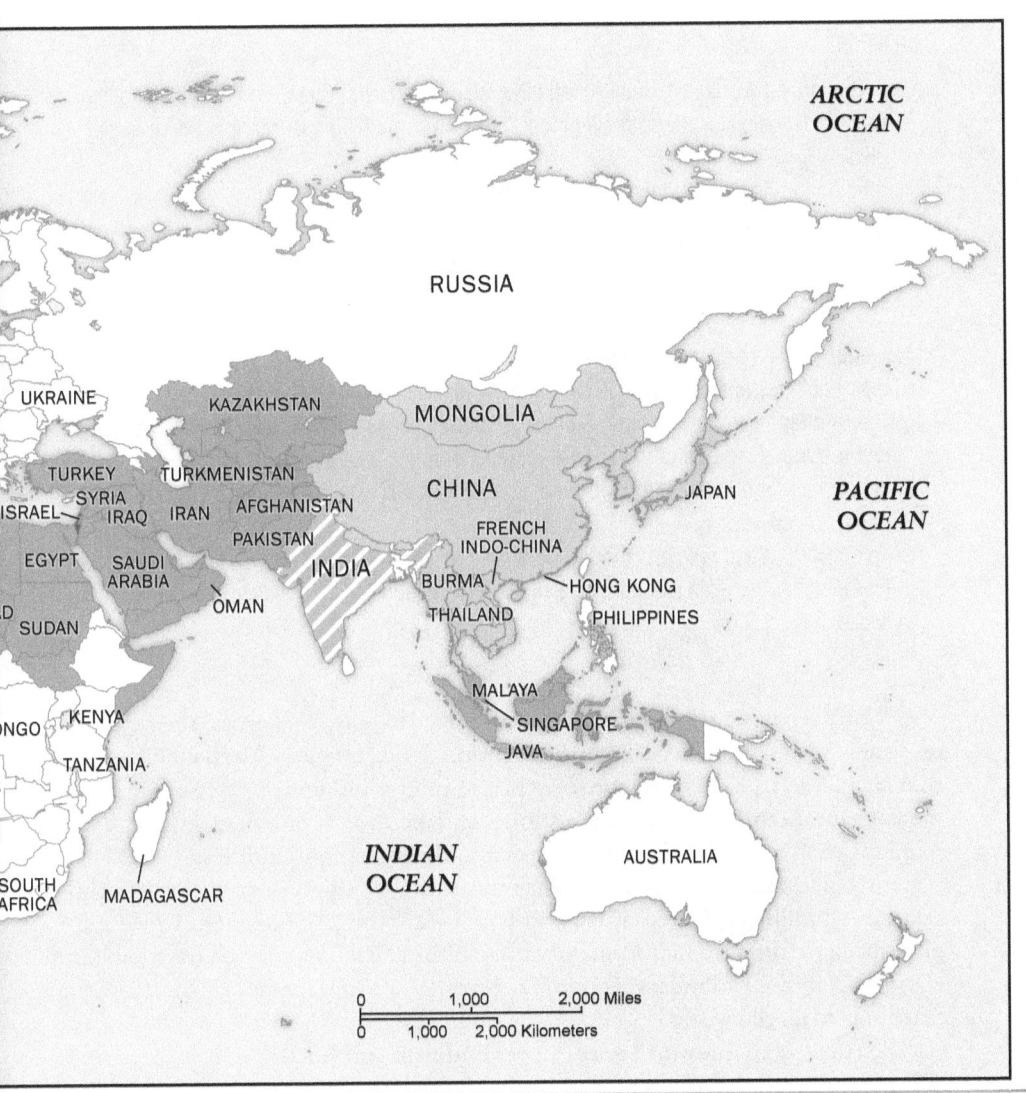

For the same reasons, they have grown "large." Four of the five world religions we describe in the pages that follow are the largest in the world: there are over two billion Christians, one and a half billion Muslims, one billion Hindus, and five hundred million Buddhists. Judaism is an exception to this demographic characteristic, for reasons noted below.

Perhaps the most important of the three characteristics is the "cross-cultural"

> **Study Aid #12**
>
> Characteristics of World Religions
>
> Demographic Characteristics
>
> > Old: The largest world religions (Christianity, Islam, Hinduism, Buddhism) are thousands of years old. Sociologists would claim that this says something positive about their social utility.
> > Large: World religions by definition tend to be large. See Study Aid #10.
> > Cross-cultural: The defining characteristic of a world religion is that it has the capacity to cross cultures and grow in cultural areas in which it did not originate.
>
> Essential Characteristics
>
> > Universal: World religions not only have the capacity to cross cultures, but also teach that their doctrines and/or practices have validity for all peoples, everywhere.
> > World-in-need-of-transformation: Generally world religions operate in a two-tier cosmology, one a spiritual realm and the other a material one. The material realm is to be merely coped with (or denied, or transformed) so that navigation to the more desired spiritual realm is achieved.
> > Differentiated: World religions tend to have defined sectors in complex, differentiated societies, and operate alongside the other sectors, such as the political, economic, and social.

one. World religions are religions that have spread extensively beyond their culture of origin. Such spread has been both intentional (i.e., missional) and incidental—that is, a largely unintended consequence of migration, military actions, and/or mercantile enterprises. In both intentional and incidental spreading, however, the religions took root in their new cultures in indigenous communities.

One could make the argument that three of the religions we include in this section—Buddhism, Christianity, and Islam—are the quintessential world religions because they are intentionally cross-cultural. That is, they all have explicit charges from their founders, Gautama, Jesus, and Muhammad, to spread their teachings to all the world.

The two remaining world religions—Hinduism and Judaism—have been and still are ambivalent as to whether they should make explicit attempts to gain new adherents. It is probably accurate to say that over the years, as India has modernized, Hinduism has increasingly seen cross-cultural growth. Judaism's ambivalence toward proselytizing or missional activity has resulted in a declining world population (the only world religion so declining) and raises the question of whether it should really be called a world religion. It has spread largely as a result of the Diaspora, the worldwide spread of the Jewish community when its community of origin, Palestine, fell to Roman conquerors. Due to persecution,

Jews have often been forced to live in close, closed communities. And due to the identity Jewish people insist on between biblical religion and culture, Judaism has to a large extent not broken out of that culture.

The distinguishing characteristic of world religions is their shift from the essentially world-affirming posture of indigenous religions to a world-in-need-of-transformation posture. A pluralistic outlook emerged contrasting a positive, transcendent, spiritual realm of goodness and light (heaven, *nirvana*, *moksha*) with the everyday, mundane, material world of darkness in which we live.

This switch in cosmological understanding was accompanied by a switch in anthropological understanding. The self, the individual human self, became the principal religious actor, whose religious job, so to speak, was to relate positively to the transcendent realm, however defined. The goal was not harmony with the world but salvation from the material world or enlightenment from a world of delusion.

Practically, this resulted in a separation of the political and religious institutions, if not in fact then at least in function. Social actors differed not only in terms of elite and folk but also in terms of political and religious. Fourfold social structures (political, religious, elite, folk) became common.

The social implications of these new structures loomed large. Political rulers became subject to judgment by religions and religious standards. Such judgments could lead to legitimation and affirmation but also to rebellion and reform.

When Christianity comes in contact with a world religion such as Hinduism, Buddhism, Judaism, or Islam, a major cultural clash occurs. In the following sections we deal with each of these clashes—Christianity with Hinduism, Buddhism, Judaism, Islam—with a package of five essays for each religion.

Study Aid #13

The Five Essays

Each of the world religions has five essays devoted to it:

- History, Beliefs, Practices: A short summary of the essential facts of the religious tradition in question.
- Christian Contacts: An outline of the primary contacts of this religious tradition with Christianity. Each contact is briefly described.
- Theological Exchanges: Overall, this religion's contacts with Christianity have tended to produce similar results in terms of theological issues that arose as a result of the contact.
- Current Issues: The key issues (theological, social, psychological, political) that surround Christianity's contact with this religion in today's world.
- Adherent Essay: This essay is written by a scholarly devotee of the religious tradition in question. We have asked him or her to be both scholarly and personal in describing the religion's relationships with Christianity.

We begin with a brief description of the "History, Beliefs, and Practices" of the religious tradition in question. Our essayists have only been given a couple thousand words to sum up the most complex religions in the world. Thus, they have focused on what would be most common to the diverse sects and denominations each religion encompasses.

The second essay, "Christian Contacts," outlines the history of Christianity's contact with the specific religion. The authors highlight the major historical contacts between the traditions, conveying a sense of how the contact came about and what the outcome was.

The collective outcomes of the contacts/clashes produced a set of theological exchanges that have become characteristic of other contacts between Christianity and this particular religion. The third essay, "Theological Exchanges," summarizes these theological questions, most of which are operative in some form today.

The fourth essay, "Current Issues," recognizes that not all of the issues have strict theological roots. Politics, economics, and culture all produce their own spin on Christian–non-Christian contacts. Sometimes theological language masks these more mundane roots.

Each of these first four essays is written by an expert religious studies scholar. The fifth, however—the "Adherent Essay"—is written by a person who belongs to the tradition. These individuals express in personal terms what it means to be a member of their religious tradition, focusing on their religion's relationship with Christianity.

6

Hinduism: History, Beliefs, Practices

RICHARD FOX YOUNG

Years ago, when I began my studies of "Hinduism" (quotation marks seem called for, since many things go by that name), I wanted to get inside of it (insofar as I possibly could) through the life of an individual whom I felt that I knew rather intimately. This, perhaps, was my historian's conceit. The individual had long since passed on, but I had ample material to work with, biographically, opening a window (widely, I thought) onto what it was to be a "traditional" Hindu in Varanasi, the most sacred site of all in Indian geography. The individual I have in mind lived in the nineteenth century and was called Nilakantha, a name for Shiva. Born into a Shaiva family surnamed Goreh, he was a Brahmin of impeccably high status, a Chitpavana. Raised religiously, Nilakantha immersed himself in the Ganges each morning, recited prayers invoking divine blessing, and spent his days mastering a vast corpus of sacred texts, the Vedas. Akin to Greek and Latin, Sanskrit is the language of divinity; for Vedic hermeneutics, Nilakantha needed linguistic tools, grammar, and lexicography. Though born Shaiva, through his studies he became concerned that Shiva lacked virtues that the divine ought to have and devoted himself to Vishnu instead. True to form, his was a life lived Vedically (as a Christian might aspire to live biblically).

Later, I learned of another Hinduism, less Sanskritic, more vernacular, and as enthusiastically Shaiva in orientation as Nilakantha's had been Vaishnava. Here, my historical interlocutor was Arumuka Pillai, a contemporary of Nilakantha's down on the northern tip of Sri Lanka (Jaffna), where Brahmins of any kind were few and far between. As a Vellala of the cultivator caste (which ranks near the bottom of the Hindu social hierarchy), Arumuka was ineligible for Vedic studies,

49

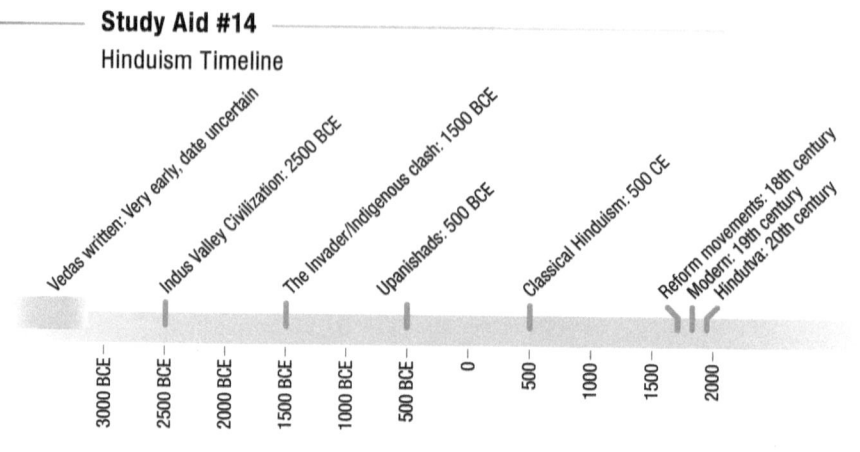

Study Aid #14
Hinduism Timeline

technically. Regionally, however, the Vellala were dominant (being propertied landowners) and pretty much able to do as they pleased. As assiduous in his ablutions as Nilakantha, Arumuka (whose name also gives him away as a Shaivite) immersed himself in a different corpus of sacred texts; these were largely vernacular texts, in Tamil: the *Agamas*. Centered on Shiva, the apical divinity who will brook no rival, they prescribe a temple-based worship that Arumuka was an avid proponent of. This was an alternative universe of *Agama*-centric Tamil Hinduism, unlike Nilakantha's Vedic, Sanskritic universe, and it had quite a different kind of gravitational pull.

Later still, back to the north, in a village off the beaten track near Jaipur in Rajasthan, I became acquainted (this time personally) with a woman known locally as Bhawani Ma (Mother Bhawani). Here, outside a small, brightly painted shrine, tended by her husband, a truck driver, in his off-hours, Bhawani Ma enters a deep state of trance, possessed by a goddess, originally (no one can say when) a woman of the Rajput (warrior) caste who had immolated herself on the funeral pyre of her husband, a casualty of snakebite. Villagers approach Bhawani Ma for help; finding lost objects is a specialty of hers, but so too is advice on lost affections. After all, as the perfect wife (perfectly devoted, that is, to her husband), Bhawani Ma knows a thing or two (when possessed) about keeping husbands and wives together. Rajasthan knows of many women like her. Vehicles of the divine, as it were, they embody Shaktism (from *shakti*, literally, "power," associated with goddess worship), the third of India's most prevalent theisms after Vaishnavism and Shaivism.

Much as I would like, one simply cannot cover, globally, all that wears the label "Hinduism" in the overview above. And so, before anything else, one needs clarity on how the phenomena are to be sorted out, which things included and which excluded. Like any religion, Hinduism lives only in the concrete, temporally, and not in the abstract, timelessly. In striving to be an unbiased observer (who, alas, is never fully transparent, even to himself), I aspire to rise above all Hindu normativities by which other Hinduisms are judged (Vaishnava versus Shaiva versus Shakta). That being said, the believer's self-understanding provides an indispensible point of departure; naturally, one's perspective may pose a challenge (and probably will) to one's self-understanding, theologically. One must reflect on such differences, deeply, once the possibility of interreligious understanding exists. Until that point, the rules of engagement are to be construed empirically. Accordingly, when Hindus find it difficult to recognize themselves in each other, I am much impressed (and feel that I may have something to learn from them) that they do not utterly and absolutely deny that the Vaishnava, Shaiva, or Shakta "other" is a Hindu. But I am also content to think of Hinduism (as I do of Christianity) as an agglomeration of things (beliefs, practices, etc.) that can be named "Hinduism" for convenience, but ought not to be treated as an invariable substance. Substance (or essence) is a philosophical concept and, as such, is best left to philosophers; as a historian of religions, I am agnostic on all such questions. In a brief overview, one must also avoid an abracadabra approach, as if the doors of comprehension might magically open up if one could only get the password right. Sufficient unto itself is the task of disagglomeration, and being clear on how it is to be accomplished.

Of my three Hinduisms, here I can include only two, that of Nilakantha and Arumuka; Bhawani Ma cannot make the cut, but only because her "Hinduism" centers on beliefs and practices that have no "orthodox" analogue. Having such analogues is why Hinduisms of the other two escape being cut. In history of religions, orthodoxy simply has to be situational and variable; on another occasion, it might be a good exercise to have a second look at orthodoxy, from Bhawani Ma's point of view. That cannot happen here, however, which is unfortunate. Though not of the mainstream in terms of Vedic respectability, her orthodox rivals, Nilakantha and Arumuka, are clearly a sideshow, demographically. From the time of Robert Redfield, social science and religious studies scholars have denominated Bhawani Ma's "Hinduism" the "Little Tradition," reserving the "Great Tradition" for the likes of my two other "specimen" Hindus. Numberwise, the nomenclature might be reversed; between them, one might imagine the Little Tradition as an ocean, out of which, here and there, Great Tradition islands rise. To go with that image, it helps to think of Great Tradition Hinduism as Sanskritic as opposed to the vernacular Little Tradition; as pan-Indian instead of local; and as a tradition that fosters ambitious goals, soteriologically (e.g., *moksha*, release from transmigration), instead of conjugal harmony and other lesser goods that Bhawani Ma is good at arranging. Neither, though, is sealed off from the other hermetically, and between the two their relationship might be described as a loose-fitting hypostatic union. Hereafter, however, I leave Bhawani Ma aside (but with brief comments, later, on goddesses in "traditional" Hinduism). And with these clarifications, the quotation marks around "Hinduism" can come off.

In one's approach, it helps to be alert to the uneven playing field Hinduism competes on, as it were, when taken out of its natural linguistic medium (Sanskrit or any of the Indian vernaculars). English is up to the task, but any interreligious literacy is going to need a foreign-language vocabulary. To start with, talk of Hinduism as a "religion" seems unavoidable; the very term, however, skews our understanding in ways that are actually very European (and, indeed, Christian). Having used the term, I need to backtrack and correct the misapprehension that Hinduism is about holding Hindu beliefs in a correct—that is, orthodox—way. Nothing could be further from the truth, although Hinduism is not utterly laissez-faire, beliefwise. "Faith," if one can call it that (*shraddha*), has a grammar, and religious claims cannot be made willy-nilly. Still, one has to understand that orthodoxy in Hinduism is mainly about orthopraxy, the norms of right conduct. Behavior is, or ought to be, guided and regulated, punished and rewarded by *dharma* (from a verb meaning to "uphold" or "sustain"), making it a poor candidate to carry the heavily cognitive, belief-oriented burden of the word "religion." This, however, it has been made to do (Hinduism now being called *Hindudharma*, Christianity *Khrishtadharma*, etc.), and so to recover a clear sense of it, one needs to strip it of any vestige of normativity with respect to belief. There is pushback from this in the complaint one often hears from Hindus who say that Hinduism is not so much a religion as a "way of life."

Norms for the Hindu "way of life" have been derived from the sacred corpus called Veda ("knowledge"), of hoary antiquity. The oldest collection, dating to the early second millennium BCE, is the *Rig*, containing "hymns" of praise to gods (*deva*) and goddesses (*devi*). In today's pantheon, few of these retain a place. Nor are the later collections, the *Sama* (songs), *Yajur* (ritual formulas), and *Atharva* (hymns and incantations) living texts, except in a rather attenuated sense. The priestly (brahminical) cultus of which they were the mainstay found itself gradually superseded by the Hinduisms remaining to be mentioned. Still, the basic morphology of Hinduism is discernible in the Veda. One can trace back to this—including the Upanishads, the last stratum of all, which predates the Christian era—the origin of notions having to do with *karma* (the postmortem fruition of human actions, good and evil), of beginningless rebirth and redeath (*samsara*), and of final liberation or release (*moksha*) from, as it were, a cosmic merry-go-round that never stops, eschatologically. Populating this cosmos, the Veda talks of four categories

Study Aid #15
Hindu Divisions

Vaishnava	642 million
Shaiva	250 million
Shaktism	30 million
Neo-Hinduism	20 million
Reform Hinduisms	5 million

of persons (*varnas*): the quartet of Brahmins (ritualists), Kshatriyas (warriors and rulers), Vaishyas (commoners), and Shudras (serfs). Ideally, life was envisioned as involving, sequentially, youth and study, adulthood and householdership, old age and renunciation in quest of final liberation. Note, though, that *dharma* was unexchangeable; neither universal nor individualized, one's *dharma* was defined by birth. Therefore, there was no single Hindu "way of life."

Impressive as it looks, a society of this description may not have existed, actually; the description is less a real morphology *of* ancient India than an ideal morphology *for* it. Hinduisms taking shape from the Christian era onward began to emerge with specificities of their own. One myth that has to be punctured is that the Veda offers a template for understanding Hindu society today. To start with, the social hierarchy on the ground is vastly more complicated than one might imagine, extrapolating from ancient texts. Overall, castes number in the thousands; in any locality, one finds several dozen. Interactions between them (involving commensality, marriage, etc.) are regulated, biosocially, by complex notions based on purity and impurity unrelated to the social functions of priest, warrior or ruler, commoner, and serf. The textual prototype omits any mention of "untouchability," even though much of the Indian population still carries that stigma (modern constitutional safeguards notwithstanding).

Hugely important for the impact it had on Hinduism's social profile, the exclusion of "untouchables" from the temple-based cultus was mitigated by the rise to prominence of *bhakti*, a less structured form of devotional theism more open to all and less regulatable, brahminically. Arising in tandem are three sectarian formations (called *sampradayas*) oriented toward one of the three divinities already alluded to, whose rise to prominence can be seen in the Veda: Vishnu; Shiva; and Devi, the goddess (whose followers are called, respectively, Vaishnavas, Shaivas, and Shaktas). Though deeply sectarian, such Hinduisms are monolatric, overall; that is to say, though centered on a particular divinity, the reality and even the limited efficacy of other divinities are not absolutely denied (yet they may be inferiorized, intentionally and more or less publicly, depending on context).

A last difference of note is the existence of an extensive body of extra-Vedic sacred texts barnacled onto each of the three sectarian formations already mentioned, but playing a huge role in Hindu religious life, down to the present. Of my three "specimen" Hindus, Nilakantha and Arumuka lived largely within this extra-Vedic realm (Arumuka more than Nilakantha); Bhawani Ma's ties even to extra-Vedic texts are far looser. Best of all would be to dispense with the notion of "canon" as too restrictive (and Christian). The Bhagavad Gita ("Song of the Blessed Lord") is a case in point. Nowadays considered the Hindu scripture par excellence, the Gita is actually a chapter in the Mahabharata, one of the great Vaishnava epics in which Krishna, one of Vishnu's *avatars* (from a verb meaning "descend"), instructs Arjuna, a warrior, on the indestructibility of the *atman* (literally, "self," derivatively, "soul"). Being extra-Vedic makes no difference to its popularity, even beyond Vaishnavism.

> **Study Aid #16**
>
> Hindu Beliefs
>
> *Brahman*: The Oneness of all.
> *Brahman-atman*: The division of the world we see into *Brahman* and individual selves; or a unity that includes all.
> *Samsara*: The endless round of rebirths that all experience.
> *Karma*: The value (positive and negative) one accrues for doing (or not doing) one's duty.
> *Dharma*: Duty, determined by birth, caste, *jati*.
> *Moksha*: Freedom or release from *samsara*.

Time rolls on, but religions do too, and among the newer Hinduisms having distinctive orientations, neo-Hinduism is perhaps the foremost. Emerging first in Calcutta (Kolkata) in Bengal in the early 1800s (but also elsewhere on the Indian periphery where Europe converged on India most palpably), neo-Hinduism pushes beyond the parameters of Vedic and even extra-Vedic sacred texts and manifests a remarkable receptivity to religions that, historically, were altogether extra-Hindu—Islam and Christianity in particular. Beginning with Ram Mohun Roy (1772–1833), who acted as a conduit for both Islamic and Christian influence, a movement gained momentum that came to be called the Bengal Renaissance, an efflorescence of cross-cultural and interreligious interaction. An ardent proponent of Hindu "reform," Roy called on Hindus to renounce their monolatric ways and worship the *one* true God, the Unconditioned *Brahman*, aniconically. Though his "Society of [Friends of] Brahman" (the Brahmo Samaj) lasted but a few years, Roy was a seminal figure who inspired many, including the preeminent neo-Hindu of all, Mahatma K. Gandhi (1867–1947). Genealogically, all neo-Hinduism enjoys an affinity of outlook that might be called universalistic to the nth degree, making it averse to being labeled an "ordinary" religion on a par with others. As Wilhelm Halbfass (1991, 51) observes:

> Instead, it is—according to this view—a framework, a concordance and unifying totality of sects. . . . It is said to be the "eternal religion," religion in or behind all religions, a kind of "metareligion," a structure potentially ready to comprise and reconcile within itself all the religions of the world, just as it contains and reconciles the so-called Hindu sects, such as Shaivism or Vaishnavism and their subordinate "sectarian" formations.

Nowadays, most of the Hinduisms introduced above flourish abroad wherever the South Asian Diaspora is found. That being so, an exclusively book-based—even or especially an iHindu internet-based—interreligious literacy ought to be discouraged. Around the corner or down the block, one has in one's neighborhood unparalleled opportunities for observing "living" texts—believers themselves—making theology "visible" in worship at the different temples that now dot our landscapes. "The history of religions," as Diana Eck (2001, 22) says, "is unfolding before our eyes."

Sources

Wendy Doniger. *Hindu Myths*. Penguin, 2004.

Diana Eck. *A New Religious America: How a "Christian Country" Has Become the World's Most Religiously Diverse Nation*. HarperSanFrancisco, 2001.

Wilhelm Halbfass. *Tradition and Reflection: Explorations in Indian Thought*. SUNY Press, 1991.

Arvind Sharma. *Classical Hindu Thought: An Introduction*. Oxford University Press, 2001.

7

Hinduism: Christian Contacts

RICHARD FOX YOUNG

Historically and phenomenologically, one finds a multiplicity of Hinduisms; "Christianity," likewise, is hardly an undifferentiated unity. When thinking of how these religions have interacted, diachronically, it makes a great deal of difference *whose* Hinduism and *whose* Christianity one has in one's sights. There ought to be no ambiguity; the pairings need to make sense. Today's neo-Hindus interact with Christians quite differently from the way orthodox Hindus did in earlier centuries. Then again, one ought to avoid simplistic generalizations about a consistently "Christian" way of interacting with Hindus, as if Syro-Malabar Christians of the fourth or fifth century interacted with Hindus in the same way as the sixteenth-century Italian Jesuits, the eighteenth-century German Pietists, or the nineteenth-century British Anglicans did. Each encounter had its own irreducible specificity; accordingly, my overview is primarily focused on instances of interactions involving cognitive exchange of a religio-theological kind.

Regrettably, the earliest Hindu-Christian encounters are mostly undocumentable. Despite the continuous existence of Syro-Malabar Christianity in southern India since antiquity, virtually nothing is known of how Hindus might have regarded their Christian neighbors (known as Thomas Christians, after the apostle who evangelized India, as their tradition holds). Here and hereafter, there is a silence toward Christianity (Christianity as variously confessed and practiced by Christians, indigenous or exogenous) that might be described as deafening. Insofar as Indian literatures are concerned, this silence was tentatively broken only in the eighteenth century, although silence in and of itself was a kind of response, loud and clear. As one Vitthal Shastri (d. 1867), an eminent Hindu of Varanasi, once explained to a British friend (Ballantyne 1860, xli): "Our silence is not a sign of our admission of defeat, which the Missionaries think [it is]." Such silence, he added, was a gesture of Hindu civility in the face of Christian provocation.

Over time, consciences became aggrieved and quarrels broke out. Among those who rose up in defense were Hindus of remarkable epistemic integrity, trained in the ancient traditions of Hindu apologetics honed in conflict with Jains, Buddhists, and Materialists. Naturally, however, intellectual confrontations did not occur in a vacuum; India's relations with Europe were a huge complication. So conflicted were they throughout much of the colonial period that missionaries had a hard time convincing Indian onlookers of Christianity's religious bona fides: only at a point as recent as the second half of the nineteenth century was it commonly acknowledged that people who called themselves Christians could be credibly understood to actually have a religion (here, Hindus would invoke the term *dharma*). Under colonialism, the asymmetry in Hindu-Christian relations meant that encounters in the public realm were often fraught with risk.

An instance illustrating how difficult it could be for Hindus to recognize in Christianity a properly normative code of conduct (that is, a *dharma*), not to mention the difficulty of recognizing in Christianity a system of cognitively coherent beliefs that could be called a religion or faith (a more recent meaning of the term, dating to India's encounter with Europe), comes from Tiruchendur, a Shaivite temple town on the southeastern coast in the mid-sixteenth century when Francis Xavier (1506–52), a Jesuit, was catechizing the Paravas. This was a downtrodden convert community living on the Fishery Coast, where they had traditionally provided cheap labor for the lucrative annual pearl harvest. Elbowing in, the Portuguese had broken the monopoly of local merchants, who traditionally had strong ties of patronage to Tiruchendur, where the six-headed, twelve-armed Tamil god, Murukan, was enshrined. Some fifty years after Xavier, the Portuguese sacked the temple and desecrated the sanctum sanctorum by the slaughter of a cow.

Already, however, the Portuguese were notorious for their flagrant misbehavior, which explains why Xavier found himself unwelcome in 1543 when he arrived uninvited and proclaimed the gospel to the temple's Brahmin officiants. In return, Xavier was subjected to a barrage of questions (Young 1989, 73): "Does the soul," went one, "die with the body as it does in the case of brute beasts?" In effect, Xavier's interlocutors were accusing him of being a Materialist (Carvaka), an adherent of the most deviant sect known to ancient India. Materialists were despised for denying the existence of an eternal self (*atman*) distinct from the body, and for having a devil-may-care attitude toward life that encouraged culinary excess and sexual laxity. This was not a good start for Christianity, and yet the situation was still very much the same in the early seventeenth century when Roberto de Nobili (1577–1656) joined the Jesuit mission at Madurai in the South Indian interior. Much more culturally adroit and linguistically gifted than Xavier, de Nobili attempted to de-Europeanize Catholicism. Long afterward, however, the indigeneity of Christianity remained in doubt.

Study Aid #17

Spread of Hinduism

At the beginning of the eighteenth century, when Protestant missionaries were active in the South, such doubts were still alive. Asked why the Tamil people kept Christians at arm's length socially, a Hindu replied (Grafe 1972, 51): "Christianity is despised by us ... because Christians slaughter cows and eat them." This already-familiar motif was only the first in a litany of complaints about European cultural abominations that heightened the "otherness" of the new religion. Remarkable, then, is that any interest in Christianity was evinced at all. Indeed, instead of utter incompatibility, some voices emphasized complementarity. We hear of this development thanks to the empathic listening and insatiable curiosity of Bartholomäus Ziegenbalg (1682–1719), a German Pietist commissioned by Frederick IV of Denmark to initiate a Lutheran mission in the kingdom of Tanjore at Tranquebar, a Danish enclave on the southeast coast (then called Malabar). One voice was that of a Vaishnava, who approached Ziegenbalg to say that "he desir'd to confer with me amicably about the great Things and Matters of Religion." His interlocutor's robust defense of Vaishnava inclusivism is of considerable interest (Philipps 1719, 14).

> I believe all you say of God's Dealings with you White Europeans, to be true; but his Appearances and Revelations among us Black Malabarians, have been quite otherwise. And the Revelations he made of himself in this Land are as firmly believ'd here to be true, as you believe those made in your Country: For as Christ in Europe was made Man, so here our God [Vishnu] was born among us Malabarians; And as you hope for Salvation through Christ, so we hope for Salvation through [Vishnu]; and to save you one way, and us another, is one of the Pastimes and Diversions of Almighty God.

That is to say, no *dharma*—or, in today's parlance, no "religion"—can be *the* Dharma; diversity ought to be celebrated, and Christians overreach themselves when they talk of Christianity as the *one true* religion.

There is, however, a less-familiar but equally representative anti-Christian Vaishnava exclusivism that also needs to be recognized, first found in the nineteenth century, the first century when full-scale theological texts on Christianity are found in any Indian language. One of the first comes from Varanasi in North India, where missionaries proclaimed the good news on the banks of the Ganges. Among the many who heard them envision for India a new identity grounded in a different *dharma* was Nilakantha Goreh (1825–95), a young Vaishnava Brahmin. As a Sanskritically literate, orthodox Hindu who had been taught that reason ought to conform to revelation, Nilakantha was deeply troubled by the missionaries' appeal to reason in their criticism of the scriptures he believed were sacred and self-validating. Their discourses reminded him of a story in the Vishnu Purana (one of the same texts being criticized) about the origins of heresy. Aeons ago in a cosmic conflict between gods (*devas*) and demons (*asuras*), the gods were losing until Vishnu conjured up a magical figure called Mayamoha, who tricked the demons into embracing a *dharma* based on nonviolence (*ahimsa*). Naturally, this turned out to be a good thing for the gods, who then triumphed over their former rivals. Actually, the *dharma* depicted by the Vishnu Purana is a kind of anti-*dharma*; traditionally, it has been identified as Buddhism. To Nilakantha, however, the story seems a plausible foreshadowing of Christianity, which he accordingly condemns as a fraudulent *dharma*. And so, rephrasing things, *to damn you one way and to save us another* is just as acceptably Vaishnava as to say, unconditionally, that God saves all people of faith and people of all faiths.

Against this background, one can understand why Nilakantha was unwilling to learn *from* Christianity as Christianity. He was, however, at least willing to learn *about* it—the better to oppose it—until eventually it worked itself into him so deeply that he embraced it himself, becoming first an evangelical Anglican and later an Anglo-Catholic. Actually, Nilakantha was living on the cusp of major religious developments in the interior of India that were gradually radiating outward from their epicenter in the cosmopolitan cultures of metropolitan India (Calcutta [Kolkata], Madras [Chennai], and Bombay [Mumbai]). On the periphery of India, constraints on extra-Vedic religious and theological inquiry had been loosened up already by the emergence of neo-Hinduism. One can take the "neo" in neo-Hinduism to describe an intellectual orientation more open to European thought and Christianity than that of traditionalists like Varanasi's Nilakantha. Neo-Hindus no longer felt obliged to maintain the old dogma that without the Veda to reveal it there could be no *moksha* (release from rebirth into blessedness). Along with this, all the assumptions came tumbling down that used to go unquestioned about the soteriological disqualification of Christians and followers of other non-Indic religions.

The primary catalyst of these far-reaching changes was Ram Mohun Roy (1772–1833), a Bengali religious reformer who found in the Jesus of Christianity an exemplar of the ethical ideals that he believed India ought to emulate. The Jesus he envisions in *The Precepts of Jesus* (1820), however, is a detheologized Jesus, unrecognizable as God the Son known to trinitarian Christianity. For this, Roy was mercilessly excoriated by the Baptist missionaries of Calcutta, who thought of him as an in-between figure, neither Hindu nor Christian. From him, a lineage of neo-Hindu New Testament exegesis commenced, which extends down through prominent figures such as Vivekananda (1862–1902) and Gandhi (1867–1947), among others who are known to the world outside India in no small part because of their mastery of English and other European languages.

Regardless of its high Western profile, neo-Hinduism's vitality in India itself at present can be doubted. The thaw was real but elicited a backlash from another variant of nineteenth-century Hindu reformism called the Arya Samaj. The Samaj was known for its biting criticisms of Christianity, voiced in the Hindi-language *Satyarth Prakash* (*Light of Truth*) by its founder, the Gujarati scholar-activist Dayananda Sarasvati (1824–83). Despite its polemical overkill (or because of it), the book remains popular and is widely distributed by the politically powerful organization that Dayananda founded in order to preserve, protect, and perpetuate

> **Study Aid #18**
> Christian-Hindu Contacts
>
> St. Thomas to India: 1st century
> Syro-Malabar Christians: 4th century
> Jesuits to India: 16th century
>   Francis Xavier (1506–52)
>   Roberto de Nobili (1577–1656)
> German Pietists: 18th century
>   Bartholomäus Ziegenbalg (1682–1719)
> Anglicans-Methodists-Baptists: 19th century
>   William Carey (1761–1834)
> Bramho Samaj, Arya Samaj: 19th century
>   Ram Mohan Roy (1772–1833)
>   Dayananda Sarasvati (1824–83)
> Vivekananda (1862–1902) to Chicago Parliament of World Religions: 1893
> Mahatma Gandhi's (1867–1947) nationalistic campaign: 20th century
> Hindutva, Hindu/Indian nationalism: 20th century
>   V. D. Savarkar (1883–1966)

the religion he named Arya Dharm (the "noble" *dharma*, i.e., the *dharma* he felt he had rediscovered in the most ancient strata of the Vedas). Unlike Ram Mohun Roy, Dayananda interpreted Gospel stories about Jesus at the most literal and superficial level of meaning (perhaps as payback to the missionaries who had dogged his heels and traduced the texts he held sacred as he itinerated across northern India propagating his vision of a repristinated Hinduism). A typical example is the *Satyarth Prakash*'s commentary on Matthew 17, in which Jesus cures a boy possessed by a demon and tells his disciples that they could have done the same if only they had had "faith the size of a mustard seed." Here, Dayananda castigates Jesus as an uncultured yokel (literally, in Hindi, *jangali admi*, "jungle-ish man"; Dayananda 1994, 625).

> Had Christ possessed even a little knowledge, why would he have talked such nonsense like a savage. However, as it has been said, "In a country where no trees are seen to grow, even the castor oil plant is considered to be the biggest and the best tree," in like manner in a country where none but the most ignorant savages lived, Christ was rightly considered a great man but Christ can be of no count among the learned and wise men of the present day.

Thus far, we have heard mainly from persons who were literate in the best traditions of religio-theological thought that India had to offer; formidably skilled proponents of specific, highly systematized Hinduisms, they endeavored to rigorously and vigorously defend and represent the truths to which they were epistemically committed. Naturally, their Christian interlocutors, missionaries who believed themselves and their religion to be indefeasible, were usually just as convinced and argumentative, if not more so (it was, after all, at their initiative that Hindu-Christian relations had become conflicted). To leave things here, however, would give the wrong impression. Factually and historically, one can adduce good evidence that Hindus and Christians have also coexisted peacefully, especially when the affinity they feel for each other expresses itself at the level of a simple faith grounded in theistic devotionalism. This can be either Hindu or Christian, although *bhakti*, the term used for describing it, is germane mainly to Indic religions.

Very movingly, I recall learning of how a Bengali Hindu named Ramacandra, language tutor to William Hodge Mill (1792–1853), a Cambridge divine sent out to Calcutta as the principal of India's first Anglican theological institution (Bishop's College, Calcutta), composed for him a lovely piece of epic poetry in Sanskrit on Christ (Khrishta) as the incarnation (*avatara*) of the Word (*Shabda* [= Logos]). This was in the 1820s, and until then, the scholarly and scholastic Mill had been trying to convert India with dense translations of the Christian creeds. The uncomplicated affection felt by Ramacandra for the figure at the very heart of Christian faith was for Mill transformative, almost conversion-like in its intensity. The long-term consequences were actually quite profound: having done with debate, diatribe, and polemics, Mill devoted the ensuing years of his life to composing a great epic in Sanskrit, the *Song of the Blessed Christ* (*Shrikhrishtasangita*), which is deeply redolent of the same fervent love of God that Ramacandra exemplified without having to be a Christian to express it. In short, although the frictions and incongruities that one finds in the encounter between Hindus and Christians are not to be flattened out or smoothed over, Hindu views on Christianity and Christian views on Hinduism have by no means always been, invariably and irreducibly, belligerent toward or subordinating of the religious "other."

Sources

James Robert Ballantyne. *The Bible for Pandits*. Benares, 1860.

H. Grafe. "Hindu Apologetics at the Beginning of the Protestant Mission Era in India." *Indian Church History Review* 6, no. 1 (June 1972): 43–69.

J. T. Philipps, ed. and trans. *Thirty-Four Conferences between the Danish Missionaries and the Malabarian Bramans (or, Heathen Priests) in the East Indies, Concerning the Truth of the Christian Religion*. H. Clements, 1719.

Dayananda Saraswati. *Light of Truth* [*Satyarth Prakash*]. Sarvadeshik Arya Pratinidhi Sabha, 1994.

Richard Fox Young. "Francis Xavier in the Perspective of the Shaivite Brahmins of Tiruchendur Temple." In *Hindu-Christian Dialogue: Perspectives and Encounters*, edited by Harold Coward, 64–79. Orbis Books, 1989.

8

Hinduism: Theological Exchanges

RICHARD FOX YOUNG

Around 1710, the Lutheran divines of Copenhagen received a letter of a most unusual kind. Sent from Tranquebar, a Danish enclave on the southeastern coast of India, it was in Tamil and addressed to them as *mahatmas* ("Great-Souled Ones"), learned in systematics (*shastra*). The author, a young Hindu called Kanapati (whose name reveals that he was a Shaiva), aspired to understand, profoundly, the religion of the Sovereign Lord (*sarveshvara*), as Christianity was called. Kanapati had been told by Bartholomäus Ziegenbalg (1682–1719), the Pietist missionary of Tranquebar, that in Europe there were theologians who were acquainted with wisdom (*jñana*). Accordingly, a letter was drafted (it survives, written Indian-fashion, on palmyra leaves), making it the oldest Indian-language document on record that offers insight into which aspects of Christianity stood in need of clarification to a person of Hindu outlook. Theologically, one sees here an opening for an almost unprecedented chapter in the history of intercultural interaction. Sadly, the Copenhagen divines failed to hold up their end of the conversation. Granted, Kanapati was asking of them a lot—648 questions in all!—but Kanapati's speaking into the void seems sadly emblematic of how much prodding it takes to elicit an interest in Hindu-Christian theological exchange, whichever side a theologian stands on.

For their part, Hindus could be equally indifferent, which makes Kanapati truly exceptional for his era. Only as recently as the sixteenth century, Madhusudana Sarasvati, a renowned systematic theologian, had smugly excluded all religions of non-Indic peoples from a treatise of his (otherwise encyclopedic with respect to religions of Indian origin). None of them, he claimed, could be salvific, for all of them were "outside the Veda." If one hears in this a resonance of *extra ecclesia nulla salus*, the medieval Roman Catholic dictum about the impossibility of salvation outside the church, that would not be off the mark. Behind the Indocentrism there lies a xenophobia, which, likewise, lurks behind Eurocentrism. The difference is that systematicians like Madhusudana were soteriological restrictivists even with respect to Hindus different from themselves. The difference that counted was actually less theological than, as it were, biosocial. Without being of the Brahmin caste, chances are that one would not even aspire to higher things, including salvation. This being the case, what could be expected of Europeans and other non-Hindus? From either perspective, that any exchange of a theological nature actually occurred ought to be thought of as a promising development.

Diachronically, the centuries from the late sixteenth through the first half of the eighteenth were a time of profoundly creative theological exchange, interculturally. How it came to be doubted, subsequently, that such a thing exists as Hindu "theology" (or, correlatively, that "philosophy" can be Indian) is really quite hard to fathom, given the deep knowledge of Hindu thought evinced by the European missionaries of the era, both Catholic and Protestant. One was Ziegenbalg, already mentioned, who literally marveled at the wisdom of the Tamils, which he thought of as superior to that of the Greeks. Definitely, the conversation that he envisioned Kanapati having with the divines of Copenhagen would have been a lively one. Still, one wonders; without linguistic skills, much gets lost in translation, as was painfully obvious when Francis Xavier tried to communicate with the Brahmins of Tiruchendur (for which, see my companion essay on "Christian Contacts"). It simply did not register that he was being subjected to a theological litmus test. On the whole, however, Xavier's Jesuit confrères did what he was too impatient to do: master the requisite languages, including Sanskrit, which is to Hindu theology what Greek or Latin is to the church. Preeminent among them was Roberto de Nobili (1577–1656), a formidable controversialist and innovative inculturationist, whose mastery of Tamil and Sanskrit literature equipped him for "preaching wisdom to the wise" (Amaladass and Clooney 2000). For a European, his writings are perhaps the earliest that accurately differentiate between the major schools of Hindu theology.

De Nobili left to his successors the task of reconfiguring Hindu theology, constructively, for Christian purposes, including liturgics. Had they not done this, how would Indian Christians think theologically, act liturgically, or pray spiritually, without a vocabulary that was truly indigenous linguistically? For India, the pre-Christian Hindu heritage is as indispensible as the Hellenistic is to Europe. Accordingly, a Jesuit is to be thanked, one Pierre Calmette (1693–1740), for coming up with a Christianized term for "theology," *brahmavidya*, literally meaning "knowledge having *Brahman* as its subject." Here, taken as a technical term of Hindu theology, *Brahman* signifies Unconditioned Being; in this sense, it seems a perfect fit for the Thomistic way of conceptualizing divinity prevalent in Jesuit theology. Still today, *brahmavidya* (alternating with *brahmavijñana*) has wide

> **Study Aid #19**
>
> Hindu-Christian Theological Exchanges
>
> Universality: Which religion, Hinduism or Christianity, is truly the universal one?
>
> Jesus as *avatar*: Is Jesus an incarnation (*avatar*) of Vishnu? Can he helpfully be considered one?
>
> *Brahman* and God: How do the two ultimate principles relate?
>
> Caste and church: Which "community" is more important: specificity of birth duty or the universality of the church?
>
> *Moksha* and salvation: What is the path to our final state?

currency throughout Indian languages in Catholic circles and beyond. One would like, though, to say that progress has continued, theologically, after this promising beginning, but that would be false. From the sublime to the ridiculous, one sees it all in the history of intercultural interaction hereafter. A prevalent fallacy, one that dies a million deaths, is that Hindu theology is reducible to a kind of pantheism. No school holds such a view, and the distinction between conditioned and unconditioned being is as sharp as any drawn by Thomas Aquinas.

Even though Indian Christians can hardly think a theological thought, celebrate the sacraments, or pray a prayer without falling back on a vocabulary preshaped by Hindu belief and practice, the fact of the matter is that informed theological reflection on this heritage has virtually ground to a halt, except among academic theologians (preponderantly of non-Indian nationalities). Fr. Dr. K. P. Aleaz, a Christian from an ancient Syro-Malabar church, is one of few Indian theologians who constructively engage the classical schools of Hindu theology as living theologies. Whether they actually are (except for the Vedanta) can be argued, just as it might be reasonably wondered whether Stoicism is alive outside of Greek and Latin literature. In any event, like all living theologies, Indian Christian theology must address on-the-ground realities of Indians who are Christians. As all but a minority come from marginalized castes that Sanskritic Hinduism excluded from temple-based religious life (and, as mentioned, from salvation itself), one sees an understandable reluctance among Dalit theologians (*dalit*, "oppressed," refers to persons of such communities) to invest themselves in studying the very theologies that legitimized their subaltern status in the first place. Insofar as Dalit theology is a liberation theology, finding a Hindu corollary is not an easy task; classically, liberation (*moksha*) has been understood transempirically, that is, as final, unrepeatable release from the entrapment of rebirth in earthly existences (*samsara*).

It is not quite true, historically, that Christian reflection on Hindu theology peaked in the eighteenth century and then went downhill thereafter. Encouraging signs of change are in the air. First, however, Hindus who themselves engaged Christianity theologically deserve recognition. As an observer who comes at this from a perspective shaped by the Reformed faith, I leave soteriology aside (other peoples' salvation, after all, is a divine prerogative), the better to understand other faiths on their terms. On this, however, my primary Hindu interlocutor of the mid-nineteenth century, the Sanskritically literate, orthodox Brahmin called Nilakantha Goreh (introduced in my previous essays), saw matters differently. For him, the thing most on his mind about Christianity was *salvation* (appropriate theological adjustments considered, from a Hindu standpoint). It would therefore be inappropriate of me if I toned him down on this. Unsurprisingly, Nilakantha's theology of religions (for that is what it amounts to; Young 1981, 153–65) falls well short of anything like a flat or absolute denial of Christianity being on a soteriological par with his own variety of Hinduism (Vedanta). Nor is it discomfiting to him that the manyness of religions includes enough room for some that are totally bogus, which included Christianity (a corollary, perhaps, to Christians who claim that other religions are deceptively foisted upon them by the devil?). Actually, Nilakantha believed that a plurality of religions was a good thing, intrinsically, and purposeful: "Just as God made the religions distinct from each other, so is it also the case that people have different kinds of capacities [qualifications, abilities, *adhikara*]." Here, then, is the reason why Nilakantha dismissed the claim that Christianity alone could be *the* one true religion, without feeling compelled also to make a counterclaim of the opposite kind on behalf of his own religion. In short, all religions (all *dharmas*, that is) have salvific potential, although unequally.

Still, a further clarification is called for, since Nilakantha needed to differentiate the religious goal he sought—*moksha* (liberation or release from rebirth through identification with *Brahman*, the Unconditioned)—from that which was the Christian goal in his understanding of it: *svarga* ("heaven"), an endless felicity in the presence of God. Again, this is different from denying, categorically, that Christianity can be salvific for Christians. That he cannot say. What he does say takes for granted the real possibility of many salvations, ranked hierarchically under *moksha* at the apex, over and above the ability of Christians as Christians even to imagine. For him, accordingly, trifling with another believer's identity would be a cardinal sin; ipso facto, this forecloses on the possibility of Hindu missions (these do occur, eventually, but postdate the era under discussion). Nilakantha argues that Hindus are Hindus and Christians are Christians because (as quoted above) "God made the religions distinct from each other." Here, unpacking is needed, for it is an axiom of Hindu thought that God acts utterly justly in creation (cyclically, of course) in that the conditions of life are all predetermined, karmically, and are the outcome of rebirths over aeons. Only in a short-term, one-life perspective can it be said that salvific prerogatives are distributed unequally. From the vantage of *samsara* (repeated rebirth), *moksha* is eventually attainable by all, though not by Christians as Christians; they simply have to endure the karmic repercussions of their actions, and make the best of their opportunities for growth in goodness and wisdom. Clearly, the tenor of the whole conceptual complex is resoundingly anticonversionistic. One simply cannot take religion off or put it on, as if it were a set of clothes.

Beneath his hard exterior, one finds in Nilakantha a kind of inclusivism that has recognizable corollaries in Christian theologies of religion. Here, though, salvation almost always lies on the far horizon, beyond this life; neither is salvation (or final liberation, *moksha*) indiscriminately available (in any single span of time, at least). Salvation is only for those karmically rewarded folk born into castes at the pinnacle of the Hindu social hierarchy who enjoy access to the Veda's salvific truth. No one is excluded from this inclusivism; time, though, is of the essence, and lots of it will be needed. Unless, that is, one looks at the manyness of religions the way neo-Hindus do. Preponderantly English-educated and found in the middle and upper Indian social classes (NB: "class" and "caste" are different statuses, difficult to correlate), neo-Hindus are "neo" in being nonrestrictionists, soteriologically. For them, salvific competence and eligibility are universalized properties enjoyed by all. Scripturally, one might think of them as Hindu "modernists." Gone, here, is the old dogma that salvific truth can only be revealed by the Veda. Instead of the Veda being truth, truth is in the Veda, but can be ferreted out from other sacred texts as well, including the Bible (a text often so familiar to the English-educated that neo-Hindu discourse can sound as if it had been calqued on it). Evidence of neo-Hinduism's openness to extra-Hindu religions can be found in its wholesale appropriation of a de-trinitarianized Jesus (Barker and Gregg 2010, 153–214). In Hindu Christology, as it were, one should not expect Jesus to be what Jesus is in Christian faith, God the Son. Rather, Jesus becomes, say, the Perfection of Virtue revered by Ram Mohun Roy (1772–1833), India's earliest neo-Hindu, or Jesus the "Eastern Seer" venerated by Sarvepalli Radhakrishnan (1888–1975).

Now, of these two orientations, the "traditionalist" and the "modernist," one might imagine that a constructive theological conversation with the latter might be the easier one to have. Search any good library and it will not take long to reach critical mass for a study on, say, points of contact between Hinduism and Christianity in Roy, Vivekananda, Radhakrishnan, and other neo-Hindus. And if the exchange takes place between a "modernist" Hindu and a "modernist" Christian (for whom, say, instead of the Bible being truth, truth is in the Bible, which in this view is not *the* only Word of God), one gets a dialogue that looks quite different from one in which the interlocutors are both "traditionalists." And while any Barthian would abjure the label "traditionalist," the contrast with "modernist" is provisionally helpful for drawing attention to the unrealized potential for constructive dialogue between Karl Barth, a Swiss theologian of the Reformed faith, and others like him, Christian *or* Hindu (indeed, Barth does have Hindu analogues!). Distinctive of such theologies is that they premise themselves on "revelation" as a self-validating authority source. And they are suspicious of "points of contact" (Barth calls them *Anknüpfungspunkt*). In his *Church Dogmatics* (I/2, §17, "The Revelation of God as the Sublimation of Religion"), Barth stakes out a position on the religions that subsumes them all under God's judgment (including Christianity and other religions of grace). Far from thinking of grace in Christianity as sui generis, Barth acknowledges, phenomenologically, that grace has extra-Christian counterparts. Here, he launches into a discourse on Hindu *bhakti* (theistic devotionalism) against his best instincts, only to conclude that religious similarities cannot have theological significance (in *bhakti*, Barth concludes, the one thing missing is the name "Jesus").

There is irony here: Barth simply cannot help himself, even though, in the end, he "can appropriate nothing of fundamental value through his study of another theistic system." This observation, by historian of religion John Carman, ends with a lament that Barthian theologies "close the door to scholarly inquiry and dialogue" (1974, 268–70, and passim). Recently, however, the pendulum has swung in the opposite direction. Francis Clooney, a Catholic pioneer of "comparative" theology, is one of the more optimistic: "Claims about revelation," he says (2001, 162), "do not stifle comparison and dialogue but infuse and inspire them." In the interval since Carman, comparativist methodologies have emerged, involving scriptural reading projects (one text off the other, for stereoscopic effect), the success of which depends in good part on having mastered the requisite languages. Such activity bodes well for the kind of theological exchange hoped for back in the early eighteenth century. For this to happen, though, one has to start with the premise that religious similarities may indeed have theological significance.

Sources

Anand Amaladass and Francis Clooney, eds. and trans. *Preaching Wisdom to the Wise: Three Treatises by Roberto de Nobili, S.J., Missionary and Scholar in 17th Century India*. Institute of Jesuit Resources, 2000.

Gregory Barker and Stephen Gregg, eds. *Jesus beyond Christianity: The Classic Texts*. Oxford University Press, 2010.

John Braisted Carman. *The Theology of Ramanuja: An Essay in Interreligious Understanding*. Yale University Press, 1974.

Francis X. Clooney. *Hindu God, Christian God: How Reason Helps Break Down the Boundaries between Religions*. Oxford University Press, 2001.

Richard Fox Young. *Resistant Hinduism: Sanskrit Sources on Anti-Christian Apologetics in Early Nineteenth-Century India*. Brill, 1981.

9

Hinduism: Current Issues

RICHARD FOX YOUNG

Since 1947 (the year of India's independence), one of the most contentious issues debated in the Indian public square has surely revolved around "conversion," as Hindus and Christians (but also other population cohorts, including Muslims) take sides on the question: Is India Hindu? The persistence of the quarrel and the acrimony it engenders makes interreligious amity almost impossible to achieve. Compounding the problem is the memory, still raw, of asymmetrical relations between religious communities in the pre-independence period and the indelible (mis)perception that Christians were a favored community on whom privilege was heaped. For British India, such a reading seems inexcusably reductionistic, but even a solid, academically sophisticated counterargument (e.g., Mallampalli 2004) is unlikely to rectify the error when politicians aspire to power by stoking the embers of resentment. The difficulty is partly that a truth lies in the falsehood. Under the Portuguese, Goa (a colonial enclave on India's west coast) was a most uncongenial place for anyone of integrity who was a Hindu. There, for some 250 years, mercy, as it were, had a heartless rigor that the Inquisition enforced relentlessly (until 1812).

Recently, public intellectuals of the conservative Hindu parties began demanding that the Vatican apologize for the excesses committed in Goa. Such demands are not simply shrugged off by Catholic theologians; not yet as a body, but individually, some have spoken up for a "wholehearted and unconditional apology" (Klostermaier 2009). While good could surely come of this (a papal apology issued to China in 2001 on similar grounds on the occasion of the four hundredth anniversary of the Jesuit Matteo Ricci's arrival in Beijing is a possible precedent),

> **Study Aid #20**
>
> Current Hindu and Hindu-Christian Issues
>
> Conversion: Can Hindus become Christian? Can Christians become Hindus?
> Civil religion: How do politics and religion relate? How should they?
> Diaspora Hinduism: How can one be a Hindu in noncaste cultures?
> Hinduism as a religion: In what sense can Hinduism be called a world religion?

there is also a downside. For one, an apology from the Vatican would not let Protestants off the hook, even though their missional excesses bear no comparison with the draconian systems of coercion that prevailed earlier. Other doubts about the wisdom of such a move have less to do with interreligious geopolitics. Might an apology abet the mistaken assumption that "conversion" is alien to India and that India would have no Christians were it not for the intervention of colonialism? For clarity, two things are crucial: first, that Hindus who become Christians (or Muslims, etc.) be recognized as having an agency of their own; and second, that religious identity not be misunderstood as timeless, ready-made, or "given," but rather as something constantly constructed and reconstructed.

On the face of it, "conversion" indeed does appear to cut across the grain of Hindu belief and practice. Indian-language lexicons have few words of a generic kind corresponding to "conversion," which can be used multidirectionally (e.g., *to* Christianity but, equally, *from* Christianity). Instead, artificial-sounding, fill-in-the-blank circumlocutions are used (as in Hindi, "to become [*hona*] a Christian," Muslim, etc.), as if all such changes were irreducibly sui generis and foreign to the way things are or should be, normatively. Accordingly, all that one cannot become is a Hindu; one must be born into the fold (and then reborn again, ritually). There is no rite corresponding to, say, a profession of faith followed by baptism (or taking refuge in the Buddha, *dharma*, and *sangha*, as in Buddhism; or reciting the *shahada* as in Islam, etc.). Historically, such a rite was unneeded. People groups outside the Hindu fold who emulated its worship ideals and social practices were gradually folded in, as it were. (Technically called Sanskritization, the process occurs over generations, not overnight.) The case is dissimilar for those who are born Hindu; such folk can indeed undergo a "conversion"-like reconfiguration of identity. Intra-Hindu sectarianism is often rife, competition keen, and the rhetoric polemical; still, the line is ordinarily drawn at denying, absolutely, any salvific efficacy to the beliefs and practices of other Hindus. In the Indian context, the single-minded adherence that Christians think of as being proof of faithfulness often seems intolerantly exclusivistic.

By whom, though, are these Christian behaviors perceived of as a betrayal of traits that are broadly regarded as "Indian" (usually by the Hindu majority)? Not by the vast population of India's still largely village-based society who live in organic relationships of unity with people of all faiths and not only Christians

(Muslims especially). While Christians may or may not participate in Hindu ritual activity, or even turn out for seasonal festivals, Hindus will at least come to theirs, uninhibitedly. Protestantism is often too austerely aniconic to elicit any considerable interest from Hindu neighbors; Catholicism, of course, is iconic, and boundary crossing is not at all uncommon at times of pilgrimage to, say, a Marian shrine. Locally, Christians can grate on the nerves of the majority community when they remain aloof and disinterested in reciprocity. A fine line has to be walked, for sure, but familiarity breeds respect, as it were, and it is basically only at the national level that all of this breaks down nowadays, thanks to the power politics of majoritarianism that imperils democracies like India's. The dilemmas engendered are modern, though ostensibly primordial, and the ideologizing is transparently political as the manyness of India's religions is ignored or trivialized and subordinated to a politically concocted Indian variant of the civil religion phenomenon.

Without an "uncivil" other to demonize, civil religions find it hard to flourish, and India's is no different. Still a smallish community overall, Christians nowadays are increasingly cast in the role of the other within (a role earlier imposed on India's sizeable Muslim minority, but with less success). To that end, a narrative gets constructed, having a basis of sorts in history (the Goa Inquisition story is regularly trotted out), from which one variant or another of a "foreign-hand" type of conspiracy theory is then conjured up. Other versions place the accent on subtler forms of unethical activity; accusations abound of fraud (heavenly rewards, promises of healing, etc.) or of inducement (waivers, say, of tuition in exchange for church attendance), perpetrated by missionaries (who today are more likely to be Indian than foreign). Risible as they seem, such claims may in fact be well founded; missionary practices have not always been above reproach, and in a society as impoverished as India's where much-needed resources (education, medical care, etc.) are difficult to access, it seems almost inevitable that converts will be suspected of having sold their birthright for a "mess of pottage." In any event, "conversion" is not a single, aoristic event but rather a process, generally lifelong, that usually looks forthrightly utilitarian toward the beginning and only assumes a more cognitive quality over time; the convert has not lived who figured everything out ahead of time, intellectually, and then decided on a change of religion. Conversion comes in all gradations and is usually preceded by a phase of try-it-out partial adhesion of variable duration. Almost always, the needs of the heart trump those of the mind. Ordinarily, these are simply the fiercely urgent needs of health and well-being, material and spiritual (Bauman 2008a, 71–100).

In former times, missionaries were the ones who found the utilitarian motivations of "conversion" disconcerting (for one thing, "conversion" was supposed to be about postmortem salvation). Ironically, and for reasons that seem narrowly un-Indian, Hindu ideologues now insist on a singularity of identity that seems virtually missionary in definition (and in point of origin, historically, may actually be). Likewise, the unboundedness of Hindu identity is at risk of being replaced by a different way of being Hindu, one that draws lines between the religions where none existed before, insisting on their not being trespassed. Hence the breakdown of interactions that were organic, historically, as politicians exploit local conflicts, making them into headline-grabbing national crises that allegedly confirm the incompatibility of Christianity (Islam, and other religions) in a nation now defined, ahistorically, as timelessly Hindu. Lost in the uproar is the voice of Christians themselves (and Muslims, etc.), who are only thought of as being acted upon, against their own best interests (and ostensibly, those of India's), by manipulative alien "outsiders." Nothing could be more false, elitist, or condescending. Nonetheless, there is a basis here, ideologically, for a kind of "protective" interventionism on the part of Hindu activists, whose real concerns may have more to do with dominance and its preservation in a society undergoing change "from below" (from, say, newly empowered Dalit communities, which provide the bulk of converts to Christianity).

And so, despite the *Indianness* of Christianity looked at from the "bottom up," dominant groups viewing things from the "top down" see Christianity mainly in terms of its *foreignness*. Beginning with Madhya Pradesh, a state in Central India, and its *Christian Missionary Activities Inquiry Committee Report* of 1956 (called the "Niyogi Report" after the high court justice who authored it), legislation has been proposed or enacted that prohibits and penalizes "conversion" by "force," "fraud," "inducement," and "allurement" (on which, see Bauman 2008b). Thanks to guarantees in the Constitution of India on the free practice of religion (including propagation), such legislation is often struck down or simply ignored as impractical of implementation. Still, the caricature of converts as victims, witless and hapless, has considerable currency; indeed, it is regrettable that the hue and cry drowns out the important truth that Hindus and Christians have coexisted, historically, and continue to enjoy organic interconnectedness when left to themselves. One must also see behind the most contemporary uptick of violence against Christians in the eastern state of Orissa to the fundamentally economic nature of local conflicts that only appear to be about religion. India's growing economy craves coal; it so happens that in these remote regions the communities who live there—and stand in the way of commercial exploitation—are Christian (mainly *adivāsis*, tribal communities that were never Hindu in the first place).

As intractable as the issues look, "conversion" has a flip side, equally fraught with consequence for the overall trajectory of Hinduism, though less for Hindus

---

Study Aid #21

Hindu Demographics

Number of Hindus in the world: 1 billion
Percentage of world population: 14 percent
Number of countries where Hindus make up more than 50 percent of population: 3 (India, Nepal, Mauritius)

of the homeland than Hindus of the Diaspora living abroad in ever-increasing numbers, in the Anglo-American world especially (Brown 2006). The subject on this side might be called *conservation*; it too involves the reconstruction of identity but is more concerned with the preservation of "tradition." Naturally, the public-square controversies of India turn out to be highly portable and get argued out in Diaspora temples and churches (McDermott 2008); just as (some) Irish in America funded the IRA, (some) Diaspora Hindus fund Indian organizations implicated in anti-Christian violence. Still, much of the most interesting action involving Hinduism in the Diaspora happens abroad for the simple reason that *transplantation* entails *transformation* (Yang and Ebaugh 2001, 270). Being Hindu in the American context (less so the European), except in a symptomatically Protestant way, turns out to be virtually impossible, sociologically.

By "Protestantization," one should understand that a reconfiguration of identity is signified, both individual and collective, which has three kinds of outcome: scripturalization, creedalization, and laicization. Without a specifiable sacred text comparable to the Bible, being Hindu in America becomes exceedingly difficult; here, if anything, religion has to be textual in order to earn recognition and respect. In practical terms, out of the amorphous Hindu scriptural corpus, a process of selectivity usually singles out the Bhagavad Gita, which is both easy to read and yet profound in meaning. Without a pronounced belief profile, as it were, one can feel downright ill at ease in America, religiously; believers are expected to have beliefs, not only practices, and where religious commitments are understood to be creedal, the question is sure to be asked, what is it that you Hindus believe? And, because of formidable legal hurdles that religious bodies have to cross over in order to earn their coveted tax-exempt status, funds must be raised and trustees appointed before ground can be broken for a new building of worship. Accordingly, the laity gets to be involved in temple life—and in charge!—in ways for which Indian antiquity offers hardly any precedent. The ensuing activity, comparable in scope and intensity to that of most Christian churches, suggests that Diaspora Hindus do not wear themselves ragged on behalf of their communities out of any mere sense of obligation; that might have been so in India, because one's kith and kin were temple-goers. Here, for that to happen, one has to be *motivated*. For this reason alone, Diaspora Hinduism seems intrinsically worth watching in the future, for the considerable impact on India it will surely have (many Diaspora Hindus are translocal, dual-nationality citizens, shuttling back and forth, country to country, with ties to temples in both).

Whose Hinduism, though, and *which* tradition are to be chosen from among the many? And who are the intrepid pioneers on the American frontier of Hinduism that will carry the burden of interpretation to the next generation? The responsibility is huge; Hindus born abroad may or may not feel either obligated or motivated to be born again, ritually, in the manner of their ancestors. Though distanced from Hinduism as a living, ambient religion, the several elders I know of personally in the temples of my New Jersey neighborhood tackle the problem innovatively and

> **Study Aid #22**
> Countries with Hindu Populations
>
> | | |
> |---|---|
> | India | 891 million |
> | Nepal | 21 million |
> | Bangladesh | 16 million |
> | Indonesia | 4.5 million |
> | Sri Lanka | 2.5 million |
> | Pakistan | 2.2 million |
> | Malaysia | 1.7 million |
> | United States | 1.4 million |
> | South Africa | 1.2 million |
> | Myanmar | 1 million |

yet with deep concern for what they imagine to be the "true" or "real" Hinduism. Often, it's a Sanskritic Hinduism that they have in mind, not a vernacular variety, though that might have been what they were raised on. A case in point would be a temple in my vicinity where worship is conducted in a typically Protestant way, congregationally. Liturgically, however, the "service" is performed in Sanskrit, a language more foreign to virtually every participant than English or, naturally, their respective Indian mother tongues. Without romanization, the prayers would be unrecitable, and with this rejection of vernacular worship Protestantization obviously fails as a tool for understanding one of the most interesting developments in Diaspora Hinduism. Also, Diaspora temples are almost invariably ecumenical in a distinctly Hindu way; Protestantization would predictably entail a simplification of the pantheon, and the rise to preeminence of a single divinity. Instead, a kind of pantheon complexification occurs, and divinities of all sectarian groupings (Vaishnava, Shaiva, Shakta) find enshrinement here. Inclusivity precludes selectivity, and in uniting all Hindus in worship under the finial of one temple, something new is occurring in the Diaspora that India itself is yet to witness, but may.

Sources

Chad Bauman. *Christian Identity and Dalit Religion in Hindu India, 1868–1947*. Eerdmans, 2008a.

———. "Postcolonial Anxiety and Anti-conversion Sentiment in the Report of the Christian Missionary Activities Enquiry Committee." *International Journal of Hindu Studies* 12, no. 2 (2008b): 181–213.

Judith Brown. *Global South Asians: Introducing the Modern Diaspora*. Cambridge University Press, 2006.

Klaus Klostermaier. "Facing Hindu Critique of Christianity." *Journal of Ecumenical Studies* 44, no. 3 (2009): 461–66.

Chandra Mallampalli. *Christians and Public Life in Colonial South India, 1863–1937: Contending with Marginality*. RoutledgeCurzon, 2004.

Rachel McDermott. "From Hinduism to Christianity, from India to New York: Bondage and Exodus Experience in the Lives of Dalit Christians in the Diaspora." In *South Asian Christian Diaspora*, edited by Knut Jacobsen and Selva Raj, 223–48. Ashgate, 2008.

Fenggang Yang and Helen Rose Ebaugh. "Transformations in New Immigrant Religions and Their Global Implications." *American Sociological Review* 66 (2001): 269–88.

10

Hinduism: Adherent Essay

Arvind Sharma

I had a colleague by the name of Scotty McLennan in graduate school. He is now the dean of religious life at Stanford University and published a book a few years back (2009) titled *Jesus Was a Liberal: Reclaiming Christianity for All*. This is how it begins:

> A Hindu priest with whom I spent a college-era summer in India used to speak of avatars: people with clear mystical awareness who have direct knowledge of the infinite spirit that infuses the universe. In other words, they have true God-consciousness. Avatars, he said, help the rest of us see what God is like in human form. They are sons or daughters of God in a uniquely pure way.
>
> The priest's avatar was Ramakrishna, a nineteenth-century saint who inspired an order and mission in India that has come to be known in America as the Vedanta Society. At the end of the summer, when I expressed a strong interest in becoming a Hindu, the Hindu priest said no. Ramakrishna, he said, taught that avatars have had different impacts from culture to culture and era to era. Yet, ultimately—although they use different names and different religious methodologies—they all point to the same God. So Ramakrishna advised seekers not to look outside their own tradition, but to follow the path they know best with wholehearted devotion. Ramakrishna counseled, "A Christian should follow Christianity, a Muslim should follow Islam, and so on." The priest directed me back to the Christianity with which I had grown up. He insisted that Jesus was my avatar, not Ramakrishna nor the Buddha nor anyone else. It was in Jesus's footsteps that I should walk to know God better.

This attitude of the Hindu priest may now be compared to that of a Christian minister.

What would the Christian minister do when approached by someone saying that he or she wanted to become a Christian? In all likelihood, such a person would be welcomed, not turned back to his or her own tradition. This stark difference in the attitudes of the two religious traditions—the Hindu and the Christian—toward conversion is a basic cause of friction between the two. I would like to emphasize that modern Hinduism, as it is lived, is vigorously opposed to conversion from one religion to another on the ground mentioned above, and that this is the mainline and not a marginal view within it (Sharma 1998, 8). No less a person than Mahatma Gandhi was a vigorous advocate of this view, as is apparent from the following dialogue between him and Charles Andrews.

C. F. Andrews: "What would you say to a man who after considerable thought and prayer said that he could not have his peace and salvation except by becoming a Christian?"

Gandhiji: "I would say if a non-Christian (say a Hindu) came to a Christian and made that statement, he should ask him to become a good Hindu rather than find goodness in change of faith."

C. F. Andrews: "I cannot in this go the whole length with you, though you know my position. I discarded the position that there is no salvation except through Christ long ago. But supposing the Oxford Group Movement people changed the life of your son, and he felt like being converted, what would you say?"

Gandhiji: "I would say that the Oxford Group may change the lives of as many people as they like, but not their religion. They can draw their attention to the best in their respective religions and change their lives by asking them to live according to them. There came to me a man, the son of *brahmana* parents, who said his reading of your book had led him to embrace Christianity. I asked him if he thought that the religion of his forefathers was wrong. He said, 'No.' Then I said: 'Is there any difficulty about your accepting the Bible as one of the great books of the world and Christ as one of the great teachers?' I said to him that you never through your books asked Indians to take up the Bible and embrace Christianity, and that he had misread your book—unless of course your position is like that of the late M. Mahomed Ali's, viz. that 'a believing Mussulman however bad his life, is better than a good Hindu.'"

C.F.A.: "I do not accept M. Mahomed Ali's position at all. But I do say that if a person really needs a change of faith I should not stand in his way."

Gandhiji: "But don't you see that you do not even give him a chance? You do not even cross-examine him. Supposing a Christian came to me and said he wanted to declare himself a Hindu, I should say to him: 'No.' What the *Bhagawata* offers the Bible also offers. You have not yet made the attempt to find it out. Make the attempt and be a good Christian."

C.F.A.: "I don't know. If someone earnestly says he will become a good Christian, I should say, 'You may become one,' though you know that I have in my own life strongly dissuaded ardent enthusiasts who came to me. I said to them, 'Certainly not on *my* account will you do anything of the kind.' But human nature does require a concrete faith."

Gandhiji: "If a person wants to believe in the Bible let him say so, but why should he discard his own religion? This *proselytization will mean no peace in the world*. Religion is a very personal matter. We should by living the life according to our lights share the best with one another, thus adding to the sum total of human efforts to reach God." "Consider," continued Gandhiji, "whether you are going to accept the position of mutual toleration or of equality of all religions. My position is that all the great religions are fundamentally equal. We must have innate respect for other religions as we have for our own. Mind you, not mutual toleration, but equal respect." (Gandhi 1950, 231–32; editor's italics)

If we analyze this conversation carefully, we will detect two grounds for Hindu opposition to Christian proselytization, one doctrinal and the other procedural. The first objection is that no change of religion is required even if one accepted the truth of Christianity, because of the pervasive acceptance of the doctrine within modern Hinduism that all religions are valid. The second is that the procedures adopted for propagating Christianity are not considered acceptable. The procedure, according to modern Hindus, is morally dubious—for at least two reasons. The desire to convert someone leads to two interconnected developments, which may be called the approbative imperative and the pejorative imperative. That is to say, one must project a picture of one's tradition rosier than it is, and must run down the other person's tradition as worse than it is, to facilitate conversion. Thus one is led into falsifying both the realities, and truth is compromised. Besides, the church missions are often accused of offering material allurements to would-be converts. From the Hindu point of view, if conversion is to have any basis, it has to be spiritual. Thus, if one is convinced that one's salvation lies only through Christianity, then the modern Hindu may reluctantly concede it as a ground for conversion, but the use of material allurement to change one's spiritual alignment is considered unworthy of an authentic religion. Thus both truth and honesty are compromised. Both the goal and the means to attain the goal, that of conversion, become suspect.

The counterposition is stated forcefully by the Indian Christian Rev. R. C. Das, who rejects the distinction between propagation and proselytization, when the former is supposed to mean proclaiming one's religions *without* seeking converts.

> The statements that one may preach but not convert, or that in serving one should not be actuated by motives of conversion, show confusion of thought and a lack of knowledge of psychology and normal human behaviour. Why is something preached? And when convinced, are they not inwardly converted? The word "conversion" simply means "change." . . . The Hindu does not object to conversion in politics, a new attitude in science, history, or philosophy. How then is objection to religious conversion valid where a man's happiness and welfare are even more at stake? (Smith 1963, 173–74)

How might one elaborate on this issue further from a Christian point of view? It needs to be recognized that the idea that there is no need for religious conversion is a Hindu doctrine and not a universal one. Many *other* religions allow for conversion. This would constitute a religious objection to the Hindu position.

It also needs to be recognized that human rights discourse emphasizes the right to religious freedom, which according to article 18 of the Universal Declaration of Human Rights specifically includes the "freedom to change . . . religion or belief" (Brownlie 1994 [1971], 25). This would constitute a secular objection to the Hindu position.

It could also be argued that Christian exclusivism, which is what the Hindu is really objecting to, comes in different shades. One might take an absolutist stand that Christianity alone is true. However, within Christianity itself there is the acceptance of the transcendental nature of the transcendent, that one can possess only relative knowledge of it. This perspective is shared by many religions of the world, along with Christianity. However, Christianity could still claim that out of all these *relative* formulations, its *own relative formulation* is *relatively* the best. So there is still a case to be made for conversion to Christianity. This could constitute a philosophical objection to the Hindu position (Sugirtharaja 2003, 62).

If any one of us suddenly found oneself in possession of what one thinks is the ultimate truth, is it humanly possible for one *not* to want to share it with others? It may not be right to construe Christian mission always as an attempt to *impose* one's religious views on others, or to *tempt* or *coerce* others into accepting it (leading to such developments as those represented by "Rice Christians"). The underlying motive could as well be the desire to *share* it with others. This may be called the psychological objection to the Hindu position.

It is clear therefore that there are good religious, secular, philosophical, and psychological grounds for allowing Christians to *seek* conversion. Where the Hindu critique becomes relevant is in the realm of procedure, when such conversion is sought. Thus, religiously speaking, a Hindu has as much a right to *object* to conversion as those who have a right to seek it; secularly speaking, a person has as much a right to *retain* one's religion as to change it; philosophically speaking, *each* religion can claim that it is in a relatively superior position; and psychologically speaking, it is quite valid for a person to say, "Who are you to ask me to change my religion, even if you think you have the truth? I shall make up my own mind."

In the end, then, we are left with valid arguments from both sides, and our task is to create guidelines for missionary activity that will best address the issues as viewed from both sides. The task is complicated by the fact that we are dealing with two basic human emotions. On the one hand, if someone has the truth or has found salvation, one can hardly be expected to keep it to himself or herself; and on the other hand, everyone has the right not to be interfered with by others in the pursuit of truth or salvation.

Sources

Ian Brownlie, ed. *Basic Documents of Human Rights*. Clarendon, 1994 (1971).

Mahatma K. Gandhi. *Hindu Dharma*. Navajivan, 1950.

Scotty McLennan. *Jesus Was a Liberal: Reclaiming Christianity for All*. Palgrave Macmillan, 2009.

Arvind Sharma. *The Concept of Universal Religion in Modern Hindu Thought*. St. Martin's Press, 1998.

Donald Eugene Smith. *India as a Secular State*. Princeton University Press, 1963.

Sharada Sugirtharaja. *Imagining Hinduism: A Postcolonial Perspective*. Routledge, 2003.

11

Buddhism: History, Beliefs, Practices

Terry C. Muck

History

Buddhism is a cross-cultural religion founded in India by a man named Siddhartha Gautama (563–483 BCE). After extensive sampling of all the religions India of his day had to offer, from high-caste Hindu wealth and privilege to a wide range of ascetic practices in the forest with other holy men (*sannyasin*), he discovered the Middle Way. Henceforth known as the Buddha (the Enlightened One), he spent the remaining fifty years of his life as a traveling mendicant preacher, teaching and preaching in the northeastern Indian and Nepali provinces of his birth and early life.

Gautama Buddha's teaching was successful. He quickly gained a following that continued to grow after his death. His immediate followers held two councils shortly after his death, one to rehearse all they could remember of his teaching and his rules for monastic practice, the other to discuss divergent opinions that had arisen as to teaching and practice since his death. This second council is usually seen as the beginnings of sectarian Buddhist schools developing. This diversity was both a response to the shape the teaching took as it spread into cultures different from its culture of origin and also an enabler of that same geographical spread.

Buddhism's widest diffusion, however, came as a result of the coming to power of the Mauryan political dynasty, which managed to unify much of the Indian subcontinent. The third ascender to the dynastic throne, Asoka, advertised his beloved Buddhism by chiseling messages on rock pillars throughout and especially on the borders of his kingdom. He culminated this work by calling a council of Buddhist leaders, a meeting that resulted in the sending of Buddhist missionaries, called *mahadhammarakkhitas* or *dharmadhatus*, to the surrounding countries such as Sri Lanka, Myanmar, Thailand, Cambodia, Pakistan, and central Asia.

In the succeeding centuries, Buddhism continued its spread into central, northern, and East Asia. It reached China in 40 CE, Korea in 350, Japan in 575, Tibet in 640, and Mongolia in the 1300s. The Buddha's teaching had obvious cross-cultural appeal, and its capacity, typical of Asian religious systems, to form relatively functional partnerships with whatever indigenous religions it came in contact with—Taoism and Confucianism in China, shamanism in Korea, Shinto in Japan, Bon in Tibet—proved to be uniquely effective.

Buddhist ideas spread to Europe and the West (during and after the eighteenth century) by means of two of the three traditional modes of religious diffusion: military, merchants, and missionaries. (The diffusion of Buddhism has been remarkably free of military attachments, at least when compared with the other missionary religions of the world.) The British East India Company came in contact with Buddhists in India and Southeast Asia. Roman Catholic, Reformed, and Wesleyan missionaries followed in the traces dug by Portuguese, Dutch, and British traders. Missionaries did the first translations of Buddhist texts, and their influence created a demand for "Oriental" studies at Cambridge and Oxford. Soon after those academic programs were established, Ivy League universities in the United States followed suit, teaching courses in Eastern philosophies and religious ideas, resulting in a form of philosophical thinking called transcendentalism.

In the twentieth century it wasn't just Buddhist ideas that came West, but Buddhists themselves. Three waves of Asian immigrants washed across American shores. The first came as laborers necessary to build the infrastructure to support the California gold rush in the late nineteenth and early twentieth centuries. The second wave, in the post–World War I years, was so successful that it created a backlash in the form of a series of restrictive immigration laws in the 1920s. The third wave came as a result of a revising of those immigration laws. The New Immigration Act of 1965 was Asian-immigrant friendly and had the effect of encouraging migration from Asian countries. Of course, a steady growth of South and Southeast Asian, Chinese, and East Asian immigrants in the last quarter of the twentieth century made United States Buddhism in the twenty-first century a religious denomination of significant size, perhaps two to three million strong.

Beliefs

What Siddhartha Gautama discovered sitting in deep meditation under the Bo-Tree at the age of thirty—what made him a Buddha, an Enlightened One—was based on the common Indian worldview that assumed everyone is enmeshed in a series of rebirths (*samsara*) that are based in quality on the positive or negative value of one's actions (*karma*). But whereas most Indian religious traditions taught that the value of one's *karma* was based on strict adherence to caste duty (*dharma*), the

Study Aid #23
Buddhist Timeline

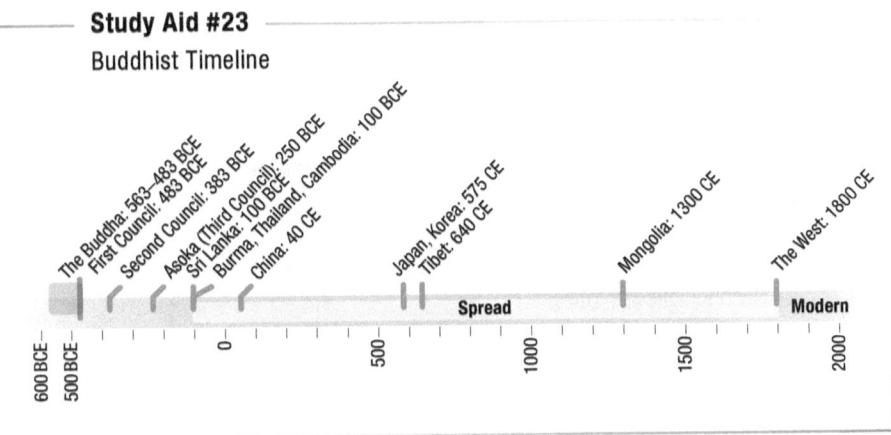

Buddha taught that it was recognition through trial and error of the truth of his teachings—what came to be known as the Four Noble Truths—that determined the positive or negative value of one's karmic deeds.

The First Noble Truth—that all is suffering (*dukkha*)—is the linchpin of the entire system. We suffer, the Buddha taught, because we see permanence where there is only impermanence (*anicca*). We want to rely on things—fame, money, honor, achievement—that only have fleeting value. Even if we retreat to belief in only one enduring entity, our human self or soul, we are mistaken. Gautama Buddha taught that even our own selves, while real, are only temporary constructs, or no-self (*anatta*). Everything is impermanent. But because we desperately want to cling to some enduring reality, we suffer.

The Second Noble Truth explains the origin of our suffering, of our intractable desire to hold on to something lasting. We are caught, the Buddha said, in an ongoing spiral of existence that operates on the simple basis of cause and effect. He called the spiral *paticca samuppada*, the circle of dependent origination. Our existence is made up of a repeating cycle of twelve links in a chain of cause and effect, moving from birth to becoming to craving to clinging, through personhood to ignorance and death—and back to birth again. The cycle of dependent origination displays a sophisticated understanding of human psychology unmatched in the other cultures of the world.

The Third Noble Truth teaches a way out of the endless round of rebirths. One breaks the cycle of existence by controlling one of the links of the chain, the desire (*tanha*) link. A full intuitive understanding of suffering and impermanence leads to a cessation of desire for an eternal self. Once desire for such an existence ceases, rebirth ends. The state that follows is called enlightenment when referring to an individual. But since the enlightened individual ceases, another term, *nirvana*, sometimes translated as "emptiness," is used to designate the eventual end of karmic existence.

> **Study Aid #24**
>
> **Buddhist Beliefs**
>
> *Buddha*: Fully enlightened being who can show others the way; Gautama Buddha, the teaching Buddha of our age.
> *Dukkha*: Suffering born of longing for permanence and eternal essence.
> *Anicca*: Impermanence. Recognition of constant change.
> *Anatta*: No-self. All is vanity.
> *Paticca samuppada*: Conditioned existence, fueled by thirst for being.
> *Nirvana*: Unconditioned emptiness.

The Fourth Noble Truth, the Noble Eightfold Path, implicitly acknowledges that most of us do not become enlightened in this lifetime and continue on in conditioned existence. We are reborn. The dynamics for living in conditioned existence sometimes seem at odds with the overall goal of *nirvana*. One lives as if this life matters, as if a good rebirth based on acquiring good *karma* through merit-making activity leads to a permanent, enduring existence. But the Noble Eightfold Path—right livelihood, speech, action, energy, concentration, mindfulness, thought, and wisdom—is an interim ethic, a way of living here and now that will most likely enable us to make spiritual progress in understanding the first three Noble Truths, and will eventually in some future life lead to enlightenment.

Three different schools of Buddhism have traditionally been identified, although each of these three major schools has many subschools. *Theravada* Buddhism is the Buddhism of Southeast Asia, countries such as Sri Lanka, Thailand, Burma (Myanmar), Cambodia, and Laos. Theravada means "words of the elders," and Theravadins often claim—with some justification—that they are the oldest of the Buddhist schools. *Mahayana* means "great vehicle" and is the Buddhism of China, Japan, and Korea. Their defining characteristic is the *bodhisattva* ideal (see below). *Vajrayana* means Diamond Vehicle and is the school primarily located in Tibet and Mongolia.

Practices

In practice, then, Buddhists seem to cope with existence on two levels, the level of *samsara*, or conditioned existence (rebirth), and the level of *nirvana*, or enlightenment (release from rebirth). At the samsaric level, Buddhist laypeople do things that earn them positive *karma* (merit) such as feeding and clothing monks (*bhikkhus*), and attending temple services for protection and veneration of the images of the Buddha. Such merit-making activities, if assiduously followed, lead to better rebirths, the theoretical aim of which is to enable the people leading those lives to continue to work on the more important problem of their enlightenment.

In order to do the more ethereal work of enlightenment, meditative skill is required. Two dominant schools of meditation have developed. In Theravada (southern) Buddhist countries, insight (*vipassana*) meditative practice was/is the method of choice. In the Mahayana (northern) Buddhist countries of China, Japan, and Korea, an a-rational approach called Zen meditation became popular. In Vajrayana, Tibetan, and Mongolian countries, other types of meditative practice utilizing mandalas and visualization developed. Although quite distinctive in terms of practice, all Buddhist meditative practices aim at enabling the practitioner to enter into the oneness of being—or the nothingness of nonbeing. All of these various types of meditation have become mainstays of Buddhism in Western countries, where it appears a lack of sophisticated meditative traditions have made Buddhism appealing.

In Mahayana Buddhist countries, an important social ethic of sorts grew up around a concept known as the *bodhisattva* ideal. The *bodhisattva* is an almost-enlightened person who instead of going on to achieve the final extinction within his or her grasp chooses to devote his or her considerable spiritual resources to helping others make progress on the spiritual path. *Bodhisattvas* take on the aura of divine helpers to whom one can turn for spiritual succor. They tend to become known for particular core virtues such as compassion (e.g., Kuan Yin) or wisdom (e.g., Manjusri).

Historically Buddhism flourished under political monarchies where a symbiotic relationship between king and religion flourished. Monarchs provided Buddhist monastic orders with patronage and protection. Monks provided kings with religio-spiritual advice and, when necessary, divine mandates for rule. This traditional partnership has been tested in more modern democratic pluralisms and nationalisms where religious plurality has replaced established religions. A similar symbiosis has traditionally existed between laypersons and monastics, who together formed the spiritual hierarchy. Again, in modern egalitarian Western cultures, privileged monastic orders are not seen as a benefit to societal function. Laypersons, therefore, have had to find alternative arenas for gaining merit and spiritual altruistic outlets. Some have turned to social service in a movement known as Engaged Buddhism.

As a cross-cultural, missionary religion, Buddhism has always exhibited an exemplary capacity to shape itself to fit into an existing culture and its mores without

---

Study Aid #25

Buddhist Divisions

Theravada: 177 million
Mahayana: 264 million
Vajrayana: 28 million
Western: 10 million

losing its essential core. In modern times, a globalized, urbanized Buddhism has taken root across the globe; it is a Buddhism that is characterized by individualized meditative practice, a portable metaphysic congenial to global culture, and an epistemology that fits postmodern thought very well. This has not been done to the exclusion, however, of more culturally specific Buddhisms across Asia.

Buddhism is a growing religion in the world today. Although it is not growing as fast as Islam and Christianity, it has spread into the traditionally Christian populations of Europe and North America. It is probably the fourth-largest religion in the world (behind Christianity, Islam, and Hinduism) with as many as 350 million members worldwide (excluding Chinese Buddhists, who are difficult to count). It is the dominant religion (more than 50 percent of the population) in eight countries around the world.

Sources

Edward Conze, ed. *Buddhist Scriptures*. Penguin, 1959.
Peter Harvey. *An Introduction to Buddhism*. Cambridge University Press, 1990.
Damien Keown. *Buddhism: A Very Short Introduction*. Oxford University Press, 2000.
Donald Lopez, ed. *Buddhism in Practice*. Princeton University Press, 1995.
John Powers. *Introduction to Tibetan Buddhism*. Snow Lion, 1995.
Walpola Rahula. *What the Buddha Taught*. Grove, 1974.
Paul Williams. *Mahayana Buddhism*. Routledge, 1989.

12

Buddhism: Christian Contacts

Terry C. Muck

Almost from their beginnings, Buddhist-Christian contacts have been missionary. Both founders, Gautama Buddha and Jesus Christ, charged their followers with going out to all the world and preaching and teaching the *dhamma* and gospel to all who would listen.

The Buddha put it this way: "For the good of many folk, for the happiness of many, out of compassion for the world, preach the truth. Don't two of you go by one road, but preach the truth, monks, which is lovely at the beginning, middle and end, in the letter and the spirit. Demonstrate the purified holy life which is fully complete" (Vinaya Pitaka: Mahavagga 11).

The Christ, in his most famous charge to his disciples, said, "Therefore go and make disciples of all nations, baptizing them in the name of the Father and of the Son and of the Holy Spirit, and teaching them to obey everything I have commanded you" (Matt. 28:19–20).

The effects of both these charges upon the early followers of Gautama and Jesus have been determinative. Both teachings were successful in reaching out beyond their cultures of origin to diverse cultures worldwide.

As a result, contacts between Buddhists and Christians have not been characterized by what one might call one-way missions but by what might be called reciprocal missions: Buddhists teaching the *dhamma* to Christians and Christians preaching the gospel to Buddhists. By and large these competing missions have been peaceful, although as we shall see in what follows, on occasion the contacts have resulted in conflict, even persecution.

The following pages will identify and briefly describe eight Buddhist-Christian historical contacts. In some cases they were initiated by Buddhists, in other cases by Christians. Some were intentionally missionary, some incidental to other pursuits. These eight incidents could be multiplied many times over—the Buddhist-Christian interaction has been rich and deep.

King Asoka

It is likely that the systematic Buddhist mission effort was the result of actions taken by an early Indian ruler named Asoka (304–232 BCE). Asoka completed a military unification of most of India begun by his grandfather and father. After a life of such conquests, however, Asoka rededicated his life and rule to promoting religion—his own Buddhism, but also other religions represented in his domain.

One of his principal acts was to call a meeting of Buddhist leaders and teachers, the Third Buddhist Council, at which a decision was made to send missionaries to surrounding countries and areas. Asoka, for example, sent his son Mahinda to Sri Lanka, and eventually his daughter, Sanghamitta, joined her brother there in the task of founding the Buddhist *sasana* (teaching) in Sri Lanka.

It is likely that Buddhist missionaries (*dharmadhatus*) were also sent to Thailand, Burma, Cambodia, and up into central Asia, where they connected with merchants on a trading route, the Silk Road, that ran all the way from the Middle East to China. Evidence of this contact abounds in written sources of the day, ranging from mentions of Indian religious, *samaneras*, in the writings of Clement of Alexandria to Philo of Alexandria to the Therapeutae in Egypt. Central Asian rulers such as Kanishka (78–102 CE) and Basiledes promoted Buddhist-Christian thinking. There is even a legend in Christian sources of two "saints," Josaphat and Barlaam, that some have suggested refers to the Buddha himself.

That our knowledge of these early contacts in central Asia is scattered is probably due to the fact that peaceful trading contacts rarely make the same splash in historical "news" as do the more flamboyant wars and rumors of wars. Merchants are typically more publicity shy than military and political leaders.

Nestorian Christians

Nestorian Christians made contact with Buddhists in China early in the seventh century. Nestorian Christianity is inspired by the teachings of a man named Nestorius. Although his teachings on the nature of Christ were deemed by most to be unorthodox, this Syrian Christianity had a powerful mission urge and early on penetrated China.

Northern China in the seventh century had the three traditional Chinese religions—Taoism, Confucianism, Buddhism—but Buddhism was especially strong. The emperors of the early Tang Dynasty favored Buddhism. Thus, the Nestorian

Study Aid #26
Spread of Buddhism

missionaries aimed their proclamations at what they determined to be the dominant religion at this time, Buddhism. Two evidences of these proclamations stand out.

One is what is called the Nestorian Stele, probably inscribed in 781, discovered in Xian in 1623, and translated shortly thereafter. The Nestorian Stele (its official title on the inscribed limestone rock is "Memorial of the Propagation in China of the Luminous Religion from the Roman Empire") tells us much of what we know about the nature of Buddhist-Christian relations in China (and, later, Mongolia and Korea) during this period. It shows that sophisticated contextualization of the gospel into Chinese Buddhist forms was a hallmark of Syrian Christianity in China. Consider this from the stele, for example: "Right principles have no invariable name, holy men have no invariable station; instruction is established in accordance with the locality, with the object of benefiting the people at large" (Palmer 2001, 23)

A second evidence is a writing probably under the direction of the most well-known of the Nestorian missionaries, Alopen. The writing is called the "Sutra of Jesus the Messiah." A *sutra* is the name given to a Buddhist religious text. It is obvious that Alopen was concerned to show that there was nothing about the story of Jesus, the gospel, that was subversive to the ancient Chinese traditions, including Mahayana Buddhism. Consider, for example, a short passage from the *sutra*: "The Messiah was surrounded by the Buddhas and Buddhist holy men, and looking down he saw the suffering of all that is born, and so he began to teach" (Palmer 2001, 78).

The Nestorian mission withered toward the end of the Tang Dynasty, probably for two reasons: (1) a systematic persecution of both Buddhists and Christians by Emperor Wuzong (840–46), who favored Confucian teaching; and (2) a dwindling support from the Nestorian home base in Syria.

Matteo Ricci

One of the most well-known of the historical contacts between Buddhists and Christians was that led by Matteo Ricci in China. Ricci was an Italian Jesuit who went to China in 1583 to teach the Christian gospel. He initially thought that the most effective way to approach the Chinese was to adopt the dress and customs of Buddhist monks. His purpose was to show the Chinese people that Christianity was a religion like Buddhism and had much in common with a system of thinking and behaving that the Chinese trusted.

Unfortunately, Ricci and his companions quickly discovered that in China of the sixteenth century, Buddhism was not held in high repute by many, particularly the Chinese upper classes. Buddhism, like Christianity, was viewed as a foreign religion, having come to China from India in 40 CE, brought, legend suggested, by an Indian Buddhist missionary named Bodhidharma. Not only that, many Chinese literati thought the monastic Buddhist clergy were lazy noncontributors to overall social functioning. In short, by dressing as a Buddhist, Ricci was associating Christianity with a negative element of Chinese society, not a positive one. When he realized his mistake, Ricci changed his strategy. He began to dress and talk like a Confucian not a Buddhist.

Ricci's approach was contextual and pre-evangelistic. He thought that the first steps in the Christian-Buddhist context should be devoted to building trust. He was not trying to show that Buddhism and Christianity were the same. But he did want to show that their common elements could bridge the cultural gap between European Christian cultures and Asian Buddhist ones. Ironically, he ended up succeeding in this by using Confucian thought, not Buddhist thought.

Ricci's ecclesiastical superiors back in Rome did not agree with his approach. After a debate that has come to be called the Rites Controversy, they ordered Ricci's successors to return to using Western Latin religious and cultural forms. For three and a half centuries this ruling stood, until the twentieth century, when Ricci's strategy was finally vindicated by church authorities.

Mongolia

The story of Buddhism's contact with Christianity in Mongolia is an intriguing one. The time frame probably coincides with the Nestorian entry into China in the seventh century.

In the area that is now Mongolia, it was the time of the Khans, a succession of rulers who managed through cunning and guile, warfare and diplomacy, to unify much of central Asia under their rule. Actually, this conquest and unification did not stop with central Asia. Under one or another of the great Khans, it included China, Eastern Europe, and parts of the Middle East. At its height, the Mongol Empire controlled the largest amount of land of any empire in human history.

One intriguing part of the story is how the Khans ended up choosing their religion. Of course they began with the central Asian shamanism that worshiped the sun as a high god. But through their wandering, conquesting ways, they came in contact with both Buddhism and Christianity, among others.

One of the Khans, Guyuk Khan (grandson of Genghis Khan), for example, became interested in Christianity (probably because his wife was a Christian) and sent a letter to the pope in Rome asking for missionaries to be sent to him and his people for conversations. Unfortunately, Pope Innocent IV misunderstood the request and responded politically, not missionally. In 1242, he sent an emissary, Friar Giovanni (John) of Plano Carpini, who failed to respond to Guyuk's rather sophisticated religious request.

As a result, the Mongols ended up adopting Tibetan Buddhism as their religion. The Khans decreed that Buddhism become the official religion of the Mongol Empire, although as long as Christians did not threaten the political rule and civic order mandated by the rulers, they were free to practice their religion.

Japan and Korea

Buddhism and Christianity were both foreign religions in Japan. Buddhism got there first. It came as part of a package of Chinese cultural forms, which included a system of writing, social order (Confucian), and religion. Because of its proclivity for seeking out religious partnerships with indigenous religions, accommodations were reached with Shinto, the Japanese nationalistic myth. Buddhism thrived in Japan.

Christianity was a latecomer to Japan. In the sixteenth century, Roman Catholic missioners accompanied their Dutch, Portuguese, and Spanish trading confrères and attempted to build Christian communities on the Japanese mainland. Some met with significant success. This initial success, however, created a religious and nationalistic backlash that eventually led to severe persecution of Christian converts. The Japanese associated growing Christian churches with a danger of Western colonization and decided to act to prevent Christian growth.

In the mission endeavors of Buddhism and Christianity in Japan, Buddhism won the day. The Christian population of Japan is less than 5 percent of the total. The situation in Korea, however, was not as clear-cut a victory for Buddhism. As in Japan, Buddhism came first and successfully planted itself as an important religious force. Christianity came later but also was successful in establishing the church and Christian institutions. Current religious demographics put the Buddhist population at 25 percent of the total population, the Christian population at just below that (22 percent).

Today Japan and Korea may seem to be indigenous Buddhist cultures. In fact, both are the products of successful Buddhist missions. In these two cases, the Buddhist mission methodology of seeking to partner with indigenous religious teachings (Shinto in Japan, shamanism in Korea), rather than to supplant those religions, has allowed Buddhism to become more successfully indigenized than Christianity, which in both countries is still seen as a Western, colonizing religion.

Southeast Asia

In most parts of Buddhist Asia, Roman Catholic Jesuits broke mission ground, to be followed later by Protestant missioners from Dutch, British, and then American

---

Study Aid #27

Christian-Buddhist Contacts

Nestorian Christians in China: 7th century
  Alopen
Mongolia: 12th century
  Guyuk Khan
Jesuits in China: 16th century
  Matteo Ricci
Japan and Korea: 16th century
Southeast Asia: 17th–18th centuries
  Spain, Portugal, Netherlands, Great Britain
West: 19th–20th centuries
  Academics, economic migrations, competing missions

mission-sending agencies. That was mostly true in the Southeast Asian Buddhist countries of Sri Lanka, Thailand, Burma, Cambodia, and Laos, although in some of those places non-Jesuit Catholic missionaries from Portugal and France had an early presence, usually as religious companions of traders from those early colonial powers. In terms of long-lasting effects, it was the later Protestant missionaries who did the heavy lifting.

All of these Christian groups found in these cultures the Buddhist *sangha* as established by the *dharmadhatus* sent by Asoka after the Third Buddhist Council in India. Like their experiences in China, Japan, and Korea, Christian missioners found themselves playing catch-up to Buddhist witnesses to the teachings of Gautama Buddha. In all of these countries, the Christian missioners have never caught up with the work done by the Buddhists; in none of them, with the exception of Korea, is the Christian population more than 5 percent of the population.

That is not to say that the Christian church has not been planted in Sri Lanka, Thailand, Burma, Cambodia, and Laos. It has. In Sri Lanka and Thailand, especially, an active presence is maintained by Presbyterian, Methodist, Baptist, Anglican, and Roman Catholic Churches. The church is planted and in no danger of disappearing. One cannot gainsay the faithfulness and dedication of the church planters.

Yet over two hundred years of intense mission effort has not produced the results that would make Christianity a significant cultural force in any of these Southeast Asian countries. By and large Christianity remains a foreign religion, interlopers on turf well staked out by Buddhist *dharmadhatus*. Perhaps this is a commentary on the relative power of trading empires and religions. The full force of colonial empire, both economic and military, was brought to bear upon these cultures and was not only defeated by the extant Buddhist cultures but in most places also managed to sully the corresponding power of Christian culture.

Buddhist Mission to the West

Buddhists came to Europe and North America as a result of contact with colonial missionaries. These missionaries studied Buddhist ideas and languages, making their study popular in Rome, Oxford and Cambridge, and American Ivy League universities, all of whom began "Oriental studies" departments.

In 1893 in Chicago, a Parliament of World Religions gathered together for the first time representatives of the major world religions. The representatives gave addresses explaining the basic teachings of their religions. Buddhist representatives from both Sri Lanka (Anagarika Dharmapala) and Japan (Soyen Shaku) gave talks that were well received and led to permanent Zen and Theravada Buddhist missions being established in the United States.

Just a couple of decades earlier, the California gold rush had indirectly led to the establishment of Chinese Buddhist groups on the West Coast. The explosive population growth created by the rush to find gold created a need for cheap labor to build the infrastructure of this new society, particularly to build railroads to connect California to the rest of the country. Workers from China especially were invited to come for this work—and of course they brought their Buddhist religions with them.

If the nineteenth century was the great century of Protestant mission to the East, the twentieth century could be called the great century of Buddhist mission to the West. In addition to the buddhalogians who came to the World Parliament of Religions in Chicago in 1893 and the workers who came to California, meditation centers, temples, and even Buddhist universities have sprung up in most major cities of the United States. One of the leaders of Tibetan Buddhism, the Dalai Lama, began to do both political and religious missions in Western countries.

By century's end, even Western converts to Buddhism, such as Jack Kerouac and Robert Thurman, were doing active Buddhist mission work in the United States. Overall this mission work has created a strong Buddhist presence in the West (perhaps two to three million strong in the United States, for example). It has also created an active dialogue between Buddhists and Christians that has enlightened, among other things, awareness of the rationales for one another's missions.

Reciprocal Mission Relationship

The two-thousand-year history of Buddhist-Christian interaction is intriguing for a number of reasons. First and foremost, it is a case study of what happens when two religions with clear mission mandates from their founders meet on the "mission" pitch repeatedly over the years. Since both religions, technically speaking, are "indigenous" to only one culture (India for Buddhism, Israel for Christianity), many comparative exercises are possible for meetings: for example, what happens when one mission force meets another mission force in a religiously different culture? In general, the history of such interactions indicates that the first religion to missionize a new place dominates.

Second are the lessons to be learned from the interactions and the fact that they have been largely peaceful. One can speculate on the reasons for this. Perhaps it was due to the fortuitous lack of political intrigue associated with their contacts. Or could the reason be economic? Perhaps their meetings were not complicated by frustrated material wants, and the relative economic prosperity that accompanied their contacts contributed to peace. Although it would be hard to assign religious virtue to either side, Buddhism's willingness, relatively speaking, to cooperate with other religions may be some indicator of why the Buddhist-Christian relationship has been a model one.

Sources

Elizabeth Harris. *Theravada Buddhism and the British Encounter*. Routledge, 2006.

Ann Heirman and Stephen Peter Bumbacher. *The Spread of Buddhism*. Brill, 2007.

Linda Learman, ed. *Buddhist Missionaries in the Era of Globalization*. University of Hawaii Press, 2005.

Samuel Hugh Moffett. *A History of Christianity in Asia*. 2 vols. Orbis Books, 1998–2005.

Martin Palmer. *The Jesus Sutras*. Ballantine, 2001.

Matteo Ricci. *China in the Sixteenth Century: The Journals of Matthew Ricci, 1583–1610*. Translated by Louis J. Gallagher. Random House, 1953.

13

Buddhism: Theological Exchanges

Terry C. Muck

The interaction between Christian theology and Buddhist philosophy has been rich from the very first contacts in Asia, probably in India, to the first mission to China in the seventh century, with increasing frequency until today. The motivation for the theological interactions varied, of course, with the motivations of the Christian and Buddhist theologians involved. Many were looking for intellectual leverage in presenting the claims of Christ over against the claims of the teachings of the Buddha (Moffett 1998). Others, however, studied Buddhism and made comparisons with Christianity in order to satisfy a deep-seated curiosity about what at first seemed a very strange way of looking at the world. And still others were intrigued about the possibility of discovering a perennial philosophy (Leibniz's term), a common underlying way of understanding the world that, they postulated, lay at the heart of all the human cognitive systems of the world (Cracknell 1995).

At the same time, one quickly becomes aware that these quests tended to produce the same comparative exercises, whether the motivation for the comparison was to discover a point of contact for mission witness, a similar teaching for deeper understanding, or a structural root of human cognition. The discovery that the Buddha's teaching on *dukkha* (suffering), for example, had much in common with Christ's teaching on suffering for righteousness' sake appears in the writings of conversion-minded missionaries, academic researchers, and Christian philosophers. Sometimes the scantiness of the evidence makes identification of motivation of the comparison difficult, but careful historical study usually reveals it. The resulting effect on the indigenous Christian theologies developed in each of these areas dominated by Buddhism was liable to come from any and all contacts, missionary or otherwise.

It is also important to acknowledge the dialectical nature of these contacts with Buddhists in Burma (Myanmar), Bhutan, Cambodia, China (and Tibet), India (and Nepal), Japan, Korea, Laos, Mongolia, Singapore, Sri Lanka, Thailand, Vietnam, and, later, in the West. Contacts initiated by incoming Christians invariably produced reactions from resident Buddhists, reactions that often imitated the nature of the Christian initiatives, and heavily influenced, for good or ill, the nature of future interactions between Buddhist and Christian thinkers. In Sri Lanka, for example, the aggressive debating tactics of early Christian missionaries sometimes misrepresented the teachings of the Buddha in order to gain apologetic advantage. This led to responses in kind from Buddhist *bhikkhus* regarding the teachings of the Christ, and has left a residue of ill will toward Christians that poisons interactions to this day.

Not all Buddhist actions, however, were simply reactions. Buddhism is a missionary religion not unlike Christianity. Modern-day intellectual engagements between Christians and Buddhists must acknowledge this. Buddhists in Europe and North America are as mission-minded as are Christians sent from the West to Asia. Buddhists in the West differ in their motivations toward Christian thinking in ways similar to the three quests of Christians, described above, in regard to the *buddhadhamma*. Some Buddhists participate in this intellectual engagement in order to gain competitive advantage, some to satisfy intellectual curiosity, and some to uncover facets of our common cognitive nature. And as is the case with the three Christian quests, the motivations all seem to produce comparisons similar in nature.

One of the results, then, of over fifteen hundred years of contact between Buddhist cultural forces and Christian cultural forces has been the development of indigenous Christian theological thinking that is distinctive precisely because of the contact with Buddhist thinking. It is worthwhile to ask the question: What kinds of Christian theology emerge as a result of contacts with Buddhism? We might suggest that three distinctives characterize such theologies.

Compassion Theology

An eighteenth-century religious studies scholar, Rudolf Otto, after studying Buddhism in Asia, was so struck by the teachings of Pure Land Buddhism and its understanding of how Amita Buddha reached out from his heavenly abode to help aspiring *bodhisattvas* attain *nirvana* that he wrote a book about how closely this belief and action resembled the Christian understanding of grace. In *India's Religion of Grace* (1930) he tried to make the case that what had been uncovered here was nothing less than a nearly identical teaching to Christian teaching on grace.

> **Study Aid #28**
>
> Buddhist-Christian Theological Exchanges
>
> Compassion theologies: Christian grace and Buddhist *karuna*.
> Jesus Christ and Gautama Buddha: Comparison of life and teachings.
> Dogma and practice: Different fundamental orientations of the two religious traditions.
> Holiness and selflessness: The nature of the self and its relationship to the transcendent (God and emptiness).
> Meditation: Buddhist practices adapted for Christian use.

Otto's argument, whatever its merits, highlights the fact that the ideal of compassion runs across the Buddhist sectarian spectrum. In Chinese and southern Mahayana Buddhism (in Singapore, for example), the most popular *bodhisattva* by far is the female Kuan Yin, *bodhisattva* of compassion. In Theravada countries, one of the greatest of all virtues is that of *dana*, or gift giving to the needy. One of the most successful Christian mission workers to Tibet, Albert Shelton, brought a gospel of compassion shaped by medical care (Wissing 2004).

Literally hundreds of Asian, especially Japanese, Christian theologians have picked up on this theological commonality and devoted large parts of their contextualized theologies to emphasizing the importance of reaching out to the poor and marginalized with the compassion of Christ. Perhaps the most well-known of these theologians in the West is Kosuke Koyama, who wrote the book *Water Buffalo Theology* after years of mission work among poor villagers in northern Thailand. God's presence and grace in the midst of human suffering finds resonances not just with the poor but also with the underlying buddhalogical instincts of Asian Buddhists. Indeed, a Christian theology that does not place the grace of God front and center (especially as it relates to compassion) has little chance of succeeding in Buddhist cultures.

Buddhist teachings on compassion, however, cannot be separated from the underlying cycle of rebirth (*samsara*) based on merit (*karma*). *Karma* is accumulated by doing good for others. Good *karma* leads to a better rebirth. This means that compassion for others has a not-so-hidden benefit to the doing of good deeds—a better rebirth. For Christians, on the other hand, grace is defined as free gift. God does not benefit from giving us the gift of salvation; God is not forced to do it because of some human action, some merit-accumulating mechanism.

To Christians, the Buddhist view of merit smacks of earning one's salvation. The Buddhist would be quick to point out that earning merit for a better rebirth is not synonymous with enlightenment. Still, the implications of better rebirths are that one is put in material positions more likely to produce spiritual progress than regressive rebirths are likely to produce. For the Christian, then, Buddhist compassion is admirable, but grace, because it is free of the encumbrances of *samsara*, is even more admirable.

Yet one cannot gainsay the positive effects of this mutual emphasis on grace/*karuna*/*metta*. Christians and Buddhists have by and large together produced a relatively conflict-free history in their interactions. Mission done out of compassion, not conquest, tends to produce better social effects than what we see in other, clashing missions. Both Buddhists and Christians have done their share of conquest-oriented missions to nonadherents, though not toward each other.

Has Buddhism been similarly affected in the producing of its indigenous buddhologies by its contact with Christian grace? An answer to this must first acknowledge that Buddhists recognize two levels of truth, *samsaric* and *nirvanic*. *Samsaric* truth has to do with those teachings that allow us to operate in the material world here and now, even though we know that this world is ultimately unreal. *Nirvanic* truths are those truths that have to do with final liberation from the processes of *samsara*—that is, rebirth. The ultimate result of intuiting *nirvanic* truth is enlightenment.

One might speculate that Buddhist understandings of *samsaric* truth have been influenced by Christian models of both teaching and practice regarding compassionate action. Modern Engaged Buddhists in South Asian countries have been busily developing a Buddhist social consciousness that takes into account textual teachings and traditional Buddhist village values in contexts heavily affected by urbanization, modernization, and globalization. As one example, in 1966 a Taiwanese Buddhist nun started a Buddhist social service agency, Tzu Chi, that has raised millions of dollars for relief and development work, with offices in over thirty countries across Asia and worldwide.

Practice-Oriented Ecclesiology

There is truth in the cliché that Christianity favors orthodoxy (correct thinking) while Buddhism favors orthopraxy (correct practice). "Practice" in Buddhist terms means meditation. "Correct meditation" means any meditation that furthers one's progress toward enlightenment; thus, using skillful means (*upaya*) of several different categories of meditation are all considered productive.

Meditation

Meditation in Buddhism varies in method, not goal. The goal is *nirvana*, suchness, emptiness, the recognition that the independent, eternal soul or self is a

---
Study Aid #29
Meditation Styles

Vipassana: Insight meditation, characteristic of Theravada.
Zen: Using a-rational methodologies such as koans. Mahayana especially.
Visualizations: Tibetan Vajrayana methodologies such as mandalas.

chimera, a recognition that results in a blissful escape from the endless round of rebirths (*samsara*) into an ineffable, undefined state beyond all distinctions.

Skillful Means

Upaya, or skillful means, is the Buddhist way of saying that the "ortho" in "orthopraxy" is not a single correct method, but a variety of methods measured by utilitarian measures. If a practice, particularly meditation, is successful in bringing a person spiritual progress, then it is "correct." If it does not bring one success, then it is to be abandoned or changed. Usually what one changes in Buddhism is the teacher one is following in order to make progress.

Come and See

The Buddha was adamant that one should not follow his teaching (*dhamma*) simply because he said so. He preached. He persuaded. But he did so in order to entice people to give his way a try. Faith (*saddha*) for the Buddha was a sort of confidence that what they heard in the *dhamma* made sense and was worth investing a bit of energy (*viriya*) in order to try it and see.

This practice orientation strongly influenced the Christian theologies that have grown up in Buddhist cultures. Such emphasis on practice can be accentuated in situations where for political reasons Christians are forced to witness through deeds, not words, as in the second half of the twentieth century in Burma or Myanmar. An indigenous theologian and scholar of great repute, Pe Maung Tin, used his great scholarship to write Christian theology that used the practice orientation of Buddhist cultures to teach the gospel. His book *Prayer and Meditation* (1960) shows the practices of both traditions in their finest form.

In China, the writings of Watchman Nee (Ni Tuosheng), founder of the Local Church Movement (also called the Little Flocks and the Christian Assemblies), demonstrate an almost obsessive concern with holiness and individual spiritual commitment. Since public life is lived according to state dictates and largely Confucian cultural ideals, interior spirituality is prized. Again one sees a confluence between the practice orientation of Buddhism and the religious privatization required of one living in a totalitarian state.

To what extent might we say that Buddhism has been affected by the indigenous Christian theologies of Asia in this area of practice? Perhaps the most obvious way has been the wholesale adoption of Christian mission methods. In Singapore, large Buddhist temples have adopted methods that make them largely indistinguishable from nondenominational megachurches in the United States. From sophisticated websites to youth programs that include basketball leagues and outings to public "worship" that looks suspiciously like Protestant seeker services, the wholesale adoption of market-oriented forms shows the extent to which Buddhist outreach has been affected by globalization.

Humble Holiness

A third characteristic of indigenous Christian theologies that have grown up in the context of Buddhist cultures is what one might call an emphasis on humble holiness. Maseo Abe, a Japanese Buddhist of the Kyoto school, was one of the first to make explicit the parallels between the signature doctrine of Buddhism, the no-self (or *anatta*) teaching, and the teachings on selflessness in the New Testament, particularly the kenosis passage in Philippians. Both traditions, according to these teachings, seem designed to fight against the excessive individualism of the modern, globalized world.

In the end, the selfless teachings of the New Testament don't approach the radical nature of the no-self doctrine of Buddhism. The Buddha taught that no permanent enduring self or soul exists. We live as if we are individuals, but spiritual progress is predicated on the recognition of the no-self doctrine. It is not too much to say that once we really understand, at the deepest intuitive level, this truth, we are enlightened.

The Christian Bible by contrast teaches that an enduring, permanent soul exists. We are enduring souls created by God for relationship with God. Yet this relationship with God is not an equal partnership. God is Creator and we are created. Problems develop when we think more of our "selves" than is proper in such a relationship—thus the New Testament teachings, particularly in Paul's Letters, on the importance of a selfless nature, a nonselfish attitude toward life in general.

In the practice of everyday life these two traditions look very much the same. The lived life of a Buddhist who is trying to grasp the radical nature of *anatta* (no-self) and the Christian attempting to overcome the temptation to pride of self are remarkably similar. Both extol what the world would consider relatively useless virtues such as meekness, humility, and altruistic love. Christian theologies that have a chance of succeeding in Buddhist cultures must relate to this congruence. Some examples follow.

Ham Sok Hon has been called the Gandhi of Korea because he articulated a spiritual vision for Korea not unlike the one Gandhi articulated for an independent India. Whereas Gandhi's vision originated in his understanding of Hindu Vedic thought, however, Ham Sok Hon's originated in his understanding of Christianity (and later Buddhism, Confucianism, and shamanism). In retelling the history of Korea from this perspective in his book *Queen of Suffering: A Spiritual History of Korea* (1985), the author identifies Korea's spiritual fate to be suffering and its calling to be to show the world how to bear that suffering "without grumbling, without evading, and with determination and seriousness" (27). This is what will help lead the world to salvation.

In a similar way, Shusaku Endo captures the essence of what Christianity probably will have to look like in Japan to succeed. Particularly in his novel *Silence* (1966), Endo shows that the aggressive, triumphalistic Western versions of Christianity have only achieved short-term successes in Japan before being rolled back by indigenous reactions. To put it in Confucian terms, theological systems dominated by the too-heavily masculine forces of yang will have to give way to yin-dominated theological expressions if they are to succeed in Japan.

In Thailand, Nantachai and Ubolwon Mejuhon have worked with a Christian mission approach they call meekness theology. Theravada Buddhist cultures like Thailand's, they argue, do not respond well to traditional Western mission approaches if those approaches are antithetical to the affective dimension of the Thai people. That affective dimension they call meekness. Their Maung Thai Church in Bangkok is testament to the effectiveness of this approach, as are the eighteen daughter churches Maung Thai has planted around Thailand.

Buddhism in the Modern West

In Western Europe and North America, one can observe a set of related indigenizing movements that are the mirror image of those described above—Buddhist mission workers attempting to develop indigenized versions of buddhology appropriate to Western contexts. Two areas of emphasis tend to stand out.

Meditation

In keeping with the individualizing emphases of Western cultures, one of the most attractive things about traditional Buddhism is its effective meditative practices. When Westerners who have to some degree or another adopted Buddhism as a way of being in the world are asked what first attracted them to this tradition, meditation is far and away the most frequently mentioned feature. Of course, in the West, meditative practice must be wrenched from its embeddedness in Asian cultures in both the *sangha* (the monastic order of monks and nuns) and village life.

Engaged Buddhism

The Engaged Buddhist movement gained a toehold in Western culture through the initiatives of world-Buddhists such as Thich Nhat Hanh and the Dalai Lama, who have captured the attention of a certain slice of Western academia with a form of Buddhism tailored to what Christians might call the gospel of social action. By emphasizing the importance of the religions of the world needing to step up to the issues of poverty, disease, and injustice, a form of Buddhism has arisen that is doing just that (King and Queen 1996).

Sources

Kenneth Cracknell. *Justice, Courtesy and Love: Theologians and Missionaries Encountering World Religions, 1846–1914.* Epworth, 1995.

Shusaku Endo. *Silence*. Taplinger, 1966.

Thich Nhat Hanh. *Peace Is Every Step*. Bantam, 1992.

William Hart. *The Art of Living: Vipassana Meditation as Taught by S. N. Goenka*. HarperSanFrancisco, 1987.

Ham Sok Hon. *Queen of Suffering: A Spiritual History of Korea*. Friends World Committee, 1985.

Sallie B. King and Christopher Queen. *Engaged Buddhism: Buddhist Liberation Movements*. SUNY, 1996.

Kosuke Koyama. *Water Buffalo Theology*. Orbis Books, 1999.

Samuel Hugh Moffett. *A History of Christianity in Asia*. 2 vols. Orbis Books, 1998–2005.

Watchman Nee. *Spiritual Man*. Tyndale, 1968.

Rudolf Otto. *India's Religion of Grace and Christianity Compared and Contrasted*. Macmillan, 1930.

Pe Maung Tin. *Prayer and Meditation*. Burma Christian Literature Society, 1960.

Douglas A. Wissing. *Pioneer in Tibet: The Life and Perils of Albert Shelton*. Palgrave Macmillan, 2004.

14

Buddhism: Current Issues

Terry C. Muck

Relationships today between Buddhists and Christians worldwide are good. This is in keeping with the roughly fifteen hundred years of interactions, which in general have been peaceful and constructive.

Much if not most of the credit for this relatively peaceful set of interactions must go to Buddhism if for no other reason than that, while Buddhism has had peaceful interactions with the other world religions, Christianity's interactions with the other world religions have been less than peaceful. And as we have seen, Buddhism's capacity to coexist with other religious systems is one of the keys to its cross-cultural spread.

This is not to say that there have not been issues, or that there are no issues today. Below we identify four important interactions in the world today. Not all of the issues we identify are negative. On the contrary, some hold great promise for future healthy missional interactions.

Issue: Conversion. Location: Sri Lanka

It is almost inevitable that two of the world's most noted missionary religions would at some points clash over their mutual search for converts. Historically it is probably the case that Buddhism has most often been on the receiving end of Christian attempts at converting Buddhists. Christians came early to Asian Buddhist countries—as early as the Nestorian Christian entry into China in the seventh century. In our day, however, Buddhism gives as much as it gets. Energetic mission efforts to the traditionally Christian strongholds of Europe and North America have resulted in significant Buddhist communities developing in both places.

In most places today where both Buddhists and Christians seek new members, the competition is peaceful and healthy. Such is the case in Europe and North America in the West, and Thailand and Singapore in Asia. It is notable that all of these places are heavily influenced by globalized markets and political systems that provide at least neutral conditions for religious pluralism. When the religious playing field is reasonably level, Buddhists and Christians tend to coexist well.

When such is not the case, two reasons seem to be the culprits. The first has to do with the history of the interaction. How contact was originally made, the methods used to do mission, and the nature of the response from the indigenous population create a historical context that is often determinative for what is going on today. A second telling factor is the current political and economic context. Christianity, for example, is often seen as a threat to political stability and local economic interests, and when that is the case, conflict often results.

A case in point is the important island country of Sri Lanka. Christian missionaries to Sri Lanka followed the merchants of Portugal (Roman Catholic), the Netherlands (Reformed), and Great Britain (Methodist and Baptist). The methods of these early Christian missionaries were not always exemplary. In their attempts to champion the superiority of Christianity, they sometimes misrepresented Buddhism and its founder, the Buddha. This became most noticeable in a number of nineteenth-century public debates between representatives of the two traditions.

In a debate, like begets like. Soon, misrepresentations were common on both sides. And not just in debates but also in publications. An atmosphere of not-very-healthy competition developed, an atmosphere that exists today in Sri Lanka. Christian missionaries are not highly thought of by the general Buddhist populace. At best, relationships between Buddhists and Christians are strained; at worst, violent.

A general principle emerges. Be careful what mission method you choose, because it is likely that the same method will be adopted by the religion on the receiving end of it—and will be used in their approaches to you. And if there are excesses, you will eventually be subject to the same excesses.

Issue: Dual Belonging. Location: United States

A common feature of human religious systems is that they ask for change and choice. In general, people would not be religious if they did not perceive a lack in their life and the desirability of change. And since there are many religious options available in most countries of the world today, a choice must be made in terms of what religion to choose.

> **Study Aid #30**
>
> Current Buddhist and Buddhist-Christian Issues
>
> Social engagement: Engaged Buddhism and Christian social action.
> Reciprocal missions: The different ways of doing mission.
> Dual belonging: Being both Buddhist and Christian?
> Religion and politics: The religiously endorsed models.

Buddhism and Christianity have different approaches in how they advise people to make these choices. Of course, both teach that their religious system is the best one and, all things being equal, the choice should be clear. But guidance in just what such a choice looks like diverges from there.

For Buddhists, choosing the *buddhadhamma* does not necessarily mean giving up what one already believes—nor does it mean that choosing the *buddhadhamma* precludes one from taking advantage of the good things other religious systems have to offer. For Christians, choosing the gospel has traditionally meant both those things—giving up one's previous religion and finding religious succor in Christianity alone.

One possible solution to this is what has become known as dual belonging—Buddhists who decide to add elements of Christianity to their religious quivers, and Christians who decide to add elements of Buddhism to their religious quivers. If it can be called a modern movement, it seems to have started in the United States with academics initially interested in studying Buddhism as an academic discipline, then with those same scholars becoming interested in interreligious dialogue between the two faith traditions, and finally with some making dual-faith commitments. One of the organizations that have actively studied and discussed dual belonging in their meetings and their journal is the Society for Buddhist-Christian Studies.

Although the ways of combining the two religious traditions can vary widely, a common configuration is for Christians to add elements of Buddhist practice, particularly meditation, to their religious repertoire. Their belief structure remains essentially Christianity of a mystical sort, but uses the spiritual technologies of Buddhism to access the deeper levels of experience/belief.

Occasionally the borrowing goes the other way. Buddhists find the reflective aspects of Christian theology appealing, begin to do some philosophical comparison of the two systems, and develop syntheses of one sort or another. As I mentioned, this kind of combining is second nature to Asian Buddhists and produces some interesting theological constructs that have influenced both Buddhism and Christianity.

A general principle emerges here also: two religions in proximity experience two competing drives. One, to define as clearly as possible differences between the two traditions, and two, to look for as many similarities and complementarities as possible.

Issue: Engagement. Location: Southeast Asia

One of the ways Christians and Buddhists are coming together is through their mutual recognition of the needs of the poor and the needs of the planet. Although Christians have been known from their very beginning as the "people who cared for one another," such activity, at least on an organized, theorized scale, has come lately to Buddhists.

In the 1960s a Vietnamese Buddhist monk, Thich Nhat Hanh, coined the phrase "engaged Buddhism." By that he meant Buddhism that encouraged not only personal meditative practice but also care for the environment and activities that aided the poor, oppressed, and sick. His teaching has taken root. Consider a case study, the recent tsunami disaster in Southeast Asia.

When a tsunami-like disaster strikes, people expect their religion to help them answer two questions: *Why did this happen?* and *What should we do about it?* Call the first the meaning-question and the second the action-question.

As we watched postdisaster events unfold in Sri Lanka and Thailand, dominantly Buddhist countries, some have been struck by the way Buddhists have enlisted their religion in answering both the meaning-question and the action-question. Those observations have become especially intriguing when compared with the way religious persons in predominantly Christian countries attempt to answer the same questions.

Consider the meaning-question. Although different Christians might answer the meaning-question using slightly different formulations, almost all would consider it mandatory to develop the answer out of their ethical, monotheistic tradition. Christians believe in a single, powerful God who desires good for the created world, including human beings. The Christian response to disaster, then, is to pray. *Why, God, did you let this happen? How can this possibly be in your plan for us?* Apparently God answers Christians differently when asked this question; a theological conundrum called theodicy—the problem of evil—has resulted from the disagreements over the way God seems to speak. Yet although the answers (or at least what we hear as answers) may differ, the act of going to God with the question in the first place is the quintessential Christian act, an act of acknowledging God's power that somehow brings succor to the devastated.

Buddhists approach the meaning-question with a different set of constructs. Buddhism, like Christianity, has no single party line in answering the meaning-question. Almost all, however, would answer it in the context of the Buddha's teachings on suffering, impermanence, and *karma*. We suffer because everything is impermanent, changing. The world changes according to the laws of *karma*, an overall web of good and bad deeds by persons and human-created institutions. One effects change not by praying to God but by meditating on the complexity of karmic events that are responsible for the moment-to-moment changes that continually alter our world. The problem is that no one of us can fully account for the entire karmic web. Thus, the specific "why" eludes us. The quintessential

> **Study Aid #31**
>
> **Buddhist Demographics**
>
> Number of Buddhists in the world: 469 million
> Percentage of world population: 7 percent
> Number of countries where Buddhists make up more than 50 percent of population: 8 (Thailand, Cambodia, Myanmar, Sri Lanka, Bhutan, Japan, Laos, Vietnam)

Buddhist act is to acknowledge impermanence and the resulting suffering, and vow to contribute positively what each of us can to the ever-changing karmic web. A certain peace—equanimity—is the result.

The differences between these two systems are profound. One believes in a single, all-powerful God who determines the destinies of the world; the other, if it believes in gods at all, sees them as divine helpers (such as Kuan Yin, the goddess/*bodhisattva* of compassion) rather than all-powerful determiners. One sees cause and effect as operative only as mitigated by divine fiat and human free will; the other elevates cause and effect to absolute status—in the samsaric world at least.

Yet the profound differences in these two religious contexts do not produce radical divergences in answer to the second question, the action-question, but rather an awesome congruity. What should we do in the face of unprecedented disaster? First, help the suffering; second, correct what can be identified as causative factors.

As we watched the events unfold on CNN, we saw Buddhists and Christians shoulder to shoulder helping those in need. We saw Western, religiously based aid agencies like World Vision, Catholic Relief Services, and Church World Service working side by side with Asian, religiously based aid agencies like Sarvodaya in Sri Lanka and Tzu Chi in Malaysia, Thailand, Indonesia, Taiwan, and elsewhere, to provide help.

Make no mistake. It is the respective answers to the meaning-questions that motivate Buddhists and Christians to act. Without those specific answers, their good deeds would be nothing more than human attempts to be good. It is the religious contexts that sanctify the deeds. Neither Buddhists nor Christians see their answers to the meaning-questions as irrelevant or interchangeable.

But the hopeful side of the response to the tsunami disaster is that perhaps the religions of the world can acknowledge that we can both hold to our religious commitments and at the same time join hands with those who have different commitments for the purpose of promoting human flourishing. Agreeing for the sake of the present and future to disagree may not be the easiest thing in the world to do; but it is what is required for all our hopes for peace.

Issue: Religion and Politics. Location: Tibet—and the West

The extent to which the Dalai Lama has captured the imagination of the Western intelligentsia can probably be ascribed to a unique set of circumstances that would be hard to imagine in any other religion today. It is not that the other religions have not had similar characters in the twentieth century. Islam had the Ayatollah Khomeini, Roman Catholicism had Pope John Paul II and Lech Walesa in Poland, and the United States had its evangelical, fundamentalist, and Pentecostal televangelists. Each of these, in addition to their religious leadership, has had enormous political influence.

The Dalai Lama, however, seems unique for a number of reasons. The first is his charismatic personality. He has exceptional intelligence, but it is an intelligence filtered through an ability to be clear and down to earth. His books, for example, are a model of communicative skill. In public he displays that universal lubricant, a sense of humor, that can establish common human ground, or turn an awkward confrontation into a feel-good interaction. He is the one religious leader that you can invite to a public podium and not be afraid of an out-of-place comment or an embarrassing faux pas. His presence is invariably flawless.

The second reason the Dalai Lama is unique is in his religious role. There is no mistaking his primary identity as the religious leader of Tibetan Buddhists. He does not apologize for that primary role, nor does he try to camouflage it in his presentations. Yet he focuses on that which unites rather than that which divides. He encourages both his followers and those of other religions he meets to think about what they have in common in their humanity, without ever denigrating the very obvious differences between Tibetan Buddhism and Christianity, Hinduism, Islam, Judaism, and other religions. This is not just a feature of his particular religion. He comes from one of the most sectarian of all religions, Tibetan Buddhism, which in his home country has competing factions. Yet the Dalai Lama seems to rise above the fray—at least in his public persona.

Study Aid #32
Countries with Buddhist Populations

China	190 million
Japan	71 million
Thailand	56 million
Vietnam	44 million
Myanmar	37 million
Sri Lanka	13 million
Cambodia	13 million
India	8.5 million
South Korea	7.3 million
Taiwan	6.2 million
United States	3 million

Third is his political savvy. The place where he affects Buddhist and Christian interactions the most is in his political leadership. He is considered the de facto leader of indigenous Tibetan people and has demonstrated great wisdom in attempting to champion the rights of his political charges without offending either China, who also claims political leadership over those same charges, and the other political leaders of the Western world, who must balance their respect for him with the health of their relations with China. He has lived in exile in India for many years, but he has not sacrificed his moral, religious, or political standing in his homeland. A remarkable achievement.

Is there a general, interreligious, Buddhist-Christian principle evident in the life and teachings of the Dalai Lama? Try this. There are within each of our religious traditions similarities to the other tradition—and differences. Whenever a religious leader, Buddhist or Christian, speaks out, he or she can choose to emphasize one or the other. There is a way to maintain one's faith and beliefs in the uniqueness of one's tradition without eschewing the value of humanity's common religious heritage.

Sources

Sebastian Kim. *In Search of Identity: Debates on Religious Conversion in India.* Oxford University Press, 2003.

Whalen Lai and Michael von Bruck. *Christianity and Buddhism: A Multi-Cultural History of Their Dialogue.* Orbis Books, 2001.

R. F. Young and G. P. V. Somaratna. *Vain Debates: The Buddhist Christian Controversies of Nineteenth-Century Ceylon.* Vienna, 1996.

15

Buddhism: Adherent Essay

Rita M. Gross

I am both a convert to Buddhism and a longtime practitioner of Buddhism. I consider that I became a Buddhist in 1973, when I was thirty years old, though I had knowledge of Buddhism for some years before that time and did not go through a ceremony of "Going for Refuge," the point at which one formally becomes a Buddhist, for some years after that time. Though I was brought up Christian, that religion and I had parted ways, quite unhappily, some years before I began to be personally interested in Buddhism.

As a college philosophy major, I decided that I wanted to devote my life and career to studying a discipline that truly dealt with answers to life's fundamental questions, and I decided that discipline would be religious studies, not philosophy. At the same time, even though I had no cross-cultural experience at all, I also decided that it made no sense to assume that culturally familiar religions had all the good and relevant answers to those fundamental life question, which led me to the PhD program in the discipline of history of religions, called comparative religions by many, at the University of Chicago. There I was first exposed to the study of Buddhism in a thorough way, though I do remember that I first heard of Buddhism in a philosophy of religion class as a college sophomore, and that even before that, somehow I had some knowledge of Tibet, despite no formal exposure at all to the study of such material. I suspect that my unhappy childhood relationship with Christianity had something to do with the decision to look beyond the Western orbit in my studies. Any intellectual curiosity at all was quite forbidden in the branch of Christianity in which I had been brought up. Suffice it to report that when I was excommunicated for the heresy of not being willing to believe that only Christians could go to heaven, I was told by the excommunicating pastor: "I knew even when you were a kid that I'd have trouble with you someday. You asked too many questions!"

Initially, I did not find Buddhism very appealing. As is the case for many, when I first tried to understand Buddhism, it seemed incomprehensible and backward to me. I was much more interested in Hinduism and also became embroiled in the early emergence of feminist studies in religion. But in 1965, when I began these studies, I didn't see either Buddhism or Hinduism as a relevant option for personal practice. In those days, it was frowned upon for scholars to have any personal interest in the religions they studied, at least if they were "Eastern" religions. Furthermore, at that time there really was no way to *practice* an Asian religion in North America as opposed to simply learning information about it.

My own conversion experience came early in my teaching career. Teaching a university-level course on Buddhism for the second time, I felt that I did not yet have a good understanding of the Buddhist worldview. I was also experiencing tremendous personal pain. As I struggled with my own pain while simultaneously struggling to understand the Four Truths of Buddhism, suddenly things came into perspective. I was suffering so deeply because of my own desire for things to be different than they were; the Four Truths of Buddhism were *true*. They explained my experience as nothing else ever had. In that moment I resolved to learn to meditate as soon as I could find a way to do so.

Since that time, my commitment to Buddhist principles has been unfaltering, and I have become a Buddhist *dharma* teacher myself with a somewhat noteworthy title. I practice and teach in the Tibetan Vajrayana tradition of Buddhism, though my approach to Buddhism, and to religion itself, is nonsectarian. In the many years since I became a Buddhist, I have thought about and published articles on many of the contemporary issues facing Buddhists. One of the most important areas has been my work on gender and Buddhism. I am the author of an important book on that topic: *Buddhism after Patriarchy: A Feminist History, Analysis, and Reconstruction of Buddhism* (SUNY Press, 1993). I have also devoted significant attention to Buddhist-Christian dialogue, having been a president of the Society for Buddhist-Christian Studies, coeditor of its journal for ten years, and coeditor of two books on the topic.

Buddhism and Christianity belong to two very different families of religions and have had relatively little interaction, historically. Christianity is a theistic tradition, while Buddhism is one of the world's few nontheistic religions. Christianity posits personal immortality as the goal of religious life, while Buddhists seek enlightenment and regard personal immortality as impossible. Both religions are alike in that they have spread far and wide beyond their places of historical origin, and both are universalizing religions that regard their message as relevant for all people regardless of culture or ethnicity. However, their methods of gaining converts and spreading have been quite different.

For much of their histories, Buddhism and Christianity have operated in different parts of the globe. Because there was little interaction between them until the era of European colonialism and Christian missionary expansion, these two universalizing religions do not have the long history of mutual warfare and violence that characterizes the history of Christian relationships with Christianity's monotheistic cousins. Though Christians have sought to missionize traditionally Buddhist countries and cultures for centuries, Buddhism is still strong in most of its traditional homelands. In the twentieth century, Communism has had a much more deleterious effect on Buddhism than has Christianity, especially in China and Tibet. Korea, however, has seen a much more successful Christian missionary movement. This traditionally Buddhist country has become about half Christian quite rapidly. Historically, Islam has probably been more damaging to Buddhism than has Christianity. Islam now holds sway in areas that formerly were home to large Buddhist populations, from Afghanistan to Indonesia, including much of India, Buddhism's homeland, where it has been only a minor religion for the last eight hundred years.

Westerners have had some knowledge of Buddhism for about one hundred and fifty years, but only in the last fifty years has Buddhism become widely established as a viable and visible religion in the West, due both to large numbers of Western converts to Buddhism and to large numbers of Asian immigrants who are at least nominally Buddhist. Buddhism has had a large impact on every aspect of Western elite culture, from psychotherapy to the arts. In some circles it has become almost fashionable to claim that one is a Buddhist. There has also been a significant international dialogue movement between Buddhists and Christians, with several international societies operating on at least three continents devoted to this endeavor. Because these two traditions, for the most part, do not have a difficult history with each other and because they are so different theologically in many ways, a mutually interesting and beneficial dialogue between these two traditions is quite possible. The large number of significant publications in this area attests to the success of the dialogue.

Some difficulties between these two traditions are also quite possible and are prevalent in some parts of the world. Both religions are successful missionary religions, and both believe that their core messages could be relevant for anyone of any cultural background. However, their attitudes toward potential converts are very different and can cause significant problems when the two religions must coexist within the same territory, as is now the case in our global village. To state the contrast most sharply, large segments of Christianity still adhere to *exclusive* truth claims, which are different from *universal* truth claims, while Buddhists usually claim that there is a variety of *skillful means or methods* for arriving at universal truths. Those who make exclusive truth claims insist that there is one exclusive route to the universal truth. Thus, for those who make exclusive truth claims, religious diversity is a mistake to be corrected as soon as possible by the conversion of the entire world to the one exclusive truth. By contrast, those who value the teaching that there are different skillful methods recognize that because of peoples' psychological diversity and differing personal histories (what Buddhists call *karma*), no single *method* or style of religious belief and practice will ever be effective or possible for everyone. Thus, religious diversity is inevitable and natural, which seems to me to be a much more reasonable and compassionate way of thinking about religious diversity than its alternative.

Today, Buddhists in parts of the world that are subjected to intensive Christian missionizing are deeply resentful of the intensity of that effort. Buddhists recognize that some people may be drawn to a religion that is so different from the religion into which they were born; that is, in part, what the teaching of skillful means is all about. But Buddhists also think that personal affinities and differing *karma* among individuals can be left to do their work without any need for aggressive, intensive proselytizing efforts on behalf of exclusive truth claims. Such efforts, we Buddhists would claim, are misguided and lacking in basic compassion and respect. The fact that Buddhism has done so well as a missionary religion relying on skillful means rather than exclusive truth claims, including in the Christian stronghold of the West, should demonstrate to Christians that there are viable and successful alternatives to their heavy-handed, traditional, exclusive truth claims. It would be very helpful if Buddhist-Christian dialogue on skillful means and religious diversity could reach those segments of Christianity that still believe they have an exclusive monopoly on religious truth that they must spread around the globe at any and all costs, including the tragedy of the eradication of religious diversity.

16

Judaism: History, Beliefs, Practices

RICHARD ROBINSON

History

The term "Judaism" is sometimes applied to the faith of the Jewish people going back as far as Moses and Abraham, considered as the seminal figures of Judaism. More specifically, Judaism refers to the Jewish faith since 70 CE, when a reconstruction of the religion took place in response to the loss of the temple and, not long after, the loss of the land as well. One also sees references to "intertestamental Judaism" and also a variety of "Judaisms" in the first century. For this article, I will be referring to the post–70 CE religion as reconstructed by the rabbis. Its antecedents are found in the Pharisees, the surviving sect after 70 CE.

It is impossible to separate the religion of Judaism from the Jewish people, or the history of Judaism from Jewish history. The Jewish people were from the beginning constituted as a nation of faith. It is also impossible to separate Judaism from its books and literature; it is for good reason that the Jews have been known as the People of the Book. The following history can only recap certain highlights.

The Reconstruction of Judaism

According to the generally accepted view, after the catastrophe of 70 CE, the Council of Yavneh convened to deal with the aftermath. At this time, rabbinic Judaism reconstructed the religion as one without temple, sacrifices, or priests. The daily times of sacrifice were replaced by times of prayer; atonement was now said to be secured through repentance, *tzedakah* (charity), and fasting. The synagogue, already well established as an institution perhaps even from the time of the Babylonian captivity, now became the central place of worship, and the institution of the rabbi as well as many elements of the synagogue liturgy were solidified.

The Development of the Oral Law

From intertestamental times on (with antecedents in the Hebrew Bible), various streams of interpretation arose concerning how to observe the law of Moses in practice and adapt it to changing conditions. This, in fact, was one of the differences between the conservative Sadducees and the more adaptable Pharisees. At around 200 CE, Judah *haNasi* (the Prince) set down much of this tradition in the Mishnah, until then transmitted orally but now put in writing from fear that the oral tradition would become lost. From around 200 to 550 CE, the much larger Gemaras, consisting of further oral legal discussions as well as ethics and folklore, were also set down in writing. One Gemara was compiled in Babylonia, which became the leading center of Jewish life in around 200 CE and remained so for the next thousand years. However, a Jewish community continued in Galilee, producing another and less authoritative Gemara. The Mishnah together with the two Gemaras formed respectively the Babylonian Talmud and the Jerusalem, or Palestinian, Talmud, the former constituting the foundation of all ensuing Jewish law. Sometime in the first centuries CE, the doctrine of the Oral Law, according to which God gave not only the Written Law (the Torah) but also its inspired oral interpretation to Moses, was solidified. Judaism increasingly became a religion in which daily life was guided by Jewish law, or *halakhah*, under the authority of the rabbis.

Times of Prosperity, Times of Conflict

From about the eighth century to the twelfth century CE is considered to be the golden age of Jewry in Spain (some date the period more narrowly), a period of intellectual flourishing and relative peace vis-à-vis non-Jews. Influenced by Arabic philosophy as well as by Aristotelian philosophy, sages such as Maimonides wrote works of philosophy and dogma, poetry, and law codes that sought to make accessible the teaching of the Talmud. To Maimonides we owe the Thirteen Articles of Faith, the nearest thing in Judaism to a statement of beliefs. Meanwhile, French and German Jewry during the latter part of this period produced Bible commentaries, preeminently those by Rashi as well as by Ibn Ezra and others. While Spanish Jewry had primarily Arabic contact until the Christian reconquest of Spain was complete, in northern and Eastern Europe the contact was with Christians (see next article). From this time too can be traced the different streams of culture and religious customs of Ashkenazic (Eastern European) and Sephardic (Spanish and Mediterranean) Jewry. In later medieval times, the Jewish center moved to Eastern Europe, where life was characterized by far more conflict with Christian

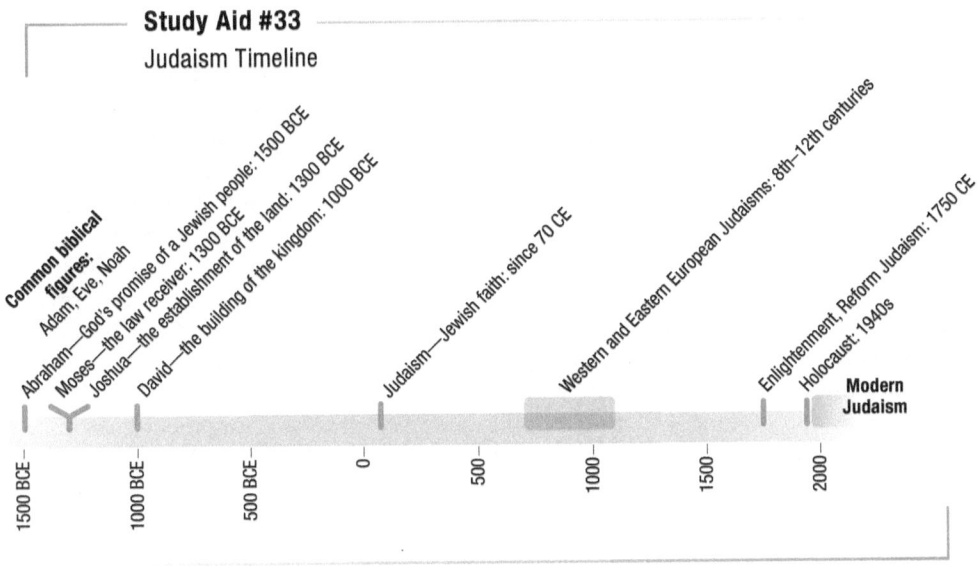

Study Aid #33
Judaism Timeline

society and a less vigorous intellectual life; and under Christian rule in Spain, France, and Germany, Jewish life was regularly punctuated by persecution and anti-Semitism (see next article).

The Kabbalah

In medieval times, the Kabbalah became prominent through the teaching of the book known as the *Zohar*. Kabbalah is the system of Jewish mysticism. According to one stream of kabbalistic thought, God exists in ten emanations (*sefirot*); at creation the divine light shattered its containing vessels, raining sparks down upon the earth. Now, by keeping the *mitzvot* (divine commandments), we can raise the sparks and redeem the universe. This "version" of the Kabbalah continues to influence both Jews and non-Jews today in art and popular culture, and it exists side by side with serious study.

Rise of Hasidic Judaism

From 1750 on, the sect of the Hasidim arose as a response to what was seen as lifeless orthodoxy. The Hasidim emphasized expressive joy along with the keeping of the commandments, and saw their leader, the *tzaddik* or *rebbe*, as variously a teacher, healer, and conduit to God. Today there exist a number of Hasidic groups, often termed ultra-Orthodox, each named after its town of origin and each with its own *rebbe*. The best-known is the Lubavitcher Hasidim, known for their vigorous worldwide outreach to non-Orthodox Jews via their network of Chabad houses.

The Enlightenment and Its Aftermath

From 1750 on is also the period of the Enlightenment, known in Judaism as the Haskalah. From this period we trace Reform Judaism, German in origin, as a movement that not only abandoned much traditional belief and behavior but also sought to assimilate into general society partly as (it was thought) a way of addressing anti-Semitism. Reform Judaism today is much less radical than when it began. Conservative Judaism, a middle ground between Reform and traditional (now called Orthodox) Judaism, has German roots but is primarily an American movement. Additional offshoots such as Reconstructionist Judaism exist, and Judaism today comprises ultra-Orthodox, modern Orthodox, Conservative, Reform, and secular, forming a pluralistic spectrum. In the United States, about one-third of Jews identify as Reform, about as many as Conservative, and about 10 percent as Orthodox (with many of the rest seeing themselves as "nonreligious" Jews). Since 1948, Israel (5.4 million Jewish people) has become a center of world Jewry and is poised to outnumber North American Jews (6 million) in the near future. Despite a strong influence of Orthodox Judaism in the government of Israel, the majority of Israelis are secular, with varying senses of tradition and observance.

Beliefs

It is often said that Judaism is a religion of deed, not creed. Indeed, it is possible to be a religious (observant) Jew in *practice* and yet have no clear *ideas* about the afterlife, the nature of humanity, or even God. Nevertheless, there are some non-negotiable beliefs that have characterized Judaism. If there is any "cardinal doctrine" of Judaism, it is the oneness (or unity) of God as formulated in the Shema (Deut. 6:4), recited three times a day and integral to the synagogue liturgy. The oneness of God has been understood since medieval times to disallow the possibility that God could be a Trinity or that God could become human. The medieval period uniquely saw the rise of statements of "dogma," the best known of which is Maimonides's Thirteen Principles of Faith, still an authoritative source. These statements, philosophical and logical in nature, specified among other things which doctrines must be believed to be included in the "world to come." Not before or since has doctrine been so much emphasized in Judaism as in the medieval period, nor tied so closely to one's eternal fate.

In general, the traditional Jewish belief is that Israel is required to live by the *mitzvot* (the divine commandments, traditionally enumerated as 613), while non-Jews need only follow the so-called Seven Laws of Noah.

Since the rise of Reform and Conservative Judaism, some "official" differences of belief can be noted—"official" in the sense that one can sometimes find statements outlining these beliefs in the platforms of the various branches of Judaism, or at least in books that are written to explain the particularities of each branch.

Orthodox Judaism—the only kind of Judaism that existed prior to the Enlightenment—believes in a personal God who entered into a covenant with the people of Israel, a people who are now obligated to follow God's Torah (Law). This Torah consists of not only the Written Law found in Genesis through Deuteronomy but also the Oral Law, comprising divinely given interpretation of the Written Law, which was also delivered to Moses on Mount Sinai. This Oral Law was finally written down lest it be forgotten. Orthodox Judaism also stresses the authority of the rabbis, basing this upon Deuteronomy 17:8–13. It is through the rabbis that the *halakhah* has developed, which applies Jewish law to new situations. While non-Jews sometimes see this process as "legalism," it actually reflects the need to adjust law to changing needs and circumstances, as well as to spell out in detail what the law may say only in generalities. In Orthodox Judaism, ideas of the future and the afterlife remain vague. A personal, human (not divine) Messiah is expected, who will accomplish the gathering of the Jewish people to Israel from the worldwide dispersion (the Diaspora or *galut*), the rebuilding of the temple in Jerusalem, and the ushering in of world peace.

In contrast, Reform Judaism allows for wide latitude of views about God, the afterlife, sin, and other beliefs. Reform Jews treat the Bible as a repository of history and story mixed with folklore, superstition, and outdated customs, but not as a divine product. The Bible is, however, mined for its ethical teachings, with particular emphasis placed on the Prophets, in contrast to the Orthodox, who treat both written and oral law as of divine origin and emphasize the Torah and law. For many Reform Jews, Jewish identity—the Jewish people—is what is central, as opposed to faith in God; observance of traditions, Jewish holidays, and so forth is useful only insofar as it allows for an expression of ethnic identity, not because of any divine force behind that observance.

Conservative Judaism takes a middle-ground position, sometimes closer to the Orthodox view than to the Reform.

Apart from theological beliefs, we can note that among all Jews there is the belief in the need for Jewish survival. Even in the best of situations, Jews have generally seen the world in terms of "us" and "them." Jews have been subjected to anti-Semitism and horrific persecutions, and for many it has become clear that wherever Jewish people live, survival as a people—which includes passing on

---

Study Aid #34

Jewish Beliefs

Monotheism: There is only one God.
Covenant: God and humanity's mutual agreement.
Torah: Life is to be lived by the law.
Land: God's promises of a land for all time.
Survival: The need for God's people to survive.

ethnic and/or religious Jewish identity, not simply physical survival—is an ongoing goal. The widespread support for the nation of Israel among Jews worldwide is an expression of this belief, as is the idea that Jews—who in today's world may be found exploring a wide variety of spiritualities—cannot believe in Jesus, for to do so would mean ceasing to be a Jew. It is sometimes remarked, not entirely tongue-in-cheek, that today's Jewish world is so pluralistic that the only thing that all Jews can agree on is nonbelief in Jesus as the Messiah.

Practices

Orthodox Jews live according to Orthodox rabbinic *halakhah*, or Jewish law, which guides all situations of life. *Halakhah* is an ongoing process, for new life situations always arise, but it is always based on rabbinic authority and precedent going back to the time of the Talmud or even earlier. When questions of practice arise, therefore, a rabbi is consulted. Conservative Judaism follows a more flexible *halakhah*, while Reform relies on voluntary desire to observe as one sees fit.

As an example, Orthodox and Conservative observe the Sabbath according to rabbinic *halakhah*. The prohibition of "lighting a fire" on the Sabbath (based on Exod. 35:3) extends to the prohibition on not driving on the Sabbath—since a spark is created when starting the engine—as well as to not turning electricity on or off. Reform Jews, on the other hand, will freely drive on the Sabbath. The Orthodox and Conservative movements, also in varying degrees, observe among other things purification and marriage laws and rabbinic kosher laws (*kashrut*, which mandates using different dishes at Passover and at other times, as well as no meat and milk at the same meal, etc.).

The Holidays

Holidays are important for most Jews. For many Jews who do not observe *halakhah* in daily life, holidays have become one of the main ways of expressing Jewish identity. Chief among these are the weekly Sabbath. Then there are the biblical festivals: Passover (combined with the Feast of Unleavened Bread into one holiday since the first century or earlier); Shavuot (Weeks or Pentecost); Rosh Hashanah (the Jewish New Year); Yom Kippur, the Day of Atonement; and Sukkot, or Tabernacles. What is often referred to as a seventh biblical holiday, First Fruits, is not observed as such by most Jews. To this should be added Purim, based on the events of the book of Esther, and Hanukkah, celebrating the recapture of the Jerusalem temple by the Maccabees around 165 BCE. Most Jewish people, though fewer than formerly, observe Passover and Hanukkah, though with less ritual and no reliance on rabbinic authority. Various minor festivals and fasts are observed; the best known is Tishah-b'Ab, a remembrance of the destruction of the first and second temples as well as other tragedies in Jewish history. For many Jews, these holidays are social more than religious occasions, particularly Passover, which becomes the occasion for a large family gathering. Even nonreligious Jews will often participate to some extent in the holidays, adapting them and seeing them as vehicles to express ethnicity more than religious faith.

Life-Cycle Events

Circumcision of eight-day-old boys remains almost universally observed as a mark of Jewishness. At age thirteen, boys will have their *bar mitzvah*, a ceremony at which time (according to Orthodox Judaism) they become responsible for observing the *mitzvot*, or commandments, or which is (for Reform or other nonobservant Jews) a coming-of-age ceremony. In non-Orthodox Judaism, girls may also have their *bat mitzvah* at age twelve. Weddings are usually performed by a rabbi under a canopy, the *huppah*, and include as a highlight the breaking of a glass wrapped in a cloth under the heel of the groom, variously interpreted as a memory of the temple's destruction, or a symbol that life has its sorrows as well as its joys. At death, most Jews still bury rather than cremate, and on the anniversary of the death of a family member, a *yahrzeit* candle may be lit, which burns for twenty-four hours. Again, for many Jews these occasions function more socially than religiously.

The Synagogue

Worship takes place in the synagogue, though fewer Jews are affiliated than in the past. Orthodox sit men and women separately; the service is largely in Hebrew; and *yarmulkas* or *kippot* (head coverings for the men) and *tallitot* (prayer shawls) are worn, the latter at certain services only. Reform synagogues are called temples, originally so styled in conscious opposition to the Orthodox belief that the Jerusalem temple must be rebuilt. Here there is mixed seating. Services are shorter, fewer, and mostly in English; in some temples no *kippot* or *tallitot* are worn.

Current Demographics

The Jewish population currently stands at about 14 million worldwide. Of this, some 5.4 million live in Israel, which at the current growth rate (largely through immigration) stands poised to outpace the 6 million in North America. The remaining population is spread throughout the world, with Europe and the former Soviet Union being the chief centers, though substantial Jewish populations are also found in South Africa, Australia, and Latin America.

Sources

Dan Cohn-Sherbok. *Judaism: History, Belief and Practice.* Routledge, 2003.

Hayim H. Donin. *To Be a Jew: A Guide to Jewish Observance in Contemporary Life.* Basic Books, 1991 (1972).

Dana Evan Kaplan. *American Reform Judaism: An Introduction.* Rutgers, 2003.

Jacob Neusner and Alan Avery-Peck, eds. *The Blackwell Companion to Judaism.* Wiley-Blackwell, 2003.

Jonathan D. Sarna. *American Judaism: A History.* Yale University Press, 2005.

Joseph Telushkin. *Jewish Literacy: The Most Important Things to Know about the Jewish Religion, Its People, and Its History.* William Morrow, 1991.

Herman Wouk. *This Is My God.* Doubleday, 1959.

17

Judaism: Christian Contacts

RICHARD ROBINSON

Early Period (to circa 550 CE, the Close of the Talmud)

Regarding the earliest period, when "Jewish" and "Christian" border lines had not hardened, it is better to speak of contacts between the mainstream Jewish community and Jewish and/or gentile believers in Jesus. The evidence is sparser than we might like. Generally the contacts we do know of (Justin Martyr; Jewish believers mentioned in the Talmud) are religious in nature (see next article), although the existence of these contacts indicates a degree of social intercourse. Also, however, we note several other points of contact. The church fathers' knowledge of Hebrew came via Jewish teachers, making them the first Christian Hebraists (a phenomenon usually spoken of in connection with the Renaissance and beyond). Second, after the official establishment of Christianity under Constantine, anti-Jewish legal enactments, along with the delivery of anti-Jewish sermons, became something of a norm. It should be noted that this came in response to popular attraction to the Jewish way of life; Christians were attending synagogues and worshiping on Jewish holidays. There is then a background of popular philo-Semitism that underlies the attempts on the part of church leadership to shore up the "border lines."

Early Medieval Period (circa 550 CE–1492, the Expulsion from Spain)

In contrast to the usual "lachrymose conception" of Jewish history (a phrase coined by Jewish historian Salo Baron), which views Jewish-Christian interaction as almost exclusively a history of pogroms and persecutions, there is a more

> **Study Aid #35**
>
> **Jewish Divisions**
>
> Orthodox: 10 percent
> Reform: 32 percent
> Conservative: 37 percent
> Other (Reconstructionist, Zionist, Cultural): 20 percent

positive side to Jewish-Christian contact that is receiving increasing recognition. Specifically, the positive contacts involved (1) social and economic intercourse and (2) specifically religious influence (see next article). To be sure, these were often contacts of convenience rather than of mutual respect, but a relatively peaceable coexistence seems to have been the daily norm at many times. Nevertheless, anti-Jewish actions, even if not the stuff of everyday life, were, when they occurred, virulent, systemic, and with long-lasting effects.

In the early part of this period, the Jewish community flourished in Arab Spain. While not the focus of this article, it must be noted that in contrast to relations with Christians, this era of Jewish history is known as the "Golden Age of Spain," in which something of a "Jewish Renaissance" took place with landmark cultural achievements in philosophy, language, and poetry.

Toward the end of the Arab period, however, and also following the Christian reconquest, a new environment enveloped the Jewish people. Regarding social and economic intercourse, Jews were often invited to settle in particular areas, bringing economic benefit to the region due to a growing expertise in international trade and an ability to act as a buffer or intermediary between Christian and Muslim lands. Legislation benefiting the Jews as well as society in general was enacted by the Carolingians, Alfonso of Aragon, Pope Innocent III (both twelfth century), and others. Increasingly in the centuries following the Golden Age of Spain, the Jewish people were proving themselves necessary for the economic welfare of the lands of European Christendom, especially in Eastern Europe. This was already true in the fiefdoms of the late first millennium, and grew to the point where the Jewish people became what Paul Kriwaczek calls the "indispensable lubricant." This sometimes worked itself out ironically, when a Christian ruler would expel Jews from an area only to have the local ruler invite them back in short notice. Besides international finance, moneylending became a chief trade, as both Christians and Muslims forbade lending at interest (though not always enforced in the church). Here is an example of the symbiotic relationship: Jews could prosper, while their prosperity meant additional tax money for the locality.

It is, however, the virulent incidents of anti-Semitism that have colored historical views of this period. We can mention the Crusades, during which synagogues were burned and Jewish communities slaughtered by passionate, if not pious, pilgrims en route to the Holy Land. The "blood libel"—the accusation that Jews used Christian blood to bake Passover *matzahs*—originated in this period, beginning in 1144 in Norwich (England), as did the charge, beginning in the thirteenth century, of the "desecration of the host"—that is, that Jews stole the consecrated host and then reenacted Jesus's crucifixion by stabbing it. Jewish communities became convenient targets during the Black Plague, when Jews were accused of poisoning wells. At the same time, Pope Clement VI issued a bull in light of events to prevent wholesale massacre of Jews, but without much effect. In 1492 the Jews were expelled from Spain and Portugal, except for those who accepted forced conversion to Catholicism. Even then, the Inquisition throughout Europe ferreted out those who secretly continued to live as Jews. In general, we may say that the uneasy coexistence that was often the norm of daily life gave way to anti-Jewish sentiments and actions when Christian communities encountered difficulties—with an intensity and residual effect that far outweighed anything that occurred in the "normal" times.

Contact occurred not just among the common people but also among scholars. As early as the twelfth century, such contacts were fruitfully taking place in the area of manuscript study and in the context of the scholastic movement's establishment of schools. Mostly this occurred in the later medieval period, to which we now turn.

Late Medieval Period (1492–circa 1750, the Start of the Enlightenment)

By the late medieval period, Eastern European Jewry had a semi-independent status recognized both by large swaths of European Jewry and by Christian rulers, a status culminating in the Jewish institution of the Council of the Four Lands and lasting until the mid-eighteenth century.

Scholarly contact, begun earlier, blossomed in the Renaissance and Reformation ages. With the sixteenth century revival of the classics, Christian Hebraists sought out Jewish teachers for the study of Hebrew grammar and exegesis. By the seventeenth century, Jewish history and rabbinics were on the table as well, integrated into the study of Christian theology and sometimes with a missionary view. Not everyone thought highly of such close contact with Jews, but this was outweighed by the belief that demonstration of the truth of Christianity could come through Hebrew literature. (Eventually the more or less philo-Semitic attitudes declined as the study of Hebrew waned in favor of studying ancient Near Eastern languages more broadly.) Maimonides's *Mishneh Torah*, a code of law systematizing the Talmud, was of special interest as being an entrée into understanding "normative" Judaism.

As a subset of Christian Hebraists, there were the Christian Kabbalists. Pico della Mirandola (fifteenth century) and Reuchlin (sixteenth century) thought to demonstrate the deity of Christ through the Kabbalah and magic. The amalgam that was the Renaissance produced the notion that the Kabbalah—but not the Talmud!—was a part of God's revelation to Moses on Mount Sinai. On the Continent this interest waned with the Counter-Reformation but remained strong in England. Related to this may be the group known as the Hutchinsonians, who found new meanings in the Bible by working with the consonantal text alone and creatively revocalizing it.

Along with these phenomena, Puritan England saw an interest in the divine restoration of the Jews to the Holy Land, and as elsewhere in the seventeenth century, a tendency toward adopting Jewish practices, including the seventh-day Sabbath.

The Enlightenment and Beyond (circa 1750–1945, the Close of World War II)

The Enlightenment—in Hebrew, Haskalah—marked a watershed in Western civilization. In Germany, France, and England, Jews were granted emancipation and became full citizens of those nations, a status not previously achieved. For their part, Jews in these countries considered themselves to be not part of the Jewish people or nation, but part of the German, French, or English people, with "Judaism" as an optional private faith. In effect there was a tradeoff: Jews could receive emancipation and equality by declaring themselves first and foremost citizens of their country of residence. This was welcomed and encouraged within the Jewish community, for assimilation and becoming no more than a Frenchman or an Englishman who happened to practice Judaism was seen as a way of ending anti-Semitism and the so-called Jewish question. On the Christian side, the increasing secularism and new Enlightenment values aided this process as well. Certainly in countries such as England and later the United States, the Jewish people fared far better than they ever had before vis-à-vis their Christian neighbors.

Meanwhile, in Eastern Europe and Russia, the Haskalah took root differently. Even the assimilated Jews of Western Europe often practiced a modernized version of Judaism; Jews of Eastern Europe tended to be more hard-line secularists, often adopting socialism as their philosophy. (It was with the help of such Jews that the labor movement in the United States gained momentum.) Also in these lands there remained a core of religious Jews who rejected the Enlightenment philosophy entirely. The relationship of both to the Christian governments was not a pleasant one. *Pogroms*—organized pillages and massacres—took place frequently, and in Czarist Russia harsh measures were put in place with regard to the Jews, such as the forced conscription of Jewish youths into the Russian army under Czar Nicholas I. Furthermore, even among the secular Jews of Eastern Europe, there was no question of being a "citizen just like any other" of those nations. The ideals of Western Europe did not penetrate east. Secular and religious Jews alike considered themselves part of the Jewish people, not merely Poles or Ukrainians or Russians.

As a result of this bifurcation, the Jews of Western Europe coexisted more or less peaceably with their Christian neighbors, at the expense of shedding ethnic identity, while religion in these countries had become a matter of private choice.

Study Aid #36

Spread of Judaism, 1000–1500

The Jews of Eastern Europe, on the other hand, did not enjoy the same relations with their host countries and maintained Jewish ethnic identity much more tenaciously, whether expressed religiously or not.

Then came immigration to America: by the German Jews in the 1840s and the Eastern European Jews in the 1880s. The former were already assimilated and often people of means (made possible by the new Enlightenment societies of Western Europe). The latter were impoverished, crowded into tenements for new immigrants, and for a generation or so retained their ethnic identity, until the forces of life in America—similar to those earlier in Western Europe—led to greater integration into American society.

As it turned out, however, the Enlightenment did not put an end to anti-Semitism. In 1890s France, the Dreyfus affair showed that being a "Frenchmen" did

> **Study Aid #37**
>
> **Christian-Jewish Contacts**
>
> Early: To 550 CE (close of the Talmud)
> Early/Middle: 550–1492 (expulsion from Spain)
> Late/Middle: 1492–1750 (the beginning of the Enlightenment)
> Enlightenment: 1750–1945 (close of World War II)
> Modern: 1945–present

not mean that one could not single out Jews as Jews. The final nail in the coffin of the Enlightenment outlook came with the Holocaust, in which the destruction of one-third of world Jewry—six million—put the lie to the idea that Jews in "civilized" Europe could be guaranteed acceptance just as any other people. Already in the nineteenth century, especially with the treatment of Jews in Eastern Europe, it was felt that without a homeland of their own, the Jews would never truly be at home in any other land, thus giving impetus to the burgeoning Zionist movement. The Holocaust cemented that viewpoint, and three years following the Liberation of 1945 at the end of World War II, Israel was established as a nation in May of 1948.

The Modern Period (1945–Present)

As just indicated, one of the key events of this period was the formation of the State of Israel in 1948, with the backing of many of the nations of "Christian" civilization, not least the United States. Not many American Jews made *aliyah*, or immigration, to Israel, despite being ardent supporters of the state. As the years went on, though, many Soviet (later, Russian/Ukrainian) Jews did come to live permanently in Israel, though their right to immigrate was initially heavily restricted by the Soviet Union. Many Russian Jews have more recently also made their home in Germany, an ironic counterpoint to the conditions prevailing for German Jewry prior to 1945. Jews continue to reside throughout Europe, North America, South Africa, Australia, and part of Latin America—that is, largely in Christian-influenced countries. (In contrast, Jews from Iran, Iraq, and many lands now part of the Islamic world have by and large left their host country.) Of note, the Jewish Israeli population now stands at 5.4 million compared to 6 million in North America and 14 million worldwide—and at the present rate, is poised to rival North America as the largest world Jewish community, largely due to immigration.

In terms of general relationships with Christians, the current climate both celebrates diversity and encourages tolerance. This has meant generally good relations between Jews and Christians, though anti-Semitism remains an ongoing concern. The current climate has also meant that many of the Jewish distinctives that characterized earlier generations have eroded away, leading to a situation in the West, at least, that partly resembles that of the earlier Enlightenment period. Of note, the intermarriage rate in the American Jewish community today is more than 50 percent—that is, over half of American Jews are marrying non-Jews, mostly those who would identify themselves as Christian. At least in America, there remains a significant number of Jews, including younger generations, who believe it important to identify as Jewish, variously understood, though they relate more comfortably to non-Jewish society than their parents or grandparents would have.

Of special concern for contemporary Jewry is the State of Israel. Those perceived to be enemies of Israel and of the Jewish people are no longer primarily Christian but Islamic. However, there has emerged among "Christian" nations—that is, largely in Europe and North America—a strong undercurrent of opposition to Israel's policies vis-à-vis the Palestinians. Sometimes this undercurrent informs the actions of Christian denominations, such as when a denomination advocates for divestment in Israel, that counters the earlier supportive trend among mainline Christian denominations in the early days of Israel's existence as a state. In stark contrast, though, there is the phenomenon of "Christian Zionism," a movement largely of American evangelical Christians who embrace enthusiastic support for the State of Israel. Within the Jewish community, there is debate as to whether such Christian Zionists are true friends of the Jewish people or whether their support for Israel comes with a conversionary motive, though general opinion leans toward the former, if a bit uncomfortably. In some cases Christian Zionists have gone beyond support of Israel to embrace a theology that downplays or disavows a need to evangelize Jewish people, a position that sits more comfortably with Jewish people, though it stands in contrast with the typical evangelical position that affirms gospel proclamation to all.

Sources

Daniel Boyarin. *Border Lines: The Partition of Judaeo-Christianity*. University of Pennsylvania Press, 2004.

Jonathan Elukin. *Living Together, Living Apart: Rethinking Jewish-Christian Relations in the Middle Ages*. Princeton University Press, 2007.

Paul Kriwaczek. *Yiddish Civilisation: The Rise and Fall of a Forgotten Nation*. Vintage, 2006.

Paul Merkley. *Christian Attitudes towards the State of Israel*. McGill-Queen's University Press, 2001.

William Nicholls. *Christian Antisemitism: A History of Hate*. Jason Aronson, 1993.

Howard M. Sachar. *The Course of Modern Jewish History*. Rev. ed. Vintage, 1990 (1977).

Israel Yuval. *Two Nations in Your Womb: Perceptions of Jews and Christians in Late Antiquity and the Middle Ages*. University of California Press, 2006.

18

Judaism: Theological Exchanges

RICHARD ROBINSON

Early Period

Initially the gospel was an internal Jewish matter, the dividing issue being the messiahship of Jesus and related matters such as questions of authority and Jesus's alleged blasphemy. With the solidification of "border lines" over the next few centuries—a gradual process rather than a moment—"Christianity" and "Judaism" became recognizable contrasting entities, and from then on we can speak more clearly of theological exchanges "between Christians and Jews," though Jesus-believing Jews and other Jews interacted from the earliest times.

Already as early as the second century, many Christians viewed the Jews as abandoned by God and replaced by a new people—namely, the church—a theological model known as *supersessionism*. Justin Martyr, for example, famously enunciated in his *Dialogue with Trypho* that the Jews were preparers for the gospel but without any current role in God's plan; for him the church was the "true spiritual Israel." He further suggests that the law of Moses, especially circumcision, was designed to mark out the Jewish people for their sin and for crucifying Christ. By the fourth century, as Christianity became the state religion under Constantine and the Council of Nicaea was convened, anti-Jewish enactments prohibited the celebration of Easter at the same time as Passover, as well as Christian worship on the seventh-day Sabbath. Augustine (fourth–fifth century) articulated the view that the wanderings and sufferings of the Jewish people were a kind of negative witness to the gospel; the Jews' observance of the Torah indicated its authenticity as a testimony to Christ. Thus in both belief and practice, the Jewish people were cast in a negative light, the result being the institutionalization of anti-Semitism in the church as well as a failure to value the Jewish origins—we might even say the Jewish nature—of Christianity.

As the same time, missionary outreach continued through the genre of apologetic *contra Iudaeos* literature (alongside similar *contra* literature aimed at non-Jews), though colored by supersessionist theology and the post-Constantine anti-Jewish enactments. At least in this arena, argumentation rather than coercion was the rule, and discussions centered largely on texts from the Hebrew Bible or in the form of dialogues. (Justin's is the most well-known but hardly the only one.)

The Jewish community developed its own responses to the challenge of Christianity. One response was apologetic, aimed both at Christians and for internal consumption, arguing exegesis and theology against the Christian positions, especially regarding matters pertaining to Christian understanding of the Hebrew Bible. This is already seen in Justin's second-century *Dialogue with Trypho*. By the mid-fourth century, Christianity had become the state religion, and rabbinic Judaism had solidified its self-identity. Now when polemics emerged, it was against clearly demarcated opponents, and earlier Jewish arguments became more specifically directed against Christianity. Thus the term *min*, "heretic," obtained a more specific usage referring to Jesus-believing Jews. The late first-century *Birkat Ha-Minim*—instituted as an additional synagogue prayer directed against the *minim*—was now understood specifically to refer to Christians. Disputes centered on correct scriptural interpretation and theology (disputes on the "Two Powers in Heaven" in response to claims of the deity of Christ), and took place in the realm of "power encounters," as both rabbinic Judaism and Christianity in this period saw the rise of wonder-workers who competed for the allegiance of the people.

The second main response was Judaism's development of internal theologies, rather than apologetic arguments, as well as liturgical moves that offered a "counterstory" to the Christian one. While the field of apologetics was often live debates or written arguments, and from the Jewish vantage point defensive, in contrast, internal theology and liturgy were proactive, a way to internalize the Jewish narrative by teaching and repetition. Tracing these moves historically is a classic chicken-and-egg problem; did the Jewish narrative develop first? Was it independent of the Christian narrative or a conscious response to the latter? The same could be asked of the Christian side. But it is not always necessary to arrive at a decision to see that, in fact, two separate narratives were unfolding.

Importantly, in the narrative of Judaism was embedded a response to Christian supersessionism. For instance, the claim that the church superseded Israel as Jacob had superseded Esau was met with the counterclaim that Esau really represented the church. Equally important, Judaism began to solidify the doctrine of the "two Torahs," that is, the Written and Oral Laws, thus shoring up rabbinic authority and traditions vis-à-vis Christian claims regarding apostolic authority and Jesus's claims about his own authority.

In the area of liturgy, the Passover Haggadah story may have also developed as it did to emphasize the Jewish narrative vis-à-vis the Christian one, as the *haftarah* reading for Passover (Ezek. 37) is also used on Palm Sunday in reference to the resurrection. The idea of a Messiah son of Joseph who would meet his death in battle (in addition to the triumphantly reigning Messiah son of David) may be a Jewish countermove against the story of Jesus the son of Joseph who died as an atonement. Many more possible examples could be adduced.

As a counterstory, the *Toledot Yeshu* stands out par excellence, for in this case there is no question of the direction of development. The *Toledot Yeshu*, crystallized by medieval times, was a parody of the life of Jesus—*Yeshu* being an acronym for the Hebrew of *may his name and memory be blotted out*, the name by which he is still known in modern Israel even among secular Jews who do not understand its origins. The *Toledot Yeshu* became the main "source" of the life of Jesus for many Jews in medieval times. According to the *Toledot Yeshu*, Jesus was born illegitimately from Mary and a Roman soldier. He was hanged on Passover after being convicted of blasphemy for sewing God's name into his leg and thereby being enabled to do miracles. In addition, he was a sorcerer. The vitriolic nature of the account goes beyond a mere counternarrative, but reflects a view of Christianity brought on by Christians themselves in their actions and attitudes toward the Jewish people.

In daily life Jews continued to turn to the gospel and Christians continued to socialize with Jews and utilize Jewish customs, but the responses of leaders and institutions on both sides precisely fought against this and continued to solidify lines. By post-Constantine times, we can hardly speak of theological exchanges as much as counterstories and hardening borders.

Medieval Period

In the thirteenth century, missionary work took on new impetus with the Dominican and Franciscan orders of the church. Some of their methods, such as production of apologetic manuals and establishment of training schools, were recognizably similar to those found in later Protestant missions, even if the specific content differed. On the other hand, as far as the Jews were concerned, what has remained indelibly in the Jewish memory are the instances of forced sermons and disputations between church officials and prominent Jews, the most well-known being that under James I in 1263 in Barcelona with Nachmanides, and which drew on the new contributions of the Dominicans. These disputations were hardly what we would think of as missionary, but rather a means for the church to retain power over Jews or to provide rationale for persecution, and the church leaders invariably "won" them. The topics largely centered on theology and scripture.

Of special note is the new turn that missionary argumentation took in the thirteenth century: selective use of the rabbinic writings themselves became part of the arsenal of argumentation for Christianity, forming an important point of contact with Jewish audiences. The Barcelona disputation was the first important

> **Study Aid #38**
>
> **Jewish-Christian Theological Exchanges**
> The messiahship of Jesus
> Supersessionism
> Polemic and counterpolemic
> Dual covenants

instance of this new approach that was quintessentially represented by Raymundus Martini's *Pugio Fidei*, which Richard Harvey terms the "magnum opus of medieval Christian missionizing among the Jews." Martini's use of rabbinic material fueled the apologetics of later generations of Christians and, in turn, the development of additional Jewish responses. Ironically, Martini's careful attention to the scholarship of texts also helped contribute to the ensuing burgeoning of Christian Hebraists and Christian Kabbalists in the Renaissance.

Also in this period, on the Christian side, there developed anti-Jewish calumnies that were theological or religious in nature. From this time we derive the accusations of the blood libel—that Jews needed the blood of Christian children to bake *matzah* for Passover—and the accusations of host desecration (see preceding article). On the southern front in Spain and Portugal, but eventually extending to large parts of Europe, the Inquisition ferreted out those Jews who had escaped persecution by pretending to be Christians but continued to secretly live as Jews. These were the New Christians, crypto-Jews, or as a slur, *marranos*, a term meaning "swine."

On the Jewish side, in this period Jewish theology became highly philosophical in interaction with Aristotelian philosophy and Arabic *Kalam* philosophy. The conclusions reached argued against Christian doctrines such as the Trinity and the incarnation. Maimonides proclaimed God to be *yahid* rather than using the biblical word *echad*, thus forestalling any idea that God could be three-in-one. These theological moves were more for internal consumption; those who disagreed with this or that idea forfeited a place in "the world to come," perhaps the only time in Jewish history when salvation was so dependent on articles of belief rather than on actions alone. Of special interest is the somewhat later *Hizzuk Emunah* ("Faith Strengthened") by Isaac of Troki, who was a Karaite and hence relied solely on scripture, not rabbinic material, for his counterargumentation. Troki has been called the father of modern countermissionary polemic literature; his work is still available and his arguments still widely used.

Interestingly, in spite of anti-Judaism at both official and popular levels, as a nation/culture/religion, Judaism sometimes continued to hold a unique attraction for outsiders, especially in Eastern Europe. We have seen the phenomenon of philo-Semitism in the early period. Agobard, bishop of Lyons in the mid-ninth century, wrote letters against the "Judaizers" in response to King Louis the Pious's favorable treatment of Jews. Slavic church leaders similarly complained of "Judaizing" in the fifteenth century, while Jewish-like Sabbath observers, some of whom also observed Jewish dietary laws, were found through the eighteenth century. When all but Catholicism was outlawed in the Habsburg Empire, there were not a few—according to Kriwaczek, entire communities, in fact—who chose conversion to Judaism over being exiled or becoming Catholic. Clearly, at the grassroots level, philo-Semitism did not die out, though it remains a largely untold story.

We again take note of the Christian use of Kabbalah and the phenomenon of Christian Hebraism (see also previous article). On the one hand, these endeavors represented genuine interest and respect for Jewish tradition, a kind of philo-Semitism. On the other hand, the Kabbalah became part of the Christian apologetic system, whereby Jewish mystical ideas of God were seen to proclaim Christian truths.

The history of Jewish-Christian theological exchanges, therefore, remained largely one of polemic and counterpolemic. While the earlier period saw this expressed in the development of counternarratives, sporadic encounters, and—from the side of those who held power—anti-Jewish legislation, the medieval period saw in addition the growth of detailed theological arguments, which often required each side to learn more about the thinking of the other. But argumentation meant little in the face of institutionalized anti-Semitism and social oppression. Nor did the latter diminish after the Reformation. Martin Luther, having begun with generous sympathy for Jews, famously ended up vitriolically anti-Jewish.

Early Modern Period (to 1945)

With the arrival of the Enlightenment (see previous article), we also encounter the rise of modern Protestant Jewish missions. From about 1750 on, but especially in the nineteenth century, institutionalized missions to the Jews burgeoned within the Protestant denominations and independent mission societies. The theological impetus for this movement lay with the Puritans of the sixteenth century, whose optimistic eschatology included hope in, and prayer for, a future conversion of the Jews. With the emergence of modern evangelicalism and the rise of modern missions, the elements were in place for a program of organized missionary work among the Jews. In this connection, the "Christian Hebraism" of the Renaissance resurfaced in training schools for missionaries, such as the Institutum Judaicum in Germany, in which knowledge of Judaism and Jewish writings was considered part and parcel of missionary preparation. By and large, the method was argumentation from the Hebrew Bible and from rabbinic writings, with counterarguments continuing to be offered by the Jewish community, both sides often drawing on material with a long pedigree in polemical writings.

At the same time, the Enlightenment in Western Europe played havoc with traditional religious faith in general. In many Christian circles, Jesus came to be regarded as merely a human being, although particularly in touch with the divine, and no longer posed a challenge to Jewish sensibilities. Some Jews began to speak positively of Jesus as a great Jew, while Reform Judaism in its earliest manifestation in Germany borrowed extensively in its worship from Christian trappings, at the same time jettisoning many traditional Jewish beliefs in the Messiah and in the return to the land of Israel. Thus as theology was "watered down" and religion tended to become something for the private sphere, little theological exchange was deemed necessary. It was primarily the Jewish missions that continued to press the theological issues in the Jewish community; Judaism was otherwise busy reconfiguring itself with experiments in Reform Judaism, Positive Historical Judaism, and other movements.

Recent Modern Period (1945–Present)

In the face of the Holocaust and the development of postmodern sensibilities, Jewish mission activity has frequently given way in the post–World War II period to an emphasis on dialogue and mutual understanding, with the issue of "conversion" off the table. The landmark 1965 Catholic document *Nostra Aetate* repudiated the charge of deicide and also made moves to disavow a supersessionist reading of history. Since that time, there has been a plethora of statements and dialogues between Jews and Christians that repudiate supersessionism and maintain the ongoing "validity" of God's covenant with the Jewish people. In many instances, the theological underpinnings of this go back to Franz Rosenzweig's early twentieth-century formulation of two covenants, one for the Jews and one for the non-Jews. This "dual covenant" theology has informed much of the recent dialogue movement, in which missionary efforts are seen as precisely failing to recognize this ongoing divine covenant with the Jewish people. At the same time, the church at large, not least through the filtering down of scholarly efforts, has begun to re-recognize the Jewishness of Christianity.

On the Jewish side, although theology has never played the role it has among Christians, "post-Holocaust theology" has become significant as Jewish thinkers have searched for ways to think about God in the wake of the horrors of the Holocaust. Some Christians too have embraced the dialogue movement and the disavowal of evangelization as the proper Christian response to the destruction of six million Jews.

Finally, we should note attitudes toward the State of Israel. Embraced by mainline church denominations at its founding, today many of the same church bodies find Israel to be problematic for them. While this is more a social than a theological issue for many Christians (see previous article), among the "Christian Zionists" a theological underpinning—ranging from dispensational belief to a more general high view of the place of Israel in God's plan—has led to widespread support for the State of Israel.

We should add that missions to the Jews remains on the agenda of evangelical churches, represented in various agencies as well as umbrella organizations such as the Lausanne Consultation on Jewish Evangelism (an offshoot of the Lausanne Consultation on World Evangelization), which has worked to affirm evangelical theological underpinnings of Jewish missions. Though polemics still marks much missionary apologetics—arguing *against* rabbinic Judaism—the trend has increasingly been to argue *for* the Jewishness of Jesus and the continued Jewish identity of those who follow him. Lastly, the Hebrew Christian or Messianic Jewish movement, in which Jewish Jesus-believers to one degree or another integrate their faith with their ethnicity in a very self-aware way, became a significant factor in the nineteenth through the twenty-first centuries. The rise of Messianic congregations, integrating faith in Jesus with a (at least partly) Jewish style of worship, is one of the more visible elements of this movement. Still largely excluded from the Jewish-Christian dialogues, Messianic Jews nevertheless bring a critical factor into the theological arena that is yet to be fully addressed by mainstream Jews and Christians.

Sources

Yaakov Ariel. *Evangelizing the Chosen People: Missions to the Jews in America, 1880–2000.* University of North Carolina Press, 2000.

Alan L. Berger, David Patterson, David P. Gushee, John Pawlikowski, and John K. Roth. *Jewish Christian Dialogue: Drawing Honey from the Rock.* Paragon, 2008.

Robert Chazan. *Daggers of Faith: Thirteenth-Century Christian Missionizing and Jewish Response.* University of California Press, 1989.

Richard S. Harvey. "Raymundus Martini and the *Pugio Fidei*: A Survey of the Life and Works of a Medieval Controversialist." MA Thesis, University College, London, 1991.

Mark Kinzer. *Post-Missionary Messianic Judaism.* Brazos, 2005.

Daniel J. Lasker. *Jewish Philosophical Polemics against Christianity in the Middle Ages.* Littman Library of Jewish Civilization, 2007.

Peter Schäfer. *Jesus in the Talmud.* Princeton University Press, 2007.

Oskar Skarsaune. *In the Shadow of the Temple: Jewish Influences on Early Christianity.* InterVarsity, 2008 (2002).

Oskar Skarsaune and Reidar Hvalvik, eds. *Jewish Believers in Jesus: The Early Centuries.* Hendrickson, 2007.

R. Kendall Soulen. *The God of Israel and Christian Theology.* Fortress, 1996.

Israel Yuval. *Two Nations in Your Womb: Perceptions of Jews and Christians in Late Antiquity and the Middle Ages.* University of California Press, 2006.

19

Judaism: Current Issues

RICHARD ROBINSON

As the twenty-first century is now well underway, several issues are high on the agenda of Jewish-Christian relationships and within the Jewish community itself.

Dialogue

In the area of Jewish-Christian relations, one of the key issues remains the desire on both sides for continued dialogue, acceptance, and respect. On the Jewish side, this is understood to include a renunciation of efforts by Christians to evangelize or "proselytize" Jews and a recognition of the validity of Judaism. The seminal influential statement in this area was *Nostra Aetate* (*In Our Time*), promulgated by the Catholic Church in 1965, which repudiated the charge against the Jewish people of deicide and affirmed the connection of Christianity to the Jewish people as well as the ongoing chosenness of the Jews. Since then, numerous dialogues and statements have ensued, melding a call for mutual respect, recognition of the place of the Jewish people in God's covenants, and cessation of missionary activity directed toward Jews.

This perspective has been fueled by several factors. First, there is the acknowledgment on the part of the church of the history of Jewish-Christian relations, in which forced conversions, anti-Jewish legislation, anti-Semitism, and ultimately the Holocaust all stand in the Jewish mind as emblematic of Christian attitudes and actions.

Second, there is the history of Christian theology, in much of which the church becomes the "new Israel" to the exclusion of the historical Jewish people, and

> **Study Aid #39**
>
> Current Jewish and Jewish-Christian Issues
>
> Anti-Semitism
> Post-Holocaust
> Israel and Palestine
> Messianic Jews
> Intermarriage

furthermore in which the Jewish people are said to abide under God's curse. Therefore, part of the theological project of the modern Jewish-Christian dialogue movement has been to distance Christians from this so-called replacement theology and to affirm God's ongoing covenant with the Jewish people. Indeed, from Puritan times onward in many segments of Christianity, especially those that are evangelical, there has been an affirmation of the ongoing place of the Jewish people within God's plan. For evangelicals, this has not stood in contradiction with the call to evangelize all peoples, Jews included. For other Christians, the affirmation of God's continued covenant obviates any obligation to evangelize Jews or indeed its propriety; since the early twentieth century the so-called dual covenant theology has, in its various forms, postulated separate divine covenants with Jews and with others. According to this perspective, it is only non-Jews who need to embrace faith in Jesus.

Third, there is what we might call the postmodern celebration of diversity and the recognition—aided by the internet, ease of travel, and increasing intersection of cultures—that our world is more pluralistic than what previous generations may have imagined. Therefore there is pressure, even within the evangelical Christian community, to relativize belief systems and to play off persuasion/evangelism against respect/understanding. Importantly, however, we note that at the official level, the Jewish community does not grant "legitimacy" to Jewish believers in Jesus, which is to say, does not offer a "seat at the table" to them. This is true even though the pluralistic climate allows for movements such as that of Buddhist Jews. The occasional exception stands out: almost alone, Dan Cohn-Sherbok, the British scholar and Reform rabbi, has advocated a pluralistic model of Judaism in which Jesus-believing Jews are one strand. Other writers, such as Michael Kogan, wish for Jews and Christians to have a mutually beneficial influence, and to recognize God's activity in both religions—but categorically rules out even the possibility of dialogue if either party continues to affirm ultimate, exclusivistic truth.

The State of Israel

For many, if not most, Jews, another litmus test of Christian-Jewish relations is attitudes toward the State of Israel. Though the Zionist movement, defined here as a belief in and activity directed toward establishment of a Jewish homeland, began in the late nineteenth century, following the Holocaust Jews worldwide embraced as a firm conviction the idea that without a land of their own, the Jewish people would forever be subject to anti-Semitism and attempts at annihilation. The State of Israel thus became both the reality and the symbol of Jewish survival and flourishing, in which, in its early days, the image of the courageous and hardworking Jewish pioneer replaced that of the victimized, ever-wandering Jewish ghetto-dweller. In the first years of its existence, the state of Israel enjoyed widespread support from mainstream Christian denominations, as well as from others.

Recent years have seen a realignment of Christian sympathies in many quarters. Spurred variously by an emphasis on justice issues and, it could be argued, a degree of historical amnesia, many mainstream Christian denominations have advocated divestment in companies doing business with Israel, with some at the same time condemning Israel as racist or practicing apartheid. At the opposite end of the spectrum, so-called Christian Zionists, largely from segments of the evangelical church, have mobilized support for Israel and for the Jewish people. In between, one finds both mainstream Christian support for the State of Israel and also evangelicals, notably Stephen Sizer, who have written in opposition to "Christian Zionism" and have promoted what many would consider to be anti-Israel views. Simultaneously, threats to Israel's existence and to the West have emerged from the more radical wings of Islam, making Christian support for Israel all the more valued, and lack of such support all the more disappointing.

The Jewish community has responded to the Christian realignment in various ways. To those who have advocated divestment or anti-Zionism, Jewish organizations have expressed their disappointment and made overtures to counter such positions, while the support of Christian Zionists is cautiously welcomed, not without misgivings that its support may be a cover for, or a prelude to, proselytization. Interestingly, some Christian Zionists who enjoy widespread evangelical Christian support, such as the Texas pastor John Hagee, have downplayed or denied any need for evangelization among Jewish people.

The extreme criticism of Israel that has come from such corners as the two Durban conferences on racism sponsored by the United Nations (2001 and 2009), or from notable figures such as Jimmy Carter, has left many Jews feeling embattled. Christian support for the State of Israel remains high on the agenda for most Jews, regardless of their internal differences on Israeli policies and the future of the Palestinian people.

Demographically, we note that the population of Israel currently stands at about 5.4 million Jews (there are a minority of other peoples—Palestinian Arabs, Druze, etc., who are Israeli citizens) out of a worldwide population of over 14 million. Much of this growth has come through immigration of Russian/Ukrainian and Ethiopian Jews. At the current rate of growth, Israel stands poised in the near future to be the largest Jewish population center in the world, outpacing the nearly 6 million Jews of North America.

Internally, twenty-first-century Israeli culture is a long way from that of the secular pioneers of the early days. No longer a nation of uniform ideals, Israel is an amalgam of internal conflicts, in which the secular, the ultrareligious, and those in between coexist and often come into conflict. Because of the nature of the Israeli government system, religious Jews exercise an influence in policy making beyond their numbers, often leading to internal discussions concerning the nature of Israel as a democratic society. As far as Jewish-Christian relations are concerned, efforts have been repeatedly made, so far without success, to restrict missionary activity in Israel. Though unusual, several violent incidents have taken place against Jesus-believing Jews in Israel that have made headlines. On the other hand, the secular complexion of most Israeli culture and the openness to spiritual exploration among young Israelis has proved to be an open door to discussions about the gospel. It remains to be seen what the future of missionary work in Israel will bring.

The Future of Judaism and the Jewish People

Several trends can be noted under this category. First is the increasing diversity of Jewish belief and lifestyle. The Enlightenment brought Reform and other varieties of Judaism (see previous articles); even though Judaism has never been monolithic, the postmodern world has seen further fragmentation of Jewish faith. Thus we see the rise of movements such as the so-called JUBUs (Jewish Buddhists), and the deliberate pushing of boundaries in publications such as *Heeb*, which adopted a name usually considered offensive and has offered articles such as those on Jews with tattoos, which are traditionally forbidden. New liturgies have been written, for example, for gay Jewish weddings. All of these trends exist alongside the continued vibrancy of traditional Judaism, which nevertheless remains in the minority. Faith in Jesus remains the big "no" in a Jewish community that seems ready to accept virtually any other expression of Jewishness.

The second trend concerns intermarriage and the feared dissolution of the Jewish people. In North America, over 50 percent of Jews marry non-Jewish spouses. (Prior to 1970, the rate was around 13 percent and has steadily risen over the last decades.) Jewish community leadership has expressed fear that the Jewish people will be "lost" if the children of such marriages do not identify as Jewish. We note

---

Study Aid #40

Jewish Demographics

Number of Jews in the world: 14,641,000
Percentage of world population: 0.2 percent
Number of countries where Jews make up more than 50 percent of the population: 1 (Israel)

that Orthodox Judaism considers a child Jewish if the mother is Jewish; Reform Judaism accepts both patrilineal and matrilineal descent; but this is a moot point if ensuing generations do not engage with being Jewish.

The third trend has to do with Israel. As previously stated, Israel stands poised to overtake North America in the near future as the largest Jewish population center. At the same time, the Israeli populace is highly secular. Israeli Jews often consider that they are Jewish by virtue of living in a Jewish state and feel no need to demarcate their Jewishness vis-à-vis Christian neighbors.

The relevance of these internal considerations for Jewish-Christian interaction points in two directions. On the one hand, the fear that Jewish identity and the Jewish people will be lost to future generations may ensure that Jesus remains off-limits for most Jews. Jewish survival, whether physically, demographically, or culturally, remains high on the agenda. Faith in Jesus is seen as leaving the Jewish people for the "other"; it has sometimes been depicted in the Jewish community by the image of "switching teams." On the other hand, the increasing diversity in the Jewish community will make the gospel a live option for many Jews. This will be the case particularly in Israel, where Jewish identity is a "given" by virtue of one's being Israeli. However, the strong religious influence in Israeli policies and the lack of constitutional protections such as we have in the United States may mean that gospel proclamation in Israel will encounter opposition more strongly than elsewhere.

Pluralism, the Uniqueness of Christ, and Evangelization of Jewish People

On the Christian side, social and theological pressures have led to downplaying the exclusivistic claims of the gospel in favor of advocating for mutual respect (a false either/or proposition). Additionally they have led Christians to affirm not only that God still maintains covenant with the Jewish people—a proposition with a long history—but also that God is in fact working salvifically (however that is defined) among both Jews and Christians in their respective faiths. These sorts of pressures have affected evangelical Christian thinking as well as that of mainline churches. There are a multitude of books and articles addressing the issues of pluralism and the uniqueness of Christ in relation to the Christian faith, and we do not need to rehearse the viewpoints here. But as far as these issues relate to the evangelization of the Jewish people, the challenge will be that of balancing, on the one side, (1) renunciation of anti-Semitism, (2) affirmation of mutual respect, and (3) affirmation of God's continuing covenant with the Jewish people with, on the other side, (4) exclusivistic truth claims, and (5) affirmation that Jesus is the Messiah for all peoples, Jews included. It will be apparent that these sorts of concerns readily relate to evangelization of *any* peoples in the postmodern world. They impinge on Jewish evangelization particularly because, in the light of past Christian treatment of the Jewish people, the pluralistic framework provides a

> **Study Aid #41**
> **Countries with Jewish Populations**
>
> | | |
> |---|---|
> | United States | 6 million |
> | Israel | 5.4 million |
> | France | 600,000 |
> | Palestine | 510,000 |
> | Argentina | 494,000 |
> | Canada | 435,000 |
> | Britain | 280,000 |
> | Germany | 230,000 |
> | Russia | 180,000 |
> | Ukraine | 175,000 |

ready means to disengage from gospel proclamation almost as a form of reparation for a history of anti-Semitism.

Messianic Jews

While standing at only around half of 1 percent, the voice of Jesus-believing Jews, or Messianic Jews, is increasingly being heard in the church and in the public arena, both in Israel and in the Diaspora. This increased visibility and the theological undertakings of Messianic Jews will need to be taken into consideration in any thinking about Jewish-Christian relations and theological formulations. But the movement of Jesus-believing Jews is not monolithic; there is as much diversity as elsewhere. Some of the most sophisticated theological thinking is coming from those who would likely not identify as evangelical; Mark Kinzer's book *Postmissionary Messianic Judaism*, while offering much valuable insight, has been notable for its Barthian and Catholic influences, its departure from traditional Christian theology in its ideas about ecclesiology, and the questions it raises in other doctrinal areas as well. Messianic Jewish theology, however, has a history that goes back to the nineteenth century, in the past tending to focus more often on polemics, and more recently broadening its range of interests. Despite being for all intents and purposes marginalized by the dialogue and ecumenical movements, the reality of Jesus-believing Jews cannot be ignored forever.

Sources

Tsvi Bisk and Moshe Dror. *Futurizing the Jews: Alternative Futures for Meaningful Jewish Existence in the Twenty-First Century*. Praeger, 2003.

Richard Harvey. *Mapping Messianic Jewish Theology: A Constructive Approach*. Authentic Media/Paternoster, 2009.

Jewish-Christian Relations. http://www.jcrelations.net/.

"Jewish Evangelism: A Call to the Church." Lausanne Occasional Paper No. 60. Lausanne Committee for World Evangelization, 2005. http://www.lausanne.org/documents/2004forum/LOP60_IG31.pdf.

Walter Laqueur. *A History of Zionism: From the French Revolution to the Establishment of the State of Israel*. Shocken, 2003 (1972).

Paul Merkley. *Christian Attitudes towards the State of Israel*. McGill-Queen's University Press, 2001.

20

Judaism: Adherent Essay

Yaakov Ariel

Since the early generations of Christianity, the relations between Christians and Jews have been particularly important for both communities. The highly complex attitudes and interactions that developed between adherents of the two faiths have stirred strong, yet varied, reactions. For Jews, these relationships have been of vital significance, determining the degree of tolerance they could expect as a minority group in Christian lands; for Christians, their relationship with Judaism was important for defining their identity, often as "true Israel."

This essay offers one person's evaluation of Jewish-Christian relations through the centuries. I have both a personal and academic interest in the topic. Growing up in Israel of the 1950s and 1960s, one learned about the often-harsh realities of the history of Jewish-Christian relations. Living in Jerusalem, where dozens of Christian groups build churches and other institutions, I was also aware of the diversity of Christian expressions and attitudes. I decided to study Christianity and its role in shaping Jewish history. Studying the history of Christianity at the University of Chicago, I took particular interest in the relationship between Protestant groups and Jews.

The History

It is my observation that the path of Christian-Jewish relations has been neither consistent nor uniform. Relations have changed and evolved, varying by era and area. Different Christians and Jews have expressed different opinions and taken different actions. At the same time, one can discern some salient features that have characterized the relations over long centuries. The relationship remained intensive and complex, and often helped shape Christian and Jewish identities and self-perceptions. Both religious traditions have developed alongside, and often in response to, each other's theological, communal, and liturgical claims. Even Jews outside Christian lands had to contend with Christian dogma, which posed an alternative both to the manner in which Jews approach God and to the ways Jews read their sacred scriptures. In defining their tradition, Christian thinkers have almost always seen it necessary to relate to God's covenant with Israel, the Old Testament, and the Jewish community of their time.

Both Christians and Jews have considered the God of Israel to be their deity. Both religious traditions have claimed to be the legitimate, if not exclusive, heirs to the covenant between God and his people and the object of God's promises to Israel. Christians and Jews have shared sacred texts, although Christians considered the Hebrew Bible to be the early part of their canon of sacred texts. Because of the closeness of the two traditions, observers have often described the relationship between the two traditions as siblings' rivalry.

Christianity was one of a series of Jewish movements that proclaimed the imminent arrival of the messianic age, when humanity would be redeemed. Jesus of Nazareth, the group's leader, also taught of the need to treat fellow human beings decently. Scholars point to similarities between Christian teachings and those of other Jewish groups of the period, primarily the Pharisees and the Essenes. Some Christian sources blame the Jewish establishment, and at times Jews in general, for persecuting its leaders, Jesus first and foremost. These Christian accusations against the Jews would prove of long-lasting significance. Although Jews were at the mercy of Christians for most of their mutual history, Christians have nurtured resentment against Jews, viewing them as having wronged Christians.

As Christians enlarged their ranks, establishing communities in other parts of the Mediterranean region, they developed their tradition further, often redefining their relation to the Jewish people and to Judaism. Paul transformed Jesus from the preacher of imminent redemption into the subject of the group's preaching and the means of attaining redemption. Faith in Jesus as the redeemer replaced the observance of Jewish rites, although at this early stage Jewish Christians continued to observe the commandments. Scholars differ in their evaluation of Paul's project. Some consider his theology to have created a wall of separation between Judaism and Christianity, while others believe that he saw himself as a bona fide Jew.

It seems that the Christian option attracted an increased Jewish following after the Jewish revolt against the Romans and the destruction of the temple in 70 CE. While the priestly class was crushed, both the rabbinical Pharisee tradition and Christianity became viable options for Jews, even as Christianity gained the allegiance of many non-Jews as well. Contrary to a popular perception that "Jews do not convert to Christianity," masses of Jews around the Mediterranean, including Palestine, became Christians. Meanwhile, rabbinical Judaism gradually took over as normative Judaism, and as such competed with Christianity for recognition as the legitimate continuation of the Israelite heritage. Christian writers began differentiating even more emphatically between what they considered to be their true faith and the erroneous persistence of non-Christian forms of Judaism. The fathers of the church often expressed negative opinions of the Jews, who, they claimed, were misinterpreting their own sacred texts. Judaism was under attack in the pagan Greco-Roman world, and some of the hostile language of those attacks passed into Christian literature. "Jewish" became an accusation in intra-Christian debates. In recent years, some scholars point to Jewish comments about Jesus and Christianity in early rabbinical texts. In hundreds of thousands of words of talmudic texts and other rabbinical writings from the first centuries of the Common Era, one can find few instances that refer to Jesus. However, most Jewish anti-Christian polemics did not come about until the later centuries of the Middle Ages.

By the turn of the fifth century, Christianity had obtained an almost exclusive standing in the Roman Empire. Jews found themselves living as a minority under Christian rule. Judaism, however, did not become a prohibited faith, and something of a Christian theology of inclusion of Jews developed. Following in Paul's footsteps, Augustine, bishop of Hippo, held that the Jews would eventually accept Christianity. In the meantime, they should remain a protected, albeit humiliated, minority in Christian lands.

In general, the Augustinian formula served as a semiofficial Christian policy toward the Jews. Christian thinkers and leaders through the Christian Middle Ages, such as Bernard of Clairvaux in the mid-twelfth century, reiterated Augustine's position. This does not mean that policies toward the Jews always followed Augustinian lines. These realities differed from region to region and from one period to another, depending on rulers' economic interests and popular sentiment, among other factors. Christians tolerated the presence of Jews for centuries in many areas where they would not tolerate other non-Christian groups. This unique and surprising situation suggests again the dysfunctional family model. Even if barely tolerated, Jews were granted an unusual status, that of the awkward straying relation. It is a remarkable fact that Jews lived religiously and intellectually creative lives under Christian rule in various parts of Europe well into late modern times. The history of Jewish-Christian coexistence therefore cannot be evaluated through the prism of brutal anti-Jewish policies, such as those carried out by the Nazis during the early 1940s.

The later Middle Ages witnessed, however, serious breaches of the Augustinian formula. The papacy upheld the policy, but many other authorities and popular leaders did not. Pope Urban II's call for a Crusade in 1095 stirred not only a mass movement of warriors making their way to fight the Muslims in the Holy Land but also massacres of Jewish communities along the Rhine. Massacres of Jews also accompanied popular preaching in support of the Second and Third Crusades in 1144–46 and 1187–89. At this stage, Jewish popular writings and prayers began to reflect bitterness against Christian persecution. Startlingly, one popular Jewish hymn that originated in the twelfth century (*Maoz Tsur*) calls upon God to strengthen the hand of the pope in his struggle against the Holy Roman emperor Frederick Barbarossa.

Popular conceptions of Jews among European Christians deteriorated in the later Middle Ages. England of the mid-twelfth century became the site of the first blood libel, the accusation that Jewish communities, on a premeditated basis, kidnapped and murdered Christian children for ritual purposes. Such accusations later spread to the Continent. In the fourteenth century, Christians blamed Jews for plagues, claiming that they were poisoning wells. Hostile images of Jews were mingled into Christian popular religion. Religious festivals included passion plays that depicted Jews as the willing killers of Jesus. Such popular images would prove more difficult to eradicate than negative judgments of Jews by theologians. The Mendicants, a new breed of Christian monastic orders, differed drastically from Augustine in their ideas about Jews. The very existence of Jews as a community separated from the Christian church seemed to threaten Christian thinkers. Stirred by the Mendicants, Christian rulers ordered Christian-Jewish disputations in which Jewish rabbis were compelled to defend their tradition. In Western Europe, the tide turned against Jews. England, France, and parts of Germany expelled many Jews. More than anywhere else, the fate of Jews in Spain demonstrated the precariousness of life under Christian rule. In Jewish memory, "Sepharad" (mentioned in the Bible and which they believed to be Spain) was a great Jewish center, where Jews had thrived. However, there, too, large-scale massacres and forced conversions began at the end of the fourteenth century, and in 1492, the "Catholic monarchs" decided to expel the Jews. Portugal forced its Jews to convert en masse in 1497, enlarging the number of *conversos* of Jewish descent.

While most *conversos* accepted their new faith, long-time Christians remained suspicious. The Inquisition uprooted "Judaizing" tendencies, and thousands of allegedly lapsed Christians were interrogated and punished. Spain also enacted laws of "purity of blood" that excluded people of Jewish descent from civic and ecclesiastical position. Ironically, although very few retained their Jewish identity, the plight of the *conversos* became in the Jewish collective memory a demonstration of Christian hostility against Jews. I grew up reading stories on the *conversos* and their suffering.

While major Christian nations banished Jews or forced them to convert and uprooted their culture, other Christian regions welcomed them, allowing for the creation of new centers of Jewish livelihood and creativity. In the early modern era, Eastern Europe became a major hub of Jewish communal, religious, and intellectual life. An important Jewish center also emerged in the more tolerant atmosphere of Holland. In the seventeenth and eighteenth centuries, Jews began resettling in some countries that had expelled them earlier, such as England and its overseas colonies. Christian attitudes toward Jews may have been at times hostile, but they were never uniform. Jews continued to live in Christian lands.

Jewish-Christian relations became yet more diverse with the rise of Protestantism in the sixteenth century. Many Protestants followed in the older Christian paradigm, according to which Christianity inherited the historical role of Israel. However, a number of Protestant groups, especially those influenced by the Reformed tradition, came to regard the Jews as the continuation of biblical Israel, a nation that in the fullness of time would be redeemed and resume its ancient role as a chosen people. Such opinions were voiced by English Puritans, French Huguenots, Dutch Reformed, Lutheran Pietists, and, later on, evangelical Christians. However, even if they distanced themselves theologically from Catholics, Protestants inherited heavy baggage from medieval European society, where Jews and their culture were viewed with suspicion. Nevertheless, already by the mid-seventeenth century, Protestant lands had become preferred destinations for Jewish immigrants, most of them making their way from Eastern European Catholic and Orthodox Christian regions. Many Protestants took a renewed interest in the Jews; Pietists and evangelical Christians especially have invested time and effort in trying to evangelize Jews, efforts that they have considered to be expressions of goodwill.

As the Christian West began to modernize, the nature of Christian influence in civic and cultural spheres was transformed. Christian nations increasingly emancipated their Jews, allowing them more educational and professional opportunities, but many Christians still held stigmatizing attitudes toward Jews, and many resented their relative success at integrating into commercial and professional urban settings. Now the Jews were blamed for the harsh consequences of modernity and for disrupting older Christian orders. Modern anti-Semitism, a collective condemnation of Jews on the basis of alleged inherent moral depravities, utilized pseudoscientific theories of racial classifications that offered seemingly rationalized bases for old hostilities and paranoia. This does not mean that all Christian thinkers expressed negative ideas about Jews. An examination of Protestant attitudes, for example, reveals a whole range of attitudes, from condemnation to goodwill, including concerns for Jewish safety and sympathy for Jewish aspirations. A number of Protestants, moved by a biblically messianic faith, advocated the restoration of the Jews in Palestine.

Three factors brought Jews to reevaluate their tradition and reconstruct their identity: the Enlightenment, modernity, and renewed encounters with Christian cultures and European nationalisms. Among other things, Jewish thinkers have come to reconsider Jesus, often attempting to reclaim him as a reformer of Judaism whose teachings should be appreciated.

Following World War I and the destruction and chaos it brought with it, anti-Jewish sentiments reached a zenith. Nazi Germany was not the only nation proactively working to remove Jews from its midst. While the Nazis held officially to a secular ideology, many committed Christians supported them. In most of Europe, neither the removal of Jews from their jobs and homes nor the mass killings were condemned or resisted by churches or their leaders. However, the same years that brought Jewish-Christian relations to perhaps an all-time low point also saw the beginnings of a historical transformation that brought greater mutual recognition and cooperation between Christians and Jews.

The Dawn of a New Era?

New attitudes in the English-speaking world began even before World War II. In the 1920s, Reinhold Niebuhr, a socially and politically liberal Protestant thinker, asserted that Judaism offered adequate moral guidance and spiritual meaning to its adherents. While at this stage Niebuhr's was a minority voice, interfaith dialogue and cooperation increased after the war, with Judaism receiving growing legitimacy in America as well as in a growing number of other Western nations. A major breakthrough took place in the early 1960s in connection with Vatican II, the Catholic ecumenical council that met intermittently between 1961 and 1965. *Nostra Aetate*, the council's declaration on the subject, cited the debt that Christianity owed the Jews and declared that Jews following Jesus's generation could not be blamed for killing him. In the aftermath of the council, Protestant groups issued similar, often more radical, declarations. Such dramatic changes in Christian attitudes reflected, at least partially, Western Christians' realization that the horrors unleashed on Jews during World War II were the fruit of long-held hostilities nurtured by Christians against Judaism and Jews. Both Catholics and mainstream Protestants have worked since the 1960s to revise their religious texts to eliminate negative depiction of Jews. Christian theologians have also made efforts to amend Christian theologies to make room for Jews as standing, alongside the church, in a covenant with God.

The attitudes of evangelical Christians, who for the most part have refrained from participating in interfaith dialogues, also underwent major changes. In the later decades of the twentieth century, evangelicals' understanding of the special role of the Jewish people in God's plans for the end times began to translate into a more favorable day-to-day attitude toward Jews. Following the birth of the State of Israel in 1948, Christian relations with Israel have entered a time of equilibrium. At times Christians and Jews tie relationships with Israel to a positive or negative attitude toward Judaism and Jews. The improvement in Western Christian attitudes toward the Jews gave rise to communities of Messianic Jews and Hebrew Catholics, Jews who have accepted the Christian faith but have chosen to maintain their Jewish identity and heritage.

In my opinion, the changes that have taken place in the last decades in Jewish-Christian relations are particularly encouraging when compared to the atmosphere that prevailed two generations ago. However, not all Christians have joined the movement toward reconciliation and dialogue. Those attitudes are found mostly among American and European Christians and have not made headway in third world or Middle Eastern churches. Even in Western nations, "classical" hostile Christian attitudes pop up from time to time, as in the case of Mel Gibson's movie

The Passion of the Christ, produced and screened in 2004–5. Such incidents may invite doubt about whether the ancient siblings' rivalry between Christians and Jews can be fully eradicated. One can be quite certain, in any case, that Jews and Christians will continue to feel strongly about each other and that their relationship will never be neutral and aloof.

21

Islam: History, Beliefs, Practices

LARRY POSTON

History

To Muslims, Islam is the *din al-fitr*—the "natural religion." Islam was the religion of Adam, Abraham, Moses, David, and Jesus. "Muslim" is what everyone would be if each were left to his or her own natural inclinations.

From the standpoint of scholars of religion, however, Islam begins with the Prophet Muhammad. Born in 570 CE near Mecca in Arabia, he was orphaned early and was passed between relatives during his early years. A gifted administrator, he was employed as a camel caravan organizer by a wealthy widow named Khadija. He proved so efficient and trustworthy that Khadija, though fifteen years his elder, married him. Dissatisfied with the polytheism of the Arabs and now with a measure of free time, Muhammad turned to spiritual matters.

At the age of forty, while meditating in a cave outside of Mecca, he encountered an angel who called himself Jibril (Gabriel) and who forced him to "recite" specific pronouncements. These "recitations" (*qur'an*) were unpopular at first because they condemned polytheism, materialism, and immorality. Muhammad warned that the judgment of Allah—the One True God—would fall upon the people if they did not repent of their sin and worship Allah alone. Few were interested. Persecution broke out against Muhammad and his followers to such an extent that by 622 he found it prudent to move to a neighboring town called Yathrib (known today as Medina—"the town"). This journey is called the Hijra, and it is from this point that Muslims begin their calendar.

In Medina, Muhammad developed a devoted following and united the tribes of Arabia. In 628 he returned to Mecca and burned the pagan idols in the shrine known as the Ka'ba. This shrine became the central worship location for the world's Muslims.

Upon Muhammad's death there was controversy concerning a successor. One group favored appointing Ali, Muhammad's designated heir. This group became known as "the party of Ali"—in Arabic the "Shi'at Ali"—shortened today to the "Shi'ites," who constitute approximately 12 percent of Muslims.

The majority, however, felt that the most qualified person should lead regardless of heritage. This group was named for its belief that the "path" (*sunna*) established by Muhammad should be maintained. These "Sunnis" prevailed, and Muhammad's first successor was Abu Bakr, his uncle and father of his favorite wife A'isha.

The first four caliphs ("successors") were the Rashidun ("the rightly guided ones"). Abu Bakr (r. 632–34), Umar (r. 634–44), Uthman (r. 644–56), and Ali (r. 656–61) are noteworthy for their accomplishments, including the collection and canonization of the Qur'an and a massive expansion of the religion.

Upon Ali's death, Mu'awiya, governor of Damascus and member of the Ummayad tribe, became caliph. After consolidating power by disposing of Ali's sons Hasan and Husayn, he set about expanding Islam's borders. From 661 to 732, the religion spread westward to Spain and eastward to India. People groups throughout the Middle East and North Africa were issued an invitation (*da'wah*) to become adherents or supporters of Islam. They were promised a reduction in their taxes; the retention of all monotheistic (i.e., Christian and Jewish) religious institutions, educational institutions, and court systems; and dismissal of all "heretic" labels. Nearly all peoples accepted the *da'wah*, and bloodshed was kept to a minimum.

In the year 750 a tribe known as the Abbasids came to power and headquartered in a new capital called Baghdad. The Abbasids emphasized the arts and sciences, leading to a civilization that became the most advanced of the then-known world. Development of such disciplines as *al-jabr* (algebra) and *al-kimiya* (chemistry) marked this period. The six major collections of *hadith* ("religious traditions") were collected during this time, and four "schools of law" dealing with the interpretation of the Qur'an were also established: the *Maliki, Shafi'i, Hanafi,* and *Hanbali*. Some followers—known as Sufis—rejected the increasing "worldliness" of the faith and turned inward to become mystics.

The Mongol invasions of the thirteenth century ended the Abbasid dynasty and presented the Muslims with a theological dilemma. Why had Allah allowed barbarian invaders to conquer his people? The Muslims decided that Allah was punishing them for having become preoccupied with "worldly" thinking. While Muslims chose to lay aside their liberal arts heritage, Europeans were developing the Islamic advances brought back by the Crusaders as spoils of war.

After the fall of Baghdad and the death of the last Abbasid caliph in 1258, the caliphate was assumed by the leader of a small tribe in western Turkey. Usuman (or Osman) and his followers eventually joined with Middle Eastern Arab tribes

Study Aid #42
Muslim Timeline

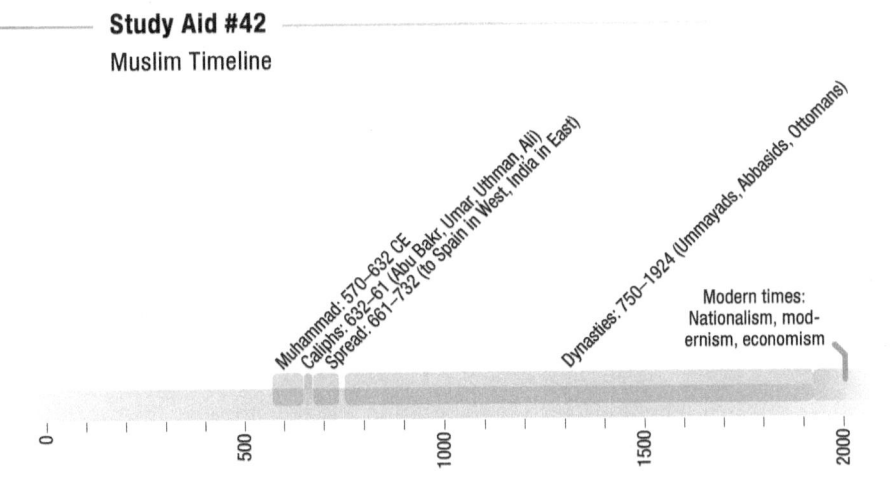

and formed the Ottoman Empire, conquering Constantinople (Istanbul) in 1453 and making this city their new capital.

The sixteenth and seventeenth centuries saw a brief period of advance, but the Ottomans were mainly occupied with holding on to as much of the Muslim world as they could. Their empire lasted until 1924, when Mustafa Kemal Ataturk took over Turkey and ended the caliphate. Today Islam has devolved into a variety of nation-states, and *nationalism* is one of the four main "-isms" with which contemporary Muslims must contend. How does a modern Egyptian view himself? As a "Muslim *Egyptian*?" Or as an "Egyptian *Muslim*?"

Modernism presents another thorny issue. Should Muslims join in the technological and scientific progress that has resulted in globalization, or should they distance themselves from it, fearing that Allah will judge them if they participate? For many, associating with anything that has a Western origin is difficult due to the residual effects of colonialism. Muslims are unable to forget that for many centuries the Islamic world was parceled out among various Western nations.

Islamic *fundamentalism* is popular in media reports, but fundamentalists (if defined by membership in one of the Muslim Brotherhood organizations) actually constitute no more than a tiny fraction of the world's Muslims. Fundamentalists insist that the community of Muhammad and the Rashidun was the only *pure* community, and every effort must be made to return the Muslim world to this pristine state.

As of 2009, Islamic sources claim that there are approximately 1.6 billion Muslims in the world, residing in nearly every country on earth. The largest populations are found in Indonesia (196 million), India (133 million), Pakistan (125 million), and Bangladesh (104 million). There are between three and six million Muslims in the United States.

Beliefs

Muslims view the Qur'an as the only true word of God. These scriptures originated in heaven, where they exist as an uncreated aspect of Allah himself. The angel Jibril revealed the Qur'an piecemeal to Muhammad, whose "recitations" became the culmination of a long series of revelations to various prophets appearing throughout history.

The Qur'an teaches absolute monotheism (*tawhid*). Allah is One and does not share his divinity with any other being; to believe that he does so is *shirk*, the greatest sin in Islam. Allah is the Creator of all things. He is absolutely sovereign over the affairs of all humans. He is loving—to those who love him. He is merciful—to those who exercise compassion toward others.

Adam, the first human, yielded to temptation and fell into sin. There is, however, no inherited "sin nature" in Islam; people are responsible for their own sins. Unfortunately humans easily yield to the temptations that surround them.

In the past, Allah sent prophets to warn the various peoples of earth, but since the time of Muhammad, the Muslim community has been responsible to act as "witnesses" of Allah's requirements for obedience to the laws revealed in the Qur'an. These laws, together with the exemplary lifestyle of Muhammad, are known as the *shari'a*—the "way" that a Muslim is to live. On judgment day, if one's good deeds outweigh the bad, one will enter *al-Janna* ("the garden"). But if one fails to submit (*aslama*) to the laws of Allah and live as a *muslim* ("a submitted one"), one will enter *al-Nar* ("the fire"). There are no mediators in Islam; the concept of a substitutionary atonement for human sin is largely lacking.

The Qur'an reveals the existence of spirit beings known as angels, such as Mikhail and Jibril. There are no "fallen angels," but there are *jinn* ("genies"), created of fire. The *jinn* can be good or evil, though most tend toward the latter. They have a fiery nature, great physical powers, the ability to make themselves invisible, and a proneness to impishness. Iblis (or Shaytan) is their leader, who seeks to lead humans into rebellion against Allah's commands.

Study Aid #43

Muslim Beliefs

Creed: "There is no God but Allah, and Muhammad is God's prophet."
Allah: The One God (monotheism).
Muhammad: God's final prophet.
Qur'an (Koran): The Holy Book, revealed by God to Muhammad.
Prayer: Muslims pray five times a day; prescribed times, prescribed prayers.
Alms: Muslims donate annually 2.5 percent of their net worth.
Fasting: One lunar month a year, Muslims fast from dawn to dusk.
Pilgrimage: Once a lifetime Muslims take an eight-day trip to Mecca in Saudi Arabia.

Islamic eschatology is essentially "premillennial." The Sunnis believe that the "last days" will be followed by a seven-year *fitna* ("tribulation"). At this time the Mahdi will appear to call the peoples of earth to repentance. Opposing the Mahdi will be the Dajjal, the "deceiver" or "antichrist." At the end of the tribulation, 'Isa (Jesus) will return to earth and destroy the antichrist and his followers. 'Isa will then rule the earth for forty years, during which time he will marry and have children. At the end of his reign, all life will come to an end. Every human being will then be resurrected in a physical body and will be judged.

Practices

The primary rituals of Islam are called the Five Pillars.

(1) *Shahada*—the "testimony" or "witness." The *shahada* is the foundational confession of every Muslim: "There is no God but Allah, and Muhammad is his messenger." The first phrase is a declaration of *absolute* monotheism; an adamant refusal to practice any form of idolatry. The second phrase is an acknowledgment that Muhammad was a true prophet, and his life is to be a model for all. Since his message was directly from Allah, one is to obey it in its entirety. *Shahada* involves *the discipline of one's spiritual self and one's worldview.*

(2) *Salat*—"prayer." Devout Muslims pray five times daily. These times punctuate the day as a means of bringing the mind and heart back to God on a consistent basis. *Salat* represents *the discipline of one's focus upon God.* Prior to prayers, the Muslim performs *wudu*, a ceremonial washing, or *ghusl*, a full bath or shower. The prayers are formal and prescribed, but each session also allows time for *du'a*, or informal prayer.

(3) *Seeyam* (or *Sawn*)—"fasting." Muslims fast each day during the month of Ramadan from two hours before sunrise until sunset. One may not eat, drink, smoke, or have sexual relations during this time. The fast is broken each evening after sunset by a light meal called the *iftar*. This is followed by the last prayer of the day and then a full dinner. One of the two Muslim holidays, the Eid al-Fitr, marks the end of Ramadan with a day of celebration. *Seeyam* involves *the discipline of one's body and sensual appetites.*

(4) *Hajj*—"pilgrimage." All Muslims who can afford to do so are to make the Hajj at least once in their lifetime. The pilgrimage is made to the Ka'ba in Mecca during Dhul-Hijjah (the twelfth month). During the Hajj, there is a time of consecration, after which one circles the Ka'ba seven times. One touches the Black Stone, a rock of meteoric origin set into a corner. The second day involves journeying to two separate locations in the vicinity of Mecca, and the third day includes a ritual known as "the stoning of the devil." At the end of this day comes the second great holiday of Islam: Eid al-Adha, which involves the symbolic sacrifice of a sheep, goat, or camel in memory of Abraham's sacrifice of Ishmael. Hajj represents *the discipline of one's nationalistic, tribalistic, racial, and/or ethnocentric tendencies.*

(5) *Zakat*—"charitable giving." *Zakat* is an obligation prescribed by God for Muslim men and women to distribute a percentage of their capital among the poor and needy. It is *discipline of one's finances and possessions*. The minimum rate of giving is 2.5 percent; there is no upper limit. Giving in this manner purifies the heart of the giver from selfishness and greed and develops sympathy for the poor. Receiving purifies the heart of the recipient from envy and hatred of the rich and prosperous.

Sources

Karen Armstrong. *Islam: A Short History*. Rev. ed. Modern Library, 2002.
Frederick Denny. *An Introduction to Islam*. 3rd ed. Prentice Hall, 2005.
John L. Esposito. *Islam: The Straight Path*. 3rd ed. Oxford University Press, 2004.
Marshall G. S. Hodgson. *The Venture of Islam*. University of Chicago Press, 1977.
Seyyed Hossein Nasr. *Islam: Religion, History and Civilization*. HarperOne, 2001.
Fazlur Rahman. *Major Themes of the Qur'an*. 2nd ed. University of Chicago Press, 2009.

22

Islam: Christian Contacts

LARRY POSTON

The first Christians with whom Muslims had contact were designated "heretical" by the Roman Catholic Church. These were the Monophysites (i.e., Jacobites and Copts) and the Nestorians. It was the latter sect that was most likely found in Mecca during Muhammad's lifetime. Nestorius believed that the *humanity* of Jesus should be clearly distinguished from his divinity. That the Nestorians seemingly downplayed any alleged "divine" attributes of Jesus may well have been the source for Muhammad's conclusion that "nearest among [men] in love to the Believers wilt thou find those who say, 'We are Christians': because amongst these are men devoted to learning and men who have renounced the world, and they are not arrogant" (Sura 5:82).

The above passage, along with Sura 2:62—"Surely those who believe and those who are Jews and Christians and Sabaens . . . shall be rewarded by their Lord; they have nothing to fear or regret"—led to the concept of the *ahl al-dhimma*—"the people of protection." Monotheists (i.e., Jews and Christians) were permitted to retain their respective religious systems. Treaties were drawn up such as that established between the caliph Umar and the Christians living in Jerusalem when it fell in 638 CE. This treaty pledged that neither Christians nor their churches would be impoverished, destroyed, or injured in any way.

During the Abbasid period (ca. 750–1258 CE) letters were often exchanged between Christian and Muslim theologians, and on occasion debates were held such as those between Abraham of Tiberias and members of the *ahl al-nazar* under the auspices of the Amir Abd al-Rahman al-Hashim of Jerusalem. There were three significant Christian apologists during these early years. Theodore Abu

> **Study Aid #44**
> Muslim Divisions
>
> | | |
> |---|---|
> | Sunni | 1.329 billion |
> | Sufi | 310 million |
> | Shi'a | 200 million |
> | Schismatic | 20 million |

Qurra (d. 830 CE) wrote that Christianity was the only true religion and defended the doctrines of the Trinity and the incarnation. Habib Abu Ra'ita (d. 855 CE) and Ammar al-Basri (d. 850) wrote apologetical works to prevent Christians from converting to Islam.

Farther along in the Abbasid period, the Risala fi al-radd ala al-nasara (Letter about the Refutation of the Christians) by al-Jahiz (d. 869) and Radd ala al-nasara (Refutation of the Christians) by Ali ibn Rabban al-Tabari were penned. Debates appear to have been held relatively often. But not all Christians were convinced that debating was helpful. John of Damascus (ca. 676–749) claimed that Islam was simply a Christian heresy that needed correction. A few decades later the Nestorian patriarch Timothy I was asked by the caliph al-Mahdi what he thought of the Prophet Muhammad. Timothy's reply was that Muhammad was a true prophet and a lover of God, as evidenced by his teaching concerning the oneness of God and his preaching against immorality and sin.

Such views did not last, however. Under the caliph al-Mutawakkil (r. 817–61), debates were halted due to their alleged disruption of society. New laws were passed that required Christians (as well as other *dhimmis*) to wear honey-colored hoods (*taylasan*) and girdles (*zunnar*) and to ride on saddles with wooden stirrups. The caliph also ordered that newly built churches be destroyed.

During the Middle Ages, relations between Christians and Muslims were defined mainly by the Crusades. The brutality of the conquest of Jerusalem in 1099 left a deep bitterness in the hearts of Muslims that continues to the present. Muslims the world over consider the establishment of Israel in 1948 to be a resumption of the Crusades, and conservative Christian support for Israel coupled with so-called neglect of Palestinian Muslims has created harsh feelings toward Western Christianity in general.

Distinct from the Crusades was a more "academic" engagement on the part of Christian theologians. These scholars portrayed Islam as a religion established by a false prophet who was one of the "anti-Christs" mentioned by the apostle John. The Qur'an was dismissed as a cut-and-paste document consisting of distorted versions of Bible narratives along with demonically inspired lies propagated by Muhammad and his followers.

Perhaps the only exception to this negative portrayal was the view developed by the Christian and Muslim residents of the Iberian Peninsula who lived and worked side by side for centuries. In 1108, Pedro de Alfonso, a Spanish Jew who had converted to Christianity, wrote one of his *Dialogues* as an attempt to portray Muslims more accurately than his forebearers and peers had done. A few years later Peter the Venerable wrote that the Crusades were misguided and that Christians should convert Muslims rather than destroy them.

Peter's work inspired Thomas Aquinas, who wrote of Muslims in *Summa contra Gentiles* and *De rationibus fidei contra Saracenos, Graecos et Armenos ad Cantorem Antiochenum*. Aquinas and his contemporaries developed a view of Islam that consisted of four main propositions: Islam is false and a deliberate perversion of truth; it is a religion spread by violence and the sword; it is a religion of self-indulgence; and it is a religion founded by Muhammad the antichrist. Aquinas believed, however, that the Crusades were misguided. Roger Bacon concurred, convinced that Muslims remained unconverted because they had not been taught the doctrines of the Catholic Church in their native tongue. Consequently, early in the fourteenth century the Council of Vienna opened the doors for several universities to establish chairs of Oriental languages.

The Franciscan and Dominican orders were the first to engage in strictly missionary activity to Muslims. Francis himself went on three missions to "the Saracens," and his followers went to Spain, Egypt, Syria, Tunisia, and Morocco. Closely connected with the Franciscans was Ramon Lull (1232–1315), who taught himself Arabic and founded a school in Majorca for the training of missionaries. In 1292 he debated Muslims in Tunis but was arrested and deported. This scenario was repeated in Algiers in 1307, and on a final trip to the same area in 1315 he was martyred.

In 1540 Ignatius of Loyola founded the Society of Jesus as an elite missionary force capable of confronting and defeating Muslim arguments against Christianity. Had it not been for the papacy's decision to use the Jesuits as frontline troops for the Counter-Reformation, Loyola's men would have concentrated their work in the Middle East.

The post-Reformation colonialist endeavors resulted in the conquest of nearly all the Muslim world by the "Christian West." India's Mogul Empire fell to the British, Malaysia and Indonesia to the Dutch, and North and West Africa were divided up piecemeal among various European colonizers.

The Christian minorities residing in the Muslim world were, in many cases, pleased to have Westerners in power. But many of these groups' leaders were resentful that their own influence was greatly diminished as a result. They also feared that a backlash might eventually arise against them should the colonizers be forced out or leave voluntarily. This proved to be the case in more than one situation. Persecutions, however, produced an outcry in the West against the Muslim "barbarians," who in turn became even more convinced that Christian nations were joined in an all-out conspiracy against the Muslim world.

The nineteenth century saw a massive outpouring of Protestant missionaries all over the globe. Most of these retained the view of Islam as a religion of false

Study Aid #45
Spread of Islam

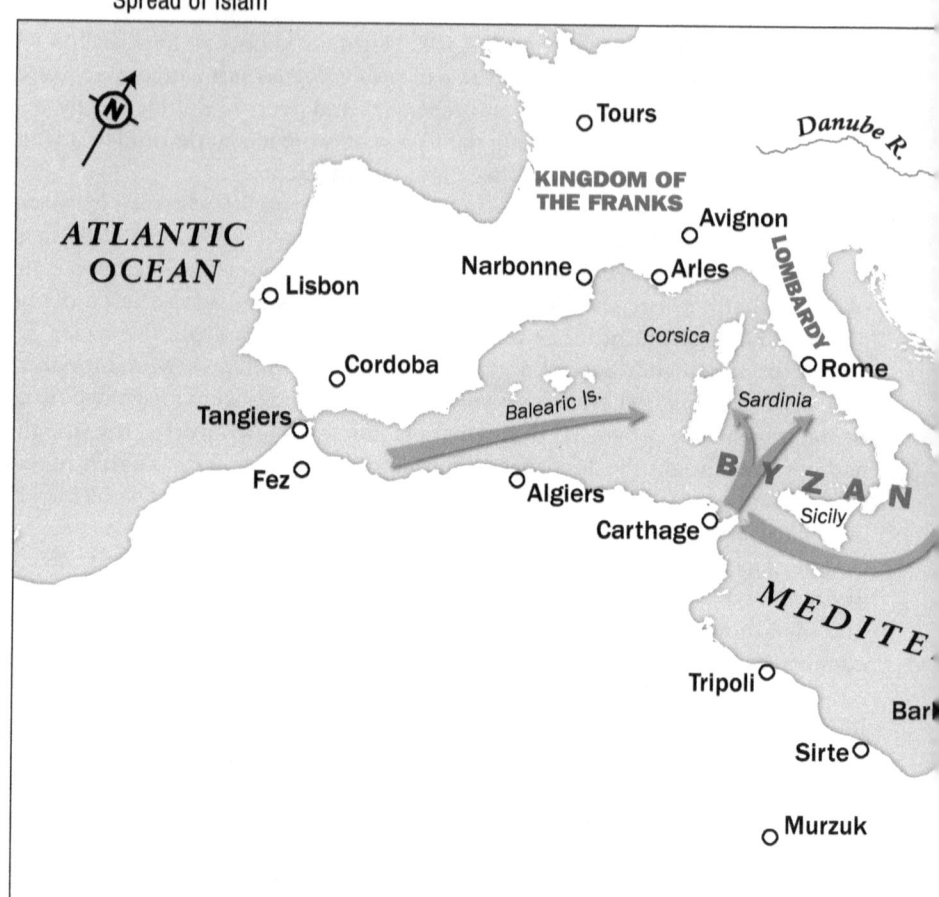

doctrine, violence, and sexual indulgence. Two of the more notable missionaries of this era were Carl Gottlieb Pfander, whose *Mizan ul-Haqq* (*The Balance of Truth*) was widely distributed in Iran, and Temple Gairdner, who functioned as a missionary scholar in Cairo.

In the early twentieth century, the last bastion of Islamic imperialism—the Ottoman Empire—was defeated by the Allies in World War I and was dismantled over the next several years. In 1924, Mustafa Kemal Ataturk deposed the last of the Ottoman caliphs, leaving the Muslim world with no central authority. Since most of this territory was now under Western hegemony, Muslim resentment toward all things Western—including Christianity—continued apace.

Muslims found ways to retaliate. One of their main weapons has been *The Gospel of Barnabas*, a work that appeared in 1709 and was translated into Arabic in 1908. The book supports Islam at the expense of Christianity, going so far as to have Jesus speak of Muhammad as the Messiah. By mid-century, debates between Muslims and Christians had again become popular. Throughout the latter half of the 1900s, such notables as the Muslim apologist Ahmed Deedat held forth, debating (among others) his Christian counterpart Josh McDowell. Deedat's many booklets with titles such as *Is the Bible the Word of God?* and *Crucifixion or Cruci-fiction?* inspired an entire generation of young Muslim imitators. As a result, since the 1960s many Muslim immigrants to the West have considered themselves *da'is* (missionaries) seeking to bring the "gospel of Islam" to the godless, materialistic, and debauched societies of Western civilization.

The 1960s also saw a change in the Roman Catholic Church's view of Islam. The Second Vatican Council published *Lumen Gentium* in 1964, proclaiming that "the plan of salvation also includes those who acknowledge the Creator, in the first place amongst whom are the Muslims: these profess to hold the faith of Abraham, and together with us they adore the one, merciful God, mankind's judge on the last day." A year later *Nostra Aetate* noted that "the Church has

---

Study Aid #46

Christian-Muslim Contacts

622	Muhammad and Christians (Nestorians) and Jews in Medina
638	Umar declares Christians (and Jews) "People of the Book"
1099	Crusades and conquest of Jerusalem
1200	Franciscan and Dominican missions to Muslims
1500	Ignatius and Jesuits begin mission to Muslims
1800	Empire missionaries
1924	Ottoman Empire defeated by West
1960s	Oil economy revives Islam as world force
2006	"A Common Word between Us and You" published

also a high regard for Muslims. They worship God, who is one.... Although not acknowledging him as God, they venerate Jesus as a prophet, his virgin Mother they also honor."

One of the most recent exchanges between Muslims and Christians began in 2006. In September of that year Pope Benedict XVI gave an address at the University of Regensburg on the topic "Faith, Reason, and the University." A quotation early in the speech elicited a negative reaction from Muslims around the world. In a discussion with a Persian scholar concerning Christianity and Islam, the Byzantine emperor Manuel II Paleologus challenged his Muslim colleague to "show . . . just what Muhammad brought that was new, and there you will find things only evil and inhuman, such as his command to spread by the sword the faith he preached." The citation was meant to be the preface to a plea for rational discussion regarding religion, but many Muslims were incensed.

In September of 2007, 138 Muslim scholars and clergymen issued a response to the Regensburg address. "A Common Word between Us and You" was designed to promote "open intellectual exchange and mutual understanding" between the world's Christian and Muslim communities. A website was established (see http://www.acommonword.com/), and to this site has been added a variety of responses from Christian individuals and groups. One of the more notable of these was issued by Yale Divinity School's Center for Faith and Culture. This document, "Loving God and Neighbor Together," was published in the *New York Times* along with the names of 135 Christians who endorsed its sentiments.

"A Common Word" proposes that the basis for peace and understanding between Christianity and Islam has always existed: "the Unity of God, love of Him, and love of the Neighbor form a common ground upon which Islam and Christianity . . . are founded." The Muslim *shahada* ("There is no God but Allah, and Muhammad is his messenger") and one of Islam's traditions ("None of you has faith until you love for your neighbor what you love for yourself") are considered the Islamic equivalents of Jesus's teaching regarding the two greatest commandments ("Love the Lord your God with all your heart and with all your soul and with all your mind and with all your strength" and "Love your neighbor as yourself"; Mark 12:30–31).

The authors claim that "through inspiration" Muhammad was repeating the Bible's greatest commandment, and he thus "brought nothing fundamentally or essentially new" to humankind. Islam recognizes Jesus as the Messiah; Muslims are therefore with Christians, not against them. Concluding the document is an invitation to recognize and honor this "common ground" and to "vie with each other only in righteousness and good works," respecting each other, being fair, just, and kind to one another, and living in "sincere peace, harmony, and mutual goodwill."

Such exchanges bode well for the future of Christian-Muslim dialogue, and as globalization continues apace, it is likely that an increasing number of such exchanges will be seen.

Sources

Clinton Bennett. *Understanding Christian-Muslim Relations*. Continuum, 2008.

Hugh Goddard. *A History of Christian-Muslim Relations*. New Amsterdam, 2001.

Anthony O'Mahony and Emma Loosley. *Christian Responses to Islam: Muslim-Christian Relations in the Modern World*. Manchester University Press, 2008.

William Montgomery Watt. *Muslim-Christian Encounters: Perceptions and Misperceptions*. Routledge, 1991.

J. Dudley Woodberry and Robin Basselin, eds. *Resources for Peacemaking in Muslim-Christian Relations: Contributions from the Conflict Transformation Project*. Fuller Seminary Press, 2006.

23

Islam: Theological Exchanges

Larry Poston

When comparing religions, we see two different philosophies. One emphasizes the *similarities* between faiths; the other highlights *differences* between them. When comparing Islam and Christianity, for instance, proponents of the first category would point out that Muslims and Christians both

1. worship only one God;
2. are devoted to a scripture they believe is divinely inspired;
3. believe that the Torah and the Gospels are inspired by God;
4. believe similar creation stories;
5. recognize the patriarchs and prophets of the Old Testament;
6. believe in Jesus's virgin birth;
7. confess that Jesus was the Messiah;
8. believe that Jesus is returning to earth to defeat an antichrist and establish an earthly kingdom;
9. believe in the Holy Spirit;
10. believe in angels;
11. believe that all people need to repent of sin; and
12. believe that prayer, fasting, and charitable giving are scripturally prescribed means of serving God.

For those whose major emphasis is contrasts, however, significant differences are noted:

1. For Christians the oneness of God is expressed as a divine threeness; Muslims insist upon a consistent monotheism.
2. The Bible *alone* is the Word of God for most Christians, as the Qur'an is for Muslims.
3. Jesus was the incarnation of God to Christians; for Muslims he was a great prophet but not divine.
4. For Muslims, Allah created Jesus in Mary's womb; Christians believe Jesus was an "incarnation" of God.
5. For Muslims, the Holy Spirit is the highest angel, not a member of the Trinity.
6. For Christians, salvation is acquired by grace through faith; Muslims believe they must earn their salvation through obedience to Allah.
7. In Islam, Adam's sin did not affect the entire human race; for Christians, atonement for inherited sin is essential.
8. Islam is externally and institutionally oriented; New Testament Christianity is internally and personally oriented.
9. In Islam, Jesus returns to complete his prophetic ministry, destroy all churches and synagogues, and marry and have children. He reigns for forty years—as opposed to the one-thousand-year kingdom of Christian premillennialists.
10. While New Testament Christianity espouses a distinction between "God and Caesar," Muslims have historically espoused theocracy.

Jesus has always been the focal point of controversy. For Christians, he is the incarnation of the One True God, the second member of the Triune Godhead, the Son of God, the Messiah, the sacrificial atonement for the sins of humankind, the resurrected Savior, the Prophet promised through Moses, the Great High Priest who intercedes for his people, and the King from David's line.

For Muslims, trinitarianism is blasphemy, and "sonship" implies that God had sexual relations with Mary. The crucifixion is denied, and "resurrection" will occur for Jesus at the same time as for all other human beings. No one can atone for another person's sins. Jesus was a prophet—a *rasul* like Muhammad—but he was neither a "priest" nor a "king."

The *ultimate* point of contention between the two groups is the issue of *authority*: the Qur'an versus the Bible. The resurrection is a nonnegotiable tenet of Christianity because the Bible teaches that "if Christ has not been raised, your faith is futile; you are still in your sins" (1 Cor. 15:17). The Bible also teaches that "no one who denies the Son has the Father" (1 John 2:23); thus to reject Jesus's Sonship is to reject God the Father. The apostle John also taught that "[Jesus] is the atoning sacrifice for our sins" (1 John 2:2), so when Muslims deny the concept of atonement, they undercut the Bible's authority.

The Qur'an, on the other hand, states that "Christians call Christ the Son of God.... (In this) they but imitate what the Unbelievers of old used to say. Allah's

> **Study Aid #47**
>
> **Muslim-Christian Theological Exchanges**
>
> Shared history
> Monotheism
> Jesus and Muhammad
> Bible and Qur'an
> Modern interreligious dialogue

curse be on them: how they are deluded from the Truth!" (Sura 9:30). Concerning the incarnation and the Trinity, the Qur'an is condemnatory: "In blasphemy indeed are those who say that Allah is Christ the Son of Mary. . . . They do blaspheme who say: Allah is one of three in a Trinity; for there is no god except one God. If they desist not from their word of blasphemy, verily a grievous penalty will befall the blasphemers among them" (Sura 5:17, 73). And with respect to vicarious atonement, the Qur'an teaches that "no bearer of burdens can bear the burden of another" (Sura 39:7). In short, Christians are convinced that the Bible is the verbally inspired and completely inerrant revelation of God to humankind, and Muslims are convinced of the same regarding the Qur'an.

Despite such obstacles, dialogue has taken place between the two religions for centuries. Saint Francis of Assisi (1182–1226), for instance, believed that Muslims were not receptive to the gospel because they had never heard it in an understandable form. He wrote his *Canticle of All Creatures* in imitation of the Qur'an's style. Intrigued by the Muslim calls to prayer, he arranged to have bells perform a similar function for church services.

Associated with the Franciscans was Ramon Lull (1235–1315), whose novel *Blanquerna* praises Islam's belief in the oneness of God. He also commended the Sufis' practice of *dhikr* as a form of meditation upon the attributes of God and expressed appreciation for the veneration given to Mary.

In the thirteenth century, the Dominican order produced William of Tripoli (1220–73) and Ricoldo de Monte-Crucis (1243–1320), both of whom learned Arabic and read Muslim literature extensively. William's *On the Condition of the Saracens* contains an analysis of the two faiths that emphasizes their similarities. Ricoldo in his *Confutatio Alcorani* praises Muslims for their studiousness, reverence for God, and charity to the poor.

As contact between the Muslim world and the "Christian" West increased during the colonial period, ways were sought to coexist peacefully. Historically when such motivations come to the fore, exclusivistic theological precepts are submerged or interpreted in new ways.

Many modern theological discussions take a "lowest common denominator" approach, usually centering on Abraham—the "neutral" progenitor of the three Western monotheistic faiths. These regard Abraham as their spiritual ancestor, and the more "liberal" adherents of each believe that he represents a stream of thought that holds that worshiping the One True God can take several forms. Enmity between the expressions of Abraham's faith is unwarranted, as noted in Sura 3:65: "Ye People of the Book! Why dispute ye about Abraham, when the Law and the Gospel were not revealed till after him?" The three religions should emphasize similarities in their thinking rather than differences, these being allegedly few and insignificant.

Proponents of this approach emphasize the Qur'an's statements regarding the validity of the Torah and the Injil (i.e., the Bible). Sura 3:84 claims that "we [Muslims] believe . . . in the books given to Moses, Jesus, and the Prophets from their Lord; we make no distinction between one and another among them." Thus through the nineteenth and twentieth centuries one finds increasing emphasis on such passages as the following.

In the Qur'an:

> Surely those who believe and those who are Jews and Christians and Sabaens—whoever believes in God and the Last Day and does what is right—shall be rewarded by their Lord; they have nothing to fear or regret. (Sura 2:62)

> And nearest among them in love to the Believers wilt thou find those who say, "We are Christians": because amongst these are men devoted to learning and men who have renounced the world, and they are not arrogant. . . . And for this their prayer hath Allah rewarded them with Gardens with rivers flowing underneath—their eternal Home. (Sura 5:82–85)

In the Bible:

> I have other sheep that are not of this sheep pen. I must bring them also. They too will listen to my voice, and there shall be one flock and one shepherd. (John 10:16)

> Then Peter began to speak: "I now realize how true it is that God does not show favoritism but accepts from every nation the one who fears him and does what is right." (Acts 10:34–35)

Emphasizing such passages—and suppressing the exclusivistic passages in both scriptures—has enabled theologians on both sides to suggest that Christianity and Islam are both equally valid ways of knowing the One True God.

Exclusivistic Muslims, however, believe that the Bible in its current form was rewritten by later religious figures to put forth their own agendas. Christians adhere to false doctrines that rob them of the salvation available only in Islam. Exclusivistic Christians, on the other hand, believe that the Qur'an was inspired by a demonic angel and that Muslims stand condemned. Exclusivists point to the following as evidence for their position:

In the Qur'an:

> It is [Allah] Who has sent His Messenger with guidance, and the Religion of Truth, to proclaim it over all religion: and enough is Allah for a witness. (Sura 48:28)

> Our religion is the Baptism of Allah. And who can baptize better than Allah? It is He whom we worship.... Or do ye say that Abraham, Ishmael, Isaac, Jacob and the Tribes were Jews or Christians? (Sura 2:138–40)

In the Bible:

> Jesus answered, "I am the way and the truth and the life. No one comes to the Father except through me." (John 14:6)

> Salvation is found in no one else, for there is no other name under heaven given to mankind by which we must be saved. (Acts 4:12)

Late in the twentieth century, Christian missiologists developed a new strategy for evangelizing Muslims. It was observed that apostasy from Islam usually results in excommunication from families, loss of jobs and social status, forced separation from one's spouse, and, in extreme cases, execution. While many in history have converted to Christianity despite such consequences, relatively few in the Muslim world have done so.

A new form of contextualization has been developed that takes into account the difficulties converts from Islam face. This strategy acknowledges six different kinds of "Christ-centered communities" (Travis 1998). C1 refers to a traditional church using an "Outsider" language; C2 to a traditional church using an "Insider" language; C3 to "contextualized Christ-centered communities using Insider language and religiously neutral Insider cultural forms"; and C4 to "contextualized Christ-centered communities using Insider language and biblically permissible cultural and Islamic forms." Converts from Islam in these categories call themselves Christians and meet in buildings designated as churches.

C5 refers to "Christ-centered communities of 'Messianic Muslims' who have accepted Jesus as Lord and Savior"; and C6 includes "small Christ-centered communities of Secret/Underground Believers." Converts in these categories continue to call themselves "Muslims," remain fully within the Muslim community, participate in the five daily prayers, attend mosque services, and, in the case of C6 adherents, do not generally share their faith with Muslims.

Opponents of the C5 and C6 approaches assert that the gospel message is compromised by the secrecy involved. The New Testament requires a forthright declaration of one's conversion, even if persecution and a martyr's death are the result.

Advocates claim that C5 and C6 converts are not denying Christ but are obeying Jesus's directive to be "as shrewd as snakes and as innocent as doves" (Matt. 10:16).

Churches can never be planted in areas where a frank declaration of conversion to Christianity results in immediate death. Subterfuge is necessary to fulfill the Great Commission. It is hypocritical for "armchair missiologists" in the West to advocate martyrdom for others when they themselves are in no danger.

What can be expected in the future? From a sociological standpoint, attempts to find common ground may gain momentum. The 2007 invitation to Christians by Muslim scholars and clerics titled "A Common Word between Us and You" gave grounds for hope that the two faiths might be able to cooperate in some settings.

Theologically, however, overcoming the mutual exclusivity of Islam and Christianity appears impossible. The most fundamental precepts of these groups' respective scriptures are incompatible. Therefore, movement toward an inclusivist position is possible only for those who have abandoned a literal interpretation of their Holy Book.

Sources

Norman Geisler and Abdul Saleeb. *Answering Islam: The Crescent in Light of the Cross*. 2nd ed. Baker Books, 2002.

Ovey Mohammed. *Muslim-Christian Relations: Past, Present, Future*. Orbis Books, 1999.

Phil Parshall. "Danger! New Directions in Contextualization." *Evangelical Missions Quarterly* (October 1998): 404–17.

Fazlur Rahman. *Major Themes of the Qur'an*. 2nd ed. University of Chicago Press, 2009.

John Travis. "Christ-Centered Communities." *Evangelical Missions Quarterly* (October 1998): 407–8.

24

Islam: Current Issues

LARRY POSTON

The Middle East versus the West

Muslims believe that Islamic culture and religion are superior to those of Europe and, in particular, North America. Because Muslims are generally unable to distinguish between a religion and the culture in which adherents of that religion reside, they believe that it is European and American "Christians" who are guilty of exporting the most despicable forms of immorality imaginable through television, movies, magazines, and other forms of mass media.

Muslims point out that it is the "Christian" societies of the West that are characterized by drunkenness, drug addiction, pornography, sexual promiscuity, homosexuality, divorce, and the collapse of traditional family structures. Violent crime is rampant, social injustice occurs at every level, racial and ethnic prejudice is endemic, and women are treated as mere sex objects for the satisfaction of men's lusts.

In addition, American foreign policy—fomented by Bible-carrying and church-attending presidents—is perceived as, at best, misguided and, at worst, completely hypocritical. For instance, during the 1980s the United States was the chief supporter of Saddam Hussein (who opposed the Iranians after their hostage-taking of Americans in 1979) and of Osama bin Laden (who was supportive of resistance to the Soviet Union's invasion of Afghanistan). When these men had served America's needs, they were simply discarded. All in all, many Muslims today believe that the world would be a much finer place if the United States simply ceased to exist.

> **Study Aid #48**
>
> Current Muslim and Muslim-Christian Issues
>
> Petroleum: Political and economic issues
> Israel
> Muslim background believers
> Islamicization
> Role of women

This being the case, evangelical Christians find that the number of Muslims willing to consider claims concerning the gospel of Christ is small. Truth and righteousness are found in Islam, not in Christianity. Therefore it is the responsibility of Muslims everywhere to "invite unto the way of our Lord with beautiful preaching" (Sura 16:125).

Islam, however, has its own "public relations" problems. Just as Christians are portrayed in the Muslim world as godless and immoral, Muslims are portrayed in the "Christian" West as fanatical terrorists. Much of this reputation is traceable to historic attempts to resolve theological conundrums. During the first century of Islam (632–732 CE), more territory was won to the faith in a shorter period of time than had ever occurred in history. Muslims interpreted this as Allah's blessing. A long period of "consolidation and maintenance" followed, during which Islamic civilization reached the pinnacle of sophistication as extraordinary progress was made in the sciences, the humanities, and the arts. The Mongol invasions of the thirteenth century, however, led to a theological crisis: how could Allah allow shamanistic barbarians to decimate his people? The Muslims concluded that the invaders were a punishment for Islam's exaltation of "worldly" interests, and as a result many advances were abandoned as Muslims simplified their civilization along more religiously oriented lines.

As the West advanced through its Renaissance and Enlightenment, Muslims became divided over the issue of modernism. Some openly questioned whether the Mongol invasions had been correctly interpreted and resented that the West—building upon Muslim thinking brought back from the Crusades—had surpassed Islamic civilization. If Muslims were Allah's chosen, should they not be the leaders of the world? Proponents of this way of thinking began to relate to Westerners and sought to acquire the technological and scientific advancements enjoyed by Western "Christians."

Another element within Islam, however, saw things differently. "Fundamentalists" were convinced that Muslims had made the correct decision regarding the Mongol invasions, and believed that a return to the kind of "classical" civilization the Islamic world enjoyed during the Abbasids' reign would invite a renewal of Allah's disciplinary actions. This issue is without apparent resolution, and therefore Muslims will continue to be ambivalent about the West.

Nationalism

One of Muhammad's chief goals was to *unite* the Arabian Peninsula's tribes into a single *umma* (community). Nationalism, however, produces the opposite effect. Since the advent of Western colonialism—and particularly since the caliphate's demise in 1924—Islam's adherents have identified themselves primarily as "Turks," "Egyptians," "Moroccans," "Libyans," "Lebanese," "Pakistanis," and the like rather than as "Muslims." A majority take their Islamicity for granted; only the fundamentalists believe that being "Muslim" should be at the core of their identity. At this point in time, a unified global Islam is no more than an elusive dream.

The same is true with respect to religious belief and practice. While Muslim apologists delight to point out the overwhelming number of denominations that exist within Christianity, contemporary Islam is characterized by the same phenomenon. Saudi Arabia would like to consider itself the arbiter of true Islam, but Arabian culture is actually a hybrid composed of a conservative form of Islam combined with a dynastic monarchy utilizing Western-educated persons as ministers. This form of Islam is quite distinct from that of Western African nations, which in many cases have developed syncretisms that combine Islam with indigenous pagan beliefs and practices. Turkish Islam is yet another variety, identifying with European cultures rather than Asian. East African Islam has been strongly influenced by mystical Sufism, while Indonesian Islam bears traces of Hinduism, Buddhism, and Chinese religions. The millions of Muslims living in Europe and North America have adapted to the beliefs and practices of "Christian" majorities within a matrix of pluralistic, secular democracies. Attempting to speak of "Islam" as a single entity is as ludicrous as seeking to identify an exemplary form of "Christianity."

The Arab-Israeli Conflict

During the last several decades, Christian-Muslim relations have been strained by another issue. The establishment of the nation of Israel in the Islamic heartland has been a point of contention between Muslims and Jews especially, but due to certain forms of theology, Christians have also been drawn into the struggle.

For centuries the area known as "Palestine" was part of the Ottoman Empire. It was fought over during the Crusades (1096–1291 CE), with the Muslims emerging as the undisputed victors. No one contested the ownership of the land until the twentieth century, when the Ottoman Empire joined the Germans and Italians and ended up on the losing side of World War I. Palestine became a British protectorate "by right of conquest." The Balfour Declaration (1917) and the San Remo Peace Conference (1920) established a basis for the return of the Jewish people to what had once been their homeland. During the 1920s, Jews fleeing from Stalin's pogroms upset the carefully planned immigration policies, and the outpouring of sympathy for the Jews following World War II's Holocaust led to the establishment of Israel in 1948. For Muslims, this was nothing less than a continuation of the Crusades. They protested this incursion from the beginning, fighting four major wars (1948, 1956, 1967, and 1973) along with innumerable smaller skirmishes.

A large proportion of conservative American Christians have supported Israel and either directly or implicitly denied Muslims' claims to the land. These Christians have interpreted the founding of modern Israel as a sign of the imminent return of Christ and believe that failure to align themselves with the Jewish nation would invite God's judgment upon the United States. Extensive lobbying campaigns have been undertaken on behalf of Israel, all of which have been interpreted by Muslims as disrespect for the rights of the Palestinian people.

Some Christians have attempted to be more evenhanded, publicly apologizing for the Crusades and seeking to establish reconciliation with the Palestinian Muslims. These have been a minority, however, and their rhetoric has been subdued.

The Status and Role of Women

During the last several decades, Muslims have been forced to deal with the issue of the role of women in religious contexts and in society. Adherents of Islam are stereotypically perceived as abusive in their treatment of Muslimas (female Muslims). The media regularly exhibit fully veiled women who are allegedly in complete subjugation to men. In certain countries women are not allowed outside their homes unless accompanied by a male relative, and in many locations they are not allowed to drive a car—or even attend school. Islam permits a Muslim man to marry up to four wives, and he may choose between Muslim, Christian, and Jewish women—while a Muslim female may only marry a Muslim. Children always belong to the father, and a daughter inherits only half of what a son receives upon the death of parents. The "Christian" West uses such items in its attempts to demonstrate the superiority of Christianity due to its "liberation" of females from patriarchy. The fact that women are now ordained in many denominations and serve as pastors and bishops is believed to be a good apologetic for Christianity.

But in actuality the liberation of women within Christianity is neither universal nor long-standing. Relatively few Christian contexts afford women leadership privileges. In neither Roman Catholicism nor Eastern Orthodoxy—which together constitute two-thirds of the world's Christians—is such liberty available. Even

---

Study Aid #49

Muslim Demographics

Number of Muslims in the world: 1,549,444,000
Percentage of world population: 22.4 percent
There are 50 countries where Muslims make up more than 50 percent of population

> **Study Aid #50**
> Countries with Muslim Populations
>
> | | |
> |---|---|
> | Indonesia | 188,164,000 |
> | India | 168,250,000 |
> | Pakistan | 166,576,000 |
> | Bangladesh | 148,078,000 |
> | Turkey | 75,670,000 |
> | Iran | 73,276,000 |
> | Nigeria | 72,306,000 |
> | Egypt | 68,804,000 |
> | Algeria | 34,712,000 |
> | Morocco | 31,845,000 |
> | United States | 5,000,000 |

Protestant denominations that condone egalitarianism have done so for only a few decades.

Muslims, on the other hand, point out that women have enjoyed a great deal of power and autonomy in Islamic history. They note the allegedly tremendous political influence that Muhammad's wife A'isha exercised during the era of the first caliphs. They refer to the subtle power that females exercised from the *harems* of the Ummayad and Abbasid caliphates. They speak fondly of the great female mystics of Islam, such as Rabia al-Adawiyya, who were instrumental in the formation of Sufism. They boast about modern Islam's progressiveness as seen in the election of women to the position of prime minister in such nations as Turkey and Pakistan.

Additionally, female Muslims write of their preference for the traditional Muslim coverings that protect them from the lustful stares of evil men. Polygamy is considered a social welfare system provided by a loving God who understands that in most societies women outnumber men. Polygamy provides the security of a husband and a home for all women as opposed to the loneliness and insecurity that monogamy imposes on those who are unable to marry.

A Muslima will point out that upon her marriage she will receive a dowry that she retains if her husband dies or divorces her. The combination of the dowry with an inheritance from her parents provides her with a form of "social security." The man, on the other hand, needs his larger share of inheritance to use as a dowry for a wife. This system has the added benefit of making a husband think carefully before divorcing, because in doing so he would forfeit his original dowry and would need to obtain additional funds should he wish to marry another. Given the divorce rates extant among both non-Christians and Christians in the United

States, Americans would be extremely unwise to criticize a system that functions much better than the "no-fault" divorce procedures available in most states.

Minority Rights

One of the greatest issues today concerns the status and rights of minority Christian communities living in Muslim-majority countries. How, for instance, should such communities interface with Christians from the West, many of whom are taking an active interest in the Muslim world for the purposes of ministry? Muslim governments are entirely opposed to evangelistic activities and seek to expel any Western citizen involved in such practices. This puts indigenous Christians in a bind. If they cooperate with Western Christians who are subsequently deported, they can bring persecution upon themselves from the Muslim government. If they refuse to fellowship with Western Christians to preserve their *dhimmi* (protected) status, they are accused by Westerners of being nominal, compromised, and cowardly "Christians" who are disobedient to the Great Commission.

The only real basis for hope regarding any of these issues is the fact that for much of the Muslim world, encroaching globalization is having a slow but significant "secularizing" effect. As young Muslims become increasingly networked through mass media and computer technologies, change is inevitable. Familiarity with pluralism, human rights, religious freedom, tolerance, and mutual respect will have a leavening effect. This may not occur as rapidly as some would like, but an eventual democratization of religion in the Muslim world seems highly likely.

Sources

Gary M. Burge. *Who Are God's People in the Middle East?* Zondervan, 1993.
John Esposito and Dalia Mogahed. *Who Speaks for Islam?* Gallup, 2007.
John Esposito and John Voll. *Islam and Democracy.* Oxford University Press, 1996.
Seyyed Hossein Nasr. *A Young Muslim's Guide to the Modern World.* Kazi, 1994.
J. Dudley Woodberry. *Muslims and Christians on the Emmaus Road.* MARC, 1989.

25

Islam: Adherent Essay

SARMAD QUTUB AND MUSA QUTUB

Islam (literally meaning "submission" in the Arabic language) is the faith of the One True God (called *Allah* in the Arabic language, meaning "The God"), a religion that began with the onset of creation. It is the true form of what one comes to think of when pondering *monotheism*—that is, one being without partner, alone without equal, ultimate without opposite. He is one pre-eternal, beginninglessly uncreated, everlastingly abiding, unceasingly existent, eternally limitless, the ever self-subsisting through whom all else subsists, ever enduring, without end. He possesses all attributes of majesty and is complete and perfect in each and every one. He is the First and the Last, the Outward and the Inward, and he has knowledge of everything. This is monotheism in its purest form. Although Christianity claims to practice a monotheistic doctrine, in reality they have fractured God into the trinity. Such beliefs are blasphemous according to Islam for, as can be seen above, salvation is through belief and submission to the One who is transcendent beyond divisibility and fraction. The ascription of a partner to God is believed to be the mightiest of sins, and the only one that God will not forgive. He, Most High, says in the Qur'an:

> Verily, God does not forgive the ascribing of divinity to any beside Him, although He forgives any lesser sin unto whomever He wills: for he who ascribes divinity to any beside God has indeed contrived an awesome sin. (Qur'an 4:48)

God sent prophets to call humankind to worship the One True God, and to call them to perform good works in preparation for the reckoning in the hereafter—where whosoever's scales are tipped in favor of the good will enter into the eternal bliss of paradise, and whosoever's scales are tipped otherwise will suffer, for at least a time if they are believers, in the mighty fire of hell.

> Say (O Muhammad): "I am but a man like all of you. It has been revealed to me that your God is the One and Only God. Hence, whoever looks forward [with hope and awe] to meeting his Sustainer [on Judgment Day], let him do righteous deeds, and let him not ascribe unto anyone or anything a share in the worship due to his Sustainer!" (Qur'an 18:110)

This fraternity of prophets began with the father of all humankind, Adam, and ended with the seal of all prophets, Muhammad (God bless them and give them peace). Muslims acknowledge the prophethood of Adam, Noah, Abraham, Isaac, Ishmael, Jacob, Joseph, Moses, Jesus, John the Baptist, and other figures found in the books of the Abrahamic traditions. Muslims believe that all these men of God were called to the sincere worship of the same one God and the performing of good words, encouraging the good and forbidding the evil. Islam is certainly not something new, for Muslims believe that all prophets and all divinely revealed scripture in their unadulterated form (such as the original Torah, Psalms, and Gospels, which Muslims also believe to be the Word of God) were part of a continuous reminder to humankind to unite in the worship of God.

The divine book of Islam is the Qur'an, which was revealed to Muhammad, an unlettered orphan in the middle of the deserts of Arabia, over a period of twenty-three years. It is the speech of God, as was the gospel in its unaltered form, to remain with humankind until the end of time, forever calling them to the worship of the One.

Muslims believe that Jesus was one of the mightiest of the messengers of God, and he did many miracles as are narrated in the Qur'an and the prophetic traditions (*hadith*). However, Muslims do not ascribe divinity to Christ, as he was a man (who functioned like all other men) sent by God to the children of Israel to confirm the message of Moses and call people to the worship of God. As mentioned before, the ascription of divinity to other than God is an act of disbelief, which automatically takes one out of the mercy of God into eternal damnation if one does not repent before death. Muslims certainly believe that those who followed Jesus as a prophet of God as his early disciples did were Muslims (meaning submitted to the will of God) and will be in the eternal bliss of paradise. However, those who took Jesus Christ as their Lord instead of the One True God or made Jesus to be the Son of God (and died in this belief) will have no share of that divine mercy and will receive God's wrath on judgment day.

This, however, does not bar us from living in peace as our ancestors did for hundreds of years, with the exception of the Crusades, in which Muslim blood was spilled in the streets of Jerusalem. Islam and Christianity lived in peace in the early days. When the second caliph, Umar bin al-Khattab, conquered Jerusalem, he allowed the Christians to have churches, perform their sacred rituals, and travel freely through the land. Likewise, when Salahuddin reconquered Jerusalem after defeating the Crusaders, he granted them access to all their religious sites, and their soldiers safe entry into Jerusalem. History shows that blood was not spilled under Muslim rule, but rather it was Christian rule that brought bloodshed between the two faiths.

Muslims and Christians together make up well over half of the world's population. The basis for peace and understanding between our two faiths already exists, as it is the foundational principle of both faiths: love of the One God, and love of the neighbor. These principles are emphasized over and over in the sacred texts of Islam and Christianity. The Unity of God, the necessity of love for him, and necessity of love for others is the common ground between the faiths. The principle of unity is universal throughout the Qur'an and is shown most strongly in God Most High's distinct words in the Holy Qur'an where he says:

> Say: He is God, the One!
> God, the Self-Sufficient Besought of All!
> He begets not, nor is he begotten!
> And there is nothing comparable to Him!
> Qur'an 112:1–4

The principle of love is shown by God's words, "So remember the name of thy Lord and devote thyself with a complete devotion" (Qur'an 73:8), and "The believing are overflowing in their love for God" (Qur'an 2:165).

God Most High tells Muslims to issue the following call to the Christians and Jews, the "People of the Scripture":

> Say: O People of the Scripture! Come to a common word between us and you: that we shall worship none but God, and that we shall ascribe no partner unto Him, and that none of us shall take others for lords beside God. And if they turn away, then say: Bear witness that we are they who have surrendered (unto Him). (Qur'an 3:64)

Clearly, the words "we shall ascribe no partner unto him" relate to the divine unity of God. These words also clearly relate to being totally devoted to God, and hence to the first and greatest commandment. According to one of the greatest commentators on the Qur'an, Abu Ja'far Muhammad bin Jarir al-Tabari, the words "that none of us shall take others for lords beside God" means that none of us should be in disobedience to what God has commanded, nor glorify the other false deities by prostrating to them in the same way as we prostrate to God. In other words, Muslims, Christians, and Jews should be free to each follow what God has commanded them, for God says elsewhere in the Holy Qur'an:

> Let there be no compulsion in religion. (Al-Baqarah 2:256)

The verse clearly shows that no person can be forced into the acceptance or belief of faith, and this is manifest in the rich history of Islam: where a few Muslim merchants went into new lands, and within a few decades, the entire country would have entered the folds of Islam. God says:

> Call unto the way of thy Lord with wisdom and beautiful preaching, and reason with them in the better way. For your Lord knows best of him who strays from His way, and who is rightly guided. (Al-Nahl 16:125)

God commanded the call to faith by wisdom and beautiful speech as opposed to the present-day misconception of the calling by the sword.

Let this common ground be the basis of all future dialogue between faiths, for common ground is that on which hangs "all the Law and the Prophets" (Matt. 22:40). God Most High says in the Qur'an,

> Say (O Muslims): We believe in God and that which is revealed to us and that which was revealed unto Abraham, and Ishmael, and Isaac, and Jacob, and the Tribes, and that which Moses and Jesus received, and that which the Prophet received from their Lord. We make no distinction between any of them, and unto Him we have surrendered. And if they believe in the like of that which you believe, then they are rightly guided. But if they turn away, then they are in schism, and God will suffice against them. He is the Hearer, the Knower. (Al-Baqarah 2:136–37)

We invite you to the worship of the One God and encourage the windows of dialogue to open between us. One's perception and understanding of Islam can easily be misconstrued with the media blitz against the faith in recent times, but we encourage you to come and experience and ask about Islam firsthand from the people who practice this way of life day in and day out. Let our differences not cause hatred and strife between us. Let us vie with each other only in righteousness and good works. Let us respect each other; be fair, just, and kind to one another; and live in sincere peace, harmony, and mutual goodwill. God says in the Holy Qur'an:

> And unto thee have We revealed the Scripture with the truth, confirming whatever Scripture was before it, and a watcher over it. So judge between them by that which God hath revealed, and follow not their desires away from the truth which hath come unto thee. For each We have appointed a law and a way. Had God willed He could have made you one community. But that He may try you by that which He has given you (He hath made you as ye are). So vie one with another in good works. Unto God ye will all return, and He will then inform you of that wherein you differ. (Qur'an 5:48)

Part 3

Indigenous Religions

26

Indigenous Religions Introduction

TERRY C. MUCK

Indigenous religions are religions that are the province of a single tribe or ethnic or cultural group. In structure they tend to be undifferentiated; that is, economics, politics, and culture, including religion, tend to be part of a single, seamless whole. Because they are restricted to a single cultural group, indigenous religions tend to be small, or at least smaller than world religions.

By definition, indigenous religions are not cross-cultural. In general they have no interest in making their religious story the story of other people groups. They believe their story is true. They hope their story is the most powerful one. They have a place in their story for other people groups, but only as supporting actors. They are exclusivistic without being universalistic.

The term "indigenous" has a history. Other terms such as "primitive" and "archaic" have been used to describe them. But "primitive" and "archaic" have a judgmental feel to them. Scholars who study these religions in depth often make the point that one discovers in indigenous (or "tribal" or "folk," other acceptable terms) religions a sophistication of thought and belief that escapes a less discerning eye.

One might say that the defining characteristic of indigenous religions is their world-affirming nature. Members in an indigenous religious group live in the present, the here and now, and celebrate the remarkable similarities between the worlds of the gods or spirits and the world of their tribe. The more they can do to reinforce the identification between the two the better. They name valleys and hills and rivers after the valleys and hills and rivers in "heaven," where the gods roam. They imitate the acts of the gods. They embrace the values their gods represent.

> **Study Aid #51**
>
> Characteristics of Indigenous Religion
>
> 1. Not cross-cultural: Indigenous religions tend to remain restricted to their culture of origin.
> 2. Smaller rather than larger: Because of this lack of "missionary" urge, they tend to be smaller.
> 3. World-affirming: Indigenists see the world as an imitation of the gods' world, therefore good and to be affirmed, imitated, and lived with in harmony.
> 4. Undifferentiated: Religion among indigenous peoples tends not to be separated or compartmentalized from political, economic, and cultural functions.
> 5. Exclusive, but not universal: Truth for indigenists is represented by their people and their story, but they have little desire for other groups to either accept or adopt that truth.

Of course, world affirming does not mean an unreflective endorsement of all things. People of indigenous traditions live in real fear of evil spirits and demons, sometimes even of the gods and spirits they otherwise endorse, but who can be capricious in their dealings with human beings. Evil spirits especially can bring illnesses, ruin crops, and cause death.

In most indigenous religious groups, harmony between gods and themselves is enhanced by acts of worship, especially sacrifice and magic. Successful worship and sacrifice are measured by the degree of harmony in the tribe that they display toward the realm of the gods. Disharmony and conflict are signs that something or someone has intruded on this peaceful identification through thoughts, words, or deeds, which are at variance with the thoughts, words, and deeds represented by the myth.

Since so little distinction is made between the political, economic, social, cultural, and religious spheres, human responsibilities to gods and other humans are uniform across all of these spheres. Put another way, there is very little tension between religious duty and social conformity.

The reader will note that this section of the handbook is divided not by named religious traditions (as in the previous world religion section) but by geographical area. Since indigenous religions are not interested in geographical spread nor even self-identifying as a distinct religious group, they are best identified by tribal and cultural groups clustered in distinct geographical areas.

In some cases such a division is relatively easy to make. In others it is more difficult. Dividing Asia, for example, into North Asia and South Asia misses some important boundaries and distinctions, and creates others where they may not exist. Nevertheless, we have divided the world into ten areas: North America, Meso- and South America, Europe, Middle East, Africa, North Asia, South Asia, China, India, and Oceania. But other divisions are possible. Several factors complicate attempts to dissolve the world into indigenous religious regions.

One is the influence of the so-called world religions on indigenous religions. Although there was once a time in human history when indigenous religions were all there was, such is no longer the case. With the spread of Hinduism, Buddhism, Christianity, and Islam, there are few places in the world where an indigenous religious group does not exist alongside of or in partnership with one or more world religions.

This coexistence takes many forms. One form might be called "side by side." Both the world religion(s) and the indigenous religious practices continue to exist in recognizable form. Another form might be called "major-minor," with either the world religion or the indigenous religion dominating the other, but both still existing in recognizable forms. A third pattern might be called the "extinction pattern," where the world religion has become so ubiquitous that indigenous religious practices seem to have disappeared.

A caution is needed regarding the extinction patterns. Even in situations where a world religion has come to dominate the indigenous religious traditions to the point of extinction, one can safely assume that indigenous practices still influence the culture. Once a value with religious warrant becomes part of a culture, it rarely, if ever, disappears completely. Sometimes it goes underground; sometimes it becomes part of the major religious tradition itself.

A second factor that complicates attempts to divide the world into indigenous religious regions is the modern-traditional-postmodern split in most of today's world cultures. Modernity complicates religious identification enormously. Urbanization, migration, and industrialization—the engines of modernity—favor a seeming loss of traditional religions, a process sometimes called secularization. More often it leads to the formation of what we will be calling in the next section "new religious movements."

The changes wrought by modernization across the world are unevenly spread and do not correspond to continental, regional, and/or local boundaries. They do not correspond to our ten-sector, geographical division of the world. One cannot say, for example, that North America is modern and Africa is traditional.

A third factor that complicates the identification of indigenous religious groups with geographical areas still further is migration. Peoples from Africa and Asia

---

Study Aid #52

Ten Geographical Areas

North America	North Asia
Meso- and South America	South Asia
	China
Europe	India
Middle East	Oceania
Africa	

are migrating to Europe and North America, bringing their indigenous religions with them in what is commonly called religious diasporas. This complicates the geographical identification, although diaspora groups typically maintain contact with their countries of origin in many ways.

Still, the principle that there are groupings of indigenous religious groups in the areas we have identified is a sound one for heuristic and analytical purposes. Yet it also expresses why we have in the "world religions" sections a set of essays on Hinduism and in the "indigenous religions" section a set of essays on the religions of India. As you will see, the essays on Hinduism acknowledge the importance of an underlying indigenous Indian worldview on Hinduism itself; and the essays on religions of India acknowledge that emergence of a world religion called Hinduism in modernity has influenced and to an important extent modified the same indigenous worldview now.

In each geographical region of this section, the reader will find four essays:

1. A "History, Beliefs, and Practices" essay that summarizes the religious worldview common to that area
2. A "Christian Contact" essay that outlines the coming of Christianity to that part of the world
3. A "Theological Exchange" essay that lists the principal theological issues that have characterized Christian indigenous contacts in that part of the world
4. A "Current Issues" essay that identifies issues Christians have today in that part of the world, especially with the religious elements of those cultures

27

India: History, Beliefs, Practices

ELOISE HIEBERT MENESES

History

India has been the birthplace of two world religions—Hinduism and Buddhism—and has received significant influence from a third—Islam. It is also the primary locale of a number of midsized religions, including Sikhism, Jainism, and Parsiism (Zoroastrianism), as well as of a multitude of smaller tribal religions. Throughout its history, the current of what has come to be called "Hinduism" today has held the center, requiring all other world or indigenous religions to interact with its beliefs and practices. (See chaps. 6–10 in this volume.) But new ideas that were spawned at the margins, along with invasions from outside the subcontinent, have required Hinduism to continually adjust or lose ground to competitors.

Hinduism is one of the oldest religions in the world. Archaeological remains from the Indus Valley Civilization show evidence of gods, priests, and purification rituals as early as 3000–2500 BCE. With the arrival of the Aryans from central Asia in 1500 BCE and their establishment over local populations (collectively termed "Dravidians"), an early pantheon of gods and goddesses was constructed, and the first outlines of a caste structure were put into place. This history has become legitimizing mythology to contemporary conservative Hindus in the defense of the superiority of high castes over low (Aryan over Dravidian), and Hinduism over other religions.

Early Hinduism was dominated by the Brahmin (priestly) caste. Brahmins had a cosmology that included an impersonal supernatural force, *Brahman*, that could be manipulated through the magical use of sound. Chanting verses of poetry and sacrificing animals to the gods were the means of influencing life's circumstances.

Study Aid #53
Map of Indian Subcontinent

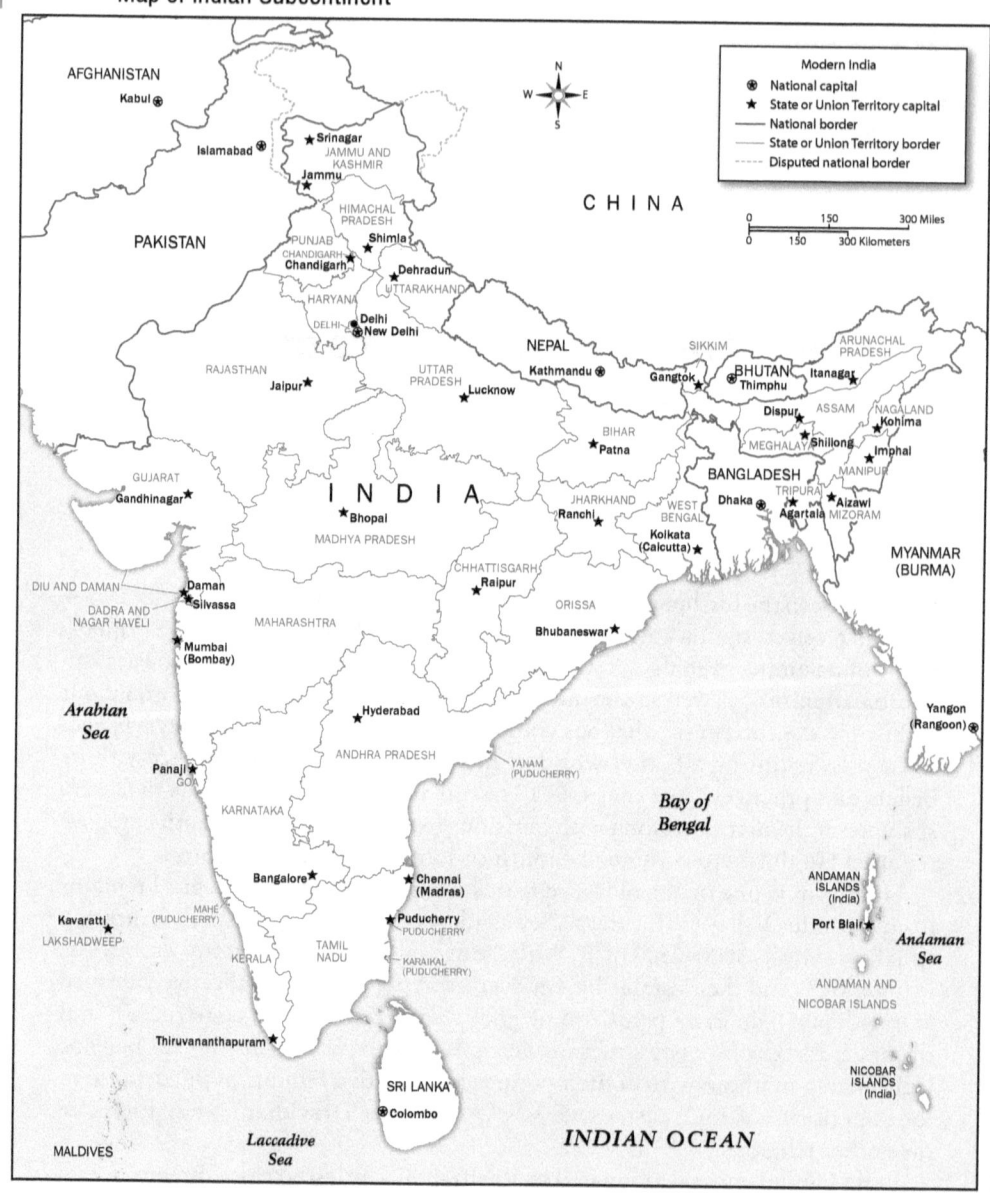

These verses were eventually codified in the Vedas (twelfth–eighth centuries BCE). Later, in a period of disillusionment with magic, the Upanishads were written (seventh–fifth centuries BCE), providing the philosophical foundation for much of contemporary Hindu belief and practice. The Upanishads declared attachment to earthly life to be the cause of suffering, equated the soul with God, and commended various forms of asceticism to release the soul from this life.

In the sixth century BCE, Buddhism was founded in North India by Siddhartha Gautama, in part as a reaction against excessive asceticism. Buddhism thrived in India for over seventeen centuries. But following a period of decline, it was largely driven out by the Muslim invasions of the twelfth century CE. It remains the dominant religion of Sri Lanka. Also in the sixth century BCE, Jainism was founded by Mahavira, in a strong affirmation of asceticism. Jains are found throughout India living side by side with Hindus now. Later, in the tenth century CE, India received the followers of Zoroastrianism when they were driven out of their homeland by the Muslim invasions of Persia. Known as "Parsis," they are now a highly respected and indigenized community in the western part of the country.

Following a few peripheral trading contacts by sea, Islam entered India in the tenth–eleventh centuries CE with the invading armies of the Turko-Afghans (including Mahmud of Ghazni). Over the next five centuries, successive waves of Muslims from central Asia raided, established kingdoms, overthrew one another, and ruled the Hindu populace of North India. The greatest of these kingdoms was the Mughal Empire, one of the largest and wealthiest empires in the world at the time. Muslim overlords were variously ruthless or relaxed in their treatment of their non-Muslim subjects. But resentment was strong in the Hindu population and continues to this day.

Caught between the influences of Hinduism and Islam, Guru Nanak (1469–1539) founded Sikhism in the fifteenth century CE. The Sikhs were initially peaceful but gradually developed a militant stance after centuries of persecution that included the torture deaths of two of their leaders at the hands of the Mughals. Currently, they are a politically organized and wealthy community concentrated in the northern state of the Punjab.

Throughout this history, there have been tribal peoples living in the mountainous areas of the country who have retained their traditional religions. They are known by Hindus on the plains as *adivāsis*. Some have been progressively absorbed into Hinduism as Dalits, or "untouchables" (*āvarnas*), at the bottom of the caste structure (see Bailey 1960). But significant pockets remain, especially in the far northeast of the country (Nagas, Assamese, Tripuris, Mizos) in the central Vindhya Mountains (Santals, Khonds, Bhils), and in the Andaman and Nicobar Islands. Virtually every part of India still has *adivāsis* practicing traditional religions, sometimes in syncretism with popular Hinduism.

The following sections will segment religious belief and practice by categories: (1) popular Hinduism, (2) Jainism, (3) Parsi, (4) Sikhism, and (5) tribal religions. But it is important to note that there is tremendous diversity within each category,

> **Study Aid #54**
>
> **Nations of Indian Subcontinent**
>
> India: 80 percent Hindu
> Pakistan: 96 percent Muslim
> Bangladesh: 88 percent Muslim
> Sri Lanka: 70 percent Buddhist
> Nepal: largely Hindu
> Bhutan: Buddhism state religion
> Maldives: Islam state religion

and a great deal of syncretism at the local level, even between Hinduism and Islam (see Beals 1980).

Beliefs

Popular Hindu beliefs are focused on village life. Local cosmology is replete with a wide variety of spirits, ghosts, demons, and *devas* (gods). Propitiation of low-level goddesses is particularly important because they are believed to cause disease. Over time, local gods and goddesses become incorporated into the larger Hindu pantheon. For example, Murugan, a regional warrior god of the south, has come to be identified as the "first" son of Shiva and Parvati, despite the prior claim of the elephant god, Ganesh, for that role in mythology. Such contradictions do not disturb ordinary people, but over time some consistency is achieved by the simple device of identifying the same god as having different forms. The result is that nearly every village and town claims the epic events of the Hindu gods to have happened in their own place, and local beliefs and practices have become increasingly "Sanskritized"—that is, dominated by the ubiquitous language of the epics, Sanskrit, which in some ways is the "ecclesiastical" language of India.

Jain cosmology shares much with Hinduism, including modified beliefs in *dharma*, *karma*, and reincarnation. Mahavira (599–526 BCE) taught that the world consists of a multiplicity of souls (*jīvas*) at various levels (gods, humans, animals, plants, even microbes), weighed down by *karma*, but moving upward toward release into *moksha*, or blissful omniscience. Three "jewels" are needed to get there: right knowledge, right faith, and right conduct. Time is eternal and cyclical. Those souls who have purified themselves through severe asceticism are known as *tīrthaṅkaras* and can become *gurus* or teachers before they die and are released. Jains value education and have a well-defined philosophy of multiple perspectives on the truth.

Zoroaster, the founder of the Parsi religion, lived in Iran at about the time of Abraham, 1400–1200 BCE (Boyce 1988, 18). The religious environment shared features with early Brahminism such as polytheism, fire sacrifice, and religious intoxication. But Zoroaster preached monotheism and a radical distinction between good (order, truth) and evil (chaos, falsehood). He declared one of the gods, Ahura Mazda, to have been the Creator and predicted his triumph over evil at the end of time, along with a new creation. In the meanwhile, humans are caught up in a cosmic battle and have a responsibility to actively promote the created good over the uncreated evil and decay.

Guru Nanak (1469–1539 CE), founder of Sikhism, rejected the polytheism, idolatry, and caste hierarchy of the Hinduism into which he was born. He taught that God is one and should be worshiped by that name, *Ek* ("One"). Rejecting excessive asceticism and ritual, and possibly influenced by Hindu *bhakti* (see below) and Muslim Sufism, Nanak stressed devotionalism and purity of heart toward God. By such worship, the soul might be released from its attachment to worldly desires, and attain *mukti*, or release from reincarnation and union with God.

Tribal peoples (*adivāsis*) have a wide variety of indigenous religions, but there are some commonalities that are the result of tribal social organization and relationship to the environment. Unlike the ranked Hindu castes, tribes are egalitarian. And unlike the highly specialized agricultural villages and urban areas of the plains, tribal communities involve all members equally in productive work. Religious beliefs tend to be animistic and closely linked to the forest environment. In addition to spirits in nature, there may be ancestor spirits, gods and goddesses, and a remote supreme God. Mythology centers on the origins of the group, legendary figures, and animal stories. Tribals typically do not believe in reincarnation unless they have been in contact with Hindu beliefs. Their lives are circumscribed by the day-to-day practical needs and events of their foraging, horticultural, or pastoral economies.

Practices

Popular Hindu religious practice is centered on a magical notion of worship. That is, gods are propitiated in order to bring good luck and avoid bad luck. *Puja* (worship) is conducted at home by offerings of food, incense, vermillion, lamplight, and prayers to *murtis* (idols) in household shrines or to iconic posters on the walls. By visiting temples, near and far, pilgrims can contribute to the *puja* being offered by priests. Both the offerings (often money) and the *darshan* (seeing the god) return blessings to the devotee. Propitiation at small local shrines, and to ant- and snake-hills, is also done. Astrologers are consulted for every major occasion and many minor ones. Rites of passage are numerous and are celebrated with prescribed rituals conducted by priests. And *bhakti*, or devotionalism, includes singing, poetry, and impassioned prayer to personally chosen gods.

A Jain's life is circumscribed by the purity rules that will ultimately release his or her soul from karmic bondage. Five vows must be taken: nonpossession (of

> **Study Aid #55**
> Religions of India
> Hinduism: 2500 BCE?
> Tribal religions: 2500 BCE?
> Buddhism: 6th century BCE
> Jainism: 6th century BCE
> Christianity: 1st or 2nd century CE
> Parsiism: 10th century CE
> Islam: 11th century CE
> Sikhism: 15th century CE

material goods), truthfulness, nonstealing, celibacy, and nonviolence. Because of the stringency of the vows, the community is divided into monastics and laity, with the latter performing the vows only in modified form. The vow of nonviolence requires all Jains to be vegetarians. Monastics (male and female) take more extreme measures, such as wearing masks to avoid breathing in insects. They are strictly celibate and wear only simple white clothing, or none at all, to avoid having possessions (Mahavira wandered naked). Fasting is highly valued, potentially culminating in the supreme ascetic act of *santhara*, or suicide by starvation. Laity give alms to monastics and venerate icons of *tīrthaṅkaras* in order to meditate on their purity and to emulate them in life.

Parsis are a close community, widely respected in India, but segmented off by their endogamous marriages and rejection of conversion. Because human action is needed to defend creation against the forces of decay, asceticism is frowned upon as an irresponsible fleeing from the world. What is needed are good thoughts, words, and deeds. Earth, fire, and water, as parts of creation, are sacred. Fire is particularly important, in homes and in temples, as a center of worship. Regular daily prayers and purification rites allow humans to advance the cause of good in the world. Traditionally, at death, bodies are laid on the top of "Towers of Silence" (round, open-air stone structures) to protect the earth from pollution. The scriptures, the Avesta, consist of a compilation of hymns for liturgical use. Parsi communities in India have relative gender equality and are active in education, industry, and philanthropy.

Unlike Hindus, Sikhs create local congregations through the practice of having communal meals eaten at *gurdwaras* (temples). Sikh communities stress relative caste and gender equality. Worship is centered on reverence for the scriptures, the Guru Granth Sahib ("the last *guru*"), verses of which are sung as hymns and memorized. Guru Nanak was succeeded by nine other gurus. The tenth, Guru Gobind (1666–1708), declared himself the last, left behind the scriptures, and formed a brotherhood of warriors, the Khalsa. Members of the Khalsa must be baptized, take the name "Singh" ("lion"), and wear the "Five K's": *kesh* (uncut hair), *kangha* (wooden comb), *kara* (metal bangle), *kachera* (cotton underclothes), and *kirpan* (dagger). The center of Sikh religion is the Golden Temple in Amritsar.

Tribals hold feasts, sing and dance, and sacrifice to spirits. They celebrate the rites of passage (especially for boys), perform rituals to appease and control nature, and prepare for war with magical means. The cult of manhood can be strong, as in the far northeast where head-hunting was once practiced. Many tribals are now converted to Christianity, and some are in conflict with the government of India over their marginalization by the Hindu majority.

The Indian subcontinent consists of India, Pakistan, Bangladesh, Sri Lanka, Nepal, Bhutan, and the Maldives. India itself is 80.5 percent Hindu, 13.4 percent Muslim, 2.3 percent Christian, 1.9 percent Sikh, 0.8 percent Buddhist, 0.4 percent Jain, and 0.7 percent other (2001 Census of India). Pakistan, which was formed to be an Islamic state, is largely Muslim now (96 percent). Bangladesh, the former East Pakistan, is also predominantly Muslim (88 percent). Sri Lanka has been tragically divided by a civil war and its aftermath between the Sinhala Buddhists (70 percent) and the Tamil Hindus (15 percent). The smaller countries have state religions: Hinduism in Nepal, Buddhism in Bhutan, and Islam in the Maldives.

Sources

F. G. Bailey. *Tribe, Caste and Nation*. Manchester University Press, 1960.

Alan R. Beals. *Gopalpur: A South Indian Village*. Harcourt Brace, 1980.

Mary Boyce. *Zoroastrians: Their Religious Beliefs and Practices*. Routledge, 1988.

Fred W. Clothey. *Religion in India*. Routledge, 2006.

Paul Dundas. *The Jains*. Routledge, 2002.

Ainslie Embree, ed. *Sources of Indian Tradition*. Vol. 1. Columbia University Press, 1988.

C. J. Fuller. *The Camphor Flame: Popular Hinduism and Society in India*. Princeton University Press, 2004.

Eleanor Nesbitt. *Sikhism: A Very Short Introduction*. Oxford University Press, 2005.

28

India: Christian Contacts

ELOISE HIEBERT MENESES

The first news of Jesus's life, death, and resurrection was brought to India by the apostle Thomas within twenty-five years after Jesus's death. Subsequent messengers of various types—merchants, colonizers, and missionaries—confirmed the story of the man Jesus, who willingly sacrificed his own life for others, and who was declared to be God by the miracle of his resurrection. Reaction to the news in India was mixed, varying from violent hostility and persecution of both messengers and converts, to wholesale acceptance, particularly by those at the bottom of the sacred social hierarchy. The news of Jesus was both challenging and liberating at the same time. This essay will trace the history of the church in India over the nearly two thousand years of its existence.

The Apostle Thomas

According to the descendant churches of the ones that he founded, Saint Thomas arrived on the Kerala (southwestern) coast in the year 52 CE. Accounts vary as to how he got there. Some say he came directly to Kerala as a slave on a merchant ship and was bought by a local king to be the architect for a new palace. When Thomas risked his own life by giving the money for the palace to the poor, the king was converted by the example of his generosity. Others say Thomas traveled part of the way by land, spending time in Bactria (modern-day Afghanistan), where the same story of the king is told. In any case, there is strong evidence for the existence of the church in Kerala from the first century, including second-century stone crosses that can still be found there (Frykenberg 2009, 99). According to local tradition, Thomas planted seven churches in Kerala before traveling to the

Tamil Nadu (southeastern) coast, where he was martyred in 73 CE by a Hindu king after twenty years of missionary work.

The historical record is somewhat sketchy over the next fourteen hundred years. But the Christian community in India retained its identity and developed its own particular forms of expression, including an Aramaic liturgy and families with lineages traced from the very first converts. The Gospel of Matthew arrived within a century or two of Thomas's death (ibid., 103). And enough contact was maintained with the eastern Christians for the "St. Thomas Christians" to receive their patriarchs from Baghdad and to generally consider themselves under the authority of the Syrian church until the arrival of the Catholics in the fifteenth century.

Yet there were long periods of isolation in which the Indian church's ability to adapt to the larger Hindu society was crucial to its very survival. Conversions, always a volatile matter, slowed to a halt as the church refrained from provocative evangelism. And Christian social life came increasingly to mirror the Hindu caste structure. Hindu notions of purity and pollution were adopted, families and congregations segregated themselves by caste, and high-caste Christians became no better than their Hindu counterparts in the mistreatment of the lower castes. "Untouchables" at the time were virtual slaves, required to live apart from villages, and even restricted to nighttime activity so that the sight of them might not pollute higher-caste people. Christians accommodated these practices, even forbidding intermarriage between castes in the church. The observance of Hindu pollution rules brought respite from persecution, but at the price of un-Christlike behavior (as has happened in many other parts of the world under similar circumstances).

In the nineteenth century, due in part to contact with Anglican missionaries, a renewal movement emerged out of the Saint Thomas community that was enthusiastic for both evangelism and social justice. The "Mar Thomas," as they are called, emphasize Bible study, the use of the vernacular language in liturgy (Malayalam), and missions to the lower castes. They send missionaries to other parts of India and have churches around the world.

Portuguese Catholic Missions: Roberto de Nobili

The first European colonial power to reach India was Portugal. Vasco de Gama landed on the Kerala coast in 1498, where he purchased spices from a trading industry partly under the control of wealthy, high-caste Christians. By 1510, Goa was established as a Portuguese colony, opening the sea routes to Catholic missions. Both the Franciscans and the Jesuits sent missionaries, one of whom was Francis Xavier. Initially, relations were fraternal between the Portuguese Catholics and the St. Thomas Christians. But they soured quickly over both doctrinal and ecclesiastical differences. The Keralites were offended by the looseness of Portuguese morality—eating meat, drinking alcohol, and marrying locally; and the Catholics were offended by the St. Thomas Christians' refusal to venerate the saints or acknowledge Mary as the "Mother of God" (Frykenberg 2009, 131). Most seriously, the refusal by the Kerala Christians to acknowledge the Roman pope resulted in forced conversions and a local inquisition.

Yet Catholic missions were far more penetrating in their encounter with India than the St. Thomas Christians had been to date. Their approach combined a willingness to adapt to local custom with an energetic engagement in philosophical discussion. Roberto de Nobili (1577–1656), an Italian Jesuit, moved to the temple city of Madurai in 1605, dressed as a Hindu ascetic, rigorously adopted high-caste dietary restrictions, and became fluent in Tamil, Telugu, and Sanskrit. He engaged scholarly, high-caste Hindus in direct debate over the merits of Christian ideas, winning a significant number of converts from the highly resistant Brahmin community. De Nobili's approach was controversial in the church, but it was affirmed by Pope Gregory XV in his 1659 propaganda to missionaries, which instructed them, "Do not regard it as your task . . . to change their manners, customs, and uses, unless they are evidently contrary to religion and sound morals. . . . Do your utmost to adapt to them."

Yet, once again, accommodation had its price. De Nobili's churches permitted the segregation of congregations by caste, including dividing walls in sanctuaries and a separate Eucharist. The pollution rules that protected high-caste purity inevitably stigmatized low-caste converts at the same time. And eventually, when Brahmin converts realized the necessity of associating with low-caste Christians, many reconverted to Hinduism.

Early Protestant Missions: William Carey

By the middle of the seventeenth century, the English had outcompeted the Portuguese for access to the Indian Ocean and begun the long process of building their enormous empire, with India as "the Jewel in the Crown." The first Protestant missionaries were German Pietists who arrived on the Tamil Nadu coast with the Danish-Halle Mission. They were followed by American Baptists and Anglicans, all working closely together. Protestant missionaries also took a scholarly approach, becoming fluent in south Indian languages and starting schools. But their response to caste was less accommodating. Churches were required to be integrated, the Lord's Supper was taken in common (a practice that is particularly anathema in India, where food is potentially ritually contaminating), and even intermarriage was encouraged. Lower-caste Hindus, *adivāsis* (tribals), and other marginalized groups were quick to notice. Not only were they welcome in churches, but they were also treated with a level of respect and encouragement that they had not previously known. One lower-caste convert remarked, "Christ has given me a turban in the place of dust" (Webster 1992, 53). The result was mass movements of "untouchable" peoples into Christianity in the nineteenth and early twentieth centuries, with thousands being baptized at a time.

> **Study Aid #56**
> **Christianity to India**
> Apostle Thomas: 52 CE
> Roman Catholic missionaries: 15th century
>   Francis Xavier
>   Roberto de Nobili
> Protestant missionaries: 17th century
>   Ziegenbalg
>   William Carey
> Anglican missionaries: 18th century

But baptisms brought controversy. The Hindu community responded violently to the loss of "their" untouchables. And the colonial government clamped down repeatedly in attempts to keep the peace and avoid disruption of the highly lucrative colonial system of trade. William Carey (1761–1834) arrived in Calcutta incognito in 1793 and spent the next few years evading the East Indian Company police due to a ban on missionary activities. It was not until 1833 that the Christian lobby in London was able to persuade parliament to lift the ban. Over the forty years of his missionary service, Carey and his associates translated the Bible into nearly forty languages and founded Serampore University.

Carey is remembered as the "Father of Modern Missions" both for his scholarly work and for his efforts to promote social reform. Carey's first campaign was to eliminate *sati*, the Hindu rite of burning widows on the funeral pyres of their husbands. His horror at the practice led him to research the Hindu scriptures to demonstrate its illegitimacy, and then to petition the government to have it banned. Later, Protestant Christians objected to traditional Indian injustices such as female infanticide, child marriage, and untouchability, and to colonial forms of oppression such as slavery, child labor, and poor working conditions. The addition of a social agenda to the proclamation of the gospel was a natural outflow of concern for the people being reached.

Hindu Social Reform: Ram Mohan Roy

The Christian social critique was primarily of practices that had been legitimized by high-caste Hindus. Low-caste Hindus, *adivāsis*, and women were the primary beneficiaries of the critique. And other religions, such as Buddhism, Jainism, and Sikhism, had already departed from the strong caste- and gender-based hierarchal notions of Brahminism. But the Brahmin community, which on the one hand was enrolling enthusiastically in Western style schools to prepare themselves for jobs in the civil service, on the other hand was maintaining the traditional form of the Hindu community in villages, neighborhoods, and homes.

Some Brahmins resisted the critique entirely. In villages, converts to Christianity were regularly threatened, beaten, and killed by conservative Hindus. "Riots" were organized to protest Dalits wearing respectable clothing, restrictions on women's marriage age (to twelve and older), and other changes in the civic law. The Arya Samaj, or "Noble Society," was founded to defend Hinduism and the Vedas to the public. It established its own schools, responded to Christian critique in pamphlets and books, and tried to disrupt evangelistic meetings (Webster 2007, 141). The status of lower-caste people and women in Hinduism was defended as a benevolent incorporation into a natural and harmonious social whole. Even *sati* was defended.

But other Brahmins, generally the more educated ones, responded to the Christian critique by encouraging social reform within Hinduism. Ram Mohan Roy (1774–1833) was educated in a missionary school. He rejected conversion to Christianity but worked tirelessly alongside his friend William Carey to abolish *sati*, female infanticide, polygamy, child marriage, patrilineal inheritance laws, and other practices related to the ill treatment of women. "What I lament," he wrote, "is that, seeing the women thus dependent and exposed to every misery, you feel for them no compassion that might exempt them from being tied down and burnt to death" (Hay 1988, 29). Roy acknowledged the superiority of Jesus's ethical teachings, but refused the doctrine of the incarnation. Together with other educated Brahmins, he founded the Brahmo Samaj, or "Society of Brahma," dedicated to constructing an enlightened and reformed Hinduism. He is widely remembered now as "the Father of Modern India."

Colonial Indian Christianity: Ramabai, Azariah, and Singh

Protestant missions produced an indigenous church that was known to defend the marginalized. As a result, Dalits compose the bulk of the church now, and the

---
Study Aid #57

Indian Responses to Christianity

Conversion
  Thomas Christians
  Dalits
Reform
  Ram Mohan Roy
  Brahmo Samaj
Reaction
  Dayananda Sarasvati and Arya Samaj
  Hindutva

Christian community has the highest female-to-male ratio in the country. Under British colonialism, however, the church allowed itself to be divided between European and Indian believers, colonizers and colonized. Indian Christians were caught in the unpleasant circumstance of having to acknowledge the abuses of their own traditional past, while at the same time being forced to accept European prejudice and oppression. Too many European Christians failed to make the connection between the evils of caste and the evils of racism. Yet the faith flourished in the transformed hearts of sometimes dramatically converted Indian Christians. Three examples will illustrate the power of Indian Christianity under colonialism.

Pandita Ramabai (1858–1922) was raised by a mendicant Brahmin family, with a priestly father who believed that women should be educated. Having been trained extensively in the Sanskrit scriptures, Ramabai first fell in with members of the Brahmo Samaj, but then became disillusioned with their failure to actually practice a different treatment of women. In 1883, she converted to Christianity because of its enlightened treatment of "fallen" women. She began her social work by opening a religiously neutral school for Hindu widows, who traditionally are not permitted remarriage or any outside employment. When her students began to convert of their own choice, hostilities from the Hindu community forced Ramabai to move the school and to declare it to be openly Christian. She then experienced a second and more powerful conversion herself, as the school was swept up in a charismatic renewal movement. For nearly forty years, she provided a steady prophetic voice for women not only to Indians but to the Western church as well.

Vedanayagam Samuel Azariah (1874–1945) was the first Indian Christian to be ordained a bishop in the Anglican Church. Azariah's life was primarily characterized by compassionate and humble service to the Christian community that he led. But he recognized the detrimental effects of Hindu values on the church, remarking, "How sad to find Christians eaten up with pride of caste and wealth" (Harper 2000, 57). And he gently chided Europeans for their unchristian behavior toward Indian counterparts. In his speech to the 1910 World Missionary Conference in Edinburgh, he reminded his listeners that the abolition of racism was "one of the deepest needs of our time" (ibid., 149).

Finally, Sadhu Sundar Singh (1889–1929) was born into a Sikh family and educated in a missionary school. When his mother died, Singh expressed his grief in an impassioned attack on Christianity as a "foreign" religion. On the morning that he intended to commit suicide, Singh encountered Christ in a lucid waking vision. Jesus asked him, "How long are you going to persecute me? I died for thee. For thee I gave my life" (Singh 1956). Singh became a Christian and immediately had to run for his life when it was threatened by his family. In order to emphasize the indigenousness of his faith, Singh rejected all personal wealth and dressed in the ochre robe of a *sadhu*. He became a missionary to Tibet, where on numerous occasions he escaped miraculously from attempts on his life, causing him to be remembered now as "the apostle Paul of India."

The Postindependence Church

India achieved its independence from Britain in 1947. After nearly three centuries of colonial exploitation, the country not surprisingly closed its borders to outside influence. Visas for foreign missionaries were heavily restricted, with the result that church leadership became fully indigenized. European denominationalism was put aside in the formation of the Church of North India (CNI) and the Church of South India (CSI) out of the former Anglican, Congregational, Methodist, Presbyterian, and Reformed dioceses. New missionary efforts and agencies emerged from local churches, doing development work in villages to alleviate poverty and practicing evangelism in remote tribal regions. Currently, there are "scores if not hundreds" of Indian missionary agencies working within the country (Frykenberg 2009, 468), and an All India Christian Council (AICC) to coordinate church-wide efforts.

In the far northeast, the non-Hindu tribal peoples of the mountainous border with Myanmar have converted to Christianity en masse. Over 90 percent of the powerful Nagas, for instance, are now Christians. Protestant missions to the area began in the early nineteenth century and produced a trickle of converts. These new Christians witnessed to their faith from village to village, producing a flood of further conversions and a truly indigenous church (ibid., 443). The Naga church now sends pastors, professors, and missionaries to the West.

The history of Christianity in India illustrates an essential feature of the gospel of Jesus Christ. Evangelism and social justice must go hand in hand. Ancient Hindu society was built on a conception of the moral order that made hierarchy necessary to stability. Attempts by missionaries, both foreign and indigenous, to promote conversions without disturbing society failed when lower-caste and female converts understood the true nature of their new identity in Christ. And efforts to promote social justice without conversion were far less effective over the long run. So, contrary to Western notions, the gospel does not divide these things: it transforms hearts and reforms societies at the same time.

Sources and Further Reading

> Uma Chakravarti. *Rewriting History: The Life and Times of Pandita Ramabai*. Kali for Women, 2000.
>
> Duncan Forrester. *Caste and Christianity: Attitudes and Policies on Caste of Anglo-Saxon Protestant Missions in India*. Curzon, 1980.
>
> Robert Eric Frykenberg. *Christianity in India: From Beginnings to the Present*. Oxford University Press, 2009.
>
> Robert Hardgrave Jr. *The Nadars of Tamilnadu: The Political Culture of a Community of Change*. Center for South and Southeast Asia Studies, University of California, 1969.
>
> Susan Billington Harper. *In the Shadow of the Mahatma: Bishop V. S. Azariah and the Travails of Christianity in British India*. Eerdmans, 2000.
>
> Stephen Hay, ed. *Sources of Indian Tradition*. Vol. 2. Columbia University Press, 1988.

Sadhu Sundar Singh. *The Cross Is Heaven: The Life and Writings of Sadhu Sundar Singh*. Lutterworth, 1956.

John C. B. Webster. *A History of the Dalit Christians in India*. Mellen Research, 1992.

———. *A Social History of Christianity: North-West India Since 1800*. Oxford University Press, 2007.

Stanley Wolpert. *A New History of India*. Oxford University Press, 2009.

29

India:
Theological Exchanges

ELOISE HIEBERT MENESES

Taken together, the indigenous religions of the Great Traditions of India (Hinduism, Buddhism, Jainism, and Sikhism) have proposed that suffering is the result of attachment to the illusions of this life, and that justice is accomplished through a cycle of rebirths. Salvation consists in escape from rebirth and union with God (or bliss). The religions differ in terms of the moral and spiritual path to salvation, with teachings that vary along a continuum from hedonism (in Tantricism), through the "middle way" (in Buddhism), to the strictest asceticism (in Jainism). But all propose a religious life that denies the value of the phenomenal world in favor of transcendence.

In contrast, the indigenous religions of the Little Traditions (that is, tribal religions) are focused on the practical problems of this life and the value of life over death. They stress the importance of ritual in the relationship to nature, the value of society for protecting people from harm, and the role of the supernatural in the battle against sickness, death, and decay. Morality is deeply rooted in kinship obligations and in conformity to society's norms. And religion serves the purpose of defining ethnic identity and contrasting it with the other groups in the area. There is a perceived war against evil forces in nature, and a parallel real one with neighbors.

Not surprisingly, then, the nature of the encounter between Christianity and the religions of India has depended heavily upon which of these two types of traditions was being engaged. This essay will describe the two types of encounter separately, drawing different conclusions for missionary efforts.

The Great Traditions

The bulk of Christian missionary efforts in India have been directed to Hindus. In general, members of the Great Tradition religions live in the fertile plains and high deserts, while the tribals who adhere to the Little Traditions live in remote, mountainous regions. Thus, relatively few missionaries have gone directly to the *adivāsis* (tribals). Buddhists, who fled the country at the time of the Muslim invasions, have been largely absent from the subcontinent (apart from Sri Lanka) since the fourteenth century. Jains and Sikhs are members of smaller religions that have not always been recognized as distinct from Hinduism. So the primary missionary engagement has been with Hindu religion and culture.

The terms "Hindu" and "Hinduism" are English words, constructed to capture the major themes running through a variety of beliefs and practices found across the country. The themes themselves are real enough, but they are made most evident by way of contrast with the themes in Middle Eastern religions such as Judaism, Christianity, and Islam. Furthermore, most of the analytical literature on Hinduism in modern times has been written by Westerners. Still, Western scholars have had plenty of indigenous philosophical literature to work with. Writings within the Hindu tradition are some of the oldest in the world. And the contrast they provide with the Christian tradition, especially in terms of ontological assumptions, is profound.

Christianity views this life as real; Hinduism describes it as *maya*, an illusion. Christianity believes that time is linear, that there was a beginning, is a progression, and will be an end to time; Hinduism views time as infinite and cyclical. Christianity describes a complex but single and personal God who created the phenomenal world and will ultimately redeem it; Hinduism describes an impersonal force behind reality, *Brahman*, which neither knows nor cares for human joy or suffering. And, as a result of these different depictions of God,

---

Study Aid #58

Theological Exchanges with Great Traditions

Contrasts
    Life: Real vs. illusion
    Time: Linear vs. cyclical
    Divinity: Incarnation vs. *avatar*
    Goal: Forgiveness vs. payment
    Mode: Love vs. purity
    Morality: Change vs. duty
Positive Exchanges
    Social Reform: Caste, *sati*
    Political Reform: Democracy

Christianity offers forgiveness for sin, while Hinduism requires full payment through rebirth.

Differences in ontological assumptions lead to differences in morality and religious practice. Christianity upholds love as the supreme value and commends a life of transformative change, while Hinduism values purity most and commends the acceptance of one's station in life and its associated *dharma* (duties, life paths, moralities). In fact, Hindus view change as threatening to both the social and cosmic orders, and conversion as a kind of treason. Christian morality is relatively flexible, resting more on principles than on specific injunctions, and its ritual practices are translatable into different cultural forms. Hindu morality is highly prescriptive, involving specific duties to family, caste, and community, and its ritual practice is rooted deeply and specifically in Indian history and culture. Thus, Christians may view Hindus as rigid and ritualistic, while Hindus may view Christians as morally loose and disloyal to community and country.

Still, Western Christians have had a kind of fascination with Hinduism and its intricate logic that has facilitated real engagement between the two religions. Their scholarly interest, along with a willingness to learn vernacular languages, has encouraged the contextualization of the gospel, especially through education. Missionaries were the first to start public schools in India, including schools for women and the lower castes. Their painstaking work on vernaculars resulted in the first and best dictionaries and grammars of modern Indian languages and of Sanskrit, and in the first translations of Hindu texts into European languages. The indigenization of the gospel took the form of presenting the story not only as literature but also as drama, a popular Indian art form, and as theological debate, an ancient Indian philosophical practice. So, with missionary intent, Christians have been willing to penetrate deeply into the Hindu worldview, to understand it in its own terms, and then to translate the gospel within it.

Still, the Christian message is fundamentally "other" to any human culture and, not surprisingly, sparks a strong reaction when it is correctly understood (John 15:18–25). Certainly this has been true in India. Perhaps the greatest difficulty for Hindus is in the Christian emphasis on a unique historical event, the incarnation, and the consequent particularity and exclusivity of the truth that that event demands. Hinduism views itself as a highly tolerant religion due to its acceptance of multiple paths to truth. Its gods engage in both good and evil acts and incarnate themselves freely for various purposes. And its members are expected to follow the different *dharmas* of their different stations. Christian insistence on Jesus's uniqueness, then, produces two objections: (1) it denies the validity of other conceptions of God and the truth, and (2) it levels the moral playing field by expecting the same *dharma* of everyone. The message of Jesus is at once overly particular as regards the truth and overly inclusive and egalitarian as regards society.

In an attempt to soften the message, some Christian theologians in India have tried to bridge the gap by linking Western liberal theology to Hindu philosophical thought. This attempt, perhaps stronger in Catholicism than in Protestantism,

> **Study Aid #59**
> Theological Exchanges with Little Traditions
>
> Contrasts
>   Deity: High gods vs. nature spirits
>   Social: Individual vs. communal
>   Cultural value: Legal vs. relational
> Positive Exchanges
>   Ontology: Reality of spiritual power
>   Divinity: Focus on Creator God

has equated the incarnation of Jesus with the Hindu concept of *avatar*, described God in the monistic manner of the Upanishads, and permitted diverse depictions of him by the laity as accommodations to finite human understanding. In the most liberal forms, Christianity is functionally subsumed under a larger Hindu philosophical framework, with prayer to the Christ within you and worship of the Great Soul, *Brahman*, becoming virtually indistinguishable. Evangelicalism, with its emphasis on conversion, is denounced as offensive compared to the purportedly more "tolerant" liberal view of God and salvation.

Yet one thing is clear. For most ordinary Hindus, the commitment to philosophical tolerance is not for the purpose of permitting individuals to choose their own religious communities. It is, in fact, the primary means of reinforcing the societal status quo. Other peoples having other points of view elsewhere may be acceptable to Hindus, but the conversion of their own neighbors and kin to those other points of view is not. Hinduism rests less on dogma than on communal loyalty and ritual practice. So the gospel of Jesus is offensive not because it requires a renunciation of the social order to follow a spiritual teaching (a practice with an ancient history in India) but because it requires the transformation of society into the kingdom of God. It is the social movements spawned by Christians, foreign and indigenous, that have produced the most hostile reactions—reactions violent enough to qualify Indian Christians now as members of the persecuted church.

Hinduism's resistance to the gospel has been successful if measured in terms of numbers of conversions. After two millennia of witness, Christians constitute less than 3 percent of the population of the subcontinent. But the argument could be made that the cultural impact of Christianity on Indian history has been very significant. Despite its ancient cosmology of hierarchy and stasis, India has a political system, a democracy, that is founded on the notion of human equality. And it has codified into law many social reforms that have their roots in the nineteenth-century Christian campaigns for the marginalized. Hindus are feeling a greater threat to their traditional way of life than ever, and not without reason. They are having to engage with Christian thought and values simply to participate in their own country's governance.

Democracy is not necessarily a Christian political system. Christians have been able to live cooperatively under, and to challenge, multiple forms of government. Furthermore, democracy was brought to India by a colonial power that engaged in a kind of apartheid. It took a nationalist campaign, and much suffering under injustice, to achieve true democracy in India. Not surprisingly, the perception that Christianity was the handmaiden of colonialism has been deeply damaging to the Indian church. And even now, Indian Christians are viewed as adherents of a foreign religion, traitorous to their own national identity. Yet the church's support for social reform has demonstrated a compassion for "the least of these" that has shaped the minds and hearts of many Indians who have not become Christians. And the country as a whole has benefited from the church's presence as a beacon of hope for all people.

The Little Traditions

As mentioned above, the tribal peoples of India live in the forested, mountainous regions of the country. They are especially concentrated in the Vindhya Mountains that divide the north from the south, and in the foothills of the Himalaya Mountains of the far northeast. The indigenous populations of these regions are thought to be the oldest in the country, having arrived in India prior to the Aryans (as evidenced by the fact that their languages are Sino-Tibetan and Austro-Asiatic rather than Indo-European). In addition, the populations of the Andaman and Nicobar Islands are entirely tribal.

In general, anthropologists have termed tribal religions "animistic." That is to say, tribal peoples, who are defined by a form of social and political organization that rests on extended kin connections, tend to have religious beliefs in spirits in nature. The link is most clear with ancestor worship. Since membership in lineages is a total identity in life, the worship of ancestral spirits is a natural consequence of death. The reverence for ancestors reinforces the solidarity within the lineage that is necessary to communal life. In some cases, ancestors are welcomed back into society as benevolent protectors, and in others they are feared for the residual resentments they may carry against the living and are ritually driven out. But in either case, they are the focal point of ritual activity designed to confirm the importance of kin relations.

In addition to ancestors, there are nonhuman spirits in nature. These may be variously associated with good and bad luck, agricultural cycles, and the use of supernatural power for one's own purposes. Witchcraft is commonly cited as the reason for disease and death, and it requires the intervention of a shaman (witch doctor) who will do divination to discover and punish the witch. Lower-level ghosts and spirits must be appeased, sometimes with animal sacrifice; and *mana*, an impersonal force, can be used in sorcery to further one's own ends or to thwart the purposes of one's enemies. Over all of this multiplicity of supernatural beings there is not uncommonly a supreme deity who created the earth but no longer interacts with it. The Creator is generally considered too high a power to be personally concerned with human beings and so is rarely petitioned for help.

For Christians, engagement with tribal religions has the advantage of a number of points of agreement on ontology (Ponraj 1996, 80). In contrast to the Great Traditions of the East, Christians and tribals agree (1) that this world is real, not an illusion; (2) that this life is the only one and therefore has intrinsic value; (3) that the world was created by a supreme deity with at least some personal characteristics; and (4) that human beings have angered the Creator (or the gods) and must therefore make blood sacrifices to avoid punishment. In fact, tribal people are more able than many Westerners to comprehend some aspects of the atonement. They understand that God's willingness to sacrifice himself for us, rather than to continue to demand our sacrifices, is revolutionary. And, unlike Western theology's use of legal terms, tribals describe Jesus's sacrifice in relational terms that closely mirror the biblical focus on reconciliation. So, in the broad sweep, theological engagement between Christianity and tribal religions has been mutually beneficial, with Western Christians gaining a more relational understanding of their own theology, and tribals gaining the understanding that the Creator has a real interest in their welfare.

It is in the arena of religious practice that there has been difficulty between Christianity and tribal religions. The immediacy that tribal peoples feel with the supernatural world, and the beliefs they hold in human abilities to manipulate that world through sorcery and witchcraft, cause them to be chronically fearful and deeply entrenched in magic. Christianity forbids both the fear and the magic. The spiritual dangers are real enough. But Christianity requires that they be addressed with a deep dependence on God expressed in simple prayer. Missionaries have sometimes attempted to force a break with shamanistic practices through dramatic means such as "power encounters," with mixed results. Other times they have tried to take the long view, slowly educating people out of animism, with the result that magical practices simply go underground. Animism, with its emphasis on the practical problems of life, and its blend of natural with supernatural means of finding help, is not easily replaced by the kind of trust in God that Christianity demands (Hiebert 2008, 105).

It is worth remembering that quasi-animistic practices occur even now in the West, such as New Age or Wicca. This has happened despite the fact that most

---

Study Aid #60

Basic Indian Religious Outlook

Samsara: Rebirth or reincarnation
Karma: Ethical principle that determines rebirth
Dharma: Duty or teachings that guide actions

Westerners have renounced the supernatural world so thoroughly that even the Christians among them only minimally believe in the Trinity, the angels, Satan, or the demons. So, once again, tribals and Westerners can assist one another to understand the Christian faith. Tribals must be prepared to embrace a Christian theology of evil along with the gospel of sin and salvation. And Westerners must reawaken their sensitivity to the supernatural world and to the cosmic battle in which we are all engaged.

Sources

Judith M. Brown and Robert Eric Frykenberg, eds. *Christians, Cultural Interactions, and India's Religious Traditions*. Eerdmans, 2002.

Robert Eric Frykenberg, ed. *Christians and Missionaries in India*. Eerdmans, 2003.

Paul G. Hiebert. *Transforming Worldviews: An Anthropological Understanding of How People Change*. Baker Academic, 2008.

Samuel Jayakumar. *Dalit Consciousness and Christian Conversion*. Regnum, 1999.

David M. Knipe. *Hinduism: Experiments in the Sacred*. Waveland, 1998.

Ken Christoph Miyamoto. *God's Mission in Asia: A Comparative and Contextual Study of This-Worldly Holiness and the Theology of Missio Dei in M. M. Thomas and C. S. Song*. American Society of Missiology Monograph, 2007.

Pamela Moro and James Myers. *Magic, Witchcraft, and Religion: A Reader in the Anthropology of Religion*. McGraw Hill, 2009.

J. Waskom Pickett. *Christian Mass Movements in India*. Abingdon, 1933.

S. D. Ponraj. *Tribal Challenge and the Church's Response*. Mission Educational Books, 1996.

Richard Fox Young, ed. *India and the Indianness of Christianity*. Eerdmans, 2009.

30

India: Current Issues

ELOISE HIEBERT MENESES

The history of the relationship between Christianity and the Indian subcontinent has been long and varied. Successive waves of missionaries over the centuries have encountered hostility, followed by the persecution of new converts. By accommodating itself to Indian social structure, the church has been able to purchase a more peaceful coexistence with Hindus. But that choice has been at the expense of the biblical mandate to defend the marginalized. Of course, on a daily basis, Hindus, Buddhists, Muslims, Jains, Sikhs, Parsis, *adivāsis*, and Christians interact peaceably and cooperate for work and other public purposes. But neighborhoods are largely segregated, and private life is communally organized. And even in the public arena, interreligious riots break out regularly, particularly between Hindus and Muslims, over perceived control of the country. Unlike in the apathetic West, religion is a serious matter in India. And religious identity is a total commitment: social, political, and cultural, as well as spiritual.

Hindu Nationalism (Hindutva)

In India, as elsewhere, globalization has produced a struggle over ethnic identity. This struggle can be traced back to colonialism, which brought peoples from various parts of the world into common empires, and to the subsequent nationalism that broke up the empires by creating a sense of common identity among sometimes previously very disparate peoples. Certainly the identity "Indian" had no meaning before the British consolidated the country and would carry little

> **Study Aid #61**
>
> **Current India-Christian Issues**
>
> Hindu nationalism (Hindutva)
> Minority groups and religion
> Caste in the church
> Globalization
> Mission to tribals
> Indian Diaspora

sense of pride now had not the nationalists formulated it in contradistinction to the Western world.

The major figures in the nationalist movement, such as Jawaharlal Nehru (the first prime minister), were nonviolent and promoted the formation of a secular state. But there were others who more readily associated Indian identity with Hinduism. The most radical of these formed associations that engaged in sometimes violent campaigns. It was a Hindu radical, Nathuram Godse, who assassinated Mahatma Gandhi in 1948 for the latter's perceived sellout to Muslim interests. The Hindu nationalists follow a dogma that was first laid out by V. D. Savarkar in his 1923 book *Hindutva* ("Hindu-ness"). Savarkar fully equated Indian identity with Hinduism, Aryanism, and Sanskritic culture. He named India "Hindustan," the sacred place of the Hindus, and declared Islam and Christianity to be foreign religions with sacred places elsewhere (in Arabia and Palestine).

Savarkar is certainly a controversial figure in India now, with many moderate Hindus eschewing his sectarian, even racist, notions. Yet the Hindutva movement has broad support and makes public claims that Hinduism is an essential element in Indian national identity. In so doing, it has legitimized a rise in violent acts against Christians, such as church desecrations and burnings, threats and harassments, and calculated, clandestine killings. In 1998, a Hindutva-based political party, the Bharatiya Janata Party (BJP), took the central government by popular election and immediately attempted to introduce a constitutional ban on all religious conversion. It failed at this and lost the position in 2004. But the BJP continues to wield significant influence in local and state politics across the country, and to encourage a climate of defensiveness in the Hindu community. The bulk of this hostility is aimed at Muslims. But Christians too are seen as a threat to national identity, and the church continues to pay the price of being viewed as a foreign institution.

The Indian church has responded well to this wave of persecution. It has refrained from violent responses and is working through legal means to defend the Christian community and to insist upon justice. There have been notable examples of publicly proclaimed forgiveness for the crimes committed. Meanwhile, the international church has been less aware than it should be of the suffering being endured bravely by Christian sisters and brothers in India, much less of the constant difficulties they face in trying to be recognized as true Indians. A general principle is that Christians in easy political circumstances should not forget those in difficult ones, and that Christians in difficult political circumstances should follow the example of the Indian church in demonstrating the love of Christ.

Minority Groups and Religions

In his definition of Hinduism, Savarkar included the few remaining Buddhists in India, along with the Jains, Sikhs, and other smaller religions. This was in line with a centuries-long Hindu tradition of incorporating members of other religions into their own cosmology by declaring them to be another caste. Western scholarship, too, has tended to subsume smaller Indian religions under the term "Hinduism" for the convenience of simplifying a very complex situation. Serious adherents of these smaller religions do not appreciate the loss of their own distinct identity. And Christian missionaries to them must be careful not to stereotype all Indians as Hindus.

The religious affiliation of low-caste and tribal peoples has also been contested. Under colonialism, some protection from local forms of oppression was provided for these groups by the creation of a list of "backward castes." When independence came, the backward castes were awarded special status and given entitlements such as free education, job quotas, and reserved seats in government. In a highly publicized debate, Dalits (former "untouchables") were declared to be Hindus, with the result that Christian Dalits could no longer receive benefits. So to this day, conversion to Christianity means a loss of government benefits for those who need them the most.

The general principle is a complex one. Christians throughout history have faced discrimination. Simple justice would demand that the church in India should address this discrimination through legal means and attempt to have it reversed. Many such efforts have been both proper and effective (Meneses 2007). Yet there have been two valuable results of the loss of government benefits: the first is the increased reliance on the church as the primary source of help in times of need, and the second is the clear and unmistakable shift that converts must make out of a previously stigmatized identity. Relying too heavily on the state for justice is always a mistake for Christians. Our justice comes from God through the work of the kingdom—only a part of which may be administered by the government.

Caste in the Church

No problem in Indian culture has been more difficult for Christians to resolve than that of caste. At the village level, caste is both an ingenious and holistic form of organization and an insidious form of oppression. Caste provides for everyone, but allows no one to escape. And it offers highly differential rewards to those at the top versus the bottom of the sacred hierarchy. So it is not surprising that the relatively few Brahmins who have converted to Christianity have tended to keep their new faith a secret, while the relatively large number of lower-caste people who have converted have willingly announced their faith, sometimes in highly political terms.

Caste—that is, *jati*, the corporate group that functions as a trade union, a voting block, and an extended family all rolled into one—has many of the benefits that Western people feel they lack when they express a longing for "community." But *jatis* inspire such strong loyalties that they can interfere with full fellowship within the body of Christ. This dynamic is certainly not unique to India. Race, ethnicity, and nationalism have produced similar trouble in the West. Yet acquiescence to social institutions that divide Christians from one another should never be acceptable. And the Indian church itself recognizes the problem.

Intermarriage is the touchstone of the matter. Not a few Christian parents would prefer to marry their sons and daughters within the *jati*, even if it means marrying outside the church. A lack of eligible matches is sometimes the reason cited, especially in the case of Christians from high-caste backgrounds. Christian young people marrying outside their *jati* may lose their previous standing in society entirely. Yet the preference for intra-*jati* marriage amounts to a subordination of the body of Christ to society. A general principle, applicable to Christians everywhere, is that the price paid for church membership is part of the sacrifice we all must make to follow Jesus. This principle is easy to promote when sacrifices are few. But those in easy circumstances should remember that social situations can change quickly, and that Christians are to be prepared at all times to suffer for their commitment.

Globalization

India is the second-largest emerging economy in the world, after China, and since its liberalization of trade laws, it has been growing at over 7 percent GDP per year. This follows on a half century of stable socialist government and strong protective policies. The opening of India's markets has resulted in an influx of investment and high returns in fields such as steel manufacturing, textiles, and the computer industry. As a result, there is a new middle class that is able to afford apartments, cars, electronics, and other consumer goods beyond their previous dreams. But the loss of economic protection has also resulted in a severe threat to the livelihood of millions of small-scale farmers (60 percent of the country) and to the working poor in cities. In 2003 alone, over seventeen thousand farmers committed suicide because they were bankrupted by high prices (*New York Times*, September 19, 2006). The full result of economic liberalization, then, has been to create deep divergences between a few super-rich industrial titans, an emerging middle class, and the mass of desperately poor people at the bottom.

> **Study Aid #62**
>
> Contrasting Views of Religious Conversion in India
>
> It is no exaggeration to say that when it comes to interreligious interchanges in modern India, the issue of conversion heads the list. A summary of the differing views follows.
>
> 1. The Indian constitutional view: Full freedom both to change religions and to propagate one's religious viewpoints
> 2. The Indian states' view: Growing number of anticonversion laws
> 3. Traditional Hindu view: Reversion not conversion; that is, all people are born "Hindu" and all should ideally revert to that natural state
> 4. Hindutva view: Hindu conversion to another religion is anathema
> 5. Non-Indian religious view (Christianity, Islam, etc.): People should be free to change from Hinduism to another religion

Christians are in a unique circumstance within the economy in India. Most come from backgrounds of rural poverty. Yet their access through the church to education, to economic assistance, and to an improved sense of self-respect has enabled them to take advantage of new opportunities. In the cities, many are members of the emerging middle class. And even in rural areas, Christians' relatively high level of education allows them to take up positions as teachers and local administrators. The simple willingness of the church to take care of its own members has meant that Christians are rarely among the most desperate poor in the country.

Western Christians are inclined to view the spread of global markets as an unmitigated good. Some may even equate globalization with the growth of the kingdom of God. But global markets do not share Christianity's concern for the poor, nor its strong warnings to the rich. So, a general principle to be observed is that Christians must not associate themselves too closely with the ideologies of any political or economic system. The cause of Christ is larger than them all. And the responsibility of Christians is, on the one hand, to work cooperatively where there is true benefit to be had but, on the other hand, to challenge structural evil and to mitigate its worst effects by caring for those being harmed.

Missions to Tribals

For all the failures of Western missionaries of the colonial era, perhaps the most encouraging result of their efforts, and of the Holy Spirit's work, has been an increasingly strong and vibrant indigenous missionary movement. There is ongoing witness to Hindus and to members of the other Great Tradition religions by the Indian church. And there is a strong and vibrant missionary movement to tribal peoples. Indian missionaries experience all the difficulties that Western ones do, but without the financial resources that the latter have. They must learn new languages, live uncomfortably in strange environments, survive endemic diseases, and endure the absence of their children in boarding schools. Their lives are filled with sacrifice. And, like centuries of missionaries before them, they are beginning to engage in good scholarship of the peoples whom they serve (e.g., Ponraj 1996).

The fruit of this labor is evident not only in increasingly large numbers of conversions, but also in improved living conditions from economic development projects, and in greater empowerment from literacy and local advocacy work. Even environmental efforts may benefit from Indian missions to tribals (ibid., 235). The principle at work here constitutes the history of the church: wherever Christianity has been successfully planted, it has moved to reproduce itself by planting further seeds beyond its own soil.

Indians Abroad

Most Indians living abroad are Hindus who maintain strong ties to India. They communicate with and visit India frequently, observe Hindu rites at home, and attempt to marry their Western-born and -educated children to members of their original communities. Expatriate Hindus are politically aware and commonly are strong nationalists. In fact, a significant portion of the funding for the Hindutva movement in India comes from outside of the country.

Second- and third-generation expatriate young people, however, do not have the same level of commitment to the home country that their parents have. In America, for instance, they attend public schools, speak English as their first language, expect to marry by courtship, and generally have American tastes and values. The pain and struggle this causes in the normally very close and mutually supportive Indian family is well depicted in films such as *Mississippi Masala*. The Indian Diaspora is broad, with significant concentrations in Singapore, east and southern Africa, Canada, Latin America, and elsewhere. It is the result of the history of Indian indentured service under colonialism, followed by the expansion of the business community under globalization. And the ability of these various communities to retain their coherence over centuries has been truly remarkable. Yet some assimilation into indigenous cultures is necessary to live in them, and the loss of traditional values is an especially poignant problem for Indian parents and children.

Christian Indian families living abroad have perhaps felt this pain less acutely. In part, this is because expatriate churches provide their members with a linguistic and cultural home away from home, while at the same time maintaining links to other denominational or area churches and bridging to the local culture. Once again, a Christian identity that supersedes ethnic and national affiliations can be the means of cultural reconciliation. The general principle is, to quote Bishop Azariah of Dornakal:

Christianity ... is a scheme of life in a society; it is an organism, a family; a fellowship, a brotherhood—whose center, radius and circumference is Christ. In fellowship with all others who are attached to the Lord, bound together by outward rules and rites and throbbing with one inward pulse and purpose, men and women of all ages, races, tongues, colours and nationalities have accepted this scheme of life, and separated from all others are more and more experiencing in this fellowship the impetus and power issuing from the Spirit who is its indweller and life-giver. (Harper 2000, 248)

To the followers of Jesus, the church is their home, and the whole world is a mission field.

Sources

Michael Burgunder. *The South Indian Pentecostal Movement in the Twentieth Century.* Studies in the History of Christian Missions. Eerdmans, 2008.

Susan Billington Harper. *In the Shadow of the Mahatma: Bishop V. S. Azariah and the Travails of Christianity in British India.* Eerdmans, 2000.

Christophe Jaffrelot. *The Hindu Nationalist Movement in India.* Columbia University Press, 1996.

Eloise Hiebert Meneses. *Love and Revolutions: Market Women and Social Change in India.* University Press of America, 2007.

V. S. Naipaul. *India: A Wounded Civilization.* Vintage, 2003.

S. D. Ponraj. *Tribal Challenge and the Church's Response.* Mission Educational Books, 1996.

V. D. Savarkar. *Hindutva: Who Is a Hindu?* Hindi Sahitya Sadhan, 2003.

31

China: History, Beliefs, Practices

Jonathan Seitz

"Chinese" may describe a nation, civilization, ethnic group, or one of many linguistic groups; and Chinese religions include most of the major world religions, as well as a variety of local, popular, or folk religions. In popular culture and some scholarship, it is common to speak of the "three religions" or "three teachings" (*sanjiao*): Confucianism (or Ruism), Daoism, and Buddhism (*rujiao, daojiao, fojiao*). These traditions find parallels in Korea and Japan, where Daoism as the indigenous religion is replaced by the system of mediums or Shinto. Chinese themselves often describe the three teachings as complementary, using expressions such as *sanjiao guiyi* ("the three teachings derive from the same source"). Chinese religion more broadly is shaped by shared life rituals, a coherent Chinese cosmology, and family and government traditions that have shaped contemporary Chinese religion.

History and Beliefs

One of the earliest records of Chinese religious practice was oracle bones, which dated to the Shang dynasty and were used for divination. The bones provide much of the earliest information on Chinese writing. During the following centuries a rich religious culture grew and developed. Chinese religion is sometimes seen as being based on *qi* (breath, air, or energy), complementary duality (*yin* and *yang*), and the five elements that were seen as constituting life. Early writings, including the Yijing or Book of Changes, were eventually incorporated into a Ruist/Confucian

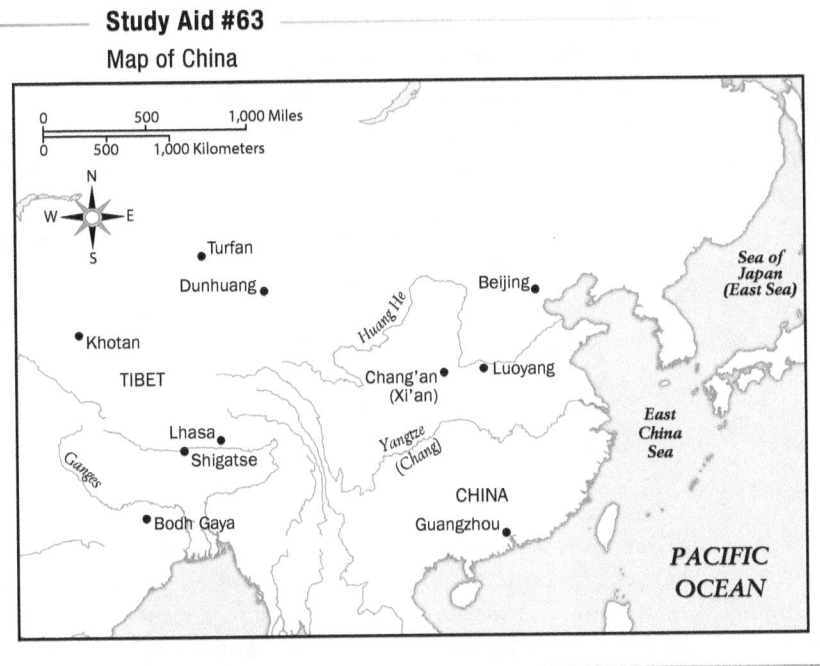

Study Aid #63
Map of China

canon. Other practices, including purification rituals, healing rites, and regional festivals, were aggregated into Daoist and popular religious schools or sects.

Confucianism is the Jesuit Latinized rendering of the name of Confucius (Kongzi), which may give the mistaken impression that Confucianism is the distillation of a single person's teachings. Scholars now often prefer Ruism ("the learned or scholarly teaching"), which better respects the diversity of Confucian belief and practice. Kongzi (Confucius: 551–479 BCE) helped systematize the Chinese classics and according to tradition assembled the five classics (wujing), composed of the Book of Changes, the Book of Poetry, the Book of Rituals, the Book of History, and the Spring and Autumn Annals. His own writings, collected in the *Analects* (Lunyu), provided greater coherence to the project. Kongzi developed a number of earlier concepts, most notably humanity (*ren*), righteousness (*yi*), loyalty (*zhong*), reciprocity (*shu*), and propriety (*li*).

Near contemporaries Mengzi (Mencius: 372–289 BCE) and Xunzi (312–230 BCE) became associated with Confucius as part of a shared school or approach. By the Han dynasty (206 BCE–220 CE), Confucianism garnered political support and became associated with the state ideology of the dynastic system. Later movements are sometimes dubbed neo-Confucianism, and Confucianism is understood to include practically any system related to the state or Chinese culture. While it has often been associated with a single ethnicity, Confucianism also profited from the innovation of foreign-led dynasties, such as the Yuan, which created the

> **Study Aid #64**
>
> Provinces of the People's Republic of China (PRC)
>
> China has thirty-three official political units, classified as twenty-two provinces, four municipalities (Beijing, Tianjin, Shanghai, Chonqing), five autonomous regions (Inner Mongolia, Guanxi Zhuang, Tibet, Xinjiang Uyghur, Ningxia Hui), and two special administrative regions (Hong Kong, Machau). The People's Republic of China considers Taiwan to be the twenty-third province, while the Republic of China (Taiwan) considers it to be under their administration. The twenty-two provinces are
>
> | | | | |
> |---|---|---|---|
> | Anhui | Hebei | Jiangxi | Shanxi |
> | Fujian | Heilongjiang | Jilin | Sichuan |
> | Gansu | Henan | Liaoning | Yunnan |
> | Guangdong | Hubei | Qinghai | Zhejiang |
> | Guizhou | Hunan | Shaanxi | |
> | Hainan | Jiangsu | Shandong | |

national examination system, China's version of civil service exams. Confucianism is closely aligned with state ideology, but in the modern period, advocates have employed it in seeking an ethnic identity that is not dependent on communist ideology or in expressing an authentic identity apart from a single government. The Confucian program took on renewed vigor with the neo-Confucianism of Zhuxi, Wang Yangming, and the Cheng brothers. Under Zhuxi (1130–1200), the four books were codified alongside the five classics. The four books are *The Great Learning*, *The Doctrine of the Mean*, *The Analects* (of Confucius), and the *Mencius*.

Daoism ("the teaching of the way") drew on earlier Chinese cosmology, including the ideas of yin-yang complementary duality and a physical world composed of five elements. The two principal works of the formative period were Laozi's *Daodejing* (*Classic of the Way and Righteousness*) and the *Zhuangzi* (named after its author). Both books include Confucius as a minor character, and Daoism is often seen, in contrast to Confucianism, as a return to the pristine natural order that exists apart from civilization. Daoism is sometimes separated into philosophical and religious Daoism (*Daojia* and *Daojiao*), although such a distinction should not be overdrawn. Significantly, religious Daoism grew out of a set of early cosmology, rituals, and practices, often seeking to deal with the daily concerns of life, life transitions, or the ideal of a long life. In time, Daoism was organized into schools. The Daoist canon, once passed down exclusively through ritual communication and ordination, is now available in libraries, although it includes nearly five thousand texts.

Buddhism ("teaching of the Buddha") has existed in China for almost two millennia; it was carried along the Silk Road during the Eastern Han dynasty (25–220 CE). Buddhism is unique among the three teachings in its foreign origins, a fact that made it an occasional object of censorship or persecution (early notable persecutions occurred 452–66 and 547–78). The name of the Buddha is the transliteration of a non-Chinese word. Buddhism arrived in China in several successive waves, bringing missionaries from south and central Asia who gradually translated the scriptures. Chinese Buddhism, even from the early years, was largely Mahayana. Monastic structures and the written canon helped institutionalize Buddhism in China, but ideals of celibacy and poverty (including relying on others for alms) added to the foreign association. Nonetheless, Buddhism found patrons and developed key forms of devotion, including festivals, pilgrimages, the construction of monasteries and stupas, and the printing of tracts and other materials. Translation was a prized activity and accompanied the proliferation of texts, from the smaller Pali and Sanskrit canons to the much larger Chinese and Tibetan canons.

Scholars of Chinese religions have sometimes challenged the three teachings emphasis. The *sanjiao* approach is itself an innovation of an earlier *erjiao* approach that predated Buddhism, and there have been proposals for a *wujiao* understanding of the religions, adding Christianity and Islam to the traditional three religions. There has also been major debate within these traditions. The complexity of Chinese religion may also be reflected in the difference between

---

Study Aid #65

Dynasties of China

Ancient
  Xia: 2100–1600 BCE
  Shang: 1600–1046
  Zhou: 1045–256
Imperial
  Qin: 221–206
  Han: 206 BCE–220 CE
  Three Kingdoms: 220–80
  Jin: 265–420
  Southern/Northern: 420–589
  Sui: 581–618
  Tang: 618–907
  Five Dynasties and Ten Kingdoms: 907–60
  Song: 960–1279
  Yuan: 1279–1368
  Ming: 1368–1644
  Qing: 1644–1911
Modern
  Republic of China: 1912–49
  People's Republic of China: 1949–present

what Robert Redfield called the great and little traditions. An early influential essay by Arthur Wolf spoke of Chinese religion as including "gods, ghosts, and ancestors." Gods were beings who could answer petitions or respond to needs and problems. Ghosts were usually malevolent beings. Ancestors, if well cared for, could protect and preserve the present generation. Each was seen as a distinct category of supernatural activity.

There is considerable debate over the "Protestantization" of Chinese religions, including the tendency of modern interpreters to philosophize and textualize Chinese religions, prioritizing or creating a canon that may not reflect the broad sweep of Chinese religions.

Practices

With massive canons and a high tolerance for heterodoxy, Chinese religion has rarely taken a creedal form. Instead, official schools, local practice, and mystic rites sometimes coalesce. China is often described as having a coherent cosmology. Chinese practices draw heavily on the yin-yang, five-elements cosmology. Consequently, years follow a sixty-year cycle (twelve months or elements repeated five times). Rituals may be based in the family system (veneration of ancestors) as well as the human life cycle (birth, death) or various community rituals (anything related to temple life, especially festivals). There are also important days during the year when the ancestors deserve special attention. The major traditional Chinese holiday is the New Year, which is still based on the lunar calendar.

Chinese gods—Buddhist, Daoist, or other—are organized within pantheons, or collections of gods, which vary according to geography and period. The pantheon system mirrors the broader Chinese bureaucracy, with gods holding distinct rank and positions in the larger pantheon. Appeals may be made to a god to help with specific problems or tasks, to reduce suffering in hell, or to aid the ancestors. Major Buddhist buddhas and bodhisatvas, including Mañjuśrī, Avalokiteśvara, and Maitreya, all became subjects of devotion in China. Historical figures from the religions have developed popular cults also, and there are often temples or statues to figures such as Kongzi, a popular figure for students taking exams; or to Guangong, the Daoist god of war; or Mazu, a popular goddess for sailors and those by the ocean.

Chinese Buddhism is principally Mahayana, with a wide variety of tantric practices included. An important minority movement is tantric Buddhism of Tibet (arrived in the seventh century CE) and Mongolia (where it was adopted by the Mongol rulers of China in the thirteenth century). Beyond the contemporary implications, central Asian Buddhism exerted a strong influence on China proper through empire (Mongol and Manchu), tribute relations (where vassal nations brought tribute to the emperor), and pilgrimage. Tibetan Buddhism includes several distinct practices, including lineages of enlightened beings (the lamas), as well as a Tibetan canon and a variety of monastic and lay traditions.

There are a variety of pantheons (collections of gods) that may be influenced by time, geography, or tradition. Thus Buddhist and Daoist canons have substantial overlap. In one exceptional case, Jesus and Mary were interpolated into an eighteenth-century Daoist book of gods. Daoists also perform a wide range of rituals, including the *jiao*, a community-based purification rite. Priests might also perform rituals for the dead, help with healing and health issues, or assist in divining the best response to a problem.

Because of the size of China (as civilization, empire, or nation), communities from virtually all world religions have been present in China, including the Abrahamic religions as well as transplant communities from central Asian religions. Jews, Christians, and Muslims have all had major communities in China, although usually they have been understood as different ethnically from the Han majority. There are now two major Muslim populations, the Hui, who live throughout China, and the Uyghur, who tend to live in the northwest (Xinjiang). Today the People's Republic of China religion bureau regulates five official religions (Buddhism, Catholicism, Daoism, Islam, and Protestantism).

Sources

Catherine Bell. "Religion and Chinese Culture: Toward an Assessment of 'Popular Religion.'" *History of Religions* 29, no. 1 (August 1989): 35–57.

Kenneth Ch'en. *Buddhism in China: A Historical Survey*. Princeton University Press, 1964.

Donald Lopez, ed. *Religions of China in Practice*. Princeton University Press, 1996.

Daniel Overmyer, with Gary Arbuckle, Dru Gladney, John McRae, Rodney Taylor, Stephen Teiser, and Franciscus Verellen. "Chinese Religions: The State of the Field. Part II, Living Religious Traditions: Taoism, Confucianism, Buddhism, Islam, and Popular Religion." *The Journal of Asian Studies* 54, no. 2 (May 1995): 314–21.

Daniel Overmyer, with David Kneightley, Edward Shaugnessy, Constance Cook, and Donald Harper. "Chinese Religions: The State of the Field. Part I, Early Religious Traditions: The Neolithic Period through the Han Dynasty (ca. 4000 BCE to 220 CE)." *The Journal of Asian Studies* 54, no. 1 (February 1995): 124–60.

N. Standaert, ed. *Handbook of Christianity in China*. Vol. 1. Brill, 2001.

C. K. Yang. *Religion in Chinese Society: A Study of Contemporary Social Functions of Religion and Some of Their Historical Factors*. University of California Press, 1961.

Fenggang Yang. *Religion in China: Survival and Revival under Communist Rule*. Oxford University Press, 2011.

32

China: Christian Contacts

Jonathan Seitz

The history of Christianity in China is sometimes told through the so-called four encounters: the arrival of the Church of the East during the Tang period, the arrival of Catholics during the Yuan, the major Catholic encounter of the Ming-Qing period, and then Protestantism in the Qing, Republican, and communist eras. Each encounter brought its own challenges and struggles. The Church of the East never found a lasting home; Catholicism found a gathering of hundreds of thousands but was then suppressed. The Protestant association with the colonial powers muffled its impact initially. After the relaxation of communist controls from the late 1970s, Christianity appears stronger than at any point in its history. Each encounter was limited to a specific period but has contributed methods of indigenization and allowed for continuing witness and dialogue.

The Church of the East (sometimes known as the Nestorians) sent the first known Christian missionaries to China. According to tradition, the Persian Alopen arrived in the Tang capital of Changan in 635 and received some official sanction. The church experienced a brief period of trial under Empress Wu Zetian and came to an end not long after Emperor Wuzong, attempting to diminish Buddhist influence, prohibited foreign religions including Christianity and Buddhism (845). Nestorianism gradually receded. Less is known about this encounter than any other, and there is considerable debate over the causes of the death of the Church of the East. Christianity in this iteration made few inroads into broader Chinese communities, remaining primarily a religion of traders.

Another episodic encounter occurred during the early years of the medieval orders and the Mongol-led Yuan dynasty in China (1260–1368). The Mongolian conquests of the thirteenth and fourteenth centuries opened up exchange throughout Asia and Europe. Kublai Khan's mother was a Church of the East Christian, and different parts of the Mongol Empire adopted a range of religious traditions. In China, the Mongols adopted the Chinese bureaucracy and imperial ideology, although they retained Buddhism. During this period Nestorians also experienced modest growth in China, and there was the creation of a metropolitan seat in 1275.

In the thirteenth century, the rise of new religious orders encouraged a broader interest in the East. Franciscan John of Plano Carpini visited the Mongol capital in 1245, and fellow Franciscan William of Rubruck went in 1253 and was even part of a dialogue between religions organized by the Mongol court. The Christian presence was buttressed by the sending of a formal missionary, another Franciscan, John of Montecrovino, in 1307. Medieval European-inspired Christianity would grow for the next century, with adherents numbering at least in the tens of thousands. However, along with the Church of the East, it seems to have faded with the end of the Mongol period.

Christianity spread enduring roots with the major Catholic encounter that began in the Ming Dynasty during the sixteenth century and extends into the present. The missionary orders experienced new rigor during the period of Catholic reformation and began to send missionaries in major numbers. Following in the wake of Francis Xavier, Italian Matteo Ricci (1552–1610) arrived in China in 1588 and settled in Beijing in 1600, beginning the Jesuit mission to China. Ricci famously first adopted the garb of Buddhist clergy but then rejected it in favor of the robes of the literati. Ricci sought imperial patronage and toleration, and labored to learn Chinese. He is often credited with beginning a Christian engagement with Confucianism. For Ricci, the elite ideology represented a possible secular complement to Christianity, and so began an emphasis on "accommodation," or the attempt to use Confucian terms and tropes in expressing Christian faith. Ricci's teaching appealed to a number of Chinese scholars, including Xu Guangqi, Li Zhizao, and Yang Tingyun. Ming and Qing courts recognized the value of exchange with foreigners, and Catholic and Protestant missionaries became sources for scientific learning, the arts, and industry. There were several periods of mild persecution: the martyrdom of a Chinese Jesuit in 1606 and forced deportation of some missionaries in 1616 and 1622. In 1631, other orders were granted access to missionaries, notably the Dominicans and Franciscans, who built communities in southern China. Missionary competition reached its height in the rites controversy, where rival orders contended for papal favor and authority before the Chinese court. The issue is a compelling (and enduring) one for Christianity in China. At issue, among other things, was whether Chinese Christians could venerate the ancestors. (In Chinese, the word for venerate can also be understood as "worship" or "respect.") Appeals went back and forth between the orders, the court, and the pope. Eventually, the pope rejected ancestor veneration, and the Chinese emperor Kangxi forbade foreign missionaries in China in 1721. The bitter encounter anticipated a number of future questions: government authority

> **Study Aid #66**
>
> **The Four Encounters**
>
> 1. Arrival of the Nestorians: 7th century
> 2. Arrival of the Roman Catholics: 13th century
> 3. The Jesuit mission: 16th century
> 4. Protestant missions: 19th century

over religion, the competition between popular and elite behavior, the problem of missionary conflict, and the divide between religious and secular.

The first Protestant missionary to China was Robert Morrison, sent by the London Missionary Society in 1807. Morrison also worked for the British East India Company as a translator (giving him legal status in China) and assisted the Lord Amherst mission (1817) and the Lord Napier mission (1834). Initially, missionaries were barred from entering China, but Morrison gained access through his connection to the company. Soon, gunboats forced open treaty ports, and not long after, the interior was also opened. The rise of the Protestant missionary movement occurred during China's "century of humiliation," which lasted from the opium wars around 1840 until the founding of the People's Republic of China in 1949. This century also saw the high tide of Protestant missionary efforts. Protestant missionaries opened secondary schools and colleges, hospitals, relief associations, and churches. The Protestant movement coincided with what K. S. Latourette called "the Great Century," when Christianity began laying new roads throughout the world.

A notable development of this period was the Taiping Rebellion (1850–64), initiated by Hong Xiuquan, a would-be scholar who received Christian tracts while taking the imperial exams. Although he initially shelved the materials, several years later he took ill and had visions that led him to believe that he was Jesus's younger brother. Hong saw one of the characters in his name in the Christian scriptures and came to believe that God would use him to establish a "great kingdom of heavenly peace." Hong's rebellion gained power throughout southern China, especially among his ethnic group, the Hakka. Soon, Hong and the Taiping took the southern capital, Nanjing, and instituted a theocracy. Missionaries initially expressed optimism about the rebellion, but soon they also turned against it. Eventually, Western forces helped assist the Qing in quelling the rebellion. The Taiping rebellion was the largest revolution before the twentieth century, and it left upward of twenty million dead. The nature of the Taiping continues to prompt study. Was it a failed effort at inculturation? Does it show the dangers of syncretism (for Christians) or sectarianism (for the Chinese authorities)? The Boxer Rebellion of 1900 presents an interesting foil. In this case the Qing court protected itself from anti-Manchu sentiment by channeling the Boxers to attack foreigners and missionaries. The Boxer Rebellion had a religious aspect also, with followers believing that martial arts training and special rituals would protect them from bullets. Eight nations put down the rebellion and created a new system of indemnities.

During this period, Catholicism also grew. The growth of treaty ports and extraterritorial properties granted through unequal treaties allowed missionaries legal leverage. Circa 1800 there were probably two hundred thousand Catholics in China, but this number grew during the modern period. The proliferation of sending orders and the growth of missionary institutions all propelled the movement forward.

Protestant missionary organization included the work of both denominational and nondenominational missionary organizations. Groups like the London Missionary Society brought together largely Reformed groups. Before long, new forms of organization arrived. J. Hudson Taylor's (1832–1905) China Inland Mission (continued today by the Overseas Missionary Fellowship, which is still the largest Protestant missionary body in East Asia) contributed to Protestant expansion in China. Missionaries divided China into a variety of regions through comity agreements, which attempted to avoid denominational competition. In some cases, Chinese religions copied existing institutions, creating, for instance, a Red Swastika Association (the swastika is an ancient Buddhist symbol that was misappropriated by the Nazis). In other cases, Christians created essentially parallel relief or humanitarian organizations that sometimes competed with the Chinese government.

In the early twentieth century, several major Chinese evangelists rose to prominence. John Sung (1901–44), Wang Mingdao (1900–1991), and Watchman Nee (1903–72) still form a popular pantheon in Chinese Protestantism. They began a ministry that was distinctively Chinese, and while some cooperated with missionaries, others sought a totally indigenized church. Indigenous churches, such as the True Jesus Church (1917), were free of missionary control and established a new form of Christianity that was freer of foreign connections and associations. Meanwhile, the traditional denominations moved toward a greater ecumenism with the first general assembly of the Church of Christ in China (1927). The famous *Re-Thinking Missions* project (published 1932) urged new attitudes toward evangelism and the world religions. Protestant encounter in the twentieth century saw new efforts to understand Christianity in light of Chinese culture. Scholars like Zhao Zichen (TC Chao) attempted creative syntheses.

The new PRC government quickly nationalized the churches in China. At least four hundred thousand quickly signed on to a "Christian Manifesto," which declared support for the new denomination and rejected imperialism. Many missionaries had left during World War II. While some returned during the Chinese Civil War (1945–49), most left with liberation in 1949, and the rest left during the hostilities of the Korean War. The Catholic encounter faced stronger challenges with the Communist Revolution of 1949. The pope was stridently anticommunist, and the church took a formal stance against cooperation with the new regime. The Catholic Church in China missed out on Vatican II and other modernizing

> **Study Aid #67**
>
> **Religions of China**
>
> Indigenous beliefs (30 percent with Daoists)
>   Yin-Yang, ancestors, divination
> Daoism (30 percent with indigenous)
>   The Dao, Lao Tzu, Daodejing
> Confucianism (6th century BCE)
>   Five Classics, Five Relationships, Five Virtues
> Buddhism (18 percent)
>   The Buddha, Mahayana, Bodhisattva ideal
> Christianity (4 percent)
> Islam (2 percent)
> Secularism/Nominalism (42 percent)

tendencies, which posed other problems during the liberalization that began in China in the late 1970s.

The communists quickly established a Religious Affairs Office, which assisted with religious questions and centralized national religious organization and campaigns. "Three-self" movements (self-governing, self-supporting, self-propagating) were created for Protestants and Catholics. The Protestant association eventually became known as the Three-Self Patriotic Movement, and the Catholic Church became known as the Chinese Catholic Patriotic Association. The relationship between the Vatican and the Chinese government turned increasingly tense. Soon there was a formal break, and Chinese Catholics began recognizing government-supported bishops (1958).

Each Christian encounter with China layered on what came beforehand. Today many seminaries around the world include a rubbing of the Tang stele, and the first Protestant Bible translations drew heavily on Catholic Gospel translations. During this period, Chinese religion also grew and shifted. The sporadic persecution of earlier periods gave way to guarded practice of later years. The Qing attempted to negotiate with the Catholic Church but ultimately feared it would compete for its subjects' loyalty. The nineteenth and twentieth centuries saw a proliferation of sects and teachings, propelled by the collapse of the Qing and the rise of new presses and methods of communication. The harsh persecution of the earlier communist years has given way to closely watched, but thriving, churches and temples. The future of Christianity in China, and its relationship to more dominant religions, is still unclear.

Sources

Daniel Bays. *Christianity in China: From the Eighteenth Century to the Present.* Stanford University Press, 1996.

Liam Matthew Brockey. *Journey to the East: The Jesuit Mission to China, 1579–1724*. Belknap Press of Harvard University Press, 2007.

Lars Laaman. *Christian Heretics in Late Imperial China*. Routledge, 2006.

Kenneth Scott Latourette. *A History of Christian Missions in China*. Macmillan, 1929.

Roman Malek. *The Chinese Face of Jesus Christ*. Vols. 1–3b. Institut Monumenta Serica and China-Zentrum, 2002–.

Jonathan Spence. *God's Chinese Son: The Taiping Heavenly Kingdom of Hong Xiuquan*. Norton, 1997.

Scott Sunquist, ed. *A Dictionary of Asian Christianity*. Eerdmans, 2001.

Stephen Uhalley and Xiaoxin Wu. *China and Christianity: Burdened Past, Hopeful Future*. M. E. Sharpe, 2001.

Philip Wickeri. *Seeking the Common Ground: Protestant Christianity, the Three-Self Movement, and China's United Front*. Orbis Books, 1988.

Richard Fox Young. "*Deus Unus* or *Dei Plures Sunt*? The Function of Inclusivism in the Buddhist Defense of Mongol Folk Religion against William of Rubruck (1254)." *Journal of Ecumenical Studies* 26 (1989): 100–137.

33

China: Theological Exchanges

Jonathan Seitz

The historical issues above hint at many of the most enduring issues between Christians and Chinese religious practitioners. At one end of the spectrum was a famous work by the French sinologist Jacques Gernet, which argued that the cultural difference between Christianity and Chinese culture is such that conflict is inevitable and the likelihood of enduring amity between the two is unlikely. Gernet subtitled his study a "Conflict of Cultures" and saw Christianity as culturally distant and incompatible with Chinese culture. At another extreme have been those who continuously have foreseen the imminent conversion of China. Nonetheless, a variety of scholars deem that Christianity has often found a home in Chinese language and culture, and this essay examines the existing data.

There are many theological issues that flow from the historical relationship between the two. Christianity failed as a primarily ethnic immigrant religion with the Church of the East, was banned or persecuted after a period of toleration in the late Ming and early Qing, and was often associated with colonialism during the first century of Protestant encounter. During the early years of the communist period, Christianity disappeared from public view. In each period, the religious conversation partner shifted, ranging from the multireligious framework of the Mongols, to the neo-Confucian elites of the Ming, to the Communist Revolution of the mid-twentieth century.

The foreign study of the twentieth century could probably be told effectively through a survey of some of the more famous mission histories of China, as in Arthur Smith's *China in a Convulsion* during the 1900 Boxer Rebellion; Milton Stauffer's memorably titled *The Christian Occupation of China* (1922), written

> **Study Aid #68**
> **Basic Chinese Religious Outlook**
> Dao: The Path or Way (both moral and cosmological)
> Yin-Yang: The dynamic of religious life, the interaction between energy forces
> Ancestors: Centrality of filial piety

after the Republic Revolution but before the anti-Christian movement (1922–27); David Patton's 1953 *Christian Mission and the Judgment of God*, written shortly after the Communist Revolution; or even David Aikman's 2003 book *Jesus in Beijing*, which heralds a new wave of expected conversions. During each of these periods, "China hands" living in China or abroad weighed in, studied the situation, anticipated conversion or rejection, and read the proverbial tea leaves to understand China's Christian potential.

Issues brought to the table by missionaries included the naming of God, the relationship between the ancestors and the living, idolatry, the relationship of Christianity to indigenous religions, and so on. Issues brought to the table by Chinese critics include the foreign entanglement of Christianity and government authority (how much influence did the pope, orders, or missionary societies have?), family relations, the name of God, and death rituals and the afterlife.

Idol or Image?

Since Christianity's arrival came relatively late, one theme that has underscored Christianity has been the question of idolatry. This marked both the Ming-Qing Catholic encounter and the modern encounter of the last two centuries. Christians often used religious polemic to distinguish their teachings from popular religion. For Protestants the iconoclastic tendency was especially strong, reinforced initially by a strong anti-Catholic tendency, and early tracts and catechisms often carried public denunciations of idolatry. Missionaries tended to emphasize the Ten Commandments and the prohibition against graven images. Converts often saw the destruction of family altars or ancestral tablets as part of becoming Christians. Chinese religionists also critiqued Christianity for the images it used. An interesting image of the Jesuit period by anti-Christian polemicists puns on the similarity between Jesus's name and the Chinese word "pig" and shows a crucified pig.

The Naming of God

The naming of God was an early problem, and words that are undifferentiated in English are often differentiated in Chinese due to Christian sectarianism. Catholicism (*Tianzhujiao*, "Heavenly Lord Teaching") is seen as distinct from

Protestantism (*Jidujiao*, "The Christ Teaching"). The naming of God was especially contentious in missionary circles. Catholics early disputed what name to give to God, and Protestants also feuded over the name of God. There were several options, including *Shen* (god, ghost, spirit), *Shangdi* (Lord on High), and *Tianzhu* (Heavenly Lord). This may, however, have been more of a missionary theological debate. In practice, Christians often interchanged the terms in daily life and worship. An interesting proposal for the name of God was Liang Fa's *Shentian Shangdi* ("The God of Heaven, the Lord on High"), which put together the three main contenders into a four-word name for God, in the same way that some Chinese gods are named. James Legge wrote an important tract arguing for *Shangdi* against William Boone's preference for *Shen*. Today there are still "dueling Bibles," which use different words for *Elohim* in the Old Testament or *Theos* in the New Testament. Similar controversies arise over the names for baptism (is it a "washing ritual" or an "immersion ritual"?). Protestants placed a major emphasis on Bible translation, whereas Catholics emphasized catechism. (Interestingly, Catholics translated the Bible into Chinese in total for the first time between 1946 and 1961.)

At issue in these debates was whether to use indigenous names for God, and which names to use. Translators have typically chosen among three options when translating Christian materials, using either a general term or category, selecting a specific term from the tradition's past, or offering a transliteration ("Jehovah," "Messiah"). Missionaries and Chinese Christians struggled also. In the case of the Church of the East, translators often had used Daoist or Buddhist terms or phrases. Catholics and Protestants repeated these conundrums. Should Christians apply the term "Lord on High" or "Heaven," as used in the Chinese classics, or a generic term like "god," or something else entirely? Each term had something to commend it but also posed distinct dangers. Another interesting question was the translation of *logos*, as in the first chapter of the Gospel of John. Christians eventually adopted *Dao*, which echoes an important Chinese religious concept. Catholics typically used the phrase "Lord" for God in the Hebrew scriptures, whereas Protestants sometimes used the transliteration "Yehehua" for "Yahweh." Like the Buddhist encounter of earlier generations, translation is one of the first steps in encounter.

Christian Practices, Social Vices

As with early church history, doctrine presented a challenge for many Christians. Trinitarianism was often baffling to Chinese listeners. Chinese Christians struggled to translate new categories of spiritual description. Christianity had a closed canon and accepted a number of creeds, which collectively defined orthodoxy. Christian piety (variable depending on sect) included prohibitions that were challenging for initial converts. This included keeping the Sabbath, church regulations about

> **Study Aid #69**
>
> Recurrent Theological Themes in China
>
> 1. Religious symbols: Idols or images?
> 2. Naming of God: *Shen, Shangdi, Tianzhu,* or unique terms?
> 3. Morality: Christian or Confucian?
> 4. Syncretism: One or many?
> 5. Filiality: Worship or veneration?
> 6. Public theology: State supervision or underground?

marriage and concubinage, and rules on vice (especially alcohol and opium, but also debates over things like gambling and foot-binding).

The non-Christian past has been a topic of some concern. Early missionaries often struggled to align Christian belief with Chinese history, by appealing to deistic ideas in the Chinese past, finding parallels to biblical stories such as Noah's flood, or, even today, locating biblical stories in Chinese characters. Often these affinities were artificially constructed, but they showed creative ways in which God's actions could be read in Chinese historical tradition.

China as a civilization or nation has typically regulated religious life. In this sense, Christianity posed a major challenge since it was carried by missionaries who collaborated with the colonial authorities and soon had extraterritoriality. A Christian sectarian movement, the Taiping, was the biggest internal revolt of the Qing, and the Boxer Rebellion (in part a Chinese religious reaction to the presence of missionaries and Chinese Christians) and subsequent indemnities were associated with the Christian presence. Today, the Chinese government, with such precedents, continues to be wary over how Christian sectarianism might affect Chinese national life.

Syncretism, Dualism, or Something Else?

Jacques Gernet conceived of a "conflict of cultures." While a number of subsequent studies rejected Gernet's findings, the issues he raised highlighted concerns that had been identified by Chinese Christians. The cycling of anti-Christian movements, the multiple re-introductions, and the creative conflict spoke to a tense relationship. How to conceive of this relationship has often been challenging. With Christians seeking to safeguard their orthodoxy and converts struggling to integrate their culture with their newfound faith, some measure of tension was unavoidable.

For Christians, an enduring theological question has concerned the possibilities and limits of contextualization, accommodation, or enculturation. The cautionary watchword has often been syncretism, where Christianity is co-opted by indigenous religious systems. In China, which was known for the absorption and sinicization of foreign peoples and religions, the risk seemed especially high.

Movements like the Taiping also pointed to the theological dangers Christianity faced in becoming Chinese. However, "dualism" has also been a problem. The sociologist Nicole Constable studied Hakka Christians in Hong Kong and found that Christians often adopted a dual system, with a set of specifically Christian rules and norms for Sundays, major lifestyles, and Christian contexts, and another set of rules that governed day-to-day life. Certainly it is appropriate that social scientists, historians, theologians, and practitioners often use different models to explain this interaction.

The nesting of Christian belief in a Chinese context often inspired hopes for a larger synthesis. Fulfillment theology was one form of this approach. Here, some Catholic missionaries saw the faith as perfecting the ideals expressed in an earlier time. In the twentieth century, liberal Chinese Christians sometimes saw Christian modernism meshing with a Confucian ideal of ordered society, progressive education, and social uplift. Other times, the expressed ideal was a philosophical accommodation, with Chinese philosophical categories replacing the Hellenistic approach of the early church or the Latin culture of the medieval period.

Cultural Ideals of Society and the Family

Another fascinating area for encounter has been conflicting views on social or cultural practices, which has been a defining feature of Christianity's modern encounter with other religions. Since Christianity was wedded to ideals of universal education, the uplift of women, and a new ideal of citizenship, Christians often associated faith with specific social practices. Missionaries and Christian converts railed against opium, gambling, foot-binding, concubinage, and child labor. In many cases, such crusades were reflexive criticisms of Chinese society, but missionaries also were arguing for egalitarian ideals that were either not present in Chinese society or were relatively weak.

Another major problem has been the question of family life and Christianity. Like the earlier Buddhist encounter, Christians struggled to rearticulate their teachings to appeal to the Chinese emphasis on filiality, or *xiao*. Christian missionaries always stressed respect for parents in their preaching (usually citing the second commandment). During periods of conflict, Christians sometimes encountered rumors that they engaged in unlawful sex acts or ate children (in their orphanages). A major theological concern in Christianity has often been the failure to

---

Study Aid #70

The Indigenous Chinese Evangelists

John Sung (1901–44)
Wang Mingdao (1900–1991)
Watchman Nee (1903–72)

make offerings to deceased ancestors. Because the consequences are so extreme (ancestors are denied offerings and become hungry ghosts), this has often been a flashpoint for converts to Christianity.

National Cooperation or Resistance

Throughout China's modern period, beginning with the 1911 revolution that ended the Qing Empire, Chinese intellectuals have criticized traditional modes of religion or philosophy. The famous May Fourth–movement author Lu Xun, in the short story "Diary of a Madman," read Confucius's *Analects*, seeing the word "devours people" on every page. He believed that the conservative traditional beliefs and practices ate away at the individual.

Christians sometimes saw such a system as oppressive but were just as likely to see a secularized, de-ritualized Confucianism as an ideal conversation partner. Protestants idealized Confucianism as a secular conversation partner, imbued with natural ethics and the hope of a just society.

In a real sense, all religions suffered during the Cultural Revolution (1966–76), during which a youth revolutionary movement, sponsored by Mao Zedong, waged war against traditional culture, foreign influence, and party corruption. Most religious bodies were shuttered during the Cultural Revolution, and many temples, churches, and traditional historical sites were destroyed. Mao and his followers included a campaign against Confucianism as part of a 1973 campaign. While Mao himself was something of a lay classicist, the movement he spawned was thoroughly anti-intellectual and antireligious. In the aftermath of the revolution, religious organizations struggled to rebuild.

The policies of several of the "little dragons" (South Korea, Taiwan, Hong Kong, and Singapore) provided one model for political liberalization. Both South Korea and Taiwan experienced several decades of totalitarian rule before undergoing waves of political liberalization. During this period, trenchant criticisms were offered by theologians like contextual theologian C.-S. Song.

Since 1900 Buddhism has declined as a percentage of the world's population. The largest stated reason for this decline was the forced secularization of China in the twentieth century. Nonetheless, such statistical analyses are approximate, and this may be a misreading of the current religious context. Today there is reason to believe that all of the world religions are growing in China. While the government carefully guards against outside influence, in practice there are likely more foreign missionaries in China than at any point in the past.

Not all of the above may seem like theological topics, and certainly many more theological themes could be introduced. For instance, there are some fascinating dialogues that have occurred between Christians and Confucianists over human nature, between Buddhists and Christians over concepts of the self or the nature of deity, and between popular practitioners over healing, possession, or the ancestors.

Theological dialogue has occurred at a variety of levels and will no doubt continue to merit formal and informal discussion. The questions posed by popular religion are especially vexing, since almost by nature, lacking major organization and institutionalization, they cannot be represented in formal dialogues. The broader response to these issues will be worked out through formal discussion, but also through ordinary people trying to find meaning.

Sources

> Nicole Constable. *Guest People: Hakka Identity in China and Abroad*. University of Washington Press, 2005.
>
> Ralph Covell. *Confucius, the Buddha, and Christ: A History of the Gospel in Chinese*. Orbis Books, 1986.
>
> Jacques Gernet. *China and the Christian Impact: A Conflict of Cultures*. Cambridge University Press, 1985.
>
> Norman Girardot. *The Victorian Translation of China: James Legge's Oriental Pilgrimage*. University of California Press, 2002.
>
> Thomas Alan Harvey, *Acquainted with Grief: Wang Mingdao's Stand for the Persecuted Church in China*. Brazos, 2002.
>
> Pui-lan Kwok. *Chinese Women and Christianity, 1860–1927*. Scholars Press, 1992.

34

China: Current Issues

JONATHAN SEITZ

The contemporary relationship between Christianity and Chinese religions is marked by the changing attitude toward religion in the People's Republic of China, the spread of Christianity into the Diaspora, and public intellectual exchange among the religions. The majority of Chinese live in China proper, and thus the question of state control is perhaps the dominant issue, as different religious groups come out of hiding and enter the public realm. Christianity and Chinese religions probably face fewer pressing issues than other religions. This may be due to Christians' efforts to keep a lower profile and the more diffused organizational structure of many Chinese religions.

The Revival of Religion in the People's Republic of China

Christianity now takes a number of forms in China proper, complicating efforts to discuss its relationship to Chinese religion. It is common to distinguish several categories of Christian practice in contemporary China: (1) state-sponsored Catholicism, (2) underground Catholicism, (3) state-sponsored Protestantism, (4) underground Protestantism, and possibly (5) "cultural Christianity." Underground and official churches may compete, but they also in some ways overlap and often share resources. Some Catholic priests, for instance, may have received a state ordination and an underground ordination, and Protestants may buy Bibles from the patriotic churches, download resources produced abroad from the internet, and attend an unregistered Bible study or church group. "Cultural Christianity" refers to academic communities' interest in the social benefits that Christianity may confer; it is common to see Christianity as a modernizing religion that emphasizes individual and social morality but that also respects some traditional aspects of society. These categories are not absolute. There are also parallels among Buddhism, Daoism, and local religions. Many temples have been reopened, and popular religion also appears to be flourishing.

The Ongoing Question of Sectarian Movements

A controversial question that affects Chinese religion generally as well as Christianity is how to respond to sectarian movements. In 2006, for instance, the *New York Times* carried a story about Xu Shuangfu, the leader of a large underground church, the Three Grades Servants Church. Xu and eleven followers were executed for involvement in the murders of a competing Christian sect. Since the Falun Gong was banned in the late 1990s, such sectarian movements have been cautiously watched. Underground churches are typically nonviolent and apolitical, but their capacity to organize followers is disconcerting to Chinese leaders and unfortunately plays into a long tradition of government control, violent sectarian movements, and sporadic persecution of religious movements.

Ethnically Chinese governments have also expressed reservations over marginal groups. Singapore has banned some religious movements with Chinese connections, including the Jehovah's Witnesses and the Unification Church.

While it is clearly a minority movement within the overall tradition, the birth of "socially engaged Buddhism" has prompted new forms of cooperation and challenge. Such socially engaged Buddhism includes themes of ecological justice, an emphasis on human rights, concerns over gender relations, and other issues. Within China and its Diaspora, Buddhist organizations are increasingly taking the lead. In Taiwan, the country's major humanitarian organization is Tzu Chi, which is Buddhist and also maintains connections throughout the world and participates in humanitarian activities in China.

The missionary movement is for all intents and purposes flourishing today in China. There are likely thousands or tens of thousands of foreign missionaries in China, teaching English, studying, working in tent-making ministries, or serving directly with churches. They reflect many of the classical structures of mission, serving as conduits to foreign knowledge and seeking the conversion of followers.

Ethnic Minorities and Christianity

Ethnic minorities provide another important topic. China has some fifty-five ethnic minorities, which officially make up around 8 percent of the population. The five stars on China's flag are sometimes said to represent five of the largest ethnicities. While some minorities align heavily with Buddhism (Tibetans) or Islam (Hui, Uighur), many are converting to Christianity, and there is sometimes interchange

> **Study Aid #71**
>
> **Current Issues**
>
> 1. Religious revival
> 2. Sectarianism
> 3. Ethnic minorities
> 4. The Chinese Diaspora
> 5. Dialogue and cooperation

between the ethnic groups of southwest China and the minority groups in Southeast Asia. An interesting pan-Asian phenomenon has been the growth of ethnic-minority Christianities. While only a few nations, notably the Philippines and South Korea, have large Christian populations, many countries throughout South, Southeast, and East Asia possess substantial Christian minorities. Often these are "hill people" in Southeast Asia, Dalits in India, or ethnic minorities in China and Chinese-speaking contexts. The "aboriginals" of Taiwan are majority Christian, and minorities in other parts of Asia (Myanmar, India) often became Christian at a higher rate. (A natural parallel is the relationship between Buddhism and counterculture in many Western countries.) Conversion to Christianity likely comes from several sources: (1) the desire to align with a religion different from the majority culture; (2) the vernacularizing tendency of Christianity, which embraces local languages and provides resources in the target language; (3) the lack of an established, accepted world religion within the community; or (4) the abundant resources connected to Christianity as a world religion that sends missionaries. These explanations cannot be complete, but they highlight the significance of a broad trend throughout the Chinese world that has given Christianity a special status among ethnic minorities. In some cases, this introduces an element of tension or conflict into existing communities. What role these minority Christianities will play in Chinese religion remains unclear. Rodney Stark has argued that conversion tends to be rare under severe or systematic persecution or in contexts where a strong religious rival already exists.

The Diaspora

Another major issue involves the presence of the broad Chinese Diaspora, which includes all of those people (Chinese speaking or not) who relate to ideas of Chinese culture. Chinese religion is sometimes regarded as an ethnic, in contrast to a missionary, religion. However, it has largely spread through migration networks that now extend throughout the world, and Chinese Buddhists now send missionaries to Southeast Asia and operate universities in the United States. They distribute tracts and broadcast radio and television shows. Among Christians, Diaspora kinship networks often spread Christianity back to the People's Republic of China or to other countries. The rate of conversion to Christianity among overseas or

> **Study Aid #72**
>
> **The Chinese Diaspora**
>
> Approximately fifty million Chinese live outside China. One nation-state, Singapore, has a majority Chinese population—almost three million Chinese live in Singapore. Ten other countries have Chinese populations over one million.
>
> | | |
> |---|---|
> | Thailand: 9.3 million | Canada: 1.4 million |
> | Indonesia: 8.8 million | Peru: 1.3 million |
> | Malaysia: 7 million | Philippines: 1.2 million |
> | United States: 3.8 million | Vietnam: 1 million |
> | Burma: 1.6 million | Russia: 1 million |

Diaspora Chinese is almost certainly higher than in China proper, and this has led to the creation of seminaries and missionary networks that connect Chinese across many time zones. In Taiwan, the Christian population in cities appears to be higher than in the countryside, with around 9 percent of Taipei residents identified as Christian. Rates given for Christianity among the Diaspora are on the following order: China, 3–4 percent; Taiwan, 4.5 percent; Singapore, 9.8 percent; Hong Kong, 10 percent; Malaysia, 9.1 percent. It thus becomes clear that while the rate is currently lowest in China, it is substantially higher in the Diaspora. In some of the multiethnic contexts (Singapore, Malaysia), the percentage of Christians is much higher among ethnic Chinese.

Formal Dialogues and State-Sponsored Cooperation

Formal religious dialogues are notable for their influence. For instance, theologians such as Hans Küng have conducted major studies of the relationship between Christian theology and Confucian philosophy or cosmology. Buddhist-Christian dialogues similarly take a variety of forms, from academic symposia to neighbor-to-neighbor conversations. Forums like the World Parliament of Religions or the World Council of Churches have hosted discussions that include Chinese religions. In some cases, conversations have also occurred at the national level. Singapore's former prime minister Lee Kuan-Yew famously toyed with the idea of implementing Confucianism as a formal state ideology for the tiny island nation. Tu Wei-Ming and others have argued for Confucianism as a pan-Asian and possibly global philosophical framework. Christians have typically been religious minorities in East Asia and so have struggled with how to relate to such approaches, sometimes seeking points of commonality, other times asserting the distinctiveness of Christianity. In fact, a distinctive aspect of religion in East Asia is that there appears to be no likelihood of a broad territorial religion on the order of Indian religion or ancient Christendom.

Conclusions

The future prospects of Chinese-Christian encounter remain hazy. The latest iteration of Christianity in China and among ethnic Chinese abroad seems durable but coexists along with a broader revival of religion. Classical issues of Chinese culture remain (filiality, the nature of God, etc.), but have often been overwhelmed by more pressing modern concerns, especially those relating to the role of the state, "Chinese-ness," and globalization. Indeed, it is the social changes just mentioned (changes in the nation-state, the growth of the Diaspora, and the importance of the nation-state), which are remaking the relationship between Christianity and Chinese religion. Because Chinese religions are more diffuse, the creedal conflicts that mark other religions are much less common among Chinese practitioners. The past shows how unpredictable current or future encounters may be, even as it points toward many fruitful areas for discussion.

Sources

David Aikman. *Jesus in Beijing*. Regnery, 2003.

Julia Ching. *Confucianism and Christianity: A Comparative Study*. Kodansha, 1977.

Alan Hunter and Kim-Kwong Chan. *Protestantism in Contemporary China*. Cambridge University Press, 2007.

Beatrice Leung and John D. Young. *Christianity in China: Foundations for Dialogue*. Centre of Asian Studies, University of Hong Kong, 1993.

Richard Madsen. *China's Catholics: Tragedy and Hope in an Emerging Civil Society*. University of California Press, 1998.

Ku Wei-ying and Koen De Ridder, eds. *Authentic Chinese Christianity: Preludes to Its Development*. Leuven University Press/Ferdinand Verbiest Foundation, 2001.

James Whitehead, Yu-Ming Shaw, and Norman J. Girardot. *China and Christianity: Historical and Future Encounters*. Center for Pastoral and Social Ministry, University of Notre Dame, 1979.

Lian Xi. *Redeemed by Fire: The Rise of Popular Christianity in Modern China*. Yale University Press, 2010.

35

Southeast Asia: History, Beliefs, Practices

Russell H. Bowers

History

Peninsular Southeast Asia includes the modern countries of Myanmar, Thailand, Cambodia, Laos, Vietnam, peninsular Malaysia, and Singapore. Where peninsular Southeast Asia's first inhabitants originated is unknown. Northwestern Cambodia, for example, has been occupied for at least six thousand years. People throughout this region likely developed the same survival skills and practiced animism contemporaneously and in a similar manner. Today traditional Southeast Asian religions interweave varied strands—animism, popular Hinduism, Brahmanism, Theravada and Mahayana Buddhism, Chinese beliefs, Catholic and Protestant Christianity, and Islam. Which ones predominate and how they interact vary by country and region.

Animism, or *folk religion*, predates and serves as warp and woof for the others, and remains the dominant religious strand in many rural regions. It differs from organized religion in that it lacks a clearly identifiable founder, systematic doctrine, and significant institutional organization. Animistic practices pervade rural life and primarily attempt to address present, mundane needs.

Buddhism possibly entered Myanmar through Asoka's third-century-BCE emissaries. Indian thought also began to influence Southeast Asia from the second century CE as a result of trade, and powerfully so from the seventh century. Myths describe the arrival of Indian prince Kaundinya and his marriage to the daughter of the king of the Nagas (supernatural water-serpents). Kaundinya became king of Cambodia; successive rulers maintain the nation's prosperity by mystically uniting with the queen of the waters; the nine-headed Naga has become a symbol of the country. Before Kaundinya's arrival, the Cambodians reputedly lived naked, suggesting that significant Indian ideological and cultural input followed the arrival of the Indians.

Such Indianization brought a mixture of Hindu and Buddhist practices. The influence of Brahmanism, with its investiture rituals and deference to royalty as *avatars* of Vishnu or Shiva, underlies reverence for kings that persists to this day (particularly in Thailand). Brahmanism's emphasis on the power of the king as a *cakravartin* or *devaraja* (world ruler), combined with Mahayana's savior figures (especially Lokesvara), supported the flourishing Angkor Empire, centered on the world's largest preindustrial city. In 1181 Jayavarman VII established Mahayana as its religion. Indravarman III (1295–1307) replaced Mahayana (and a resurgent Brahmanism) with Theravada, weakening the Brahmanistic hierarchical ideology upon which Angkorian society had been built and possibly contributing to its decline. Similarly, Theravada arrived in Malaysia in the early centuries CE and was displaced by Mahayana in the eighth through thirteenth centuries. In Malaysia's case, however, Islam (rather than Theravada) superseded Mahayana in the fourteenth and fifteenth centuries.

As Buddhism entered the region, it melded with local spirit cults. State sponsorship of Buddhism in Myanmar, Thailand, Laos, and Cambodia, beginning in the eleventh century, led to the assimilation or decline of competing faiths. These four nations looked to India for cultural influence; then, as contact with northern Indian Buddhism waned because of the influx there of Islam, they adopted Sri Lankan Theravada. Malaysia turned from Buddhism to Islam. Vietnam was influenced more by China than by India, so Vietnamese Buddhism is chiefly Mahayana. Singapore is consciously multireligious. Buddhists of many varieties coexist there, but because of Chinese influences most are Mahayana, and often syncretized with Confucian, Daoist, and other Chinese beliefs. Buddhism is Singapore's fastest-growing religion. In recent decades, modernization has prompted the emergence of "Reformist Buddhism," with renewed attention to scriptures and social contribution rather than simply the observance of rites. Other regional Buddhist movements of the past half century stressing greater social involvement include the work of Vietnam's Thich Nhat Hanh, Thailand's Sulak Sivaraksa, and the "Gandhi of Cambodia," Supreme Patriarch Ghosananada.

The changing nature of Thai rice myths illustrates adjustments that occurred as Buddhism encountered traditional animism and vied for popular allegiance. In a first type of myth, rice long ago grew by itself; people did not need to cultivate it. But a widow beat a large grain pile, humiliating the rice goddess, and since then people have had to invite her back into their homes. In a second type, Grandmother Rice was offended when the Buddha did not realize how long she had been feeding people. So after she flew away, the Buddha had to seek her out and implore her to return. In a third, rice fed the first four Buddhas, though the grain size progressively diminished over the years. The first myth genre explains the need for animistic ritual to ensure a good crop; the second suggests conflict

Study Aid #73

Map of Southeast Asia

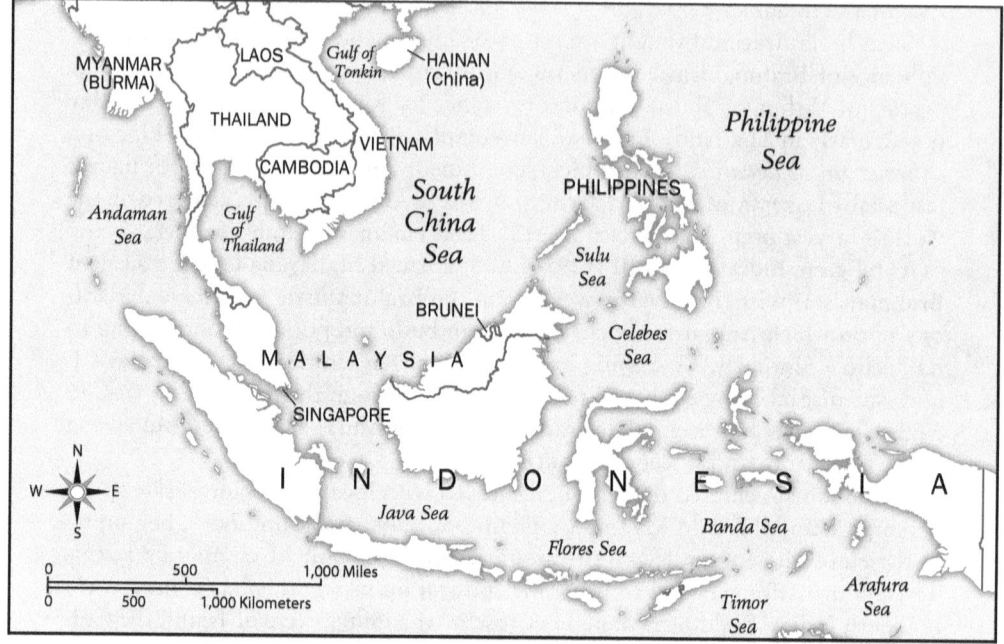

between the older animism and the newer Buddhism; the third depicts peaceful integration of animism and Buddhism.

In the nineteenth century, Vietnam, Laos, and Cambodia constituted French Indochina; Malaysia, Singapore, and Myanmar were British; only Thailand remained independent ("Thai" meaning "free"). The colonial powers imposed secular governments, weakening both the semidivine status of kings and the influence of the monks. Twentieth-century wars, occupations, military governments, and communism have furthered this change, forcing Buddhism to assume a less political role than it exercised previously.

Popular *Hinduism* was carried southwest by sea merchants from India to Java, from Java to Cambodia, and from Cambodia overland to Thailand, Laos, and southern Vietnam. Another route was across the Isthmus of Kra, then down and up the coast to southern China. Although today Hinduism per se is little practiced in Southeast Asia outside Bali and certain isolated locations, it still underlies regional thought and ritual. Images of Hanuman throughout Cambodia, the large statues of Vishnu and the churning of the Milk Ocean in Bangkok's Suvarnabhumi Airport, various local adaptations of the Ramayana, the festival of Thaipusam, and Sanskrit loanwords in several languages, for example, make this clear.

At the same time that Indian traders were developing sea routes to China, Chinese were sailing west, seeking to replace the land roads to India that had become blocked by central Asian nomadic tribes. Chinese thought, blending Daoism, Confucianism, ancestor veneration, and the search for auspiciousness, entered Southeast Asia (particularly Vietnam) as it accompanied trade. This influx increased with later Chinese immigration to mercantile centers where it thrives today, such as Bangkok, Ho Chi Minh City, Kuala Lumpur, and Singapore.

The relatively late importation and statistical insignificance of Christianity means that its themes and imagery influence the bedrock beliefs and mythology of the region less than those of Hinduism, Buddhism, and Islam.

Arabs and Persians traded in Southeast Asia long before they converted to *Islam*. But as the Middle East became increasingly Muslim, so did its merchants. By the eighth century India's shipping was increasingly controlled by Muslims, whose beliefs began to penetrate Southeast Asia's trading centers and a few royal courts. After the thirteenth-century collapse of the Malay Buddhist empire Shrivijaya, the door opened for more intentional Islamic proselytization. Ports on the north coast of Sumatra were converted and became centers from which Islam crossed the straits to Malacca and elsewhere in Malaysia. In 1413 Malacca's ruler converted, shifting local religion from a core of indigenous animism overlaid with Buddhist-influenced Hinduism to Islam. Elements of Shrivijaya Buddhist court etiquette, however, did continue and are still practiced today.

Conversion to Islam in Southeast Asia generally proceeded peacefully, as merchants and sailors introduced their faith. Once key port cities converted, others did as well to enhance business connections. Bali (with deep popular Hindu roots) and most of peninsular Southeast Asia (long committed to Theravada) largely resisted the encroachment of Islam. But the wealth and confidence of the Arab traders proved persuasive to many Malays.

In the late 1970s, about 100,000 of the 250,000 Muslims (mostly Chams) then living in Cambodia were killed by the Khmer Rouge. But aided by Indonesia, Saudi Arabia, and Brunei, the Cham community is again growing. Islamic minorities are also found today in Vietnam and Singapore; Islam is the majority faith in Malaysia, southern Thailand, and northwestern Myanmar.

Beliefs

Influence from China is stronger in the north and east; from India in the south and west. But practices from both permeate the region. As elsewhere, some local traditions recall distant memories of a high, Creator God. But (s)he has withdrawn and become inaccessible, leaving people with lesser spirits—particularly those of the land and of ancestors—to consult or appease, which animists believe they must do to secure protection and enjoy a satisfying present life. It is with the present life that animists are primarily concerned—with what works more than

> **Study Aid #74**
>
> Countries in Southeast Asia
>
> | | | | |
> |---|---|---|---|
> | Cambodia | Malaysia | Singapore | Vietnam |
> | Laos | Myanmar | Thailand | |

with abstract philosophical "truth." Holism is key to Asian spirituality. No clear division separates between the visible and invisible worlds. Spiritual forces are feared rather than loved, placated and manipulated rather than adored. Spirits are served corporately at the village level, rather than either individually or nationally.

The beliefs of any particular nation, village, or individual are frequently syncretistic and, to Western eyes, unsystematic and contradictory. Strands from diverse ideologies are woven into a fabric that cannot be unthreaded without destroying the whole cloth. Villagers who identify themselves as Buddhist typically, when pressed, explain that their first concern is to appease the spirits of ancestors; second, to appease the local (earth) spirits; and third, to honor the Buddha. This hierarchy does not strike those who hold it as either contradictory or disloyal to any whom they revere. As long as the ancestors, for example, receive their due, they do not mind that the *nats* or *neak ta* are also served; there seems to be little concept of an exclusive or jealous God.

Not only do diverse faiths intertwine, but great differences exist within a single tradition as well. For example, at the pass between Cambodia's Phnom Penh and Kompong Som stand many shrines to *Yiey Maw*. Conflicting stories describe who she was and why phallic-shaped offerings should be made to her in order to ensure a safe trip. But the fact that the stories are mutually exclusive neither generates disputes among those who stop to offer their bananas nor discourages the practice of presenting those offerings.

Chinese Confucianism, which promoted sagacity, family, and relationships; Daoism, which originally proposed a relaxed coexistence with nature but later attempted magical manipulation of it; and spirit and ancestor veneration, which tried to secure auspiciousness and avoid misfortune—all focus on harmony in this world. Such a focus complemented rather than competed with the Buddhist search for positive future rebecoming and ultimate *nirvana*. A blend migrated south into Vietnam, where it further assimilated with local beliefs.

Sufis accompanied Muslim traders into Southeast Asia. Their mysticism and devotionalism resonated with the local *bhakti* Hinduism; their role in introducing Islam helps explain the mysticism and relative tolerance of this region's version of that faith. Southeast Asia was never conquered and politically united by Muslim tribes as in Africa and the Near East but rather was developed in a decentralized manner around popular teachers or village councils. Preexisting practices were therefore not only permitted to continue but sometimes incorporated into Muslim ceremonies. Society is more egalitarian, and women enjoy more rights here than in the Middle East. Malaysia's constitution reads: "Islam is the religion of the Federation; but other religions may be practiced in peace and harmony in any part of the Federation." Thus although most of its citizens are Muslims, Malaysia is not an Islamic state. Some hope that this pluralized, nonmonolithic Islam of Muslim-majority Malaysia and Indonesia will help moderate the appeal of more radical groups elsewhere.

This does not mean that Southeast Asia is free from Islamic unrest. Ethnic divides remain. Early twentieth-century Malay Muslim reformers, focusing on preserving their particular cultural heritage, marginalized local Arab and Indian Muslims within Malaysia. But deeper still simmer religious divides—a broad distrust of the non-Muslim world in general. In their colonial years in Malaysia, the British encouraged an Islamic bureaucracy that exercised authority over Muslim civil matters. In the late nineteenth century, reform movements urged less compromise with the West and a return to putatively pure Islamic roots. This "modernist" and "revivalist" Islam presses for and has won significant legal concessions for the Muslim community at the expense of non-Muslims. Tensions over Christian use of "Allah" for God, for example, continue both in the courts and on the streets. Similarly, among the causes of the ongoing violence that re-erupted in southern Thailand in 2004 is long-simmering unrest over (perceived) marginalization of and threats to Muslim Malay religious and cultural uniqueness. One avowed objective is the secession of the southern Muslim provinces from a predominately Buddhist Thailand.

Southern Vietnam is home to the originally political-religious faith of Cao Đài. With strong roots in spiritism, Cao Đài proposes that while all religions are based on divine revelations, in the 1920s God revealed himself in a fresh way to Ngô Văn Chiêu. Not surprisingly, its creed and practices are syncretistic. A large eye, often enclosed in a triangle, is a primary image employed in this faith. Another recent syncretistic faith is Dejiao, the "teaching of moral uplifting," which emerged in southern China in 1939 and has spread to Hong Kong, Thailand, Malaysia, and Singapore. The patriotic though weakened Hòa Hảo Buddhism retains a following in Vietnam.

Practices

In regions where Theravada predominates, ancient monastic practices continue. Shaved, robed monks silently progress through village and city streets bearing alms bowls. Faithful laity *wai* (bow with folded hands in front of chest), lower their heads respectfully below those of the monks, and scoop cooked rice into their bowls. The monks neither make eye contact with nor thank the laity (since through seeking alms they are benefiting the latter by providing them an opportunity to earn merit), but will often briefly chant some scriptures. *Wats* (Buddhist compounds typically including a recitation and/or image hall, monks' quarters, and stupas) are scattered throughout the cities and in many villages. In the latter they may still serve as community centers, schools, hostels, and crematoria. Boys

Study Aid #75

Religious Percentages in Southeast Asian Countries (rounded numbers)

	Buddhism	Ethno-religion	Islam	Chinese folk	Hinduism	New religion	Non-relig/atheist	Christian
Cambodia	85	5	2	5			3	1
Laos	49	42		2			6	2
Malaysia	7	3	48	24	7	1	1	8
Myanmar	73	13	2		2		1	8
Singapore	15		18	43	5	2	5	12
Thailand	85	2	7	1			2	2*
Vietnam	50	9	1	1		11	21	8

*some consider this figure inflated

and young men are often ordained as monks—even if only for a short time—to earn merit for their parents (e.g., to pay their mothers back for their milk) or for a deceased relative. Vesak is an important holiday. Monks may be called upon to chant at weddings, funerals, and other important occasions.

But even in Theravada regions many animistic practices continue. Spirit houses outside homes and businesses provide sites for offering rice, flowers, incense, and so on. In Cambodia such offerings are made to the *neak ta* (the "Ancient People," spirits of dead or mythological village founders). In Myanmar coconuts and red cloth are presented to *nats*. Even on the streets of Bangkok stand many spirit houses for the *phii*. Laos reveres the *nak* serpent spirit. In the countryside, significant natural phenomena such as waterfalls and large trees will often sport shrines where offerings are presented to the resident spirits. The most important religious festival in Theravada Cambodia is not a Buddhist celebration but Pchum Ben, an occasion to feed and placate the hungry spirits released temporarily from hell. Khmer New Year in April is a time to bid farewell to the *devada* of the previous year and welcome its replacement. Although these are not Buddhist occasions, celebrations (particularly of Pchum Ben) often take place in *wats* and incorporate monastic participation. Wearing strings, tattoos, and amulets for good luck is widespread.

Malays strongly profess a form of Islam, not Buddhism, which is mingled with non-Muslim beliefs and rituals. Many of these invoke spirits and magic in an attempt to secure success in the present life.

In Vietnam a small-mirrored octagonal disc, adorned with the Daoist yin-yang and other symbols, and placed above the doors of homes and shops, is thought to keep out wandering ghosts. Seasonal worship of the land has caused many Vietnamese peasants to be radically attached to their nourishing birthplace.

Thailand annually celebrates many ceremonies and festivals that blend Buddhist and local animist beliefs. The most important Buddhist festival is *Visaka Bucha*, commemorating the birth, enlightenment, and *parinirvana* of the Buddha. The laity bring food for the monks, circumambulate the temple, and listen to recitations. Northeast Thailand performs fertility ceremonies to persuade the spirits to allow good crops. In the Royal Plowing Ceremony (held in both Thailand and Cambodia), two sacred oxen guided by the king or his emissary plow a furrow into which rice seed is sown by court Brahmins. The oxen are then offered various foods and, depending on what they eat, soothsayers predict the nature of the approaching growing season. Rockets are launched during the Rocket Festival in an attempt to induce adequate rainfall. During the annual Loy Krathong festival, offerings are set afloat to ask forgiveness from the goddess of the waters for polluting the water the previous year. Loy Krathong is syncretistic in that it reflects animistic elements in its honoring of water spirits; the Chinese Water Festival, in which candles are floated to guide home the spirits of the drowned; Hindu Diwali, which commemorates the return of Rama and Sita to Ayodhya; and occasions in the life of Siddhartha Gautama before his enlightenment when he floated a bowl upstream and left a footprint on the Nammathanati River beach in India.

Many Singaporean Chinese practice folk Daoism—a blend of ancestor veneration, Confucian ethics, devotion to local deities (but not a transcendent God), and concern for fortune-telling, divination, auspiciousness, magic, and sorcery. Finding luck is very important; feng shui, shamanism, charms, and astrology are typical methods of pursuing it. The most popular Chinese deity is doubtless Guanyin, who is thought to save from misfortune and capable particularly of granting conception to infertile women. The kitchen god (Zao Wang), who observes the family members' conduct from a kitchen wall or hearth mantel and annually reports to the heavenly Jade Emperor, is a commonly worshiped household deity. The previously mentioned Reformist Buddhism seeks to eliminate such practices and could possibly polarize Singaporean Buddhists into traditionalists and reformists.

Sources

Maung Htin Aung. *Folk Elements in Burmese Buddhism*. Oxford University Press, 1962.

David B. Barrett, George T. Kurian, and Todd M. Johnson, eds. *World Christian Encyclopedia: A Comparative Survey of Churches and Religions in the Modern World*. 2nd ed. Oxford University Press, 2001.

Ruth Gerson. *Traditional Festivals in Thailand*. Oxford University Press, 1996.

Paul Hiebert, Daniel Shaw, and Tite Tiénou. *Understanding Folk Religion: A Christian Response to Popular Beliefs and Practices*. Baker, 1999.

Jan Knappert. *Mythology and Folklore in South-East Asia*. Oxford University Press, 1999.

Siraporn Nathalang, ed. *Thai Folklore: Insights into Thai Culture*. Chulalongkorn University Press, 2000.

B. J. Terwiel. *Monks and Magic: An Analysis of Religious Ceremonies in Central Thailand*. 3rd rev. ed. White Lotus, 1994.

36

Southeast Asia: Christian Contacts

RUSSELL H. BOWERS

Christianity is a relatively new and minority faith in Southeast Asia. Only recently has it begun to make a cultural impact. But it has done so—to a degree disproportionately large in comparison with its numbers—especially in education and health care.

Beginnings to Sixteenth Century

As early as 100 BCE a trade route between India and Vietnam passed through the Straits of Malacca. Persian Nestorian and Syrian Monophysite Christians sailed among the merchants, at times accompanied by monks. Archaeology suggests the presence of such Christians as early as the seventh century in Malacca, the eleventh in central and northern Myanmar, and perhaps Thailand.

The growth of sea trade in the early sixteenth century accelerated the rate of imperial and religious change throughout Asia. Previously, empires had risen and fallen slowly, as armies conquered via land routes. But after Vasco de Gama reached India in 1498, merchants, followed by military ships, increasingly plied South and Southeast Asian waters. European merchants and military forces washed over Southeast Asia in three waves: the Portuguese in the sixteenth century, the Dutch in the seventeenth, and the British and French in the nineteenth.

In 1511 the Portuguese captured Malacca from the Muslims. A fortress guarding the strait between peninsular Malaysia and Sumatra, Malacca was key to the sea-lanes between the Indian Ocean and the China Sea. The city had served as a base for Islamic expansion to Indonesia and the southern Philippines. Now

Portuguese Catholic priests would similarly employ it, reaching as well to Japan and China. But decades were to pass before the Catholic Church began to purposefully penetrate farther south.

Catholics, Sixteenth to Nineteenth Centuries

Catholics long preceded Protestants in evangelizing Southeast Asia, and Catholicism remains the largest Christian denomination in most of its nations. Starting in 1554 they made sporadic efforts to establish missions in Myanmar, which consisted of several small Buddhist kingdoms. By the time the missionaries were forced out around 1800, they left behind two churches in Rangoon and about three thousand adherents. The Buddhists in Myanmar's south proved resistant, and the Catholics had not yet reached the more responsive animist north.

Vietnam similarly consisted of several small kingdoms, notably Tonkin in the north and Cochinchina in the south. Tonkin became the most responsive region in Southeast Asia to Christianity during this period. Fleeing persecution in Japan, Jesuit refugees arrived in 1615. Alexandre de Rhodes, who served intermittently in both Tonkin and Cochinchina in 1624–45, was preeminent among French Jesuit missionaries to Vietnam. By the time he was finally banished and persecution took hold, an estimated three hundred thousand Christians inhabited Tonkin (some consider this number inflated), and by 1680 the Catholic Church claimed eight hundred thousand adherents throughout Vietnam. La Société des Missions Étrangères de Paris, formed in 1659, helped facilitate the transition in the region from Portuguese Catholic to French influence, and from the imperial *padroado* system (in which government patronage of the church blended missions and colonialism) to one of ecclesiastical control. Despite an influx of new converts, persecution during the next two centuries cut deeply into the Christian population. Such persecution provided the pretext for French military and political intervention in the later nineteenth century.

The Jesuits entered Laos in 1642 but were forced to leave five years later. Catholic mission to Laos was not resumed until the 1870s. Progress was made, but a number of priests were killed in the following decade. An apostolic vicariate was established in 1899.

Portuguese Dominicans arrived in Cambodia in 1555. But for well over a century the few Catholics living in Cambodia were mostly expatriates—Portuguese, Japanese fleeing persecution at home, and some Vietnamese. A 1659 missionary charter directed that three apostolic bishops be sent to Asia to create a local clergy, keep in close contact with Rome, avoid meddling in politics, and adapt to local customs. But there was little effort to convert the Khmers; that would not take place for another century.

The first resident Catholic missionaries to Thailand arrived in 1567. Thailand tended to be no more receptive of Christianity than was Myanmar, though less overtly hostile. It is sometimes said that nowhere has there been less opposition to presenting the gospel than in Thailand, and nowhere has there been less response. Nevertheless, Muslim agitators, Burmese invaders, and Thai resentment against Spanish piracy led to the martyrdom of several missionaries over the next half century. But by 1665 an official attitude of religious toleration allowed the founding of a seminary for Southeast Asia. By the end of the nineteenth century Thailand was home to about thirty thousand Catholics.

Portuguese Catholics arrived in Malaysia in 1511, Xavier himself serving occasionally between 1545–52. When the Dutch took over in 1641, the bishop and priests were forced to flee to Timor. Britain replaced Holland in 1826, and the diocese of Malacca was reestablished in 1888. By the end of the nineteenth century twenty thousand Catholics lived in Malaysia.

Catholics entered British Singapore in 1821, primarily to minister to expatriate Europeans and Chinese. Shortly before mid-century, the Church of the Good Shepherd was opened, followed by the founding of mission schools.

The Catholic Church suffered a half century of significant decline throughout Asia beginning near the end of the eighteenth century. Causes were varied: the Rites Controversy in China, which caused division among the Catholic missionaries and alienation of Christian faith from local cultures; the loss of support for the church after the 1789 French Revolution; the ascendency of Protestant Britain; the church's suppression of the Jesuits and consequent loss of missionary personnel; and popular equation in some places of Christianity and Western colonialism and depravity.

Protestants, Nineteenth Century

The bulk of Protestant missions took place from the late nineteenth century onward. Private English and Dutch companies operating in Southeast Asia primarily pursued profits and often discouraged missionary work as being potentially disruptive. Later, when more comprehensive colonial governments were established,

---

Study Aid #76

Christian Contacts in Southeast Asia

Nestorians: 7th century
  Strait of Malacca
Roman Catholic Missions: 16th century
  From Portugal
  From France
Protestant Missions: 19th century
  From the Netherlands
  From England

missionaries enjoyed greater freedom to work and consequent success in their efforts. The European governments did not compel conversion of the local people but provided the political stability that allowed mission work to flourish.

English Baptists extended their Indian mission eastward to Myanmar in 1813 through Adoniram and Ann Judson. Anglicans followed in 1826 after the first Anglo-Burmese war, but their early ministry was directed to expatriate British nationals. Presbyterians arrived in 1852; Methodists, in 1879.

Anglicans also arrived in Singapore after its founding as a British port in 1819. Here as in Myanmar, their work was primarily directed toward the English community. The Presbyterians established a church in 1843; the Methodists arrived in 1885. The Anglicans and Methodists established schools for the children of immigrant workers. These, as well as those established by the Catholics, proved key to indigenizing Christianity in Singapore.

The earliest Protestant efforts in Thailand were directed primarily at resident Chinese immigrants. Sometimes missions abandoned their efforts to reach the ethnic Siamese to focus instead on the more responsive Chinese. American Presbyterian medical doctor Dan Bradley served from 1835–73; as a testimony to his impact, missionaries to Thailand are still often called *moh* (medical doctor). Medical and educational work have done more than anything else to open Thais to Christianity. The first known ethnic Siamese convert was won by the Presbyterians in 1859. By the end of the century only five thousand Protestants lived in Thailand.

A Presbyterian mission to Laos was founded in 1868. Within a year, six converts had been made, but two were killed and the rest scattered. Certain civil rights were granted to Christians in 1878.

The London Missionary Society entered Malacca in 1815 but focused its ministry on the British community. The British policy of minimal interference with local customs and affairs, and the 1874 Treaty of Pangkor with the Malay Sultans, resulted in little effort for many years to evangelize the ethnic, Islamic Malays. When the attention of missionaries finally turned outside of the expatriate community, it zeroed in instead on Chinese and Indian immigrants. As in Singapore, educational ministries to the children of these immigrants proved the most fruitful in establishing Christianity among local non-Westerners.

Twentieth Century and Beyond

The 30,000 Catholics in Thailand at the close of the nineteenth century grew to 255,000 at the close of the twentieth. Most are Vietnamese and Chinese, and about one-third live in Bangkok. The Church of Christ in Thailand, started in 1934 and today associated with the World Council of Churches, is the largest Protestant organization, with about 120,000 members. Mission schools have not been as effective in indigenizing Christianity in Thailand as they have in the former British colonies of Malaysia and Singapore. Protestants number 303,000; independents, 779,000.

> **Study Aid #77**
>
> **Southeast Asian Heroes of the Faith**
>
> Alexandre de Rhodes (Vietnam): Contextualized catechism
> Adoniram Judson (Myanmar): Indigenous church architecture
> Kosuke Koyama (Thailand): *Water Buffalo Theology*

The Christian and Missionary Alliance (CAMA) arrived in Danang, central Vietnam, in 1911. Following the mid-century rise of communism in Vietnam, many Christians, Catholic and Protestant, migrated south. After 1975 all religious groups throughout the nation faced government restrictions. Organizations such as the Institute for Global Engagement are making some progress in improving freedom to worship in the nation. But despite their efforts, persecution and repression continue, especially among the Protestant Montagnards of the Central Highlands. Examples include the 2009 middle-of-the-night destruction of the historic stone church at Buon Ma Thuot. The US State Department removed Vietnam from its list of Countries of Particular Concern in 2006. But in its 2009 annual report, the US Commission on International Religious Freedom (USCIRF) recommended its inclusion, stating that "there continue to be far too many serious abuses and restrictions of religious freedom in the country." Despite difficulties, the church continues to grow.

In 1923 the CAMA also entered Cambodia. Protestantism grew slowly until shortly before the takeover by the Khmer Rouge in 1975, then subsequently suffered great loss along with the rest of the country. A significant number of Cambodians were won to Christ in Thai refugee camps. Upon their repatriation after 1979, and particularly since the 1990 de facto legalization of Christianity, their witness has blunted the objection that Christianity is foreign. Thousands have consequently come to the faith. Many denominations, parachurch organizations, and NGOs also now work in the country. The Catholic Church, which numbered over one hundred thousand in 1950, was not very indigenized and consisted largely of Vietnamese and expatriate Westerners. It therefore suffered significant losses in the Khmer Rouge era, and numbers only about fifteen thousand today. Influences from outside Cambodia continue to foster denominational division.

Karen and other tribespeople of northern Myanmar have been more receptive to Christianity than have the southern Burmese, who are more deeply committed to Theravada. In fact, Christianity may be said to be integral to the identity not only of the Karen, but also of the Chin, Lahu, and other tribes in Myanmar and northern Thailand. Foreign missionaries were expelled from Myanmar after the military coup of 1962. Myanmar (listed as Burma) is one of eight Countries of Particular Concern. The government is accused of favoring Buddhism in an attempt to garner popular support. The Myanmar Baptist Convention is by far the largest Christian denomination, though Anglicans, Methodists, and Catholics remain active.

The Lao Evangelical Church resulted from the union in 1956 of the Swedish Protestants, the Swiss Brethren, and the CAMA. All foreign missionaries were expelled in 1975, and no contact with the outside world was permitted until 1990. Since then, membership has grown, estimated in 2006 to have reached one hundred thousand, with three hundred churches. It is the largest Protestant denomination recognized by the government. Most believers and churches are found in the rural areas. A Bible school program has been established in the capital. Persecution in Laos did not reach the intensity that it did in Vietnam or in Cambodia under the Khmer Rouge; nevertheless it remains on the "watch list" of the USCIRF. The government has labeled Christianity as an imperialist foreign religion and Christians as the number-one enemy of the state. There are credible reports of forced renunciations of Christian faith.

The important and continuing role of mission schools in Singapore has contributed to Christianity's disproportionately strong representation among the well-educated, professionals, middle class, English speakers, and private-housing dwellers. The relative wealth of both nation and church; its number of mature, educated leaders; the relatively high percentage of Christians (14.6 percent, and growing at 3.2 percent per year); the constraints of the Racial Harmony Act, which prohibits offensive action against religion; and the strong governmental social and political roles—all combine to often direct the church's ministry efforts outside Singapore's borders, particularly within the region. Both insiders and outsiders sometimes characterize the Singaporean church as the Asian Antioch. Singapore and Malaysia are the chief missionary-sending nations of this region.

Christians in Malaysia constitute 8 percent of the population (Catholics and Protestants each 3 percent; Anglicans and independents each 1 percent). But the percentage is lower in peninsular Malaysia—which is ethnically more Malay and therefore Muslim—than in East Malaysia. Because of its ethnicity, Malaysia in significant ways has more in common with Indonesia and the Philippines than it does with the rest of peninsular Southeast Asia. Peninsular Malaysians who are Christians are mostly Chinese or Indian; few are Malay.

Mission agencies in some parts of the region developed comity agreements with each other in the early twentieth century, whereby different denominations would assume responsibility for certain areas and vacate others. These agreements often worked well but are not widely observed today. The Southeast Asian Christian community has thus grown in its first centuries despite opposition from trading companies, Buddhism, Islam, and denominational rivalries.

Sources

Don Cormack. *Killing Fields, Living Fields: An Unfinished Portrait of the Cambodian Church—the Church That Would Not Die.* OMF/MARC, 1997.

Ian Gillman and Hans-Joachim Klimkeit. *Christians in Asia before 1500*. University of Michigan Press, 1999.

Robbie Goh. *Christianity in Southeast Asia*. Institute of Southeast Asian Studies, 2005.

Samuel Hugh Moffett. *A History of Christianity in Asia*. 2 vols. Orbis Books, 1998–2005.

Peter C. Phan. *Mission and Catechesis: Alexandre de Rhodes and Inculturation in Seventeenth-Century Vietnam*. Orbis Books, 1998.

Alex G. Smith. *Siamese Gold: The Church in Thailand*. Kanok Bannasan, 1981.

Scott Sunquist, ed. *A Dictionary of Asian Christianity*. Eerdmans, 2001.

37

Southeast Asia: Theological Exchanges

RUSSELL H. BOWERS

Nestorian Influence?

Scholars speculate regarding the early impact of Nestorian Christianity upon Southeast Asia. Some deny any substantial influence. Others suggest that Nestorianism may have been more spiritual and acceptable than the later Western Christianity associated with colonialists preoccupied with trade and economic exploitation. Because of the latter, Christianity came to be regarded in the minds of many as a Western, conqueror's religion. The number of Nestorians may have been relatively small, and the connection between them and present-day Christianity is obscure. But nevertheless their presence in Southeast Asia means both that the Christian faith is not as new to the region as some would argue and that Christianity was first practiced in an Asian and not a European form. The "Tradition of the Elders" regarding a Creator God and savior that predisposed the Karen to the gospel, and that is still found among other tribes in Myanmar and northeastern India, may recall Nestorian influence. But until more evidence emerges, speculations regarding Nestorian influence are likely to remain speculations.

Attempts at Contextualization

Today's statistically weak Christian presence in much of Southeast Asia results from, at least in part, disinclination on the part of Christians in the early years to enthusiastically study local culture and contextualize the Christian faith. Although some missionaries produced valuable anthropological studies, most found little

> **Study Aid #78**
> Theological Influences
> Nestorian theology
> Attempts at contextualization
> Christian social service
> Effects of colonialism

of worth in local culture and religion. The region itself was perhaps devalued—some early Protestant missionaries served in Southeast Asia only because their intended destinations (particularly China and Japan) were closed. The earliest missionaries to Thailand did not seek to win the Thais but immigrant Chinese. In Malaysia little effort was made to reach Malays compared to Chinese (and Indian) immigrants. Immigrant communities proved more receptive to the gospel than indigenous populations. In several nations earliest efforts focused first on serving the expatriate European rather than indigenous communities. Although there are exceptions, too frequently Christianity has been presented, particularly in Thailand, in forms unnecessarily Western—architecture, hymnody, structure of church services, and so on. Even Bible translation and distribution lagged. Nineteenth-century Protestant mission in Thailand has been described as characterized by attack, not accommodation, on the part of missionaries whose self-confidence doubtless struck the Thais as arrogance. Such an approach is rarely welcomed anywhere, particularly so in Thailand, where much is tolerated from foreigners except disrespect for Buddhism or the king. It violates "The Thai Way of Meekness." Even the preoccupation of the predominant Presbyterian missionaries with orthodoxy conflicted at a deep level with Thai Buddhism's stress on orthopraxis. Christianity then and now is thus often perceived as non- or even anti-Thai; conversion wrests new Christians from family, friends, and culture.

Vietnam is a different story, at least as far as the Roman Catholic Church is concerned. Key elements in Alexandre de Rhodes's strategy were respecting the good in indigenous culture, mastering the Vietnamese language, and training local converts for both evangelism and clerical ordination. His contextualized approach made Christianity understandable and acceptable to the Vietnamese people. Rhodes published a Portuguese-Latin-Vietnamese dictionary that was later used to create the romanized alphabet still used today. His statue was erected in Hanoi in 1940 (taken down in 1956), commemorating him as the creator of the national script. He urged, in Paris and Rome, that to secure lasting results, indigenous Vietnamese clergy must be appointed. The numerical success in his lifetime has been noted. And despite bouts of intense persecutions since his time, the Catholic Church remains a significant religious presence in Vietnam, with 5.3 million adherents, or 6.7 percent of the population. In addition, expatriate Vietnamese constitute significant percentages of Roman Catholics in neighboring

Cambodia and elsewhere. By contrast, an inside criticism of the Protestant Evangelical Church of Vietnam and its parent, the Christian and Missionary Alliance (CAMA), is that their theology and practice of disengagement with society, and failure to actively promote social justice, contravene Vietnamese values and have retarded the advance of the church. Such Protestantism has appeared less holistic than Vietnamese indigenous faith or even Islam.

Another exception is Myanmar, and the work of Adoniram and Ann Judson. Their decision to open a traditional *zayat* brought people in who would not have entered a mission house, and the church was born. Local converts took on the responsibility of evangelism. Adoniram Judson invested years in mastering Burmese and translating the Bible into that language. His goal was to make Christianity understandable to the Burmese mind without compromising it; part of his strategy to do this was "to preach the gospel, and *not anti-Boodhism* [emphasis in the original], and to persuade our assistants to do the same" (Wayland 1854, 112). As with Catholicism in Vietnam, despite ongoing persecution, the Protestant church in Myanmar continues in a higher percentage than elsewhere in the region; it is home to 3.7 million Christians, most of them Baptists, comprising 8.2 percent of the population.

Not all attempts at contextualization are welcomed. Some Catholic attempts at contextualization in Thailand following Vatican II, such as the use of the Buddhist term "temple" for "church," were not well received by Christian church officials.

Social Service

The church has grown not only when it has sat with local people to listen, learn, and contextualize but also when it has knelt to serve.

Singapore and Malaysia are today home to a significantly higher percentage of Christians than are Thailand, Cambodia, and Laos. In these first two the influential factor may have been the church's social services more than its contextualization efforts, as was the case in Vietnam and Myanmar. First among these are the schools it established for children of immigrant (often Chinese) workers. In 1852 the Roman Catholic Church opened Saint Joseph's Institution, a secondary school for boys, followed two years later by the Convent of the Holy Infant Jesus for girls. These (and other) schools were attended by both Catholics and non-Catholics, many of whom converted. Saint Joseph's remains one of the top secondary schools in Singapore. The Anglicans founded St. Margaret's, possibly the oldest functioning girls' school in East Asia, in 1842, followed by St. Andrew's School for boys in 1862. Methodist schools opened in 1886 and 1887 also carried on significant ministries and continue in operation today. All of these played a key role in indigenizing the Christian faith in Singapore. Similar stories could be told of schools in Malaysia. A second significant social service was medical ministry.

Cambodia provides another example of the fruitfulness of service. Church growth, particularly among the Protestants, was minimal until the eve of the Khmer Rouge takeover in 1975. During the subsequent Khmer Rouge and Vietnamese years, many Cambodians fled to Thailand. The service that Christians rendered in Thai refugee camps won many to Christ. Upon their return to Cambodia, these new and trained Christians evangelized their fellow Khmer. Ongoing outside aid after the reopening of Cambodia also broke down barriers. Stan Mooneyham (the founder of the Christian relief and development agency World Vision) once cut his arm to demonstrate to a hostile Hun Sen that under his white skin he bled the same as Cambodians; this is a classic combination of contextualization and service. The trauma of 1975–90, combined with Cambodians now hearing the message from returning Khmers rather than foreigners, led to explosive church growth—from at most one thousand Christians in 1990 to more than three hundred thousand in 2004.

Effects of Colonialism

Southeast Asian religion cannot be understood apart from some reference to colonialism. Before the coming of the West to the region, semidivine kings ruled, legitimized by the Buddhist *sangha* (the order of Buddhist monks). Colonial overlords disenfranchised the *sangha* and imposed secular governments. Twentieth-century wars, military governments, and communism further politically weakened Southeast Asian Buddhism. Nevertheless, the *sangha* remains a force. Monks were key to the downfall of Vietnam's Ngo Dimh Diem in 1963 and continued to stir political instability there for another two years. Buddhism became a unifying force against the British in early twentieth-century Myanmar and continues to oppose the present military junta.

But colonialism's interrelationship with Christianity is even more profound and complex. It has been neither wholly negative nor wholly positive. On the one hand, the greed, rapacity, and debauchery of some people associated with the "Christian" West long tainted the faith in the region. In an apt analogy, the evils of that era cling to Christians as does stale cigarette smoke to the coat of a

---

Study Aid #79

Distinctive Features of Theravada Buddhism

An emphasis on monastic life and the *arahat* (sage or saint) ideal
Pali as the liturgical language
The historical Buddha
Use of the Pali commentaries on scripture
The scholastic Abhidhamma Pitaka (part of the Theravada scriptures)
Symbiotic relationship between monarchy and monastery

> **Study Aid #80**
>
> Nestorianism
>
> Definition: A christological doctrine advanced by Nestorius, patriarch of Constantinople from 428 to 431.
>
> Key doctrine: Dyophysitism, which teaches that Jesus had two natures, one human, one divine, whereas Monophysitism teaches that he had only one nature.
>
> Heterodoxy: Nestorianism was declared a heresy by the Council of Chalcedon in 451.
>
> Mission spread: Early to Syria, then to China, India, and Southeast Asia.

nonsmoker who has spent hours closeted with those who do. To many people, even Islam, foreign as it is, is a more spiritual and legitimate religion because it came by persuasion and not at the end of a musket. The insufferable sense of Western cultural superiority exuded by some has not sat well, least of all with local Confucianists. Significant indigenous Christian leadership had difficulty emerging before the latter twentieth century.

But on the other hand, Europe did not compel conversion. The closest would be the Dutch attempts to dismantle the Catholicism left by the Portuguese. Rather, the colonial political structures in time gave missionaries a relatively safe context in which to do their work. Western linear thinking, which accords greater significance to the individual and individual choices than does typical Eastern cyclical, karmic thought, made Christianity both more understandable and desirable. This may be one reason why Christianity has done better in regions that have had extensive interaction with Western thought and that have not been long under dogmatic Theravada or Islam, such as Singapore, than those that have not. In addition, the West brought welcomed advances in education, medicine, economic development, and democracy. These, rather than colonialism's negative influences, became increasingly associated with Christianity in the years leading up to the post–World War II end of colonialism.

Religious Tendencies

Regional conversions to Christianity have also come easier from animists, Hindus (except in Bali), and practitioners of Chinese traditional religions than from convinced Buddhists or Muslims. There are complex reasons for this, ranging from the latter's genuine conviction regarding the truth or goodness of their faiths, to their desire to promote ethnic or national identity (especially when threatened from the outside). As already discussed, a summary dismissal of Buddhism as idolatrous, for example, has generally stifled rather than promoted communication and understanding. Some Protestants (as mentioned above) took this tack, but there were Catholics who did as well. Jean Baptiste Pallegoix's 1846 attack on Buddhism, *Pudcha Wischana*, is an example. To be fair, at times Buddhist hearers have displayed what could be taken as a premature, dismissive misunderstanding of Christianity. Ponchaud describes how a Buddhist superior turned from a conversation to tell a nearby elder that Catholics evidently venerated Indra and naively believed myths. Mistrusting metaphysics and theology, some Thai Buddhists misinterpret Christianity to be, at least in part, animistic. At any rate, although a few Thais, Burmese, Khmer, and Malays have become Christians, their percentages are few in comparison with the Karens or Montagnards.

Religions that successfully establish themselves in new areas generally accept and adapt at least some paradigms and values of the ideologies they displace. Tribal and other groups in Southeast Asia that assume the existence of the spirit world are thus in some ways primed to hear the Christian message, particularly as presented by charismatics. It is not surprising that charismatic Christianity constitutes a significant and growing sector of the church in the region. A holism that embraces this life's concerns, which generally is practiced in the charismatic church, also resonates with local values more than does preoccupation with only right thinking. In 2000 CE, charismatics constituted 24 percent of the Christian community in Southeast Asia. If mostly Catholic Vietnam is excluded, the number jumps to 34 percent.

Cultures that have been subject to unaccountable authoritarian rule (such as Cambodia during the Khmer Rouge era) may find themselves accepting of similar church rule. In recent decades the church of South Korea has increasingly sent missionaries overseas, including to Southeast Asia. Hope has been expressed that as Korean missionaries come with all their commitment and significant contributions, they will not repeat the errors of European and American missionaries of a century ago, who often imposed their culture as they presented the gospel.

Sources

John R. Davis. *Poles Apart? Contextualizing the Gospel in Asia*. Theological Book Trust, 1998.

Paul Hattaway. *Peoples of the Buddhist World*. Piquant, 2004.

David Lim, Steve Spaulding, and Paul De Neui, eds. *Sharing Jesus Effectively in the Buddhist World*. William Carey Library, 2005.

François Ponchaud. *The Cathedral of the Rice Paddy: 450 Years of History of the Church in Cambodia*. Fayard, 1990.

Poh Boon Sing. *The Christian in the Chinese Culture*. 2nd ed. Good News Enterprise, 1989.

Bobby E. K. Sng and Chee Pang Choong, eds. *Church and Culture: Singapore Context*. Graduates' Christian Fellowship, 1991.

Stephen Taylor. "A Prolegomena for the Thai Context: A Starting Point for Thai Theology." ThD dissertation, International Theological Seminary, Los Angeles, CA, 2003.

David Hock Tey. *Chinese Culture and the Bible*. Here's Life Books, 1988.

Tu Thien Van Truong. "Mệnh Trời: Toward a Vietnamese Theology of Mission." PhD dissertation, Graduate Theological Union, Berkeley, CA, 2009.

Francis Wayland. *A Memoir of the Life and Labors of the Rev. Adoniram Judson, D.D.* 2 vols. Phillips, Sampson, 1854.

38

Southeast Asia: Current Issues

Russell H. Bowers

Internal Issues

The church in Southeast Asia needs to press ahead with increasing its theological sophistication. At present, Singapore seems poised to continue to lead. The nation's theological and philosophical accomplishments are impressive and increasing. Malaysian and other regional theologians have contributed, of course, as well. But Singapore and Malaysia are not typical of the entire region. Each nation's church ministers in an individually distinctive situation. Each must understand, articulate, and practice the Christian faith in its unique terms and ways. Translation of Western theologies and commentaries continues in the region, which is fine. But developing local, contextualized theology, a project much discussed and universally agreed upon, must be more aggressively accomplished. It must go beyond putting an Asian face on Western content, since outside theologies often miss whole genres of local thought; Southeast Asian theological and practical concerns are not easily pigeonholed into others' categories.

Premier interdenominational theological institutions include Singapore's Trinity Bible College, whose faculty has published significantly, and Seminari Theoloji Malaysia. The faculties of both schools hold terminal degrees from institutions around the world. About half of the faculty members are Methodist, and more than a quarter are either Anglican or Presbyterian.

For millennia Southeast Asia has had an oral culture, whose traditions have only recently been reduced to print. As well, some Christians are more concerned with the practical living out of their faith than with reflecting on and writing about it. Theological writing is done in a wide range of formats, and not exclusively in books and journal articles. In places where relationship and the affective are valued more than data and the cognitive, world*feel* might trump world*view*. For these reasons it would be premature to conclude that paucity of writing reflects poverty of Christian experience. But a thoughtful, written intra-Asian Christian dialogue would enrich all parties—those who write and those who read. Indigenous theology will demonstrate that Christianity is not foreign; one can be thoroughly Asian and truly Christian.

Rich, contextual thought has been produced throughout the years, from Theodore Thanbyah's writings on Karen themes, to "Banana Theology" in Malaysia and "Water Buffalo Theology" in Thailand, to Batumalai Satayandy's work in "neighborology" and "goodwill," to Vietnam's doctrine of the "Three Fathers" (relating, in this land of Confucian filial piety, father, king, and creator), and the poetry of Hàn Mac Tu. One can only hope such creative work continues.

Not unique to Southeast Asia, but nevertheless an issue here, is the task of *understanding and assuming its place in the worldwide church*. In places where struggling congregations stagnate out of deference to foreign missionary culture, locally appropriate leaders and practices must replace inherited ones. By contrast, where local ministries have achieved great maturity, they need not divorce themselves from all outside input. The "body of Christ" metaphor applies to nations as well as congregations: each part has both strengths and weaknesses. In short, the Southeast Asian church must continue down the path of viewing itself and functioning as a partner in the universal church—neither a junior nor a senior partner, but a partner.

One specific way in which Singapore in particular has increasingly participated in the universal church's mandate is missions. In part because Singapore's strong government has taken responsibility for the nation's social needs, the church's attention has focused outside national borders. Numerous missions projects continue to be undertaken—mostly within the region. Whether working in inner-city slums or remote mountain villages, such efforts are as cross-cultural for Singaporeans as they would be for anyone else. The Malaysian church also undertakes significant cross-cultural missions. One may find, for example, Malaysian missionaries working among Cambodian slum dwellers.

Another issue southeast Asian churches grapple with is unity. When Cambodia reopened to outsiders in 1990, a problem developed of certain denominations entering and "buying" local churches, possibly to pad the buying denomination's statistics. Not infrequently, another denomination might later make a better offer, and those congregations might again switch their allegiance. One hopes that such unbiblical practices are few and decreasing, but where they persist they must be weeded out. Aside from such blatant abuses, competition rather than cooperation characterizes some areas. It can be confusing and discouraging for people simultaneously hearing of the Christian faith for the first time from different sources, each claiming to be truer than the others. Some denominations struggle to maintain small training schools, resulting in inefficiency and duplication of effort. The comity agreements of the last century might again be explored as one solution; charity is another.

A third internal need remains *leadership development.* Whether because of explosive numerical growth in some areas, government persecution of leaders in others, or the influx of cults in still others, more trained pastors are needed. The best training for most pastoral situations is that which is done within the local context, includes practical service, and does not end up exalting the graduate to an economic or social tier above that of the congregation.

It would not be possible for someone outside the region to say this, but the assessment of one respected senior Asian leader is that the church's most basic problems are its own internal weakness and spiritual poverty—the nominal commitment of second- and third-generation Christians, disunity that wastes resources, confused theology, and the twin but opposite dangers of demonizing and uncritically accepting competing world religions.

External Issues

The church must address the following *philosophical and religious* issues in its interaction with non-Christians: (1) Clearer articulation of the Christian message in images and terms that resonate with the local people. Although there were exceptions, many early missionaries viewed Southeast Asian culture and beliefs negatively and made little attempt to understand them or contextualize their message. There are still those—whether Western or now Korean—who continue this approach. Misunderstandings still occur at the deepest levels. Hence the gospel must be articulated in terms that make sense to the hearers. Because Christians sometimes cocoon after conversions, second- and third-generation churches often do not know how to introduce themselves or relate to non-Christians of their own culture. (2) The development of a variety of unique apologetic works that address

---

Study Aid #81
Current Issues

Internal issues
  Developing contextual theologies
  Local vs. global church
  Unity of the church
  Leadership development
External issues
  Competing missions, Christian and Muslim
  Overcoming polemical attacks gracefully
  Living in religiously plural cultures

each community's faith and worldview. For example, while officially the Malaysian government discourages the denigration of any religion, increasingly nuanced polemics against Christianity are regularly made. These call not for a rehearsal of general apologetics but for specific Christian responses. Interaction at this level is not easy in Malaysia, where government support for Islam is so strong. But it must be done. Ng Kam Weng of Malaysia's Kairos Research Centre is one of those leading the way in this. For another example, the church needs to work to understand the link between postmodernism and Buddhism, and then formulate a response. Postmodern nihilism's deconstruction of the human person into nothing more than a bundle of "desires" with no underlying permanent substance resonates with the classic Buddhist view. A consequent search for a wisdom that transcends the spiritual emptiness, frenetic activity, and meaninglessness of much of modern life may therefore easily lead to Buddhism. This may be one reason behind that faith's recent rapid growth in Taiwan, China, and Singapore. The church must articulate its own answer to this viewpoint, particularly for the sake of more thoughtful Buddhists such as university students. Again, these examples point to the need of specific, focused, regional apologetic work. (3) A frank appraisal of the tension between the Christian Great Commission and Islamic *da'wa*, the mandate to call outsiders to Islam. *Da'wa* is a major preoccupation of the Islamic resurgence in Malaysia. Such mission brings Islam and Christianity into competition and, too often, conflict. Christians and Muslims need to honestly admit this tension and formulate what the ground rules will be. (4) Further work on defining the principles governing Christian participation in, or avoidance of, local Buddhist, Chinese, or folk ceremonies, including holidays, weddings, and funerals. This is a practical concern frequently voiced by grassroots Christian leaders. It is part of the larger question of what should be the Christian's philosophy of interaction with members of non-Christian faiths in a pluralist society. (5) Development of a theology of the spirit world. (6) Navigation of the tension between increasing pluralism, secularism, and religious openness on the one hand, and the resurgence of Buddhism, Islam, and various fundamentalist sects on the other.

Cultural matters of concern include the following: (1) Strengthening marriage and the home. An extreme example is the dysfunctionality foisted upon Cambodian families during the Pol Pot years, when the communists destroyed all sense of community. But voices throughout the region agree that the attitude toward family needs to be strengthened in the face of undermining cultural currents. One specific recurring question asked is, since there are so few Christian men, whom are Christian women to marry? A second is, in societies where deference to the aged is the norm, how should a Christian young person respond to a parent who insists that he or she marry a Buddhist? And a third is, how can the practice of family members selling their daughters and nieces into prostitution be stopped? (2) Clarifying the distinctions between Christianity and the West, and between Christianity and colonialism. Many Southeast Asians view Jesus as the Western god and the Buddha as theirs. Many Muslims equate (perceived) Western materialism, decadence, and exploitation with Christianity. Asians, who view life holistically regardless of their religious affiliation, often look with disdain upon the moral depravity and practical atheism of powerful professing Christians in their midst, both past and present. Memories of the greed and immorality of some colonialists cause Christianity to be perceived as lacking the authenticity of Islam, Buddhism, and primal folk religion. It will be helpful to remind local people of Christianity's Asian provenance and early expressions, as well as its distinction from Western accretions and aberrations. (3) Discussing what Christian conduct should be in those cultures where bribery is expected.

The *political* environments among the Southeast Asian nations vary, and each nation's church must adapt appropriately. In 1992, Singapore's Maintenance of Religious Harmony Bill, under which the state may restrain anyone who causes ill feelings among the various religious groups or who under the guise of religion promotes a political cause, took effect. Singapore also employs censorship to preempt religious tensions, having barred, for example, the film *The Last Temptation of Christ* and the book *The Satanic Verses*. Because Christianity is the most recent of the major religions to arrive in force in Southeast Asia, and because it has greater ties than do Buddhism and Islam to foreign ideas and input, it is sometimes suspected of being a destabilizing force. Islamic societies, such as Malaysia, and countries that have sustained ideological or military conflict with America, such as Vietnam, Laos, and Myanmar, are particularly wary of Western influence, perceived or actual. In Malaysia the church may face a cold shoulder or hostility, but in parts of Vietnam, Laos, and Myanmar, very real persecution.

Social concerns include poverty and exploitation, including the above-mentioned problem of families selling children into prostitution and the corruption that turns a blind eye to it. Malaysia Baptist Theological Seminary's 2001 development of its MA degree in holistic child development may help with this. Rapid urbanization, environmental degradation, HIV and AIDS, and drug use are other social problems that the church must address. Socially, Christianity could provide a unique model for Malaysia. That nation is not so much a melting pot as it is a collection of distinct, self-contained cultures. Islam is 99 percent ethnically Malay (and other *bumiputras*); Buddhism, 98 percent Chinese; Hinduism, 99 percent Indian; Chinese traditional religions, 99 percent Chinese. The Christian church is different: it embraces members from all of these ethnicities. If it could do this well, the church could provide a model for the nation of a genuine unity that embraces multiracial diversity.

Interreligious Dialogue

Islamic revivalism has intensified the need for Christian-Muslim dialogue in Malaysia. Nineteenth- through mid-twentieth-century Christian failure to target ethnic Malays confirmed and strengthened their self-understanding as Muslims.

> **Study Aid #82**
>
> Indigenous Asian Theologies
>
> Karen Theology
>   Theodore Thanbyah, Burma
> Banana Theology
>   Hwa Yung, Malaysia
> Water Buffalo Theology
>   Kosuke Koyama, Thailand
> Neighborology
>   Batumalai Satayandy, Malaysia
> Three Fathers Theology
>   Han Muc Tu, Vietnam
> Meekness Theology
>   Ubolwon and Nantachai Medjuhon

Islam's social and political force in Malaysia positions it as a potential threat to the minority Christian community. Unfortunately, the Malaysian church has invested inadequate attention to understanding and engaging its larger context, including Islam, often because of preoccupation with denominational differences and with addressing aspects of the charismatic movement that resemble local spirit-medium cults. The push to produce evangelistic workers has inclined theological schools toward methodological and "practical" studies rather than theological reflection and dialogue. The nation needs more scholars with expertise in Islamic studies and relations. Because of the intimidation that flows out of Malay Muslim sensitivities and political dominance, Christian educators find it less stressful to focus on internal Christian theological concerns. Unfortunately, such self-imposed marginalization will render the Christian community increasingly irrelevant.

Reluctance to aggressively dialogue may grow out of Christian fear of losing rights and freedom of movement within the country, and Muslim fear of losing numerical ground. Malaysian ambivalence toward non-Muslim use of the national language stems partly from desire to protect Malays from Christian influence, but it results in isolating Christians from national life and culture. Malaysian Christians tend to make little use of local art, since what is Malaysian is often perceived as Islamic, and Muslims prefer the lines of demarcation to be clear. This equation of Malay identity and Islam makes contextualization difficult. Church architecture resorts to quasi-European forms, while Christian art remains undeveloped. As a regional contrast to the social strictures under which the Malaysian church operates, in the nearby and largely Catholic Philippines, the church supported the 1986 overthrow of Ferdinand Marcos. The political realities of peninsular Southeast Asia are quite different: the Malaysian, Singaporean, and other churches must be much more circumspect.

Similarly in southern Thailand, Buddhist-Muslim dialogue is weak; there seems to be little effort on the part of Christians and Muslims there to understand each other.

Southeast Asia in general is characterized by openness to nonmaterial realities, but difficulty in accepting exclusive claims. In many of its subcultures lies embedded a preference for bending truth so as not to lose face or cause another to lose face. Cultures influenced by Confucianism are likely to display particular respect for authority and the family. There is a great deal of local ethnic, cultural, and religious diversity. There are also a great many people yet to be reached. Dialogue that is built on respect and a genuine effort to hear as well as speak may prove one of the more culturally appropriate means of communication.

Sources

Saphir Athyal, ed. *Church in Asia Today: Challenges and Opportunities.* Lausanne, 1996.

Russell H. Bowers, ed. *Folk Buddhism in Southeast Asia.* Phnom Penh, 2004.

John C. England, ed. *Asian Christian Theologies: A Research Guide to Authors, Movements, Sources.* Vol. 2, Southeast Asia. SPCK, 2003.

Listening to Voices from Inside: Myanmar Civil Society's Response to Cyclone Nargis. Centre for Peace and Conflict Studies, 2009.

Robert Day McAmis. *Malay Muslims: The History and Challenge of Resurgent Islam in Southeast Asia.* Eerdmans, 2002.

Kam Weng Ng. *The Quest for Covenant Community and Pluralist Democracy in an Islamic Context.* Edited by Mark L. Y. Chan. Trinity Theological College, 2008.

39

North Asia: History, Beliefs, Practices

SEBASTIAN KIM

Although major religious traditions in Japan and Korea, which include Buddhism, Confucianism, and Daoism, have been very much influenced by China until the modern period, both countries have developed their own indigenous religions: Shinto in Japan and shamanism in Korea, among other folk religions. The major institutionalized religions in Japan are Shintoism and Buddhism, with 83.3 percent and 71.4 percent, respectively, of the population of 126 million. The total number of adherents exceed 100 percent because some people regard themselves as affiliated with both religious traditions. Sixty percent of people have either a Buddhist altar or a Shinto shrine in their house, or both. Christians constitute 2 percent of the population, and other religions, mainly from migrant and ethnic groups, make up 7.8 percent. In South Korea, Christianity is 29.2 percent (Protestants, 18.3 percent; Catholics, 10.9 percent), Buddhists 22.8 percent, and other religions 1.3 percent of the population of 48 million. Any religious activity in North Korea is severely restricted, and there is little known about religious practice there.

Shinto, Buddhism, and Folk Religions in Japan

As early as the third century, the Japanese people had formulated a degree of common identity and culture along the lines of clan and their *kami* (spirits or deities), which were manifested through myths and folk stories. The collection of these myths established some of the foundational ideas for the institutionalization of Shintoism, providing motifs for worship, rituals, and concepts of deities. These

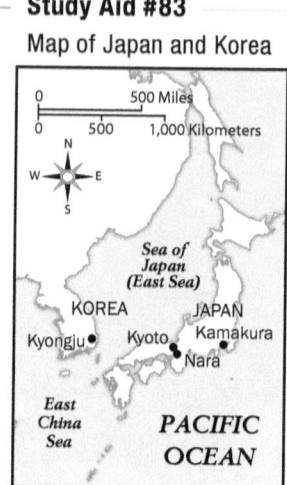

Study Aid #83
Map of Japan and Korea

gradually developed through nationwide religious tradition in the seventh century and the establishment of the regulations of Shinto in the tenth century. After the arrival of Buddhism in the sixth century, the two religions coexisted in an uneasy relationship of mutual accommodation, with each tradition being influenced by the other. But in 1868, with the restoration of imperial rule, Shinto became the official state religion, separate from Buddhism, and Shinto nationalistic ideology became a guiding principle of the Japanese people. State Shinto was abolished in 1945, although unofficial links between Shinto, the imperial family, and the government remain. Shinto religion takes several forms: Shrine Shinto, which represents the vast majority; sect Shinto, a movement arising out of the Tokugawa and Meiji periods, which promised to produce worldly benefits such as healing, wealth, and success; folk Shinto, practiced by a wide range of common people, and incorporating various superstitions, taboos, and magical aspects; and the Shinto of the imperial household, focused on the rites for imperial ancestors. Shinto is closely related to national unity and identity. Shrines serve as community centers. Currently, there are about eighty thousand Shinto shrines in Japan.

The Mahayana form of Buddhism arrived in the sixth century, via Korea. After initial resistance from Shinto authorities, the Japanese rulers embraced the new religion and built many temples in the capital city of Nara. Japanese Buddhism developed during three eras: Nara, Heian, and Kamakura. Kamakara was especially creative, with Buddhist innovators such as Honen, Shinran, Dogen, and Nichiren emerging from its ranks. There have been various sects within Buddhist traditions as well as new forms such as Zen Buddhism, Jodo-kyo Buddhism, and Nichiren Buddhism. Zen Buddhism was the most popular form of Mahayana Buddhism in its initial introduction to Japan and later became two different groups: Rinzai and Soto. Jodo-kyo Buddhism, or Pure Land Buddhism, emphasized the Buddha who leads to the "pure land" and then on to *nirvana*. Nichiren Buddhism was initiated by the monk Nichiren, who was a progressive thinker, and it later split into several groups, including a controversial movement called Soka Gakkai, started in 1930. Soka Gakkai currently has ten million followers, and the conservative New Komeito Party is its political wing.

Shinto—"the way of the gods"—originated in prehistoric times and is characterized by the worshiping of *kami*. Shinto has no founder, no official sacred scriptures, and no systematic doctrines. *Kami* are associated with various supernatural and sacred forms of life, including human ancestors, spirit figures, and the natural forces of mountains, rivers, trees, and rocks. They are not separated from humans, but closely related, and share intimate interactions. A baby's early birthdays are celebrated in the local Shinto shrine, and also the beginning of adulthood at the age of twenty. Wedding ceremonies are traditionally conducted by Shinto priests, but Western and other forms of weddings are also popular, and the majority of weddings take place in wedding halls. Most of Japanese funerals are conducted by Buddhist priests. Noted Buddhist scholars developed Japanese art and culture.

Religious doctrines are not emphasized by most Japanese, but they manifest high levels of religious participation in daily life through family rituals and visits to shrines and temples. In the history of Japanese religion, different religions are inclusive and complementary, as the Japanese incorporated and assimilated various religious faiths and practices into their daily lives. Japanese religious practice includes multiple belonging, typically between Shinto and Buddhism, but can be extended to other religious practices as well. There are large numbers of religious organizations and sects, and people often have multiple memberships in these traditions. In particular, visiting local shrines and temples for prayers and good fortune at specific times of the year or at the time of annual festivals is very common in Japanese religious patterns. The two most important occasions are the New Year festival (Hatsumode), when people visit shrines and temples to pray for good fortune in the coming year, and the summer festival of Obon, which is the occasion of families getting together to honor their ancestors and visit the family temple. About 80 percent of the whole population participates in these two festivals, which are cultural and social as well as religious activities characterized by celebration, regeneration, and purification. Rituals of purification are a vital part of Shinto. They are believed to be cleansing the impurity accumulated by daily life and are performed on a regular basis. Ritual purification is done at a shrine daily as a ceremony of offerings and prayers. This is also done by water purification while reciting prayers and simultaneously washing one's hands and mouth under a waterfall, river, or other running water.

The traditional role of community and belonging determines individual affiliation to either a Shinto shrine or a Buddhist temple. Though in recent years the units of family, local community, and village have loosened, the bond of the household still remains very strong, and the religious activities, while not necessarily holding

> **Study Aid #84**
> Religions of Korea and Japan
>
> Japan
> Shinto: 83 percent
> Buddhism: 72 percent
> Christianity: 2 percent
> Other: 8 percent
> South Korea
> Shamanism: 9 percent (100 percent influence)
> Confucianism: 0.2 percent (100 percent influence)
> Christianity: 29 percent
> Buddhism: 23 percent
> Other: 1 percent

religious significance, reinforce the social and cultural bonds within and outside family ties. Buddhism is often associated with the rites relating to funerals; Shinto, with nationalist militarism—especially during the Second World War, but even today for many. Christianity and other religions with exclusive approaches to other religions and active evangelism are not in keeping with Japanese religious traditions. In general, Japanese are willing to be involved in religious activities and events but do not wish to be associated with institutionalized religion or zealous approaches to faith. People perform the rituals with sincerity and purity of mind, which are very important to Japanese religiosity, but in the main, religion is situational and complementary to contexts of birth, death, marriage, and other passages of life. This does not mean that beliefs are not important but rather that action precedes beliefs and gives meaning to the latter. There is an experimental attitude and fluidity to religion, and the concepts of deities are not necessarily cognitive beliefs but rather are bound by cultural and social traditions and the sense of belonging.

In addition to the two major established religions of Shinto and Buddhism, there are various folk religions, which are very much integrated into the lives of people through family, society and festivals, ceremonies, magic, and taboos. These are very much shamanistic in nature, seeking for the good fortune and well-being of the individual and family. In general, Japanese religions evince an emphasis on filial piety, an inclusive approach to different religious traditions, and a strong connection with ancestor worship.

Shamanism, Buddhism, and Confucianism in Korea

The dominant belief system in ancient Korea was shamanistic; shamans were intermediaries who contacted the ancestors, who, with the spirits and demons, were regarded as present in every object in the world, seen and unseen. With the introduction of Buddhism and Confucianism, shamanism faded away from the public domain, but the beliefs were assimilated into the organized religions and became deeply rooted in the religiosity of Koreans. The Korean primal or folk religion is regarded as influenced by Siberian shamanism, along with the patterns of early indigenous agricultural society. The belief in Hanullim, a supreme and heavenly divine figure, was elaborated in Korea's creation myth, Dangun, in the time of ancient Chouson, and various versions of this were developed according to different kingdoms as the kings of Puyo, Koguryo, Kaya, and Silla all claimed their divine right to rule. In the tribal period, religious practices were concentrated on the offering of prayers for a good harvest, for healing of disease and casting out evil spirits, and for dealing with ancestors and the souls of family members who died recently.

In modern South Korea, the activities of shamans, ritual leaders, and fortune-tellers continue to be deeply rooted among ordinary people. Their presence is not very obvious, however, as they are not respectable, and their practice is regarded as superstitious and premodern. Female shamans often play the role of calling the spirit of a dead person, mediating between the living and the dead, and predicting the future of customers. Among various activities, *kut*, or exorcism, ceremonies are held as large-scale village events or on a small scale in houses, and there are various types, according to clients' requests and needs. Various colors of costumes and flags are used. The color white refers to the supreme heavenly divine being, red to the mountain god, blue to the heavenly generals, and yellow to the ancestors. Drums and other musical instruments are played, and food and traditional liquors are offered. There has been increasing interest among the general public about *kut* in Korean political and cultural life as a part of the revival of Korean national identity.

Buddhism was introduced in 327 CE. It soon became the state religion of the Three Kingdoms and was regarded as giving spiritual endorsement to the authorities. During the Koryo Dynasty, when Korea was united, Buddhism received strong support from the monarchy and the aristocrats, and it inspired rich art, literature, and architecture. Although Buddhism suffered under the policies of the Confucian leaders of Chosun, and was forced to the periphery of political and urban life, it has remained a dominant religion for Koreans. In

Study Aid #85

Korean Shamanism

Muism: Indigenous term for Korean shamanism, also called Sinism.

Mudang: A Korean shaman, often a woman, who acts as intermediary between adherents and the spirit world.

Kut: Various rituals seeking blessings of the spirits for human subjects.

more recent years, Buddhism has been experiencing a revival among the younger generation. Buddhism is stronger in the east of South Korea, in the Youngnam and Kangwon provinces, and the most dominant group (about 90 percent) is the Chogye Order.

Although Confucianism was introduced to Korea as early as the Three Kingdoms period, it became the official ideology only in the Chosun Dynasty, which developed a Confucian system of education, ceremony, and civil administration. Toward the end of the dynasty there was criticism of the close integration of government officials and Confucian scholars, which was contributing to corruption, and of the internal rivalry among different schools, which hampered the smooth operation of government. Confucianism, with its philosophical and cultural vigor, had recently been reintroduced into the modern and diverse society of South Korea and was adopted by the new rulers. Only 0.2 percent of contemporary South Koreans identify themselves as belonging to Confucianism as a religion, but the influence of Confucian ethical and social teachings is very significant in the private, family, village, and national lives of Koreans.

There is also an indigenous religion, Cheondogyo (the religion of the heavenly way), which was related to the Donghak movement, a reform movement among the poor peasants in the southwest region in the mid-nineteenth century, and which upholds one supreme God, Hanullim, in response to foreign influence in Korean society. It incorporates ideas from Confucianism, Buddhism, shamanism, Daoism, and Catholicism, and it played a major role, along with Christianity, in the Korean nationalist movement against Japanese rule. Cheondogyo's essential beliefs include the equality of human beings, the belief in a supreme being, and the deity's healing power. Followers believe that believers are identified with the supreme being through reverencing the spirit and that humans are identical with heaven and with God. They also hold that the manifestation of heaven can be achieved here and now by means of social and political action. All members take part in private daily morning prayer in front of an altar.

Sources

Robert E. Buswell Jr., ed. *Religions of Korea in Practice*. Princeton University Press, 2007.

James Huntley Grayson. *Korea: A Religious History*. Rev. ed. Routledge, 2002.

Helen Hardacre. *Shintō and the State, 1868–1988*. Princeton University Press, 1989.

Ichiro Hori. *Folk Religion in Japan: Continuity and Change*. University of Chicago Press, 1983.

Chongho Kim. *Korean Shamanism: The Cultural Paradox*. Ashgate, 2003.

Lewis R. Lancaster and Richard K. Payne, eds. *Religion and Society in Contemporary Korea*. Institute of East Asian Studies, University of California, 1997.

Earl H. Phillips and Eui-Young Yu, eds. *Religions in Korea: Beliefs and Cultural Values*. Center for Korean-American and Korean Studies, California State University, 1982.

Ian Reader. *Religion in Contemporary Japan*. University of Hawaii Press, 1990.

Ian Reader and George Tanabe Jr. *Practically Religious: Worldly Benefits and the Common Religion of Japan*. University of Hawaii Press, 1998.

Paul Swanson and Clark Chilson, eds. *Nanzan Guide to Japanese Religions*. University of Hawaii Press, 2006.

40

North Asia: Christian Contacts

SEBASTIAN KIM

In North Asia, Catholic Christianity was first introduced to Japan through Western missionaries and to Korea through a Korean who visited China, and then by foreign missionaries. Both countries witnessed severe persecutions of Catholic Christians by the government authorities, from which the communities took centuries to recover. Missionaries of Protestant and other denominations who arrived in the late nineteenth century were relatively well accepted by the governments and the general public, though they too went through a difficult time during the Pacific War in both Japan and Korea, and during the Korean War. Christian activities in both nations were strongly controlled by the Japanese authorities in the early twentieth century, but since the 1950s, believers have experienced religious freedom, except under the harsh atheistic regime of North Korea.

Introduction of Catholic and Protestant Christianity in Japan

The first Japanese to respond to the message of Jesus Christ was a fugitive named Anjiro, who searched Southeast Asia to find the great Jesuit missionary Francis Xavier and persuaded him to come to Japan. The Christian message was well received at the court of the Daimyo Ouchi Yoshitaka, who traded with the Portuguese through the port of Nagasaki. During the following "Christian century," a faith that was adapted to Japan spread to the capital city Kyoto, and by 1614 there was probably a larger proportion of Christians in Japan than there is estimated to be now. However, subsequent rulers persecuted Christians; all churches were closed, all Christian practice—in public or in secret—was prohibited, and Christians were tortured in order to produce apostasy—often by treading on an image of Christ. The suffering of the period has been captured by Shusaku Endo in his novel *Silence*, which has been very widely read in Japan and around the world. According to one estimate, about half of the Catholics in Japan today are descendants of those who hid their faith for the next two centuries. When Catholic missionaries reentered the country in 1859, now led by the Paris Missionary Society, they made contact with the "hidden Christians," especially around Nagasaki. While many rejoined the Roman Catholic Church, a much larger proportion—mainly islanders—chose to keep attending the Buddhist temples and to maintain the practices they had evolved while keeping their faith secret. About thirty thousand remain today.

Protestant churches were planted after Japan opened selected ports to foreign settlement, at first by American missionaries: Episcopalians, Presbyterians, (Dutch) Reformed, Methodists, and some independent Baptists. Most Japanese continued to be suspicious of foreigners, and anti-Christian edicts were still in place, so very few converted. A Russian Orthodox mission that began in 1861 made better progress; by 1875 there were already two Japanese priests. Educational work attracted more and helped to produce some outstanding leaders, who were formed in the Student Christian Bands. Progressive thinkers understood Christianity to be the secret of the West's success, but the enthusiasm for Christianity soon cooled with the rise of Japanese nationalism. During the next fifty-five years, as Japan built up its military power and expanded its empire across East Asia, Christians sometimes resisted but more often accommodated the growing militarization and imperial conquest. Churches sent missionaries to help Christians in occupied countries. Most Catholics and Protestants also complied with the requirements for Shinto shrine worship and observance of the emperor cult, even making theological justification for the practice.

Church Unity and Ecumenical Movement in Japan

From as early as 1877, some of the mission churches had united in an ecumenical spirit, but it was the threat of organizational extinction by the government, as war threatened and the regulations on denominations tightened, that resulted in almost all the Protestant churches joining together in 1941 to make a single United Church of Christ in Japan (Nihon Kirisuto Kyodan). The church retains the core of the union—Reformed, Methodist, and Congregational churches—and remains the largest single denomination today. After the end of the Pacific War, several thousand foreign missionaries entered the country, leading to a proliferation of smaller churches, but not to significant long-term increases in the proportion of Christians.

The Protestant churches in Japan have spawned many indigenous groups. The earliest, the Nonchurch Movement founded by Uchimura Kanzo in 1901, was primarily a prophetic reaction against the foisting of foreign denominational divisions and extrabiblical practices on Japanese Christians. The founders of the Way (1907)

> **Study Aid #86**
>
> **Christian Contacts in Japan**
>
> Early Catholic: 17th century
>   Jesuits the first to actively do mission work in Japan
>   Frances Xavier, persecutions
> Indigenous: Early 19th century
>   Uchimura Kanzo starts indigenous movement
> Protestants: Late 19th century
>   Western missionaries gain access to country

and Christ Heart Church (1927) rebelled against the institutionalism of Western religion and its exclusivism, insisting that the scriptures of various Asian religions were also vehicles of revelation and adopting traditional Japanese religious practices. Later indigenous churches have been more oriented to popular religiosity and were more Pentecostal or charismatic in nature, such as the Restorationist-style Spirit of Jesus Church (1941). This church and some others have evolved ways of relating to the world of the dead, which was the function of traditional ancestor veneration. Japan has its share of neo-Pentecostal movements; some of these come from among the substantial Korean minority and from South Korea itself. There are now more than three times as many Protestants as Catholics in Japan.

Although Japanese Christians are numerically a small minority, their contribution to the modernization of Japan is commonly acknowledged. Disproportionate numbers of Christians have contributed to education and social welfare. Tetsu Katayama became Japan's first socialist (and Christian) prime minister in 1947. As a Christian pacifist he effectively put a stop to the remilitarization desired by the Americans and some other Japanese. Christians have also campaigned for the rights of minorities such as the indigenous Ainu people in Hokkaido. Although the Kyodan (the United Church of Christ) and other churches began in 1967 to admit their wartime collaboration, they have yet to succeed in persuading the wider society to deal with it to the satisfaction of neighboring countries.

Establishment of Catholic and Protestant Churches in Korea

The mountainous and tightly controlled Korean peninsula was difficult for foreign missionaries to penetrate and not high on their agenda, but in both the Protestant and the Catholic cases, Koreans took the initiative to bring Christianity to their homeland. In 1784 Yi Seung-Hun, a Korean student in Beijing, was baptized by a Catholic priest and returned home to start a church himself. In this period after the Chinese Rites Controversy, Korean converts were instructed to stop their traditions of ancestor worship. This set them at odds with their rulers, and Catholics were subjected to several waves of persecution, culminating in 1866 with the deaths of at least a quarter of the Catholic population. In 1984 eight thousand Korean martyrs were canonized en masse, giving Korea the fourth largest number of martyrs of any country in the world.

Almost one hundred years after Yi's baptism, a Protestant convert named Suh Sang-Yun risked his life to carry copies of a translation of Luke's Gospel into Korea. In this highly Confucian culture, the new book was read avidly, and the first Protestant church began. A year or so later, in 1885, under pressure from foreign powers, the government permitted the first foreign missionaries to enter. The "three-self" (self-governing, self-supporting, and self-propagating) missionary policy shared by all the main missions from 1893 was taken equally seriously by Korean Christians, who started local congregations, schools, and hospitals across the country. Much of the pioneer work was done by women's fellowships and by "Bible women"—lay women evangelists. In a transitional period they represented the forces of modernization, and as the rapid rise of Japan threatened Korean independence, this offered a sign of hope.

In 1907 a revival broke out in Pyongyang, now capital of North Korea, and an indigenous Christianity was born. The chief characteristic of Korean Christianity was its unquestioning approach to the biblical text, employing Confucian methods of repeated reading and memorization to study it. Reading the Bible, Christian converts saw parallels between their situation of subjection to Japan and the experience of the Israelites, and revival leader Kil Son-Ju and other Christians initiated the independence movement of March 1, 1919. The movement failed, but it sealed the Protestant churches' association with nationalism. During the period of Japanese occupation (1910–45), the churches kept the millennial hope of liberation alive, especially through another revival movement led by Lee Yong-Do from 1928 to 1933. Some Christians resisted the imposition of Shinto shrine worship, believing it contravened the first commandment; at least fifty were killed and others imprisoned.

In the aftermath of the Second World War, atheistic communism took hold in the North, although the revolutionary leader Kim Il Sung had come from a Christian family. All religious activity was prohibited, and today little is known for certain about the state of Christianity in North Korea, which remains a closed state. Many Christian men fled south and founded new churches among the displaced there, but reconstruction of church and nation was halted by the outbreak of North-South hostilities in 1950. After the war, under leaders such as Presbyterian pastor Han Kyung-Chik—one of the refugees from the North—the mainline evangelical churches committed themselves to evangelistic and social work, for which Han Kyung-Chik was awarded the Templeton Prize in 1992. Because they shared the government's fear of communism and looked favorably on the United States, pastors in South Korea encouraged their congregations to support the government in its drive for modernization. Remembering the suffering of Jesus Christ on the cross, which they believed lifted the burden from their back, Christians were willing to work hard and make sacrifices for the national good.

> **Study Aid #87**
>
> **Christian Contacts in Korea**
>
> Chinese Catholic convert Yi Seung-Hun brings gospel: 1784
> Protestant convert from China Suh Sang-Yun brings gospel: 1885
> Revival in Pyongyang: 1907
> "Market" Christianity: 20th century
> Fusion of Western economic influences with Christianity

However, their uncritical support for military government was denounced by radical Christians, who were influenced by theologies of humanization and liberation and the earlier Christian role in the independence movement. Although imprisoned and tortured for their political activities, Suh Nam Dong and other first-generation "*minjung* theologians" took the side of poor people and oppressed workers (*minjung*). Roman Catholics were also active in the *minjung* movement, and Protestant theologians were inspired by the writings of the Catholic activist Kim Chi Ha. During the 1970s and '80s these Christians made a significant contribution to workers and human rights and to the eventual achievement of democratic government in South Korea in 1988.

From the 1970s, South Korea built up its industrial base to become by 1997 the eleventh-largest economy in the world, and during this period the churches also grew rapidly. Most of the growth in the peak period took place in the mainstream Presbyterian and Methodist churches. In urban areas, particularly, the churches offered networks for pastoral support and for business purposes, together with opportunities to develop skills in English, for example, and leadership. Those who put themselves under the discipline of the church testified to its benefits and spread the message of salvation (and judgment) both spontaneously and in systematic evangelistic campaigns. Korea became famous for its megachurches, the most famous of which is the Full Gospel Church of Cho Yonggi, which now claims more than three-quarters of a million members. Based on 3 John 2, Cho developed techniques of prayer and evangelism that would guarantee a "threefold blessing" of health, well-being, and prosperity, which outwardly resemble both practices of the ancient shamanistic religion of the Korean people and the "positive thinking" of late capitalism. Although Cho's church is neo-Pentecostal, all the mainstream churches look back to the Korean revivals, which they seek to reproduce through annual revival meetings, and therefore have a strongly charismatic stream, especially among the women. However, this is under the control of the (overwhelmingly) male leadership and their preferred Confucian style of operating, which is ordered and disciplined. Korean churches thus combine two complementary faces that meet both elite and popular religious needs. This is comprehensible in the context of the *yin-yang* balance between female and male principles; however, *yin-yang* is experienced by many women as oppressive, so

Korean feminists have sought an alternative framework of traditional religion for their theologizing.

In South Korea, Christians tend to be urban and middle class. Postwar Korean churches are built in modern styles and make use of the latest technology to convey a future-oriented message of good news. Korean Christians regard the growth of the church and the economic miracle of twentieth-century Korea as blessings from God—and understand a close connection between the two. This confidence has led to a huge overseas missionary movement from South Korea. Through the widespread Korean Diaspora—there are particularly large Korean communities in the United States, China, Russia, and parts of central Asia, Japan, and Brazil—and through the sending of missionary families and single women for long-term work and groups for short-term mission trips, the Korean gospel is exported across the globe. Missionaries, who, like all Koreans, are very well educated, bring not only their religious practices but also their business and practical skills, especially medical skills, both Western and Eastern (such as acupuncture).

As Korea moves rapidly from modernity into postmodernity, the mainstream Protestant churches have been losing ground, but numbers of Christians have remained high because of the growth in the number of Roman Catholics, now 40 percent of all Christians. Because Catholicism became perceived as antinational, Catholics had something of a "ghetto mentality" until the 1970s, but since then they have grown, for several possible reasons. First, tastes in spirituality seem to be moving toward more traditional forms of both Christianity (Anglo-Catholics are also growing) and Korean religions. Second, under Cardinal Stephen Kim, the Catholic Church took a strong stand on human rights, which enhanced its credibility in the public mind. Third, the Catholic Church has remained above the allegations of corruption and scandal that have damaged some Protestant leaders. Since 2002, when the soccer World Cup was played in Korea, a Korean, or Hallyu, wave of cultural influence has spread across Asia, and particularly China, and in this low-key way, Christian influence is also being spread from Korea.

Sources

> Robert E. Buswell Jr. and Timothy S. Lee, eds. *Christianity in Korea*. University of Hawaii Press, 2006.
>
> Otis Cary. *A History of Christianity in Japan*. London, 1995 (1909).
>
> Neil S. Fujita. *Japan's Encounter with Christianity: The Catholic Mission in Pre-modern Japan*. Paulist Press, 1991.
>
> Ikuo Higashibaba. *Christianity in Early Modern Japan: Kirishitan Belief and Practice*. Brill, 2001.
>
> Samuel H. Moffett. *A History of Christianity in Asia*. 2 vols. Orbis Books, 1998–2005.
>
> Mark R. Mullins. *Christianity Made in Japan: A Study of Indigenous Movements*. University of Hawaii Press, 1998.
>
> Chai-Shin Yu, ed. *Korea and Christianity*. Asian Humanities Press, 2004.

41

North Asia: Theological Exchanges

SEBASTIAN KIM

The theological issues facing North Asia are not dissimilar to those faced in other contexts, but the most pertinent ones are the following: theological responses to religious traditions of Buddhism, Confucianism, Shintoism, and shamanism; the political turmoil of North Asia in recent years; and the problems of injustice and division within each nation.

Integration with Buddhism and Confucianism in Korea

Due to the close association of a particular religion with the political authority in any given historical period, there has been relatively less interaction and conflict between the different religious communities in Korea. Furthermore, the majority of Korean Protestant Christians, due to their evangelical and conservative orientation, have had very little experience of interacting with and expressing interest in other religions—although they are subconsciously influenced by Confucianism, Buddhism, and shamanism in their beliefs and practice. There have been various theological explorations by progressive theologians to relate Christianity with other religions, or to translate the Christian message into the concepts of other religions, but their theologies have not made much impact on the life of the church or have been harshly rejected by the majority of Christians.

The integration of Christianity and Korean religiosity was much discussed in the 1960s; the two foremost theologians in this field were Ryu Dong-Shik and Yoon Sung-Bum. Ryu in his thesis "Dao and Logos" suggested that the use of the Eastern philosophy of the Way is necessary for conveying the message of the

> **Study Aid #88**
> Theological Exchanges
> Theological responses to other religions
>   Buddhism
>   Confucianism
>   Shintoism
>   Shamanism
> Political turmoil and theology
>   *Minjung* theology (liberation)
> Injustice and economic divisions
>   Blessing theology (*bok*)

Christian gospel in Asia. According to him, Koreans have maintained in their ancient culture and religiosity the three aspects of *han* (oneness), *mot* (beauty), and *sam* (life), which are essential to the Korean spirit. These were integrated in the classical philosophy of *pungnyu-do* in the sixth century, from which he takes his *pungnyu* theology. *Pungnyu* literally means "wind and flow," evoking the inspiration of Korean thinkers through creative retreat in the fresh air and by the pure streams of the beautiful mountains. Ryu also describes the dynamics of the development of Korean theology as the result of constant interaction between paternal and maternal movements of the Holy Spirit, where the former is rooted in the Confucian tradition and leads to the conservative and hierarchical aspects of Korean church life, and the latter embraces a shamanistic approach to the faith and is closely related to the revival movements and Pentecostal churches in Korea.

Yoon Sung-Bum believed that Korean theology would blossom through creative exploration of the religious meaning of the Dangun myth—the story of the origin of the Korean people from the union of the son of heaven and a female bear—in the light of Christianity. He then further argued that there are elements of the Trinity in the myth because there are three figures referred to in the story. He insists that Confucianism provides the background of Korean thinking and so is an indispensable tool for Korean theology. In his "theology of sincerity," the Chinese word *seong* refers to a combination of word and deed. He regarded sincerity as having the meaning of *logos* or revelation. Yoon argued that sincerity can integrate dichotomic concepts in traditional theology, such as law and gospel, sacred and secular.

There are various other approaches to the interaction of Christian theology with the different religions in Korea. One of the most dramatic and creative was the incorporation of Korean shamanism into Christian theology in the presentation by Hyun Kyung Chung at the Canberra Assembly of the World Council of Churches (1991), which called forth varied responses. As she invoked the Holy Spirit, Chung also called on the spirits of people in the past and even the spirits of nature. Chung has opened a creative possibility of exploring Korean religiosity in Christian theology, but she also drew much criticism from within Korea and thus demonstrated the difficulties of dealing with the issue of religious pluralism in the Korean context.

Dealing with Poverty: Seeking Blessing or Liberation of *Minjung*?

Revival has been described as a key characteristic of Korean churches; anyone wishing to understand the Korean church has to understand its revivals. A series of revivals, led by Kil Sun-Joo and other evangelists from the early twentieth century, sought spiritual blessings, such as forgiveness of sins and personal and national salvation. These revivals have resulted in several dynamics in the practices of the Korean church in which Korean Christians experience an outpouring of the Holy Spirit, genuine repentance, and forgiveness, and this gives them confidence to preach the gospel and keep the faith in times of difficulty. One of the most distinctive characteristics of Korean churches, resulting from the revivals, is the prayer meeting with *tongsung kido* (the whole congregation praying aloud separately but simultaneously). These take place daily in the early morning, in weekly house groups, and all night long on Fridays.

The man who epitomizes this approach to seeking revival is David (formerly known as Paul) Yonggi Cho of Full Gospel Church in Seoul. His story is one of remarkable transformation of a church that started meeting in a tent in 1958. Yonggi Cho, in his often-quoted book *The Fourth Dimension*, described the struggle of hundreds of thousands of Koreans who were living in extreme poverty after the Korean War and saw their poverty as the work of Satan. The gospel of holistic blessing is not limited to the Full Gospel Church; indeed, it is found across whole sections of Korean churches. As revival is characteristic of the Korean church regardless of denomination, so the message of the expected blessings for those who seek is common to most mainline Korean churches.

Study Aid #89

Minjung Theology (Korean Liberation Theology)

Minjung: The people, or the oppressed.
Han: The anger at oppression turned inward.
Dan: To cut off *han* and its deleterious effects.
The four stages:
  Invite God into the heart.
  Let God grow in the body.
  Struggle to embody God.
  Live as humble champions of the oppressed.

Korean Christianity has a tendency to stress pietistic living and separation from politics, but we also must note the contribution to society of *minjung* theology, or Korean liberation theology. In the 1970s Korea experienced a need for a new understanding of Christian faith that would meet the needs of the urban poor, who were victims of highly competitive, capitalist market practices. The *minjung* movement was sparked when Jun Tae-ill died by self-immolation in November 1970 in a protest against the exploitation of fellow factory workers. Christian leaders took up this problem as a major issue and began standing for, and with, the poor and exploited. *Minjung* theologians, both Catholic and Protestant, captured people's imagination and brought the issue of poverty and exploitation to public attention.

Suh Nam Dong, among the most well-known of *minjung* theologians, presented his thesis arguing that Jesus identified with the poor, sick, and oppressed and that the gospel of Jesus is the gospel of salvation and liberation. For him, this is manifested in struggle with those evil powers, and so liberation is not individual or spiritual but rather communal and political. Suh systematized his *minjung* theology in the following years, seeing the *minjung* as subjects of history and introducing *han*, or anguish and despair, as the key theme for theology in the Korean context. Ahn Byeung-Moo, another well-known *minjung* theologian, asserted that Jesus identified in such a way that "Jesus is *minjung* and *minjung* is Jesus." He shared his life with the *minjung* to such an extent that he endured the cross as the climax of the suffering of the *minjung*. Therefore the presence of Christ is not when the word is preached nor when the sacrament is conducted but when we participate with or in the suffering of *minjung*. Jesus is God becoming flesh and body, which is a matter of material being and reality in everyday life, not of ideology or philosophy. Therefore he argued that the *minjung* is the owner of the Jesus community. This is fundamentally a "food community"—a community sharing food; the concept of a worshiping community came later.

Minjung theology has made a significant contribution to the Korean church and society through its understanding of liberation and justice, which showed the poor and oppressed that they should not be the objects of exploitation and that their protest was legitimate. *Minjung* theology was a major instrument of the *minjung*, or civil rights, movement, which challenged both church and society to deal with the problems of socioeconomic and political injustice; it also contributed to the democratization of Korean politics in the late 1980s.

Nonchurch Movement and Indigenization of Christianity in Japan

Theological exploration in the early Catholic period was largely led by Jesuit missionaries, who established Catholic schools and Bible colleges, and also by a few Japanese intellectuals. One of the major works was the publication of the *Catechismus Iaponesis* in Latin in 1586, a catechism designed to explain Christian

> **Study Aid #90**
>
> Indigenous Christian Movements in Japan
>
> Common characteristics
>   Freedom from Western institutions
>   No ordained clergy—priesthood of believers
>   No sacraments
>   Pacifism—spiritual warriors
>   Bible study
> Examples
>   Nonchurch Movement
>   The Way
>   Christ Heart Church
>   Glorious Gospel Christian Church
>   Living Christ One Ear of Wheat Church
>   Christian Canaan Church
>   Japan Ecclesia of Christ
>   Spirit of Jesus Church
>   Holy Ecclesia of Jesus
>   Sanctifying Christ Church
>   Original Gospel (Tabernacle)
>   Life-Giving Christ
>   Okinawa Christian Gospel

doctrines to the ordinary Japanese by using Buddhist and other religious terminologies and Japanese traditional customs. Thereafter there appeared a series of catechisms and instructions for Christians, including *Myote mondo* (1605), a dialogue between a Buddhist nun and a Christian woman arguing for the rationality of Christian faith over Buddhism and Shintoism. Written by Fucan Fabian, the dialogue was among the numerous early attempts to present Christian faith to Japanese people.

Protestant Christianity actively engaged in exploring Christian theology from a Japanese perspective. Masahisa Uemura, a pastor and evangelist, published a number of books and booklets explaining the nature of religious truth, the existence of God, and human spirituality. He founded Bancho Ichi Church in 1887 and became a leading figure in Japanese Protestant Christianity. In 1904 he also founded Tokyo Theological School (later Tokyo Union Theological Seminary), which is still a major theological institute in Japan.

With very different theological and ideological orientation, including a nationalistic and Confucian emphasis, the "Kumamato group" was formed in 1876. Danjo Ebina became the leading figure in this group, which started various theological journals with particular emphasis on the realization of the kingdom of God and on Christ as the ideal human character of God-human union. In the aftermath of Japan's defeat and the dropping of the atom bombs, theologian Kazoh Kitamori wrote his groundbreaking work *Theology of the Pain of God*, which was published in Japan in 1946. Kitamori used the words of Jeremiah 31:20 to encourage the Japanese people that the "transcendent pain of God is immanent in the painful reality of the world." The book reached a worldwide audience and influenced German theologians particularly, including Jürgen Moltmann. However, Kitamori did not address the issue of Japanese complicity in their own suffering and the suffering they caused other Asian nations during their imperial rule.

Japan has integrated theology and church structures from the Western churches and missionaries, but at the same time, the church there has produced various indigenous theologies and movements. The Jesuit missionaries were very successful in their initial mission work since the time of their arrival in 1549, what is known as "the Christian century in Japan." This growth of Christianity was soon followed by the severe persecution of Christians by the government for the next two centuries, and Christians became "hidden Christians" (*kakure krishitan*) in order to survive the harsh period of persecution. In 1859 Japan reopened its door to Christian missions, and both Protestant and Catholic missionaries began their work. The Protestant movement of Japan was initiated in three "band" areas: Yokohama, Kumamoto, and Sapporo. The latter two were led by lay Christian leaders and represented a distinctive approach to Protestant faith differing from the churches with a denominational emphasis established by missionaries. Although they were started by Western lay Christians teaching the Bible to students, they soon became Japanese-led movements. Some of their characteristics include making a "covenant" to commit themselves to read the Bible and live an ethical life, and not to belong to any denominational churches or abide by doctrines and creeds.

The Nonchurch Movement has had significant influence on the indigenization of Christianity in Japan. Uchimura Kanzo is the most prominent leader of this movement, as he sought for "pure" and "spiritual" religion of Jesus Christ, free from institutional boundaries and dogmas developed in the West. Uchimura was influenced by Puritanism and Quakerism from the United States. Insisting on the priesthood of all believers, he rejected ordained clergy as standing in between believers and God. He also rejected the sacraments of baptism and the Lord's Supper and emphasized the importance of salvation by faith alone. Later in his life, he espoused pacifism and preached the second coming of Christ. Although he had initially supported the Japanese government's war efforts in the Sino-Japanese War, he later criticized subsequent wars and the colonization of Asian nations. The ethical understanding of Uchimura was guided by his warrior-class background and Confucianism, which led him to emphasize loyalty, duty, and filial piety plus an educational system based on a teacher-and-disciple model. The Nonchurch Movement has taken Bible studies (*seisho no kenkyu*) as the key component in their meetings and largely rely on charismatic leaders, Bible study magazines, and the publication of special lectures, which are used for evangelism. For Uchimura, *bushido* (way of the warrior) coupled with Confucian ethics and ardent study of the Bible is the foundation of Christianity in Japan. He and his followers tend to be from an intellectual background. The Nonchurch Movement has not really become a mass movement, but their prophetic role toward mainstream churches in Japan and wider society has made a significant impact.

Kosuke Koyama became well known through his articulation of a theory of contextualization of Christian theology in Asian contexts. A student of Kitamori, Koyama highlighted in his *Water Buffalo Theology* the "glory of the crucified Lord" and sought to present an Asian theology carrying the "marks" of Jesus in the plurality and suffering of the people. Koyama connects the image of the broken Christ with the Lord's Supper, as Christ gives himself as a sacrifice. He utilizes stories in an imaginative manner as he reflects on his own missionary experiences in Thailand. His theological focus is the cross, and this becomes the platform for engaging in interreligious dialogue with the people in Asia as he presents the "crucified mind" over against the "crusade mind" of many Christian approaches to the people of other faiths. Although his theological resources and the audience of his theology are not limited to Japan, he draws his theological exploration from his identity as Japanese and his theological training in Japan.

Sources

Yonggi Cho. *The Fourth Dimension*. Bridge-Logos, 1979.

Christian Conference of Asia/Commission on Theological Concerns. *Minjung Theology: People as the Subjects of History*. Orbis Books, 1983.

John C. England et al., eds. *Asian Christian Theologies: A Research Guide to Authors, Movements, Sources*. 3 vols. ISPCK, 2002–4.

Yasuo Furuya, ed. *A History of Japanese Theology*. Eerdmans, 1997.

Heup Young Kim. *Christ and the Tao*. Christian Conference of Asia, 2003.

Sebastian C. H. Kim, ed. *Christian Theology in Asia*. Cambridge University Press, 2008.

Kazoh Kitamori. *Theology of the Pain of God*. John Knox, 1965.

Kosuke Koyama. *Water Buffalo Theology*. SCM, 1974.

Wonsuk Ma, William Menzies, and Hyeon-sung Bae, eds. *David Yonggi Cho: A Close Look at His Theology and Ministry*. APTS, 2004.

David Kwang-Sun Suh. *The Korean Minjung in Christ*. Christian Conference of Asia/Commission on Theological Concerns, 1991.

Notto R. Thelle. *Buddhism and Christianity in Japan: From Conflict to Dialogue, 1854–1899*. University of Hawaii Press, 1987.

42

North Asia: Current Issues

SEBASTIAN KIM

Although both Japan and Korea share much of their cultural, religious, and political histories, the contemporary situations and issues facing Christianity in each nation are significantly different. This is not only because of different problems in wider society but also because the reception of Christianity in each country has been very different, resulting in a contrasting church life: in South Korea, Christianity is a highly visible part of national life to which more than a quarter of the population adheres, whereas in Japan, Christians make up a tiny portion of the population.

Ethical Issues in South Korean Christianity

The growth of Korean churches within just a few decades has been remarkable, and today visitors can witness churches everywhere in major cities as well as in villages in South Korea. South Korean Protestant churches also have not shied away from being involved in the sociopolitical and economic life of the people throughout their relatively short history. They have been very active for the common good, especially in the times of Japanese occupation, postindependence, and the military-backed governments, and have made significant contributions to the public life of the nation during times of great turmoil in Korean history.

However, the socio-ethical conduct of Christians, particularly of Protestants, has been questioned both within and outside of the churches. At the same time that the church was growing, the South Korean economy flourished. It grew from being one of the poorest countries in the world after the Korean War to becoming the world's eleventh-largest economy. Seven out of ten of the world's largest churches are located in Seoul, and there are numerous other large churches all over the country. Seoul has been described as the "second Jerusalem." As the number of churches grew in this period, so did the influence of Protestants in most parts of public life in Korea. For example, two out of four recent democratically elected presidents have been Protestants (including the present one), and 119 out of 299 members of parliament are Protestants (39 percent—compared to Protestants making up 18.3 percent of the population). Protestants often claim these changes of demography and influence are due to blessing from God; however, this increasingly dominant position of Protestants in Korean public life has not been received as a blessing for all.

There are some aspects of the Protestant church that may have contributed to a lack of credibility among the general public. First, Korean Protestant churches tend to hold a church-centered theology. This could be a result of the "three-self" method and the denominationalism brought by the early missionaries. This self-sufficiency of the local church has been the strength of Korean Christianity in terms of its sustained growth and financial independence. But it has also resulted in the churches becoming highly competitive with one another by employing aggressive methods of evangelism and building large and extravagant buildings. The political closeness to the democratic and capitalist system has been fully exploited as churches seek numerical growth. This prohibits any ecumenical work among the churches in a similar area, between different denominations, and even between churches within the same denomination. The church has been operating on the principles of the capitalist market economy.

Second, the majority of Protestants hold an exclusive theology toward people of other faiths and of no faith. Often this exclusive theology creates an exclusivistic attitude that tends to lead to rejection of others and unwillingness to enter into dialogue. This becomes particularly problematic when the church is closely

---

Study Aid #91

Current Issues in South Korea

Challenges
 Social conduct of Christians
 Religious intolerance
 Personal morality rather than social ethics
 Reunification
Contributions
 Revivals
 Prayer
 Church organization
 Missions

associated with political power and enjoys economic strength. The Protestant churches have become increasingly confident, to the extent that they are arrogant toward people of other faiths. Recently, there have been a number of high-profile incidents of physical attacks by Christians on Buddhist temples and shrines of Dangun, the mythical founder of Korea. This reflects a lack of sensitivity to Korean religious plurality on the part of Christians. Social care and involvement are often used as part of evangelistic campaigns, and this has damaged their credibility in spite of a real desire on the part of many Christians to serve others.

Third, Protestants tend to emphasize personal morality rather than social ethics. From the beginning of the introduction of Protestantism to Korea, there has been great interest in personal Bible study, prayer, revival, and spiritual blessing. At the same time, there has been a lack of teaching about conduct in public life, and there is a deep gap between personal and public life, sacred and secular, and the spiritual and the material spheres. This dualism also reflects the gap between the minister and the congregation. Protestant churches tend to focus on the minister's sermon and his charismatic leadership, but sometimes this may encourage the abuse of their authority in areas such as the handling of finances and personnel.

The above areas of concern have in common certain dualistic tendencies of church versus world, Christian truth versus untruth, sacred versus secular, faith versus works, and personal versus communal life of individual Christians and churches. These are reinforced by the traditional Korean dualistic philosophy and also the rival political and economic polarizations of democracy versus communism and capitalism versus socialism. Perhaps the greatest challenge for Protestant Christians in Korea is to overcome unhealthy dualism and move into a more integrated and mature Christian life in private, in the church, and in the wider society.

Seeking Blessings in South Korea

Revival meetings are often conducted on the basis of the gospel of holistic blessing, commonly known as *kibock sinang*, or seeking blessings, but this has been criticized from both moderate and conservative sections of the Korean church. They have various reasons: First, they see it as unbiblical and influenced by shamanism, which they regard as this-worldly, unethical, antihistorical, and temporal. Second, they object to *kibock sinang*'s belief that poverty is a curse and the result of wrong actions and attitudes toward God. Third, they interpret *kibock sinang* worship, offerings to God and good deeds, as performed in expectation of receiving from God something in return. Fourth, they blame *kibock sinang* for contributing to the lack of political participation of the Korean church and slowness to share resources with others. It has been described as a "corrupted faith" and "making Christianity a lower religion." The critics focus on the negative outcome of excessive seeking of blessings, seen in the revival meetings and services. They criticize the revival preachers for their unethical approaches, such as offering material blessings and healing. It is not uncommon to see revival meetings dominated by stories and testimonies of those who have received blessings of wealth, healing, and success. There is an excessive drive to increase church membership and construct new church buildings or church prayer halls in the mountains, often by borrowing money from the bank in "faith" that God will fulfill his promise. The critics are right in that the extravagant demonstration of material blessings in church buildings and membership has become a problem in the Korean church. It encourages a materialistic and mechanical approach to faith.

Korean Reconciliation

The conflict between the two Koreas is certainly the dominant concern for Koreans and has affected the lives of Koreans ever since the country was divided. Though the desire for reunification has been the most important agenda for political leaders, the ways to achieve the goal have differed widely, as the two Koreas were at the forefront of the Cold War ideological conflict. Until the early 1980s, most churches in South Korea either took a conservative, anticommunist position, or kept the policy of separation from politics. The most significant contribution of the churches to reconciliation was in 1988, when the Korean National Council of Churches issued the Declaration toward the Unification and Peace of the Korean People, which made a significant impact both within the church and on the whole nation. The document made practical suggestions to both governments, including the withdrawal of the US army and the dismantling of the UN head office in South Korea. The declaration also proclaimed the year 1995 as a jubilee year for peace and unification, when Koreans could celebrate the fiftieth anniversary of the liberation from Japan. More recently, the churches have been involved in various ecumenical humanitarian projects such as the South-North Sharing Campaign, founded in 1993.

The churches in Korea went through severe persecutions during the nineteenth century, the Japanese occupation, and the Korean War; they have not merely survived but also grown in significant numbers. The challenge to the church in South Korea remains whether it can meet the needs not only of its members but also of the wider public and therefore genuinely become "salt and light" in the midst of the dynamic and yet diverse contemporary societies on the Korean peninsula.

Indigenization of Japanese Christianity and Maintaining Integrity in Sociocultural Contexts

Some Japanese Christian leaders and theologians, particularly in the Kyodan (the United Church of Christ), have been very interested in integrating Christianity into Japanese cultural and religious traditions, as they see there is a clear continuity between them. Many indigenous Christian groups in Japan exhibit sincere

> **Study Aid #92**
> **Current Issues in Japan**
>
> Challenges
>   Confucian values?
>   Militarism
>   Ethnic minorities
> Contributions
>   Life transition rites (e.g., weddings, funerals)
>   Personal counseling
>   Positive public perceptions

attempts to acculturate Christianity and to set it free from Western dominance and traditions. Others in the church have not been as eager to do this. Most movements, however, have been unable to maintain long-term growth in spite of their attempts to adapt and incorporate Japanese social and cultural patterns. A difficulty faced by leaders and theologians is the task of identifying Japanese culture, since it is not single but consists of a complex of subcultures. The indigenous Christian movements differ in their theological understanding, worship patterns, daily Christian practices, organization, leadership, and group dynamics. Many indigenous movements have applied a Confucian model of a male-dominated, teacher-disciple relationship as the basis of organization and an emphasis on lay leadership, rejecting clergy and the importance of the sacraments. However, other more recently developed charismatic movements tend to accept the distinction between clergy and laity, and to be more egalitarian in terms of gender participation in their leadership. However, because of informal arrangements of leadership training and education, there is a shortage of leaders to succeed. Movements often disband due to lack of continuity of development and eventually die out. The size of these groups reduces considerably as the generations go by. There are also problems of pastoral care of the group members, such as in regular meetings, care for the elderly, or funeral help, when there are no responsible leaders for such ministries. To respond to these problems, many groups now seek out formal theological education and hence move toward institutionalization as they meet the changing contexts of contemporary Japan.

There are various concerns facing Christianity in Japan. One is a gradual increase of militarism in Japanese society and in politics, which Christians are called to respond to. Another is the treatment of *Burakumins* (social outcasts) and ethnic minorities in the country. A third is Japan's wartime role in neighboring Asian countries. There have been various attempts from Japanese Christians for reconciliation, and this is an ongoing project, as economic, political, and social interactions have been complex in East and Southeast Asia both past and present.

Japanese churches are very small—the average attendance is about twenty to thirty—and Christians are often under pressure to conform to the cultural and religious customs of family and society, involving attending Shinto shrines and Buddhist temples and participating in cultural ceremonies, which some Christians regard as rooted in religious understandings. However, there have been some encouraging aspects of Christianity in Japan. In 1981, the NHK (Japan Broadcasting Cooperation) conducted a survey of "Japanese Religious Consciousness" through interviews with more than thirty-six hundred adults across Japan. In that survey 20 percent of respondents expressed their empathy toward Christianity. A more recent 2006 Gallup survey showed the same thing. It is interesting to note that among young people, Christian weddings are increasing in popularity. This does not directly relate to faith in Christianity. However, this new trend may be regarded as expressing a positive attitude toward Christianity among the new generation of Japanese and may result in an embracing of Christianity as a part of their life passage rather than as an imported Western religion. There is also a growing interest in Christianity among college and university students, and the activities of Christian societies are a very positive sign of acceptance of Christianity among young people. Other encouraging signs include growing Christian involvement in personal counseling through telephone services and counseling centers; active lay volunteer work by Christians; the ministry of Christian social workers; involvement in peace action and human rights advocacy; the work of Christian artists, dancers, and writers; and the dedicated work of Christian teachers.

Sources

John Breen and Mark Williams, eds. *Japan and Christianity: Impacts and Responses*. Macmillan, 1995.

Hyun Kyung Chung. *Struggle to Be the Sun Again*. SCM, 1990.

Philip Jenkins. *The Next Christendom: The Coming of Global Christianity*. Oxford University Press, 2002.

Jung Young Lee, ed. *An Emerging Theology in World Perspective: Commentary on Korean Minjung Theology*. Twenty-Third Publications, 1988.

Mark R. Mullins and Richard Fox Young, eds. *Perspectives on Christianity in Korea and Japan: Gospel and Culture in East Asia*. Mellen, 1995.

Jong-Sun Noh. *God of Reunification: Toward a Theology of Reunification*. Seoul, 1988.

James M. Phillips. *From the Rising of the Sun: Christians and Society in Contemporary Japan*. Orbis Books, 1981.

David Reid. *New Wine: The Cultural Shaping of Japanese Christianity*. Asian Humanities, 1991.

43

Europe: History, Beliefs, Practices

RICHARD SHAW

Christianity is a global religion founded in Palestine by a small group of followers of Jesus, a first-century Jew who demonstrated a uniquely compassionate (though assertive) ethic and nuanced resistance to the prevailing Judaic system of the day. Although brief in his ministry (one year by Synoptic writers and three years by Johannine sources), Jesus galvanized the movement he had initiated through his proclamation of the advent of the now-but-not-yet kingdom of God, and his insistence upon faith in himself, substantiated by his own alleged resurrection from the dead.

Jesus's teaching was successful. The messianic revitalization movement he spawned spread rapidly throughout the Roman Empire, abruptly confronting religious practices and challenging both long-entrenched and newer ways of thinking, acting, and living. Several eyewitnesses intimately associated with Jesus recorded their experiences with him, detailing events and repeating sermons, sayings, blessings, curses, and integral stories they remembered their teacher professing. Second-generation adherents added to this growing body of collective memory. Others, including Paul the apostle, claimed to have had supernatural, mystical experiences with Jesus and became propagators of the faith.

The apostle Paul reached the farthest southeastern shore of Europe (present-day Turkey) between 49 and 51 CE. As Paul and others proclaimed the news of Jesus the Messiah in Europe, they encountered other religious beliefs and systems active there. Primary among these was Judaism, Diaspora adherents of which had established communities in present-day Macedonia, Greece, and Italy. Judaism, a religion that has its origins in profound acts of human obedience, traces its roots to the eighteenth

Study Aid #93

Map of Europe

or nineteenth century BCE, to the Sumerian Abram, with whom Yahweh established a covenant. That the founder of Christianity—Jesus—was ethnically and religiously Jewish demonstrates the continuity of this newer faith with that of the older.

But Judaism was but one of the prevailing systems of religious practice and devotion. Remnants of Greek mythology lingered among Hellenistic peoples. Greek philosophy, albeit of similar roots as Greek mythology, often challenged the morality and inconsistency of Greek narrative and consequently served as a moral and ethical framework for action and thought. The twin Greek ideologies of Neoplatonism and gnosticism presented particular tests to Christianity, as did Stoicism, Pythagoreanism, and Peripateticism. Much Greek thought assumed a reality of ideas distinct from, and superior to, the material world, which was considered transient, imperfect, and illusory.

Roman religion, founded, according to legend, by Numa, the second of Rome's early kings, centered upon four foundational concepts:

1. a reverent fear of the gods expressed through a contractual or juridical pragmatism, *do ut des* (I give so that you [god] may in turn give to me);
2. a practical theological framework of gods and goddesses, demonstrated through the assignation of specific major/minor deities;
3. the paramount locus of state affairs, thus ensuring the strength of community; and
4. the tandem dynamics of conservatism—respect of old Roman gods—and openness to syncretic addition.

This state religion, based upon the preexistent paterfamilias (head of family) pattern, later added additional deities, adapted to those of the Greek pantheon.

Although the Roman Empire was extensive in its geography and hegemony, other powerful tribes and kingdoms fought for survival, identity, and community. Celtic culture, once dominant in present-day western Germany and eastern France, was eventually pushed to Wales, Scotland, Ireland, and Brittany. Indigenous Celtic religion boasted its own pantheon of deities, including Llow in Gaul and Lug in Ireland; Celts maintained that all things in life happened according to the will of the gods. As an oral religious culture, labeled by outside observers as "emotional" and "volatile," the Celtic faith system observed elaborate ceremonies and, according to some sources, human sacrifice. The Celtic priestly class of Druids enjoyed an exalted status and was open to both men and women. Conducting religious rituals in groves of trees, Celtic Druids' theologies asserted correlative relationships between the earth, the stars, and humankind.

The Roman Christian missionaries Augustine, Columba, and Patrick were instrumental in the spread of the gospel among Celtic peoples, but the existence and practice of Celtic Druid ritual continues to the present day. The dynamic of fertility was rudimentary to indigenous Celtic religion, as well as Druidism, but was also expressed in fertility cults. The communicative interface between the material, natural world and the spiritual world was accessed through caves, streams, sacred trees, and other numinous places. Christianity, whether well contextualized or Roman, submerged many expressions of these ancient faiths, though it did not annihilate them.

The religious environment that Christianity encountered among Germanic and Scandinavian tribes was much less orderly, instead characterized by a sense of danger, capriciousness, and belligerence. The major Scandinavian and Germanic deities were Woden (Odin), Donar (Thor), and Tiw (Ty). This triad played a functional role of magician, warmonger, and worker-producer, respectively. In addition to these deities were the two aggregates of the Vanir and the Aesir. In Asgard, the splendorous paradise of the gods, Woden had a great hall, Valhalla, from which he surveyed the cosmos with his single, piercing eye. The beliefs associated with

> **Study Aid #94**
>
> Countries of Europe
>
> | | | | |
> |---|---|---|---|
> | Albania | Denmark | Liechtenstein | Russia |
> | Andorra | Estonia | Lithuania | San Marino |
> | Armenia | Finland | Luxemborg | Serbia |
> | Austria | France | Macedonia | Slovakia |
> | Azerbaijan | Georgia | Malta | Slovenia |
> | Belarus | Germany | Moldova | Spain |
> | Belgium | Greece | Monaco | Sweden |
> | Bosnia/ Herzegovina | Hungary | Montenegro | Switzerland |
> | | Iceland | Netherlands | Turkey |
> | Bulgaria | Ireland | Norway | Ukraine |
> | Croatia | Italy | Poland | United Kingdom |
> | Cyrus | Kazakhstan | Portugal | Vatican |
> | Czech Republic | Latvia | Romania | |

these deities, their home, and their functions waned as Christianity continued its burgeoning expansion. The Danes were converted in about 905 CE; the Norwegians and Icelanders followed in about 1000 CE. The Swedes were more tenacious in clinging to their fertility rites and religio-cultural compulsives of valor in battle, honor, and family allegiance, until the first decade after 1100 CE.

When Christian faith first reached the Baltic nations of present-day Estonia, Latvia, and Lithuania, missioners discovered a worldview focused upon the construct of the World-Tree, Cosmic-Tree, or Life-Tree. Atop the uppermost branches of this tree were the heavenly bodies, including birds, and especially eagles. Under the boughs of the tree lived humans and animals, and below them, snakes and other crawling and creeping beings. The roots of the massive tree reached deep into the earth, from which, it was believed, flowed springs of life and wisdom. This World-Tree represented the earth, including humankind and animals, as an indivisible holism. Ancient Balts maintained that the sun was drawn across the sky by two magical steeds—the Ašvienlai—pulling a chariot. The Latvian cosmogram Auseklitis showed the directions of the earth. Christianity came to Latvia and Estonia in 1180 CE and to Lithuania in 1249 CE.

The ancient Thracians were predecessors of present-day Bulgarians. These Balkan people were a conglomerate of divergent tribes, whose religion was akin to that of adjacent Greeks and Macedonians. The eastern and Egyptian gods—Mithras, Sarapis, Osiris, Isis, Harpokranes, and Anubis—were venerated in cultic ritual and festival, as was Dionysus. One aspect of Thracian religion was its close association with astronomical phenomena. Another facet highlighted the infamous Thracian Horseman, given the Greek name "Heros" in many reliefs and inscriptions. The Horseman evolved in both popular and scholarly thought to become an almost universal deity of hunting, fertility, life, and death, and was believed to be all-knowing and all-powerful. The cultural memory of the Thracian Horseman has been preserved in over fifteen hundred stone reliefs and over one hundred bronze statuettes.

Christianity began to permeate the land known today as Bulgaria through the missionary efforts of Cyril and Methodius, two ninth-century monks who allegedly created the Glagolitic, or ancient Slavonic, alphabet. Threatened by the Byzantine Empire to the south and the east and the Great Moravian Empire to the north, Bulgarian leader Knyaz Boris deemed it politically and militarily advantageous to convert to Christianity, the religion of both opponents. Baptized in 864 CE, the Bulgarian leader adopted Christianity for himself and his people, initiating the destruction of old pagan shrines and monuments. Because of the translatability of the kerygma into any and all cultures, Christian faith developed a symbiotic relationship with political powers in the eastern Balkans.

The peoples of the Iberian Peninsula were conquered by the Roman Empire between 39 and 19 BCE. Although many members of the predominantly three tribes of Lusitani, Celtiberians, and Iberians accepted the religion of their Roman invaders, the pre-Roman cults of Endovelicus and Trebaruna continued to practice well into Roman times. These ancient henotheistic cults, as well as Roman religion, were tolerant of the addition of other deities and accepted Germanic, Egyptian, and Greek gods and goddesses into their existing pantheon. While the New Testament canon articulates the apostle Paul's desire to visit Spain in his missionary ventures, it is doubtful that he ever reached Western Europe. The missionary was well informed of the progress of the Romanization of Spain, and the presence of Greek populations, especially along the coast. But events in his own life precluded the mission-hearted Paul from westward travel. It was most likely merchants and traders who initially brought the Christian faith to the Iberian Peninsula.

Upon the collapse of Rome, the Visigoths filled the power vacuum. The Christianity they brought was of such a cruel and barbaric nature, however, that the minority populations of Jews, slaves, and serfs aided the Islamic Moors in their overthrow of the Goths. The reconquest of the Iberian Peninsula was achieved through the leadership of Afonso I (Afonso Henriques) in Portugal in 1064 CE and the Asturians in Spain, beginning in 711 CE and completed in 1492 CE.

The area now known as Russia was initially inhabited by many divergent clans and tribes. These tribespeople paid homage to water-dwelling succubi and other

---

Study Aid #95

Christianity's Early European Conversation Partners

Greek philosophy
Roman religion
Celtic religion
Scandinavian/Germanic pantheons

Latvian religion
Slavic religion
Iberian religion
Visigoth divinities

female spirits, who allegedly made their homes in sacred trees. Scandinavian merchants, in search of wealth and trade partners, were causative in nation building among these different groups. Influenced by the Byzantine Empire—especially through Patriarch Photius of Constantinople—the Russians were overtly unresponsive to evangelization. Princess Olga, following the death of her husband, Igor, was the initial change agent in the Christianization of the Russians. Converted around 950 CE, this Russian ruler was baptized by Germanic missionaries. Olga's grandson Vladimir requested missionaries from the Byzantine Empire to come and work among the numerous Slavic tribes and clans. Distancing himself and his peoples from the Roman Church, Vladimir may have coerced many of his subjects to convert through political and/or military pressure. Although conquered by the Mongols in 1240 CE, the Russian nation maintained cohesion through the stabilizing and unifying power of the Christian faith throughout the period of its occupation.

The Eastern European nation of Poland's initial encounter with Christian faith was triggered by the conversion of Duke Mieszka, who through his wife, Dobrawa, sister of Boleslav II of Bohemia, responded to the gospel of Jesus Christ. Immediately following Mieszka's baptism in 966 CE, an episcopal see for Poland was established, probably under the ecclesial jurisdiction of Magdeburg. The Poles' new national Christian identity brought them within the sphere of Western Christianity, including direct affiliation with the Western church in Rome. While Christian faith provided military and political strength, pre-Christian mythologies surrounding Rusalkas continued to prevail in both imagination and daily life. Rusalkas were believed to dwell in forests and lakes of western Poland; these spirits were the ghosts of murdered girls who sought to satisfy their unfulfilled desires. Pre-Christian Poles also venerated the natural elements of the earth—water, fire, soil, and air—and observed rituals in their honor.

While the Christian church has long been established within European countries and among European peoples, dating from the earliest contact of the Christian gospel with the ancient Macedonian Lydia, Christianity has not always flourished. Many early conversions were military or political in nature, and the Christian faith was rarely deep in its penetration of cultural patterns. But the translation of the Christian scriptures into Latin, the language of the Roman Empire, and much later into the vernaculars of ethnic groups, whether Slavic, Germanic, Celtic, Romantic, Scandinavian, or another, propelled the gospel of Jesus Christ and the concomitant ethic and values deeply into civilizations. The resurgence of pre-Christian paganism, in tandem with a Christianity-resistant secularism, is on the rise in many places in Europe. Notwithstanding, the future of Christian faith is not as bleak as some may predict. Immigration of Christians from the global South—who bring with them a vibrant and robust Christian faith into decaying European cities—is beginning to challenge pre-Christian paganism in fresh new ways.

44

Europe: Christian Contacts

Richard Shaw

Christian contact with the people of Europe and their religions has come in different ways, through divergent forms and relationships. In some cases, Christian-European religious contact has been primarily missionary. In other cases, the interface of religious systems has been developed through less intentional means, including relationships focused upon trade, commerce, industry, migration, empire building, military maneuvers, and education. Jesus Christ's missionary mandate, "Therefore go and make disciples of all nations, baptizing them in the name of the Father and of the Son and of the Holy Spirit, and teaching them to obey everything I have commanded you" (Matt. 28:19–20), has been assumed by many of his followers, whether they be intentionally missionary or predominantly laypersons engaged in their professions, giving witness to Christ's transformative power.

Notwithstanding, Christianity, in its nascent contact with the Roman Empire, was tragically rooted in martyrdom. Bishop Felix of North Africa refused to worship the Roman emperor Diocletian in 304 CE. Though given multiple opportunities to comply with Roman law, the Christian leader maintained his singular allegiance to Jesus Christ, suffering the fatal consequence of his civil disobedience. The larcenous crime with which Felix was charged was his failure to turn over Holy Scriptures by imperial mandate. Citing Acts 5:29, "We must obey God rather than men," Felix was beheaded for his rejection of imperial deity. Christian faith and emperor worship were clearly mutually exclusive (Ehrman and Jacobs 2004, 10–11).

A second example of Christian contact with indigenous European pre-Christian religion is the sterling witness Martin of Tours. Bishop Martin's methods of evangelism and mission were divergent, though singularly focused on spiritual ends, manifested in cultural demonstration. The pattern of proclamation, the performance of wonders, and the willingness of hearers to convert were sustained during the bishopric of Martin, with ancillary actions of the destruction of sacred objects, including temples and sacred trees (Cusack 1998, 63–64). Though reports indicate that many persons accepted Christian faith, there also exist accounts of European first peoples who resisted Martin's actions on occasion. Martin, bishop of Tours from 371 to 397 CE, can be described as an exorcist, a healer, one devoted to prayer and asceticism, and a defender of orthodox Christian faith.

A third example, though intensely distinct from Martin, is Clovis, king of the Franks. Royalty and nobility played highly influential roles in the lives of early European peoples and societies, with public, spiritual transformation of both *duces* and *reges* leading to mass conversions of ethnic groups, including tribes. Clovis, of royal blood and the first of the Merovingian kings, was introduced to faith in Jesus Christ through his wife, Clotild. Perhaps due to his own framework of power and identity, Clovis was reluctant to accept the faith of his wife, though her Christian witness and constant presence undoubtedly contributed to his knowledge of the faith. Clovis's conversion, a Gideon's fleece–like experience, is reported to have been the fulfillment of a pledge in which the Frankish king vowed that he would be baptized a Christian if the victory over the Alamanni came to him. "'Jesus Christ,' he [Clovis] said, 'you whom Clotild maintains to be the Son of the living God . . . if you will give me victory over my enemies, . . . then I will believe in you and I will be baptized in your name'" (Gregory of Tours 1974, 8). The subsequent battle at Tolbiac was a decisive victory for the Franks, and though there is debate as to the time elapsed, Clovis was indeed baptized. This public conversion to Christian faith was initiated clearly by his Christian wife, Clotild, and the contact was highly intentional.

A fourth example of Christian contact with indigenous European pre-Christian religion is Hilda of Whitby (614–80 CE), who, responding to the preaching of Saint Paulinus in 627 CE, converted to Christian faith and pledged her life in commitment to Jesus Christ. Hilda lived in the world as a married woman for thirty-three years, followed by life as the abbess of a double monastery for an additional thirty-three years (Brown 2003, 376). Reports about Abbess Hilda's wisdom drew persons from near and far to hear her render decisions and provide counsel. The Venerable Bede, in his *Ecclesiastical History of the English People*, notes that those persons under Hilda's tutelage were required to study the Holy Scriptures and to engage themselves in good works (Bede 1955, 247). Contact between Christianity and pre-Christian European religions was thus bidirectional—that is, centrifugal through those going out of the monastery, and centripetal through those drawn to the Christian center, seeking wisdom and advice.

Cyril (Constantine) and Methodius brought Christian faith to persons dwelling in central and Eastern Europe beginning shortly before 862 CE. These brothers' first interface with pre-Christian European religion was among the Khazar people,

> **Study Aid #96**
> Modes of Christian Contact in Europe
> Missionary   Mercantile
> Martyrdom/persecution   Migration
> Military

who had requested that someone come and teach them about Christianity (Evans 2008, 73). The Moravian Duke Ratislav broadened these Macedonians' mission when he expressed the desire to have missionaries come to teach his subjects in their own language. Although prior Christian contact had been made through German missionaries, Methodius and Cyril were greatly influential in the conversion of many Slavic peoples, in that these missionaries were diligent in learning the indigenous languages, customs, traditions, and mores. Through the invention of the Glagolitic alphabet, and the translation of parts of the Christian scriptures and liturgy into the language of the people, the rate of acceptance of Christian faith was greatly accelerated. Such intentional contact was through invitation by rulers of ethnic groups and kingdoms. Cyril and Methodius's contact is identified today by many as contextual—highly respectful of and relevant to culture, and transformative—interfacing the gospel of Jesus Christ with human need.

A sixth example of Christian contact with religions extant in Europe is Urban II, elected pope in 1088 CE, though he was in exile at the time. Notwithstanding that he is often vilified by Muslims, Jews, and Christians alike, Urban II, in his inimitable manner, was diligently responding to an urgent request made by Byzantine emperor Alexius I Comnenus for mercenary forces to be sent to assist in the conflict with Muslim Seljuk Turks. Urban received Alexius's ambassadors at the Council of Piacenza in northern Italy in March 1095 CE, and shortly thereafter announced another council, this one at Clermont in the Auvergne region of France (González 1999, 293). In a meadow outside the French city, the pope, continuing the reformative revitalization movement begun by his predecessor, Gregory VII, read the letter detailing gruesome tortures of Christian pilgrims at the hands of recently converted Seljuks. The call given combined Urban's intent to bring to an end the chronic warfare of medieval times with a "true pretext . . . [for] the glory of dying in the very same place as Jesus Christ" (Michaud 1855, 51). This Christian contact was military and intentional, advocating a forceful apologetic against a hegemonic power.

An alternative approach to Christian contact with Muslims was offered by Francis of Assisi, born 1181 CE. This Italian mendicant's method was rooted in a serious illness and a life-changing encounter with a leper. Following a spiritual experience during prayer before a crucifix in San Damiano, Francis renounced wealth, status, and position in order to imitate the Crucified Christ (Bevans and Schroeder 2004, 142). Francis's contact with pre-Christian peoples was missionary in nature, through the medium of preaching and ministry to the poor, particularly to those afflicted with leprosy. Initially the mendicant alone engaged in this contact, but he later was accompanied by other devoted men. When Francis's preaching was only partially accepted, he turned from those living in and around Assisi to "the Saracens," Muslims of other eastern and southern regions. Unintentionally, the missionary landed on the Dalmatian coast (present-day Croatia) in 1212 CE (Farmer 1997, 192). In 1219 CE he departed on a mission of nonviolence to Egypt, where, after crossing the line between Muslim armies and Crusaders at Damietta, he engaged in interfaith dialogue with Sultan Melek-el-Kamel. His Christian apologetic was more extensive than rhetoric, however, in that Francis challenged the Muslim scholars to a trial by fire. Upon the scholars' hasty retreat from the challenge, the mendicant proposed that he enter the fire first, and if, like the three Hebrew children of Daniel's prophecy, he exited the fire un-singed, the sultan would accept the veracity of Francis's faith claims. Although divergent accounts relate the reactions to the proposal in contrary terms, it is agreed that Francis's contact with Muslims, and particularly the sultan, can be characterized as initiatory, intentional, missionary, and bold, though without military or political support or innuendo (Tolan 2002, 216).

An eighth example of Christian contact with pre-Christian European religion is the sterling Swiss Reformer John Calvin. Born in Noyon, France, in 1509 CE, Calvin adopted an approach to mission that has been identified as theocratic and covenantal. In January 1537, the Reformer presented to the Little Council of Geneva a set of articles concerning reform. Interpreting God's will as directing him to set up the evangelical standard in this Swiss city, Calvin emphasized strong church discipline, children's education, and a system of inspectors—composed of laypersons—to enforce ecclesiastical compliance, all to implement a moral code grounded in axial values. Although banished from Geneva for four years, eventually the Reformer was welcomed back and given inordinate control over the city and its social affairs (Baker and Landers 2005, 230). Christian believers from other lands, particularly England, France, Scotland, and the Netherlands, sought refuge in Calvin's Swiss city, assured that religious freedom would be guaranteed. Calvin's theological system, although resisted during his time and through the present day, guided his actions and directives, commensurate with his conception of the sovereignty of God. Undoubtedly, the reforms initiated and employed by

---

Study Aid #97

Models of Christian Contact in Europe

Bishop Felix of North Africa	Pope Urban II
Martin of Tours	Francis of Assisi
Clovis, king of the Franks	John Calvin
Hilda of Whitby	John Wesley
Cyril and Methodius	Pedro Okoro

John Calvin were the products of theological and social evolutionary process, most audaciously advocated first by Martin Luther and second by Ulrich Zwingli. But one must argue that this Swiss Reformer's praxis—the unswerving discharge of the evangelical insistence on holism—has left the most enduring legacy of Christian contact with pre-Christian peoples. Though criticized as antimission, Calvin insisted upon evangelism unrelentingly: "It befits us so to feel as to wish that all be saved. So it will come about that, whoever we come across, we shall study to make him a sharer . . . of peace. . . . Even severe rebuke will be administered like medicine, lest they should perish or cause others to perish" (Chadwick 1990, 138). Calvin's contact, thus, with pre-Christian European religion was calculated, missionary, and enduring.

Occurrences in the British Isles, particularly in England, accelerated by the Industrial Revolution and events on the European Continent, eventuated in the demise of religious life, evidenced in both public worship and social morality. Abject poverty, unrestrained urbanization, and economic stringency caused many persons, especially those of common birth and a peasant lifestyle, to languish in bewilderment. Real-life issues, unaddressed by formal religion, went unanswered, and Christian faith, although introduced centuries before, was at its lowest ebb. Such was the environment into which the ninth example of Christian contact with pre-Christian European religion was born: the evangelical revivalist John Wesley. Born in 1703 CE in Epworth, England, Wesley underwent a transformative spiritual experience in his early years.

In 1735 Wesley and his brother Charles sailed for the colonies in America, at the request of Governor James Oglethorpe, to minister to the British colonists in the province of Georgia. On his sea voyage Wesley was deeply and profoundly influenced by the pietistic faith of the Moravians, especially their "sweet spirit and excellent discipline" (Tomkins 2003, 43). The young British missionary understood his calling to the province of Georgia to be one of evangelism among the Native Americans. Though Wesley was diligent in his witness, the mission was a resounding defeat. Upon returning to England, the Anglican attended a prayer meeting among the Moravians at Aldersgate Street. It was about this experience that Wesley would later write, "I felt my heart strangely warmed."

Convinced that people in London and the British Isles were perishing in their sins and suffering injustice, the zealous itinerant "field" preacher underwent persecution, opposition, and resistance, most often from government magistrates and clergy. Impervious to such hostility, Wesley continued refining his message and his delivery, with many coming to faith immediately upon hearing the message. Such was the response to Wesley's contact with pre-Christian Europeans that he is credited with initiating one of the most profound movements within English history, averting rebellion and revolution through reaching those persons and populations untouched by the Anglican and Roman Catholic Churches.

A tenth and final example of Christian contact with European religion is through such persons as Pedro Okoro of the African and Caribbean Evangelical Alliance.

Okoro, along with many others throughout the European continent, has led in mission and evangelism among immigrant communities from Africa, South America, the Caribbean, and Asia. The increase of immigrant communities within Europe, particularly from Africa, South America, and Asia, has catapulted the growth of Black Majority Churches and other Diaspora congregations, bolstering the continuing mission from everywhere to everywhere. As in the cases of John Wesley, John Calvin, Saint Francis of Assisi, and Cyril and Methodius, the contact between Christian faith and European religion is intentionally missionary, initiated by the agents of Christianity.

These ten paragons of contact—Felix, Martin, Clovis, Hilda, Pope Urban II, the five missionary entities of Cyril and Methodius, Saint Francis of Assisi, John Calvin, John Wesley, and Pedro Okoro—serve as watersheds each in the history of Christian contact. Though each association was distinct, nonetheless in most cases the contact was intentional, missionary, and strategic.

Sources

Robert Baker and John Landers. *A Summary of Christian History*. 3rd ed. Broadman & Holman, 2005.

Venerable Bede. *Ecclesiastical History of the English People*. Penguin, 1955.

Stephen Bevans and Roger Schroeder. *Constants in Context*. Orbis Books, 2004.

Peter Brown. *The Rise of Western Christendom*. Blackwell, 2003.

Owen Chadwick. *The Reformation*. Penguin, 1990.

Carole Cusack. *The Rise of Christianity in Northern Europe, 300–1000*. Cassell, 1998.

Bart Ehrman and Andrews Jacobs. *Christianity in Late Antiquity, 300–450 CE*. Oxford University Press, 2004.

G. R. Evans. *The History of Christian Europe*. Lion Hudson, 2008.

David Hugh Farmer. *Oxford Dictionary of the Saints*. Oxford University Press, 1997.

Justo González. *The Story of Christianity*. Hendrickson, 1999.

Gregory of Tours. *History of the Franks*. Penguin, 1974.

J. F. Michaud. *The History of the Crusades*. Redfield, 1855.

John Victor Tolan. *Islam in Late Medieval European Imagination*. Columbia University Press, 2002.

Stephen Tomkins. *John Wesley: A Biography*. Eerdmans, 2003.

45

Europe: Theological Exchanges

RICHARD SHAW

The interaction between Christian theology and pre-Christian theologies and philosophies in Europe has been characterized by the dialectics of militarism and pacifism, contextualization and strict uniformity, and hegemony and subaltern subversion, from early days until today. Some scholars have approached the dialogue with intellectually fervent debate, as in the case of the apostle Paul in Athens (Acts 17). Others, such as Bonaventure and Thomas Aquinas, though equally as fervent, bifurcated theology and philosophy, insisting upon faith as both essential and superior to reason. Subalterns such as John Huss and Isidore of Seville demonstrated the pacific nature of Christian theology, and other missionary theologians such as Patrick and Boniface opted for more indigenous and spiritually powerful means of engagement. Christian theology's encounter with twenty-first-century philosophies and theologies in Europe continues to both reinforce past dialectical polarities and stimulate new arenas of debate and dissension.

Stoicism thrived before and during the nascent Christian movement. As Christian theology burgeoned and matured, the over-three-hundred-year-old philosophy of Stoicism was compelled to respond, often doing so through its appeal to physical theory, logic, and causal determinism. The Stoic tenets of modality and bivalence, often illustrated through Chrysippus's analogy of a rolling cylinder, were rooted in the central tenet of corporeality—that is, that only matter exists. Not atheistic, Stoicism maintained that all that is real, including God and the human soul, is material. God exists panentheistically, permeating all matter as a divine fire. The Stoic maxim "Live according to nature" epitomized the tandem Stoic ethical principles of absolute law and the centrality of reason within human existence.

Much of the theological thinking of pre-Christian Celtic and Germanic peoples focused upon the motifs of foreknowledge and destiny. Middle-ground issues rooted in existential questions—of the here and now, the living not the dead, success and failure, and power needed to control the exigencies of life—drove many to postulate that certain men and women possessed skills necessary to discover mysterious knowledge. Early Christian missionaries to peoples motivated by such concerns were forced to contend with strongly held beliefs in superstitions and omens, and to locate those nuances of the Christian gospel that foreground faith in contrast to hidden knowledge. Though unrelated to ancient Gnostic thought, pre-Christian Europeans maintained similar theologies and, when confronted with gospel claims, were challenged to either abandon life ways and rituals centered on magic or to syncretize the old and the new.

Christian mission history seems to pivot upon the fulcrum balancing uniformity with long-standing church tradition, and contextualization with indigenous cultural forms. Thus when Gregory the Great (540–604 CE) dispatched the Roman Catholic monk Augustine to Britain, the mission methodology employed by the Roman centered on the Romanness of Christian faith. Indigenous forms were subverted, though not emasculated, and continued on, even though clandestine. Patrick and other Celtic missionaries, however, accommodated themselves—and the gospel they proclaimed—to the residents, discovering that, indeed, the truth of the Christian scriptures was true, that the created order, including cultural lore, philosophy, and ideology, was already giving witness to God's prevenient grace. Such a dialectic of mission practice, though perplexing, forced interaction between Christian theology and pre-Christian understandings in northwestern Europe.

In addition to the motifs of foreknowledge and destiny, the mystical theme of interaction with the supernatural world was integral to Christianity's encounter with pre-Christian beliefs. The enigma of the supernatural, particularly in the interpretation of dreams, caused early Europeans to attempt to establish intentional relationships with gods and goddesses. Scandinavian legendry and lore point to the early belief in the gods Freyr and Thor appearing in dreams, sending messages to leaders. Land spirits, often either incarnated in or possessing domestic livestock such as cows, were alleged to communicate with the living, bringing messages from ancestors or other deceased human beings. Such communications occurred

---

Study Aid #98

European Mission Dialectics

Militarism and pacifism
Contextualization and uniformity
Hegemony and heterogeneity
Providence and divination
Early mission practice and later mission practice

through dreams, not as omens, but as visitations. Icelandic legendry posits the belief in foreknowledge through dreams, often mediated through symbols.

When Christian faith was introduced to Scandinavian peoples, there was no discontinuity with the affirmation of beliefs in dreams, nor of communication of the divine through dreams. Perhaps the most discontinuous aspect of dreams and their interpretation came with the content of dreams. The biblical canon certainly assumed the validity of dreams as interaction with the supernatural world, and the acquisition of foreknowledge through them in, for example, Joseph's dreams of sheaves in the field and the heavenly bodies (Gen. 37). Ireland's great fifth-century missionary Patrick had dreams of his own, of such gravity and import that he credits them with both his conversion to Christian faith and his missionary calling.

In addition to the motifs of foreknowledge/destiny and mystical interaction with the supernatural, a third common theme of pre-Christian Europe was the relationship between divination and war. Much Albanian legendry, for example, centers upon the warriors Mujo and Halil and their encounters with the mythical *Kulshedra*, or dragon. Although veneered with both Islamic and Christian vocabularies and other cultural accoutrements, a pre-extant maintenance of belief in the relationship between secret prophetic knowledge and the outcome of battle was omnipresent. In pre-Christian Greece, great attention was paid to celestial movements and events, while diviners were held in high regard and their predictions trusted as immortally reliable. In the post-Hellenic Roman Empire, embarking on war was predicated upon divination, normally conducted through sacrifice. However, with the advent of Christian faith, divination was adroitly suppressed in many cases and anathematized in others. Divination and its concomitant hegemony upon warfare was so influential that the early Christian leaders expressly addressed it in church councils and synods, including Laodicea around 360 CE, Vannes in 461 CE, Agde in 506 CE, and Orléans in 511 CE. Forms of augury, including necromancy, hydromancy, geomancy, and omens through haruspicy—the study of the entrails of animals—were interpreted by Christian missionaries and clerics as absolutely discontinuous with scripture and hence forbidden.

The uses of divination, and particularly its coupling with warfare, were to diagnose causes of defeat and loss, to determine proper courses of action leading to military victory, to avoid dangers posed by potential enemies and opponents, to determine the guilt of one's warriors prior to the onset of battle, to select commanders, to find weapons and other instruments of war temporarily misplaced, and to gain supernatural knowledge, often perceived as secret and known only to a lucky, chosen few. The Christian gospel, when encountering adherents of divination, sought to demonstrate a theology of providential guidance, believing in spiritual discernment available to all who follow and trust Jesus Christ.

Perhaps one of the most appealing facts of the Christian narrative to pre-Christian Europeans, particularly rulers, such as the fifth-century king of the Franks Clovis, was the belief that the God of the Christians was a more powerful and beneficent ally in battle than another god or gods. The alignment of military

> **Study Aid #99**
> **The European Islamic Challenge**
> The history
> Vehicles
>   Immigration
>   Intermarriage
>   Conversion
> Issues
>   De facto pluralism
>   Ecumenism
>   Syncretism
> "Eurabia"?

victory with a triumphalistic faith may have persuaded earthly sovereigns to jettison previously held faith commitments, or at least to syncretize them. Notwithstanding, the moral holiness of the gospel story—including the ethic verbalized and demonstrated by Jesus Christ—served as the compelling factor to conversion for others. Willibrord and the younger Columba, often called Columban, preached the uncompromising morality of the Christian narrative with such boldness that both were often persecuted. Such abuse aside, the consequent beneficial effects to society and culture, however, secured both missionaries' temporal success, obviated through the establishment of a strong church in Frisia and northern Italy, respectively.

A third nuance of the Christian story discovered to appeal at both individual and societal levels has been labeled *erudition* (instruction); Christianization—appropriating Christian faith at multiple levels—was perceived as leading from darkness to light, from ignorance and unbelief to civilization, from backwardness and obscurity to progress and development. Though misinterpreted at times within Christian history, including tragic cases of the use of violence, coerced conversion was at some points forbidden, glossed as a breach of the rules and as a disregard of the will of the recipient. That powerful rulers not only gave ear to the story, but also committed themselves to it, was potent and significant enough for others to become sympathetic with the newfound faith.

Sociological aspects of the Christian story and those who came to embrace it also served as compelling factors in the rise of Christianity. The story of Jesus Christ and his power to transform lives and societies was particularly irresistible to religious skeptics, most prevalent among the more privileged social classes, drawn to a new culture. The plausibility of existing religious faith within pre-Christian European arenas had eroded, leading those who had substantial privilege, though less than they felt they deserved, to abandon their perceptions of deprivation. Though much of what these skeptics turned to was theologically innovative and pristine, the force of its central message was both consoling and ambitious.

Escape from or reduction of marginality, a second sociological phenomenon relevant to the Christian gospel, drew many persons to the new faith in Jesus Christ. While some Jews attempted to become a new kind of Jew, others defined Christianity as the fulfillment of centuries-long Judaism. Christianity, whether interpreted as continuous with historic Jewish faith or discontinuous with entrenched Judaism, was compelling because of its cultural familiarity with the first position, and its newness with the second. Congruent with sociological axioms, converts to the Christian gospel were drawn primarily from the ranks of the religiously inactive and discontent. These were individuals who saw within the Jesus story both a fulfillment of Jewish promise and prophecy, and a correspondence with traditional convention. That marginalized persons found moral authority; community solidarity; empowerment regardless of gender; compassionate, prescriptive action in response to epidemics and warfare; and a countercultural alternative to urban blight and misery was integral to the growth of Christian faith and acceptance of its message and ethic.

Undoubtedly the greatest contest to Christian faith on the European continent has been, and continues to be, Islam. While other religions and philosophies—including Judaism, Druidism, and divergent new religious movements—have challenged the perceived hegemony of European Christendom, Muslim ideologies and agendas demonstrate daunting, remarkable potency. By 711 CE a small band of Muslims, advancing out of North Africa, crossed the Strait of Gibraltar and discovered the Visigothic kingdom on the Iberian Peninsula so internally weakened that they quickly overran it. This band, under the leadership of Tarik, continued to emasculate rulers and kingdoms until they were finally defeated by Charles Martel in 732 CE, at the Battle of Tours. Though repelled in France, Muslim forces continued to gain ground, primarily in southern Europe, with Rome being sacked in 864 CE and Pisa in 1004 CE. Balkan states in southeastern Europe, though providing robust defense against the new faith through leaders such as the Albanian George Kastriot Skendërbeg, were finally subdued in the Battle of Kosovo Polje in 1389 CE. The Islamic faith was thus extended and propagated through the Ottoman Empire until its collapse in the early twentieth century.

Notwithstanding, the resurgence of Islam on the European continent is well documented. Scholars including Bernard Lewis, demographer Jean-Claude Chesnais, Spanish journalist Silva Taulés, and European commissioner Frits Bolkestein have predicted the (re-)Islamization of Europe. Philip Jenkins and others use the term "Eurabia" to describe this demographic and religious phenomenon. Though the vast majority of Muslims on the European continent are immigrants (and their descendants) from former British and French colonies, religious conversion is recognized, with the single most common factor being the marriage of European women to Muslim men. Other identified factors, all creditable, include the intellectual and spiritual appeal of Islam, the glamour of Islamic history and culture, and close involvement with Muslim communities. Some conversions have been labeled "protest conversions"—that is, a change of fiduciary commitment due to a rejection of mainstream culture, including its worldview and values.

While many Christians have sought to embrace tenets of Islamic faith—particularly those values that lead to a global ethic—others have denounced such interreligiosity as breaking the limits of ecumenism to the point of syncretism. Increasingly marginalized by secularized systems with compelling political will, Christian faith nonetheless, as history has demonstrated, responds most robustly when oppressed. The dialectic polarity thus established, Islamic resurgence and the revival of Christianity seem poised for continuing encounter.

46

Europe: Current Issues

RICHARD SHAW

While for many decades many, if not most, people in Europe had considered issues of tolerance and minority rights long settled, in many places such assumptions are being tested, if not discredited. Scholars, journalists, political leaders, clergy, and others have, for centuries, maintained the notion that the European continent is "God's Continent" (Jenkins 2009, 2) painstakingly Christianized over a period of more than a millennium. Relationships between Christians and Muslims, for example, are foregrounded in Western Europe many times each week, as adherents of each world religion seek to inculcate the values, ethic, and priorities they embrace in as many seekers, if not converts, as possible, through religious, academic, economic, and/or legal means. Eastern Europeans, with a protracted historical memory of interreligious conflict, reflect a more jaded and nuanced perspective to such conflict and controversy. Dechristianization, or more precisely, secularization, coupled with immigration and an insistence of nonassimilation among diaspora immigrant communities, has spurred critical reflection. "¿Qué Europa queremos? ¿Una sociedad postmoderna, multicultural o fiel a sus raíces?" ("What kind of Europe do we want? A postmodern, multicultural society, or one faithful to its roots?"), asks Jutta Burggraf in *Scripta Theologica* (2008, 839). In Eastern Europe, the long anti-Christian era of Marxist ideology, according to Pavel Hanes, continues to linger "under various disguises" (Hanes 2008, 29). Walter S. Ray lambasts those within Christianity who seek to identify the values of Western Europe as rooted in Christianity, with acquiescence to those who, though they would concur, would be reluctant to admit it (Hanes 2008). Additionally, a plethora of adherents of other religions—whether indigenous pre-Christian faith systems or transplanted ones—challenge both the image of

European progressiveness and the assumption of a fait accompli. Although such a bevy of polemical and contentious issues is ubiquitous and often disconcerting, there is guarded optimism regarding future missional interactions between Christianity and other faiths in Europe. Below I identify four major issues that are significant and relevant today.

Issue: Conversion. Location: Kosovo

Undoubtedly one of the major sites of cultural change within Europe is the tiny nation-state of Kosovo, once a part of Serbia, and prior to that, Yugoslavia. Historically predominantly Albanian Muslim—though with divergent ethnic and religious minorities—this flinty, landlocked Balkan country has experienced substantial conversion to Christianity, of both Roman Catholic and evangelical persuasions (Ray 2008), since the NATO-led war against Serbia in 1999. Westward-leaning and decidedly pro-American in terms of worldview, policy, economy, and education, Kosovar Albanians have demonstrated an embrace of Christian faith, both in traditional and liturgical and in celebrative and ecstatic styles, at more than a brisk pace.

Perhaps such acceleration has occurred, at least in part, because of the natural rise of new religious movements—or revitalization of old faith systems—as a response to social crises. Frequently in the history of humankind, crises produced by social or natural calamities "have been translated into crises of faith" (Stark 1997, 77). A second reason for such rapid conversion to Christianity may be that Christian missionaries—both foreign-born and indigenous—as agents of the gospel of Jesus Christ have availed themselves to Kosovar Muslim Albanians in times of need and suffering. The social ethic taught by the founder Jesus Christ,

---

Study Aid #100

Current Issues in Europe

Increased religious conversion
  Social crises
  Material need
  Women's rights
  Dual belonging/hybrid identities
Religion and politics
  Immigration
  Freedom of religion
Interreligious engagement: Two questions
  What is the meaning of increased engagement?
  What actions should engagement lead to?

understood as inherent to Christian faith and practice, has been implemented, especially beginning in the autumn of 1998 and continuing to the present. A third reason suggested is the role of women in Christianity, among both evangelical and Roman Catholic communities. Like their Christian sisters in the Southern Hemisphere, female Muslim-Background Believers have articulated the emancipating power of the Christian message, juxtaposed with more restrictive roles in Islam.

The liberal "Islam lite" version of faith espoused and practiced in Kosovo has brought accolades from Western observers who fear a militant Islamic fundamentalism seen elsewhere. But reaction to Christian conversion has been evidenced in cities such as Gjakova, in the southwestern corner, near the border with Albania. In a November 2007 posting on the website of the Gjakova branch of the Kosovo Islamic Community, a list of Protestant ministers—both indigenous Kosovar Albanians and foreign workers—was provided (Bureau 2009). According to the US State Department report, personal information including names, addresses, telephone numbers, and the names of churches or humanitarian aid organizations affiliated with these individuals or entities was available on more than one hundred private websites as well.

Although major violent clashes between Christianity and Islam are absent from the tiny, fledgling country, numerous governmental and international agencies have reported sporadic, localized interreligious conflicts. The interface between the two faiths—both of missionary nature—will continue to chafe abrasively as accelerated cultural change persists.

Issue: Dual Belonging. Location: Great Britain

A religious marketplace exists in virtually every place in Europe. One characteristic of religious marketplaces is the competitive nature of human religious systems. With so many religious options available, and with only minor, if any, negative, pernicious consequences for religious change, people, when they experience lack in their lives, express a desire to make a change in faith.

Christianity and Judaism, twin monotheistic, Abrahamic religions, both offer compelling reasons for adherence. The burgeoning Messianic Synagogue movement attempts to bridge the division between these two religions, recognizing the fulfillment of one (Judaism) in the other (Christianity). Messianic Judaism retains ancient Jewish forms and calendar, emphasizing the continuity between the faith of Abraham and the faith of Jesus, whom most Messianic Jews call "Yeshua." Insisting that Jesus Christ did not come to create a new religious system but rather to prophetically complete the ancient one, this movement traces its roots to the founder of Christianity, identifying no other human initiator. While other Jews—Orthodox, Conservative, Reform—do not accept Jesus Christ as the Messiah, nor Messianic Jews as true Jews, Messianists accept both Jesus Christ as the Promised One and their Jewish ethnic and religious identities.

One prominent location of this energetic development is Great Britain. Members of the British Messianic Jewish Alliance (BMJA), established formally in 1866, having discovered that their newfound "faith made them 'true Israelites,' emphasized their essential unity with the Jewish people and sought to demonstrate that Jews in Yeshua were vital to the healthy growth of the Church." Recognizing the claims of the Jewish community that it is impossible to believe in Jesus and be Jewish, Messianic believers are quick to self-identify as "converted sinners," rather than "Jewish converts to Christianity," asserting that Jewishness is not a sin to be repented of but rather that all people, regardless of their ethnicity, are called upon to convert from sin to Jesus Christ. Fully embracing their ethnic heritage and the religious legacy of many generations, Messianic believers urge Christian proclaimers to be diligent and sensitive to Jewish persons, to pray for the peace of Jerusalem and the salvation of the Jewish people, and to reject anti-Semitic dogma in whatever form it is embedded or expressed.

Dual belonging and hybrid identity present challenges for those engaged in public discourse, whether Christian ministers interpreting scriptures, Christian missionaries seeking to evangelize, or those involved in political affairs and policy making. Due diligence is essential for all, recognizing that the language one uses carries meanings and triggers consequences, often unintended.

Issue: Religion and Politics. Locations: Germany and Turkey

Regardless of topics permeating Western and Eastern intelligentsia and media, those themes associated with religion and politics in the Middle East and Europe are, as a matter of course, highly focal and potent. Historical events, including those of random nature as well as those of intentional purpose or design, coupled with cultural memory and the desire for ethnic retributive justice, coalesce into public opinion and, more significantly, public policy. Conflicts, addressed in discourse and dialogue, often develop into violence and warfare, infused with religious ideals and values. Of note is the curious dialectic between Germany and Turkey, as well as the wider implications in the Middle East.

Beginning in the 1950s the demand for labor resonated throughout northwestern Europe, particularly in Germany. The flow of workers from East Germany ceased with the construction of the Berlin Wall in 1961, simultaneous with the first Bilateral Recruitment Agreement reached between Germany and Turkey. By December 1961, seven thousand temporary workers from Turkey were living in Germany (Cook 2001, 985). Pressure from business leaders in Germany led to the termination of the two-year limit for Turkish workers. Although most Turks believed they would return to their homeland in time, the vast majority did not, and in mid-2010 the percentage of the German population self-identifying as Turkish stands at 2.4 percent, or 1.97 million persons. Reportedly, the German

> **Study Aid #101**
> Shifting Meaning of Mission Vocabulary
>
> Tolerance   Mission
> Pluralism   Witness
> Secularization

government has done little to assimilate these Turkish persons into the predominant culture. Perhaps this is the case because of the understanding that many of the Turks would only be temporarily in the country.

Notwithstanding, the reality of unassimilated Turks within the greater German culture, including within the political arena, with the vast majority of these Turks professing Islamic faith and the vast majority of Germans professing Christian faith or no faith, has caused interethnic and interreligious tensions. In mid-February 2010, Turkish prime minister Recep Tayyip Erdogan urged Turks living in Germany to resist assimilation and maintain their Turkish—and therefore Muslim—traditions. About six weeks later, in late March 2010, Erdogan issued a call to the German government to establish Turkish-language secondary schools in Germany. In response, German chancellor Angela Merkel replied, "I do not think this brings us forward, as I think that Turkish children and pupils should go to German schools. I do not think much of the idea of Turkish children going to Turkish school." With passionate advocates on both sides of this thorny issue at local, national, and international arenas, the interface between religion and politics will continue to abrade.

Issue: Engagement. Location: Geneva, Switzerland, and Palestinian Territories

Though the divisive situation between Germany and Turkey appears bleak, there is hope for more constructive engagement between Christians and Muslims regarding the Middle East. Though certainly not a monolithic or representative organization, the World Council of Churches (WCC) is presently seeking to work redemptively among Christians, Jews, and Muslims in Israel and the Palestinian Territories. Citing the denial of access to "land and water resources," the restriction of "their [Palestinian] freedom of movement," the diminishing of "their basic human dignity and, in many cases, their right to life," the World Council of Churches' central committee, in a September 2, 2009, public statement on Israeli settlements in the occupied Palestinian Territory, called upon the government of Israel to "urgently implement an open-ended freeze in good-faith on all settlement construction and expansion." Realizing that there are Christian and Muslim Palestinians precludes any assumption that the WCC is pandering to only one religious group. On the contrary, the deliberate engagement of the

WCC with the government of Israel and the Palestinian authority demonstrates willingness for dialogue and advocacy, delimiting the religious and ethnic claims of any *one* of the Abrahamic religions.

Such engagement among Christian, Jewish, and Muslim entities and individuals, particularly over the conflicting rights and responsibilities of those persons specifically involved, foregrounds two existential questions: the meaning question and the action question. One may ask, What is the purpose of such dialogue among differing, passionate individuals, apparently diametrically opposed at a foundational level to mutual goals and intents? Other ancillary questions related to meaning have to do with historiography, theology, and ethnic identity: To whom does this land actually belong? Whose record of history do we trust, and why? Is there sufficient goodwill to accord polarized goals?

The second question—the action question—grows out of the meaning question. What will we do to achieve a mutual peace? How much power do we relinquish in order to achieve our goal and the goal of the "other"? To whom do we listen, and to whom do we answer, in our doing? The WCC's central committee has responded to the meaning question through (1) a dialectical lens of biblically based human rights for all persons, accepting all peoples' history recordings; and (2) through a theological lens that recognizes biblical justice grounded in access of all persons to health and life. The action question, at least at this stage, is answered through verbal and physical means—advocacy by a religious entity directed toward a political one, coupled with shipments of food, medicines, and other supplies to meet human needs.

The current situation of Christianity and other religions in Europe, and how these interface with the Middle East, is tenuous at best. Future challenges posed by missionary religions and new religious movements demand vision, allowing for the uniqueness of each, while striving for cooperation for the betterment of all.

Sources

> British Messianic Jewish Alliance. "Introducing the British Messianic Jewish Alliance." http://www.bmja.net/BMJA percent20GENERAL percent2005.pdf.
>
> Bureau of Democracy, Human Rights, and Labor. "International Religious Freedom Report 2009: Kosovo." US Department of State. October 26, 2009. http://www.state.gov/g/drl/rls/irf/2009/127318.htm.
>
> Bernard Cook. *Europe since 1945: An Encyclopedia*. Garland, 2001.
>
> Jutta Burggraf. "¿Qué Europa queremos? ¿Una sociedad postmoderna, multicultural o fiel a sus raíces?" *Scripta theologica* 40 (2008): 839–58.
>
> Pavel Hanes. "Christianity in the Post-Marxist Context." *European Journal of Theology* 17, no. 1 (2008): 29.
>
> Philip Jenkins. *God's Continent*. Oxford University Press, 2009.

"Merkel Rebuffs Erdogan on Turkish Schools in Germany." Expatica.com. March 26, 2010. http://www.expatica.com/de/news/german-rss-news/merkel-rebuffs-erdogan-on-turkish-schools-in-germany_33537.html.

Walter S. Ray. Review of *Rethinking Christendom: Europe's Struggle for Christianity*, by Jonathan Luxmoore and Jolanta Babiuch. *Religion in Eastern Europe* 27, no. 1 (February 2007): 57.

———. "A Tale of Converts in Kosovo." *The Economist*, December 30, 2008. http://www.economist.com/research/articlesBySubject/displaystory.cfm?subjectid=7294978&story_id=12868180.

Rodney Stark. *The Rise of Christianity*. HarperSanFrancisco, 1997.

"WCC Calls to Freeze and Dismantle Israeli Settlements." September 3, 2009. http://globalministries.org/news/mee/wcc-calls-to-freeze-and.html.

47

Middle East: History, Beliefs, Practices

J. Andrew Dearman

History

Religion in the Middle East casts a long shadow, with material cultural remains providing evidence of religious practices millennia before writing developed. With the advent of writing in the great civilizations of Egypt and Mesopotamia (ca. 3000 BCE), there is documented evidence of complex religious systems, central to their societies, and complete with institutions such as temples, specialized personnel, and sacrificial cults to serve the gods. In addition to matters common to religious development, the region has experienced several fundamental shifts in political hegemony, cultural profile, and language usage, all of which also affected the practice of religion. The religious heritage of Egypt, Canaan, Syria, Asia Minor, and Mesopotamia, as known from the third and second millennia BCE, is now difficult to identify in the current religions of Judaism, Christianity, and Islam, each of which essentially assimilated their older counterparts and succeeded them. Judaism, which emerged from the Iron Age states of Israel and Judah during the Persian period, has its heirs in the small, modern state of Israel. Christianity, which emerged from Greco-Roman Judaism, has its heirs in most modern Middle Eastern states, but is now the majority in none of them. Islam, which emerged from the Arabian Peninsula in the seventh century CE to control the whole region, remains the majority religion in every modern Middle Eastern state with the exception of Israel. It is also the reason for the centrality of Arabic as the lingua franca, the most widely used language in the region.

The end of the second millennium BCE saw the collapse of traditional centers of power in much of the region, and in the aftermath a number of new entities

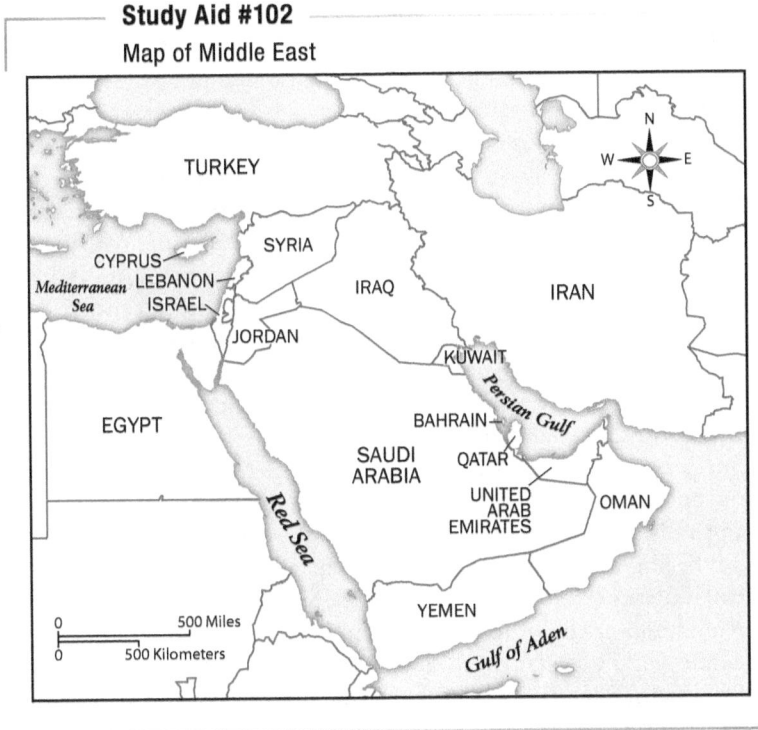

Study Aid #102
Map of Middle East

emerged into recorded history. Among these newly emerged states was Israel, whose constituent tribes and cities were heirs to the Bronze Age traditions of Canaan and Syria. In the centuries that followed, Israel and Judah produced a collection of authoritative writings now known to Jews as the Hebrew Bible and to Christians as the Old Testament. In the ninth through seventh centuries BCE, Neo-Assyrian forces expanded from their center in northern Mesopotamia, moving west into Syria-Palestine and eventually for a time into Lower (northern) Egypt. When the Neo-Assyrian Empire crumbled, it was succeeded by the Neo-Babylonian Empire and the vigorous King Nebuchadnezzar (ca. 605–539 BCE). Next came the Persian Empire under Cyrus the Great and a series of successors (ca. 539–330 BCE). As with the Assyrians, the Babylonians and Persians eventually ruled much of the ancient Near East and briefly parts of Egypt. These immense political changes brought with them cultural diffusion as well; so, for example, Assyrian astral cults and Persian dualism interacted with the religions of Syria-Palestine and Egypt.

Another immense cultural change came to the region with the military campaigns of Alexander the Great (334–323 BCE). Through military prowess he brought about a reordering of the political map of the ancient Near East. After his death in 323, his successors carved out spheres of influence and dominated the Mediterranean and Near Eastern regions for the next 175 years. Even more influential and much longer lasting was the change brought in by the Greek language and culture of the time, known today as Hellenism. Eventually a form of Greek became the common language of the region. Egyptian and Semitic deities were identified with Greek counterparts, even as new temples were built.

The arrival of Roman imperialism in Egypt and the eastern Mediterranean brought yet more change and eventually a broader cultural mix between Greco-Roman institutions and those of longer duration in the region. Christianity began as a Jewish messianic sect during Roman hegemony in Palestine. With the so-called conversion of Constantine, the Roman ruler of the eastern empire, Christianity emerged as a favored religion in the first quarter of the fourth century CE and as the official religion of the empire by the end of that century. Political power was centered in Byzantium, renamed Constantinople and located on the former land bridge between Asia and Europe at the Bosporus Strait.

The Byzantine Christian Empire lasted until the arrival of Muslim forces from Arabia, just a few years after Muhammad's death in Medina in 632. Egypt, Palestine, Syria, and Iraq were all incorporated into the Islamic sphere, and the process of creating an Islamic culture began. Two primary forms of Islam developed, the Sunni and the Shi'a. The latter looked to the male descendants of Muhammad as the rightful leaders of the community, while the Sunnis saw continuity in leadership based on maintaining the pattern of the prophet's leadership. The political center of the Islamic world varied in the following centuries. It would be located in places such as Damascus, Baghdad (a city formed initially as a capital for Muslim rulers), Cairo, and eventually Constantinople, which was captured by Muslim forces in 1453 and renamed Istanbul. The Ottoman Empire had its capital in Istanbul and ruled the Middle Eastern region from around 1520 until 1918.

The middle decades of the twentieth century saw much of the Middle Eastern political map redrawn by the British and French governments, the victors over the Ottoman Empire in World War I. In 1948, Jewish immigrants to the region declared a modern state of Israel and made Modern Hebrew one of its official languages. In the latter half of the twentieth century, other states in the region emerged from colonial influence to form national governments and identities. A Muslim identity is common to these other states, although Christianity, Druze, and Baha'i are also present.

Beliefs

The primary structure of ancient Near Eastern religions was that of polytheism. This is the case even with the diversity of regional cultures, the long history of development, and the massive syncretistic and assimilating shifts that came with the advent of Greco-Roman cultures. The deities were understood as a hierarchical interactive community, in some sense like a state or urban bureaucracy, where their tasks with weather, fertility, trade protection, crafts, and health were carried out.

> **Study Aid #103**
> **Countries of the Middle East**
>
> | | | | |
> |---|---|---|---|
> | Bahrain | Israel | Palestine | Turkey |
> | Cyprus | Jordan | (territories) | United Arab |
> | Egypt | Kuwait | Qatar | Emirates |
> | Iran | Lebanon | Saudi Arabia | Yemen |
> | Iraq | Oman | Syria | |

Indeed, the language of king and queen could be used of chief deities, as could terms like "father" or "creator of the gods." The deity Assur, for example, was the patron of the Assyrian city of the same name and was proclaimed as the divine king in the Assyrian realm. Ishtar was the Queen of Heaven among the Assyrians. In a pantheon, other deities might be understood as members of a lower rank, though important in their own sphere, and perhaps as offspring of a high or primordial deity. The creation of the world could be associated with primordial deities (as in Mesopotamia), or with a high deity such as El in parts of Bronze Age Canaan, or with a variety of deities in Egypt. The abode of the gods was understood to be heaven, even when they were associated with mountains, seas, or other earthly terrain such as particular cities or regions. Thus some deities were associated with astronomical phenomena. Shamash was the sun deity in Mesopotamia; Re was the sun deity in Egypt. In Syria-Palestine the vigorous storm deity was known as master (Baal) and rider of the clouds. With the advent of Hellenism, some new deities were added to the region and some indigenous deities were identified with Greco-Roman counterparts. Ishtar, for example, was identified with Venus, and Melqart, the patron deity of Tyre, was identified with Heracles.

There is evidence that several of the tribal societies of Syria-Palestine understood their collective identity in light of a chief or patron deity. This is not monotheism per se, which entails the denial of the existence of any other deity, but can be defined as monolatry, at least at the level of the ruling dynasty and/or the sponsored cult of a capital city. In Egypt, Pharaoh Akhenaten (fourteenth century BCE) sought to reform Egyptian religion similarly to the primary worship of Aten, although he did not deny the existence of other Egyptian deities. His reforming efforts were resisted and died with him. Israelite religious beliefs were forged in these circumstances. Israel's deity (YHWH), often pronounced Yahweh, was proclaimed Israel's sole deity. The strong prohibition in the Hebrew Bible against the worship of other deities (Exod. 20:3) assumes their potential appeal, but also that Yahweh (typically translated as "Lord") was sufficient for the needs of his people. Yahweh as Lord is carefully differentiated from the Canaanite Baal, though he wielded similar powers. Yahweh is also called (the) "God," using the common terminology for the high god El, recognized as the creator in the Canaanite realm, and he is addressed as the cosmic king.

> **Study Aid #104**
>
> **Middle East Empires, Eras, Ages**
>
> Neo-Assyrian: 9th–7th centuries BCE
> Neo-Babylonian: 6th century
> Persian: 5th–4th centuries
> Hellenism: 3rd–1st centuries
> Roman: 1st–4th centuries CE
>
> Byzantium: 5th–7th centuries
> Islam: 8th–15th centuries
> Ottoman: 16th–19th centuries
> Colonial: 20th century

It is ironic, historically speaking, that the three monotheistic religions either emerge from or take strong root in the region. Judaism is an outgrowth of the religious traditions of Israel and dependent on the Hebrew Bible and authoritative postbiblical texts such as the Mishnah, the Jerusalem and Babylonian Talmuds, and various Midrashic compositions. In the formative years of classical Judaism, Jerusalem and the Jewish temple located there were central to Jewish identity. The second temple was destroyed in 70 CE, and Jews were expelled from Jerusalem after a subsequent revolt against Roman rule. While there remained a strong Jewish presence in the region, there was no Jewish state until 1948 and the formation of the modern state of Israel.

Islam was birthed in the Arabian Peninsula and understood itself as the final and complete revelation that the only true God (Allah in Arabic) conveyed to Muhammad, having raised up prophets in previous generations beforehand. Both Christians and Jews are understood as People of the Book, with Moses understood as giver of the Torah and Jesus as giver of the gospel. Neither Torah nor gospel, however, is identified with the text by that name as preserved in Judaism and Christianity. The written revelation of Allah, given to Muhammad, is the Qur'an. "Islam" is the Arabic term for submission and characterizes the posture of a Muslim who submits his or her life to the revealed will of Allah. Abraham, known from the Hebrew Bible (the Christian Old Testament) and the New Testament, is not reckoned as a Jew, but as a prophet and one who submitted his life to Allah.

Practices

One may summarize the primary practice of ancient Near Eastern religions as the care for and service of the gods. Devotion or piety is actualized through prayer, sacrifice, testimony, and fidelity to the teaching of priests and the wisdom of sages. Temples for seasonal sacrifice and votive offerings were central institutions of society. The gods governed the affairs of the regions in which they were worshiped, and they were petitioned to bless their patron cities and lands with fertility and peace and to ward off the powers of pestilence.

Jewish monotheistic worship at the temple in Jerusalem had the basic characteristics of an ancient Near Eastern sacrificial cult and followed a calendar of festivals based on the history of God's actions on behalf of Israel. Three in particular were pilgrimage festivals. In early spring was Passover, celebrating the deliverance of Israel's ancestors from Egyptian slavery. In late spring was the Festival of Weeks, which celebrated the firstfruits of agricultural harvest and the giving of the covenant and God's instructional code at Mount Sinai. In the fall came a New Year's celebration, the Day of Atonement, and the festival known as Ingatherings or Booths. This last celebration commemorated God's care of Israel's ancestors, who wandered in the wilderness on the way from Egypt to the promised land in Canaan, and provided an occasion to give thanks for a fall agricultural harvest. Jews in dispersion from the land of Israel had also developed patterns of nonsacrificial worship on the Sabbath day (seventh day of the week), when they gathered at synagogues (= place of assembly) to read from the Law and the Prophets, to hear their significance expounded for the life of faith, and to pray. With the destruction of the temple, this pattern of worship became the norm for Jews. Classical Jewish practices include a dietary code, cessation of work and corporate worship on the Sabbath, confession that the Lord is "one" (Deut. 6:4), study of the law, circumcision of males as a sign of God's covenant with them, ritual practices designed to reflect the holiness of service to God, and acts of charity.

Classical Islamic practices are conveniently arranged as Five Pillars of the faith. They are as follows: the confession that there is no god except Allah and Muhammad is his prophet; daily prayer (a "call" to prayer is issued five times a day); pilgrimage to Mecca, the holiest city in Islam; fasting in the daylight hours during the month of Ramadan; and the giving of alms to the poor. The Muslim house of worship is known as a mosque. Daily prayers may be said in the mosque or elsewhere. Friday-noon prayers are accompanied by a sermon expounding a text from the Qur'an, delivered by a community leader. Believers prostrate themselves in the direction of Mecca, where Muhammad first received revelation from Allah.

From the time of Muhammad, there has traditionally been no distinction made between the political governance of an Islamic society and the practices of the faith. At the same time, Islam has traditionally held that there should be no compulsion in religion. Historically, Muslim rulers in the Middle East have protected the right of minority religions (e.g., Judaism, Christianity) to assemble and worship but have forbidden their proselytizing activities and reckoned conversion as apostasy to Islam and a criminal offense.

Sources

John L. Esposito, ed. *The Oxford Encyclopedia of the Islamic World*. Oxford University Press, 2005.

Richard C. Martin, ed. *Encyclopedia of Islam and the Muslim World*. Macmillan, 2004.

Jacob Neusner, Alan J. Avery-Peck, and William Scott Green, eds. *The Encyclopedia of Judaism*. Brill, 2005.

F. E. Peters. *The Monotheists: Jews, Christians, and Muslims in Conflict and Competition*. Princeton University Press, 2003.

Donald B. Redford, ed. *The Oxford Encyclopedia of Egypt*. Oxford University Press, 2001.

Jack M. Sasson, ed. *Civilizations of the Ancient Near East*. Hendrickson, 2000.

Antoine Sfeir, ed. *The Columbia World Dictionary of Islamism*. Columbia University Press, 2007.

Fred Skolnik, ed. *Encyclopedia Judaica*. Macmillan Reference, 2007.

48

Middle East: Christian Contacts

J. Andrew Dearman

Christianity originated among Jews of the eastern Mediterranean and was initially a sect of Judaism that believed Jesus of Nazareth was uniquely God's Son and Israel's anticipated Messiah. Jesus is defined in light of Judaism's scriptures and in conjunction with its fundamental claims about God and divine activity. Judaism itself emerged in an ancient Near Eastern context and in dialogue with the impact of Hellenism in the region. From its inception, therefore, Christianity had an identity linked with Judaism, but also contact with other religions of the region, and sought to make itself intelligible in that broader context.

The foundational texts of Christianity are written in Greek and found in the New Testament. The common use of the Greek language in the region was a factor in the early dissemination of Christianity. This was true of Judaism also, as it sought to present itself to gentile and pagan cultures. Hellenistic Jews had translated their scriptures into Greek, and early Christians made ready use of the translations. Jewish Christians initially went to synagogues and to "God-fearers," gentiles who found Jewish monotheism appealing, but they found converts also among pagans. With disastrous revolts against Roman control and the Christian appropriation of the "Old Testament," Jews turned increasingly back to the Hebrew form of their scriptures and related texts.

The parting of the ways between Judaism and Christianity is a complicated matter. Judaism underwent painful change in the aftermath of Jerusalem's destruction in 70 CE, and at some point after that Jewish Christians were essentially ostracized from synagogue worship. From the side of Judaism, there were difficulties with the claim that Jesus was the Messiah from David's line, that Jesus was uniquely

> **Study Aid #105**
>
> Religions of the Middle East
>
> Old Testament era
> - Baalism
> - Canaanite
> - Moabite
> - Philistine
> - Phoenician
>
> Modern era
> - Baha'i
> - Christianity
> - Druze
> - Islam
> - Judaism
> - Mandeanism
> - Yazidi
> - Zoroastrianism

God's Son, and that gentiles could enter the faith community without circumcision and certain other requirements of the Torah. It should be noted that early Jewish Christians argued about these matters as well. Though not a large percentage in the empire's population, Christianity became majority gentile a century or so after its birth. Christian writers from the first two centuries of Christianity frequently address relations with Jews (e.g., Justin Martyr, *Epistle of Barnabas*).

In the fourth century CE, Christianity was accorded favorable status by Emperor Constantine and was declared the official religion of the state by century's end. Pagan temples were demolished, and traditional holy sites were converted to Christian worship. This was a massive change from the indifference or hostility toward Christianity in the previous three centuries. Pagan criticism had portrayed Christianity as a novel superstition, essentially as atheism and bad citizenship, as it shunned traditional religions and the emperor cult, items that undergirded regional cultures and gave expression to the order established by Rome. Christianity responded in several ways. Some claimed that Hellenistic culture was God's preparation for a timely final revelation. Others sought to show by means of charity that God intended Christians to live at peace with all peoples. The rejection of pagan religion was not a hatred of humanity or indifference toward public life. Christianity was even called a "third race," neither pagan nor Jew, bound not by birth or common language, but by trust in what God had accomplished in Christ for salvation. As a result of the Constantinian legacy, Christianity developed its public profile and took its place in political structures of the Byzantine Empire.

Judaism had been officially tolerated under Roman rule, in spite of tensions and regional hostilities. It maintained a secondary status in the Byzantine Empire and developed an insular culture. In its ancestral land, churches were erected in Jerusalem, Bethlehem, and Nazareth. The hub of Jewish life eventually settled in Galilee and the city of Tiberias, as Jerusalem was in the hands of Christians. While there were contacts between Jews and Christians, the latter often portrayed Judaism as obstinate in not recognizing Jesus as the Messiah and Savior.

Islam's emergence from Arabia brought forth changes that still mark the region. In 637 CE the Christian patriarch of Jerusalem surrendered the city to Muslim forces under the leadership of Umar, who would subsequently establish his base of control in Damascus. He allowed the Christians to worship in their churches, but they had to accept subservience to Islamic rule. This would be the basic pattern established wherever the Muslim forces prevailed. Islam was not to be separated from political rule. It was, moreover, a huge change for Christianity, as it went from political power to secondary status, and over time to a demographic minority. Islam would have final say over the affairs of minorities, both religious and political.

In Jerusalem two mosques were constructed on the ruins of the Temple Mount, where the former Jewish temple was located. Christians had left the ruins in place as a sign of Jesus's words (Matt. 24:1–2). According to the Qur'an, Muhammad had been transported to a place of prayer in a far place (*al aksa*; 17:1), and this place was identified in Muslim tradition as the Jerusalem temple area. Indeed, early in his religious practices, Muhammad taught his followers to face Jerusalem in prayer, though the practice changed to the direction of Mecca. One mosque was known as the Al Aksa Mosque. The other is now known as the Dome of the Rock. In Damascus, the sacred area of the city had been the location of a series of religious practices, and most recently the site of a Byzantine church. Eventually that building was incorporated into a mosque. Associated with the mosque is a shrine that is reputed to hold the head of John the Baptist (see Mark 6:14–29). Muslim tradition holds that Jesus will return to the earth for judgment day and that he will come to the Damascus mosque.

These two examples show the complicated interaction between Islam, Christianity, and Judaism. Islam sought to show itself as the fulfillment of earlier revelation given to Jews and Christians and the restorer of the true religion practiced by Abraham. The adoption of the Jewish Temple Mount in Jerusalem or the traditions of John and Jesus in Damascus shows aspects of incorporation and reframing of significance. Islamic political institutions developed over the Middle Eastern and North African regions, even as the center of rule would change. Arabic became the common tongue in much of the region, so that eventually inhabitants would be collectively known as Arabs. As earlier with Hellenism and Greek (and then Christianity), now Islam and Arabic characterized the region as a whole. Christians faced the challenges of accommodation and the maintenance of identity, given this context. One of the ways to maintain identity was employment of their own language of liturgy and worship (Coptic, Greek, Syriac). Accommodation meant the payment of a minority tax and a prohibition against evangelism.

The Crusades inflamed relations between Muslims and Christians, even as they showed differences among Western and Eastern Christians. After the Crusades' conclusion, Islam continued to expand. In 1453 Constantinople fell to a Muslim army. The Ottoman Turks established hegemony over much of the Middle East until the conclusion of the First World War in 1918, when the Western victors dismembered the Ottoman Empire and Muslim Turkey emerged with a secular

> **Study Aid #106**
>
> Middle East Polarities
>
> Hebrew-Greek
> Hellenistic-Roman
> Jewish-Christian
>
> Indigenous-Judeo/Christian
> Judeo/Christian-Muslim

government. Great Britain and France drew borders for new political entities in the region and established direct administration or client rulers. Palestine was governed by Great Britain. Many Arabs resented the control of the Western powers, even as they were glad to be free of Turkish control. Muslims saw parallels to the Crusades.

These and other events of the twentieth century ushered in far-reaching changes in the relations between Christians and other religions in the region. At the end of the nineteenth century, European Jews began immigrating to Palestine and establishing settlements, initially by negotiating with the local population and Ottoman officials. With British control of Palestine after 1918, this process accelerated, gaining even more momentum after the rise of Hitler to power in Germany in 1933. The Muslim population, in particular, opposed Jewish immigration, and riots broke out in the 1920s. At the conclusion of World War II, with sympathy toward Jewish immigration as a result of the Nazi Holocaust, Great Britain faced severe difficulties in governing Palestine, where there was Arab opposition to accepting any more Jews and Jewish opposition to limitations placed on them by the British. The formation of the State of Israel in 1948 marked the first Jewish state in the region in two thousand years. The British had governed religious affairs in Palestine according to standards established by recognized authorities in the respective religions (e.g., the Greek patriarch, grand mufti, and chief rabbi). Essentially this established a status quo. This has been the policy of modern Israel with respect to defining religious identity and relating to the Muslim and Christian populations under its authority. For example, various Christian bodies control the affairs of the Church of the Holy Sepulchre in east Jerusalem, and, in spite of severe quarreling among the churches, the Israeli government has been hesitant to intervene. Administration of the Temple Mount area in east Jerusalem, where the two mosques are located, is in the hands of the Islamic Waqf (a religious foundation), as it was in the League of Nations mandate system.

In the last hundred years, the immigration of Middle Eastern Christians to other countries has lessened their numbers considerably. If current trends continue, Christianity will be a negligible presence in the land of its birth in fifty years' time. The Gulf Wars in Iraq have led to Islamic intimidation and violence against the Chaldean and Assyrian Christians located there.

There is a small Jewish Christian population in modern Israel. This is a sensitive matter, as Israel is the one state in the world that is Jewish. From the Israeli side it raises the question of whether Jewish Christians are to be identified as Jews, and if so, in what sense? Jewish Christians are not recognized by Israel as eligible for the law of return, which gives Jews anywhere in the world the right to immigrate to Israel. Evangelism is another sensitive matter, as there is widespread aversion to it among Israeli Jews. From various Christian sides, Jewish Christians in Israel further complicate difficult matters. How, for example, do Western Christians relate both to them and to Arab Christians, especially given the sense among the latter that they have been largely abandoned by the West? And there is the matter of the Jewish state. There are several issues here, but with regard to political relations, virtually all Middle Eastern Christians relate differently to Israel than do Jewish Christians.

Sources

Betty Jane Bailey and J. Martin Bailey. *Who Are the Christians of the Middle East?* Eerdmans, 2003.

John Bunzl, ed. *Islam, Judaism, and the Political Role of Religions in the Middle East.* University Press of Florida, 2004.

Robert Goldenberg. *The Origins of Judaism: From Canaan to the Rise of Islam.* Cambridge University Press, 2007.

Sidney Harrison Griffith. *The Church in the Shadow of the Mosque: Christians and Muslims in the World of Islam.* Princeton University Press, 2008.

Emmanouela Grypeou, Mark Swanson, and David Thomas, eds. *The Encounter of Eastern Christianity with Early Islam.* Brill, 2006.

Philip Jenkins. *The Lost History of Christianity: The Thousand-Year Golden Age of the Church in the Middle East, Africa, and Asia—and How It Died.* HarperCollins, 2008.

Xavier Levieils. *Contra Christianos: La critique sociale et religieuse du christianisme des origines au Concile de Nicée (45–325).* Walter de Gruyter, 2007.

F. E. Peters. *The Monotheists: Jews, Christians, and Muslims in Conflict and Competition.* Princeton University Press, 2003.

49

Middle East: Theological Exchanges

J. Andrew Dearman

According to the Gospel of John, Jesus engaged a Samaritan woman near Shechem in conversation and told her that "salvation is from the Jews" (John 4:22). His comment is made in the context of his self-presentation to her as the giver of "living water" and in response to her comment that Samaritans worship on one mountain and Jews on another. Jesus speaks to her as a Jew. His comments presuppose two related matters: First, that Jews and Judaism are bearers of divine revelation in ways that Samaritans are not, even though Samaritans considered themselves the true heirs of God's revelation to Moses. Judaism's role is also confirmed in his references to "living water," a phrase from the Old Testament that describes God in his relationship with his people (Jer. 2:13), and to "salvation," a comprehensive term referring to God's ultimate purpose to overcome sin, death, and evil, and to establish his eternal rule. Second, Jesus, himself a Jew, is the bearer of divine revelation. This is clear from his identification of himself as giver of "living water" (see John 7:37–39), his authoritative pronouncement that the Father (= God) seeks those who will worship him in "spirit and in truth," his identification of himself as the Messiah (= Christ) anticipated by the Jews (4:23–26), and the subsequent description of him by Samaritans as the "Savior of the world" (4:42).

One can readily see from these two matters that in origin Christianity was integrally related to Judaism, even as it presented itself as a religion of salvation for the whole world. In sociological terms, early Christianity was a messianic sect of Judaism that managed to craft its message into forms that non-Jews could also accept. The community was called by the Greek term *ekklēsia*, which refers to an

> **Study Aid #107**
>
> Middle East Theological Exchanges
>
> With Judaism
>   Jesus: Prophet or Messiah?
>   Torah: In force or superseded?
> With indigenous religions
>   Monotheism: One god or many?
>   Universalism: For us or for all?
> With Islam
>   Allah: One or three?
>   Jesus: Prophet or Son of God?
>   Muhammad: Final prophet?

assembly or gathering of people, but was also used to describe the community of Israel in the Greek translation of the Hebrew Bible. It is now commonly translated in English as "church." All of this is not to say that Judaism of the day had no interest in proselytes or in the salvation of the world that God had created. Instead, Jewish Christians took those concerns and presented them in ways, historically speaking, that Jews and non-Jews could engage.

The authoritative narrative of Judaism's origins and classical identity is derived from the Hebrew Bible. This is essentially the case with early Christianity, which takes much of its own identity in light of the Old Testament (= Hebrew Bible), interpreted through the words and deeds of Jesus. This last item is of crucial importance. When an early Christian text of the first two centuries quotes an authoritative text, it is typically from the Hebrew Bible, albeit in Greek translation, but its significance is interpreted in light of the life, death, and resurrection of Jesus. Eventually those early Christian writings of apostolic content (which concentrate on what Jesus said and accomplished) are also collected along with the Old Testament to form the Christian Bible. In particular, Christianity took its cue from the promises of God to bless the nations (Gen. 12:3), to make his people a "light to the nations," and to bring in an eternal era of peace and the forgiveness of sins (Isa. 2:2–5; 9:1–6; Jer. 31:31–34). Jesus was understood as the promised agent of God's eschatological blessings (Isa. 11:1–9), which were inaugurated in Jesus's first advent and which will be consummated in his second advent. Christianity's moral code was based on the Decalogue and the ways in which Jesus saw the will of God in the commands of the Old Testament. It parted company with Judaism over continuing the ceremonial and ritual requirements for the faithful. Christianity claimed that in the death and resurrection of Jesus, God had brought to an end the sacrificial and ceremonial requirements of the Torah. Jesus's death was the final sacrifice, and entrance into the new community formed by him was based on faith and open to Jew and gentile alike.

Two primary matters, therefore, were the dividing points between Judaism and Christianity: One centered on the person of Jesus. Was he a prophet or also Israel's Messiah and uniquely God's Son? Should his death be understood in sacrificial terms, and did God raise him from the dead to vindicate his work and message? The other was the community ethos. Should the ceremonial and ritual commands of the Torah, which were a dividing point for some gentiles otherwise attracted to Jewish monotheism, remain defining standards of the community for those who came to faith in Christ?

Christianity sought a point of contact with pagan religions by casting itself as a monotheism in which the world's Creator sent an agent of salvation, the Son of God. A "son of God" was recognized terminology in Greco-Roman culture, even though it entered Christianity first through the Old Testament. Many pagans found Christianity's social profile to be deficient, as Christians were repeatedly accused of indifference to common life. This was due primarily to Christian resistance to participation in civic rituals and the emperor cult, elements that pagans saw as fundamental to public life and citizenship in a community. Since Jesus had the title "Lord," a term used of God as well, Christians had trouble attributing it to the emperor and in offering sacrifices on his behalf. Christians countered that their community was formed as a citizenship in heaven (see Phil. 3:20), open to all, where members bore one another's burdens and maintained a common faith in a resurrected Lord. Some pagans also had difficulties with the Jewish-Christian belief in the resurrection of the body, preferring instead the eternality of the human soul. While Christianity has kept the affirmation of the resurrection of the body as an article of faith, some members have always interpreted life after physical death primarily in spiritual terms as the survival of the soul with God.

Islam is formulated as a religion of revelation bringing to final form and clarity Allah's earlier revelations to a series of prophets, many also known from the Old and New Testaments. Unfortunately, the exchanges between Muhammad and these faiths that brought Islam into being are unknown. *Allah* is the Arabic term used in the Qur'an and in Islam to refer to the divine Creator of the world and the sender of the final revelation to Muhammad. It is a generic term for deity or god, as are the Hebrew terms *'el* and *'elohim* and the Greek term *theos*; like them, Allah can also be used in direct address and function like a personal name. It remains a matter of discussion among Muslims and Christians whether Arabic-speaking Christians should use Allah as their term for "God," which is typical in Arabic translations of the Bible. Islam's first prophet was Adam, and others include Noah, Abraham, Joseph, Moses, Aaron, David, Solomon, Jesus, and John the Baptist. One can readily see the connections here to the story line of the Christian Bible, however it was mediated to Muhammad. Moses had a ministry with Jews and delivered to them the Torah (Arabic *Tawrat*). Jesus had a gospel (Arabic *Injil*) that he delivered to Christians. The Torah of Judaism (the Pentateuch), however, is not the same thing as the *Tawrat* mentioned by the Qur'an, any more than the *Injil* of Jesus is the gospel message or narrative texts of the New Testament. Moses and Jesus were muslims—that is, those who submit to God. Although Jews and Christians are known as People of the Book, Islam maintains that Jews' and Christians' scriptures are composed of truth and error, so that they can be led astray by adherence to them. In Islamic thought, this helps to account for the stubbornness shown by both in clinging to forms of their own religion when they should recognize the final revelation of the Qur'an.

Islam placed Christianity in a position analogous to that which Christianity assigned to Judaism. Christianity claimed the validity of the Hebrew scriptures as divine revelation and that Jesus was the Messiah of Israel. The logic of these claims was that Jews should recognize Jesus as the Christ and enter the fellowship formed in his name and dedicated to his worship and service. Islam affirmed the gospel represented by Jesus and that he submitted himself to God in conformity with the pattern established by Muhammad and written in the Qur'an. The logic of these claims was that Christians should recognize the finality of the Qur'an and henceforth pattern their lives in conformity with it.

Muhammad represents the basic pattern of a religious reformer and prophet, accepting elements from Judaism and Christianity, but reformulating them in light of an alternative vision. On the basis of a powerful religious experience, he sought to eradicate the polytheism and fetishism of the area, to restore the monotheistic religion of Abraham (2:125–37), who he insisted had instituted the worship of Allah in Mecca, and to reform Jewish and Christian practices accordingly. The difficulty of filling out this description, or any other account of Muhammad's intentions, starts with the lack of evidence for his experience with Judaism and Christianity. There are more records of his encounters with Jews, but these concern primarily political and social affairs rather than discussion over points of scriptural interpretation and Jewish beliefs. There is even less evidence for his encounter with Christianity, although one of his wives was a Christian. Islam holds to the tradition that Muhammad was formally illiterate. This serves to underscore the miracle of the Qur'an. Muhammad did not write it, but learned to recite the revelation given him by Allah through the angel Gabriel. All this is to say that we do not know what, if anything, Muhammad may have read in an

---

Study Aid #108
Middle East Holy Books

Ancient Near Eastern texts
Hebrew scriptures
   Talmud
Bible
   Pseudepigrapha
Qur'an
   Hadith

Arabic text regarding the Bible. It is virtually certain that he observed religious practices of both Jews and Christians, and probable that he learned about their faith traditions through oral exchange.

The Qur'an does not have a narrative core to it like the Hebrew Bible or the New Testament. It is poetic discourse, but alludes frequently to what can be called basic narrative accounts of Judaism and Christianity. It seems, for example, to reflect appreciation of the monotheistic claims of both communities, while chiding Christians for thinking that Jesus was God's biological offspring (5:116; 6:100–104; 112:3) and rejecting the worship of Jesus in addition to God (5:75; 43:63–65). Jesus is born to a chaste woman (Sura 19), but his formation is like that of Adam, who was not begotten. These claims suggest a misunderstanding of Christian teaching that Jesus was supernaturally conceived and that the one God is Triune in his being. The angel Gabriel is a figure known in both Old and New Testaments, as is the figure of Abraham, who lived before Moses. The Qur'an's appeal to Abraham as a pivotal figure is a classic reformist posture, claiming a pristine faith from the beginning that was corrupted over time by Jews and Christians, who nevertheless preserved memories of his importance. Islam's claim that Abraham and Isaac built the Ka'ba in Mecca as a monument to worship the one God is not part of Jewish or Christian tradition.

The Qur'an affirms the claims also known in Christianity that Jesus could do works of power. Interestingly, one of the examples cited (3:49) is not preserved in the New Testament but is known from noncanonical texts. Those who do not respond adequately to Jesus are chided, as if the Qur'an adopted a form of the Christian polemic against Jews for not recognizing the significance of Jesus. The allusive style of the Qur'an makes it difficult to grasp its presentation of Jesus's death. There is no support for his death as an atoning sacrifice; an opaque reference to his death essentially says Jesus's followers were confused (4:157). It should be noted that on the basis of 19:33 and 5:117, some Muslim scholars acknowledge Jesus's death and his vindication by God.

Sources

Camilla Adang. *Muslim Writers on Judaism and the Hebrew Bible: From Ibn Rabban to Ibn Hazm*. Brill, 1996.

J. K. Aitken and Edward Kessler, eds. *Challenges in Jewish-Christian Relations*. Paulist Press, 2006.

Colin G. Chapman. *Cross and Crescent: Responding to the Challenge of Islam*. InterVarsity, 2007.

C. N. Cochrane. *Christianity and Classical Culture*. Liberty Fund, 2003.

Ahmed Ginaidi. *Jesus Christ and Mary from Quranic-Islamic Perspectives: Fundamental Principles for Dialogue between Islam and Christianity*. Ibidem-Verlag, 2005.

Sidney Harrison Griffith. *The Beginnings of Christian Theology in Arabic: Muslim-Christian Encounters in the Early Islamic Period*. Ashgate, 2002.

Xavier Levieils. *Contra Christianos: La critique sociale et religieuse du christianisme des origines au Concile de Nicée (45–325)*. Walter de Gruyter, 2007.

Bernard Lewis. *The Jews of Islam*. Princeton University Press, 1987.

F. E. Peters. *The Monotheists: Jews, Christians, and Muslims in Conflict and Competition*. Princeton University Press, 2003.

David Thomas. *Christian Doctrines in Islamic Theology*. Brill, 2008.

50

Middle East: Current Issues

J. Andrew Dearman

Current issues facing Christianity in the Middle East are a combination of long-standing matters and major developments in the last one hundred years. One perennial matter revolves around the historical and theological links between Judaism, Christianity, and Islam. They have been linked for centuries as Abrahamic religions or as the three monotheistic religions. History has forced each religion to define itself, at least in part, by what it has in common with the other two and where it sees itself as a unique bearer of divine revelation. Both parts of the self-defining are important.

As discussed below, recent decades have brought new contours to the question of Christian identity vis-à-vis the other two. It is important to note how Christians of the Middle East have been and are affected by these changes, as their voices are often not heard by Christian siblings in the West.

Minority Status and Emigration

Christians are a minority in every state of the Middle East where they reside. They are a minority in at least two fundamental senses. In the first, they are a minority with regard to population percentage. This, of course, was not always the case, but it has been for the last fifty years or so. In 1900 one could point to a number of towns and villages in Palestine, Jordan, Egypt, Syria, and Iraq with majority-Christian populations. The last 110 years have reversed this statistic for all but a few villages and smaller towns. The last state to have had a majority-Christian population is Lebanon in the mid-twentieth century. Historically there had never

> **Study Aid #109**
>
> Middle East Current Issues
>
> Christian minority status: Christians are a minority in every country of the Middle East.
> The State of Israel: Whose land is it? The conflicting rights of Jews and Palestinians.

been a State of Lebanon, but France sought to support the Arab Catholic population of the area in the realignment of the Middle East in the aftermath of World War I. Lebanon's first constitution stated that the prime minister should be a Maronite Christian. In the 1970s, struggles broke out in the country as the (by then) majority-Muslim (Sunni and Shi'ite) and Druze populations protested and sought greater political control. Lebanon still experiences periodic sectarian tensions, and these are exacerbated by Syria, which has never agreed with Lebanon's formation as an independent state. The most recent census in Israel indicates approximately 150,000 Christians in Israel and no city with a Christian majority. Statistics are not available for the West Bank and Gaza, but the estimation of the Christian population is 2 percent.

In a second sense, Christians have been a minority in the Middle East due to a region-wide minority status in political and social arenas since the Islamic takeover in the mid-seventh century. Islam has historically shunned a division between religion and political order, going back to the example of Muhammad himself and the principles enshrined in the Qur'an, so that wherever Islam has held political sway, non-Muslims have had to come to terms with their secondary status. This has meant various things for Muslim-Christian relations over the centuries, alternating between cooperation and oppression, depending on circumstances.

It is a curious and important fact that the Middle East is a region with a very long cultural history, yet the states in the region are almost all twentieth-century creations by Western powers, directly or indirectly. The Western influence is seen directly in the drawing of boundaries and the "Mandate" adopted by Great Britain and France after 1918. Indirectly, the Western powers set in motion events that would lead to the formation of the modern State of Israel in 1948. These changes resulted in forms of Arab nationalism and Muslim resurgence as states acquired their independence, and also suspicion of the West in the Muslim mind, which often equates the West with Christianity. Emigration has been an increasing response of Christians to the difficulties of existence in the modern Middle East. Declining birth rates have been another. The former has meant the breaking up of families and ties of long duration. Christians have gone to various Western and other receptive communities. The 2000 census for the United States showed, for example, a Christian majority among citizens of Arab descent. A bleak outlook on the future is common to those who remain in the region.

Arab historians have stressed a rising national consciousness among Arabs, who chafed under the autocratic control of the Ottoman Empire. Indeed, Sharif

Hussein of Mecca encouraged a revolt against the Turks in 1916. It was led by his sons Abdullah and Ali, aided and abetted by the British. They were encouraged in 1915 by letters from Sir Henry McMahon, British high commissioner in Egypt, to believe that the defeat of the Ottoman Empire would result in the establishing of Arab independence in parts of the region. In 1917, the British foreign secretary wrote that "His Majesty's government views with favor the establishment in Palestine of a national home for the Jewish people, and will use their best endeavors to facilitate the achievement of this object, it being clearly understood that nothing shall be done which may prejudice the civil and religious rights of existing non-Jewish communities in Palestine" (Balfour Declaration). As noted, at the conclusion of the war, the French and British extended their mandate of victory to the division of the Middle East. Jewish immigration increased in the newly established British protectorate of Palestine. Abdullah was made the emir of Transjordan, now the State of Jordan. Ali was initially declared king in Damascus but was pushed out by the French and later made king of the newly created State of Iraq at British instigation. Neither Arabs nor Jews were satisfied with Western hegemony in the postwar Mandate period. From their perspectives Great Britain and France had overpromised and underdelivered, and both Muslims and Jews seized opportunities to take matters in their own hands. Eventually the Arab entities gained their independence from France or Great Britain, and Jewish immigration resulted in the modern State of Israel and repeated wars with Arab neighbors.

Arab nationalism in the second half of the twentieth century has had both secular and Islamic underpinnings. Generally speaking, the secular form tolerated Arab minorities such as Christians, while the Islamic resurgence has been harder on non-Muslims. The rise of a Jewish state in the Arab heartland, combined with resentment over Western maneuvers in the region, has led to a potent form of Islamic response not seen since the Crusades. Thus Christianity is in marked decline in the land of its birth and the immediately surrounding areas.

Israel and Judaism

The Israelites and their Jewish heirs originated in the ancient Near East. This history includes centuries of time when there was an Israelite or Jewish state. Neither Christianity nor Islam, however, had to deal with an independent Jewish state in the eras in which they subsequently emerged. Both movements claimed some continuity with Judaism, even as they proclaimed something new. In both cases elements of newness, replacement, completion, or even restoration of things lost were what prevailed, and political order followed suit, first with Christianity and then with Islam holding political sway. Judaism had never been without witness in the land of its birth, but an independent state in their ancestral homeland had eluded them since the period of Roman rule.

> **Study Aid #110**
> The State of Israel
>
> | Abraham | Promised land | Diaspora |
> | Jacob/Joseph | Exile | Palestinians |
> | Exodus | Return | Modern statehood |

The creation of the modern State of Israel—easily one of the most surprising and influential political events of the twentieth century—has resulted in Christian rethinking of the role of Judaism and its political expression in the Jewish state. There are several aspects to this rethinking. A classical response to Judaism has been forms of replacement theology, often called supersessionism, in which the elect roles of Judaism and Israel have been replaced in the divine economy by Christianity and the new Israel of believing Jews and gentiles (= the church). Some elements of this view are widely accepted in Christianity. For example, in various ways the New Testament claims that components (e.g., dietary restrictions, circumcision, animal sacrifices) of the Sinai covenant are no longer binding on Jews or gentiles who believe in Jesus Christ, the fulfillment of the new covenant promised in the Old Testament (Jer. 31:31–34; cf. Galatians; 2 Cor. 3; Heb. 7–10). Does this also mean the end of the elect status of Jews and of Israel as a religious community? While some have answered unequivocally yes, the matter is complicated by the mystery of eschatology. What might Paul have meant in his claim that "God's gifts and his call are irrevocable" so that in the future "all Israel will be saved" (Rom. 11:25–32)? Paul's claim seems to be that in spite of the fact that Jews have missed God's climactic revelation in Christ in the historical moment, the status of Jews as recipients of God's irrevocable calling means that in the future Jews will embrace Christ and be included in the church.

Some Christians have proposed forms of a dual covenant in the present where God embraces the responses of both Jews and Christians. This is the opposite of supersessionism and leaves a final reconciliation of Jews and Christians to an eschatological denouement. From a Christian perspective, this is tantamount to viewing Judaism as yet another form of saving faith, where Jews should no longer be evangelized. Among evangelical Protestants, particularly dispensationalists and those called Christian Zionists, there is much anticipation for the role of Jews and the modern State of Israel in fulfilling biblical prophecy. Some of this support was awakened by the formation of the modern State of Israel in 1948, which is linked to Old Testament prophecies of a restored Israel in an eschatological future.

The State of Israel is something of a watershed in Christian reflection on Judaism. Should Christians see its formation as the fulfillment of Old Testament prophecy, or perhaps as the prelude to such a fulfillment, or simply as a Jewish democratic state? And if it is linked to biblical prophecy, does this mean that areas such as the West Bank and parts of current Lebanon, Syria, and Jordan should also belong to Israel? Western Christians remain divided on these matters, as do the Christian populations of the Middle East. Few Arab and historic Eastern Christians attribute a primary role to modern Judaism or the State of Israel in their interpretation of biblical prophecy, whereas the smaller groups of Jewish Christians and Messianic Jews in Israel may well hold to forms of dispensationalist teaching or Christian Zionism. Jewish Christians are a sensitive matter in Israel and face significant cultural and religious resistance from Jewish contemporaries, quite apart from a common support of the modern state.

Sources

J. K. Aitken and Edward Kessler, eds. *Challenges in Jewish-Christian Relations*. Paulist Press, 2006.

Richard Bauckham. *Jesus and the God of Israel: God Crucified, and Other Studies on the New Testament's Christology of Divine Identity*. Eerdmans, 2008.

Elias Chacour. *Blood Brothers*. Chosen Books, 2003.

———. *We Belong to the Land: The Story of a Palestinian Israeli Who Lives for Peace and Reconciliation*. University of Notre Dame Press, 2001.

Colin G. Chapman. *Cross and Crescent: Responding to the Challenge of Islam*. InterVarsity, 2007.

Eugene B. Korn and John T. Pawlikowski, eds. *Two Faiths, One Covenant? Jewish and Christian Identity in the Presence of the Other*. Rowman & Littlefield, 2004.

Paul C. Merkley. *Christian Attitudes towards the State of Israel*. McGill-Queens University Press, 2001.

Eliezer Schweid. *The Land of Israel: National Home or Land of Destiny*. Fairleigh Dickenson University Press, 1985.

R. Kendall Soulen. *The God of Israel and Christian Theology*. Fortress, 1996.

Bat Ye'or. *The Decline of Eastern Christianity under Islam: From Jihad to Dhimmitude; Seventh–Twentieth Century*. Fairleigh Dickinson University Press, 1985.

51

Africa: History, Beliefs, Practices

Irving Hexham

The History of the Study of African Religions

Normally an introductory essay on a major religious tradition begins by providing a brief survey of the tradition's history. In the African case it is important to begin not with the history of African religions but with the place of African religion in Western scholarship. This is because the representation of African religious traditions is so distorted that we certainly need to recognize the biases that led to its neglect. Recognizing bias is the first step toward understanding African religious traditions.

For example, in 1969 one of the founders of religious studies, Ninian Smart, published *The Religious Experience of Mankind*. In it he devoted exactly five out of 576 pages to a consideration of African religion. More recently Christopher Partridge, in his edited work *Introduction to World Religions* (2005), treats African religions in a mere eight pages while devoting fourteen pages to the Baha'i and twenty-two pages to the Zoroastrian traditions, which are small and virtually extinct. Few other introductory works devote more than twenty-five pages to African traditions despite the fact that sub-Saharan Africa alone has a population of around one billion people.

The reason for this bias is to be found in history. Prior to the Enlightenment, Africans were widely regarded by Europeans as people with whom they had a lot in common. This can be seen in European works of art where one of the three kings in many nativity scenes is clearly African. Similarly, many cathedrals have medieval tombs where a knight, usually a Crusader, is African. Thus as late as the eighteenth century, a Ghanaian, Anton Wilhelm Amo (1703–59), established

Study Aid #111
Map of Africa

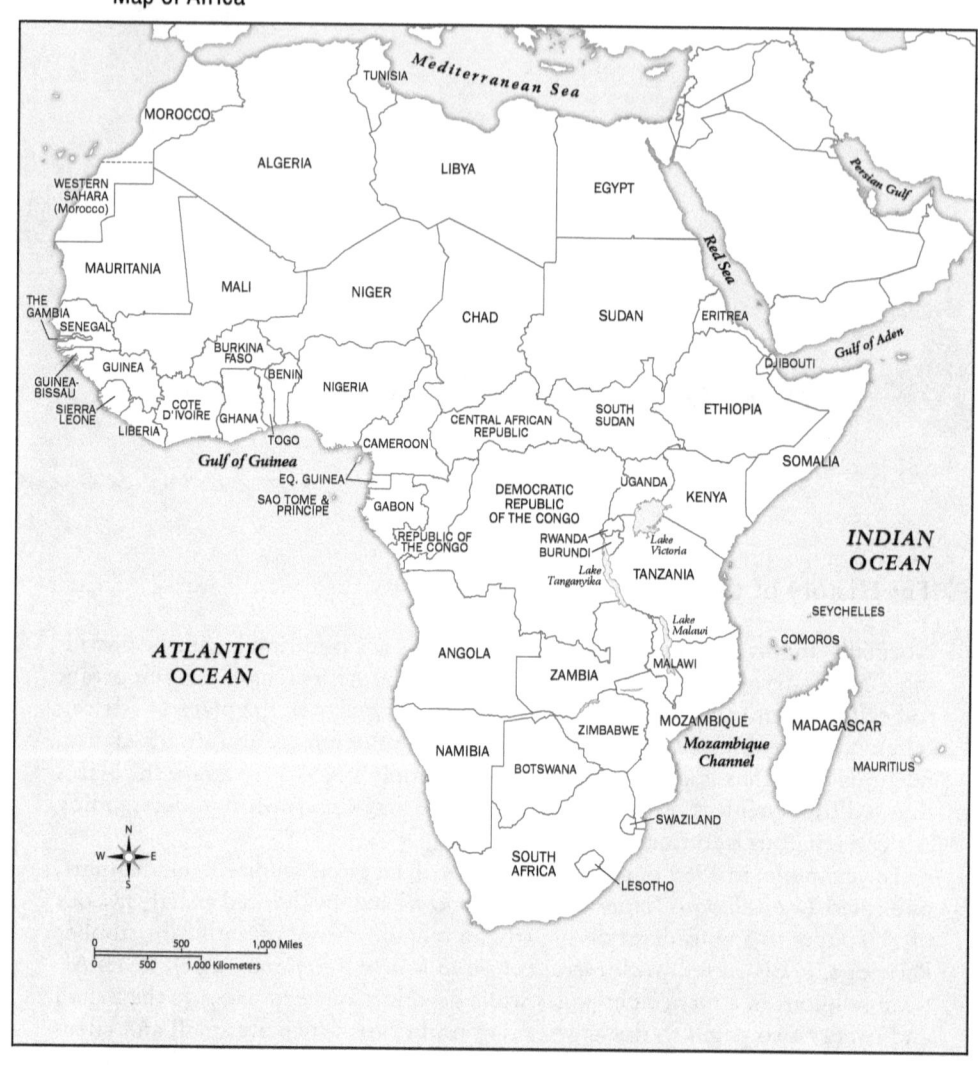

a reputation as an outstanding philosopher and worked as a professor at the German University of Halle.

Then during the Enlightenment, which is usually depicted as an era of reform and social advancement, Africans and their religions were disparaged. For Africans it was a tragedy. The French philosopher Voltaire (1694–1778) denigrated Africans as "a species of men as different from ours as the breed of spaniels is from that of greyhounds," a species who he claimed were incapable of "any great application or association of ideas, and seem informed neither of the advantages nor abuses of our philosophy." The Scot David Hume (1711–76) followed suit when he wrote, "I suspect that negroes . . . be naturally inferior to the whites. There never was a civilized nation of any other complexion than white"; Jean Jacques Rousseau (1712–78), who is usually remembered for his attack on slavery, spoke about "negroes and savages." Examples like these can be multiplied with philosophers like Immanuel Kant (1724–1804) and George Friedrich Hegel (1770–1831) expressing similar if less strident views.

The situation did not improve in the nineteenth century, and by the time "comparative religion" and later religious studies developed, African traditions were generally overlooked because, to put it crudely, they were seen as "primitive" or at least not on the same plane as other major religious traditions. Yet in reality these biases completely distort our understanding of Africa and Africans.

The History of African Religions

The truth of the matter is that due to a lack of literacy in most of Africa, particularly Africa south of the Sahara, there is a scarcity of written sources outlining the history of African religions. The major exceptions to this are North African countries: Egypt, Ethiopia, and parts of West Africa. Yet here again most of the material available to us deals with Christianity, Islam, or Judaism.

Very little written material documenting African traditional religions prior to the sixteenth century exists, and even then it is scarce. Only from the early nineteenth century onward do we find good sources dealing with African religious beliefs and practices, yet written largely by European explorers, government officials, missionaries, and traders.

Traditional African Religious Beliefs and Practices

Writing about "African religion" is very tempting and something many authors have done. Yet it is also misleading, as the works of people like John Mbiti show. European-educated Mbiti and similar African scholars, often based in American or European settings, impose a unity on African traditions that simply does not exist, as Okot P'Bitek showed long ago in his *African Religions and Western Scholarship* (1970). Unfortunately, because his book was written and published in Africa, it has not received the attention it deserves.

Writing about "African religion" as though there is a basic religious system common to the whole of Africa is rather like writing about American, Asian, European, Chinese, or Indian religion. Such enterprises, when they occur, overlook the fact that despite many similarities, for example between Buddhism and the Hindu tradition, or Christianity and Judaism, the differences are what make particular religions what they are in practice.

One simply cannot speak about African religion. Rather, it is necessary to recognize the multiplicity of African religions even though there are similarities between African peoples that are usually associated with geographic regions such as central, East, West, and southern Africa. Yet even within these regions the differences between the religious beliefs and practices of different groups are often considerable.

With this caveat, this article will attempt to summarize some general features found in many African traditions. In doing so it needs to be recognized that while these traditions share some common features, there are also considerable differences. For example, in some areas of Africa the birth of twins is celebrated and ritualized while in others the weaker twin is traditionally left to die, even though there are rituals surrounding their deaths. Thus to speak about beliefs concerning the souls of twins can be very misleading because groups differ in their attitudes so greatly.

Another source of misunderstanding is the tendency of many European scholars and missionaries, following the example set by John V. Taylor (1963), to talk about "primal" religions and experiences. This is usually done as though such experiences are unique to Africans or other peoples who somehow live closer to nature than people living in more technologically developed society. Within religious studies this trend was encouraged by the work of scholars like Mircea Eliade, who mystified the idea of myth as an expression of people living close to a now lost or almost lost transcendental reality.

Recognizing the existence of primal experiences and their role in the growth of religions is important. But this recognition needs to include all religious traditions, not simply Africans or other people living in what are presented as premodern, nonliterate societies. The realm of the primal is universal.

The basic structure and working of primal beliefs are similar to that of many scientific beliefs. Thus rather than seeing African beliefs about witchcraft as strange ideas related to nontechnical, prescientific societies, it is important to recognize that their structure is not very different from the popular understanding of things like electricity. Such beliefs are quite logical, and this logic needs to be recognized, as E. E. Evans-Pritchard argued in his classic study of witchcraft among the Azande (1937).

Religions without Scriptures

Perhaps the greatest difference between most African religious traditions and other "world religions" is their lack of scriptural traditions recorded in written texts. Although this may seem to be a major difference from most other "world religions," it has to be recognized that until recently the Hindu tradition rejected

> **Study Aid #112**
> **Countries of Africa**
>
> | | | |
> |---|---|---|
> | Algeria | Ethiopia | Nigeria |
> | Angola | Gabon | Rwanda |
> | Benin | Gambia | São Tomé and Príncipe |
> | Botswana | Ghana | Senegal |
> | Burkina Faso | Guinea | Seychelles |
> | Burundi | Guinea-Bissau | Sierra Leone |
> | Cameroon | Kenya | Somalia |
> | Cape Verdi | Lesotho | South Africa |
> | Central African Republic | Liberia | South Sudan |
> | Chad | Libya | Sudan |
> | Comoros | Madagascar | Swaziland |
> | Democratic Republic of the Congo | Malawi | Tanzania |
> | | Mali | Togo |
> | Republic of the Congo | Mauritania | Tunisia |
> | Côte d'Ivoire | Mauritius | Uganda |
> | Djibouti | Morocco | Zambia |
> | Egypt | Mozambique | Zimbabwe |
> | Equatorial Guinea | Namibia | |
> | Eritrea | Niger | |

the use of written texts, and many devout Hindus still prefer oral to written communication for religious matters. Only in the nineteenth century did the "Hindu scriptures" become readily available through the work of British and other European scholars. A similar project in Africa would have produced equally complex scriptural traditions, but this never took place.

Religions without written scriptures and recorded histories often share common features, such as the belief in evil powers identified with sorcery and witchcraft, specialized healers, psychic events, and the importance of ancestors. Given the lack of written scriptures, most African traditional religions, like most grassroots religious movements everywhere, are based on the religious experience of their founders and members. These are essentially oral traditions that give primacy to the interpretation of experience.

Anthropologist Robert Redfield called religions of this type "little traditions," because charismatic experiences, healings, prophecies, visions, and so on are the principal concern of devotees (1965). In such traditions the shamans, or similar ritual figures, communicate between this world and the next, often with the aim of placating the ancestors. At the core are vivid, life-changing experiences that defy rational explanation. Consequently, these experiences find expression in rich religious mythologies.

Explaining Primal Experiences

Fred Welbourn, in *Atoms and Ancestors* (1968), observes that until recently few Europeans or North Americans had seen bacteria. In fact, we rarely think about bacteria unless there is an outbreak of disease. We simply take the existence of bacteria on trust. Yet for at least a hundred years most people in the West have believed that bacteria are a natural part of life. They are something we normally do not think about unless they begin to cause problems through an outbreak of some kind of illness. Only then do we consult doctors, whom we trust to heal us using antibiotics.

Ancestors are as real to people living in traditional societies as bacteria are to us. Consequently Africans often claim to experience the actions of ancestors and sometimes even to encounter them. But in general many Africans do not expect to see their ancestors because ancestors work in other ways that are usually seen as part of everyday life. Thus normally people pay little attention to them unless they begin to cause problems. In most African societies, however, custom directs that the ancestors be remembered, and in many such societies there are shrines to the dead that need to be tended regularly.

Usually only when certain types of misfortune occur does anyone think about the ancestors. Otherwise they are taken for granted. Yet when there is an outbreak of disease or repeated misfortune occurs, a specialist will be consulted to discover whether the problems a person is encountering are caused by an ancestor or ancestors. Like the Western medical specialist, Africans who know how to communicate with the ancestors are usually highly trained and prized. Such training involves serving the equivalent of an apprenticeship with a recognized specialist whose abilities to heal and generally deal with the ancestors and other nonhuman causes of misfortune are well known.

Today such apprenticeships are often supplemented by correspondence and other courses offered by colleges of healing and religion. As a result, today many healers proudly display their certificates just like North American doctors often have their degree certificates on display. What this shows is the ability of so-called primal traditions to embrace the modern world and adapt to it.

The Problem of Witchcraft

One of the constants in African religious traditions is a belief in witchcraft and sorcery. Here we have to be very careful because the exact meaning of both of these terms varies from society to society. Essentially, witches and sorcerers cause harm to innocent people, and "witch doctors" are needed to free and protect people from these evils.

While all Africans see witches as evil, there is considerable disagreement as to whether witches deliberately cause evil or whether the power of witchcraft is something acquired by accident, inherited, or developed naturally. By contrast, sorcerers are people who study, usually with another sorcerer to whom they may or may not be related, to gain power over others and to cause physical harm. One difference between witchcraft and sorcery is that witchcraft is usually seen in terms of psychic powers, while sorcery often involves the use of magic potions.

Historically, both witchcraft and sorcery were countered by the work of traditional healers. Today, many African Independent, or Indigenous, Churches have incorporated the role of the traditional healer into their prophetic and healing ministries. Unlike most mission churches, these Christian groups appeal to the teachings of the Bible, which they blend with traditional healing practices to protect and heal their members. While many missionaries and members of mission churches often condemn such practices, there is a growing recognition that the people involved are genuine Christians who are seeking to apply their faith to the realities of their everyday lives.

The Question of God, Gods, and a Secular Society

One of the most difficult issues to address in relation to African religious traditions is the place of God or gods in traditional African cultures. This is a problem because numerous writers, such as John Mbiti and Geoffrey Parrinder, established the generally accepted view that behind the apparent differences between African religions, there is a common core of belief based on the recognition of a High God. The problem is that while it is possible to generalize in such a way that a High God seems obvious, close examination of the historical sources does not support the claim for Africa as a whole or even within particular regions.

A good example of the issues involved in this debate can be seen in attempts to prove that the Zulu believed in a High God. The position is taken by many scholars, including Isaac Schapera (1937), Geoffrey Parrinder (1969), John Mbiti (1969), W. D. Hammond-Tooke (1974), Axel-Iver Berglund (1989), Thomas Lawson (1984), and Benjamin Ray (2000), that the mere repetition of the idea gives it credibility. David Chidester states this position well when he writes, "At the highest degree

---

Study Aid #113

General Features of African Traditional Religion

African traditional religions are oral traditions that seek the health and well-being of both individuals and communities through ritual actions.

Oral traditions	Ancestors
Witchcraft	High God
Shamans	Interpretation of experience

of abstraction, the existence of a high god overarched all the diverse religious interests in traditional African religion. . . . In general however, no prayer, worship, or sacrifice was directed toward the high god" (1992, 6).

The problem is that while a superficial case can be made to support this argument, when the historical evidence is examined, it is far from clear (Hexham 1981). Here one needs to be very careful about what is being said. There is no doubt that today the vast majority of Zulu believe in God and that since the late nineteenth century belief in some sort of High God has grown. But this does not mean that the Zulu, or any other African people, always believed in a High God.

What the evidence suggests is that the ancestors, who were and remain distinct from God, were always important to ordinary Zulu. Yet at the same time Zulu society was remarkably secular and in a certain sense modern. The earliest missionaries, like Captain Alan Gardener, marveled at the intelligence of the Zulu, which they compared to the widespread ignorance and lack of intelligence found in their homelands. Therefore, while imposing a belief in God on traditional Zulu belief from time immemorial is unjustified, it is possible that during certain periods of history, now lost because we lack documentary evidence, there was a belief in a High God. What this means is that we need to pursue a much more cautious approach to the history of African religions that takes seriously the available evidence and refrains from generalizing.

Conclusion

The debate about a High God recognized throughout Africa brings home the fact that at present we know relatively little about African religions compared with the other great religious traditions. Therefore, there is scope for considerable work in this area.

Sources

David Chidester. *Religions of South Africa*. Routledge, 1992.

E. E. Evans-Pritchard. *Witchcraft, Oracles and Magic among the Azande*. Clarendon, 1937.

Irving Hexham. "Lord of the Sky-King of the Earth: Zulu Traditional Religion and Belief in the Sky God." *Studies in Religion/Sciences Religieuses* 10, no. 3 (September 1981): 273–85.

Thomas E. Lawson. *Religions of Africa: Traditions in Transformation*. Harper & Row, 1984.

John S. Mbiti. *African Religions and Philosophy*. Heinemann, 1969.

Edward Geoffrey Parrinder. *Religion in Africa*. Praeger, 1969.

Christopher Partridge. *Introduction to World Religions*. Fortress, 2005.

Benjamin Ray. *African Religions: Symbol, Ritual, and Community*. 2nd ed. Prentice Hall, 2000.

Robert Redfield. *The Little Community; and, Peasant Society and Culture*. University of Chicago Press, 1965.

Ninian Smart. *The Religious Experience*. 5th ed. Prentice Hall, 1996.

F. B. Welbourn. *Atoms and Ancestors*. Edward Arnold, 1968.

52

Africa: Christian Contacts

IRVING HEXHAM

Today most scholars acknowledge that the earliest recognizable human remains are to be found in Africa, which was the cradle of the earliest human civilizations. This fact fits well with the biblical account of history, where Africa and what today we call the Middle East are in continuous interaction. After the age of Abraham, his descendants took refuge in the African kingdom of Egypt, and Moses marries an Ethiopian (Num. 12:1). Numerous other Bible passages refer to Ethiopia, or Cush, as it is called in older translations. Consequently, both Christians and Jews have had long and largely undocumented contact with Africa and African religions over millennia. Thus most Christians outside of Africa are shocked when they learn that our first complete bound Bible—that is, a Bible that is bound like a modern book—was discovered in an isolated Ethiopian monastery in 2010. It dates from the sixth century and shows not only that African Christianity is ancient but also that Africans were on the cutting edge of technological innovation in the early centuries of the Christian era.

The Greek Connection

One of the things that distorts our understanding of African traditions is the maps we use. Look at almost any map of the ancient or biblical world, and Egypt is cut off slightly south of Thebes. Now compare one of these maps with an ancient Greek or Roman map, and suddenly the ancient world expands well beyond the boundaries of the Roman Empire. In fact, it included the kingdom of Nubia, which roughly corresponds to modern Sudan, and Ethiopia. This fact is very important for understanding African religious traditions because both Christian and Jewish communities thrived to the south of Egypt for centuries.

What really separated Africa from Europe, and African religious traditions from European Christianity, was the rise of Islam in the seventh century CE. The Muslim conquests of the Middle East, Egypt, and North Africa separated Christian areas of Europe from Africa and disrupted centuries-old trade routes that took Christians to India and as far away as China.

Early Christian missionaries converted many peoples in Egypt and along the North African coast. Other Christian missions made converts in what is now Arabia and areas like Yemen. As a result, Christianity spread into Africa from both the Arabian Peninsula and Egypt, with the result that shortly after the death of Christ there were thriving Christian communities in areas like Nubia and Ethiopia. Given the trade routes along the East African coast and to India, it seems very likely that Christians reached places like modern Kenya, perhaps Tanzania, and the islands of the Indian Ocean, such as Mombasa.

The Impact of Islam

All of this changed in the seventh century with the rise of Islam and the lightning-fast Muslim conquest of Egypt, North Africa, and the Arabian Peninsula. As a result, Christians living in what was then the Roman world lost touch with Christian communities in Africa and Asia. The problem this created can be seen by looking at the following maps.

Consider a map of the "Roman Empire at Its Greatest Extent," from John Harvey Robinson's *An Introduction to the History of Western Europe* (1926). This map is typical of maps found in textbooks even today. It cuts off the Roman world by showing only the Roman Empire, leaving out nearby areas with which the Romans had close contact but did not rule. As a result it creates the impression that the Romans knew nothing of Africa and had no contact with Africans.

Consider further the world as Romans knew it before the rise of Islam. In particular there were large and ancient African kingdoms south of Egypt. The Romans also had trade routes to India and China. As a result they knew far more about the world than modern people usually recognize.

Or consider the time during and after the rise of Islam. From what we learn in normal textbooks, African, Indian, and Chinese Christians had meaningful contact

---

Study Aid #114

Christian Contacts with African Religion

Pre-Christian Greek contacts	Islam
Apostle Mark	Slavery
Augustine	Modern missions

with each other. Many maps illustrate this. As Europe developed, however, maps focused on Europe and little else. According to the world as it looked to people living in Europe, the Christian kingdoms of Africa become forgotten realms, only existing in legends and as far-distant memories.

Consequently, we know very little about the history of African Christianity and, for that matter, other African religious traditions south of the Sahara before the late fifteenth century, and in many cases before the nineteenth century. Only when Portuguese, Spanish, and later Dutch and English traders began their "voyages of discovery" in the fifteenth century and onward was contact reestablished with African communities. When this happened, Christians found that Africans often quickly embraced the Bible as part of a lost tradition that they claimed belonged to their ancestors.

African Jews

Until at least the mid-nineteenth century, missionaries and scholars were inclined to believe that when Africans said that their ancestors had worshiped the God of the Bible they were telling the truth. Thus the first missionary to the Zulu in South Africa, Alan Gardiner, wrote that he had arrived in Zululand just as the traditional orally transmitted knowledge of God was dying out. He also speculated that the Zulu might be Jewish in origin. Other African groups scattered across the continent in places as far apart as South Africa, Cameroon, Ghana, Nigeria, and Uganda also claim Jewish descent.

During the twentieth century the claim that certain traditional practices proved a particular African group was descended from Jews was increasingly dismissed by scholars. Instead they argued that Africans picked up these ideas about the Jewish origin of their peoples from reading the Bible. Thus, scholars thought that claims of Jewish descent were seen as a way of resisting colonialism and imperial conquest. Consequently, such claims were "invented" histories and thus false.

In 1996, however, American researchers established a genetic link between the Lemba of South Africa, who claimed to be Jews, and Jews living in Israel, particularly those belonging to ancient priestly families. This finding has the potential to completely rewrite African history. Further genetic mapping may lead to the recognition that many African traditions can be traced back to both Christian and Jewish groups, as their members have claimed since their earliest modern contacts with Europeans.

The Kingdom of the Congo

These speculations aside, the interaction of European explorers, traders, and missionaries with Africans steadily increased from the sixteenth to the nineteenth centuries, and many Africans embraced Christianity as their own. For example, in the Congo basin there was a large and flourishing kingdom that embraced Christianity in the late fifteenth and early sixteenth centuries as a result of the work of Portuguese missionaries.

In fact, the king was baptized, and the Vatican exchanged ambassadors with the kingdom of the Congo. The Congolese king's son studied theology in Portugal and before returning home was appointed the first Christian bishop for central Africa. Unfortunately, he died before leaving Portugal. Nevertheless, the Portuguese recognized the kingdom of the Congo as an important Christian realm in Africa, and Portuguese missionaries continued their work evangelizing a large area.

For almost a hundred years the kingdom thrived as a well-governed Christian state before it collapsed. The downfall of the Congo kingdom came about partly as a result of civil war and partly as a result of the growth of both the European and Arab slave trade. The tragic story of the Christian kingdom of the Congo is well told by Richard Gray in his now-classic work *Black Christians and White Missionaries* (1990).

On the basis of archival documents, Richard Grey convincingly argues that the success of Portuguese missionaries in creating an indigenous African Christianity deep in the heart of Africa was far greater than has been recognized in the past. Distinguishing between the ways missionaries understood and practiced Christianity and the ways black Africans appropriated the faith, Gray focuses on how a highly visible but small minority of African leaders converted to Christianity before actively promoting the faith as a genuine African religion. Although he concentrates on central Africa, similar stories can be told of other parts of this vast continent.

The Curse of Slavery

As Christianity spread in sub-Saharan Africa from the fifteenth century onward, particularly in East and West Africa, so too Islam spread through missionary activities, trade, and conquest. The greatest impact on Africa prior to the nineteenth century was made by Muslim slave traders. From the seventh to the late nineteenth century, they devastated wide areas of Africa in their search for slaves. Although most people know about the transatlantic slave trade, which remains a blot on the history of the West and something Christians ought to mourn, few know anything about the internal Arab slave trade. According to the Transatlantic Slave Database, around 12.5 million African slaves were transported to the Americas between the early sixteenth and mid-nineteenth centuries. Appalling as this figure is, it is dwarfed by the number of Africans enslaved by Muslims from the seventh to the nineteenth centuries. The economic historian Ralph Austin estimates that seventeen million Africans were enslaved by Muslims. The French historian Paul Bairoch revised the number upward to around twenty-five million.

More recently, Muslim apologists have claimed that the number was minuscule. Some, like Ali Masrui, argue that if the Muslim world enslaved so many Africans, there should be a huge black population stretching from Arabia to Spain. Bernard Lewis answers this objection by observing that the Arab slave traders routinely castrated the men, while the children of the women, many of whom served as sex objects in harems, were killed at birth.

Whatever the correct figure, the truth is that by the nineteenth century, Arab slave traders roamed at will throughout Africa. Things changed in mid-century as a result of the efforts of missionaries like David Livingstone, who, whatever his faults, devoted his life to ending African slavery. During the same period the British Royal Navy patrolled the coast of Africa to prevent slave ships from moving slaves across either the Atlantic or Indian Ocean.

One of the problems in discussing the slave trade in Africa is that while the Atlantic slave trade is well documented and the subject of numerous books, very few studies exist documenting the Arab slave trade. As a result, although we know that from the seventh century onward Arab slave traders routinely captured black Africans to work as slaves, we know very little about the exact numbers or treatment of the slaves because there are few reliable records accessible to historians. This is an area that requires far more research.

The Modern Missionary Movement

Early in the nineteenth century a steady flow of Christian missionaries departed from Europe and the Americas for Africa. These people were motivated by a desire to spread the gospel and, later on, to free Africans from the curse of Arab slave traders. From the beginning, the missionary effort combined explicit evangelism with the creation of hospitals and schools. It also caused missionaries, like John Philip of the London Missionary Society, to come into conflict with white settlers.

From the outset the new wave of missionaries to Africa combined a zeal for the gospel with practical goals and humanitarian activities. Thus education both in terms of academic learning and the teaching of practical skills was a key feature of nineteenth-century missions. As a result, they established elementary schools, trade schools, and colleges of higher education, including what became the University of Fort Hare in South Africa.

Importantly, the missionaries sought out intelligent Africans whom they selected for travel overseas to both Europe and North America. Many of these people, like the South African Tiyo Soga, completed their education in Europe or North America, where they gained their degrees before returning to Africa. As Donovan Williams ably pointed out, Soga, who was the protégé of Scottish missionaries, was able to marry a young Scot whom he met during his studies in Glasgow before returning to South Africa. Back in Africa, Soga became the

> **Study Aid #115**
> Growth of African Christianity (Fifty-Four Countries)
> 1800: 4 million Christians, 6 percent of population
> 1900: 10 million Christians, 10 percent of population
> 2000: 360 million Christians, 46 percent of population

leading figure in what became black nationalism. Inspired by his example, other young Africans embraced both Christianity and the desire for self-determination. Thus the African National Congress was founded in 1912 by a group of devoted Christians who, contrary to the negative propaganda of the apartheid era, sought justice for their people inspired by the gospel and a realization that Christianity was deeply rooted in Africa.

What happened in South Africa was repeated throughout the continent as African leaders, many of whom were educated at Fort Hare, embraced both the gospel and their African heritage. Such people fought for justice, and in doing so sought to apply the gospel to everyday life. They resisted white rule and oppression, but, remarkably, they also renounced hatred and violence—although some occurred—in favor of embracing their "white brothers" as fellow believers.

On the cultural front, African converts regularly visited Europe and North America from the late nineteenth century onward. In doing so, they often embraced European ways of life, including, as Terrance Ranger points out, ballroom dancing, while introducing Europeans and Americans, particularly black Americans, to their own dance traditions and, most importantly, to music. Thus jazz grew out of the interchange between visiting African converts and black Americans, many of whom shared their deep Christian faith.

Equally important, although denied by some church historians, is the role of Africans in inspiring the Pentecostal movement, which, as Karla Poewe points out, was deeply influenced by African spirituality in both Africa and America. Later it was the South African David du Plessis who lit the spark that launched the charismatic movement of the 1960s, while du Plessis himself was deeply moved by Zulu Christianity.

Conclusion

African Christianity has a long and complex history, which is little understood and in need of extensive research. The truth is that we know little about the history of Christianity in Africa despite large volumes by people like Bengt Sundkler, Elizabeth Isichei, and C. P. Groves. Nevertheless, they laid a foundation that reminds us of Africa's rich Christian heritage that remains to be explored in greater detail.

Sources

Paul Bairoch. *Le mythe de la croissance économique rapide au 19e siècle*. Éditions de l'Institut de sociologie, 1962.

Richard Gray. *Black Christians and White Missionaries*. Yale University Press, 1990.

C. P. Groves. *The Planting of Christianity in Africa*. Lutterworth, 1948.

Elizabeth Allo Isichei. *A History of Christianity in Africa: From Antiquity to the Present*. SPCK, 1995.

Bernard Lewis. *Race and Slavery in the Middle East: An Historical Enquiry*. Oxford University Press, 1990.

R. Segal. *Islam's Black Slaves: The Other Black Diaspora*. Farrar, Straus & Giroux, 2001.

Bengt Sundkler and Christopher Steed. *A History of the Church in Africa*. Cambridge University Press, 2000.

Donovan Williams. *Umfundisi: A Biography of Tiyo Soga, 1829–1871*. Lovedale, 1978.

53

Africa: Theological Exchanges

Irving Hexham

Although many people think of Christianity as a Western, particularly European, religion, the reality is that early Christianity was nourished in Asian societies of the Middle East and the Roman world of North Africa. Consequently, Western Christianity as we know it took root in African soil. To appreciate this we need to examine the early impact of Africa on Christianity, contextualization of Christianity by modern missionaries to Africa, and the way black Africans have created their own independent or indigenous churches.

The Early Impact of Africa on Christianity

Any discussion of the contextualization of Christianity in Africa must begin with the New Testament. There we learn that on the way to Jesus's execution, Roman soldiers forced an African, Simon of Cyrene, to carry the cross of Jesus (Mark 15:21). We are not told what Simon was doing in Jerusalem, nor do we know what happened to him afterward, although from the reference to his two sons it seems that he and his family became Christians. We also hear in Acts 11:19–21 of people from Cyrene converting to Christianity and know from archaeological evidence that a thriving Christian community soon took root in the city, which was a prosperous Roman settlement in what today is Libya. The other major biblical tie to Africa is found in Acts 8:26–39, which records Christian conversations with a eunuch who was a minister in the Ethiopian government.

When Christianity burst onto the world scene, North Africa was a prosperous Romanized area that stretched from Egypt to Morocco. Along the coast of this vast area were thriving cities, making it the heart of the Roman world. Most of the trade went from east to west or north to south across the Mediterranean. But a small but significant amount of spices and other goods came north across the Sahara or along the Nile from Nubia and Ethiopia.

The population of Roman Africa was made up of the descendants of the Carthaginians and a mixture of local peoples, all of whom had intermarried Greek and Roman settlers. The cities were rich culturally, with well-established educational institutions, a strong commitment to the Roman Empire, and a thriving civic life.

In this complex society the Berbers played an important role. As a group with its own distinct language and customs, the Berbers were spread out across Roman Africa and in many places were well integrated with Roman society. Berber peoples were also to be found across the Sahara in places like modern Mali, Niger, and Burkina Faso. Thus they formed a link between North African Roman civilization and the civilizations of black African Christianity and African traditions.

One of the first great Christian theologians, Quintus Septimius Florens Tertullianus (160–225 CE), better known as Tertullian, was born in the most important of these coastal cities, Carthage. According to tradition, his father was a Roman centurion who settled in North Africa. We know nothing about his mother. We know very little about his life except that after watching Christians die heroic deaths in the arena, he studied their beliefs and was converted. On the basis of his writings it is fair to call him "the father of Western theology."

It was Tertullian who first gave expression to the Christian doctrine of the Trinity, which he described in terms of "three persons sharing one substance." He is also remembered for his insistence on the priority of revelation and his firm rejection of the influence of Platonic philosophy on Christian belief. This he summed up with the phrase "What has Athens to do with Jerusalem? The Academy with the Church?" (*Against Heretics* 7).

Study Aid #116

African Influences on Christianity

Biblical
  Mark 15:21; Acts 11:19–21; Acts 8:26–39
Tertullian
  The Trinity
  Priority of revelation
Augustine
  Dynamics of conversion
  Church and state
  Monasticism
Modern
Diaspora missionaries to the West

Interestingly, what is overlooked in most discussions of Tertullian is the African background to his work. As with Augustine, his mother was probably a local woman, because while he is a superb writer and master of Latin, throughout his works are echoes of African traditions. This is seen in his typically African attitude toward rivers, springs, streams, and the sea. It is also seen in his attitude to healing and the role of the Holy Spirit. Both of these things come together in his treatises on baptism, where he argues that waters acquire healing powers through the intervention of angels and the spirit.

After Tertullian, the second great shaker of Western Christianity was Augustine of Hippo (354–430). Once again, Augustine had a Latin name, Aurelius Augustinus Hipponensis, which distracts from his African roots. Nevertheless, he was born in the North African Roman city of Tagaste, today's Souk Ahras, in modern Algeria, which was a major Berber population center. From her name, Monica, it appears that his mother was a Berber. His father, on the other hand, was a Roman citizen, but we know nothing of his ethnic origin. What we do know is that his father was a pagan while his mother was a Christian. The story of his life and conversion to Christianity is found in his classic work *The Confessions*. From this and his other writings, Augustine appears to anyone who is familiar with African society to be thoroughly African. Like Tertullian, he delighted in stories about healings, miracles, and martyrs. Importantly, he reports his mother performing the common African rite of *refrigerium*, or leaving food and wine on the graves of the departed. Such practices continue today among Christians in places like Ghana or in Sierra Leone. Finally, it is important to note that Augustine firmly embraced monasticism, which originated in the third century in Egypt.

The importance of all this is that early Christianity, particularly those branches that spread to Western Europe, was rooted in North Africa, where there are clear signs of contextualization in terms of local beliefs and practices. The implications of this are that the Western Christian tradition was contextualized in Africa long before it spread to northern Europe. Therefore, talking about the contextualization of Christianity in Africa is actually highly complex and cannot be reduced to the way the nineteenth- and twentieth-century European missionaries introduced their form of Western Christianity to Africans.

Contextualization by Modern Missionaries to Africa

The modern missionary movement is usually dated from the founding of the Baptist Missionary Society in 1792 and the arrival of William Carey (1761–1834) in India the following year. In its wake a host of new missionary societies were founded in Britain, a number of which focused on Africa. Around the same time many others sprang up in various European countries and North America. In addition to these Protestant missions, a significant number of older Roman Catholic missions were supplemented by new Catholic missions, as well as a smaller number of missions belonging to the various branches of Eastern Orthodoxy.

A common complaint about Christian missions found in secular literature is that they "destroy indigenous cultures." Perhaps the best example of this comes from the book *The Role of Missionaries in Conquest*, which was published in 1952 in Johannesburg, South Africa. What gave this book credibility and made it very popular was that the author was named Nosipho Majeke. Thus the impression was created that this was an African response to European missionaries. Unfortunately this book set the tone for a lot of the late twentieth-century literature on Christian missions in Africa, as its message was uncritically accepted by many academics. In fact, we now know that the author was actually Doris Taylor, the wife of the University of Cape Town economics lecturer and a South African communist.

Generalizing about the role of missions and missionaries in Africa is virtually impossible. The fact is that various missions were different from each other in numerous fundamental ways. Thus many Roman Catholic and high Anglican missions, as well as a number of German Lutheran missions such as the Berlin Missionary Society, sent out missionaries who had great respect for African culture and made every effort to contextualize the message within an African context. On the other hand, many African converts and their children, for example the great South African black leader John Henderson Soga, reacted with horror at the traditional practices of their own societies. Nevertheless, in general, Protestant missions tend to be less accommodating to traditional religion than Catholic ones.

A good example of the problems of contextualization can be found in the nineteenth-century debates about polygamy in the context of South Africa. Here a wide range of opinions may be found among the missionaries. For example, the Anglican bishop of Natal, John Henry Colenso, held a nuanced position in connection with polygamy. While he believed it was the duty of the church to promote monogamy, he was prepared to tolerate modified forms of polygamy

---

Study Aid #117

African-Initiated Churches (AIC)

AICs have been widely discussed in both the history of religions and Christian mission literature. One of the most faithful guides is Harold Turner, who shows how the words used to refer to the churches reflect deeper theological understandings:

African Separatist Churches
 Allen Lea. *The Native Separatist Church Movement in South Africa* (1928)
African Independent Churches
 Bengt Sundkler. *Bantu Prophets in South Africa* (1948)
African Indigenous Churches
 G. C. Oosthuizen. *Post-Christianity in South Africa* (1968)

among new converts, arguing that one could not expect someone to divorce his wives after conversion. Nevertheless, an unmarried man or woman who became a Christian ought to remain monogamous.

While this position sounds very liberal and in touch with the realities of African life, his fellow Anglican missionary to Natal, Henry Callaway, who later became the bishop of the Transkei, held a very different position in his debates with Colenso. In Callaway's view the bishop's understanding of African life was clouded by the fact that he lived in the provincial capital of Pietermaritzburg. If only he would live among ordinary Africans well away from white towns, he would see the reality of polygamy and realize that in practice it enslaved women.

In these debates the issue was not the interpretation of the Bible or the imposition of a Victorian morality. Rather, it was the anthropological question of how polygamy actually worked in traditional African societies. Both men in fact were seeking the good of the people around them, and neither can be said to have allowed a crude ideology of white supremacy to shape his thinking.

Today debates like these continue in Africa through works like Eugene Hillman's *Polygamy Reconsidered* (1975) and Shorter's (et al.) *African Christian Marriage* (1977). In general, however, a consensus appears to have been reached by African Christians that polygamy is not the preferred, or Christian, form of marriage. Thus debates about African Christianity continue to the present, with Africans playing an important role in developing their own form of modern Christianity.

Indigenous Contextualization: African Independent/Indigenous Churches

Perhaps the most important development within the Christian traditions of Africa over the past two centuries has been the development of so-called African Independent, or Indigenous, Churches (AICs). These are churches created by Africans that either broke away from, or developed independently of, established mission churches, and they are the most dynamic aspect of modern African religion.

Initially European writers and scholars gave African Independent Churches the derogatory name "separatist churches" (Lea 1926). Perhaps the worst example of the denigration of African Independent Churches is found in John Buchan's popular novel *Prester John* (1910). In this book the black mission convert breaks away from the church that educated him to create his own violent, antiwhite religious movement with the aim of driving European settlers into the sea. The plot, of course, is foiled by the book's hero, a young Scot.

Later, largely as a result of the publication of Bengt Sundkler's now-classic work *Bantu Prophets in South Africa* (1948), attitudes among Christians toward African Independent Churches gradually began to change. Sundkler's work was followed by Katesa Schlosser's *Propheten in Africa* (1949). These pioneering works were both broad overviews. The first detailed study of specific African Independent

Churches appears to be F. B. Welbourn's *East African Rebels* (1961), which is a study of independent churches in East Africa.

According to Harold Turner, the earliest African Independent Churches developed in the Congo during the sixteenth century. But we know little about these movements. The real growth of AICs begins with the nineteenth-century Protestant missionary movement, which brought with it literacy and the Bible.

By the nineteenth century AICs had begun to develop in southern Africa and elsewhere. There appeared to be two distinct routes to the development of these movements. They first arose out of mission churches through conflicts with European missionaries, or settler groups, and disagreements about how the Bible ought to be interpreted. The second grew out of indigenous African prophetic movements that developed independently of mission churches but embraced the Bible to legitimate their ideas. One of the earliest recorded African Independent Churches that grew out of an established mission church was founded in South Africa's Transkei by the Methodist preacher Nehemiah Tile in 1834. This movement combined Christian theology with Thembu nationalism, but unfortunately it disintegrated after Tile's death in 1881. Nevertheless, from the 1880s, AICs developed rapidly throughout Africa. Many of these churches incorporated "Ethiopia" or "Ethiopian" into their name. Consequently, they soon became known as the Ethiopian movement, which had political connotations since at that time Ethiopia was the only truly independent African state on the continent. These churches then fit the pattern of reaction to European dominance. One of the most successful of this type of church is the Herero Oruuano Church of Namibia, which is essentially a Lutheran church that broke away from its parent organization.

Around the same time another type of African Independent Church, which did not grow out of existing missionary churches, developed. These churches developed as a result of the preaching of Africans who believed they had a unique call from God. In the process, they incorporated African traditions, seeing them in terms of their readings of the Bible.

Arguably the oldest continuous AIC with a sizable following is the Nazareth Baptist Church of the amaNazarites, founded in 1912 by the Zulu prophet Isaiah Shembe (1867–1935), while the largest AIC in southern Africa is the Zion Christian Church, which Ignatious Lekganyane (1885–1948) founded in 1924. In central Africa, the prophet Simon Kimbangu (d. 1951) founded an equally large and vibrant movement, the Church of Jesus Christ on Earth, which is commonly known as the Kimbangists. In West Africa, the Aladura movement comprises a number of different churches and is probably the largest movement there, while in East Africa, the African Israel Church and the Brotherhood Church are particularly important. Together, these churches far outstrip established mission churches in terms of membership and represent a dynamic development in the growth of Christianity.

Today there is a tendency for scholars, reacting against an earlier racism, to see all African Independent Churches as the Africanized form of Christianity and to view them in terms of contextualization. While this approach is attractive, it overlooks certain realities. For example, before his untimely death in 1989, Londa Shembe, the grandson of the founder of amaNazarites, Isaiah Shembe, rejected the view that his movement was simply an African form of Christianity. In his view, it might be genuinely Christian, but he was unsure and toyed with the idea that perhaps it owes more to Judaism or perhaps even the large South African Hindu community than to Christianity. On the other hand, his uncle, Amos Shembe, had no doubts that the amaNazarites were a genuinely Christian movement.

This debate about the limits of contextualization can be seen in the writings of South African G. C. Oosthuizen, who questioned whether the amaNazarites and other similar African movements should be easily identified as Christian. After Oosthuizen published his views, Western academics sensitive to racism tended to dismiss the other work by Afrikaners as influenced by the realities of apartheid.

Conclusion

The history of the interaction of African religions and society with Christianity is long and complex. From the time of the early church until the present, Africans have played an important role in the development of world Christianity. Today this interaction is entering a new phase as African missionaries are increasingly being sent to Europe and North America to evangelize what African Christians see as an increasingly pagan society. What this means for the future of Christianity remains to be seen. Nevertheless, we have a clue from the amazing success of the charismatic movement in the 1960s, which was directly linked to Africa and the African experience.

Sources

Peter Brown. *Augustine of Hippo: A Biography*. Faber & Faber, 2000.

John Buchan. *Prester John*. Thomas Nelson, 1910.

M. L. Daneel. *Zionism and Faith-Healing in Rhodesia: Aspects of African Independent Churches*. Mouton, 1970.

Rosalind I. J. Hackett. *New Religious Movements in Nigeria*. Mellen, 1987.

Eugene Hillman. *Polygamy Reconsidered: African Plural Marriage and the Christian Churches*. Orbis Books, 1975.

Benezeri Kisembo, Laurenti Magesa, and Aylward Shorter. *African Christian Marriage*. G. Chapman, 1977.

Allen Lea. *The Native Separatist Church Movement in South Africa*. Juta, 1926.

Nosipho Majeke. *The Role of the Missionaries in Conquest*. Society of Young Africa, 1952.

G. C. Oosthuizen. *Post-Christianity in Africa: A Theological and Anthropological Study*. T. Wever, 1968.

Londa Shembe and Irving Hexham. *The Scriptures of the amaNazaretha of Ekuphakameni: Selected Writings of the Zulu Prophets Isaiah and Londa Shembe*. University of Calgary Press, 1993.

Bengt Sundkler. *Bantu Prophets in South Africa*. Lutterworth, 1948.

———. *Zulu Zion and Some Swazi Zionists*. Oxford University Press, 1976.

Frederick Burkewood Welbourn. *East African Rebels: A Study of Some Independent Churches*. SCM, 1961.

Martin Elgar West. *Bishops and Prophets in a Black City: African Independent Churches in Soweto, Johannesburg*. D. Philip, 1975.

David E. Wilhite. *Tertullian the African*. Walter de Gruyter, 2007.

54

Africa: Current Issues

IRVING HEXHAM

Today sub-Saharan Africa is a poor continent rich in material and human resources with a large and growing Christian population. On the one hand, there are many hopeful signs pointing toward positive change. On the other, there is a cycle of poverty and corruption that prevents Africans from reaching their true potential. Religious fanaticism, traditional beliefs, and unhealthy mixtures of religion and politics all serve to hold Africans back. These issues are treated below in the hope that by recognizing some of the most pressing issues, change will come about to create a new Africa.

Religious Fanaticism

Religious fanaticism is often difficult to distinguish from political and other forms of fanaticism, many of which use religion as an excuse. When extremist groups claim to be acting in the name of religion and invoke such things as the imminent return of Christ or the need to wage a jihad, then it seems fair to speak of these movements as motivated in part by religious extremism. As such they may be seen to have their roots in religions like Christianity or Islam. With African traditional religions the situation is more complex. Therefore, one needs to be clear about what we mean by a traditional African religion.

For the purpose of identifying them as social phenomena, African traditional religions may be described as oral traditions that claim to seek the health and well-being of both the individual and community through ritual actions. These rituals are understood by participants in terms of movements based on beliefs about the ancestors (who are often called the living dead), sorcery, and witchcraft. As pointed out in the article on the history, beliefs, and practices of African religions, the specifics of various African traditions vary from society to society, including the ways in which they understand illness, misfortune, and the steps needed to restore normality.

What they share in common is a belief that misfortune and illness result from psychic curses and that the appropriate rituals can protect both the individual and society. Central to these beliefs is the issue of witchcraft belief, which is found throughout Africa. In some societies, witches learn their craft; in others, the powers of the witch are inherited. In all cases, Africans believe that witchcraft is evil. Such beliefs have profound social consequences, particularly in terms of witchcraft.

Witchcraft

Witchcraft-eradication movements, and efforts by individuals or small groups to free themselves from the power of witches, are the cause of hundreds of painful deaths every year of people accused of being witches. From the cape to Cairo, from Nairobi to Laos, witchcraft-eradication movements thrive, causing suffering to thousands of people annually. Although Christian ministers and Muslim clerics generally oppose such movements, as do the leaders of African Independent, or Indigenous, Churches (AICs), a great deal needs to be done to rid Africa of this curse.

Ritual murder is another prevalent problem throughout the African continent. Anyone who regularly reads African newspapers soon discovers gruesome stories detailing grotesque ritual murders performed by ritual experts to obtain body parts for their "medicines." Frequently these body parts are taken from young children, particularly boys.

In recognizing the problem of witchcraft and sorcery in Africa, it is important not to confuse them with modern Western new religious movements like Wicca.

Traditional Religions and Politics

Traditional religions have often played an important role in the political development of African societies. Historically, one of the most spectacular examples of this is the destabilization of nineteenth-century Xhosa society by the preaching of the prophet Nogqawusa, who urged the performance of certain ritual acts that he believed would enable the ancestors to drive Europeans into the sea. Of course, there was no African apocalypse that liberated the Xhosa from European influence. Instead, thousands died of starvation, and Xhosa society disintegrated.

More recently the Mau Mau movement in Kenya was inspired by spirit mediums who played a leading role in the rebellion against white rule. Similarly, in the struggle for Rhodesian independence, spirit mediums again took an active part

> **Study Aid #118**
> **Current Issues in Africa**
> Religious fanaticism
> Witchcraft
> Traditional religions
> African Indigenous Churches
> Millenarian movements
> Political leaders and religion
> Christian missionaries
> Islam

in galvanizing African rebels to fight against the white government of Ian Smith. Then during the 1990s in Mozambique, the spirit medium Manuel Antonio led a major rebellion against the government. In this instance the African government of Mozambique realized the importance of spirit mediums and recruited others to that cause.

In West Africa the government of Benin has used traditional beliefs and the power of voodoo to legitimate its rule. Similar traditionally based political movements exist in Kenya and Uganda.

The Traditionalist Accommodation with Christianity

Many traditional healers and religious movements throughout Africa have reached an accommodation with Christianity. For example, in South Africa and Zimbabwe traditional healers are often found in AICs, where they have their own distinct role within a Christian framework. Similarly, both traditional and AIC healers are deliberately encouraged by their governments to cooperate with Western-trained doctors in modern hospitals. This is done by allowing that certain diseases are what Western people would call psychological, and that these can be dealt with using traditional means of healing. In contrast, things like tuberculosis and cancer require treatment by Western-trained doctors.

Christians and traditionalists have collaborated in Kenya to have Mount Kenya declared a "national shrine." There also have been instances where Christian denominations have apologized to traditional believers after local Christians or pastors have destroyed traditional holy sites or sacred groves.

These instances of friendly cooperation need to be balanced against violent outbursts in places like Ghana, where traditional and Christian youth groups have clashed. One of the traditionalist demands in Ghana and other places is that Christians refrain from loud hymn singing and the beating of drums. A growing form of opposition to Christianity in Africa is the traditionalist claim that their own religions "never champion racism," while Christianity is a racist religion. Such propaganda overlooks the fact that many traditional religions were rooted in specific ethnic groups that saw all others as potential enemies.

Nevertheless, given the history of apartheid, such claims have made progress in recent years. For example, when the former East German historian of Christian missions Ulrich van der Heyden first visited South Africa in the early 1990s, he was surprised by how well kept the graveyards were at former mission stations, many of which were in ruins. Returning some fifteen years later, he was shocked to discover that many of these graveyards had been desecrated and that pagan symbols were spray-painted on tombstones.

Cults and Millenarian Movements

In general African governments do not seem particularly worried about so-called cults. The exceptions to this are in Uganda and Kenya, where they are seen as a problem. In other places, like West Africa, they're usually seen as more of a nuisance. Where problems arise is usually in terms of things like immunization programs or the claim by various religious leaders that they perform miraculous acts of healing. Thus various African governments have been outspoken in their criticism of healing movements as the work of charlatans.

One of the most troublesome new religions in central Africa is that of the Acholi spirit medium Alice Lakwena (1957–2007), who fomented a rebellion against the Ugandan government in 1986. Eventually, after thousands of deaths and widespread destruction, she accepted an amnesty and retired to Kenya.

The movement she founded, however, continues to exist under the guise of the Ugandan Lord's Resistance Army (LRA), led by her cousin Joseph Kony (1961–). For almost twenty years it terrorized large parts of northern Uganda, the southern Sudan, the Democratic Republic of the Congo, and the Central African Republic, frequently violating human rights. As a result, in 2005 the International Criminal Court issued warrants for the arrest of the LRA's leaders.

Subsequently, in 2006 the LRA began negotiations with the Ugandan government, and a truce was arranged. In 2008, however, Ugandan, Congolese, and Sudanese troops launched a series of attacks against the LRA. In retaliation, the LRA carried out a series of massacres and are reported to have crucified Catholic worshipers that they captured at a church in southern Sudan. Since then, further military action by government forces appears to have virtually destroyed the LRA, although people in the areas affected by the movement continue to live in fear for their lives.

Today there are conflicting claims about the fate of the LRA's leader, Joseph Kony. Some reports say he is dead, others claim he is in hiding, while still others suggest he is fighting on in the bush. Whatever the truth of the matter, this is one of the most devastating religiously inspired rebellions in African history.

African Political Leaders and Religion

African newspapers make it clear that, unlike the first generation of African political leaders who led their countries to independence from colonial rule, many today are ambivalent about their relationship to Christianity. The first-generation political leaders in newly independent African states were almost without exception educated in mission schools and, like Nelson Mandela, retained a very high respect for Christianity regardless of their personal piety or lack of it. Today, however, the situation is changing.

Nevertheless, African political leaders continue to take religion and church affairs far more seriously than European or North American politicians. Consequently, they often participate in denominational conferences and speak in churches. Most African political leaders believe that religion plays an important role in society by providing a moral compass. Thus they frequently call upon the church to become involved in social problems. For example, Robert Mugabe regularly appeals to the church to "restore morality and discipline," while Zambian political leaders have no difficulty in talking about Zambia as a Christian state.

At the same time, the cordial relations between politicians and church leaders can quickly give way to strong criticism of church affairs by politicians, particularly if Christian leaders dare to criticize political decisions. As a result, when leaders of Kenyan churches raised questions about the wording of the constitution, they were sharply rebuked by the government.

The African press often criticizes both political and church leaders with good reason. For example, one Zambian journalist, Wellington Mbofana, once declared, "Clerics who sleep with dogs shall wake up with flees." This provoked howls of outrage from politicians who were stung by his criticisms. Yet African journalists continue to bravely criticize both church and state, often on the basis of Christian moral values.

The outstanding example of African journalists standing up to political and religious hierarchies is in South Africa. During the apartheid era, journalists, many of whom would not have called themselves Christians, frequently appealed to Christian values in their criticism of apartheid. Inspired by this example, other journalists throughout Africa have taken a strong stance against corruption and perceived evil.

The Problem of Islam

Western Muslims often claim that Islam is "a religion of peace." Technically this claim is correct—Islam preaches peace. The way it is believed that peace comes about, however, is through submission to Muslim rule. Therefore, in Islamic theology, conquest for the purpose of imposing God's will is perfectly acceptable to many Muslims. This is not to argue that Muslims are particularly violent or inclined to violence. In fact, many Muslims are peaceful people who make excellent neighbors. Nevertheless, it has to be recognized that in Muslim theology and political thought, the idea of jihad, or holy war in defense of Islam, is a noble concept. It also needs to be recognized that for many Muslims the creation of a realm of peace involves the imposition of *shari'a* law. These two facts create a major problem on the African continent and require considerable thought and attention.

Having said this, it is important to note that in African Islam there is actually a pacifist tradition. Further, many traditional Muslim leaders throughout Africa have spoken out against violence and are opposed to the growth of militant Islamism. Others reject the idea of imposing *shari'a* law on entire societies where the majority of people are not Muslim.

A related issue is that of blasphemy in Muslim areas of Africa. Orthodox Muslims worship God alone and regard Muhammad as his messenger. As a result, in many areas of Africa it is very easy for Christians and others to unwittingly commit blasphemy. For example, even the claim "Jesus is Lord" is, strictly speaking, blasphemous in Muslim theology. Of course, influenced by Western multiculturalism, many people wonder why Muslims and Christians cannot simply "live together." The problem is that even a Christmas hymn like "Hark! The Herald Angels Sing" contains many lines like "Christ, the everlasting Lord" that, strictly speaking, are blasphemous in terms of Muslim theology.

Since blasphemy is a capital offense, this makes it very difficult for Christians to live in Muslim-controlled areas. Similarly, to talk about Jesus as anything other than a prophet who lived before Muhammad can be taken as blasphemy and potentially spark a riot in areas where *shari'a* law is not enforced. In other areas where *shari'a* is enforced, it can lead to imprisonment and, if the accused is proved guilty, death. These are issues that require both our attention and that of our governments if Christians and Muslims are to live together peaceably in Africa or anywhere else.

Conclusion

Today sub-Saharan Africa is a challenging place with many poor states on the verge of disintegration. Yet many states have large populations of highly committed Christians. Nigeria is particularly prone to violence and faces terrorist activities in both the Muslim north and Christian south. Despite enormous wealth, a cycle of poverty and corruption persists, while very real ecological damage is devastating offshore areas due to oil leaks and human carelessness. In this situation there is a very real need for something like the post–World War II Marshall Plan to provide not simply financial aid but also stability and expertise to help Africans help themselves and break the cycle of disintegration and violence.

Sources

Tim Allen and Koen Vlassenroot. *The Lord's Resistance Army: Myths and Realities.* Zed, 2010.

David J. Bosch. *Transforming Mission: Paradigm Shifts in Theology of Mission.* Orbis Books, 2011.

John Davis. *Terrorism in Africa: The Evolving Front in the War on Terror*. Lexington Books, 2010.

David J. Hesselgrave and Edward Rommen. *Contextualization: Meanings, Methods, and Models*. Baker, 1989.

Janet Hodgson. *Ntsikana's Great Hymn: A Xhosa Expression of Christianity in the Early Nineteenth Century Eastern Cape*. Centre for African Studies, 1980.

Isak A. Niehaus, Eliazaar Mohlala, and Kally Shokane. *Witchcraft, Power and Politics: Exploring the Occult in the South African Lowveld*. Pluto, 2001.

Edward Geoffrey Parrinder. *Witchcraft: European and African*. Faber & Faber, 1970.

J. B. Peires. *The Dead Will Arise: Nongqawuse and the Great Xhosa Cattle-Killing Movement of 1856–7*. Ravan, 1989.

Johannes Verkuyl. *Contemporary Missiology: An Introduction*. Eerdmans, 1978.

55

Oceania: History, Beliefs, Practices

Charles Farhadian

History

Oceania consists of the regions of Polynesia, Micronesia, Melanesia, Australia, and New Zealand. As one of the most ethnically, culturally, and religiously diverse areas of the world, this region is made up of more than twenty-five thousand islands that contain about a quarter of the world's distinct religions. Melanesia alone contains well over a thousand religio-linguistic groupings, with more than twelve hundred distinct languages that correspond to different cultures. The religions of Oceania are an amalgam of indigenous religious traditions with unique histories spread out over the Pacific Islands, in what some have called the "liquid continent," lying in an ocean that covers roughly 30 percent of the earth's surface. The term "Oceania" refers to a region rather than to a people—there are no "Oceanians."

Westerners introduced the term "Oceania" to describe a sociopolitical reality of the islands of the southwest Pacific and Australia. The Greek term *nesia* ("island") was used by Westerners to refer to the major island groups of Oceania, which are Polynesia ("many islands"), Micronesia ("small islands"), and Melanesia ("black islands"). Scholars suggest that people were present in Oceania tens of thousands of years ago. Evidence of early Oceanic religions has been discovered by archaeologists, who have noted significant interest of the people around death, the supernatural, and even cannibalism in some parts of the region. Our knowledge of the religions of Oceania comes mostly from the records of European explorers, beginning in the early sixteenth century with the work of Antonio Pigafetta. Early European interpretation of the religions of Oceania and its people reflected European prejudices regarding race and intelligence. For instance, Europeans held different opinions about local inhabitants, with some explorers referring to Islanders as "Noble Savages"; others saw locals as good "Children of Nature."

Such diverse interpretations were characteristic of the philosophical and religious viewpoints (and prejudices) of sixteenth- through eighteenth-century Europe. The stories of Captain Cook and other explorers during this period introduced the people of Oceania and their religions to Westerners. Within the first two years of its founding in 1795, the London Missionary Society (LMS) had permanent missionaries in Tonga, Tahiti, and the Marquesas. Early European Christian missionaries combined mission work with exploration and research, sailing on ships throughout the islands, many losing their lives to disease, sailing accidents, or martyrdom. As Christianity spread through the islands, Pacific Islanders themselves would carry the lion's share of the burden of mission throughout the rest of Oceania. By the 1900s, Oceanic missionaries were major forces of Christian witness throughout the region. In the twentieth century, many Christian denominations in Oceania sought independence from European control, thus moving from a status of "missions" to "churches." Today every major Christian denomination—Catholic, Orthodox, and Protestant, as well as countless faith mission groups, including numerous Pentecostal churches—has found a home in Oceania, making Oceania the region with one of the highest percentages of Christians worldwide.

The most reliable information we have on the early religions of Oceania comes from the records and journals of long-term Christian missionaries, European explorers, and administrators. Anthropologist E. B. Tyler, when learning about the Australian Aborigines, adopted the term "animistic" (a belief in spirits) as his theory of the origin of religion. Animism suggests that the whole cosmos is alive, animated by spiritual power. In the nineteenth and twentieth centuries, three major religious themes dominated the Western understanding of religions in Oceania—*mana, tabu,* and *totemism*. Some of the most influential social scientists (E. B. Tyler, É. Durkheim, Margaret Mead, and B. Malinowski) have investigated Oceanian religions through these themes. *Mana*, wrote missionary anthropologist R. H. Codrington, "is a power or influence, not physical, and in a way supernatural; but it shows itself in physical force, or in any kind of power or excellence which a man possesses." As a spiritual power, *mana* was a fundamental reality that struck awe in people of Oceania, permeating their religions and view of nature, human life, and the spirit world. *Tabu* (taboo) denoted a strong prohibition within society based on ethnic and religious beliefs. *Tabu* is a Tongan word that means "forbidden" or "set apart," and refers to areas that are restricted or not allowed, since they are things set apart because of their sacred nature. *Totem* is a spirit being that protects a certain group and functions as a representative of a group of people (e.g., family, clan), often embodied in such entities as the forces of nature (e.g., the spirit of the wind), animals, or plants.

Religions of Oceania consist not simply of a myriad of indigenous forms of religious life, each recognizing that spiritual powers animate material objects, but also a blending with the world religions, with the most popular world religion in Oceania being Christianity. Christianity arrived in large part during the period of European colonialism, when Protestants and Catholics introduced the Christian faith to Polynesian chiefs, whose people converted and then spread the faith westward in a chain reaction that eventually communicated Christianity to the Melanesian Islands. The history of Oceanic Christianity reflects the ecclesiastical diversity and theological accents of the kinds of churches introduced throughout the region.

The Christian mission effort in Oceania was so robust that it caused a contemporary anthropologist to claim that the people of Oceania "have been subject to more intense missionization, by European and indigenous missionaries, during the nineteenth and twentieth centuries, than almost any other peoples in the world." By 1992, about 95 percent of Pacific Islanders identified themselves as some sort of Christian, a testimony to the success of Christian missions throughout the region for the previous 150 years. The religions of Oceania are not missionary religions; neither do they seek to win converts nor convince outsiders of some universal truth. Consequently, the history of the religions of Oceania is a history of particular peoples of Oceania and

Study Aid #119

Map of Oceania

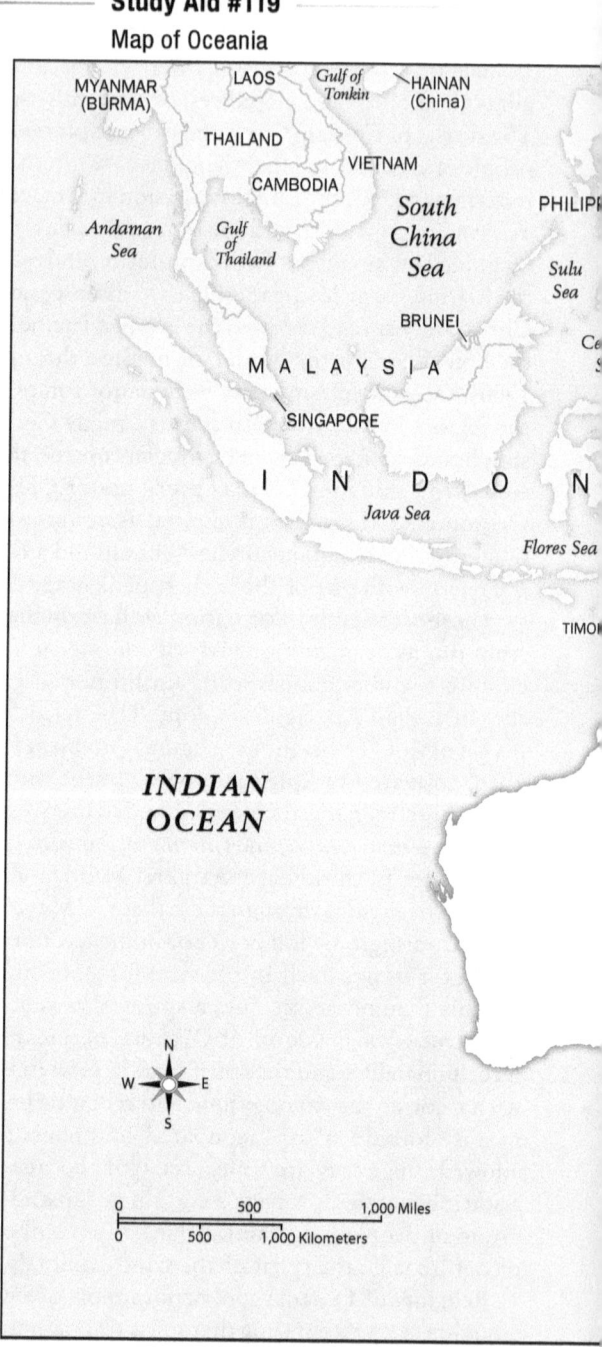

the ways in which they have blended local religious traditions with forms of Christianity, and increasingly with other new religions. While Mormon missionaries were present in small numbers in Oceania prior to the mid-twentieth century, the period following the Second World War witnessed the influx of large numbers of Mormon missionaries and eventually the conversion of many Pacific Islanders to the Church of Jesus Christ of Latter-Day Saints.

Beliefs

While it is impossible to provide a detailed introduction to the religions of Oceania because of the region's religious diversity, some themes are fairly characteristic of Oceanic religions.

Dreaming (Dreamtime)

Having access to that which springs eternally (dreamtime) is a special feature of many religious beliefs in Oceania. Dreams are an arena where visions are given and where the dreamer receives knowledge and direction. For Aboriginal Australians, dreaming focuses on events and places more than time. Events are revealed in dreamtime, and these events can reach back two generations, as one scholar notes, "just beyond the memory of specific people."

Cosmology

In the traditional religions of Oceania, the cosmos and the natural world are thought to be animated by benevolent and malevolent spirit beings. The traditional peoples of Oceania recognized both horizontal and vertical dimensions of religion. That is to say, they recognized that spirits resided on the human level (horizontal) and in the skies (vertical). However, traditional Polynesian religions emphasized the vertical dimension of religion, while the Melanesian emphasized the horizontal. Overall, there is a close connection for all peoples of Oceania between the forces of the sky (e.g., divinized sky), the human community, and the earth and underworld. Thus, while some religions of Oceania emphasized either the horizontal or vertical dimensions of the spirit world, there is nevertheless a strong sense of the vertical connection between the three domains of heavens, earth, and underworld.

Making Authorities

The traditional world of Oceanic peoples involves different strategies for legitimizing authorities according to the particular regions of Oceania. These authority systems are related to the religions of the region. For instance, in Polynesia

> **Study Aid #120**
> Countries of Oceania
>
> | | | |
> |---|---|---|
> | Australia | Marshall Islands | Samoa |
> | Melanesia | Micronesia | Tavalu |
> | Bougainville | Nauru | Tokelau |
> | Fiji | Northern Mariana Islands | Tonga |
> | New Caledonia | Palau | Wallis and Futuna |
> | Papua New Guinea | Polynesia | Islands |
> | Solomon Islands | American Samoa | New Zealand |
> | Vanuatu | Cook Islands | Christmas Island |
> | Micronesia | French Polynesia | Cocos Island |
> | Guam | Niue | Norfolk Island |
> | Kiribati | Pitcairn Islands | |

authority is inherited, so that a chief's son will usually inherit the role of chief upon the death of his father. But the Melanesian way of making authorities involves earning the position through the accumulation of trade goods, securing a person's "big-man" status through loaning material items, giving gifts, and adjudicating conflicts within a village. Making Melanesian big-men required a good deal of stiff competition; for Polynesians, inheritance was the first hurdle, since he would have to rule well. While the Polynesian chieftan pattern differs from the Melanesian big-man pattern, both statuses attach moral credibility to the leader.

Power

Undergirding the role and structure of leadership (e.g., big man or chieftain) is the notion of power. There are two sides to power—one that reflects the human-spirit encounter and the other that reflects the human-human encounter. The authority of Polynesian chiefs was legitimated on the basis of their *mana*—"spirit-authority"—which was demonstrated through actions, right decisions, and leadership ability. Even the son of a Polynesian chief could lose his chiefly status if he were not possessed by *mana*. Inherited authority was no guarantor of successful leadership. Additionally, although rare, cannibalism was practiced in some parts of Oceania as a means to absorb the *mana* of the individual victim as well as that of the victim's tribe.

Cargo Cults

Contact with early Western explorers, missionaries, and administrators helped stimulate a new, broad movement referred to generally as the cargo cults. From the early nineteenth century to the early twentieth century, the height of European

> **Study Aid #121**
> Growth of Christianity in Oceania (28 Countries)
> 1800: 100,000 Christians, 4 percent of population
> 1900: 5 million Christians, 77 percent of population
> 2000: 18 million Christians, 92 percent of population

missionary and colonial engagement with the Pacific Islands, Pacific Islanders saw the material wealth of Western colonial administrators, traders, and missionaries and sought to obtain that wealth through magic and other ritual actions. Also referred to as "prosperity cults," these cargo cults were led by charismatic individuals who preached that the missionaries and administrators had access to material goods and that such goods were also obtainable by local peoples through correct ritual action. To many people of the Pacific region, the possession of cargo was the same as the possession of power. In part of Melanesia it was touted that the missionaries and colonial administrators were hiding goods in secret locations and that cargo cult leaders had the keys to unlock the doors. Most cargo cults have since disappeared, but the John Frum cult is still active on the Melanesian island of Vanuatu.

Practices

The world of traditional Oceanic religions was a near seamless entity, where one domain of life affected other domains to the extent that one could assign blame or causation for physical illness on a broken relationship between the spirits and the people or on conflicts between spirits. In the past several decades, scholars believed that traditional Oceanic religions functioned more as technologies than as spiritual forces leading to salvation. Today there is greater appreciation for the ways in which traditional Oceanic religions perceive salvation itself differently from non-Oceanic perspectives. For instance, many Oceanic religions affirm the notion of salvation, but as located in this world rather than in some distant, heavenly location. Nevertheless, the "technology" of religion—performing religion correctly—is still quite significant to the religious people of Oceania. Generally, religious practices were geared toward averting disaster and obtaining success through prayers, sacrifices, and offerings made to a host of deities.

Appeasing the Spirits

The traditional religions of Oceania strongly emphasized actions that would appease the spirit beings. One important means of appeasing spirits was to offer spirits the highest commodity item possessed by the people, which in traditional Pacific societies usually meant certain animals or highly prized foodstuffs. Sacrifices could be offered anywhere and consisted of almost anything valuable (e.g., pigs, kava, leaves). Among highland tribes from the massive island of New Guinea (today divided between the eastern half, Papua New Guinea, and the western half, the Indonesian province of Papua), domesticated pigs were offered sacrificially, their blood shed in order to appease the spirits in times of tribal warfare, natural catastrophe, or any other major event such as a rite-of-passage ceremony. In Polynesia, high chiefs acted as mediators between the divine and human realms. In traditional Hawaii, the "great sacrifice" consisted of hundreds of pigs and a few human victims, in an effort to secure friendship with the gods.

Magic

The use of magic is virtually endemic throughout the traditional religions of Oceania. Magic refers to the human attempt to influence the spirit world in order to procure some positive or negative result in the here and now. Manipulation of plants, ritual objects, and body elements is geared toward practical benefit or harm, perhaps to divine the culprit of a crime, to deal harm to an enemy, or to secure love. Such use of magic is popular in Polynesia and Micronesia not only in traditional societies but also within contemporary societies in urban centers.

Sources

Ian Breward. *A History of the Churches in Australasia*. Oxford University Press, 2004.

Gananath Obeyesekere. *The Apotheosis of Captain Cook: European Mythmaking in the Pacific*. Princeton University Press, 1992.

Marshall Sahlins. *Islands of History*. University of Chicago Press, 1985.

56

Oceania: Christian Contacts

CHARLES FARHADIAN

The wave of Christian mission activity in Oceania began in eastern Oceania at the end of the eighteenth century, stimulated in part by the mandate of the Great Commission, "Therefore go and make disciples of all nations" (Matt. 28:19). Christian missions began in the Polynesian islands, then moved westward through Micronesia and eventually to Melanesia, communicated by Western missionaries and Pacific Islanders themselves. Although Christian missionary contact with Oceania began prior to the end of the eighteenth century, it was British explorer Captain James Cook's observations (1768, 1780) that Tahitians would never become Christians that challenged the London Missionary Society (LMS) to send a ship, the *Duff*, to Tahiti in August of 1796. Today Oceania has one of the highest percentages of Christians worldwide, and is home to every major Christian denomination, including several faith missions groups.

The Christian encounter with the religions of Oceania cannot be separated from the sociocultural patterns that functioned as carriers of the religious perspectives. European contact introduced many things to the people of Oceania, such as trade goods, firearms, steel tools, plants, new diseases, and views of nature and the body. To many people in Oceania, these new items and ideas were part and parcel of Christianity. Therefore the encounter between Christianity and Oceanic religions was not simply a meeting of theological ideas but rather one of embodied encounters. Since the religions and cultures of Oceania were so intimately connected, so much so that no Melanesian language, for instance, even had a separate word for "religion," it is not surprising that people of Oceania often interpreted the cultural and "civilizational" (social, economic, political) aspects of missionaries as Christian.

Thus the history of the encounters between European Christians and the peoples of Oceania is uneven, mixed with praise and criticism of Pacific Islanders. On the one hand, European Christians admired Pacific Islanders' skills, courage, and faithfulness. Yet on the other hand, missionaries criticized Pacific Islanders as being lazy, violent, and incompetent. History shows that Pacific Islanders were never the passive agents that missionaries may have thought, despite the social, cultural, and religious differences.

Mutual Misunderstanding

Mutual lack of understanding characterized early encounters between Western Christians and Polynesians. The views of European Christian missionaries, influenced by Enlightenment notions that assumed Western cultural superiority, the centrality of reason as a source of knowledge, and a host of perspectives regarding race, sexual activities, the body, and even agricultural practices, created obstacles for Christian witness.

Many early Western missionaries failed to understand the complex nature of the religions of Oceania, assuming that Christianity would be a facile and total replacement for the superstitions and taboos held by Islanders. In part influenced by an evolutionary perspective on religion, which interpreted religions as evolving from animism to polytheism and culminating in monotheism (i.e., Christianity), many early European missionaries in Polynesia interpreted local religious traditions (animism) as easily surmountable through the introduction of Christianity (monotheism). The fact that many of the earliest missionaries to Tahiti left the islands discouraged is a testimony to the resilience of Oceanic traditions in the face of European Christianity in the early years of mutual encounter.

Early European Christianity in all its denominational forms usually defined itself in contrast to Oceanic religions, showing little interest in local religious traditions. For instance, European missionaries rejected some Oceanic festivals, ceremonial items (e.g., kava), and sexual practices (e.g., extramarital sexual relationships). Yet as the encounter between Christianity and Oceanic religions unfolded, and as Christian faith was received, the peoples of Oceania exhibited significant agency in reinterpreting and adopting Christianity on their own terms, reflecting the dynamic nature of Christianity's engagement with the peoples and religions of the region. As mentioned earlier, European contact introduced new technologies, and too many people in Oceania, these new items and influences were part and parcel of Christianity. Consequently, the meeting of Christianity and the religions of Oceania was quite complex, given the religious, cultural, and linguistic diversity of Oceania.

Polynesian Encounters

European Christianity encountered Polynesian religions that recognized a high God, Tangaloa, who remained somewhat distant from people's lives. Polynesian gods were active in Islander dreams, visions, and trances. The missionaries' failure to understand the Polynesian virtue of reciprocity, whereby networks of belonging and mutuality were created through gift-giving and other activities, led to experiences characterized by unsymmetrical social relationships. And Christian missionaries did not recognize that Polynesian land was loaned to missionaries, not given in title, which also contributed to tensions between European Christians and Polynesians.

In Tonga, European missionaries learned that kinship relations were the primary source of material benefits and economic assistance. Ranking by birth, occupation, wealth, and education were prestige-granting criteria within Tongan and many other Polynesian communities. After Christianity was widely received in Polynesia, churches functioned as another prestige-granting institution, similar to the role that birth or wealth had played in traditional Polynesian culture; if one wanted to increase one's social status, that person would need the support of fellow congregants.

Yet despite early and in some cases long-term misunderstanding, European Christianity would eventually be interpreted on Polynesian terms, even with unforeseen consequences such as the Mamaia movement (1826–41) in Tahiti and Leewards, which sought to implement the reversion to polygamy and extramarital relations.

After some time, British missionaries permitted Polynesians to use local feasting, singing, and dancing in the light of biblical teaching as expressions of Christianity. European missionaries placed a high priority on creating educational institutions, from which they could teach literacy and the Bible.

Christianity spread rapidly in Polynesia once powerful chiefs converted, bringing their large numbers of subjects into the faith. The conversion of chiefs usually

---

Study Aid #122
Christian Contacts

Misunderstandings
- Eurocentrism
- Animism vs. monotheism
- Conflict production

Christian contributions
- Health care
- Education (and printing presses)
- Conflict resolution

required that chiefs put away all but one wife. Eventually various Polynesian chiefs, such as Pomare in 1812, converted to Christianity and led their people to follow Christianity en masse. These "group conversions," which would eventually occur throughout much of Oceania, challenged Western missionary perceptions that prioritized individual transformations over corporate conversion. Mass movements into Christian faith occurred frequently, and music and singing from particular Christian denominations would replace dancing of the traditional fertility cults.

A particularly striking encounter occurred between Christianity and traditional religious specialists. With Christian conversion, some roles of the traditional religious specialist were recast into Christian leadership roles, rather than being rejected altogether. The Ma'ohi, the indigenous people of French Polynesia, for instance, used the word *taura* ("rope," connecting the gods and humans) to refer to their traditional religious medium. However, today the Ma'ohi refer to Christian ministers as *tahu'a pure* (priests, "prayer leaders"), experts in ritual practice and sacred knowledge (Lange 2005, 38).

Resistance to Christian conversion also was present in some Polynesian islands, such as Niue, which, interestingly enough, had no tradition of hereditary chiefs, and whose five thousand people in the mid-nineteenth century fiercely rejected Christian faith. The longer missionaries were present in Polynesia, the more willing missionaries were to permit Polynesians to use local feasting, singing, and dancing as expressions of Christianity, thus encouraging Polynesian forms of Christianity to flourish.

Micronesian Encounters

Early Catholic and Protestant missions to Micronesia were negatively affected by new diseases the Europeans introduced there. Christian contact in Micronesia began in 1668, when six Jesuit priests, along with lay helpers, landed on Guam to evangelize the people of the Mariana Islands. Yet influenza, dysentery, and other diseases introduced by early missionaries decimated people in the Marianas, reducing the population from forty thousand to four thousand in a matter of a few decades. Likewise, the people of Kosrae were wracked by disease introduced by whalers, reducing its population from three thousand to about three hundred. Following the demise of island populations was the demise of chieftain authority. Thus the church became the new authority on some islands devastated by disease.

With the coming of European missionaries, new perspectives on bodily adornment and clothing were introduced by the newcomers. Micronesian female converts to Christianity adopted shirts to cover their bare breasts, while male converts wore pants, with Marshallese chiefs donning suits and top hats.

As in many other contexts worldwide, the power of the Christian God was often contrasted with the power of local deities; in some cases traditional religious specialists exclaimed that attending a church service would anger the local gods.

On some islands, flu epidemics were interpreted as just that—the punishment of Islanders by their gods. As a last gasp of chiefly authority, in the late nineteenth century Marshall Islands' chiefs began to threaten Christian converts, but that proved to be futile as people continued to embrace the Christian faith.

Melanesian Encounters

Historian Garry Trompf has written extensively about pre-Christian Melanesia, demonstrating that the integrity of Melanesian societies is based on a notion of retributive justice. That is, the stability of Melanesian society persists through exchange relationships. "Payback" and revenge against enemies, as Trompf notes, were crucial values in pre-Christian Melanesia and remain important throughout the history of European missionary encounters with Melanesian religions. When Melanesians gave major gifts, such as foodstuffs, their social and moral prestige was raised, creating a condition where the receiver was obligated to the giver. Payback and revenge required vigilant observation of "met and unmet obligations" (Trompf 2008).

Christian missionaries entered Melanesia without an appreciation of these Melanesian strategies of establishing and sustaining obligations. Most missionaries failed to recognize that the payback system pertained to virtually all aspects of Melanesian life, such as religion, violence, war, and economics. The logic of retribution undergirded both negative actions, such as violence, and positive ones, such as sacrifices to the deities. Thus payback was a "religious" idea based on moral pressures to revenge a wrong or engage in retributive justice.

Christian conversion encouraged only positive reciprocity, with such values as "unconditional love" and "compassion" becoming the new ideals. Negative reciprocity was discouraged. This reconfiguring of moral life under the banner of Christianity required a concomitant reinterpretation of positive and negative events. As a case in point, the death of a Christian known not to have engaged in retributive justice may have been interpreted as God's will rather than as a result of the refusal to pay back some malicious action. Furthermore, Christianity was appealing in part because it counterbalanced and overcame the practice of payback delivered by sorcery. In fact, in Papua New Guinea it was common for Melanesians to perceive Christian leaders as animated by a form of sorcery.

In addition, the entrance of Christian missions, replete with material goods considered simple by Western standards—such as radios, foodstuffs, and modern clothes—stimulated cargo cultism: the expectation that Melanesians will have their material expectations satisfied on conditions prophesied by a variety of cargo cult leaders. Trompf notes that going to church may have been interpreted by Melanesians as the "road to the cargo" and the second coming of Christ as its arrival. When the cargo never arrived, the anticipation for goods still found resonance among some Melanesian independent churches. Trompf states that

> **Study Aid #123**
> Oceanic Encounters, Pluses and Minuses
>
> Polynesia
>   Minuses: Reciprocity, land
>   Pluses: Mass conversions, indigenous missionaries
> Micronesia
>   Minuses: Disease, spirit encounters
>   Pluses: Clothing, gift exchanges
> Australia
>   Minuses: Time, place (land)
>   Pluses: Institutions, health care

several of the independent Melanesian churches, such as the Christian Fellowship Church (CFC) on New Georgia and the Congregation of the Poor in Fiji, are led by healer-prophets who conjoin the reception of cargo and the reception of salvation. The John Frum cargo cult in Vanuatu is still active today, promising to bring prosperity to its followers.

Australian Encounters

In 1821, the Wesleyan Missionary Society sent William Walker as the first missionary to Australian Aborigines. By the mid-nineteenth century, Christian missions were peppered throughout the Australian continent. While some European missionaries disdained Aboriginal religions, many missionaries were outspoken defenders of the Aborigines, at least to the extent that missionaries could seek to communicate Christian faith to the Aborigines.

For the first century of Christian presence among the Aborigines, European missionaries sought to regulate Aboriginal bodies and souls through the introduction of strict daily timetables, seeking to re-create Aboriginal life along the lines of a European model. In some missions, for instance, Aborigines were expected to follow specific times for breakfast, prayer, sewing, and scripture lessons, in an effort to teach Aborigines modern lifeways.

A striking difference between early Christian missionary perspectives and Aboriginal religions was their views about the relationship between God and the land. Missionaries attempted to communicate a transcendent God, one divine being revealed in the Bible, who required that human beings are to love one another just as God has loved them. Protestant missionaries prioritized the Bible and the sacraments (including worship) as mediators of God, who provided everything from above.

But Aboriginal religions had a different view, recognizing that power and sacred knowledge were attached to specific sites and people. Thus Aboriginal religions were less concerned about engaging a single, universal God. Aboriginal deities were located in specific sites on the land, giving human beings local access to the deities. Researcher Tony Swain argues that these differences of perspectives on God and the land were at the heart of the tensions between European Christianity and Aboriginal religions.

Christian Contributions

Throughout Oceania, Christian missions were the first to introduce modern health care, educational institutions, literacy, and Bible translation. Printing presses produced literature used for training Islanders in literacy and Bible study. Training centers were opened, where village children were educated, later being sent as the first Island missionaries to other islands in Oceania. Training schools also served to educate pastors and teachers to serve fellow Islanders. Usually by the second generation of Christianity in a given area, Islanders made up the vast majority of Christian missionaries to other islands. Island pastors had a reputation of serving as peacemakers during village conflict. Their role now extends beyond village life, as many Island ministers serve a mediating role between local congregations and international church boards and Western and international nongovernmental agencies. There remains today a huge need to research and explore the histories of these Oceanic missionaries and their work to benefit the churches of Oceania and the churches worldwide.

Sources

> James A. Boutilier, Daniel T. Hughes, and Sharon W. Tiffany, eds. *Mission, Church, and Sect in Oceania*. University Press of America, 1978.
>
> Ian Breward. "Christianity in Polynesia: Transforming the Islands." In *Introducing World Christianity*, edited by Charles Farhadian, 218–29. Blackwell, 2010.
>
> Francis X. Hezel. "Christianity in Micronesia: The Interplay between Church and Culture." In *Introducing World Christianity*, edited by Charles Farhadian, 230–43. Blackwell, 2010.
>
> Raeburn Lange. *Island Ministers: Indigenous Leadership in Nineteenth Century Pacific Island Christianity*. Macmillan Brown Centre for Pacific Studies, 2005.
>
> Tony Swain and Garry Trompf. *The Religions of Oceania*. Routledge, 1995.
>
> Garry Trompf. "Christianity in Melanesia: Transforming the Warrior Spirit." In *Introducing World Christianity*, edited by Charles Farhadian, 244–58. Blackwell, 2010.
>
> ———. *Payback: The Logic of Retribution in Melanesian Religions*. Cambridge University Press, 2008.

57

Oceania: Theological Exchanges

CHARLES FARHADIAN

As a general statement, prior to European missionary contact, the people of Oceania did not have a separate word for "religion." Neither did they employ the word "theology" to refer to their interactions with the world of deities. For our purposes here, theology is understood as "talking about God" or simply "God-talk." Thus, any time people from any religious tradition speak about God, they are engaged in doing theology, even if they are not paid professional theologians. In this sense, people from Oceania did engage in theological reflection—even though "theology" was not a formal discipline in the region—whenever they engaged or spoke about the world of spirits, in that they were making sense of the divine or deities or the relationship between cosmic, social, and environmental realities.

Furthermore, when approaching the theological encounter between Oceanic religions and Western Christian missions, it is important to recognize that the category of "theology"—that is, the Oceanic perspectives on the divine—was not limited to talking about God. If we consider only Oceanic *discourse* about the divine or deities, assuming those words to be the sole carriers of Oceanic theology, we lose sight of immensely diverse *nondiscursive* ways by which people of Oceania expressed their understanding of the divine. Therefore, it is worthwhile to glean Oceanic "theological perspectives" from observing such diverse, typically non-theological foci as the role of traditional religious authorities, retributive justice, conversion, and rituals of salvation.

Since traditional Oceanic religions attributed the quality of people's social, emotional, political, and economic lives to the world of the spirits, it could be argued that the people of Oceania actually had a more robustly integrated spiritual view of the cosmos, humanity, and the natural world than the views typically held by European Christian missionaries. To the people of Oceania, the spirits were the source of health and life, and great human effort, time, and resources were spent on maintaining the spiritual order. People learned the legends of their particular people (e.g., tribe, clan) that conveyed the stories of the ways that the spirits were connected to the people's history, territory, and group identity.

Consequently, it is important to keep in mind that European Christian missionaries entered immensely rich Oceanic environments, replete with spirits and stories that sustained nearly every aspect of people's lives. While it was the intention of European Christian missionaries to serve the people of Oceania, with a view of introducing them to Christian faith, it happened that Oceanic religion also blended with European Christianity, inspiring movements that transformed lives within the region and made the new faith meaningful to local lifeways, even, at times, to the dismay of the Western missionaries.

Religious and Theological Authority

European Christian missionaries in many instances sought to transform the traditional roles of religious specialists. European Christian missionaries contended with, and often benefited from, the traditional religious authorities in traditional Oceanic societies. These missionaries quickly learned that Oceanic religions acknowledged numerous active deities, with traditional religious specialists, prophets, and priests functioning as intermediaries between the human and divine. Although individuals could perform some religious rituals, such as private prayer and worship, there were identifiable religious specialists throughout Oceania. Theologically, European missionaries usually interpreted traditional religious specialists of Oceania as a testimony to Pacific Islanders' heathenism. By the nineteenth century, however, Protestant missionaries attempted to avoid long-term missionary leadership of churches, seeking to encourage a "native pastorate." Furthermore, when Christian leadership roles were introduced, the Christian chiefs and big-men issued new law codes that laid out punishments of behavior that missionaries deemed sinful. Sanctions provided by the traditional religions of Oceania were replaced by prohibitions established by Christian chiefs and big-men. As Christianity expanded throughout Oceania, the role of the traditional religious specialist was edged out in most places, losing much of its relevancy.

Who should have religious authority in the community, the traditional leaders or Christian converts (e.g., pastors)? Under what conditions would a traditional religious authority give up his or her social and religious influence? Throughout Oceania, the roles of traditional religious authorities were negotiated, with some falling out entirely and others being recast in Christian terms. For instance, the Maramatanga movement, which emerged in the 1930s among the Maori of New Zealand, identified traditional Maori prophets with the New Testament, thus

> **Study Aid #124**
> **Theological Exchanges in Oceania**
> Traditional religious authorities
>   Who has authority?
>   What authority do they have?
> Retributive justice
>   Reciprocity, payback
>   Grace
> Conversion
>   Mass conversions
>   Individual conversions
> Rituals of salvation
>   Local rituals effective
>   Local rituals not effective

attempting to legitimate themselves on biblical grounds. Furthermore, on the island of New Guinea, where mass conversions often occurred that sometimes brought hundreds of people into Christian faith based on the decision of a "big-man" (leader), there are numerous occasions when big-men refused to accept the new faith, and social tensions ensued. The demise of traditional religious specialists was also a result of other influences that appeared more effective, such as modern medicine, whereby traditional healing practices were sometimes diminished or blended with modern medical technologies.

Retributive Justice

In Melanesia, traditional big-men gained social and moral status through their own efforts, for instance, by accumulating trade goods as a demonstration of superior knowledge and courage. Writing extensively about the notion of retributive justice (i.e., payback) in Melanesia, Garry Trompf argues that a notion of reciprocity undergirds the most significant Melanesian social and religious interactions. In traditional Melanesian society, Melanesians expected some return (payback) for proper actions. As such, Melanesian converts to Christianity interpreted their new faith within their traditional understanding of payback and reciprocity. For instance, missionaries noted that when Melanesians went to church, they expected something in return. The same expectation of reciprocity remains in many parts of Melanesia, even if it has been transformed into anticipation of good things for following proper Christian ritual behavior. Fijians, for example, identified Christianity and reciprocity by using the term *loloma* ("kindly love"), referring to the reciprocity of gift-giving, to mean Christ's "grace."

Given the Melanesian belief in payback, the theological notion of Christian grace—that is, God's unmerited favor—was a new concept. But it is important to recognize that missionary talk about God and about fundamentally crucial notions like grace or salvation was perceived not simply as abstract ideas for people of Oceania. The emphasis of some faith missions on the imminent return of Jesus Christ motivated Oceanic conversions to Christianity, with an anticipation that his return would occur within their lifetime. Throughout much of highland New Guinea, converts to Christianity expected the impending return of Christ, so they waited. They did not anticipate having to learn about "worldly matters" such as business, law, politics, or economics. Yet Christ did not return to meet the first generation of believers, leaving many highlanders with the quandary of whether to wait longer, try to educate themselves to be better prepared for a this-worldly occupation, or proceed with some combination of these alternatives. Thus some churches have been left with a deficiency in training their young to tackle the hard realities of life by encouraging them to seek higher education and business knowledge.

The acceptance of Christianity was often perceived as a power encounter, with people from Oceania seeking a greater *mana* ("spiritual power") from the material goods provided by missionaries. Thus, the implied theological message was that people of Oceania did not see material goods (i.e., matter) as simply inorganic, dead material but rather as possessing a life force that could be utilized by those who possessed such objects. Such differences between Christian missionaries and the people of Oceania regarding the relationship between spirit and matter would give rise to significant misunderstanding, particularly when combined with a notion of reciprocity, where people of Oceania expected payback in the form of employable, spiritually powerful goods.

Theology of Conversion

A major theological issue emerged when missionaries had to contend with mass conversions of people of Oceania to Christian faith. Mass conversions, where large numbers of people would convert to Christianity at the same time, typified the conversion patterns throughout much of Oceania. Missionaries had to wrestle with the question of whether such conversions were legitimate. Many missionary-sending agencies and churches struggled to make sense of "people movements," where large-scale conversions to Christianity sometimes were considered invalid. Understanding mass conversions would require that missionaries reinterpret their own theology of conversion.

European missionaries to Oceania took with them their inherited notion of the autonomous individual as an independent actor, where self-sufficiency was more important than social responsibilities, and embracing a religion was a matter of personal, not corporate, choice. This Enlightenment notion about the self was quite different from what Europeans encountered throughout Oceania, where people were much more sociocentric in their orientation to one another. Sociocentric identities of the people of Oceania prioritized the social grouping within which the individual self exists; the community takes precedence over the individual. In more sociocentric cultures, the group tends to function as a social unit, so there is less emphasis on individual selves, with the aim of maintaining a harmonious community.

Throughout Oceania, then, the role of Polynesian chiefs and Melanesian big-men cannot be underestimated in terms of their influence on huge numbers of people. As chiefs and big-men converted to Christian faith, so too did the people under their authority. Even as mass conversions occurred, missionaries at once celebrated those large-scale transformations and questioned whether individuals within those movements were "fully converted." Christian Keysser (1877–1961), a German Lutheran missionary in New Guinea, argued for the importance of group conversions rather than expecting individual decisions to follow Christ.

New Rituals of Salvation

How can one be saved? What is the relationship between Christianity and local religions regarding salvation? Does Christianity eliminate all prior forms of religious tradition? Or does Christian faith build on the foundations of earlier traditions? Each mission took its own unique theologies, emphases, clergy-laity relations, and forms of worship to Oceania. Regarding the critically important theological topic of soteriology (i.e., understanding salvation), Christian missionaries positioned themselves as either continuous or discontinuous with Oceanic religions. That is to say, some Christian missions argued that Christian faith was a fulfillment of the ritual life of the people of Oceania, while other missions contended that the Christian understanding of salvation was absolutely discontinuous with local traditions of salvation.

Although there was a range of opinions on the relationship between Christianity and local religious traditions, since the missions were by no means a homogenous group, missionaries communicated, either directly or indirectly, that local Oceanic religious rituals were an ineffective means of garnering salvation. Consequently, Christian missionaries introduced new and effective rituals for salvation that reflected the theological perspectives of the missions. Generally, the more discontinuous the missions believed Christianity to be from local religions, the greater the degree of suspicion, prejudice, and doubt on the part of the people of Oceania. Perhaps it is not ironic that revival movements throughout Oceania often sought to preserve indigenous identity and values—a "custom movement"—over against European missions and colonial governments. For instance, the Marching Rule movement in post–World War II Solomon Islands, a sociopolitical and religious movement that inspired thousands, sought to retrieve indigenous custom (*kastom*), with heavily sociopolitical dimensions. The Marching Rule movement was in large part a reaction against the fundamentalist faith mission South Sea Evangelical Mission/Church, which taught that the Bible, and especially the New Testament, was the sole authority in a believer's life, thus eliminating so many sources of knowledge that had marked traditional religion in the Solomon Islands.

Hence Christian mission theology regarding salvation was quite diverse, even among the more conservative faith missions. The nineteenth-century faith mission Regions Beyond Missionary Union (RBMU), for example, began mission work among Papuan groups in Western New Guinea (i.e., Irian Jaya, Papua) beginning in the mid-twentieth century. The film and book *Peace Child* portrays the early 1960s missionary encounter with the Sawi people, who held treachery as an ideal. According to Sawi tradition, peace between clans could be established only through the gifting of a big-man's son to the big-man of the enemy's clan. Peace was guaranteed between the clans only if the child lived, for when the "peace child" died, warfare would ensue. RBMU missionary Don Richardson communicated that the God-man Jesus was the eternal Peace Child given by God so that there would be permanent peace for those who accepted him. The theology employed by Don Richardson is an example of a redemptive analogy, whereby it is believed that pre-Christian religious traditions, such as the Sawi's peace-child ceremony, can be fulfilled, rather than wiped away, by the gospel.

A variety of perspectives regarding the relationship between Christianity and local rituals of salvation continue throughout Oceania, even without the presence of Christian missionaries.

Sources

James A. Boutilier, Daniel T. Hughes, and Sharon W. Tiffany, eds. *Mission, Church, and Sect in Oceania*. University Press of America, 1978.

Wendy Flannery and Glen W. Bays, eds. *Religious Movements in Melanesia Today*. Part 3. Point Series 4. Melanesian Institute, 1984.

Charles W. Forman. "Finding Our Own Voice: The Reinterpreting of Christianity by Oceanian Theologians." *International Bulletin of Missionary Research* 29, no. 3 (July 2005): 115–22.

Jocelyn Linnekin and Lin Poyer, eds. *Cultural Identity and Ethnicity in the Pacific*. University of Hawaii Press, 1990.

Ennio Mantovani, ed. *An Introduction to Melanesian Religions*. Point Series 6. Melanesian Institute, 1984.

Don Richardson. *Peace Child*. Regal, 1974.

Joel Robbins. *Becoming Sinners: Christianity and Moral Torment in a Papua New Guinea Society*. University of California Press, 2004.

Tony Swain and Garry Trompf. *The Religions of Oceania*. Routledge, 1995.

Matt Tomlinson. *In God's Image: The Metaculture of Fijian Christianity*. University of California Press, 2009.

58

Oceania: Current Issues

Charles Farhadian

Today, most of the people of Oceania self-ascribe as some form of Christian, making the region an area with one of the highest percentages of Christianity on the globe. The *Atlas of Global Christianity: 1910–2010* (Johnson and Ross 2009) reports the following changes in the percentages of Christians in Oceania for the period of 1910 to 2010. In Melanesia, the percentage of Christians grew from 15.4 to 91.4 percent. In Micronesia, the percentage grew from 76.7 to 92.5 percent during that hundred-year period. And the percentage in Polynesia slightly declined from 99.2 to 96 percent for that same period. Australia and New Zealand are the only regions of Oceania that have experienced a significant decrease in the percentage of Christians, falling from 96.9 percent to 73.4 percent during 1910 to 2010. Despite the demographic changes of Christianity, Oceania remains a robustly Christian region of the world. Despite the high percentages of Christianity throughout Oceania, significant current issues facing the people of Oceania have also challenged the role of Christianity in the wider societies.

The World Religions and the New Religious Movements

The forces of migration, globalization, and religious conversions are reshaping the religious landscape around the globe, including that of the people and cultures of Oceania. Migrants have introduced their religions to Oceania, whether or not those religions are missionary in nature. Over time migrant groups have maintained their identities by a variety of means, with religious self-ascriptions being one important way to sustain themselves in their new contexts. For instance, in the Cocos Islands and Christmas Island, Christians are the minority populations, while Chinese and Malay Muslims form the majority. Yet the religious changes throughout Oceania are due not only to the arrival of immigrant groups who may not initially share the religion of the majority people. Religious changes are also the result of religious conversion, whereby indigenous people of Oceania embrace a new religion. Therefore, since the twentieth century, there has been a proliferation of forms of Christianity as well as the establishment of many other world religions. And the religions have diverse views on a wide range of topics that affect the daily life of their adherents and their societies. Should women be ordained? How has the divine been revealed? What role should religion play in the political arena?

In both Australia and New Zealand about 25 percent of the immigrants are from Asia, and they have introduced several forms of Hinduism, Buddhism, and Islam, among other traditions. There are large numbers of Korean, Chinese, and Indonesian churches in both Australia and New Zealand, and all the major Orthodox churches are represented in Australia. Today there are well over half a million Buddhists and a similar number of Muslims in Australia and New Zealand, with about three hundred thousand Hindus in the region. These figures contrast to the declining number of traditional religionists in Australia and New Zealand. Since the twentieth century, new challenges emerged for Christian churches in the Pacific with the vigorous growth of Christian and non-Christian religious movements, including charismatic and Pentecostal churches, the Seventh-day Adventists, and the Church of Jesus Christ of Latter-Day Saints (Mormons), some of which inspired cargo-cult expectations among Pacific Islanders. In Micronesia many islands contain over a dozen different denominations, while in Melanesia there are many more. The introduction of the "new" religions, in the form of new Christian churches and new religious movements, has given rise to new forms of ecumenical and interfaith spirituality, as well as greater tensions between groups. Therefore the influence of new religions has met with uneven results, as greater ecumenicity and conflict have both emerged.

Growing Individualism

Christianity and the colonial powers that operated in Oceania played immeasurably critical roles in introducing and sustaining—in part through their theology, bureaucracies, and economic structures—a high degree of individualism that was new for most people of Oceania. In many ways, Christian missionaries and European colonial powers shared a similar vision of individualism, even if their ultimate goals were at times quite distinct. The concept of individualism, which viewed the individual as a social, political, and economic force separate from traditional kin groups, was closely tied to the emergence of modernization. It was reported, for instance, that in the South Sea Evangelical Church, "Each individual is expected

> **Study Aid #125**
> **Current Issues in Oceania**
> Growing religious pluralism
> Growing individualism
> Role of religion in nation making
> Ecumenicity and autonomy

to resolve moral and doctrinal questions for himself by reference to the Bible, but it is assumed that reasonable minds will agree upon its interpretation" (Boutilier, Hughes, and Tiffany 1978, 172). According to Featuna'i Ben Liua'ana, vice principal of Malua Theological College, Samoa, "The emphasis on individualism and lack of Christian values has fragmented family-church allegiances. The failure to reconcile Christianity to ancestral identities and priorities has driven people to the [new religious groups] whose teachings relate to traditional prophecies and mythical expectations" (Johnson and Ross 2009, 200).

A major challenge to the church in Oceania is how to sustain Christian faith in the midst of secular competition carried by economic changes, such as market-driven capitalism, mass media, a tourist industry, and the attractions of the burgeoning cosmopolitan centers of Sydney, Auckland, and Honolulu. One option followed by some people of Oceania is to showcase aspects of their traditional culture, usually by presenting the "tribal" nature of it, decontextualized and placed within the purview of tourists, with the aim of procuring income from the stream of vacationing tourists. Tourists arriving on Pacific Islands can be welcomed by high school and college-aged students playing traditional instruments, having exchanged their school clothes for their traditional (i.e., "tribal") clothing to promote their indigenous cultures. One can see such displays in various forms throughout Oceania. In highland Papua (the western half of the island of New Guinea), some highlanders who had adopted modern Western clothing now have retrieved the penis gourd (*koteka*), since they can get paid by photographers to look so-called tribal.

The Role of Religion in Nation Making

In the postcolonial period, as island groups throughout Oceania have sought to define themselves as nations, the role of religion has often been a part of the discourse of nation making. In Fiji and Vanuatu, Christianity has been highlighted as a part of the "true nation" (Foster 1995, 262). Given that Christian missionaries usually were the first to introduce modern education and health care to Oceania, it is not surprising that Christianity itself has been drawn into the debates about nationalism. People of Oceania learned literacy, the Bible, and training for mission and ministry from Christian missionaries. Even if it were an unintended consequence, by their introduction of health care and educational institutions, Christian missionaries were introducing institutional life and forms of bureaucracy and standardization that would later function as stepping-stones to nation making.

Yet the public role of religion, and in particular a religion's relationship to nation-making strategies, varies in part according to the constitutional limitations. New Zealand, for instance, has declared, "There is no State Church here," and Australia's constitution "limits itself to a negative protection against Commonwealth interference" (Maddox, 2012). Yet among the Maori of New Zealand, Christian prayers in the Maori language are the usual way of beginning a public event. And both New Zealand and Australia continue to invoke Christian rituals in public ceremonial life, such as opening their national parliaments with prayer.

Additionally, many Pacific Island churches are struggling to address the environmental damage wrought by local, national, and international groups. What cannot be overlooked is the intimate connection Pacific Islanders have to the land, a connection that is straining under the burdens resulting from forces of modernization and globalization, yet which remains a powerful reminder of the church's challenge to care for creation. Bishop Leslie Boseto, moderator of the United Church of Papua New Guinea and the Solomon Islands and a well-respected "Voice of the Pacific," stated that "the more we love Christ, the more we love the earth" (see Forman 2005, 116). The Pacific perspective recognizes an interdependence between the natural world and human world. Charles W. Forman (2005) suggests that the close connection between Pacific Islanders and the land is an important theological motif among Pacific Island theologians, noting that they often include social ethics in their theology because of their holistic view of life.

Ecumenicity and Autonomy

Since the twentieth century, churches that were established by missionary outreach maintained some linkage with those sending churches that were based in the West, thus stimulating global connections and denominational networks. The variety of churches in Oceania—Protestant, Catholic, and Orthodox—has raised significant theological questions about the nature of the church itself. Is the church essentially one or many? How should churches relate to one another? Such questions about ecclesiology center on the nature of the local and translocal (universal) church; these are questions that all churches are called to answer as a part of their Christian witness.

There is growing concern among some church leaders and scholars in Oceania that independent churches are threatening the ecumenism sought for by churches in the region. Manfred Ernst, the director of research at Pacific Theological College, Suva, Fiji, uses the term "new religious movements" to describe the bewildering array of "new" churches (e.g., evangelical, Pentecostal) as well as the new religious movements (i.e., Mormons, Seventh-day Adventists, etc.) that have burgeoned in Oceania in the twentieth century. Ernst argues, "The United Church sees the New Religious Groups and especially the kind of theology they bring in as a real challenge to *ecumenism* and the Historic Mainline Churches" (Davidson 2004, 143). However, some independent, evangelical, and Pentecostal churches insist that the historic mainline churches have lost relevancy with the people of Oceania, thus leaving a genuine need for other ways to articulate a meaningful Christian faith.

Yet Christian ecumenism, which sees the church as essentially one, has given rise to many ecumenical organizations and educational institutions. Several ecumenical organizations have emerged since the mid-twentieth century, and they have bolstered the unity of the church by sharing ideas, theologies, mission, and worship. The major ecumenical groups include the National Council of Churches in Australia (consisting of seventeen churches), founded in 1946; the Melanesian Council of Churches, founded in 1964; and the National Council of Churches in New Zealand (consisting of ten church bodies), founded in 1941. The Pacific Conference of Churches (consisting of twenty-seven churches), which started in 1961, is the Pacific-wide ecumenical movement consisting of smaller ecumenical bodies: Fiji Council of Churches, Kiribati National Council of Churches, National Council of Churches in American Samoa, Niue National Council of Churches, Papua New Guinea Council of Churches, Samoa Council of Churches, Solomon Island Christian Association, and the Tonga National Council of Churches. Along with the ecumenical church movement, there has been cooperation in theological education throughout much of Oceania, through such institutions as the Pacific Theological College (est. 1966), the Melanesian Associations of Theological Schools (est. 1969), and the Australian and New Zealand Association of Theological Schools (est. 1968), which comprises sixty-four theological colleges and seminaries of churches in Australia and New Zealand.

Independent church groups, whether started by evangelical faith missions or charismatic or Pentecostal churches, also have theological training centers throughout the region. Many of these independent churches have their own ecumenical groupings, such as the South Pacific Association of Bible Colleges (SPABC). Established in 1969 for independent evangelical Bible colleges in Australia, Papua New Guinea, Vanuatu, and New Zealand, the SPABC is composed of more than twenty Bible colleges. Pentecostals are more loosely affiliated, but there are many Pentecostal training centers throughout Oceania, such as the Advance Ministry Training Center (Assemblies of God) in Auckland, New Zealand; Living Word School of Ministry in Sydney, Australia; Pacific Rim Bible College in Oahu, Hawaii; and Youth With A Mission (YWAM) discipleship training centers in Perth, Australia.

The future of the church in Oceania depends in large part on the ways in which the church is made meaningful locally, relates ecumenically across church divisions, and sets an example of being ecumenical with one another while being evangelical in its outreach.

Sources

James A. Boutilier, Daniel T. Hughes, and Sharon W. Tiffany, eds. *Mission, Church, and Sect in Oceania*. University Press of America, 1978.

Allan K. Davidson. "'The Pacific Is No Longer a Mission Field?': Conversion in the South Pacific in the Twentieth Century." In *Christianity Reborn: The Global Expansion of Evangelicalism in the Twentieth Century*, edited by Donald M. Lewis, 133–53. Eerdmans, 2004.

Charles W. Forman. "Finding Our Own Voice: The Reinterpreting of Christianity by Oceanian Theologians." *International Bulletin of Missionary Research* 29, no. 3 (July 2005): 115–22.

———. *The Island Churches of the South Pacific: Emergence in the Twentieth Century*. Orbis Books, 1982.

———. "The South Pacific Style in the Christian Ministry." *Missiology* 2 (1974): 421–35.

Robert J. Foster, ed. *Nation Making: Emergent Identities in Postcolonial Melanesia*. University of Michigan Press, 1995.

Todd M. Johnson and Kenneth R. Ross, eds. *Atlas of Global Christianity 1910–2010*. Edinburgh University Press, 2009.

Victoria S. Lockwood, Thomas G. Harding, and Ben J. Wallace, eds. *Contemporary Pacific Societies: Studies in Development and Change*. Prentice Hall, 1993.

Marion Maddox. "Christianity in Australia and New Zealand: Faith and Politics in Secular Soil." In *Introducing World Christianity*, edited by Charles Farhadian, 203–17. Blackwell, 2012.

Garry Trompf. "Geographical, Historical, and Intellectual Perspectives." In *The Gospel Is Not Western: Black Theologies from the Southwest Pacific*. Orbis Books, 1987.

59

North America: History, Beliefs, Practices

CHRISTOPHER VECSEY

History

The indigenous peoples of North America, who lived from the northern periphery of Mexican civilizations and beyond to the Arctic Circle, numbered perhaps as many as twelve million in 1491. Having no overarching political structure for these several hundred different peoples, who were located continent-wide and spoke a multitude of languages, cultural patterns developed locally as adaptations to particular circumstances of environment and history.

At the same time, networks of exchange carried goods, traits, persons, and ideas from one community to another; thus, one can ascertain regional commonalities and even some shared features that seem nigh universal, at least to an outsider observer.

In these contexts, it is more appropriate to refer to "religions" of North America than to a single religion, although some argue that Native North Americans lacked nomenclature for "religion," if by that we mean institutions of doctrine and worship regarding supernatural beings, or churches set apart from quotidian, civic life for the purpose of eternal salvation. In recent years it has become common to refer to Native American "spirituality" rather than "religion(s)."

Indian peoples have inhabited North America for thousands of years; however, the deep history of their religious lives is largely unknown, except as unearthed in archaeological remains. It would appear from the tens of thousands of burial, astronomical, figurative, and ceremonial mounds throughout the eastern part of North America (e.g., at Cahokia in present-day Illinois)—dating from before the time of Christ until the thirteenth century, and even beyond

Study Aid #126

Map of North America

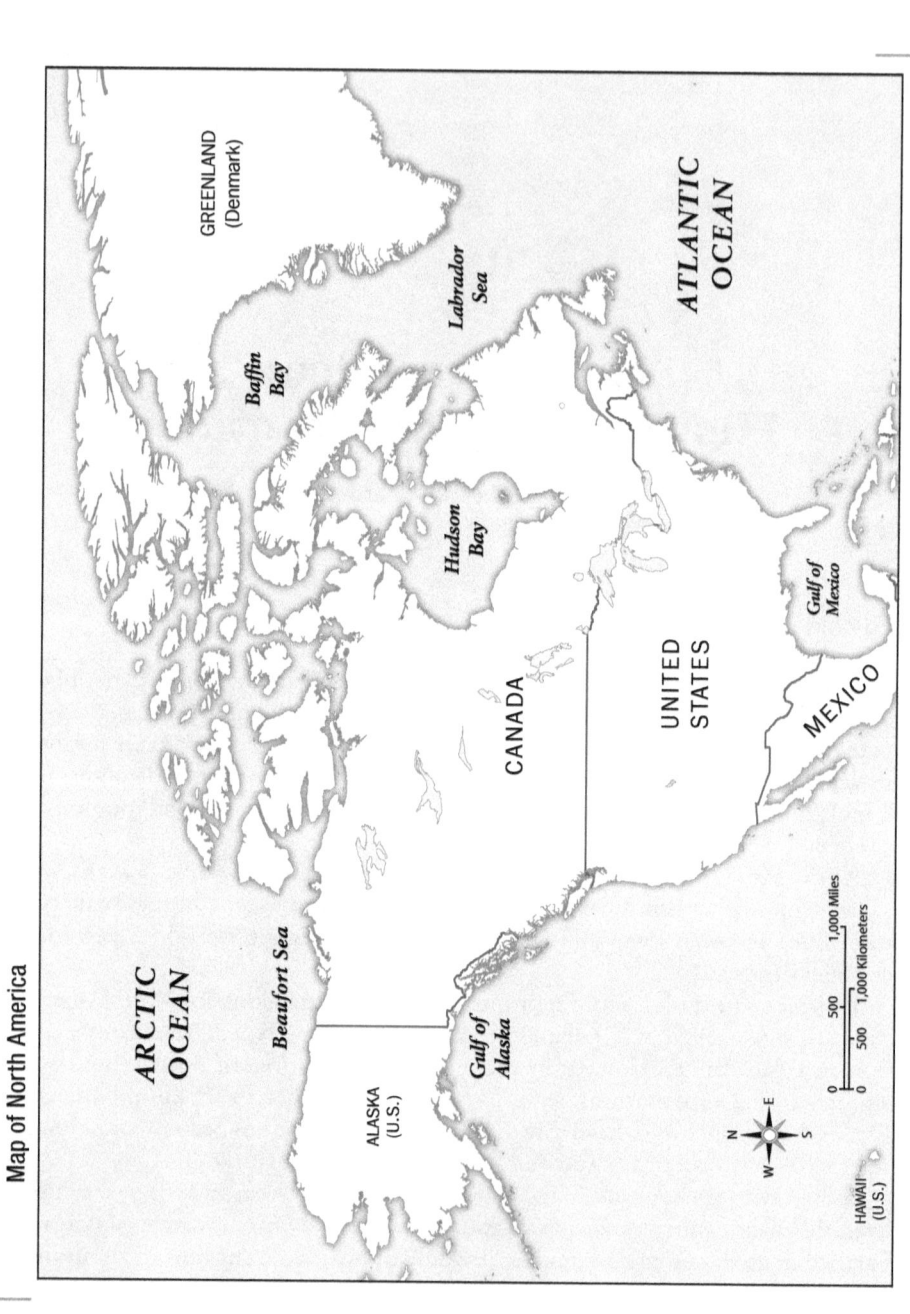

to first contact with European invaders—that robust and highly elaborated forms of religious expression had devolved into smaller scales of community practice by the 1500s. Similarly, in the American Southwest, Native populations had abandoned the grand architectural matrices of the 1200s with their ritual centers (e.g., at Chaco Canyon in today's New Mexico) for more diminutive, self-sufficient pueblos. Hence, localism came to characterize the religions of indigenous North America.

Farmers of the southern regions, gatherers of the arid west, fishers of the northwest coast, and hunters of the northern climes all developed religious practices and beliefs in keeping with their subsistence needs and societal organizations. It is not unfair to suggest that American Indians' religions were part of their cultures of adaptation to immediate conditions, possessing the function of promoting the human life of local communities.

Think of religion in this way: as beliefs in, attitudes toward, and relations with the sacred sources of life, and imagine each Native community—concerned ultimately with preserving the life of its people (often calling themselves the People)—as conceiving of beings upon whom that life depends, regarding them as sacred, and aiming to engage them in relationships, through which the People might survive and even thrive. Along the way, identifying the sacred helps each community to identify itself in relation to its sources of life.

Beliefs

Who were those beings—the objects of religious belief and relation? Although some Indians conceived of a great, transcendent, mysterious Being, beyond the capacity of human symbolism to depict, most of the sacred sources of life were perceived as aspects of the material world: sky, earth, sun, moon, thunder, lightning, mountain, wind, and so on, each imbued with a powerful spirit, an intelligence, a personality, a capacity for relationship.

Indeed, Native peoples thought of the universe as replete with life. The People sustained a healthy existence by recognizing the multiple forms of personalized life and treating them with propriety. Every crop planted and harvested, every herb extracted, every animal killed, every fish netted or speared, every eddy and whirlpool negotiated, every creature admired and emulated—even a rock, fashioned into a tool or ornament—was a person in its own right, and each possessed spiritual aspects, including an animating soul and a divinity who watched over the species or the landform.

Several observations follow. First, in the Indians' views of the world, the material and spiritual aspects were mutually implicated rather than segregated. Second, the spiritual aspects were able to change their forms, to metamorphose, to appear in various guises. Third, the sources of life included human relations, one's living kin, and their spiritual dimensions after death.

> **Study Aid #127**
> Countries of North America
>
> Canada   Greenland   Mexico   United States

Religion was a means of making relatives, of addressing the world in kinship terms, and therefore eliciting the duties wed to one's fellow beings in the web of life. Native prayers evoked Father Sky, Mother Earth, Grandmother Corn, Brother Deer, the Three Sisters (corn, beans, squash), and the Grandfathers of the Six Directions, as well as relatives in the beloved human community. One's life depended on all these, and more.

Not all was harmonious in the relations between the People and their sources of life, especially the animals. Numerous myths recounted the fractures between humans and their prey: animals caused diseases in humans in retaliation for too much killing; a contest won for humans the right to hunt, but at the cost of a shared language; marriages between humans and animals invariably soured with the realization that humans are apt to kill their bestial offspring. In general, Native American ethics posited the value of nonhuman lives, and Indians apologized ritually for killing certain game animals. At the same time, Native mythology provided an apologia for hunting nonhumans, despite their erstwhile commonality. Religions played a role in mediating the fraught relationships between humans and their animal relatives, their sources of life.

How did Native peoples come to know of their many sources of life, and how did they encounter them? Oral traditions told of the transformative powers who put the universe into its present condition: the Iroquois woman who fell from the sky and her grandson twins, who opposed one another's creativity at every turn; the white buffalo calf woman, who gave the Lakotas a sacred pipe with which to call upon the sacred beings; the woman of the deep, whose digits became the sea mammals upon whom the Inuit subsist; the changing woman, whose warrior sons rid the world of devouring monsters, and thus saved the Navajos from extinction; and so on. In each community variants might number as many as there were storytellers. Indians seemed capable of appreciating divergent testimonies concerning the events of the primordial past and variegated cosmological constructs.

Practices

Individual spiritual experience was encouraged, especially among the hunters and gatherers, with their loosely organized arrangements of social authority. Through dreams Indians experienced spiritual realities, communicating directly with their sources of life. Dreams could be means of validating, enriching, or altering the basic worldview of the People. In dreams a person might receive a vocation, commune with one's ancestors, or travel—by soul—to distant realms.

Some Native communities so valued dreaming as a religious experience that they trained themselves to achieve trance states, in order to meet the sources of life face-to-face in visions. Sometimes youths entered into lifelong relationships with the vision visitors, who vowed to guard and guide the visionary in times of want, or to share their spiritual powers for the sake of long life and happiness, for the individual or for the People at large.

Certain Native practitioners were so adept at entering ecstatic trances and at forming relationships with helpful spirits that they professionalized their talents for the sake of the People. In times of crisis—when diseases, droughts, or starvation, for example, threatened community life—the "shaman" (as this personage is called in the study of religions) stepped forward to help. He or she might call down the spirits to answer questions: Why are animals not dying for us? What is the nature of this mysterious illness? Or the shaman might travel, by soul flight, to the land of the dead to retrieve a lost soul, or to the bottom of the sea to appease the source of sea mammals. In the process, the shaman might get members of the community to confess sins and thereby restore proper relations with the sources of life.

Shamans should not be idealized as wholly beneficent religious functionaries. Persons of such spiritual prowess—approaching the powers of divinities as they accumulated helping spirits—were also a focus for anxieties among the People and could be accused of sorcery, especially when their performances failed to alleviate crises. Witchcraft accusations were a means of locating personified evil in the community, relationships gone awry.

When things went wrong, Native religions sought restoration through ritual: reciting formulaic, compelling, living words, passed down through time from mythological heroes; enacting gestures and manipulating objects, aimed at exorcising disruptive intrusions from a patient. Such symbolic healing drew upon powers originally bestowed by sacred, immune beings, who continued to serve as sources of life.

Native American ceremonialism, most fully elaborated among southern farming communities, was designed to establish regular relations between the People and their sources of life. In the course of a person's life, and in the course of any given year, Indians sought to ritualize their sense of propriety with a living, sustaining universe.

Two components of virtually every Native ritual system were smoking tobacco (or some such fumigant) and bathing in steam. Smoke and steam, ethereal substances, symbolized the mysterious interpenetration between visible and invisible,

---

Study Aid #128

Elements of North American Indigenous Religions

Animism	Shamans and tricksters
Oral traditions	Life-cycle ceremonies
Dreams, smoke, and steam	Seasonal ceremonies

material and spiritual worlds. Smoking tobacco in a pipe was a form of prayer, an offering, a sacrifice to the sources of life. Few ceremonials were complete without the tobacco's metamorphosis, by way of fire, into smoke and into the atmosphere. Steam baths were means of cleansing, curing, praying, and socializing, preparing oneself for ceremonials to come through hot vapor created by the colliding of fragrant water and roasted rocks in an enclosed space.

Over a lifetime an Indian marked stages of personal development with the help of religious rituals: receiving a name, which associated one with a particular source of life; burying one's placenta in order to establish one's place in the world; celebrating one's first menstruation by having a stand-in for the holy people to mold the girl into the shape of the divine female paradigm; undergoing a puberty fast, so as to empty oneself, then to receive a guardian spirit, in preparation for adult responsibilities; receiving wedding blessings; and of course preparing for one's journey to the otherworld at the time of death. At each stage of maturity, one's progress was fathomed in terms of relationships established.

The circular, reiterative progress of seasons and their associated economic activities provided opportunities for Native communities to express their religious attitudes toward the world in its many parts. Thus at midwinter the Iroquois recounted their dreams, and their fellows attempted to deliver on the wishes expressed therein. Throughout the rest of the year the Iroquois paid thanks to natural forms—the maple, the thunders, the wild strawberry, the green corn, and so on—upon whom they depended, as they made their bountiful presence felt in the Iroquois world. The Creeks marked their new year each summer by putting out old fires, cleansing their villages, forgiving all debts, and lighting new fires. Creek men cleansed themselves for the occasion by disgorging the contents of their stomachs via ingesting a purgative drink. At midsummer the Lakotas celebrated a ceremonial in honor of the sun, marked by the construction of a cosmic tree and the self-abnegation of young men—while others in the community made marriage arrangements and welcomed enemies for a peaceful respite. Among the Kwakiutls, human relationships were solidified each year through the institution of giveaways, which enhanced hierarchical prestige, demonstrated generosity, inculcated reciprocity, and allowed the wealthy to deplete their excess goods, which were considered morally tainted. Pueblo Indians invited deer, buffalo, and mountain sheep into their villages, by wearing mimetic costumes in their honor and copying their every move. Skagits caught and feasted on the first salmon of the season, returning from the sea to spawn upriver. In all these ceremonials the People tried to right their relations with their various sources of life, material and spiritual, combined.

Sources

Peggy V. Beck and Anna Lee Walters. *The Sacred: Ways of Knowledge, Sources of Life.* Navajo Community College, 1977.

Ruth Fulton Benedict. *The Concept of the Guardian Spirit in North America*. Memoirs of the American Anthropological Association 29. American Anthropological Association, 1923.

Ake Hultkrantz. *Belief and Worship in Native North America*. Edited by Christopher Vecsey. Syracuse University Press, 1981.

———. *The Study of American Indian Religions*. Edited by Christopher Vecsey. Crossroad, 1983.

Lawrence E. Sullivan, ed. *Native Religions and Cultures of North America: Anthropology of the Sacred*. Continuum, 2003.

Dennis Tedlock and Barbara Tedlock, eds. *Teachings from the American Earth: Indian Religion and Philosophy*. Liveright, 1975.

Christopher Vecsey. *Imagine Ourselves Richly: Mythic Narratives of North American Indians*. HarperSanFrancisco, 1991.

60

North America: Christian Contacts

CHRISTOPHER VECSEY

All manner of Christian agencies have vied to make Christians of the indigenous peoples of North America living in the lands now constituting the United States and Canada. From the first landfall to the present day, missionaries representing Roman Catholic, Russian Orthodox, Anglican, Congregationalist, Presbyterian, Baptist, Methodist, Moravian, Mennonite, Episcopal, Lutheran, Quaker, Nazarene, Mormon, Pentecostal, and numerous nondenominational and independent churches have expended energy and money and exerted influence among American Indian populations.

Since this evangelistic outreach has taken place within the context of European invasion and expansion, imperial conquest, and colonial control (still ongoing), it is difficult to separate religious factors from more secular concerns (military, economic, political, etc.), not to mention social and material conditions (such as intermarriage and disease) in evaluating the appeal of Christianity to Native peoples—or their resistance to Christian appeals.

After five hundred years of Christian presence in the New World, the majority of Indian people—several million in the United States, a million in Canada—are Christians, and it would be very difficult to find any Native person today untouched by Christian influence. What are the patterns of this Christianizing impact over time?

Establishing Missions

In the 1500s, following the conquest of Mexico and the establishment of the viceroyalty of New Spain, Catholic explorations filtered northward into Florida

> **Study Aid #129**
> **The Complexity of Christian Appeals**
> Colonial control
> Military conquest
> Religious conversion
> Economic competition
> Social change
>   Intermarriage
>   Health care/disease
>   Education

and New Mexico, securing beachheads for Spanish expansion. Missions were a means of pacifying territories and their inhabitants, in order to wrest natural resources and secure lands against colonial rivals. In the far northeast, French Catholics did the same: planting crosses as symbols of conquest and introducing the indigenes of New France to Christian belief and practice. Although English Protestants devoted far less effort to missionary activity than their Catholic rivals, their New England Praying Indian Towns of the 1600s were similarly machinery of pacification and operated under similar principles.

We must understand these two aspects—conquest and instruction—in light of one another. Founding each mission involved a process of reducing far-ranging Indian communities into centralized locales; attracting them with displays of European prowess, wealth, pageantry, generosity, and protection; and then asserting authority over their daily lives. Easier said than done, and the building of mission chains—along the Rio Grande and St. Lawrence River valleys, throughout the Great Lakes, into what is now southern Arizona, to the famous California missions of the late 1700s and early 1800s, and so on—was a slow, uneven, hazardous enterprise. As long as Indians maintained their local autonomy in economy and politics, they were not easily persuaded to submit their freedoms to the commands of foreigners. Even after joining missions, Indian neophytes (as the Spaniards termed them) were apt to escape to their home communities when mission conditions disappointed them.

Resistance

Native peoples uninterested in mission life were apt to attack the missions, perhaps to destroy them or at least to raid their stores. On several occasions missionized Indians rebelled against Catholic control—most notably in 1680 in New Mexico. In this Pueblo revolt, led by a Native religious leader named Popé, a united Indian front killed the majority of Catholic priests residing in their villages and expelled the Spaniards from New Mexico for over a decade.

What impelled the Pueblos to attack the missionaries and their Spanish associates? A series of administrative acts that the Native peoples viewed as religious persecution—the burning of numerous masks and other items of cultic devotion, the arrest of indigenous religious leaders, and the hanging of several—stoked local ire. The Pueblos blamed an extended drought and assaults by Native foes on the interruption of traditional liturgy and the alienation of aboriginal divinities. In short, the Pueblos wanted their religious autonomy restored and were willing to fight for it.

In the long run, however, as well as in the short, Christianity had its attraction to many North American Indians. Even the Pueblos, by the 1700s, reconciled themselves to Catholicism, and today most of their descendants are baptized Catholics (without necessarily forgoing their Native spiritual organizations).

Christianity's Appeal

What drew Indians to Christianity initially, and what has kept so many in association with Christian denominational faith? The persuasive rhetoric of Christian proselytizers cannot be denied. Christianity possesses a narrative grandeur—from creation by a mighty God to the drama of human sinfulness and the miraculous, salvific sacrifice of Jesus, through whom forgiveness is gained—and its ethical command to love others has great appeal to communities under stress. The book of Revelation has passages as inspiring as any vision, and it has been a popular text for many Indians.

If Indians could be convinced that they shared in Adam and Eve's fallen state (human depravity was not a concept well known to the Native mind) and if they could accept the notion of a universally applicable religious system (each tribal community had its own faith, suited to its particular circumstances), then Christianity might take hold over their convictional lives.

Missionaries reinforced their catechesis by impressing Indians with the fiery punishments awaiting them in the afterworld if they resisted Christian entreaties to convert. Moreover, preachers emphasized the gifts granted by their powerful God to the Christian faithful. When Indians suffered the epidemic diseases (smallpox, etc.) brought to the Western Hemisphere's aboriginal populations by Europeans, missionaries blamed the illnesses on Native sin and recalcitrance and boasted of their own health in the midst of deadly scourges. Some Indians took Christian ministers to be shamans and sought to submit to their revelations and commands; others accused the preachers of sorcery and despised them all the more.

Cultural Disintegration and Revitalization

As Christian missionaries persuaded Indians to embrace their forms of worship—teaching hymns and staging passion plays, processions, and so on—and instructed them in the faith, Indian communities were under multifaceted duress. Disease, warfare, alcoholism, ecological disruption, loss of sovereignty to colonizing usurpation: all these conditions drained Indian confidence and resolve. To many Natives, not only was Christianity a part of the invading force, but it also offered hope for the future to peoples in disarray.

No wonder, then, that some Indians converted to Christianity as an explanatory force and a mechanism of community building. Sometimes whole communities converted en masse. Others were wracked by factionalism as Christian and pagan parties, or Protestant and Catholic partisans, competed for the upper hand in the home ground.

And no wonder that some Indians, dead set against Euro-American Christian civilization that they interpreted as the source of their demise, took up portions of Christian cosmology and social ethics in order to construct an overall message of Nativist revitalization. The Delaware prophet Neolin in the 1760s fabricated a buckskin Bible, whose design pointed the way toward avoiding all whites in order to regain the Edenic state of precontact existence. In 1799, under Quaker inspiration, the Seneca prophet Handsome Lake began to receive a series of visions upon which he crafted a code of religio-societal behaviors, which has served the Iroquois Longhouse Religion to the present day. Other new Indian religions like the Native American Church (the Peyote religion) or the Indian Shaker Church have combined Christian and Native elements in a syncretistic harmony.

Native Christians

For some Indians, Christianity became the core of their identity, and they needed not to dwell upon opposing impulses between their Native and Christian selves. Kateri Tekakwitha (1656–80), a Mohawk convert to Catholic faith, devoted her young life at one of the Indian reductions (settlements) near Montreal to ascetic privations and mortifications of the flesh, as well as corporal acts of mercy among her fellow Indians. Her heroic virtue served as inspiration to the priests who served as her spiritual mentors. Samson Occom (1723–92), a Mohegan converted by the New Lights of the Great Awakening, dedicated his Presbyterian ministry to the edification and survival of Native communities in southern New England, even serving as Moses to his Brotherton fellows in search of refuge on the Iroquois

---

Study Aid #130

The Christian Mission Pattern

Establish a mission
Resistance
Christianity's appeal
Cultural disintegration/revitalization

Native Christians
Nationalism
Harmony/Ambivalence

frontier. The Métis Louis Riel (1844–85), part Ojibwa, part French Canadian, left the Catholic seminary to become Canada's most famous traitor. Following his millenarian visions of the Virgin Mary and the Sacred Heart of Jesus, he gathered Natives and Métis in a failed attempt to prevent Canada's annexation of his homelands, for which he was hanged. Following his conversion, the Lakota holy man Nicholas Black Elk (1863–1950) served as Catholic catechist to Indians of the northern plains, teaching the gospel from a pictorial catechism that traced the two roads (to heaven and hell), posed as a choice to all humans from the beginning of time to the last judgment. These and other Christian Indians have located their deepest spirituality where Native and Christian ways coincide.

Nationalism

The ascension of the United States and Canada as the two chief state powers of North America meant that Indian missionary efforts in the nineteenth and twentieth centuries were encased in nationalism. Some missionaries served as agents for governmental policies; others applied conscience to criticizing the excesses of Manifest Destiny. During the US Peace Policy, 1869–76, missionaries exerted their wills over reservation Indians, for good and ill. Christian "Friends of the Indians" promoted the Allotment Act of 1887, whose purpose was to "civilize" Indians by reducing their tribal landholdings to individual plots. At the behest of Christian "reformers," the US and Canadian governments in the late 1800s and early 1900s outlawed Native religious practices, like sun dances and giveaways. With the creation of denominational boarding schools (called residential schools in Canada) in the late 1800s, generations of Indian children were separated from their parents and placed under the jurisdiction of missionary bodies, who too often overstepped their authority and exercised dictatorial, often abusive, control of their young charges, with deleterious long-term effects. Under these pressures it was increasingly difficult for Indians to maintain their traditions, and Christian allegiance was thereby solidified, although not without lingering resentments and surreptitious survivals.

Harmony and Ambivalence

In situations where Indians have maintained insular control over their Christian organizations—for example, the independent Seminole Baptist churches in Oklahoma or the Narragansett Church of Rhode Island—worship appears to valorize a seamless religio-ethnic identity, made of two traditions—Native and Christian—which once were disparate, even antagonistic. Native peoples such as the Inuit of the far north have turned to Pentecostal healing circles to address their hurts and revivify their broken relationships with humans and the earth through ritualized reconciliation.

Other Indian Christians find the process of spiritual healing fraught with paradox. As the late Lakota Sister Marie-Therese Archambault, OSF, once said, "As a Native [Christian] the very faith you embrace is one that was used to destroy you, that collaborated with the government in cultural genocide.... This is the terrible irony of being Native American and [Christian]."

A Swinomish eucharistic minister tells this story, a favorite of his when addressing Catholic audiences. It always gets a knowing laugh, especially from Indians:

> A priest came to an Indian village. He performed religious instruction and baptized the whole village, except for one elder, who resisted conversion. So, the priest visited him and finally baptized him, giving him a new, Christian name.
>
> The priest told the elder that there were three rules he was compelled to follow: go to Mass on Sunday, confess your sins on Saturday, and abstain from eating meat on Friday.
>
> Pretty soon, however, the priest found the elder on a Friday, cooking venison in a pot. He asked him, "Why are you eating deer meat rather than fish?"
>
> "I am eating fish," the elder replied.
>
> "Don't lie to me," said the priest.
>
> "I'm not lying," said the elder. "This *is* fish. When I killed a deer, I took it down to the river and baptized it, and changed its name to 'fish.'"

Sources

R. Pierce Beaver, ed. *The Native Christian Community: A Directory of Indian, Aleut, and Eskimo Churches*. MARC, 1979.

Henry Warner Bowden. *American Indians and Christian Missions: Studies in Cultural Conflict*. University of Chicago Press, 1981.

John Webster Grant. *Moon of Wintertime: Missionaries and the Indians of Canada in Encounter since 1534*. University of Toronto Press, 1984.

Frederic B. Laugrand. *Inuit Shamanism and Christianity: Transitions and Transformations in the Twentieth Century*. McGill-Queen's University Press, 2010.

Christopher Vecsey. *On the Padres' Trail*. University of Notre Dame Press, 1996.

———. *The Paths of Kateri's Kin*. University of Notre Dame Press, 1997.

———. *Traditional Ojibwa Religion and Its Historical Changes*. American Philosophical Society, 1983.

61

North America: Theological Exchanges

Christopher Vecsey

It would appear that the history of Christian-Indian contact has had the quality more of a monologue than an exchange of ideas. Literate Europeans published their proclamations, recorded their observations, argued among themselves over the conduct of their imperial ventures, and created rule books for changing and controlling indigenous peoples.

Of course they conversed with Native North Americans. In Mexico some of those dialogues, real and imaginary, found their way into print in the 1500s, and in retrospect they seem like slippery miscommunications across linguistic and cultural boundaries. Catholic missionaries attempted to shape Native concepts about God, sin, redemption, and the like, yet Indians expressed these new ideas through the lens of their own traditions. The *Jesuit Relations* of New France recorded two centuries of interchange between missionaries and Indians, but even when the indigenes' supposed viewpoints were written down in the *Relations*, the Catholic clerical scribes seem—as we read their accounts—more like ventriloquists than amanuenses, putting words into the Natives' mouths.

Christian "Right of Discovery"

From the first, European authorities declared their theological prerogatives. In 1493 Pope Alexander VI granted Spain and Portugal the "right of discovery" in the New World—a theological construct of medieval Christendom that granted Christian sovereigns authority over non-Christian peoples and their territories, as if pagans possessed no sovereign rights of their own. European powers questioned papal jurisdiction. In due course Protestant countries like England and

> **Study Aid #131**
>
> **Theological Rationales for Conquest**
>
> Christian "right of discovery" "The Medicine Men and Clergy" dialogue
> Native testimonies Contemporary Native theology
> Indian rejoinders

the Netherlands paid his dicta no mind. Nonetheless, the "right of discovery" remained the metaphysical groundwork for imperial (and later national) land claims in the Americas, and in 1823 the US Supreme Court deemed American land title to derive ultimately from the Christian "right of discovery."

During the colonial era, many Europeans saw America as a demonic land, inhabited by demonic people. Even though a 1537 papal bull declared Indians to be fully human, there were thoroughgoing suspicions regarding Native capacities for ethical conduct and self-discipline. Confessional guidebooks emphasized the Natives' deviant sexuality and pagan proclivities. In the public debates in Valladolid, Spain, 1550–51, regarding the rights of Indians to justice in New Spain, a jurist argued that they were natural slaves deserving minimal protections by law, either because they lacked religion entirely, or because they were corrupted by their devil worship. The 1823 Supreme Court decision persisted in referring to Indians as savages with no right to autonomy when faced with Christian power. To this day, Indian activists have tried to persuade the Holy See to rescind its 1493 declaration and to disavow the "right of discovery," to no avail.

Spanish jurists figured how to put the theology of "discovery" into practice, through the mechanism of "The Requirement," instituted in 1513 and employed throughout the sixteenth century. Upon encountering Indian peoples, the "discoverer" was to read a declaration, proclaiming the papal donation of God's sovereignty to the Spanish Crown, and requiring—much like the summons of an Islamic jihad, from which "The Requirement" derived its form—the "discovered" to submit to Christian rule. Any resistance, or any delay, would result in punishment, including enslavement, "The Requirement" said. In 1598, for instance, the Spaniards read the decree to the Acoma Pueblo in New Mexico, and following a military engagement, the Acomans were subdued (each man had a limb severed) and put to work, building a church in their town.

Native Testimonies

This sort of one-sided theological expression typified much of the exchange between Christians and North American Indians over the centuries. Perhaps Christians who married Indians—John Rolfe and Pocahontas come to mind—entered into intimate religious conversation, beyond catechizing. Surely some Christian ministers listened to the religious ideas of the Indians to whom they preached and responded to them, as did, for example, Moravians among the Delawares in the 1700s and Jesuits among the Ontario Ojibwas in the nineteenth century. Literate Indian Protestants, such as Samson Occom (Mohegan) in the eighteenth century and William Apess (Pequot, author of *A Son of the Forest*, 1829) in the nineteenth century, made clear the value of their indigenous spirituality and the hypocritical shortcomings of the Euro-American practice of Christianity. It is not clear, however, that non-Indians paid much attention to them. With the growth of anthropology as a discipline, the genre of the Indian life history opened a way for non-Indians to learn in print about Native experiences and conceptions; see, for example, the ubiquitous *Black Elk Speaks* (1932). Indian authors like Charles Alexander Eastman (Dakota) reflected upon *The Soul of the Indian* (1911) and exhorted Christians to live up to the ideals of their divine founder.

Only in the twentieth century, however, is there a written record of theological exchange in North America between Christians and Indians, which is worth reviewing. In the epoch of the American counterculture and the New Indians proclaiming Red Power, the son of a Dakota Episcopal priest, Vine Deloria Jr., published *Custer Died for Your Sins* (1969). In this and his many books and articles to follow, Deloria captured the imagination of some Christians to an alternative Native view of the cosmos grounded in sacred nature rather than historical time, in duties rather than rights, in matter over spirit; in visions rather than logic, in relationships rather than hierarchies, in ritual rather than memorized creed, in tribalism rather than individualism, in local communities rather than universal evangelism. Deloria excoriated Christian missionaries, for certain, for their roles in subjugating American Indians to Euro-Christian rule in the United States and Canada. He went so far as to call Christianity "the chief evil ever to have been loosed on the planet." However, he also presented a Native theology (e.g., in *God Is Red*, 1973), which he thought superior to anything Christianity had to offer. In short, he aimed to challenge the basic assumptions of the Christian West.

Deloria's style of invective made him seem more adept at hurling bombast than in dialogue between faiths. Following centuries of one-way communication from Christians to Indians, Deloria avowed: *We Talk, You Listen* (1972). Nonetheless, Christian journals like *Christian Century* published his words. Although he criticized liberation theology, Christian liberals appreciated his commitment to justice and his treatment of Indian societies as covenanted base communities. In an age of growing ecological concern, Deloria's Native perspective upon a living, related universe seemed like a breath of clean air, an inspiration to some.

Medicine Men and Clergy

While Deloria engaged in a public argument with Christian theological sensibilities, interfaith dialogue was beginning to take place in private Catholic circles, moved by the ecumenical spirit of the Second Vatican Council (1962–65). In Alberta and

Ontario the church created centers for sharing theological viewpoints between Native and non-Native Catholics. The most sustained (and most thoroughly documented) dialogue, the Medicine Men and Clergy Meetings (1973–79), took place on the Rosebud Lakota Reservation in South Dakota, organized by a Jesuit, William F. Stolzman.

Like several of his fellow Jesuits, Stolzman had contemplated and experimented with "inculturation" theology: encouraging Lakota Catholics to express their Christian faith through Lakota forms, such as smoking tobacco in sacred pipes. In so doing he began to ponder the similarities between Catholic and Lakota liturgy. In 1986 he published his thoughts in *The Pipe and Christ*. In the meantime he had the opportunity, over six years of intermittent conversation, to share theological ideas with Lakota medicine men (Catholic and non-Catholic), their female relatives, and over a dozen Jesuits.

They compared their ideas about spiritual vocation, discernment of the supernatural, syncretism, salvation, prayer, liturgical efficacy, witchcraft, revelation, metaphysics, souls, reincarnation, sin, God, miracles, ethics, and the relative authority of the two religious traditions, Lakota and Catholic. The discussants compared at length the relative mediating functions of the pipe and Christ in their respective faiths, as well as the role of peyote in the Native American Church.

Some Lakotas were adamant that Lakota and Christian forms—say, the sweat lodge and the Mass—should be kept apart from one another, even if it could be argued that they constituted paths to the same relationship with God. The Jesuits, especially Stolzman, sought greater communion between the two religions, especially between the pipe and Christ. Another area of disagreement concerned human sinfulness. The Lakotas refused to accept the Christian doctrine that all humans participate in the fall of Adam and Eve and share in the condition of original sin (and therefore are in need of saving grace).

Despite their disagreements, the medicine men and priests maintained a collegial air as religious practitioners. Indeed, they praised one another for their mutual spirituality and leadership. They recognized the great change in Jesuit attitudes that would allow such a dialogue to take place. At the same time, some on each side refused to yield in their suspicions of the other. The Jesuits had plenty to apologize for—for example, violence institutionalized at their boarding schools—and apologize they did. But, as far as they hoped to understand or even appreciate Lakota religion, they were not about to consider it the equivalent of Catholicism. For his part, Stolzman appreciated the similarities between the two traditions, enough to fit them together where appropriate.

Development of Contemporary Native Theology

A paradigm shift was taking place in many centers of Christian leadership, as evidenced by the apologies for the missionary past issued to Native Americans by Christian bodies from the 1970s to the 1990s. Concurrently, Indian Christians were feeling free to express not only their criticisms of their churches but also their notions of a Christianity enriched by Native insights.

To help them in this endeavor, agencies provided a forum for discussion and pastoral education. The Indian Ecumenical Conference began in 1969 as a grassroots means to gather various Native spiritual leaders for conversation under one tent. The first conference was held in 1970, and throughout most of the 1970s and 1980s it met annually, and again in 1992—an encampment of thousands—on the Stoney Indian Reserve in Alberta. The wonder of these meetings was the relative harmony wrought from diversity, for these were gatherings of Indians often at odds with each other: Christian ministers, born-again pagans, traditionalists, Red Power activists, and so on. They shared a commitment to Indian religious self-determination and to one another, and they recognized the necessity of intertribal solidarity to a publicly recognized Native American worldview. This was a movement of pan-Indian ecumenism and spiritual politics, and it has influenced all other Indian religious developments since that time.

The Tekakwitha Conference began in 1977 as a Catholic missionary group honoring the saintly, seventeenth-century Mohawk Kateri Tekakwitha and developed into an annual gathering for thousands of Catholic Indians and non-Indians (with many local chapters), which fostered devotional inculturation, intertribal cultural sharing, and lively debate about the dynamics of being Indian and Catholic. The Native Theological Association was founded in 1977 for interdenominational Protestant catechetics with an eye toward developing a distinctive American Indian theology. The Native American Project of Theology in the Americas began in 1978 to encourage ecumenical discussion among Native Christians and traditionalists. A decade later, in 1988, the Native American Lutheran Theology Project encouraged dialogue between Indian Christians and the rest of the Christian community. Under its aegis Lutherans Paul Schultz (Ojibwa) and George Tinker (Osage) produced the first comprehensive overview of Indian Christian theology, *Rivers of Life* (1988), written by and for Native people.

Although one might say that "theology" seems to be an endeavor at odds with Indian spiritual sensibilities, Tinker and several coauthors have tried to establish a distinctive Native theology, based upon tribal and Christian traditions, and

---

Study Aid #132

Contemporary Native Theology

Indian Ecumenical Conference: 1969
Tekakwitha Conference: 1977
Native Theological Association: 1977
Native American Project of Theology: 1978
North American Institute for Indigenous Theological Studies: 1999

drawing upon their experiences and those in their communities. In contemporary collections of Christian Indian writings, recollections of personal hurt and means of societal healing are major concerns. It would appear that Native theology must address the dysfunctions of present Indian life. Emphasis is placed on the Creator's love of the world and reflection in its forms, including humans. Perhaps at odds with Christian notions of original sin and the need for redemption—both in individuals and in nature—contemporary Native theology tends to see unity, harmony, personality, and goodness in the world.

Relying on personal vision for revelation, Native theology values a plurality, even a plethora, of worldviews. Jesus is an attractive figure to Indian theologians, but for his compassion and self-sacrifice, like a sun-dancer, not because he is considered the single, divine mediator between humans and God.

Nor is the Bible held central to Native theologians. Indians do not see themselves in the history of Israel, except perhaps as the Canaanites, whose territory was usurped by the Hebrews. And they do not see themselves bound to all the teachings of an ancient book produced by other people so far away and long ago.

What positive values do contemporary Indian theologians espouse? The valorization of Native traditions, insights, communities, and elders. The importance of relations, among humans and especially between genders, with nonhuman persons of nature, and with the divine—in short, with all the sacred sources of life.

Sources

Marie-Therese Archambault, OSF, Mark G. Thiel, and Christopher Vecsey, eds. *The Crossing of Two Roads: Being Catholic and Native in the United States*. Orbis Books, 2003.

Vine Deloria Jr. *For This Land: Writings on Religion in America*. Edited by James Treat. Routledge, 1999.

Clara Sue Kidwell, Homer Noley, and George E. Tinker. *A Native American Theology*. Orbis Books, 2006.

Achiel Peelman, OMI. *Christ Is a Native American*. Novalis-Saint Paul University, 1995.

Carl Starkloff, SJ. *The People of the Center: American Indian Religion and Christianity*. Seabury, 1974.

William F. Stolzman, SJ. *The Pipe and Christ*. Red Cloud Indian School, 1986.

George E. Tinker. *Spirit and Resistance: Political Theology and American Indian Liberation*. Fortress, 2004.

James Treat. *Around the Sacred Fire: Native Religious Activism in the Red Power Era; A Narrative Map of the Indian Ecumenical Conference*. Palgrave Macmillan, 2003.

———, ed. *Native and Christian: Indigenous Voices on Religious Identity in the United States and Canada*. Routledge, 1996.

Christopher Vecsey. *Where the Two Roads Meet*. University of Notre Dame Press, 1999.

62

North America: Current Issues

CHRISTOPHER VECSEY

A century ago the prospects of North American Indians had reached their nadir. Their population had plummeted to no more than a few hundred thousand. They were impoverished, dependent, in danger of extinction, and objects of pity and contempt in mainstream North American society. Scholars engaged in "salvage anthropology," hoping to record the last fragments of a dying culture. United States and Canadian governments claimed plenary powers over their communal and individual lives. As a Protestant minister said, exhorting the US Congress to pass coercive legislation that would usurp the remnants of Indian reservation lands, "Barbarism has no rights which civilization is bound to respect."

Native religions were subject to bureaucratic prohibition. Police arrested ritual practitioners, and Courts of Indian Offenses meted out punishments. Some Indian communities protested these policies. In the 1920s, responding to government attempts to curtail their ceremonials, Pueblo leaders proclaimed, "We have a religion" deserving of First Amendment protections. In so doing, they adapted post-Enlightenment American notions of institutional religion, the right to free exercise thereof, and freedom of individual conscience. These claims, successfully asserted, raised the question of religious freedoms for Christian members of Pueblo communities who claimed that they were coerced by their Native authorities to participate in pagan rituals. Among the Pueblos, Navajos, and other Indian communities, religious factions—members of the peyote religion, Catholics, and so on—sought redress in US courts against tribal governments, which asserted residual sovereignty over their members and remaining territories.

In the Pueblo Indian Dance controversy, local artists, writers, anthropologists, tourists, and other non-Indians enamored of Native spirituality lent their influence to the Pueblo cause. A new sensibility in North America was developing: Romantic nostalgia for a primitive past, commitment to modernist liberality, cultural relativism, and a thirst for mysticism. First bohemians, then mainstream Americans, began to condone, appreciate, admire, and—in the New Age—appropriate aspects of Indian religiousness.

When several states and the US Congress tried to pass legislation forbidding all use of peyote, an anthropologist advised Indian peyotists to create a Native American Church, which could claim the First Amendment right to ingest the cactus as its communal sacrament. John Collier, one of the Pueblo promoters, became commissioner of Indian affairs in the New Deal. In 1934 he rescinded federal strictures against Native religions. Christian missionary groups complained. "Does Uncle Sam Foster Paganism?" a Protestant journal queried. Collier could reply that he was only fostering religious freedom for all American citizens (Congress bestowed citizenship on all US Indians in 1924); however, he made no secret of his high regard for Indian spiritual traditions, which he compared favorably to Christianity.

Resurgence

American Indians did not disappear. They survived, and over the course of the twentieth century became one of the fastest-growing ethnicities in the United States and Canada. Today there are several legally recognized Native peoples in North America, plus millions of people who claim some Indian heritage. In the last quarter of the 1900s—inspired by the spirit of anticolonialism worldwide and the civil rights movement in the United States—Native communities asserted their political autonomy, and in remarkable, but limited, ways, they have received recognition as nations within the federal matrices of Canada and the United States.

Study Aid #133

From "religion" to "Religion"

Indigenous Native American religion (NAR)
Attempts at eradication of NAR
Adoption of "Religion": 1920s
Rescinded Federal strictures: 1934
American Indian Religious Freedom Act: 1978
    Helped protect some sacred sites (e.g., burial grounds)
    Allowed for some exceptions for religious practices (e.g., peyote)
    Protected public practice (e.g., in schools, prisons)

Witness, for example, the many successful Indian land claims made in the United States, or the creation of the Inuit territory of Nunavut in 1999.

Concomitant with this Native political resurgence has been a religious renaissance of considerable import. Demands for fishing, hunting, water, and other treaty rights have led to expressions of spiritual self-determination and the valorization of traditional religious culture. As Indian communities have wrangled for control over their own educational systems, they have opted to teach their children "traditional" values, along with their indigenous languages (most of which are still in danger of demise). Rituals long considered defunct were performed across Native America, sometimes with the help of reference to written texts left over from the days of salvage anthropology.

Religious Freedom

The American Indian Religious Freedom Act (AIRFA) of 1978 sought to enhance the sustaining of Native religious traditions in the United States in the face of continuing legal obstacles. Although lacking mechanisms for enforcement, AIRFA directed government agencies to protect Indian religious practice when threatened by degradation or destruction of natural sites considered sacred by Indian communities, and by laws infringing upon Indian religious practices.

Indians and their lawyers began to file grievances in several types of circumstances: when their sacred sites—mountains, lakes, burial grounds, pilgrimage destinations, and so on, many of them on federal and state lands beyond the jurisdiction of reservations—were mined, dammed, polluted, developed, or otherwise exploited for non-Indian use; and when laws criminalized activities—the ingestion of peyote, primarily, but also, for example, trapping endangered species like eagles to procure feathers used in ceremonies—considered essential to Indian religions. But also, Natives decried their lack of religious freedom—the ability to hold traditional ceremonies, for example—in the confines of institutions like prisons and schools, and they expressed outrage that museums and archives held thousands upon thousands of revered artifacts—paraphernalia used in ceremonies, but also the bodily remains of beloved ancestors—against the will of Indian communities.

On its own, AIRFA has seemed ineffective. In 1988 the Supreme Court ruled (in *Lyng v. Northwest Indian Cemetery Protective Association*) that the Indian communities of Northern California could not prevent the building of a road through a public forest where they conducted vision quests. The court denied the road's negative impact on the Indians' religious practice. Nor did other legal proceedings protect several southwestern Indians' sacred sites from tourism, recreational use, and the construction of scientific facilities.

AIRFA seemed equally impotent in 1990 when the Supreme Court ruled (in the Oregon case *Employment Division v. Smith*) that minority religions like the Native American Church cannot expect special protection from general laws passed

> **Study Aid #134**
> Contemporary Religious Patterns
> Social challenges
>   Poverty, violence, suicide, alcoholism
>   Reservations, gambling, "statehood" issues
> Two religious trajectories
>   Resurgent native traditions (NAR)
>   Contextualized Christian theologies

by the states—for example, against controlled substances—and the states do not need to defend their compelling need for such laws, even when they infringe upon Indian religious practices.

When the *Smith* decision seemed to place the peyote religion in jeopardy, a public outcry ensued, not only from Indians but also from mainstream religious groups. Through the 1990s, Congress, the president, the court, and the state of Oregon all commented upon the peyote religion and Indian religious freedoms in general. The Native American Graves Protection and Repatriation Act of 1990 (NAGPRA) has proved especially effective in permitting Indian communities to negotiate with museums for the return of sacred objects for the purpose of defending Native religious integrity.

The existence of AIRFA, NAGPRA, and several other laws has created an atmosphere of contention, not only between Indians and non-Indians but also within Native communities, as differing parties make competing assertions about what is sacred and how the sacred ought to be defended. Medicine men's associations among the Lakotas, for example, have sought to regularize ceremonial procedures and codes of conduct, but their jurisdiction is often questioned by their compatriots. Iroquois Longhouse leaders in the United States have issued edicts prohibiting the display of ceremonial masks, which Canadian Iroquois have openly for sale in their territories. Some Indian people insist that the sacred must be secret and that religious matters must not be divulged to outsiders—neither academics nor New Age enthusiasts eager to emulate Native spirituality. At the same time, however, some Indian scholars and artists have published revealing analyses of their tribal ceremonialism, organization, terminology, and so on—to the ire of some communities or portions thereof. No community is uniform in belief, attitude, or behavior.

Contemporary Religious Patterns

What are the patterns of religiousness among Native North Americans today? Amid the often dire conditions of contemporary Indian life—statistics regarding poverty, violence, suicide, alcoholism, imprisonment, and so on are disturbing;

the sense of siege by an outside world bent on clear-cutting forests, strip-mining coal, damming rivers, extracting uranium, and storing radioactive wastes on Native soil is dismaying—what roles do the varieties of religious expression play in Indian lives? Here are some vignettes of recent vintage.

*A young Canadian Ojibwa chief addresses an academic conference about the catastrophic effects of mercury poisoning on his reserve. Binge drinking. Murders. Abandonment of children. Gang rapes. Glue sniffing. Despair. A scholar in the audience asks the chief what could possibly turn these conditions around. The stunned crowd hears the chief reply, "Jesus is the answer."

Two decades later the same chief reports to another symposium that his reserve has recovered its equilibrium, partially through a policy of tough love toward wayward youths and expulsion of recalcitrant malingerers, and the voluntary segregation of families avowing sobriety. Another factor in inspiring community cohesion and hope, he says, has been the renewal of traditional ceremonies, formerly banned by the Ontario provincial police and Christian missionary personnel.

*A Rio Grande Pueblo celebrates its Catholic saint's feast day in January by attending Mass before dawn, then gathering in one of its plazas to welcome the deer, buffalo, and mountain sheep. Animal impersonators come down from the surrounding hills and enter the plaza, where adorned women and male drummers constitute a welcoming chorus. Back and forth all morning, the villagers and the animals dance in honor of each other.

*On the Lummi Reservation in Washington State, various Salish people gather at a memorial for a recently deceased man. The ceremonial time is divided among Pentecostals, Indian Shakers, traditional spirit dancers, and representatives of a new religious group—a syncretism of Shakerism and spirit dancing—called the Seven Drum Religion. Each group takes its turn with its particular prayer forms, in helping send the soul of the dead to the otherworld, and in comforting the living. Then everyone shares a feast of venison and salmon.

*The Creek medicine man conducts a sweat-lodge ceremony for youths and elders on his Oklahoma property. He explains to the men, sitting naked in a circle around hot stones in a small cave, about the origin of the ritual they are about to join in. It is a return to the womb of the earth, from which humans emerged in the beginning of time. These first humans were helpless as newborns, and they cried like wolves to be reunited with their mother. The medicine man—formerly a Baptist minister—exhorts his fellows to cry like those first humans as he pours water over the stones, filling the cave with steam.

*Another sweat is performed by a Catholic priest (who is also a medicine man) at a Tekakwitha Conference in Maine. With bishops and laymen in the steamy tent, the medicine priest invokes the spirits of the earth, the ancestors, the nonhuman relatives, and the mysterious transcendent. "God equals Great Spirit equals Kitche Mainto equals Wakan Tanka equals all other names of the divine," he states, and no religion has preeminence as a spiritual expression.

*The Native chaplain tells some droll tales to the inmates in the gymnasium of a maximum security New York State prison. Then he makes some fry bread, which he sets aside for their feast. But first there are speeches and dances to perform, in honor of the Thunder, who is being welcomed back after a winter's absence. The Indian prisoners—almost all young Iroquois men—pay respectful attention as the chaplain, an Iroquois elder, preaches against the use of alcohol. Together the men recite the standard Longhouse prayer—thanksgiving to enumerated beings from the earth to the sky and beyond. Rattles in hand, they perform several dances, then eat the fry bread, corn soup, strawberry drink, and other Iroquois delicacies. Someone asks where one of their fellow Iroquois inmates is this day. He is meeting instead with a Christian prayer group. He has decided that these Native ceremonies are unholy, and he will have no further part in them.

*A Navajo storyteller is narrating a tale she learned from her mother years ago, about changing woman and the sun, and the monsters who used to devour humanity's ancestors. Switching between Navajo and English, she portrays a world in which people have forgotten their daily prayers. They no longer thank the Sun for his light-giving journey; they have lost the ability to seek divine aid from the terrors obstructing their lives. The teller can be jolly; this afternoon she is fierce, repeating a lesson she has been giving to all her Navajo audiences this winter. She recounts the gruesome details of a recent, horrific murder on the reservation. She avers that the world has gone upside-down, from lack of attention to prayer and from failure to uphold relationships with the holy people and with one another. Like other contemporary Native moralists, she calls the People back to their traditions.

Sources

Andrew Gulliford. *Sacred Objects and Sacred Places: Preserving Tribal Traditions.* University Press of Colorado, 2000.

Philip Jenkins. *Dream Catchers: How Mainstream America Discovered Native Spirituality.* Oxford University Press, 2004.

Steven T. Newcomb. *Pagans in the Promised Land: Decoding the Doctrine of Christian Discovery.* Fulcrum, 2008.

Ronald Niezer. *Spirit Wars: Native North American Religions in the Age of Nation Building.* University of California Press, 2000.

Huston Smith. *A Seat at the Table: Huston Smith in Conversation with Native Americans on Religious Freedom.* University of California Press, 2005.

Christopher Vecsey, ed. *Handbook of American Indian Religious Freedom.* Crossroad, 1991.

Tisa Wenger. *We Have a Religion: The 1920s Pueblo Indian Dance Controversy and American Religious Freedom.* University of North Carolina Press, 2009.

63

Meso- and South America: History, Beliefs, Practices

WILLIAM SVELMOE

History

On the surface, Mexico, Central America, and South America are largely Catholic countries. Certainly the Catholic Church dominates the landscape both literally and figuratively. But in reality, this area of the world has an incredibly diverse religious heritage, which continues to influence the daily lives of people across all social strata. The indigenous religions of Meso- and South America can be divided into three general groupings: the great organized traditions whose political power was largely destroyed upon European contact, African-based spiritist religions first introduced through slavery, and the animist tribal religions still practiced in the Amazon.

When the Spanish arrived in the sixteenth century, they were initially resisted by three powerful civilizations: the Aztecs (or Mexica) in central Mexico, the Maya in southern Mexico and Central America, and the Incas in the Andes. The religions practiced by these groups probably initially developed from animist traditions that primarily involved the supplication of spirits associated with various natural phenomena. From there, as cultures expanded beyond small family clusters, the religions organized into ancestor cults, then to the worship of specific ancestors of powerful families or clans, to, finally, the construction of impressive ceremonial centers devoted to tribal deities, some of whom appeared to demand universal allegiance. Eventually, the Aztecs, Maya, and Incas organized into states powerful enough to impose their religions onto numerous lesser surrounding cultures.

Maya culture emerged around 500 BCE. At its peak around 750 CE, Mayan influence may have extended over more than thirteen million people from the

Yucatan in southern Mexico to Guatemala in Central America. The Maya constructed more than eighty large ceremonial centers with pyramids, palaces, and temples, some of which attracted populations as large as forty thousand. By 1000 CE, Mayan political unity had largely collapsed. Unfortunately the deliberate destruction of Mayan cultural artifacts by the Spanish makes it difficult to accurately reconstruct their beliefs and practices. Despite this destruction, however, Mayan religious and cultural influence continues to this day among the indigenous Indian groups of Mesoamerica.

The Aztecs arrived in central Mexico from the northwest in the twelfth and thirteenth centuries CE. They were troublemakers and thieves who arrived and poached from local groups until they were driven on. They began constructing their splendid city of Tenochtitlán on the current site of Mexico City in 1325. In 1430 they began the warfare that saw them essentially become the rulers of most of Mexico.

At that point Tlacaélel, perhaps their greatest leader, essentially tore up their past and created a narrative befitting their newfound cultural power, doing away with their poor beginnings and associating their past with that of the ancient majesty of the Toltecs, upon whose civilization they built. He gave the Aztecs a new destiny as followers of the war god Huitzilopochtli, who was no longer just a tribal deity but now a divinity essential to the fate of all humanity. Together with their god they served the sun to keep it strong in its daily battle against the darkness and the moon and stars. The mission of the Aztecs became to conquer their known world in order to secure captives who would feed the sun with blood, the fluid of life.

When Montezuma came to power in 1502, the Aztecs may have ruled a population of around twenty-five million. At a time when Seville, the largest city in Spain, had a population of 70,000, Tenochtitlán had a population between 150,000 and 200,000, with another 300,000 in the suburbs. It is no wonder that the Spanish chronicler Bernal Díaz, traveling with Cortés in 1519, wrote, "It was all so wonderful that I do not know how to describe this first glimpse of things never heard of, seen or dreamed of before." Spanish wonder, however, did not prevent Spanish swords from quickly destroying the magnificent city and culture.

Sophisticated cultures developed along similar lines in the Andes Mountains and along the coastal plains of South America. In the early thirteenth century the Incas emerged as the dominant Andean culture. They also developed a highly complex and organized religion, although it is difficult to reconstruct because they left behind no written records. They also were relatively quickly overthrown by the Spanish, although many Inca folkways are still practiced by Andean cultures.

The African-based spiritist religions of Brazil and the Caribbean arrived with the eleven million slaves who were forcibly transported to the New World after 1530. By the 1820s two-thirds of Brazil was black, both slave and free. For five hundred years African religions have creatively interacted with Roman Catholicism and the animism of indigenous people to form numerous influential religions.

Study Aid #135
Map of Meso- and South America

Candomblé remains perhaps the closest to its African origins. The first known place of formal Candomblé worship emerged in Salvador on the northeast coast of Brazil in 1830. Candomblé proliferated after the end of slavery in 1888 as centers of solidarity for the newly freed blacks struggling to find their way in a still-oppressive culture.

Umbanda, a Yoruban-derived tradition that originated in Rio de Janeiro in the 1920s, is now popular in Brazil and other countries in Latin America. It combines African traditions with Catholicism, Native American traditions, and the brand of spiritist parapsychology inspired by Allan Kardec, a French medium in the mid-1800s. It has been called the first uniquely Brazilian religion.

Finally, in the Amazon, Indian tribes continue to inhabit animist traditions that date back to the first human beings to traverse the continent. While perhaps a comparative few still practice such folkways, the spirituality of these Native Americans continues to feed the vibrant forms of supernatural religion practiced by so many throughout the Americas.

Beliefs

Four core beliefs animated the sacrificial practice of the Aztecs, Maya, and Incas. For humans, sacrifice demonstrated worth and dependence. For the gods, sacrifice called them to their creative tasks and then nurtured them during their labor.

Aztec creation narratives provide a clue to how the cultures of Meso- and South America conceptualized their primary religious task. When the gods conceived the idea of the universe, they first had to prove themselves worthy of so formidable an act of creation through acts of self-sacrifice such as hurling themselves into fire. Sacrifice, then, as a means of proving one's worth, was at the heart of Aztec religious practice. So also was demonstrating dependence. Life could be unstable in the valley of Mexico. The Aztecs learned that gods could be inattentive, even capricious. Consequently, it was very important that the community continually recognize its total dependence on the gods. Sacrifice publicly acknowledged that dependence and demonstrated that humans were worthy of continued favor. But sacrifice also woke up the at-times distracted gods and challenged them to remember their duty to care for their creation. It then nurtured the gods with the food they needed to prosecute their work.

The Indians of Meso- and South America saw themselves as existing in a relationship of mutual dependence with their gods. Human beings were obviously dependent on the gods for sun, rain, harvests, victories in battle, good health, and protection through all the myriad exigencies of daily life. But the gods were also dependent on humans to provide them with the praise that called them to return to their own best vision of themselves as creators and sustainers of life on earth, and with the food that nurtured them through the challenge of these continuing acts of creation. The practices outlined below were based on this essential relationship.

> **Study Aid #136**
> Countries of Meso- and South America
>
> | Mesoamerica (8) | South America (14) | |
> |---|---|---|
> | Belize | Argentina | Guyana |
> | Costa Rica | Bolivia | Paraguay |
> | El Salvador | Brazil | Peru |
> | Guatemala | Chile | Suriname |
> | Honduras | Colombia | Uruguay |
> | Mexico | Ecuador | Venezuela |
> | Nicaragua | Falkland Islands | **Caribbean (24)** |
> | Panama | French Guiana | |

The Aztecs, Incas, and Maya all had a strong sense of destiny and fate. This destiny was intricately tied into the cycles of time, embodied in the yearly round of seasons, planting and harvest, and the larger cycles of birth and death, of rise and fall. Since fate, like time, was cyclical, it could be at least partially determined by paying close attention to the history of what had happened before on certain days or in certain years. One of the largest tasks of the priests was to use their esoteric knowledge of calendars, time, and history to divine how to achieve the maximum good and avoid the evil that clung like barnacles to specific units of time.

The Maya had both a solar calendar of roughly 365 days (eighteen months of twenty days with a nineteenth month of five unnamed and dangerously unlucky days) and a ritual calendar of 260 days (twenty named days repeating in a cycle of thirteen). Each day had certain characteristics according to its place on both calendars. It took fifty-two years for the two calendars to work through all the possible combinations of days. There were nineteen thousand different combinations of characteristics that could influence the prospects of individual days. The recurrence of the same combination of influences could be expected to produce the same effects. All of this kept priests busy calculating the best days for this or that endeavor to be undertaken by either the community or an individual. The sacrificial system, in turn, was fueled because the positive aspects of a given day might be promoted and/or the negative aspects assuaged through the proper sacrifice.

The gods of Meso- and South America were invoked for protection and guidance in this life, not to ensure a specific destiny in the afterlife. The several locations for the afterlife were determined by manner of death, not by manner of life. Everyone was doomed to wander endlessly in the nine levels of the underworld unless their manner of death, such as in war, in childbirth, or on the sacrificial altar, exempted them. Being an exceptionally good person, someone who lived in harmony with their community and the universe, might, however, ensure that one's death came in one of these honored fashions, which then would send one to a more coveted destination in the afterlife.

The central belief of the Afro-Brazilian religions was, and continues to be, that communication between the living and spirits is both possible and desirable. This communication takes place through possession, and its goal is to tap the wisdom of the spirits to provide counsel and to cure the sick. The spirits, or *orixás*, are deities (as in Candomblé) or the spirits of the dead (as in Umbanda) who wander in disembodied state while attempting to work their way to higher levels of wisdom. One way they can do so is to help humans out through acts of charity. The spirits have distinct personalities and desires, physical appetites that must be satisfied by specific foods, dances, even drumming styles. Practitioners learn how to feed the *orixás* with sacrifice and offerings, which then enables the spirit to work effectively on behalf of supplicants to help them solve all manner of everyday problems.

Finally, in Amazonian religions, long protected from contact by the difficulties presented by Amazonian geography, the core belief is that spiritual essence animates the natural world. Shamans mediate between the human and spirit worlds, using their esoteric knowledge, and drugs, to communicate with spirits on behalf of their people. Powerful shamans will move in the spirit world as naturally as they do in the physical world, conversing with spirits they know by name, even having sexual relations with favorite spirits. It can take years of initiation to become a shaman, a role often passed from father to son, mother to daughter. Lengthy prayers must be learned by heart, plants studied for their curative power, ceremonial methods memorized that can last for days. The goal is most often the healing of the sick, although in times of stress shamans will ask the spirits for guidance as to where to find food, how to escape enemies, or even how to deal with the encroachment of outsiders.

Practices

The religious practice that so shocked the Spanish and continues to both fascinate and repel even today was human sacrifice. All three of the dominant cultures at the time of the conquest practiced human sacrifice, although only the Aztecs made it a regular part of their ritual. Whereas human blood was perhaps dessert for the Maya and Inca gods, it was meat and potatoes for Huitzilopochtli.

Quite simply, shedding human blood represented the ultimate demonstration of human worth and of human dependence. It was the most powerful means of summoning the gods to their task, and it provided the most nurturing food to sustain them in that task. It is important to remember that the Aztecs were no more ashamed of their practice of human sacrifice than Christians are of participating in the Eucharist. Shedding human blood was a regular and necessary part of their religious ritual. And everybody in the nation took part, not just captured prisoners. Priests regularly shed their own blood through ritual cutting or piercing with thorns. And these were not paper cuts. After running a large thorn through

> **Study Aid #137**
>
> Indigenous Religions of Meso- and South America
>
> Great traditions
>   Aztec (Central Mexico)
>   Maya (Southern Mexico and Meso)
>   Inca (Andes in Peru)
> Animist tribal religions
> African-based slave religions

their arm, leg, chest, or even tongue or genitals, they would draw a thick knotted rope through the hole and pull it back and forth to enlarge the wound and stimulate regular blood flow. Montezuma himself would have regularly shed his blood for his people.

The cutting out of human hearts on the altar at the apex of pyramids was simply the highest form of such sacrifice, and the victims, as we think of them, often went to their deaths understanding that they were being accorded a great honor. For a captured warrior it was an opportunity to earn honor in death, to offer his life for the sustenance of the earth, and to earn a coveted position in the afterlife. Many victims were feted with celebrations lasting a week or even a year before going to their deaths. Some freely walked under their own power to the altar.

The Aztecs turned human sacrifice into performance art for the entire community. Maybe three thousand to four thousand people per year were offered at the great pyramid in Tenochtitlán, although at the dedication of the temple, whose ruins still stand in Mexico City, there may have been as many as twenty thousand killed in a slowly moving procession that stretched out of the city and onto the causeways to the mainland. Captured warriors were first tethered to platforms where, much as in a bullfight, they demonstrated their bravery while slowly being cut down by up to four opponents. After their death, their flesh was consumed by members of the community. Even little children were sacrificed to the rain-god, the tears of the onlookers stimulating the tears of the god.

Enormous spectacles such as this took place on special ceremonial days, perhaps determined by divination. But human bloodletting and lesser forms of sacrifice, both with animal blood and with various types of produce, took place regularly on a more intimate level. What we might think of as spirituality for most people probably amounted to trying to avert evil or stimulate good in their lives by earning the gods' favor through appropriate sacrificial observances. Many of these would have taken place in consultations with priests over the most propitious time, according to the complex calendars, to engage in a required or desired activity.

Insofar as these cultures had an ethical system, it was based on the connection of all humans in the community to each other and to the rest of the universe. Ethical systems were not built around specific sins that displeased a specific god, or even specific moral actions that pleased the gods. Humans kept themselves and their communities in balance by not overindulging in behaviors that might invite evil consequences by throwing the entire community out of harmony.

The Afro-Brazilian religions also have no specific moral code. The *orixás* do not demand rigid norms of conduct but do expect the faithful to meet ritual obligations, perhaps to avoid certain foods and places during specified times, and to perform required offerings and rites, all in an attempt to ameliorate the worst of what a malevolent deity might have planned and to promote the good that benevolent deities might be coaxed to engage in.

Although there is no institutional church, there are regular meetings wherein the rituals of possession and consultation take place; yet consultation can also occur during private visits. Ceremonies often begin with animal sacrifices to the *orixás*. Initiates process in costumes matching the *orixás*, which will possess the priests or priestesses. At that point the *orixá* is said to ride the human's body like a jockey on a horse, and the person possessed will often take on the characteristics of the deity possessing him or her. At some point during the ceremony, devotees approach the possessed to seek counsel. The offerings left at crossroads and throughout Brazilian cities, at times causing serious trash-collection difficulties, are often the results of such counsel.

In Amazonia, ritual is usually the practice of the shaman as he or she attempts to effect a cure. The ritual involves the chanting of memorized prayers specific to the occasion; the use of various items such as plants, rattles, and so on; and perhaps the blowing of smoke over the body of the afflicted as a means to expel the evil.

Sources

Inga Clendinnen. *Ambivalent Conquests: Maya and Spaniard in Yucatan, 1517–1570.* Cambridge University Press, 1987.

———. *Aztecs: An Interpretation.* Cambridge University Press, 1991.

John D. Early. *The Maya and Catholicism: An Encounter of Worldviews.* University Press of Florida, 2006.

Gary H. Gossen, ed. *South and Meso-American Native Spirituality: From the Cult of the Feathered Serpent to the Theology of Liberation.* Crossroad, 1993.

Charles C. Mann. *1491: New Revelations of the Americas before Columbus.* Knopf, 2006.

Joseph Page. *The Brazilians.* Da Capo, 1995.

Anna L. Peterson and Manuel A. Vásquez, eds. *Latin American Religions: Histories and Documents in Context.* New York University Press, 2008.

Mark Andrew Ritchie. *Spirit of the Rainforest: A Yanomamö Shaman's Story.* Island Lake, 1996.

64

Meso- and South America: Christian Contacts

WILLIAM SVELMOE

Catholicism and Conquest

Christianity came to Meso- and South America behind the roar of cannon fire, the crack of muskets, and the sharp blades of Spanish and Portuguese steel. The religion of the conquistadores overwhelmed the defenses of the native cultures, decimated by European diseases, bloodlust, and the hunger for gold and slaves. That these cultures bowed before the cross of Christ should surprise no one then, and indeed, on the surface statistics demonstrate that the majority of the population today calls itself Christian. What does surprise is the power of native worldviews to provide a unique shape to the continent's Christianization.

There is no necessary reason to believe that the conquistadores and the Franciscans, Dominicans, and Jesuits who followed in their wake were all unfeeling hypocrites when they Christianized native peoples at the point of a sword. The Roman Catholicism they practiced had been forged in the centuries of the reconquest (the *Reconquista*) of Spain from Muslim invaders. Violent religious conversion was simply part of their world, and their impatience with native peoples intent on following their devilish beliefs to hell was undoubtedly real. The shock on the face of Hernán Cortés, when in 1519 Montezuma ushered him into the inner room at the top of the pyramid of Huitzilopochtli and he viewed the blood-spattered walls and the gleaming gods, was real. The bloodbath that followed, after Montezuma refused to immediately agree that his gods were in truth devils, represented both a lust for gold and a religious cleansing. Within two years after initial contact, the Aztec Empire was destroyed.

It took the Spaniards another decade to conquer the now-decentralized Mayan civilization in the Yucatan, but by 1540 the Spanish ruled all of Mexico. Then in 1532, Pizarro, with 168 soldiers backing him, began the long climb into the Andes to confront the Incan Empire. Once again the initial bloodbath was followed by enforced Christianization. The process, however, would not have been a shock to any of these New World cultures. They had all gained their cultural and religious ascendance through force of arms, and they now understood that a more powerful god had subdued their gods. They would accept the new god and the new religion even as many, probably most, interpreted all that they were taught through the lens of their indigenous worldview. Essentially they adopted Christianity into, as much as over, their own religious system.

There were in essence two sides to the Spanish church's approach to Native Americans, a marked division that continues to this day. On one side was perhaps the primary instinct of the church to support the intimate connection between cross and sword, between church and conquering state. At its baldest, this approach is represented by the *Requerimiento* (the "Requirement"), a document read to the Indians before they were attacked. Essentially the document stated the rights of the crown and the church to demand native subjection, and their right to enforce those demands at the point of the sword. The amount of time Indians were given to absorb this information depended largely on the mood of the commanding officer. This side is also represented by the reaction of the Franciscan friars in the Yucatan when they discovered in 1562 that, after decades of missionary effort and seeming compliance on the native side, the Indians were continuing to practice their own religion in secret. Led by Diego de Landa, the Franciscans tortured more than 4,500 Indians and killed at least 150 in what can perhaps best be seen as the violent reaction of a betrayed lover. At its most refined, this approach is represented by the arguments of Sepúlveda in Valladolid in 1550 that the Indians were by nature inferior beings, like children, who needed to be saved from themselves, at the point of the sword if necessary. Whatever methods the church required to force religious conversion and compliance were by definition legitimate.

On the other side was the instinct of many friars to defend the Indians against the worst depredations of the Spanish settlers. Bartolomé de Las Casas is the most famous example of a priest who became a defender of the Indians. His published accounts of Spanish atrocities were read around the world. After decades of defending the Indians, he arrived in Valladolid in 1550 to debate Sepúlveda over the nature of the Indians and, consequently, over how they should be treated. Las Casas argued that Indians were human beings who, having never heard the gospel, should be won by example, not force. The famous Jesuit missions in Paraguay are an example of missionary priests defending the rights of Indians over against those of European colonists. If for no other reason, Catholic missionaries sought to save Indian lives so they might be converted to Christianity before they died.

Although ostensibly defending Indian rights, the friars were often themselves a major source of social disruption. In order to better Christianize the population,

> **Study Aid #138**
> Growth of Christianity in Meso- and South America
> **Mesoamerica**
> 1800: 5 million Christians, 77 percent of population
> 1900: 107 million Christians, 96 percent of population
> 2000: 130 million Christians, 96 percent of population
> **South America**
> 1800: 8 million Christians, 91 percent of population
> 1900: 38 million Christians, 93 percent of population
> 2000: 321 million Christians, 93 percent of population

the friars forced the Indians to relocate into settled communities constructed around a plaza and church. In such communities friars could model Spanish ways of living, enforce new sexual and marital customs, ensure regular catechization, and use Indian labor even as they protected Indians from labor-hungry colonists. Such arrangements worked in many outposts of the Spanish New World empire to regularize Indian devotions, even as many groups continued to practice their own religion away from prying eyes, or melted back into the countryside entirely at the first opportunity.

The Indigenization of Catholicism

To the friars' credit, many made serious attempts to learn Indian languages and to translate basic Christian concepts into indigenous idioms. But that Catholicism eventually thrived in Meso- and South America is perhaps largely due to the Indians themselves. The vision of an Indian peasant became the most powerful symbol of Catholicism's ability to transcend cultural barriers and become truly indigenous. This is the story or legend of Juan Diego and the Virgin of Guadalupe.

Diego's Indian name was Cuauhtlatoatzin. He was a farmer and mat weaver. In his fifties he converted to Christianity and was given the name Juan Diego. The story goes that one morning in 1531, on his way to Mexico City, the peasant was arrested by the sound of his name being called from the top of a nearby hill. It was the Virgin Mary. She asked that a shrine be built on the hill in her honor. Juan carried her message to Bishop Zumárraga, who turned him away numerous times before finally accepting Juan's message after the image of the Virgin of Guadalupe (which resides today behind bulletproof glass in the second-most-visited Catholic shrine in the world, after the Vatican) miraculously appeared on the peasant's cloak. The list of parallels between Guadalupe and Aztec religion are impressive. The Virgin appeared on an Aztec site dedicated to Tonantzin, the virgin mother of the gods. Her skin was brown, her hair dark, and she was dressed as an Aztec princess. She spoke native Nahuatl. She claimed to be the mother of the Indians and sent Juan Diego on a mission of reverse evangelism, in which an Indian attempted to convince the leading Spanish prelate of the truth of his message.

Although the Virgin of Guadalupe remains by far the most significant New World cult of the Virgin, there were many more appearances throughout the Americas by both Mary and other saints, including the Virgin of Caridad in Cuba and our Lady Aparecida in Brazil. Such symbols represented a bonanza for the friars as Indians flocked to adopt them as their own. But they also enabled native peoples to meld Christian deities into their own pantheon of gods, as the saints and Mary were easy to identify with their own preconquest deities. The friars found that the Indians were often only too willing to worship someone new, even as, at times, they were unclear on the proper ranking of such deities, as the nonplussed preachers discovered who found Indians in one village worshiping Satan. It seemed only logical to worship a powerful "deity" who, according to the friars, was intent on doing one harm and had the ability to get one cast into hell. Such a being ought to be appeased in any way possible.

In the early nineteenth century, during the violent independence movements in which Spain lost control of most of its New World colonies, the Virgin of Guadalupe and other such personages became potent symbols for the new nations. Such symbols seemed to indicate that the locus of God's attention and blessing had shifted to the New World, and shrewd commanders wed themselves closely to these images. Today the Virgin of Guadalupe is perhaps the primary mediator of popular Catholicism south of the Rio Grande. There is scarcely a bus or taxi in Mexico that doesn't have a Virgin displayed prominently somewhere. The same could be said for many Latin American countries. She even swings from rearview mirrors in the Philippines. The Catholic Church owes much of its success in Meso- and South America to her.

A similar indigenization took place as Catholic Christianity mixed with traditional African beliefs on the large slave plantations or in the backcountry communities of runaways. Catholic practices, images, saints, and deities were adopted into the prevailing African belief system. Although the mixing probably took place on a more equal level in the communities of escaped slaves, even on the large plantations African belief and ritual could easily be hidden beneath official Catholic practices. Catholic masters were generally less concerned with orthodoxy than were their North American Protestant counterparts, so a potent syncretism was perhaps the natural outcome of the mix of cultures.

Early Protestant Contact

Spain and the Catholic Church worked hard to keep Protestants out of Latin America. They were largely successful until the nineteenth century, outside of a few failed colonial enterprises by Protestant powers such as the English and the

> **Study Aid #139**
> Christian Contacts in Meso- and South America
> **Roman Catholicism**
> Spanish, Portuguese: 1500
> Three approaches
>   Anti-indigenous, e.g., Diego de Landa
>   Pro-indigenous, e.g., Bartolomé de Las Casas
>   Indigenization, e.g., Juan Diego, Virgin of Guadalupe
> **Protestants**
> British, German, American
> Three approaches
>   Evangelical—faith missions
>   Pentecostal—charismatic missions
>   Liberation—praxis missions (Catholic response)

Dutch. After Spain and Portugal lost control of their New World colonies, the Catholic Church continued to exercise tremendous power, even as political control of Latin American countries swung back and forth between liberals, who sought to weaken the church's influence, and conservatives, who saw the Catholic Church as an integral institution for cultural cohesion and elite control. Liberal governments saw religious freedom as essential to the promotion of immigration, and so the nineteenth century saw the first significant Protestant contact with Meso- and South American religions.

Most of the Protestants who came to Latin America in the nineteenth and early twentieth centuries arrived as ethnic religious communities, and as such they had little impact on the surrounding religions. British Anglicans, German Lutherans, and Mennonites had little interest in the evangelization of their hosts. They were looking for good land and guarantees that they could practice their religion in peace. Only African American immigrants to the Dominican Republic and Haiti after the Civil War in the United States saw evangelization as one of their Christian duties. Consequently they assimilated into the surrounding population, while most white Protestant immigrants remained apart from their neighbors. Significant Protestant impact on Latin America waited for evangelicals, fired with the missionary impulse, to turn their attention to a field that for much of the nineteenth century was seen as less attractive than China or Africa.

Evangelical Protestant Missionization

In the nineteenth century the same liberal governments that invited Protestant immigration also welcomed a few Protestant missionaries in an attempt to undermine the Catholic Church's hold over rural populations and over an educational system that liberal leaders felt promoted religious obscurantism. In the nineteenth century the Protestant missionary enterprise was spearheaded by the British and American Bible Societies and focused primarily on scripture distribution. By the end of the nineteenth century some North American denominational missions, primarily the Presbyterians, Methodists, and Baptists, had growing works in Central and South America, often building schools, which satisfied the desire of liberals for alternatives to Catholic education.

By the early twentieth century, independent Protestant missionary organizations, often of the "faith mission" fundamentalist and/or evangelical variety, were flooding into Latin America. Almost all of this early work was carried on in Spanish, with a focus on establishing Spanish-speaking churches. Then in the mid-twentieth century, North American missions in the mold of the Wycliffe Bible Translators and New Tribes Mission began work in the hundreds of indigenous tribal languages throughout Mexico and South America. Wycliffe focused primarily on scripture translation, although indigenous Protestant churches were often a result of such work. While throughout most of the region Protestantism was contacting what was now a largely syncretistic mix of Catholicism and native forms of worship, in remote areas missions like Wycliffe came into contact with indigenous religions and were at times quite successful at turning native peoples into evangelical Protestants, often even to the point where they adopted fundamentalistic North American cultural folkways.

Pentecostalism and Conquest

While the kinds of Protestant work described above certainly gained numbers of adherents throughout the region, the real challenge to the hegemony of the Catholic Church has come in the last fifty years from Protestant Pentecostalism. Pentecostalism, with a worldview easily adapted to indigenous worldviews, will more than likely be *the* story in the region in the twenty-first century. Spreading from North America in the early 1900s, Pentecostalism rapidly indigenized. Aggressively evangelistic, and with a worldview that encourages joyful encounters with the supernatural, Pentecostalism appeals strongly to the disadvantaged. Its spread has been startling, to the point where some estimate that currently almost half of Brazilians, for example, affiliate with a Pentecostal church. Out of a current population in Latin America of 520 million, approximately 170 million attend a Pentecostal or charismatic church.

Sources

Inga Clendinnen. *Ambivalent Conquests: Maya and Spaniard in Yucatan, 1517–1570.* Cambridge University Press, 1987.

Virginia Garrard-Burnett. *Protestantism in Guatemala: Living in the New Jerusalem.* University of Texas Press, 1998.

Ondina E. González and Justo L. González. *Christianity in Latin America: A History.* Cambridge University Press, 2008.

David Martin. *Tongues of Fire: The Explosion of Protestantism in Latin America.* Blackwell, 1990.

Timothy Steigenga and Edward Cleary, eds. *Conversion of a Continent: Contemporary Religious Change in Latin America.* Rutgers, 2007.

William Svelmoe. *A New Vision for Missions: William Cameron Townsend, The Wycliffe Bible Translators, and the Culture of Early Evangelical Faith Missions, 1917–1945.* University of Alabama Press, 2008.

65

Meso- and South America: Theological Exchanges

WILLIAM SVELMOE

The conquest culture that enveloped Meso- and South America in the centuries following the arrival of the Spanish and Portuguese left little room, at least on the surface, for a two-way exchange of theological ideas. Consequently the questions surrounding how Christianity was received, understood, and practiced by the natives has consumed scholars far more than any question of the impact of native religions on Christianity. An examination of the history of such discussions, however, reveals just how complex the relationship between Christianity and the religions native to the region has really been.

The problem of religious identity, especially in the colonial period, is usually framed around questions of success. Earlier scholars, educated from a Eurocentric perspective, asked, "How successful were European missionaries at transplanting their religion to Meso- and South America?" In the past few decades, scholars have turned the question around and asked, "How successful were the native Americans at holding on to their religion under the onslaught of European armor and Catholic culture?" Most scholars today recognize that residents of the region of indigenous or African heritage practice a religion that is both genuinely Christian and genuinely indigenous. There is no agreement, however, on which worldview reigns supreme, although many argue that native people practice a Christianity filtered through what is still a largely indigenous worldview. Mestizo culture, however, is probably largely Catholic Christian, although a Catholicism that has been forced to adapt itself to the folkways of Meso- and South America. Protestantism has made its greatest inroads through the Pentecostal movement, a fact that demonstrates the continuing power of indigenous ways of thinking to force Christian culture to move into channels of the region's own choosing.

A historical analysis of these debates reveals that earlier scholars focused on the Iberian historical actors, specifically missionaries and priests. Consequently their model of cultural flow looked strikingly like a monologue. More recently scholars have attempted to find a larger role for the Indian actors, usually hidden behind the Iberians in the historical script. They have had to use sources creatively since most of the original native material has either been destroyed or not yet deciphered. Consequently they have combed the records of Inquisitorial trials, dusty administrative documents, and even marriage records to try to piece together the remarkable story of resistance to the obliteration of Indian culture and religion. While recognizing the power of the Europeans to change both the physical and mental landscape of the New World, scholars have constructed a model of cultural flow that highlights the dialogue between the conquerors and their native subjects.

The debate may appear, as we so frequently find in the study of history, to be merely a question of emphasis. Even Robert Ricard, who at times seems an apologist for the Catholic Church, recognized that the missionaries were less than successful in many ways. He chose, however, to emphasize the areas in which they succeeded, or at least appeared to have succeeded. Writing in 1933, Ricard was optimistic about the results achieved by the missionaries, and indeed his sources seemed to justify his optimism. Using primarily letters, journals, and records kept by the orders, he found that the missionaries did indeed seem to have been remarkably successful at persuading Indians into the kingdom. Ricard did acknowledge native resistance but characterized it as consisting mainly of "the great force of inertia." He dismissed as "trivial" native objections that it would be folly to set aside the teaching of their ancestors to embrace a religion that destroyed the ancient customs of their people. The return to "sinful" practices on the part of the Mexican neophytes, therefore, did "not imply a systematic resistance" but simply ignorance (Ricard 1966, 264–69). After describing the beating of Indians who failed to attend church, he remarked, "In any event, a strict discipline seemed necessary for the guidance of indolent neophytes" (ibid., 97).

Ricard was specifically disturbed by theories of syncretism. He referred to such theories as "mixed religion," which held that the natives were not truly Catholic but had merely mixed an "entirely formal and superficial Catholicism with their ancient superstitions and traditional rites." Ricard argued that native heterodox notions were actually of European origin, not necessarily a "pagan survival." Ricard accepted that the intent of what might have been pre-Christian forms had now, postconquest, been embodied with Christian intent, so that an action which once honored a pagan god now honored the Virgin (ibid., 276–80).

Thirty years later, writing in 1966, Ricard's translator recorded that Ricard's thesis had never been seriously challenged. The monologue drowned out any opportunity to hear a dialogue.

More recently scholars have argued, however, that even where the missionaries appeared to have been successful, they failed because, lacking "all recognition of the profound and systematic otherness of others" (to use Inga Clendinnen's awkward phrase), "they could have no sense of the difficulties in the way of the reception and understanding of their message" (Clendinnen 1987, 114).

Roger Bastide, writing in 1960, was one of the first to stress the importance of religion as perhaps the one area where an oppressed culture could actively resist the encroachments of the dominant culture, even while outwardly seeming to accept that culture's ideology and forms. Working with African slaves in Brazil, he argued that syncretisms were not simply "mixtures," but were "coherent systems" organized by a repressed culture to adapt their ancient beliefs to new structures (Bastide 1960, 56). Throughout his work, Bastide emphasizes the actions taken by blacks to reinterpret Catholicism in the light of their tribal beliefs. The Catholic saints simply provided a white face for their African gods. Catholicism "superimposed" itself on African religion; it did not "penetrate" that religion. An Afro-Brazilian "visualized the saints and the Blessed Virgin . . . exactly as he visualized his gods or his ancestors, not as bestowers of celestial grace but as protectors of his earthly life." Bastide understood that the two clashing cultures were truly "other" and were therefore bound to interpret each other through their own categories, even as his interpretation perhaps lacked the nuance to be ultimately satisfying (ibid., 128, 141, 68).

More recently Sabine MacCormack approached her complex study of colonial Peru from a similar conceptual framework. She understood that the actors in this "violent confrontation" between opposing religious traditions would of necessity act within the cultural constraints dictated by those traditions. Hence the Spanish priests saw satanic delusion behind much of the native worship practices. It was only natural then for them to seek to stamp out these practices by whatever means necessary. Similarly, when Andean natives converted to Christianity, their Andean religious conceptions did not disappear. They made the new religion their own within the light of their non-Christian cognitive categories. MacCormack formulated the problem brilliantly when she wrote that "Andean conversions to Christianity should . . . be understood as a chapter in the history not only of Christianity but also of Andean religion" (MacCormack 1991, 8–11).

This represents a dynamic conceptual shift from the earlier work of historians like Ricard. Despite the difficulty of finding definitive sources, scholars are now attempting to understand the worldview of this "other" group of human beings and to reconstruct how they would have interpreted the cataclysm within which they found themselves, how they would have understood the strange new religion forced upon them by their conquerors. While they certainly reformulated their beliefs, myths, and rituals, they did not let the Spaniards "modify the categories they recognized as definitive." MacCormack found this essential dichotomy of religious perspective so central and so powerful that she concluded that Peru "became a land of two separate societies between which little cultural exchange was possible" (ibid., 8–11).

Similarly Ramón Gutiérrez doubts the effectiveness of Pueblo conversions "no matter how great the effort" of the friars. The friars interpreted external conformity as true conversion, but Gutiérrez demonstrates the ease with which Indians complied externally while their inner religious landscape remained unchanged. The revolt in 1680 that drove the Spanish from New Mexico simply underlined the deep roots of the ancient Pueblo religion. These works and others emphasize the dialogue between slaves and masters, natives and conquerors, to determine the ultimate shape of colonial society. Slaves and Indians filtered Catholicism through their own worldview, accepted an external compliance of form, but maintained an internal world peopled with their own gods. They added new gods and new ideas where these gods and ideas melded naturally with their heart religion. They rejected, or perhaps never clearly understood, gods and ideas that seemed entirely foreign. Religion provided perhaps the last opportunity for hopeful resistance to the Iberian conquerors, and the indigenous people clung to their religious identity tenaciously.

The question then is naturally raised, Was colonial Meso- and South America really Catholic, or was it its own new hybrid religion? Was it pagan Catholicism or Catholic paganism? And, of course, asking the question of the colonial period begs the question still today, especially in places like Brazil, where we see so much free mixing of all sorts of religious belief, and among indigenous people, wherever they are still found.

Here the Virgin of Guadalupe perhaps gives us some insight into these questions. While a previous essay outlined her story, it is helpful here to reexamine the contexts in which her story is best understood. The first context is the colonial struggle between native religion and Spanish Catholicism. Within a conquest culture, the original vision of Guadalupe represents a compelling attempt by the Indians to reassert the Indians' own needs and desires within their radically changing world. The "Indianness" of the original vision, the fact that the Virgin appeared on the site of one of the Indians' destroyed temples, the aspects of the painting with symbolic appeal to the native worldview, the fact that the vision

---

Study Aid #140

Theological Exchange in Meso- and South America

One-way: European Christianity to Americas
    Can lead to indigenized European theologies
One-way: Indigenous religious resistance
    Can lead to indigenized indigenousness
Two-way? Indigenized Christianity and Indigenous
    Can lead to true contextualization

was given to an Indian who then "evangelized" the Spanish, and the fact that the tradition was carried forward by 150 years of Indian oral tradition before being picked up by mestizos, all point to an Indian origin and an Indian purpose. The cult of Guadalupe served to brilliantly combine the two religious worldviews. Indian gods controlled planting and harvesting, sleeping and rising, fertility, games, indoors, outdoors, pleasure, and pain. Faced with the rather austere Catholic God wielding the theological concepts of sin, judgment, and eternal destiny, the Indians found in Guadalupe a god connected with daily life, a feminine face of concern for their this-worldly pleasure and, more frequently, pain. Moreover, the connection with Mary kept their god officially sanctioned by the church, thereby keeping the Inquisition off their backs. A "Guadalupinist Catholicism," a form of all-pervasive Catholic popular religiosity, became a peculiarly native form of religion throughout the colonial period.

Later, and in similar fashion, Mexican mestizos adopted the Virgin of Guadalupe as a vital symbol in their task of nation building during the revolutionary period, thereby setting up a second context in which the Virgin operated and continues to operate as a symbol of liberation for Mexicans and Latinos. Finally, and here the context connects the present with the past, the Virgin of Guadalupe must be seen in the context of the struggle between official and popular religion. Orlando Espin has argued that "popular Catholicism is the manner in and through which most U. S. Latinos are Catholic," an assessment that would almost certainly hold true for Catholics south of the border as well (Espin 1994, 313). Popular Catholicism today represents a worldview not unlike that of the ancient Indian Guadalupan Catholicism. It is a world largely outside of the institutional church in which the numinous is active in everyday life, in which the gods (read saints and/or Mary much more than God or Christ) are interested and deeply involved in the concerns of the most marginalized people. As Jeanette Rodriguez has argued for Mexican-American women, the religious worldview is for many the only worldview (Rodriguez 1994, 59). Guadalupe functions powerfully in this context as a symbol of a merciful god whose grace is active in everyday life. She communicates where traditional symbols of god are silent and perhaps unapproachable. She touches individual lives in all those deeply personal areas where the institutional church seems to have failed.

Throughout the history of Meso- and South America, then, Catholic Christianity has made inroads into native religious worldviews when it has managed to provide affective and experiential religion. It has struggled to connect where it has remained largely theological and concerned more with eternal destiny than with this-worldly comfort and guidance.

The conflict between religions that focus on this world and a religion that focuses on the next world remains at the core of the disconnect between religions indigenous to the area and Christianity. Insofar as Christianity focuses on one God and the work of Jesus Christ to save souls from eternal damnation, it has largely failed to overthrow the worldviews of indigenous religions that focus on the appeasement of many gods to ensure this-worldly success and community harmony. The religions indigenous to the area had no clear concept of the afterlife and, indeed, paid slight attention to any attempt to gain some sort of bliss that would mark an advanced stage in the life cycle of the soul. Many, in fact, did not view the soul in the Western sense as the individual identity of each human being. The supreme Christian focus, then, on the salvation of the soul has been, from the beginning of the interactions between the two worldviews, decidedly problematic.

Consequently, the Christian focus on the central importance of God the Father and his Son Jesus Christ has often not translated well to indigenous religions that embrace an entire pantheon of gods. If the afterlife is of little concern, it seemed better to focus on the more approachable "gods"—Mary and the saints—rather than the central Christian deity, who seemed largely concerned with an afterlife-focused salvation. For indigenous people, salvation in this life from sickness, drought, and warfare was more important than worrying about some final otherworldly destination. Hence their gods were all intimately involved in the daily exigencies of ordinary life, and, while not particularly loving gods or gods desiring of human love (another concept foreign to indigenous worldviews), they could all be approached with these immediate concerns.

The indigenous easily adopted new deities into their pantheon. They were comfortable with the idea of local and tribal gods, so had no problem adopting new and more powerful tribal gods from others, although such adoption did not of necessity lead to discarding their previous gods. In native pantheons, the more powerful gods were always the more difficult to approach, so the traditional Christian Godhead was marginalized, and the saints and Mary became much more important. The saints became the intermediaries who petitioned God on behalf of his lowly subjects and brought their daily concerns before him.

Miracle stories and myths about the saints, prevalent in medieval Catholicism, also transplanted well to indigenous belief, as did the Catholic focus on festivals and celebrations. These all had natural indigenous correspondents. Christian ethics intersected best with native belief where it focused on community harmony rather than on individual sin with its consequent punishment. Insofar as Christianity is an individual religion, its success has been impaired in native communities. Balance, harmony, outward behavior, especially excessive behaviors, are all more important than concern with the individualistic internal motivations behind behavior. Here again Christianity often struggles to connect with native worldviews.

Perhaps it is easy to see from this discussion why popular, as opposed to official, Catholicism is the primary mode of expression for Hispanics and Meso- and South Americans, and why Pentecostalism is the most powerful religious current sweeping the area today. Both subjects will be addressed in the final essay. Traditional views continue to dominate the religious outlook of indigenous, black, and even mestizo cultures in the region, and Christianity will have to be immediate, affective, sensual, and this-worldly if it hopes to effectively build on its centuries of cultural dominance to genuinely influence the people of the region.

Sources

Roger Bastide. *The African Religions of Brazil: Toward a Sociology of the Interpenetration of Civilizations*. Johns Hopkins University Press, 1960.

Inga Clendinnen. *Ambivalent Conquests: Maya and Spaniard in Yucatan, 1517–1570*. Cambridge University Press, 1987.

Orlando Espin. "Popular Catholicism among Latinos." In *Hispanic Catholic Culture in the U.S.: Issues and Concerns*, edited by Jay Dolan and Allan Figueroa Deck, 308–59. University of Notre Dame Press, 1994.

Gary H. Gossen, ed. *South and Meso-American Native Spirituality: From the Cult of the Feathered Serpent to the Theology of Liberation*. Crossroad, 1993.

Ramón Gutiérrez. *When Jesus Came the Corn Mothers Went Away: Marriage, Sexuality, and Power in New Mexico, 1500–1846*. Stanford University Press, 1991.

Sabine MacCormack. *Religion in the Andes: Vision and Imagination in Early Colonial Peru*. Princeton University Press, 1991.

Robert Ricard. *The Spiritual Conquest of Mexico: An Essay on the Apostolate and the Evangelizing Methods of the Mendicant Orders in New Spain, 1523–1572*. University of California Press, 1966 (1933).

Jeanette Rodriguez. *Our Lady of Guadalupe: Faith and Empowerment among Mexican-American Women*. University of Texas Press, 1994.

66

Meso- and South America: Current Issues

WILLIAM SVELMOE

Interest in religion in Meso- and South America is as intense as it has ever been, perhaps more so. Edward Cleary has written that "religious conversion is the single greatest social process changing Latin America and the Caribbean in the twentieth and twenty-first centuries" (Cleary 2004, 50). And Pentecostalism, while arguably *the* story in religion around the world, let alone in Meso- and South America, is not the only expanding religious movement in the area. Indian and African religions are vigorously adding new adherents. The Catholic Church has responded to its challengers by absorbing many of their worship practices. Indeed, many in the region freely move between all of the aforementioned religious movements, mixing and matching, borrowing where they will, moving as freely out the back door of the church as they did in the front. Meso- and South America seems to be, as it has always been, a region of many gods and of a people who often choose to worship their gods outside of any institutional church.

Indeed the Latin American setting is challenging the very way scholars speak about conversion. What is traditionally seen as a process involving a radical change in beliefs, values, and behaviors is, in this setting, seen by some as a much less radical and dramatic shift. The belief systems that dominate the region, whether popular Catholic, Pentecostal, African, or indigenous, all share certain essential features that have always resided at the core of the Latin American religious experience, features outlined in prior essays, so that conversion from one religion to another, such as it is, involves a much easier passage between ideological systems that share common basic assumptions, and often involves practice of what might seem to be mutually exclusive religions at the same time.

What a Brazilian evangelical pastor observed of religious practice in Brazil perhaps applies to all of Meso- and South America. He noted that, while on the surface Brazil is a Catholic nation, in reality its primary allegiance is to spiritism. Every other religious belief system overlays an essentially spiritist foundation. Or, as the wife of a Brazilian pastor wryly remarked, "People say that Brazil is real receptive to the Gospel. But what we have found is that they are really just receptive to anything. ... They will go to their Catholic Mass on Saturday and their Spiritist meeting on Tuesday. ... They just add [the Gospel] to the other things they already had" (Macharg 2000, 72).

Evangelicals, of course, are not the only group having to deal with the essential syncretism of religious culture in Meso- and South America. In Bolivia some parishioners tote revered skulls, kept year-round in their homes for protection, to a special Catholic Mass for the skulls. This devotion to skull intercession is naturally quite difficult to reconcile with traditional Catholic teaching, but if the church wants to maintain its influence, it has to accept indigenous practices and popular beliefs. As one priest remarked, "I use my time [at the Mass for the skulls] to teach them Christian values and symbols, but I have to watch what I say or the people will get upset" (Smith 2005). The Catholic Church's post–Vatican II crackdown on such popular expressions of indigenous Catholic belief and its attempt to focus devotion on Christ rather than on Mary and the saints has almost utterly failed. Such devotions are too deeply rooted. Today the church has largely abandoned such efforts and has accepted popular religious devotions as a genuine expression of the people.

Although the Catholic Church in Meso- and South America has managed to buck the disastrous decline in number of clergy seen elsewhere in the world, and has actually seen an increase in clergy by 70 percent in the last forty years, there is still a severe shortage of priests. In fact, this shortage has been a mark of the church in Latin America throughout its history. With very little presence of the institutional church in many areas of the region, it should be no surprise that a popular folk Catholicism often mixed with various African-based and indigenous religions is the primary means through which many in the region practice their faith.

The State of the Catholic Church

Throughout its history, the Catholic Church has been a political force, which, while increasing the church's power, becomes problematic when the church is seen as supporting the interests of the powerful over against the weak. Indeed, for most of its history in the region, this is exactly what the church has done. For example, the church explicitly backed Argentinian military officer and politician Juan Perón, to the extent that the belief circulated in Argentina that "true Catholicism is Peronism" (González and González 2008, 167). After that relationship soured, the church supported the military coup that overthrew Perón, but whomever it

> **Study Aid #141**
> Current Issues
>
> Catholic and Pentecostal Syncretistic theologies
> Conversion redefined Eclectic practices

supported, it usually managed to support the party in power. The church feared liberalism, communism, and Protestantism, and close alliances with governments helped to keep those isms at bay, with the result that political violence merged with religious violence in discouraging ways.

This tragic and violent history has often cut the church off from the very people who most needed it. Carolina Maria de Jesus, for example, the slum-dwelling author of *Child of the Dark*, the Brazilian diary that became a publishing phenomenon in the 1960s, was not allowed to enter her local church when she was young because she was illegitimate. Despite the fact that she probably never took the Eucharist, she continued to describe herself as a devout Catholic. As Ondina and Justo González note, "For Carolina and many like her, the church was an institution whose priests occasionally showed up in cars, handed out some food and platitudes, and then climbed back into their cars and drove away to a place far from the hunger and filth" of the favelas. Yet she often wrote of prayer and of God. "One might wonder if, for Carolina, God and the Catholic Church were entities unfamiliar with each other" (ibid., 179).

After Vatican II and the subsequent Latin American bishops' conference at Medellín, Colombia, in 1968, the Latin American church changed a great deal in its outlook. In the context of the violence unleashed on the continent because of the Cold War, and in the context of an official church that found itself alienated from the people it professed to serve, at least some factions of the church took steps to line up on the side of the vast majority of the regions' people, the poor and oppressed. Many in the church began to see the problem of poverty on a continent-wide scale, a continent dependent on foreign markets and investors, so that economic and political decisions were always made to favor foreigners and wealthy elites. They began to demand structural changes and even revolution. At Medellín some bishops broke sharply with a hierarchy that they viewed as giving lip service to solidarity with the poor. While Medellín produced documents that could be read in a number of ways, the conference seemed to commit the church to a more radical role in promoting political, economic, and social change.

One of the most profound developments was Medellín's call for the creation of "base communities," communities of the poor organized to challenge the power and control of elites. At the base communities, parishioners were taught to "see" the problems around them, to "judge" the root causes, and then to "act" to change them. They were taught to read scripture as a lens through which to understand the world around them rather than simply to learn doctrine, a process that radicalized many of the communities. What is now known around the world as liberation theology developed as theologians began to put a similar process into action and called for new ways of studying the central texts of the faith from the perspective of the poor and oppressed rather than from the perspective of elites. This process led to the church's declaring a "preferential option for the poor." God, argued liberation theologians, always sides with the poor in any conflict of interest with the wealthy.

For decades the Catholic Church hierarchy both inside and outside the region fought vigorously against liberation theology in its ranks, often led by the former pope when he was Cardinal Ratzinger. The church feared the Marxist language and tools used in the movement to organize and teach the poor. Although most of the movement's leaders rejected the charge that they were somehow communists, the result of liberation theology was that many church leaders in the region protested vigorously against the cozy relationship between the church and repressive dictatorships and also against the dictatorships themselves. Salvadoran Archbishop Óscar Romero is just the most famous of many who gave their lives in the decades of violence against liberation priests and the poor that resulted from the anticommunist purges led by powerful dictators.

Despite the hierarchy's opposition, liberation theology continues to provide energy to the efforts of priests throughout the region to organize and involve the poor in the church. In 2007 there were eighty thousand base communities in Brazil and one million "Bible circles" that met regularly to discuss scripture from a liberation viewpoint. As theologian Leonardo Boff said, "The force of Latin America's harsh social reality is stronger than Rome's ideology, so the theology of liberation still has a great deal of vitality" (Rohter 2007).

Nevertheless, the theology of liberation and the base communities are not uniformly accepted even by those they are most intended to serve. The movement has split many parishes, as many devout Catholics stubbornly look to the church to be a spiritual haven from the harsh realities of their daily lives. They do not go to church to hear sociological analyses of the structural conditions that underlie the endemic poverty in the region. Most perhaps do not even comprehend much of the message of liberation. They continue to look to their religion, as they have for centuries, to provide relief and solace from the struggles of their daily lives. Ironically this has caused many Catholics to look elsewhere for spiritual comfort, and the elsewhere to which they have often looked is Pentecostalism. As one Brazilian minister remarked in *The New York Times*, "The irony is that the Catholics opted for the poor, and the poor opted for the Evangelicals" (Page 1995, 377).

The Pentecostal Tsunami

The rise and growth of the Pentecostal movement throughout the world was the religious story of the twentieth century, and it will undoubtedly be the story of the twenty-first century as well. This is certainly true in Meso- and South America. Recent surveys suggest that 170 million of the region's 520 million people now call themselves Pentecostal or charismatic, a staggering figure considering the virtual monopoly held by the Catholic Church for centuries. Other studies demonstrate that 36 percent of Chileans and perhaps 47 percent of Brazilians attend Pentecostal churches. Even in Mexico, roughly 13 percent now claim Pentecostal allegiance. The story is primarily of the movement of nominal Catholics into Pentecostalism. In 1960 perhaps two-thirds of Catholics rarely, if ever, attended church, and in the last half century many of these nominal Catholics have either become serious Catholics or converted to Protestant Pentecostalism.

Many reasons can be cited for this impressive growth, but one is certainly primary: Pentecostalism, rather than seeking to transplant a foreign culture to the area, has rapidly indigenized. It adapts well to the folkways of the region and gives room for indigenous leaders to quickly rise. It promotes indigenous worship styles, even indigenous theologies. Pentecostalism grows in large part, in other words, because of its natural connection with the traditional religiosity of the region. It adapts well to African-based and indigenous religious worldviews. Pentecostals don't question that spiritual reality; they simply call it something different. The emphasis on spirit possession and the various manifestations of the spirit are a powerful connection to both African and indigenous worship expectations, as are worship forms involving rhythmic movements of the body and repetitive phrases.

The emphasis on religion as a central means to find physical healing, as an avenue to financial prosperity, and as a promoter of devotion to God in order to gain benefits in *this* life—these all resonate powerfully with the central tenets of the religions indigenous to the area. Pentecostalism speaks to impoverished people who need a community and a divinity that will focus on their daily needs, both psychological and physical. As one Brazilian Presbyterian pastor argued, "The main appeal [of the Pentecostals] is that they present a God that you can use. Most Presbyterians have a God that's so great, so big, that they cannot even talk with him openly, because he is far away. The Pentecostal groups have the kind of God that will solve my problems today and tomorrow. People today are looking for solutions, not for eternity" (Macharg 2000, 71). Pentecostals in the region focus much of their communal energy on resisting the devil. The devil is blamed for many physical and psychological troubles. The casting out of devils can be very therapeutic in an area where health care for the poor is extremely inadequate. Exorcising Satan blames such problems on someone else—not on unmovable government structures but on a devil who can be defeated by a community of humans united in prayer. And such a focus both competes with and complements African and indigenous religious worldviews and emphases.

The joyful, even boisterous, worship style of Pentecostalism also provides a strong attraction to religious folk who love pageantry and lively music and singing. Recognizing the importance of this, much Catholic worship now apes Pentecostal styles. A recent study estimated that roughly half of Brazilian Catholics are charismatic. Catholic Masses are often filled with dancing crowds singing and clapping. Even the mainline Protestant churches in the region that are growing are almost all involved to some extent in Pentecostal types of experiences with the Holy Spirit and fervent worship styles.

Although some recent studies seem to indicate that Pentecostal numbers have plateaued, the movement shows all the signs of continuing to be a vital player in the region's religious identity in the twenty-first century. Pentecostalism almost perfectly combines elements of traditional Christianity and indigenous religious worldviews in a way designed to attract the fervently religious people of Meso- and South America. In addition, its aggressive proselytizing promises to keep converts rushing in the front door even as, in fairly large numbers, the high demands placed on adherents keep the less than faithful slipping out the back.

Return to Indigenous Religions

The truly indigenous religions of Meso- and South America are also seeing a resurgence of popularity. Along with all manner of New Age movements, the counterculture in North America has embraced a kind of hip shamanism since the 1970s. Carlos Castaneda was only the most popular of a number of such author-practitioners.

More important in the Latin American setting has been the increasing prominence of indigenous movements seeking political rights and control of their lands and culture. As part of a struggle to recover their identity, indigenous groups have embraced their ancient religions. Mayan ruins have once again become places of worship. Traditional rituals have been revived throughout what was once the Inca Empire. Such movements have already begun to raise serious questions for Christian churches. How much of such indigenous worship practices should Christianity seek to incorporate as a way of validating indigenous peoples, especially in the context of North American colonialism? Some Protestant churches that have traditionally demanded the complete abandonment of such beliefs and practices are now struggling with the question of perhaps admitting traditional beliefs, practices, and ceremonies into their own worship. It is likely that in the years ahead, churches will split over such questions. New hybrid religions may be created, a fitting testimony to the continuing influence of the indigenous religions of Meso- and South America.

Sources

Edward L. Cleary. *How Latin America Saved the Soul of the Catholic Church*. Paulist Press, 2009.

———. "Shopping Around: Questions about Latin American Conversions." *International Bulletin of Missionary Research* 28, no. 2 (April 2004): 50–54.

Ondina E. González and Justo L. González. *Christianity in Latin America: A History*. Cambridge University Press, 2008.

Ken Macharg. "Brazil's Surging Spirituality." *Christianity Today*, December 4, 2000, 70–72.

Joseph A. Page. *The Brazilians*. Da Capo, 1995.

Larry Rohter. "As Pope Heads to Brazil, a Rival Theology Persists." *New York Times*, May 7, 2007.

Fiona Smith. "To Bolivians, Skulls Good Luck." *South Bend Tribune*, November 10, 2005.

Timothy J. Steigenga and Edward L. Cleary, eds. *Conversion of a Continent: Contemporary Religious Change in Latin America*. Rutgers University Press, 2007.

Part 4

New Religious Movements

67

New Religious Movements (NRM) Introduction

Terry C. Muck

New religious movements, as the "new" implies, refers to groups that have grown up in modern cultures in the past two hundred years. Wherever there are modern cultures, there are new religious movements; wherever there are new religious movements, there are modern cultures.

A modern culture has a number of features, including

- a reliance on rationalistic models of thinking,
- a dependence on the scientific method,
- leadership based on the authority of office, and
- a bias toward market economics.

In terms of new religious movements, however, one feature of modernity is paramount. To use a sociological term, modern cultures are differentiated. That is, modern cultures have a number of systems that are both dependent on one another and independent of one another: a political system, an economic system, a social system, a cultural system, a personality system, and a behavioral system.

New religious movements tend to find their reason for being in one or another of these six systems. The majority, of course, tend to come from the cultural system, where they are derivatives of traditional religions or world religions. Transcendental Meditation, for example, is rooted in Hinduism but transplanted to Western therapeutic culture. The Church of Jesus Christ of Latter-Day Saints is a reinterpretation (or recovery?) of Christian history, belief, and practice.

> **Study Aid #142**
> Types of New Religious Movements
>
> Christian derivatives
> World religion derivatives
> Nature religions
> A-religions
>
> Psychological religions
> Secular religions
> Social religions

Some new religions come from the social system. Their reason for being is to augment social systems designed to allow people to live together harmoniously. Freemasonry, for example, is sometimes described as a social club, where its raison d'être is to encourage community. However, it uses religious terminology, derived largely from Christianity, to build that community. As a result, Freemasons insist that they are just a social club, but others wonder about their use of religion and its terminology.

Other new religions have political emphases. Christianity and civic religion in the United States, for example, share political symbols such as flag, country, patriotism, and holidays to encourage a sharper identity between God and country. Christian Identity, on the other hand, is a new religious movement that uses political symbols as a form of resistance to prevailing political patterns.

A few new religious movements seem most at home using economic symbolism. The most outstanding twentieth-century example would be Marxism, an ideology based on an economic deprivation metaphysic. Some economic groups, such as the Landmark Forum, exist to elevate participation in market capitalism to a religious level. Some would say that all religions in modern cultures are heavily influenced by market economics. One example might be what some Christians call the prosperity gospel.

Western therapeutic cultures have tended to elevate individualism to premier status. The resulting nature of personality has led to the popularity of religions such as Scientology and the human potential movement, both of which consider peoples' health as the Holy Grail of modern living.

Finally, the revival of some ancient indigenous religions, such as neopaganism, represents attempts to reclaim an almost biological identification with nature and our genetic core. These old/new religious movements rely on instinct- and intuition-based epistemologies, and the web of all being as a metaphor of existence.

Religion in differentiated modern cultures plays a dual role. It provides both meaning and motivation. Traditionally, of course, religion has always provided meaning to human adherents. In fact, Talcott Parsons considered religion to be perhaps the first adaptive response human beings had to unexplained, seemingly random suffering: disease, death, natural disasters, and so on. And throughout human history and across human religious-symbol systems, one can see religion enabling us to better cope with and control our environment.

In the modern era, however, religion provides an additional coping function (in addition to the traditional ones), which we might encapsulate with the word "integration." Although the differentiation of modern cultures provides enormous adaptive capacity, it also creates an unintended consequence. Fragmentation of the social system leads to the loss of an integrating center, which in turn leads to a potential loss of meaning and results in growing existential anxiety.

In such a social system, religious-symbol systems succeed or fail based on the extent to which they can integrate diffuse, competing meanings and thus relieve anxiety. The economic system, for example, tells me that meaning comes from making money; the political system tells me that meaning comes from power acquisition; the cultural and personality systems tell me that meaning comes from group and personal identity formation.

Religion helps adherents cope with the confusion created by multiple meanings. Many of the new religious movements use one or another of these social systems as a centering place for integrating multiple meanings. Freemasonry, for example, addresses existential loneliness by creating a social club, using religious symbolism as a way of further stressing its importance.

In the process of interpreting meanings, new religious movements also provide motivation for social actors and their acting. Why go against my own economic or political interest to create better social conditions? The answer for some is because my religious myth describes for me the value of such an action and thus provides me with the motivation to act on it.

The ways that new religious movements create integrated meanings and motivations vary along two further axes. In addition to choosing one of the six social locations as primary (political, social, economic, cultural, personality, or behavioral), new religious movements can either embrace or resist current religious forms in these spheres (and choose to reform, revitalize, or reject them), and new religious movements can either embrace or resist the temptation to try to organize the social spheres themselves.

Consider, for example, the two new religious movements we chose to represent the economic system: Marxism and the Landmark Forum. Karl Marx saw his teachings as resisting and revolutionizing the current bourgeoisie dominance of economic production. "Workers of the world, unite!" he said, and he advocated an overthrow of current rulers. The Landmark Forum, on the other hand, fully embraces the prevailing economic form—market capitalism—and encourages adherents to take full advantage of it.

Consider another system, the cultural system, the usual location of the traditional historic religions, including Christianity. The new religious movement the Church of Jesus Christ of Latter-Day Saints (Mormons) embraces Christianity but seeks to restore it to what it sees as its original form and intent. Satanism, on the other hand, exists primarily to counter every Christian value and advocates the elevation of what could accurately be described as anti-Christianity.

New religious movements embody the trend that sees the relationship to the ultimate as no longer the monopoly of the historic religions" (Bellah 1991). Religious symbolism emerges from everywhere in the modern social system—in political speeches, in television advertisements, and in pop culture songs and imagery. Many of the religions of this system are the organizations and institutions that have emerged and are emerging from this movement moving us all toward an embrace of domesticated transcendence.

Source

Robert N. Bellah. "Religious Experience." In *Beyond Belief*. University of California Press, 1991 (1970).

68

NRM: Christian Derivatives Introduction

TERRY C. MUCK

In Western culture, particularly the United States, many of the new religious movements we encounter are derived from Christian teachings. The reason for this may seem at first simple: Christianity is the dominant religion in Western cultures, and when it comes time to think about new religions, people in such a culture naturally choose to use the religious materials available to them.

Some sociologists, such as Rodney Stark, however, have added to this commonsense truism. When people spend their lives, Stark avers, building up spiritual capital in one religious tradition, they are more likely to change to another religious system if they can take some of that hard-won religious capital and expertise with them. Most Christians, that is, who for one reason or another have decided to change religions, don't want to change *everything* about their religion. They want to retain as much as possible from the religious life they have worked all their life building.

Thus it is no mistake that when Christians in the United States decide it is time for a religious change, they tend to choose one of the three largest of the new religious movements in the United States: Mormonism, Christian Science, and Jehovah's Witnesses. These three religions teach widely different approaches to connecting our everyday, mundane worlds to the eternal realm of transcendence, but all three have deep roots in Christianity.

In fact, all three continue to consider the Christian scriptures, the Bible, as the revealed and holy word of God. In addition to the Bible, however, all three add a second book as equally authoritative. Mormons have the Book of Mormon, which they consider a revelation of God received by their founder, Joseph

> **Study Aid #143**
>
> People of the Second Book
>
> Church of Jesus Christ of Latter-Day Saints (Mormons): Book of Mormon
> Christian Science: *Science and Health with Key to the Scriptures*
> Jehovah's Witnesses: New World Translation of the Bible

Smith. Likewise, Christian Scientists believe their founder, Mary Baker Eddy, to have written a book, *Science and Health with Key to the Scriptures*, as a guide to properly understanding the Bible. Jehovah's Witnesses don't have a separate book per se, but they do have a special English translation of the Bible, the *New World Translation*, that makes clearer, they think, some of the key teachings of their faith. Because of these literary additions, sometimes these new religious movements are called Religions of the Second Book.

Another common feature of these three new religious movements: They do not consider themselves new in the sense that many of us do. Mormons, Christian Scientists, and Jehovah's Witnesses all consider themselves heirs to the original and most faithful intent of Christian teachings. They all believe, for one reason or another, that the teachings of Jesus have become corrupted, lost, or muted over time. For one reason or another, Christianity has taken a wrong turn, and these traditions get Christianity back on the right track.

69

Church of Jesus Christ of Latter-Day Saints: History, Beliefs, Practices

CRAIG BLOMBERG

In the spring of 1820, the fourteen-year-old Joseph Smith Jr., living in Palmyra, New York, in light of James 1:5–6, had been praying to God for wisdom as to which church to join, after preachers from several denominations had held revivals in the area. As he later recounted, he walked to a nearby grove and had a vision of Father and Son as separate men, but identical in appearance, telling him to join no existing church but await further revelation. An angel, Moroni, then appeared to him in 1823 and promised he would later dig up a book of golden plates, which he claimed to do in 1827 at the adjacent hill of Cumorah. Using special eyepieces for inspiration, he dictated to a scribe the meaning of the writing, which he described as in the "reformed Egyptian" language. He then had to return the plates to the angel for safekeeping. The result was the 1830 publication in English of the Book of Mormon.

The story the book narrates is of the migration of ancient Hebrew peoples across Africa and the Atlantic to settle in the Americas. Episodes of life on this continent between roughly 600 BCE and 420 CE ensue. Not long after his death and resurrection in Israel, Jesus appears in the New World as well, so that people in this hemisphere also have a chance to receive the gospel. The faithful become known as Nephites, and the rebellious as Lamanites (the supposed ancestors of the American Indians). A succession of wars between the two groups eventually leads to the extinction of the Nephites, but the plates of their history are first buried for safekeeping by Moroni, son of the last Nephite general, Mormon.

Study Aid #144
Mormon Timeline

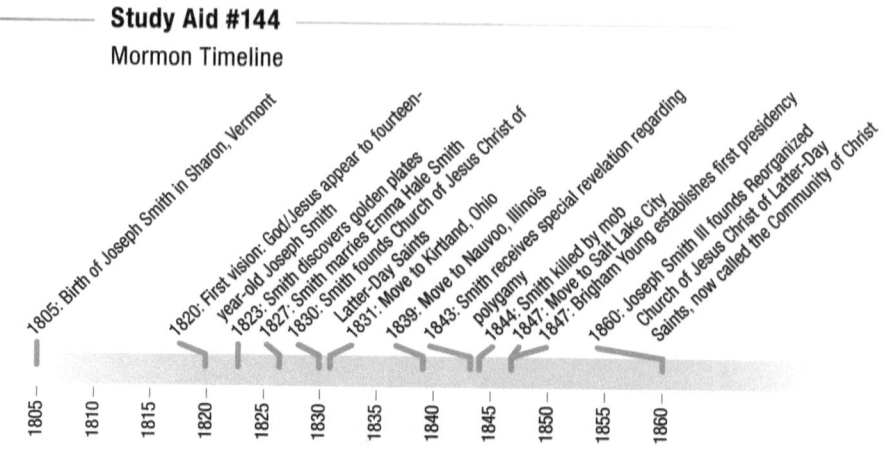

In April 1830 Smith and five followers reconstituted what they called the first Christian church on earth, with full divine authority since the twelve apostles had died. In between had come "the Great Apostasy," in which Christ's delegated priesthood had been lost. The Reformation recovered many true Christian doctrines that Eastern Orthodoxy and Roman Catholicism had corrupted, but not the "keys of the kingdom" originally given to Peter. This required the Restoration of the nineteenth century.

The decade of the 1830s proved turbulent for the fledgling Mormons, more officially known as the Church of Jesus Christ of Latter-Day Saints (LDS). LDS claims tended to polarize people; one either supported them or found them heretical, which often led to persecution. Key centers for the Mormon church moved westward—to Kirtland, Ohio; Independence, Missouri (where Christ is to return); and Nauvoo, Illinois. The movement was highly evangelistic from the outset, sending missionaries throughout the United States and Britain. Within a decade, LDS numbered around twenty thousand.

Until Smith founded Nauvoo as a theocracy that he governed as mayor, his theology, while radically Arminian, did not challenge the heart of Christianity. Because of his "First Vision," he did believe that God was embodied and that Jesus was the literal Son of his heavenly Father. He questioned the ontological unity of the persons of the Godhead and deplored that brand of salvation by grace that appears to require no substantially transformed living. But language of Father, Son, and Holy Ghost as one God and salvation by grace through faith permeates the Book of Mormon. In Nauvoo in the early 1840s, however, Smith would elaborate his beliefs, most notably in his funeral oration known as the King Follett Discourse, that God was once a man like we are and that humans could become like God is now. It was in Nauvoo that polygamy became clearly enmeshed with the church, and here that Smith increasingly distanced himself from the American government. Finally, in 1844, he was arrested, taken to the jail at Carthage, Illinois, and there murdered by a marauding mob.

Mormons subsequently split over who would succeed Smith. A small minority wanted to follow his son, Joseph III, and remained in the Midwest, forming the

---

Study Aid #145

Mormon Beliefs

Basic Mormon beliefs are expressed in the Thirteen Articles of Faith, which were listed by Joseph Smith when he was asked about the church's basic beliefs:

> We believe in God, the Eternal Father, and in His Son, Jesus Christ, and in the Holy Ghost.
>
> We believe that men will be punished for their own sins, and not for Adam's transgression.
>
> We believe that through the Atonement of Christ, all mankind may be saved, by obedience to the laws and ordinances of the Gospel.
>
> We believe that the first principles and ordinances of the Gospel are: first, Faith in the Lord Jesus Christ; second, Repentance; third, Baptism by immersion for the remission of sins; fourth, Laying on of hands for the gift of the Holy Ghost.
>
> We believe that a man must be called of God, by prophecy, and by the laying on of hands by those who are in authority, to preach the Gospel and administer in the ordinances thereof.
>
> We believe in the same organization that existed in the Primitive Church, namely, apostles, prophets, pastors, teachers, evangelists, and so forth.
>
> We believe in the gift of tongues, prophecy, revelation, visions, healing, interpretation of tongues, and so forth.
>
> We believe the Bible to be the word of God as far as it is translated correctly; we also believe the Book of Mormon to be the word of God.
>
> We believe all that God has revealed, all that He does now reveal, and we believe that He will yet reveal many great and important things pertaining to the Kingdom of God.
>
> We believe in the literal gathering of Israel and in the restoration of the Ten Tribes; that Zion (the New Jerusalem) will be built upon the American continent; that Christ will reign personally upon the earth; and, that the earth will be renewed and receive its paradisiacal glory.
>
> We claim the privilege of worshiping Almighty God according to the dictates of our own conscience, and allow all men the same privilege, let them worship how, where, or what they may.
>
> We believe in being subject to kings, presidents, rulers, and magistrates, in obeying, honoring, and sustaining the law.
>
> We believe in being honest, true, chaste, benevolent, virtuous, and in doing good to all men; indeed, we may say that we follow the admonition of Paul—We believe all things, we hope all things, we have endured many things, and hope to be able to endure all things. If there is anything virtuous, lovely, or of good report or praiseworthy, we seek after these things.

Reorganized Church of LDS (today the Community of Christ) and choosing not to accept some of Smith Jr.'s most recent and controversial emphases. The vast majority followed Brigham Young, who, beginning in 1847, led about sixteen thousand LDS on a wagon trip westward, across the Rockies. They finally settled in Utah's Great Salt Lake Basin, after hardships killed one-third of those who began the trek.

For three decades, Young ruled over the religious and political hierarchies of Utah (prior to its statehood) until his death in 1877. During these years, the prevailing vision was for the faithful worldwide to come to Utah to build "Zion" on earth—a theocratic kingdom completely obedient to God. Mormons were encouraged to become self-sufficient people in every area of life, which heavily contributed to the perception that they believed in salvation by good works. Polygamy flourished, but was increasingly opposed by the rest of Americans. In 1890, six years before Utah became a state, it was officially outlawed by the LDS church through a "revelation" from the church president and prophet Wiliford Woodruff.

The twentieth century saw the steady growth and increasing mainstreaming of Mormons into American society. With a handful of unofficial exceptions, today they strongly promote patriotism and monogamous family values, two crucial about-faces from their earlier history. From roughly two hundred thousand members in the late nineteenth century, they have grown to over fourteen million worldwide, with slightly more than half living outside the United States.

To understand the evolution of the LDS, one has to recognize that an official decree of a current church president trumps all previous "revelation." Whereas historic Christianity consistently seeks biblical support for changes it desires to make in faith or practice, returning to the canonical sources is less crucial for Mormons. Thus despite Book of Mormon teaching that blacks were cursed with their skin color for the disobedience of their ancestors and thus ineligible for the LDS priesthood, a 1978 revelation overturned that prohibition.

Current beliefs that deviate to some degree from historic Christianity on central doctrinal topics include the conviction that not only the (King James Version) Bible but also the Book of Mormon, the Doctrine and Covenants (mostly a series of revelations to Joseph Smith about circumstances related to the early years of the LDS), and the Pearl of Great Price (including the Book of Abraham, supposedly translated from ancient scrolls that Joseph Smith purchased from a traveling salesman, other parts of which have been preserved but reflect ancient Egyptian funerary prayers) are inspired, canonical authorities. As already noted, God the Father is embodied. Humans were all once disembodied spirit beings in a premortal existence. Life on earth tests people to determine what kind of eternal life they will experience.

The fall of Adam and Eve was necessary to institute this probationary period, with the freedom to choose good or evil. Those who accept the Mormon gospel, either in this life or the next, who have lived worthy lives, and are baptized into the LDS church (or by proxy by a living member if they have already died) will attain to the celestial kingdom (the most glorious of three available to resurrected humans). They will continue evolving in their godhood, though always remaining subordinate to and dependent on Jesus and God. Only a small minority of the most incorrigible will experience an eternal hell.

At the same time, the LDS shares many central doctrines with Orthodox, Catholics, and Protestants: We are sinners in need of salvation, which can come only through Jesus Christ, God's Son, who died a substitutionary, atoning death on our behalf, was bodily raised from the dead, and will return a second time in glory to end this world as we currently know it. Mormon ethics mirror conservative Christian ones and add abstinence from alcohol, coffee, and tea. Marriage is strongly encouraged and even required for greatest eternal bliss.

Mormons worship weekly, on Sunday mornings, in local churches, while temples are reserved for weddings (sealing couples for "both time and eternity"), baptisms for the dead, and temple endowments (prophetic words spoken to guide their lives). The church is elaborately hierarchical, with the president overseeing a Quorum of Twelve Apostles, under which serve regional leaders in groups of "Seventies," followed by bishops who lead a given "stake"—a geographical area composed of a number of "wards" (akin to local parishes). There are no professional clergy, but all faithful LDS men who have come of age may serve as priests, exhorting the faithful and administering the sacraments (water baptism by immersion and the Lord's Supper, using bread and water).

Today, while Utah remains the most heavily LDS part of the world, Zion is built wherever the faithful gather. Over 130 temples worldwide allow devoted Mormons to serve God fully almost wherever they reside. LDS have distinguished themselves in every branch of professional life, in politics, the arts, and education. Salt Lake City's Mormon Tabernacle Choir is internationally renowned, as is the nearly thirty-five-thousand-member Brigham Young University in Provo, Utah.

Further Reading

Book of Mormon. Church of Jesus Christ of Latter-Day Saints, 2003.

Matthew Bowman. *The Mormon People: The Making of an American Faith.* Random House, 2012.

Richard Bushman. *Mormonism: A Very Short Introduction.* Oxford University Press, 2008.

Quincey Newell, Eric Mason, and Jan Shipps. *New Perspectives in Mormon Studies.* University of Oklahoma Press, 2013.

David Rowe. *I Love Mormons.* Baker Books, 2005.

70

Church of Jesus Christ of Latter-Day Saints: Theological Exchanges, Current Issues

CRAIG BLOMBERG

History discloses a very checkered past of Mormon interaction with historic Christianity. Joseph Smith believed that God and Jesus appeared to him, instructing him to join no existing Christian denomination. In his canonized autobiography, he gave their reason: all the creeds were abominations to the Lord, and all who professed allegiance to them were corrupt (History 1:19). When he approached a local Methodist minister about this vision, he was told it was of the devil because visions and revelations from God had ceased after the time of the apostles (1:21). Mormonism, on the other hand, has always rejected "cessationism," believing in ongoing revelation and an open canon.

Not surprisingly, the main forms of theological interaction between LDS and traditional Christians during Smith's lifetime were evangelistic. Mormons sought to persuade others to join what Smith called "the only true and living church upon the face of the whole earth" (Doctrine and Covenants 1:30). On the one hand, Smith often made very magnanimous statements about elements of truth and goodness that could be found in other faith communities, and not just Christian ones. On the other hand, he insisted that only LDS had priesthood authority restored to them, and therefore only baptism into the LDS church could usher one into the highest, celestial kingdom in the life to come.

Smith's increasing support for polygamy, his mixed signals concerning his respect for the American government, and various allegations of financial malfeasance

> **Study Aid #146**
> Contacts with Other Christians
>
> Joseph Smith's early antidenominationalism
> Mormon evangelistic efforts
> Conflicts: polygamy, theocracy
> Lack of ecumenical acceptance
> Worldwide missionary proselytizing
> Recent dialogues
> From cult to sect to church

against him and other church leaders all made the early Mormons an easy target for persecution on the part of the more traditional Christian world. This persecution ranged from interpersonal hostility, to discriminatory legal practices, to occasional vigilante actions, like those culminating in Smith's murder. On occasion, Mormons returned the "favor," most notably in the 1857 Mountain Meadows massacre, in which then-president Brigham Young's orders not to interfere with non-LDS immigrants to Utah arrived too late to prevent local church leaders from killing 120 unarmed men, women, and children in an arriving wagon train.

Young's desire to rule a theocracy in Utah did not lend itself to theological dialogue with members of other denominations or religions, nor were there many nearby with whom to converse. All this began to change in the 1890s with the church's subsequent outlawing of polygamy and Utah's statehood. In 1899, the prominent Christian evangelist Dwight L. Moody even preached in the Mormon Tabernacle in Salt Lake City.

In the early part of the twentieth century, the best-known sustained "ecumenical" theological exchange involved LDS president B. H. Roberts and Catholic priest Cyril van der Donckt. The published form of their exchanges appeared as *The Mormon Doctrine of Deity*, although it was heavily skewed in the direction of Mormon theology by virtue of the amount of text given to each writer.

As the twentieth century progressed, groups like the World Council of Churches and the National Council of Churches (in the United States) came into their own, embracing almost all professing Christian denominations with the notable exceptions of most uniformly evangelical ones and sectarian groups like the LDS. Despite their willingness to broaden considerably the theological criteria for what was truly "Christian," repeated theological investigations by the mainline, conciliar churches concluded that the LDS were heterodox. Baptism into the LDS church was not sufficient for membership in historic Protestant congregations should a Mormon wish to "convert," just as no form of historic Christian baptism sufficed for membership among the LDS for proselytes to Mormonism.

For the most part, no comparable, official evangelical investigations into LDS belief and practice occurred. But the 1970s and 1980s saw the numerical growth, financial prosperity, and political influence of evangelicals catapult them into national limelight. Not coincidentally, these decades also produced the growth of numerous "countercult" ministries that targeted newer offshoots of major world

> **Study Aid #147**
> Current Issues
>
> Nature of Godhead, Trinity Salvation/exaltation Modern revelation
> Status of Jesus and deity Glorification

religions viewed as threats to historic Christian theology, not least because of the converts they were gaining from conservative Christian churches, particularly overseas. Prominent among these "cults," as they were often called, were the Mormons. Many knew them best (or only) for their missionaries—young men sent out in pairs, dressed in white shirts, ties, and name badges, riding bicycles, and going door-to-door to try to generate interest in the LDS faith. Overseas, LDS missionaries found by far their greatest success in proselytizing new evangelical Christians, still young in their faith. LDS strategy, at home and abroad, increasingly involved playing down their doctrinal distinctives, emphasizing shared moral and political concerns, promising not to take away any of the good that people had already experienced as Christians but merely to add to and complete what they had already received.

Evangelicals were understandably distraught. In the United States as many as one-quarter of new LDS converts were former members of their churches. The ministries and publications of Walter Martin and Gerald and Sandra Tanner became the best known in highlighting the heterodox doctrines of Mormonism, disputing its claim to be a fully Christian movement and refuting its insistence on being the one, true church. Smaller, like-minded ministries, often parachurch in nature, did not all prove equally accurate or charitable in their rhetoric, and tensions between evangelicals and Mormons began to heighten.

The 1990s and the 2000s brought a thaw in relationships, at least on some fronts. LDS president Gordon B. Hinckley was continuously advocating the "mainstreaming" of Mormons in the societies in which they lived. Evangelicals found LDS political candidates and platforms amenable to their own. Serious, respectful theological dialogue emerged with the publication of Stephen Robinson's and Craig Blomberg's *How Wide the Divide?* A decade-long project by liberal Protestant Donald Musser and LDS philosopher David Paulsen culminated in their coedited *Mormonism in Dialogue with Contemporary Christian Theologies*. David Rowe's *I Love Mormons* reflected a kinder, gentler evangelicalism in its desire to build bridges with the LDS world. A model of interreligious dialogue is presented in Robert Millet and Gerald McDermott's *Evangelicals and Mormons: Exploring the Boundaries*.

Perhaps most significantly, a series of semiannual private meetings gathered key Mormon and evangelical scholars for talks on most all the central issues that divided their communities. A number of resulting publications brought both LDS and evangelical writers together, some based on public conferences as well. At the forefront of many of these events were Fuller Seminary president Richard Mouw and Brigham Young University religious studies professor Robert Millet.

A key difficulty in all these gatherings and projects involved the pressure participants felt by those within their own communities to take a quite different tack. Sadly, countercult ministries deplored whatever seemed not to be overtly evangelistic, but rightly stressed that without the involvement of LDS church authorities in such clarifying conversations, no agreements among scholars necessarily counted for anything. Church authorities, for their part, did not much help the process along. While, by the end of the 2000s, a few had in fact begun to participate in some such gatherings with evangelicals, the majority did not and even occasionally took steps easily perceivable as antagonistic to the process.

Meanwhile, small LDS apologetics organizations with acronyms like FARMS and FAIR functioned as a kind of Mormon equivalent to the evangelical countercult industry. Most LDS, however, are pure fideists. They have a "testimony," a subjective conviction that the Book of Mormon is true and that therefore Joseph Smith was a true prophet of God, so that everything else they believe flows from these foundational convictions.

The situation at the beginning of the 2010s thus remains uncertain. A growing openness among evangelicals to consider at least some individual Mormons as bona fide Christians clearly exists, especially those whose views fall into what some have labeled a Mormon "neoorthodoxy": a clearer affirmation of the eternity of the Godhead, a kind of social trinitarianism, the seriousness of the fall and the depth of human sin, the sizable gap that separates Creator and creature, the full deity of Christ, substitutionary atonement and bodily resurrection, the possibility of salvation and even exaltation outside of the LDS church, the need for grace through faith to be the animating principle that saves anyone even if it must of necessity produce good works and more-godly living, and glorification as the reception of God's communicable attributes only, not confusing the ontology of deity and humanity. Evangelicals, for their part, have rediscovered patristic theology, thus leading some to recognize a proper place for the theosis ("deification") of believers, rightly defined, while serious Wesleyan-Arminian theology (much closer to LDS thought than Calvinism) has also made a comeback.

Whether anything akin to a "Vatican II" (among Catholics), on however small a scale, will ever result in official LDS clarification of which views are and are not acceptable within this church's orbit remains to be seen. Apart from some such official pronouncements, evangelical suspicion that the LDS church authorities reject the views of Robinson, Millet, and their theological kin will remain. Precisely because evangelicalism has no comparable magisterium, even with such pronouncements, some traditional Christians may never be convinced. But the analogies with evangelical-Catholic relationships suggest that a lot of good could result.

71

Church of Jesus Christ of Latter-Day Saints: Adherent Essay

ROBERT L. MILLET

My paternal grandfather met the Mormon missionaries and was baptized in the 1930s near New Orleans, Louisiana. I was born in Baton Rouge in 1947 and brought up as a Latter-Day Saint. After completing a full-time LDS mission in the late sixties, I transferred from Louisiana State University to Brigham Young University, where I received both a bachelor's and a master's degree in psychology. I later completed a PhD in religious studies at Florida State University and joined the Brigham Young University religion faculty in 1983. I have served as chair of the department of Ancient Scripture, dean of the College of Religious Education, Richard L. Evans Professor of Religious Understanding, and Abraham O. Smoot University Professor of Religious Education. In the church, I have served as a bishop (a pastor of a congregation) of two different wards (congregations) and as a stake president (with responsibility for eleven congregations).

After more than a decade of extensive reading and reflection on Christian history and theology; after hundreds of hours of stimulating and informative doctrinal conversations with some of the brightest Christian minds in the country; and after attending countless Christian academic conferences across the country, I remain an active, practicing, and deeply committed Latter-Day Saint. I have learned a great deal about the lifestyles and belief systems of what might be called more "traditional" Christians and have grown to admire and love my Christian friends far and wide. Nevertheless, I have yet to discover in the teachings of the various denominations and faith traditions anything that would move me away from dead-center Mormonism. I sincerely believe that Mormonism offers some of the deepest and most inspiring insights anywhere into such matters as the nature of God and humanity and the purpose of life; the infinite and eternal atoning sacrifice of Jesus Christ; the purpose of the church of Jesus Christ and the vital place of priesthood authority and ordinances (sacraments); the proper relationship between a salvation that comes by grace alone and an obedient discipleship characterized by faithfulness, good works, and charitable service; the state of the soul immediately following death and preceding the resurrection; the nature of a material heaven hereafter; and the purpose and everlasting continuation of the family unit.

Second, I am completely sold on day-by-day Mormon life. The New Testament affirms that the church is the outworking, the visible manifestation, of Christianity outside the chapel or beyond the weekly worship service. Few religious organizations in the world can approximate what Mormons do to meet the needs of children (the Primary); youth (Young Men/Women); single adults, married couples, men (Priesthood Quorums); and women (the Relief Society). The church's missionary program now has over fifty-one thousand full-time missionaries in over three hundred missions, with an annual convert baptism rate of approximately three hundred thousand persons. It may well be that the full-time mission, for both young men and women, does more to develop leadership skills and secure the young people within the faith (over 90 percent remain active and involved in the church after their missionary service) than any other facet of LDS living.

A close third would be the genius of the church's lay ministry—largely untrained boys and girls, men and women, learning through experience how to minister regularly to church families (through what is called home and visiting teaching), deliver a sermon, teach a class, evangelize, conduct a meeting, and preside over a group of Saints. Further, the LDS church's solid and sustained emphasis upon the family as the most important unit in time and eternity assures us that those deepest and most endearing of earthly relationships (husband and wife, parents and children, brother and sister) are not fleeting and temporary, as many Christians aver, but rather are intended to bring a piece of heaven to earth and capacitate us as families (through the sealing blessings of the temple) to span the veil of death.

The Church of Jesus Christ of Latter-Day Saints, organized officially by Joseph Smith on April 6, 1830, in Fayette, New York (a part of the "Burnt Over District"), came into being in the era of Restorationism, or Christian Primitivism. It was a time in America when earnest seekers labored to return to the "ancient order of things," to restore the first-century Christian church.

It seems never to have occurred to Joseph Smith that the movement he set in motion was anything other than restored Christianity. At the same time, he fully acknowledged that truth and goodness were to be found in the Christian churches of his day. His approach to the truth has been called a kind of independent, revelatory eclecticism. He observed: "Have the Presbyterians any truth?" "Yes. Have the Baptists, Methodists, etc., any truth? Yes. They all have a little truth mixed with error. We should gather all the good and true principles in the world and treasure them up, or we shall not come out true 'Mormons'" (Smith 1976, 316).

Sadly, as a result of the claims of Joseph Smith and his followers, Latter-Day Saints and conservative Protestants (particularly evangelicals) have been involved in a war of words, a spread of suspicion, for 180 years. Now, if we were to distill all that creates the divide between the Latter-Day Saints and their traditional Christian friends into one distinctive feature of Mormonism, it would have to be our claim to modern revelation—modern prophets, modern scripture, modern priesthood, and continual prophetic direction. All else that produces a major theological chasm (nature of God, trinitarian theology, premortal existence of man, priesthood, temples, etc.) are fruits of a faith founded on a belief in a latter-day prophet who was authorized by God to teach and interpret scripture and ordain.

Latter-Day Saints certainly consider themselves to be Christians. They believe in the Christ of the New Testament—in his virgin birth, his perfect life, his miracles, his incomparable teachings, his atoning sacrifice, his literal bodily resurrection, and his future return in glory to reign as King of kings and Lord of lords. We believe that salvation is in Christ and that it comes by and through his holy name and in no other way. And yet we as Latter-Day Saints acknowledge that we are not trinitarian Christians; we do not accept the doctrinal decisions of post–New Testament councils and creeds as scriptural or as binding on the Christian conscience.

On the one hand, we want the world to know that we worship Jesus as the Christ, the Promised Messiah, our Savior and Redeemer. For us the Jesus of history is indeed the Christ of faith. On the other hand, we must maintain our distinctiveness in the religious world if we are to be true to our history, loyal to our mission, and if we are to contribute meaningfully to major religious discussions. We are not Christians just like everyone else; we are Christian, but different. Father Richard John Neuhaus once said to me: "It is vital that Latter-Day Saint Christians and Nicene Christians listen to and learn from one another." We do not think we are the only true Christians on earth, nor do we doubt the sincerity or commitment of our Christian friends. We do take the Savior's Great Commission seriously, and so we send missionaries throughout the world to share what we feel is a distinctively Christian message. We are not troubled that other Christian groups do the same.

Given the challenges we face in our society—fatherless homes, child and spouse abuse, divorce, poverty, spreading crime and delinquency, rampant pornography and immorality, spiritual wickedness in high places—it seems foolish for men and women who claim to believe in the Lord and Savior, whose hearts and lives have been surrendered to that Savior, to allow doctrinal differences to prevent them from working together. We may never resolve our differences on the Godhead or the Trinity, on the spiritual or corporeal nature of Deity, or on the sufficiency of the Bible, but we can agree that the ultimate transformation of society will come only through the application of Christian solutions to pressing moral issues and that the regeneration of individual hearts and souls is foundational to the restoration of virtue in our communities and nations. "If I esteem mankind to be in error," Joseph Smith explained, "shall I bear them down? No. I will lift them up, and in their own way too, if I cannot persuade them my way is better; and I will not seek to compel any man to believe as I do, only by the force of reasoning, for truth will cut its own way. Do you believe in Jesus Christ and the Gospel of salvation which he revealed? So do I. Christians should cease wrangling and contending with each other, and cultivate the principles of union and friendship in their midst" (Smith 1976, 314).

Source

Joseph Smith. *Teachings of the Prophet Joseph Smith*. Salt Lake City: Deseret, 1976.

72

Jehovah's Witnesses: History, Beliefs, Practices

GEORGE CHRYSSIDES

History

The origins of Jehovah's Witnesses can be traced to Charles Taze Russell (1856–1916), who was brought up in the Presbyterian tradition but found difficulty in accepting mainstream Christian doctrines, especially predestination, eternal damnation, and the Trinity. Inspired by the Adventist preacher Jonas Wendell, he formed his own group known as the Bible Students, and established the journal *Zion's Watch Tower and the Herald of God's Presence*, now called *The Watchtower*. Zion's Watch Tower Bible and Tract Society (later renamed the Watch Tower Bible and Tract Society of Pennsylvania) was set up in 1881 for the distribution of Bibles and tracts.

Russell's main piece of writing was the six-volume *Millennium Dawn* (1886), which was renamed *Studies in the Scriptures*. The first volume, *The Divine Plan of the Ages*, claimed that the world's political and religious systems would soon come to an end and that Christ's invisible "second presence" had come in 1874, with a "harvesting period" extending to 1878. The year 1914 would mark the "end of the Gentile times," with a return of the Jews to God's favor. These dates are not "failed prophecies": Russell specified the dates 1874 and 1878 after they had passed, not before. Although there was a failed expectation that the faithful would be translated into heaven on one of these dates, it was concluded that 1914 marked an invisible occurrence—Satan was cast out of heaven and Jesus began his heavenly rule. From 1918 onward, members of the 144,000 "anointed class" have been received into his heavenly kingdom.

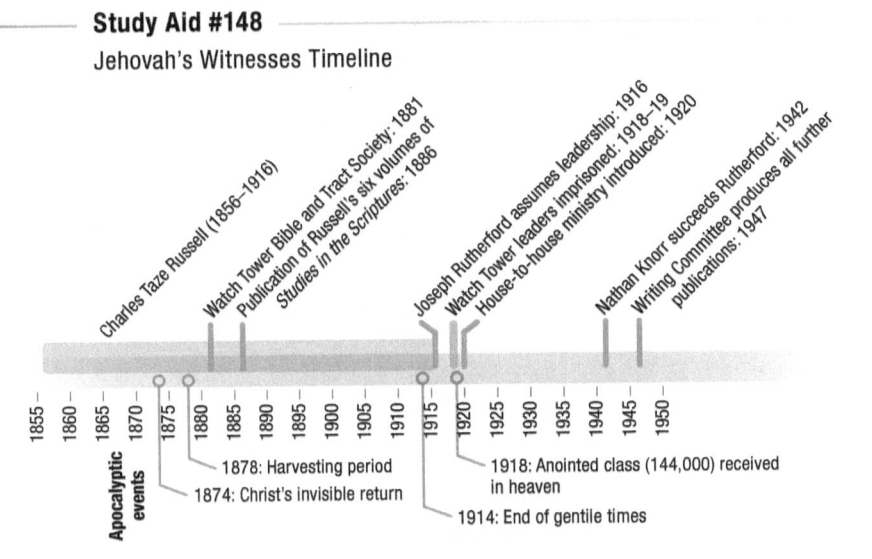

Study Aid #148
Jehovah's Witnesses Timeline

Following Russell's death in 1916, the leadership passed to Joseph Franklin ("Judge") Rutherford. His succession proved controversial, and about a quarter of the members left, forming a number of splinter groups, several of which still remain. Rutherford successfully achieved organizational uniformity in the society, ensuring that the various "ecclesia" (their name for congregations) studied the same passages of scripture and based their meetings on Watch Tower teachings. Because of the Bible Students' antiwar stance, Rutherford and a number of Watch Tower leaders were imprisoned for a period during 1918–19. Rutherford believed that the opposition was instigated by mainstream clergy, and this date marks the beginning of the society's opposition to the Christian churches. Rutherford also introduced house-to-house ministry—a practice for which present-day Witnesses are particularly known. The name "Jehovah's Witnesses" was first introduced at a convention in 1931: although this is the name by which members are best known, it does not have any legal status. It was Rutherford who introduced the distinction between the 144,000 "anointed class," who would reign with Christ in heaven, and the "great crowd"—now the majority of Jehovah's Witnesses—who expect everlasting life in a restored paradise on earth. Rutherford wrote several books; his style was more popular than Russell's, whose writings became gradually withdrawn from the society.

Rutherford died in 1942 and was succeeded by Nathan H. Knorr. Knorr emphasized the need for the training of the society's missionaries, and the organization expanded markedly under his leadership. The book *Let God Be True* (1946) was the key summary of their theology, although this is now superseded by a variety of Watch Tower publications. Russell's and Rutherford's writings are no longer used for study purposes, and since 1942 all publications have been written anonymously. A Writing Committee oversees their publication, and a Publishing Committee attends to their production: these are two of six committees responsible to the Governing Body, which is the ultimate source of authority, consisting of twelve senior Watch Tower leaders, all of whom belong to the 144,000.

Beliefs

For the Jehovah's Witnesses, the Bible is the principal authority for belief and practice. It was completed during the first century, during the lifetime of Jesus's disciples. After that period, the church became apostate, being influenced by Hellenistic beliefs and adopting pagan practices such as the celebration of Christmas and Easter. Jehovah's Witnesses do not have a creed and believe the ancient creeds, such as the Nicene Creed and the Apostles' Creed, come from the postapostolic period, when the church had become apostate. They reject the doctrine of the Trinity, holding it to be unbiblical and influenced by Hellenism. They believe that God is to be addressed by his personal name Jehovah rather than by generic names such as "God" or "the Lord." Jesus is God's Son and is subordinate to him rather than fully divine. The holy spirit (always spelled in lowercase) is not regarded as a person but as God's active force in the world.

Men and women are God's creation, not the result of evolution from a lower species, and they were given dominion over creation. Adam and Eve, the first humans, sinned through disobedience and became subject to Satan's rule and to death. However, God made redemption possible through sending his Son as the "ransom sacrifice" for sin. Witnesses subscribe to the "ransom" theory of atonement rather than any of the other mainstream soteriological theories. In common with mainstream Christian theology, Witnesses regard Christ's death as the means

---

Study Aid #149

Jehovah's Witnesses Beliefs

Bible is principal authority for belief and practice
Noncreedal
Doctrine of Trinity rejected
God to be addressed as Jehovah
Jesus is God's Son, but not fully divine
Jehovah's active force in world is holy spirit
Ransom theory of Jesus's atonement
Armageddon will commence soon
Limited progressive revelation
No professional clergy

of atonement for sin, but they insist that he was nailed to a "torture stake," not to a cross. Jesus rose as a "spirit being" and ascended into heaven after forty days.

Witnesses do not believe in an episodic "second coming," insisting that the correct translation of the Greek *parousia* is "presence." The "second presence" is held to have occurred in 1914, when Satan was cast out of heaven (Rev. 12:9). Having been cast down to the earth, Satan now rules the present world. His rule will end with the battle of Armageddon, in which Christ and the angels will defeat Satan's armies. Satan will be cast into an abyss for a thousand years, during which period the earth will be progressively restored to a paradise for the faithful. The "anointed class"—144,000 of the faithful—have already begun their rule with Christ in heaven, while the "great crowd"—now the majority of Jehovah's Witnesses—will enjoy everlasting life on paradise earth (Rev. 7).

It is a popular misunderstanding that Jehovah's Witnesses "keep changing the dates" for an "end of the world," since they believe neither in a second coming nor that the world will finally end. Their dating system is complex and has been associated with various events in human history from the time of Adam to the present. There have been occasional failed expectations, notably in 1925 and 1975, but Witnesses continue to believe that humanity is living in the last days and that Armageddon will commence soon.

Practices

Jehovah's Witnesses' lifestyle is based upon their understanding of the Bible. Their own New World Translation is the preferred version. The teachings of the Hebrew-Aramaic scriptures (their preferred name for the Old Testament) belong to the "old covenant" and are no longer binding unless they are reinforced in the "new covenant," found in the Christian Greek scriptures (the New Testament). Thus, Jesus reinforces the prohibitions on murder, theft, and adultery but not Sabbath observance. Their avoidance of blood is based on God's commandment to Noah (Gen. 9:4), which was upheld at the Council of Jerusalem (Acts 15:20).

Witnesses regard themselves as being in the world but "no longer part of the world" (John 15:19 NLT). Despite the world's being subjected to Satan's rule, they are expected to obey the law of the land, unless this conflicts with divine law. Witnesses will therefore refuse to participate in armed conflict, regarding this as contrary to Christ's teaching (John 18:36). They decline to salute national flags and sing national anthems, on the ground that such actions bestow a degree of honor that should only be given to God. A faithful member will attend five meetings each week and will undertake house-to-house ministry—known as "publishing." All members are considered "ministers": Jehovah's Witnesses do not have a separate clergy.

A person becomes a Witness through baptism by total immersion, but only after the elders of a congregation are satisfied with the candidate's lifestyle and understanding of the faith. Only adults are baptized, but care is taken to include children in worship and to bring them up in the faith. A high value is placed on family life. Mainstream Christian festivals are not celebrated—only the Memorial (sometimes called the Lord's Evening Meal), which commemorates Jesus's final meal with his disciples. Baptism and the Memorial are regarded as the only rites that Jesus instructed. Other festivals such as Christmas and Easter are regarded as pagan customs that were not observed by the first-century church. Birthday celebrations are also regarded as pagan, although families will often institute "present days" when gifts are exchanged, and wedding anniversaries may be observed.

Witnesses tend to pursue trades rather than professions. Higher education is not prohibited, but members should not pursue it for financial prosperity, and they should be careful to avoid "harmful associations" by making inappropriate friendships. Smoking, recreational drugs, gambling, and extramarital sex are forbidden; alcohol may be consumed in moderation.

Although Witnesses describe their teachings as "the truth" and believe in scriptural inerrancy, they hold that God can progressively shed "greater light" on their understanding, and hence some details in their teachings have been modified through time.

Further Reading

J. A. Beckford. *The Trumpet of Prophecy: A Sociological Study of Jehovah's Witnesses.* Blackwell, 1975.

George Chryssides. *The A to Z of Jehovah's Witnesses.* Scarecrow, 2009.

New World Translation of the Bible. Watch Tower Bible and Tract Society, 1984.

James Penton. *Apocalypse Delayed: The Story of Jehovah's Witnesses.* University of Toronto Press, 1997.

Shawn Francis Peters. *Judging Jehovah's Witnesses.* University Press of Kansas, 2002.

73

Jehovah's Witnesses: Theological Exchanges, Current Issues

GEORGE CHRYSSIDES

The Watch Tower Bible and Tract Society emerged from Christianity's Adventist tradition, and founder-leader Charles Taze Russell established it for the study of the Bible and for the distribution of Bibles and tracts. His members did not regard themselves as a body that exclusively offered salvation, teaching that the 144,000 anointed ones were gathered widely from the Christian faith. Russell approved of the setting up of the Evangelical Alliance in 1846 as a key end-time event, regarding it as a body that would purge Christianity of its imperfections. Russell viewed Roman Catholicism less favorably, regarding it as the "abomination" that Daniel prophesied, claiming that Daniel's 1,260 days referred to the 1,260 years from 539 to 1799, when Catholic rulers dominated world affairs.

Russell challenged Protestant leaders to debate his distinctive teachings, and two large debates were organized for this purpose—the first in Pittsburgh, Pennsylvania, in 1903 with the Rev. Dr. E. L. Eaton, pastor of North Avenue Methodist Episcopal Church, and the second in Cincinnati, Ohio, in 1908 with the Rev. Lloyd Smith White.

Under its second leader, Joseph Franklin Rutherford, who assumed office in 1917, attitudes to other denominations changed markedly. Other Christian leaders were opposed to the Bible Students' antiwar stance and resented the attack on mainstream clergy in *The Finished Mystery*, which was published in that year. (This book was allegedly a posthumous work by Russell, but was written under Rutherford's supervision.) The hostility led to the arrest and imprisonment of several Watch Tower leaders from 1918 to 1919.

The Finished Mystery introduced the society's current teaching that Nimrod was the initiator of false religion, since he traveled to Babylon, where he became king "in opposition to Jehovah" (Gen. 10:9). This notion is based on Alexander Hislop's *The Two Babylons* (1858). While Hislop regarded Roman Catholicism as the second Babylon and the teacher of false religion, Rutherford extended the concept to encompass all of Christendom, opposing Catholics and other Protestants alike.

In 1936 Jehovah's Witnesses adopted the practice of advertising public lectures in Glasgow, Scotland, bearing placards while distributing their leaflets. The practice was extended to London and to the United States and aroused particular attention in 1938, when the slogan "Religion is a snare and a racket" was typically displayed. "Religion" meant all "false religion" and demonstrated the Witnesses' opposition to every form of religion apart from their own.

Progressively, the Watch Tower organization has distanced itself from the mainstream churches. During the Russell era it adopted as its symbol a crown of thorns with a cross intercepting it diagonally. In 1922 the symbol was abandoned, in line with the society's belief that the cross was a pagan symbol and that the correct translation of the Greek *stauros* is not "cross" but "torture stake." Jesus, they teach, was nailed to a single upright piece of wood, not a two-piece edifice with a crossbeam for the victim's arms. The Watch Tower's hymnody started to reflect this also. Previously, the society made use of traditional Christian hymns, such as those of Isaac Watts, Philip Doddridge, and Charles Wesley, but since 1966 Jehovah's Witnesses have further distanced themselves from mainstream Christianity by exclusively using their own words and music for their songs.

Witnesses hold that mainstream Christianity has departed from the doctrines and practices of the early church. They object to the creation of a paid clergy, the appropriation of Hellenistic and other pagan ideas, and involvement with civil governments. The Watch Tower organization perceives itself as God's true organization, which endeavors to restore the Christian faith in its first-century form. It has therefore no wish to compromise its standards for ecumenical considerations, and does not accept the mainstream churches' sacraments. Anyone becoming a Jehovah's Witness must undergo their distinctive baptism, even if previously baptized in a Christian denomination.

> **Study Aid #150**
> **Jehovah's Witnesses—Christian Contacts**
>
> Traditional Christianity considered apostate
> Roman Catholicism deemed an abomination
> Traditionalists debated in 1903 and 1908
> Watch Tower leaders arrested and imprisoned by US government
> Ecumenism opposed and other church sacraments rejected
> Attendance at other churches' worship services forbidden

When the World Council of Churches (WCC) was formed in 1942, the Witnesses did not regard it as a commendable achievement. They were unimpressed by the fact that a number of member churches had emphasized a "social gospel" rather than the necessity for salvation and that the WCC appeared to display some embarrassment about proselytizing, some Christians claiming that non-Christian theists as well as Christians might be able to be saved. Additionally, the WCC sought to influence world affairs, in marked contrast to the Jehovah's Witnesses' belief that Satan rules the world. Witnesses believe that the WCC thus made itself part of Satan's kingdom.

Jehovah's Witnesses' separation from mainstream Christianity entails that members will not contribute financially to charities that are run by mainstream Christians. They are critical of the money spent on administrative costs and on salaries, and they also believe that it is more important to combat spiritual hunger than physical famine. When there is a natural disaster, they prefer to send contributions to their own congregations that are affected by disasters, allowing them to give help where it is needed. Such help is not necessarily confined to their own members.

Jehovah's Witnesses are forbidden to attend mainstream Christian places of worship, and repeated attendance could result in "disfellowshipping" (expulsion). An exception may be made for a wedding or a funeral of a friend, where one's presence is expected out of politeness. In such circumstances, Witnesses should keep their participation to a minimum. It is held that Jehovah-God does not hear the prayers of apostates; hence, when prayer is appropriate in the company of mainstream Christians—for example, if grace is said before a meal—a Jehovah's Witness will wish to say the prayer. Jehovah's Witnesses do not read religious literature written by mainstream Christian authors, although occasionally *The Watchtower* quotes them where they appear to support the Jehovah's Witnesses position. Witnesses are particularly careful to avoid reading "apostate" literature—that is, material written by those who have deliberately decided to leave the organization. When discussing the Bible in the course of their house-to-house work, Witnesses favor the Society's New World Translation of the Bible, believing that it is more reliable than others. If a householder wishes to use some other translation as the basis of their dialogue, however, they will allow this, although they will not endorse any translational errors.

Witnesses accept that they have to work beside mainstream Christians, as well as those of other faiths or none. Where work involves clear violations of their beliefs—for example, a nurse participating in an abortion, or a builder being asked to carry out repairs on a church building—they will not cooperate. There are often gray areas where cooperation with "Babylon the Great" is slight, such as a window cleaner working at a vicarage, or a supermarket assistant selling tobacco. Performing such services is left to the individual's conscience, although he or she may seek advice from an elder. In practice, Witnesses keep each other's company for recreation, although there is no objection to having friendships with those outside the organization, provided that "harmful associations" are avoided.

> **Study Aid #151**
>
> Jehovah's Witnesses—Current Issues
>
> Avoidance of blood transfusions
> Refusal to participate in armed conflicts
> Unwillingness to salute national flags, sing national anthems, or celebrate national holidays
> Desire to remain separatist as much as possible

In the course of their history Jehovah's Witnesses have attracted much opposition from mainstream Christians. In some countries this has involved active persecution, with penalties involving confiscation of property, prohibition of worship, and imprisonment. In the United States, Europe, and Australasia, opposition takes the form of books, brochures, and leaflets criticizing their beliefs and practices. Some are produced by countercult organizations. The Reachout Trust in England is one such example: it originated in 1982 when a group of individuals picketed a convention in Twickenham in London. As the protests were repeated, the group became institutionalized. Initially its prime target was the Jehovah's Witnesses, which it continues to criticize forcibly, although it now offers an evangelical Christian critique of other new religious movements and other faiths. Other Christian publications directed at Jehovah's Witnesses come from Christian publishing houses, individuals, and, frequently, apostate members. Witnesses do not reply to such critiques. When several Christian scholars criticized the New World Translation when it was first published, several *Watchtower* articles responded, but the Watch Tower Society's policy now is to ignore such criticism and to get on with its task of proclaiming the coming kingdom.

Several hundred Christian critiques of Jehovah's Witnesses have been published, and the continued proliferation of such literature seems to be more attributable to the level of hostility that the organization has attracted than to new insights on the authors' parts. The main grounds for criticism include Witnesses' interpretation of the Bible; in particular, critics accuse Jehovah's Witnesses of failed prophetic expectations, and they attempt to justify mainstream doctrines of Christ's deity, the personal nature of the Holy Spirit, and the Trinity, in the face of the Watch Tower Society's rejection of these. Other grounds for criticism include their refusal to accept blood transfusions and their nonparticipation in anniversaries such as Christmas, Easter, and birthdays.

Very occasionally, mainstream Christians have identified features from which the churches might learn. In *Meeting Jehovah's Witnesses*, Jack Roundhill suggests that Witnesses' sense of urgency, their efficient organization, their stewardship, their programs of instruction, their inclusion of children, and their emphasis on family life are all positive aspects that are worthy of consideration.

74

Jehovah's Witnesses: Adherent Essay

ROLF FURULLI

I have been one of Jehovah's Witnesses for forty-nine years, including fifteen years as a full-time preacher. I have been married for forty years, and my wife is also a Witness. We belong to the Majorstua Congregation in Oslo, Norway, where I serve as an elder. I have a PhD in Semitic linguistics; my dissertation presented a new understanding of the verbal system of Classical Hebrew. I teach Semitic languages, and I have also written two books on Bible translation and two books on the chronology of the Bible compared with the Assyrian, Babylonian, Egyptian, and Persian chronologies.

In my preaching work I am often asked: "What is the basic difference between the Witnesses and other religions?" My answer is: "In contrast to many other Christians, we believe that every word in the Bible is inspired by God. These words are our standard, and we refuse to adjust our beliefs and practices in accordance with the changing viewpoints in the secular world, as other denominations have done." The inspiration of the Bible relates to the autographs, whose text is almost identical with the text we have today. However, textual criticism is viewed as important, and the English translation of the New Testament made by linguists among the Witnesses and published in 1950 was a pioneer work in this respect, with indexes and thousands of footnotes with references to variant readings in different Greek manuscripts and in the old Bible versions in Latin, Syriac, Coptic, and other languages. The entire Bible with footnotes and indices was published in 1984. As of 2008, the New World Translation of the whole Bible is being published in forty-three languages, including three versions for blind persons, and the New

Testament is published in eighteen additional languages, with a total circulation of 143,458,577.

The most important person in the universe is Jehovah God. He exists from eternity to eternity and is the only One to be worshiped. To sanctify his name is even more important than the salvation of humankind. Our basic goal is to develop a close, personal relationship with Jehovah so that we can freely approach him in prayer through Jesus Christ. In our preaching work we speak about Jehovah's personality and wonderful attributes and about how he has promised to transform this earth into a paradise. The holy spirit is Jehovah's active force.

Jesus Christ also plays a very important role, but in contrast to most other denominations, we reject the Trinity doctrine. Jesus is viewed as God's only-begotten Son, the first one that Jehovah created, and he is both Savior and King. Although evangelical Christians view Jesus as King, I have never met one who has shown how his or her life would have been any different if the person believed in Jesus only as Savior but not as King. However, our lives would be completely different if we believed in Jesus only as Savior. Because we also believe that Jesus is King, we have accomplished something that everyone would say is excellent, but that no other group has done: ten million people from over 235 nations have been brought into a close fellowship to form one united "nation." We view ourselves as ambassadors and envoys of the kingdom of God, and we remain separate from this world; therefore, we never serve in the armed forces of any nation, and we never participate in political activities. We have voted once and for all for God's kingdom, and we have eliminated all previous barriers between the Witnesses because of differences in race, education, social background, and different political views. Moreover, each one has rejected the standards of this world and strives hard to follow the ethical and moral principles of the Bible. This united people unanimously preach the kingdom of God in every country and invite others to accept Jesus as king. In 2008, our 7,124,443 publishers used 1,488,658,249 hours in the preaching work. When we take into account a death rate of 1 percent, which is not compensated by newborn children, who are not publishers, the increase of new publishers was 3.1 percent.

The role of Jesus as Savior is also very important. In contrast with many denominations who believe that Jesus can save people because he is God, we believe that Jesus, when he was on earth, was a perfect human being, just like Adam. By using his life in a selfish way, Adam sold himself and his offspring under sin, with death in view. Jesus, the second Adam, gave his perfect human life as a ransom sacrifice, and by this he bought all the offspring of Adam. What, then, is necessary to get everlasting life? The only way is to believe in the ransom sacrifice of Jesus. In contrast with the Lutherans, who believe that God has chosen which individuals will be saved and has implanted faith in them without their own will or participation, we believe that no one is predestined for life, but every person must study the Bible, and then choose whether to believe in Jesus. In contrast with the Catholics, who believe that performing certain acts is necessary for salvation, we believe that regardless of what we do, we cannot deserve to be saved. Rather, just as God said, after Abraham had attempted to offer up Isaac, that now he knew the real faith of Abraham, Christian acts are necessary, because they prove that we have faith in Jesus—the only thing that can save a person. Of the persons who will be saved, a small group of 144,000 will serve in the heavenly government, while millions will survive the end here on earth. During a period of one thousand years, they and the resurrected ones will become perfect, and then they will live forever in the earthly paradise.

Faith in Jesus also has implications for Christian doctrine. Because we believe that we can only get everlasting life through Jesus (Rom. 6:23), we reject the belief that we already have everlasting life in the form of an immortal soul. This is a non-Christian, Greek idea not found in the Bible, and it contradicts the hope of the resurrection of the dead. We also believe that Jesus took our punishment (Isa. 53:5) instead of us. But Jesus is not undergoing eternal torment for our sake: he died for us, and this is the punishment he took away. On the basis of God's grace we are offered everlasting life. If we want life, we will get life as a free gift; if we do not want it, we will experience everlasting death, not everlasting torment.

More than 20 percent of the words of Jesus in the Gospels are eschatological, and he said that his followers would know the time period for his final judgment but not the exact day and hour (Matt. 24:32–36). He also said that we should be on the watch. On the basis of time prophecies in the Bible, we believe that Jesus began to reign as king in the year 1914 and that his judgment will come in the time in which we are now living. Therefore, we preach the good news of this kingdom all over the world (Matt. 24:14). While we are awaiting the end, we make reasonable personal plans for the future as if the end could come in one hundred years, but we live our lives as if the end could come tomorrow.

The organization has a remarkable unity in belief, although each member has great personal freedom to make decisions. No clergy exists, but each congregation is led by a body of elders. These elders recommend new elders, and these are appointed by representatives of the Governing Body. The members of the Governing Body are not inspired by God and are not prophets, but they function as teachers. They oversee the worldwide preaching, the writing of books and magazines, and the organizing of programs for teaching in the congregations. No elder has the right to make decisions on the part of others, but each member has the freedom and the right to make personal decisions on the basis of Bible principles.

Are Jehovah's Witnesses Christians? Please consider the following: A group of persons who believe that every word in the Bible is true, who believe in the ransom sacrifice of Jesus, who strive to follow closely in the footsteps of Jesus, and who are willing to die rather than to break the laws of the Bible—are they not Christians? True, we do not believe in the Trinity, but our beliefs and practices are much closer to those of the first Christian congregations than are the beliefs and practices of the major Christian denominations.

Can there be any relationship between the Witnesses and others? All over the world, as far as it depends on us, we have good relations with others on a personal level (Rom. 12:17–18). In our congregations we learn to be respectful toward others and tolerant of their religious beliefs, and we give others the right to believe what they want to believe. But tolerance does not require that we always agree with their beliefs; therefore, we do not take part in interconfessional activities, because that often involves compromising our beliefs. We are persecuted in thirty countries today because of our refusal to compromise our faith. What we desire is that others allow us to be useful and productive members of our communities, and respect our Christian beliefs and consciences.

75

Church of Christ, Scientist: History, Beliefs, Practices

JOHN K. SIMMONS

Christian Science, discovered by Mary Baker Eddy (1821–1910) in 1866, emerged in American culture during the turbulent later decades of the nineteenth century. Because it is one of only a handful of major Christian sects actually founded in the United States, the story of the Christian Science movement has as much to reveal about the spiritual yearning of Americans as it does about the complexities and nuances of American culture. The opening line in Eddy's seminal work *Science and Health with Key to the Scriptures* provides an immediate insight into a primary religious impulse of her time. "To those leaning on the sustaining infinite, to-day is big with blessings." The cultural experience of American citizens living in the late nineteenth century was anything but sustaining. In fact, day-to-day life often seemed as fractured and unstable as bedrock in California. Though all religions, to some extent, embody a spiritual search for permanence in a constantly changing world, Eddy's delineation of a "sustaining" metaphysical reality found a ready audience in believers who had lost faith in a traditional Christian worldview challenged by scientific and social revolutions. Her promise of unassailable physical well-being gave hope to many sufferers in a time when medical practices were, at best, primitive. The joining of Christian Science and anxious Americans was a marriage made in heaven. In April 1879, Eddy and ten followers founded the Church of Christ, Scientist. Three decades later, in 1906, when thirty thousand Christian Scientists celebrated the dedication of the four-thousand-seat domed Italian Renaissance/Byzantine Mother Church in Boston, it was clear that Christian Science had become one of the most successful religious organizations in America.

Study Aid #152
Christian Science Timeline

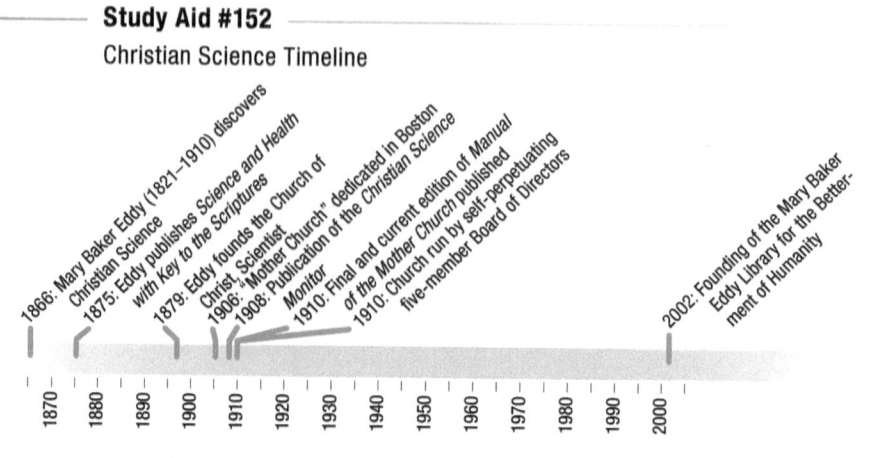

Christian Scientists understandably claim Eddy's truths to be part of a unique and final religious revelation. However, most outside observers place Christian Science in the metaphysical family of religious organizations with roots both in nineteenth-century philosophical idealism and the quest for alternative means of healing. The term "metaphysical" denotes the primacy of Divine Mind as the controlling factor in human experience. If God is Mind and the substance of being is Spirit, then human beings, as the expression of Mind, must reflect God's eternal perfection. Original sin is not the cause of human suffering. All negative experiences, including sin, disease, death, and evil, are the result of a profound error in thinking, an error Eddy termed "mortal mind." The fundamental perceptual error of mortal mind is the pernicious belief in the self-limiting reality of a material world. For Eddy, spirit was the ontological and theological universal; matter was mortal error.

While traditional Christian teaching places the kingdom of heaven in a realm beyond and hereafter, Christian Science calls for the actualization or demonstration of perfection in the here and now by knowing the truth of being. The Christian Scientist does not pray to a God for health, security, and prosperity. These are qualities of God's unchanging expression that human beings invariably will reflect, experientially, once they depart from erring, limited, mortal thinking. God, as Divine Principle, can be demonstrated scientifically by anyone who knows and affirms this principle of being. Eddy called upon her followers to reflect seven synonyms for God: Principle, Mind, Spirit, Soul, Life, Truth, and Love.

The "Christian" element in Christian Science emerges in a radical reinterpretation of Jesus's role in the Gospels. Gone is the atoning, sacrificial death on the cross. Jesus becomes the exemplar, the first and ultimate "Christian Scientist" who demonstrably overcame sin, sickness, and death through his superior perception of the allness of Spirit and the nothingness of matter. Jesus is revered by Christian

Scientists, but he is not the Messiah as defined by orthodox Christology. Christian Scientists do not believe in the deity of Jesus. Rather, Jesus is unique because he was the first human being to understand and fully express Divine Mind. Jesus's at-one-ment with God is the natural state of all human beings. Though Eddy's many detractors scoffed at her theology, claiming it was irrational and dangerous, she stressed the practical nature of her "science." It was in day-to-day challenges that Christian Scientists proved God's perfection. Thus, healing became a focus of the religion; a practical manifestation of the change in thinking from the material to the spiritual.

From 1875, the year Eddy established the first "Christian Scientists' Home" and published the first edition of *Science and Health*, up to the turn of the century, this visionary religious leader took Christian Science through several institutional mutations. The early church structure included the establishment of the Church of Christ, Scientist (1879), the Massachusetts Metaphysical College (1881), and the National Christian Science Association (1886). However, when the congregational pattern of church polity, characteristic of her first religious organization, proved too democratic, she shocked her followers by disorganizing the National Christian Science Association. When, in 1892, she reorganized the Christian Science movement around the Mother Church in Boston, her unwavering motivation must have been to secure her spiritual vision in institutional form. Eddy selected twelve "Charter Members" and twenty "First Members" as the core group within the Boston church, then urged all Christian Scientists to join this First Church of Christ, Scientist. All other Christian Science churches became "branch churches," satellites revolving around the Mother Church.

Strict rules and regulations governing the Christian Science movement are laid out in the *Manual of the Mother Church*. At Eddy's request, the first codification was undertaken by a committee in 1895 and would go through eighty-eight editions. Two weeks after her death on December 3, 1910, the board of directors came out with an eighty-ninth edition, which guides the movement to this day.

Study Aid #153

Christian Science Beliefs

Located within metaphysical family of religions
Primacy of mind (Divine Mind) over matter
Suffering not caused by sin, but error of thinking (mortal mind)
Solution is transformed way of thinking
Perfection sought "here and now," not in the hereafter
Jesus not the Messiah, but the perfect exemplar
Seven synonyms for God:
   Principle, Mind, Spirit, Soul, Life, Truth, Love
Consciousness in God, not human mind

> **Study Aid #154**
>
> Current Issues
>
> Healing outside of traditional medicine
> Allness of mind, nothingness of matter
> Womens' leadership roles
> Relationship of Christian Science to Gnosticism

Since changes cannot be made without her approval, church structure and liturgical activity have remained the same within the movement to the present time.

The *Manual* defines the organizational structure of the church, rigidly controls the propagation of Christian Science teaching, and guides the religious practices of Christian Scientists throughout the world. The Mother Church, the First Church of Christ, Scientist, in Boston, is controlled by a five-member, self-perpetuating Board of Directors of the Mother Church. The *Manual* also affirms the establishment of the Board of Trustees, which legally holds and manages church property. The Christian Science Publishing Society (CSPS), directed by the *Manual*, is responsible for the dissemination of all authorized materials on Christian Science. The Publishing Society produces the *Christian Science Monitor, Journal, Sentinel*, and *Herald* and recently has taken management of the official Christian Science website, www.spirituality.com. Unauthorized presentations about Christian Science are prohibited.

Christian Science church services are highly structured and identical in format. Lessons, chosen by the Mother Church and published in the *Christian Science Quarterly*, are based on topics originally selected by Eddy. Ministers do not conduct services in Christian Science. First and Second Readers, elected to three-year terms from within the branch church congregation, read alternating passages from the Bible and *Science and Health*. On Wednesday evenings, branch churches offer selected readings from the Bible and *Science and Health*, presented by the First Reader, and followed by voluntary testimonials of healing by audience members.

Other important positions within the movement include Christian Science teachers, lecturers, nurses, and practitioners. Teachers are board-approved educators who provide class instruction to church members who seek a deeper understanding of Christian Science. The "best of the best" may become Christian Science lecturers. Controversy arising between Christian Science and the dominant culture inevitably centers on the adherents' choice of spiritual healing over traditional medical practices. Consequently it is the Christian Science practitioner who is really on the front lines of healing within the movement. Practitioners do not diagnose illness or provide medical care. Rather, they assist the afflicted in knowing the spiritual nature of reality, helping them through the error of material thinking into the spiritual reality of health and wholeness, as God's perfect reflection. Christian Science practitioners receive nominal fees for their healing skills. There are a small number of Christian Science nurses. They do not dispense medicine but are trained to provide additional care such as bathing or dressing wounds. The seriously ill can retire to a Christian Science nursing home facility where food, basic care, and prayer are offered.

Since the height of membership in the 1950s, the Christian Science movement has been on a steady decline. The church leadership, however, is making strides to rectify the situation. In the late 1990s, the fourteen-acre Mother Church complex in Boston embarked on an extensive construction project. The $50-million Mary Baker Eddy Library for the Betterment of Humanity opened in fall 2002 for the purpose of transmitting Eddy's ideas to the general public and making her writings more available to scholars. The official website, www.spirituality.com, is state of the art, and, for the first time since Eddy's demise, the presentation of Christian Science is lively and refreshing. Christian Science is still portrayed as an extraordinary and unique spiritual revelation, and Mary Baker Eddy is revered; however, the website does something previously unheard of in the restrictive world of the Christian Science Publishing Society: it acknowledges other religious or spiritual worldviews rather than building philosophical or theological walls designed to protect Christian Science.

Further Reading

Mary Baker Eddy. *Science and Health with Key to the Scriptures*. Christian Science Board of Directors, 2006.
Stephen Gottschalk. *Rolling Away the Stone*. Indiana University Press, 2011.
Robert Peel. *Mary Baker Eddy*. 3 vols. Henry Holt, 1966, 1991.

76

Church of Christ, Scientist: Adherent Essay

Shirley Paulson

I grew up in a family of devoted Christian Scientists and never rebelled against the teachings of the church. From early childhood I learned to trust God as my best Friend, my Father-Mother, the omnipresent Love that would meet all my needs. Healing was a side effect of our faith and religious life, but it inspired me to strive for the things of God. My mother prayed for me during my youth, and her prayers healed me of a nervous habit, poison oak, flu, a fall from a horse, and other typical childhood maladies.

By my young adult years, I had to delve into my own studies and prayers to strengthen my faith. My healing experiences solidified my relationship with Christ (the eternal Word of God), as well as my understanding of the kingdom of God. Here are some quick examples: In my late teens I had a serious infection that ran up my leg. It frightened me, but I was immediately healed after a conversation with a Christian Science practitioner—an experienced healer whose practice is based on biblical models and is authorized by the Christian Science Church. He helped me turn away from fear and reminded me of biblical examples of God's power and will to heal. I remember regaining confidence in God's unconditional love for me.

Later, a relationship breakup was just as painful to my broken heart, even though it might not have seemed as critical as the infection. But again, a total surrender to God's capacity to provide good in my life healed the sorrow. Several years later, my struggle was even greater as I battled with a challenging skin disease. Though I had experienced healing with every previous physical and emotional ailment, and I knew I was gaining spiritual strength and maturity, this healing required three years of humble prayer and study, instead of three minutes. The victory was far sweeter than physical freedom, because I gained a deeper understanding and affection for God.

Now, as I come face-to-face with my human inadequacies, I am comforted to know Christ as my Savior today and forever. Christologically speaking, Christ's divinity is understood in Christian Science as being made manifest in Jesus's humanity, and therefore I see Jesus as the model for my life. I am currently a Christian Science practitioner, and the entire Bible is the basis for my Christian Science practice. The textbook *Science and Health with Key to the Scriptures*, by Mary Baker Eddy, is the primary guide I use for discerning the spiritual healing message of the Bible.

Mary Baker Eddy's understanding of the relationship between her discovery of Christian Science and Christianity is that her church was "designed to commemorate the word and works of our Master, which should reinstate primitive Christianity and its lost element of healing" (Eddy 1895, 17). Originally she thought Christians in general would welcome her discovery of this aspect of discipleship that had been mostly lost. "Heal the sick, . . . the kingdom is come nigh," Jesus instructed his disciples (Luke 10:9 KJV; see also Luke 9:2; Matt. 10:7–8). On this basis, Eddy never considered her work as in competition with or different from Christianity, but as more evidence of Christianity's validity for the benefit of humanity. She claimed that the heart and soul of Christianity was its power of love, and that its scientific understanding revealed to her would enable faithful Christians to alleviate suffering of individuals and systemic forms of oppression (Eddy 1890, 135).

However, despite the hundreds whom she healed personally or who were healed through reading her works, clerical attacks on her were merciless. Jesus warned his disciples that their power to cure diseases—as he sent them out to do—would provoke hostility (Matt. 10:1, 8, 12–18), and Eddy viewed her persecution in the same light. There were several layers of objections to Eddy's Christian Science, ranging from her attaching the term "Science" to "Christianity," to her claim to heal in opposition to medical law, plus the audacity of a nineteenth-century American woman to teach, preach, heal, and found a church so successfully. But the most grievous offense struck a deep nerve within mainstream Christianity: Christian Science's apparent proximity to Gnosticism.

Eddy's death, in 1910, preceded the discovery of the Nag Hammadi papyrus manuscripts by some thirty-five years, and therefore her only knowledge of Gnostic writings was through the church fathers' polemics. What is surprising to many Christian scholars is the fact that Docetism, dualism, asceticism, and the unreality of sin were anathemas to Eddy. She instructed that no one can claim the unreality of sin until the one who believes in and acts on sin is saved through repentance and genuine reformation (Eddy, 447:12; 461:16). The salvific power of Christ is required for all humans. Docetism, the teaching that Jesus's body only seemed to be or that he was not a human person, is a false teaching according to Christian Science. His crucifixion and resurrection would have been meaningless if his body were unlike that of other humans. Therefore she writes, "The crucifixion of Jesus and his resurrection served to uplift faith to understand eternal Life" (Eddy, 497). While there is indeed a distinction between Christian Science and orthodox Christianity, the claims of likeness to Gnosticism are misleading.

The crux of the issue is more accurately an epistemological one. Eddy uses the analogy of the relation between sun and earth to understand the cause and origin of being. As the earth appears to be at the center of the solar system, so human beings perceive themselves to be the cause of their existence. But a heliocentric viewpoint reveals the sun, not the earth, to be at the center of the universe. A geocentric view presents an exact inversion of the truth. Similarly, God, rather than humanity, is the center and cause of human conscious existence. God, the source of intelligent being, presents an exact inversion of the human mind's limited perspective—as distinctly opposite of the geocentric and heliocentric viewpoints. From this perspective, all true intelligence originates in perfect God, Mind, mandating that the human sense of limitation and evil must be corrected. It is the office of Christ to correct the sinful, sick, and dying sense of humanity. Reasoning this way, a human being can experience a Christ experience similar to other Christians (repentance from sin, physical healing, grace, redemption, salvation), but the ontological statements of being are the reverse of orthodox theology. In Christian Science, God (Mind) reveals God's self to human thought through Christ, because God is the origin of consciousness. This epistemological statement reverses a sinning mortal's failure to know the infinite goodness of God.

Understanding the origin of consciousness in God (rather than in the human brain) is essential for the successful practice of Christian Science healing, since it provides the basis for spiritual reasoning and prayer. It is also the distinguishing factor between Christian Science and other new religious movements. New Age, in particular, teaches a more subjective relationship to the divine, placing emphasis on the primacy of human thought. Sydney Ahlstrom's concept of harmonialism, an umbrella term for many nineteenth-century metaphysical religions (1019–26), wrongly includes Christian Science. The distinction would be more conspicuous by taking into account the complete rejection Christian Science makes of the human mind's self-constructed world.

This concept of the origin of consciousness is also the basis for the Christian Science objection to materialism in all its forms, from scientific materialism in Western thought, medical materialism, ecclesial materialism, and the blunt atheism of matter (Gottschalk 2011, 3). Just as Eddy saw consistency in Jesus's teaching of love through his healing the sick, she likewise encouraged her students to love enough to heal the sick in Christ's name. Christian Science does not teach disdain for the human body. As Jesus cast out "demons" in order to heal the sick, Eddy strove to destroy the demons in human thought (such as materialism) in order to bring health and peace to the human experience.

Based on contemporary research regarding some ancient so-called Gnostic texts, there is considerable justification for reassessing the meaning and role of these texts in their relation to Christianity. If, as Karen King concludes, at least some of these questionable texts are not truly docetic, ascetic, dualistic, or championing multiple creators, then there could be reason to associate Christian Science with them. King debunks both the rationale of ancient heresy and the Christian polemicists' efforts to enforce it, giving the gatekeepers of today less authority to reject Christian Science. King's analysis of the *Gospel of Mary* also reshapes the debates over ecclesial authority, women's leadership, and perhaps even the patriarchal establishment of canon, creed, and clerical authority.

If she is right, I believe Mary Baker Eddy's place in Christian history will become more relevant as modern Christianity reconsiders its relationship to the otherwise rejected ante-Nicene forms of Christianity. Patriarchal influences will be silenced, healing will be restored, and more Christians will unite in their mutual love of Christ. I am hopeful for the kind of ecumenism in which Christian fellowship welcomes the gifts of those who follow Christ, even if they do it differently.

Sources

Mary Baker Eddy. *Church Manual*. Boston: Christian Science Board of Directors, 1895.

———. *Science and Health*. Boston: Christian Science Board of Directors, 1890 (1875).

Stephen Gottschalk. *Rolling Away the Stone: Mary Baker Eddy's Challenge to Materialism*. Bloomington: Indiana University Press, 2011 (2005).

Karen King. *The Gospel of Mary of Magdala*. Salem, OR: Polebridge, 2003.

77

NRM: World Religion Derivatives Introduction

Terry C. Muck

When the non-Christian world religions, such as Hinduism, Buddhism, and Islam, take root in a Western culture and in the United States, religious traditions emerge that sometimes straddle the borderline between the original world religion and a new religious movement. That there is a category of new religious movements that can be called "world religion derivatives" seems incontrovertible. But applying the label is not always so easy. The problem is one of measuring deviance. World religion derivatives have in some sense strayed from the orthodoxy or orthopraxy of the parent religion, but in some cases the deviation is slight, in others major.

In this section we have identified three world religion derivatives, one each from Islam, Hinduism, and Buddhism. We have made the judgment that they are different enough from the parent religion to deserve the label of new religious movement, but we acknowledge that some in each of these movements might take issue with that judgment. Usually the issue would be that many, if not most, in such movements consider themselves to be *more* orthodox than that parent religion and what it has become. They see themselves as reviving or restoring the original religious movement in question, or reforming it along lines that would have been endorsed by the founder(s).

Identifying world religion derivatives is further complicated by the fact that sometimes disagreements arise not about deviancy but about whether a movement is religious at all. For example, practitioners of Transcendental Meditation usually make the claim that they are not a religion, that they are not practicing a religion,

> **Study Aid #155**
>
> **World Religion Derivatives**
>
> Nation of Islam: An Islamic movement that has taken root primarily among urban African American groups.
>
> Transcendental Meditation: A meditative technique with roots in Hindu *bhakti* movements.
>
> Soka Gakkai: A Buddhist movement with a particularly pronounced social consciousness.

that their meditative program is secular. Observers outside the movement, as you will see in the essay below, often take issue with that claim.

The three new religious movements we have chosen—the Nation of Islam, Transcendental Meditation, and Soka Gakkai—are just three of many, many manifestations of Islam, Hinduism, and Buddhism that have taken root in the West. Buddhism, in particular, has proved itself over and over again throughout history to be adaptable to any new culture with which it comes in contact, and its presence in Western culture is no exception to that phenomenon. But these three movements are three of the largest and most well known of the world religion derivatives, and the telling of their stories in many ways anticipates most of the stories of what Gordon Melton in his *Encyclopedia of American Religions* estimates to be the over fifteen hundred new religious movements in the United States.

78

Nation of Islam: History, Beliefs, Practices

Steven Tsoukalas

History

The Nation of Islam (NOI), founded by W. D. Fard (Master Fard Muhammad) and Elijah Muhammad, did not arise in a socioreligious vacuum. Founded in 1930, it arose in the context of black nationalism, which was a reaction against racism in the nineteenth and twentieth centuries in the United States.

Against racist atrocities, nineteenth-century black leaders like David Walker and Henry Highland Garnet called blacks to reject the stereotypically viewed "Uncle Tom" of Harriet Beecher Stowe's *Uncle Tom's Cabin*, wherein Uncle Tom exemplifies a false "Christian heroism" by "turning the other cheek," thereby providing context for blacks as a messianic redeemer race. Suffering, perseverance, and forgiveness, these leaders said, were not desired contexts.

Walker and Garnet authored *Walker's Appeal and Garnet's Address to the Slaves of the United States* in 1848, calling blacks out of their Uncle Tom roles, commanding them to eschew ignorance, stop forgiving white racism, and realize their superb (with some, ontologically superior) African heritage. Walker foresaw God sending a great black leader (in 1928 Robert Alexander Young's *Ethiopian Manifesto* predicted the same) and called Americans to repent or their country would be destroyed. Other black leaders followed Young, Walker, and Garnet. In this form of black nationalism was a sense of messianism, both race-wide and individual.

Walker and Garnet's views influenced black nationalist leaders of the nineteenth and early twentieth centuries: Edward W. Blyden, Martin Delaney, Alexander Crummell, W. E. B. Du Bois, and Henry Sylvester Williams.

Study Aid #156
Nation of Islam Timeline

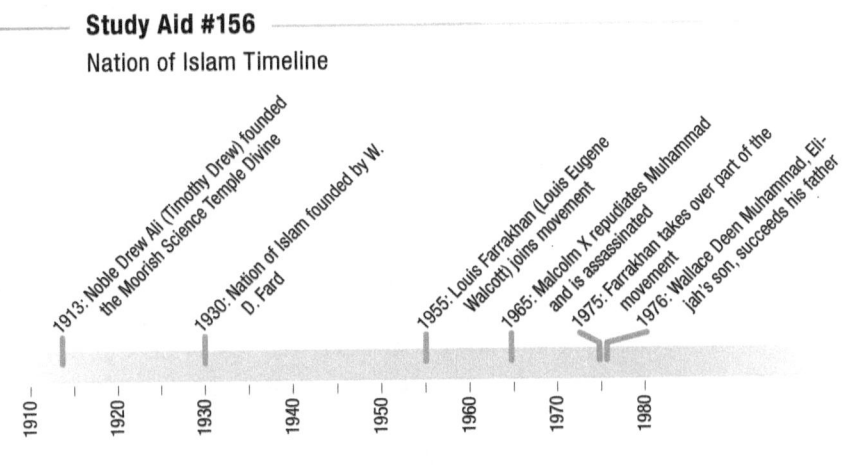

1917: Marcus Garvey founds the Universal Negro Improvement Association
1934: Elijah Muhammad (Elijah Poole) takes over leadership
1948–52: Malcolm X (Malcolm Little) joins movement

Two early twentieth-century leaders, Marcus Garvey (mainly sociological) and Noble Drew Ali (mainly religious), arose in the context of black nationalism. Both influenced Elijah Muhammad and Fard. Garvey's Universal Negro Improvement Association called for racial unity among blacks, race pride, the establishing of schools, independent commerce and industry, and a religion other than white Christianity, all grounded in color prejudice and black ontological superiority. Garvey also hoped to move all African Americans to Africa within fifty years.

Noble Drew Ali, born Timothy Drew, in 1913 claimed to receive a call from the king of Morocco to teach Islam to blacks in the United States. He formed the Moorish Science Temple Divine and National Movement of North America (later called Moorish Science Temple of America). Drew taught that Morocco was the origin of the black race (ontologically superior, Moors, descendants of the ancient Moabites, the original inhabitants of earth); Islam is the religion for blacks, and Christianity the religion for whites; Jesus was a black prophet; all whites are "colored" and unnatural; whites are European, evil, and satanic by nature; Europeans will be destroyed; racial separation; abstention from slothfulness, alcohol, infidelity, and certain types of food; separation of black women and men in meetings; no mixed marriages; and members should change their names.

By 1929 Ali was dead and Garvey deported on a mail-fraud conviction. Someone needed to fill the socioreligious gap in the industrial North, which in the early nineteenth century was seen as utopia for blacks desiring escape from the South and racism. Enter Elijah Muhammad and W. D. Fard.

Muhammad, born Elijah Poole (Middleton Poole, says Muhammad, was his American ancestors' slave master) in 1897 in Georgia, was a son of Baptist minister

William Poole. He received special treatment as a minister's son. But young Elijah witnessed racist realities. One atrocity he recalls is the murder of a black man who was hanged and riddled with bullets for allegedly raping a white woman. In search of Northern utopia, young Elijah moved to Detroit but experienced a terrible awakening—things were not so different there. Elijah again found himself facing financial hardship and racism.

For socioreligious identity, Elijah joined Garvey's movement and Prince Hall Freemasonry (for blacks). Even with affiliation in these, Elijah still longed for something. Fard was the answer. Fard (half black and half white, and, some theorize, a former inmate of West Coast prisons) appeared mysteriously in Detroit in 1930 and, selling silks, began visiting homes and sharing his message of black superiority and African heritage. Individual home meetings turned into mass meetings, and Elijah Muhammad became entranced with "Allah in the flesh." After three and a half years Fard mysteriously disappeared, and Muhammad, called the "Messenger," assumed leadership.

Two key figures arose during Muhammad's leadership—Malcolm X and Louis Farrakhan. Malcolm X ("X" refers to rejection of his slave-master name) was born Malcolm Little in 1925. In and out of jail, Malcolm was visited by Fard supernaturally during one of his incarcerations. Malcolm thereafter embraced the NOI. During a parole leave, Malcolm traveled to hear Elijah Muhammad speak and slowly gained approval and trust from Muhammad. He later became minister of Philadelphia's Temple #12 and New York's Temple #7. Later, while making an Islamic pilgrimage to Mecca, Malcolm stood beside what he believed were white devils, but they worshiped God as he did. This, coupled with charges of sexual immorality against Elijah Muhammad, led to Malcolm's disassociation with the NOI.

Louis Farrakhan, born Louis Eugene Walcott in 1933, was baptized in a Christian church and recalled conversations between his mother and friends. She lamented over the blacks' social situation and God's not sending a deliverer. In 1955 he heard Elijah Muhammad speak and in his mind joked about Muhammad's inability to speak well. Moments later, Muhammad singled out Louis from the crowd, stating that though he may not speak eloquently, it did not change the message. Elijah further stated that Louis could help free the black man. To Louis, this

---

Study Aid #157

Nation of Islam Beliefs

Monotheistic: "No God but Allah"
Nation of Islam leaders serve as prophets of Allah to blacks
Jesus is a prophet, not the Son of God
Blacks as the original created race, but whites created by Satan to persecute blacks
Nation of Islam helps blacks restore their rightful culture

confirmed a conversation he had a few years earlier with Malcolm X. Malcolm shared that Allah had come and had a Messenger to lead the black people. Walcott became Louis X and quickly rose up the ranks. Upon Elijah Muhammad's death in 1975, Louis took leadership of a portion of adherents, stating that he would sustain the teachings of Fard and Muhammad. Other adherents followed Elijah's son Wallace Deen Muhammad, who earlier had come to doubt Fardian Islam.

Beliefs

Blacks are collectively God, yet "there is no God but Allah." And Fard is Allah in the flesh, being one in a string of finite gods who have ruled separately during trillions of years. Jesus was only a prophet, not God the Son. The Bible is a "poison book," verses having been added and changed to suit the white man's needs. According to the NOI, after giving four hundred years of sweat and blood and in turn receiving horrendous treatment from whites, blacks deserve twenty to twenty-five years of reparations with needs covered by their former slave masters until reaching self-sufficiency.

Whites are inferior by nature. Collectively Satan and individually devils, whites are hybrids of the Original Black Man (a collective term for all blacks and a title for the first god). Whites came into existence about 6,000 years ago through experiments of the evil, mischievous scientist Yakub. Starting 6,600 years ago, Yakub conducted a 600-year-long series of birthing restrictions (all-black couples could not marry, all-brown couples could). If all-brown couples birthed all-black babies, the babies were killed. Brown babies were allowed to live. In 600 years brown was filtered down, producing white. The 6,000-year rule of the evil-trickster white race had begun.

According to the NOI, Elijah Muhammad did not die in 1975 but joined Fard in the "Mother of Planes," a half-mile-by-half-mile spaceship housing fifteen hundred small bombers designed to destroy whites and any "Uncle Toms" not embracing Fardian Islam. After Armageddon all will be restored to original conditions—only those who have accepted Fard's Islam will live on earth.

Practices

Adherents meet in mosques. Meetings feature talks by NOI leaders. Men and women are segregated in services. Evangelism occurs in mosques and in one-on-one encounters, including ministers visiting prison inmates. The "Fruit of Islam" (FOI) comprises young men serving in military-like fashion, protecting Louis Farrakhan and other ministers and members. The Nation of Islam celebrates "Savior's Day," an annual convention honoring the birth of Master Fard Muhammad. Members learn from the pure and holy Qur'an and the Bible. Though the latter is "poison," it nonetheless is quoted and is taught with study aids. NOI practices include diet restrictions; abstention from infidelity, alcohol, and drugs; attending NOI schools; and operating intra-NOI commerce and industry. To foster new identity, members take the surname "X" or take entirely new names. Social reform results in self-improvement, all done to honor Elijah Muhammad and to serve Master Fard Muhammad. The NOI does not publish any figures of membership. Estimates range generally from ten thousand to two hundred thousand. By far the largest number of members are in the United States.

Further Reading

Claude Andrew Clegg III. *An Original Man.* St. Martin's Press. 1997.

Mattias Gardell. *In the Name of Elijah Muhammad.* Duke University Press, 1996.

C. Eric Lincoln. *The Black Muslims in America.* Eerdmans, 1994.

Wilson Jeremiah Moses. *Black Messiahs and Uncle Toms.* Pennsylvania State University Press, 1982.

Elijah Muhammad. *Message to the Blackman in America.* Muhammad Mosque of Islam No. 2, 1965.

———. *Our Saviour Has Arrived.* Muhammad's Temple of Islam No. 2, 1974.

Steven Tsoukalas. *The Nation of Islam.* P&R, 2001.

79

Nation of Islam: Theological Exchanges, Current Issues

Steven Tsoukalas

The epithet "Nation of Islam" (NOI) suggests that the movement is a valid expression of both the Qur'an and traditional Islam, but according to orthodox Muslim apologists, such is not the case. To be sure, the NOI offers Islamic doctrines along with its emphasis on the Qur'an, but several traditional Islamic apologists have argued successfully (given the heterodox Islamic views of the NOI, such as W. D. Fard being Allah in the flesh and labeling all whites "devils") that the NOI is not true Islam. Additionally, the NOI was influenced by certain expressions of Christianity, heretical expressions of Christianity, and certain non-Christian religious groups utilizing the Bible and some of its content to certain extents.

Pre–Nation of Islam

Nineteenth- and twentieth-century black nationalism, as it engaged certain Christians' racism, played a crucial role in the subsequent rise of the NOI in the twentieth century. Figures such as David Walker and Henry Highland Garnet, Edward W. Blyden, Martin Delaney, Alexander Crummell, W. E. B. Du Bois, and Henry Sylvester Williams deserve deep consideration, for they reacted in varying ways to Christianity through their contact with Christians who claimed the name of Jesus but acted in ways unlike Jesus.

> **Study Aid #158**
> **NOI Christian Contacts**
>
> Pre–Nation of Islam: Black nationalism vs. Christian racism
> W. D. Fard: Influenced by Jehovah's Witnesses and Freemasonry
> Elijah Muhammad: From imitation to radicalization
> Malcolm X: Conversion while incarcerated
> Louis Farrakhan: Radicalized by hypocritical Christians

W. D. Fard's Contacts

Though Master Fard Muhammad ("Allah in the flesh," according to the NOI) to a large degree remains a historical mystery, some theorize that Fard was influenced by the teachings of Jehovah's Witnesses, to the point that he encouraged people to listen to radio speeches given by Joseph Rutherford, the leader and president of Jehovah's Witnesses from 1916 to 1942. Additionally, it is quite possible that Fard came into close contact with the Freemasons and with Baptist fundamentalism through the preacher Frank Norris. Though surely none of the above influenced Fard to the fullest extent, in his theology or in the theology of his spiritual offspring—Elijah Muhammad, Malcolm X, and Louis Farrakhan, all of whom, directly or indirectly, were influenced by Fard—one finds similarities with Jehovah's Witnesses and Freemasonry. For example, Fard authored the *Secret Ritual of the Nation of Islam*, which was transmitted orally to members and contains a question-and-answer format. Such transmission and question-and-answer formats characterize various Masonic rituals.

Elijah Muhammad's Contacts

Elijah Poole, later to become the Honorable Elijah Muhammad, leader of the NOI until 1975, was born to Baptist minister William Poole in Georgia in 1897. Influenced by the Christianity of his father, he envisioned himself becoming an inspiring preacher. He studied the Bible to the point of frustration for not being able to understand it as deeply as he wanted. Later he discovered certain problems with the Bible and often engaged his father in debates, which usually ended in frustration. The result was that young Elijah, who was taught that Islam was a heathen religion, thirsted to find what he thought was lacking in Christianity. In time Elijah came to doubt Christianity's teachings, in part because of the hypocrisy he witnessed among Christians. Part of this hypocrisy was "white Christians" and their treatment of blacks. Various murders of blacks took place at the hands of whites who took the law into their own hands.

The later, older Elijah Muhammad came to call these and all other whites "devils," saw Jesus as a black man, and viewed Christianity as the religion for white devils, a religion existing for the purpose of making slaves out of blacks. Rather than embracing the Christianity of his father, Elijah distanced himself and the NOI from the "spook god" of Christians. Instead, rather than being identified as Christian, Elijah wanted NOI adherents to bear one of the ninety-nine remaining names of Allah (Allah is the one-hundredth name).

Malcolm X's Contacts

Malcolm X was born to traveling Baptist preacher Earl Little. But unlike young Elijah Poole, Malcolm had virtually no time to be taught Christianity by his father. In 1931, when Malcolm was in kindergarten, his father died tragically in a streetcar accident. Growing up in the Great Depression had its effects on young Malcolm, and so did growing up in a house and environment plagued with violence. In the 1940s Malcolm Little was incarcerated in a Massachusetts prison for crimes committed. He first noticed Elijah Muhammad's teachings in prison, but Malcolm also read scores of books on Christianity, philosophy, world religions, and books published by Jehovah's Witnesses. Subsequently he converted to NOI and in the 1950s and early 1960s fervently attacked the core doctrines of the Christian faith while calling Christianity the white man's religion, the devil's religion that deceived blacks into thinking they were cursed by God because of the color of their skin.

Louis Farrakhan's Contacts

Louis Eugene Walcott, born in 1933 and raised in Roxbury, Massachusetts, was a baptized Episcopalian in his early childhood. As a youngster he confessed that he loved Jesus and loved scripture but longed for answers. Answers never came from Christians, and Louis often recalled how his mother, in conversations with friends, mentioned her hope for a deliverer that would rescue the black people from their oppression. Like Elijah and Malcolm, Louis also made mention of hypocrites who carried the name of Christ, for he was made to sit only in the balconies of churches. This, said Louis, could not have been the teaching of Jesus.

Theological Issues with Christianity

Given the above, one may find it strange that the NOI utilizes themes and trappings of Christianity. For example, there is room for the Bible in the theology and practices of the NOI, and it is often quoted, even though the movement views it as a "poison book." Moreover, Jesus is mentioned in what the NOI considers positive and respectful ways, and biblical passages, verses, and themes (including mention of Jesus) are in NOI writings.

> **Study Aid #159**
>
> Current Issues
>
> True NOI mantle of leadership, Muhammad or Farrakhan?
> True Islam or racist Islam?
> Legacy: Elijah Muhammad or Malcolm X?

NOI contact with so-called Christians and their racism was mentioned earlier, but it is still necessary to state that true Christianity takes issue with the NOI that all whites are devils, given, for example, that the grace of God is demonstrated to all regardless of skin color. Further evidences of contact arise not so much with what the NOI affirms regarding certain Christian doctrines but with what the NOI denies, causing Christian reaction against the pseudo-Christian teachings of the NOI (though in comparison with other major heretical groups engaging the Christian church, little about the NOI is written by Christians).

According to the NOI the Christian God is a "spook god," but in providing an alternate view of God, the NOI is not as systematic as some might hope. In wading through NOI publications, one finds the confession that Fard is God, "Allah in the flesh." But one also finds that Fard is one of a string of finite gods (or Allahs) that have existed throughout time, and within this string there exists only one god at any given time (perhaps this is how the NOI confession, "There is no God but Allah," on the surface appears to be an orthodox Islamic confession). Still further, the NOI teaches that the title of "God" belongs to the black race collectively.

Other NOI doctrines include Jesus as dead and forever dead, he being no more than a man and a prophet. Jesus is not the Christ; Fard is the Christ. Neither is Jesus the Son of Man; this title is reserved for Fard. Christians take issue here because of the NOI's denial of the uniqueness of Jesus as both God and man. Evidencing this denial, the NOI employs Bible verses and arguments that deny the deity of Jesus in much the same way as in Jehovah's Witnesses publications. Subsequently, there is in NOI writings a rejection of and polemic against the biblical doctrine of the Trinity. Finally, there is no resurrection of the dead in the biblical sense. "Resurrection" according to the NOI is a "mental resurrection," a resurrection of the minds of mentally dead blacks who come to knowledge of both origin and identity. This marks in NOI doctrine a refusal of biblical eschatology, for there is life only in the here and now.

Further Reading

Lewis V. Baldwin and Amiri YaSin Al-Hadid. *Between Cross and Crescent: Christian and Muslim Perspectives on Malcolm and Martin.* University Press of Florida, 2002.

Edmund Curtis. *Islam in Black America.* SUNY Press, 2002.

Carl F. Ellis Jr. *Free at Last? The Gospel in the African-American Experience.* InterVarsity, 1996.

Alex Haley. *The Autobiography of Malcolm X.* Penguin, 2001.

Martha Lee. *The Nation of Islam: An American Millenarian Movement.* Syracuse University Press, 1996.

Elijah Muhammad. *Message to the Blackman in America.* Muhammad's Temple No. 2, 1965.

80

Transcendental Meditation: History, Beliefs, Practices

Geoff Gilpin

Transcendental Meditation (TM) is a spiritual practice that involves the mental repetition of a mantra—a sound that produces a sense of relaxation and inner peace. Originally practiced in India, TM was popularized by Maharishi Mahesh Yogi (1917–2008), a key figure in the spread of Eastern spirituality throughout the world in the second half of the twentieth century.

History

As a young man, Maharishi was a disciple of Swami Brahmananda Saraswati (1868–1953), known as "Guru Dev," a prominent Indian religious leader. Maharishi began his public career shortly after the death of his master, traveling across India on a successful lecture tour. He left the subcontinent in 1958 for a decade of extensive travel in Asia, Europe, and North America.

An energetic and charismatic teacher, Maharishi attracted committed followers and established TM centers around the world. In the early days of the TM movement, people who wanted to learn meditation got their instruction directly from Maharishi. By the early 1960s, however, there was enough demand that Maharishi began training groups of meditation teachers known as "initiators." By the end of the decade, Maharishi had trained thousands of young, idealistic TM teachers and deployed them in cities across North America and Europe.

At a lecture in London, England, in August of 1967, the audience included three members of the Beatles rock group. They quickly adopted Maharishi as their spiritual teacher, learned TM, and traveled to Rishikesh, India, to join him

> **Study Aid #160**
> Transcendental Meditation Timeline
>
>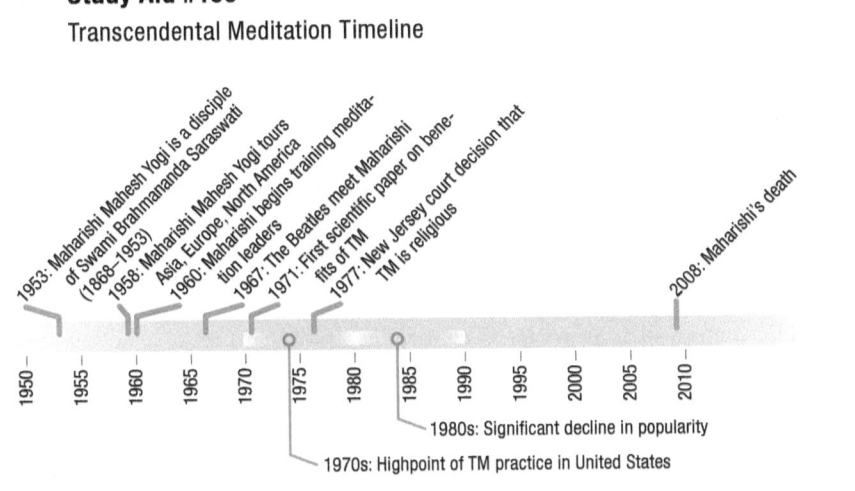

at his retreat. Although the Beatles did not remain in India or with Maharishi for long, their huge popularity and influence among young people ensured his celebrity.

Maharishi's fame came at a time when many Americans and other Westerners were interested in learning about Eastern spirituality. There were other Asian gurus and organizations teaching meditation at the time, but Maharishi was the most visible and best organized.

Another innovation involved scientific research. In 1971, the first scientific paper on the effects of TM, titled "A Wakeful Hypometabolic Physiologic State," appeared in the *American Journal of Physiology*. The researchers found that TM produces changes in respiration, brain-wave activity, and other variables. Later studies examined the effects of TM on blood pressure, anxiety, academic performance, use of alcohol and drugs, and many more physical, psychological, and social factors. Maharishi's organization collected these studies and reprinted them in widely distributed pamphlets.

The appeal of scientific authority, combined with Maharishi's fame and organizational skill, and the testimony of celebrity meditators including Clint Eastwood and talk show host Merv Griffin, made TM very popular in the late 1960s through the mid-1970s. According to the official TM website, more than five million people have learned the TM technique.

By the late 1970s, however, TM was just one of many options for Westerners interested in meditation. It was certainly one of the most expensive. (The fee increased sharply over the years, from $75 in the early 1970s to a high of $2,500 in the early 2000s.) Although the TM organization doesn't publish yearly initiation statistics, and there is no way of knowing how many people keep up with the practice, the general consensus is that the number of people learning and practicing TM has plummeted in the decades since its peak popularity.

Starting in the late 1970s, Maharishi introduced additional meditation techniques and an extensive line of consumer products and services. None of these proved popular with the general public. In his later years, Maharishi and his followers campaigned for government support and entered politics by organizing the Natural Law Party. These efforts proved largely unsuccessful.

Beliefs

In public venues, such as the introductory lectures where most people first learn about TM, Maharishi and his representatives frame his teachings in secular terms. Instead of promoting traditional Indian beliefs such as reincarnation or a pantheon of deities, they present meditation as a way to relieve stress, gain deep rest, and generally promote health and happiness. Many people who learn TM are motivated by these practical results and not by any beliefs regarding consciousness or spirituality.

However, for those who want to learn more about TM, Maharishi offers extensive teachings based on his interpretation of the Vedas, the ancient Sanskrit texts. According to Maharishi, TM practice goes back to the time of Vedic civilization.

A core principle of Maharishi's teaching is that the natural state of human life is bliss. According to Maharishi, suffering is an abnormal state caused by stress in the human nervous system. TM reduces this stress and allows the mind to follow its natural tendency toward transcendental awareness, or Being. Through regular contact with Being, the human nervous system evolves toward higher states of consciousness, eventually attaining a state of unity with the cosmos.

One of the most unusual aspects of Maharishi's teaching is an attempt to harmonize Vedic tradition with modern science. Under Maharishi's direction, physicists in his movement have discovered what they claim are correlations between the sounds of the Vedic hymns and the mathematics of advanced physics. Maharishi and his followers believe that this connection allows human consciousness to directly influence the laws governing matter and energy. By practicing the TM Sidhi program, an advanced form of meditation, they claim it is possible to develop paranormal abilities such as levitation, invisibility, and superhuman strength.

Furthermore, groups of meditators practicing the TM Sidhi program supposedly produce a phenomenon known as the Maharishi Effect. The results of this effect, which can operate over great distances, include reductions in crime and traffic accidents, less violence during wartime, growth in the stock market, and improved weather. The TM organization has published research studies that it claims provide scientific proof for the Maharishi Effect, although there seems to be little interest in the mainstream scientific community.

People who are seriously committed to Maharishi's teachings generally adopt a number of other beliefs based on his interpretations of the Vedic literature. These include Ayurveda, traditional Indian medicine, with its model of human physiology based on three governing principles known as *doshas*.

Other beliefs include traditional Indian astrology known as Jyotish, and Maharishi Sthapatya Veda, a system of architecture based on the idea that buildings should be constructed in alignment with cosmic forces. Maharishi encouraged his followers to avoid buildings with doors that face south, a direction that supposedly admits evil influences.

Practices

The process of learning TM begins with attending an introductory lecture that outlines the benefits of meditation and the basics of the practice. People who wish to continue attend a second, preparatory lecture and have a brief interview with the TM teacher. They are told of the requirements, which include abstaining from alcohol and recreational drugs for a brief period.

On initiation day, TM students report to a designated location, typically the home of a volunteer in the early days of the TM movement or, later on, one of Maharishi's educational or health facilities. Per the requirements, students bring fresh flowers, a piece of fruit, and a white handkerchief for use during the initiation ceremony.

During TM initiation, the teacher performs a *puja* ritual at an altar with a picture of Guru Dev, Maharishi's master. The teacher chants in Sanskrit and makes offerings from the flowers and other items brought by the student. After the *puja*, the initiator gives the student a mantra and guides him or her through the first period of meditation. Most TM students are instructed to meditate twice a day for twenty minutes per sitting.

After learning the basic TM technique, people who wish to pursue Maharishi's teachings have a number of options, from advanced lectures at a local TM center

---

Study Aid #161
Transcendental Meditation Beliefs

TM is a secular meditative technique
History of TM, however, goes back to the Vedas
A harmony between the Vedic tradition and modern science
Sonic theology
Paranormal abilities possible (levitation, invisibility)
The Maharishi Effect
Ayurvedic medicine

to weekend residence courses to enrollment at one of Maharishi's educational institutions. The TM Sidhi program is available to people who have practiced TM for at least two months. This program involves extended periods of meditation to accommodate the yogic techniques that purportedly lead to supernormal abilities. Practitioners, known as *sidhas*, may meditate for several hours a day.

The centerpiece of the TM Sidhi program is a practice called yogic flying. The flying technique involves meditating in a cross-legged position sitting on a foam mat. The technique leads to a hopping motion that practitioners believe is a precursor to genuine levitation.

Most members of the TM movement are vegetarians. Many rely on products and services sold by TM-related organizations, including health-food products, personal-care items, herbal remedies, astrological consultations, gemstones, and many others.

Current Status

Maharishi's death in 2008 leaves the future of his movement in question. The core members are the same baby boomers who joined in the late 1960s and early 1970s, a population that is aging and shrinking in numbers. Currently, the most visible leaders are the physicist John Hagelin, who ran for president of the United States three times on the pro-TM Natural Law Party ticket, and the film director David Lynch. Lynch has established a foundation for teaching TM in schools.

Further Reading

Herbert Benson. *The Relaxation Effect*. William Morrow, 2000.

Geoff Gilpin. *The Maharishi Effect: A Personal Journey through the Movement That Transformed American Spirituality*. Tarcher Penguin, 2006.

Maharishi Mahesh Yogi. *Maharishi Mahesh Yogi on the Bhagavad-Gita*. Penguin, 1990.

———. *Science of Being and Art of Living: Transcendental Meditation*. Plume, 2001.

Paul Mason. *The Maharishi: The Biography of the Man Who Gave Transcendental Meditation to the World*. Element, 1994.

81

Transcendental Meditation: Theological Exchanges, Current Issues

GEOFF GILPIN

Although the origins of Transcendental Meditation (TM) are obscure, the name was coined by Maharishi Mahesh Yogi (1917–2008). Maharishi combined elements of traditional Indian spiritual practice with his own teachings and a standardized method of marketing and instruction. His campaign to bring this package to a worldwide audience was remarkably successful, at least during the late 1960s through the mid-1970s. TM and Maharishi gave many Westerners—Christian and non-Christian alike—their first exposure to Eastern meditation and spirituality.

Maharishi began teaching TM in his native India, where his audience would have been mostly fellow Hindus. He achieved some success, although he was hardly unique as a meditation teacher in that culture.

Maharishi made his first trip to a predominantly Christian country, the United States, in 1958, where he established a base of operations in California with a small group of supporters. At that early stage of his career, Maharishi spread his message largely through low-tech, grassroots methods—word of mouth, advertising posters, amateur newsletters, and media coverage in the form of articles in local newspapers. Not surprisingly, his audiences remained relatively small.

His encounter with the Beatles in 1967 changed his fortunes dramatically. The Beatles lived in the glare of mass media. When Maharishi entered their orbit, he went from obscurity to celebrity sensation almost overnight.

The sudden eruption of TM into global consciousness is probably unique in religious history. Mainstream Westerners of all religious backgrounds were

> **Study Aid #162**
>
> **TM-Christian Contacts**
>
> 1958: Maharishi comes to United States
> 1977: Science of Creative Intelligence course taught in New Jersey high schools
> 1984: Cardinal Jamie Sin argues TM not compatible with Christianity
> 2005: David Lynch Foundation established
> 2008: TM benefit concert for "at-risk" students

suddenly confronted with an unexpected emissary from a strange world—an Eastern guru offering inner peace through the novel method of sitting in a chair with closed eyes.

For the duration of his celebrity, Maharishi enjoyed a pulpit that would have been the envy of the medieval popes. He spoke, and the TV, radio, and print media delivered his words to audiences around the world, whether they were interested in what he had to say or not. It was a genuine cultural shock. TM became wildly popular. Christians reacted in every possible way from enthusiasm to scorn to indifference.

When analyzing the role of TM in Christian culture, it's important to realize that the direct influence of Maharishi and his movement came and went fairly quickly. The popularity of TM peaked with Maharishi's appearance on the Merv Griffin daytime talk show in 1975 and declined steadily after that. By the end of the decade, the novelty of TM was over. People interested in pursuing an Eastern or New Age spiritual path had a smorgasbord of new gurus, groups, techniques, and therapies—far more options than they'd had when TM was the latest fad.

Maharishi himself spent the last decades of his life in seclusion. Many of the baby boomers who made up the core of his movement left to start families and careers. The momentum never came back. For most Christians, regardless of their attitudes about TM during its heyday, it hasn't been an issue for a long time.

Furthermore, any discussion of Christian contact with TM has to acknowledge that one side does not see the encounter as religious. TM itself, strictly speaking, is a meditation technique. Maharishi always stated that TM is not a religion. He and his representatives claim that TM is a neutral, secular "technology" for reducing stress in the human nervous system. They claim that people from all religious backgrounds can practice TM and benefit from it without any conflict over their beliefs.

The issue is complicated by the fact that many people use the phrase "TM" to refer to the network of organizations—such as the Students International Meditation Society—that Maharishi established over the years. As with the TM technique itself, Maharishi and others in his movement claim that these organizations exist for secular purposes, typically educational but also for economic development, health care, scientific research, and so on.

In practice, people who learn TM are welcome to observe any religion they wish. Of the millions who started TM during the 1960s and 1970s, certainly many, perhaps a majority, were professing Christians. These people were able to reconcile TM practice with their religious beliefs. Even some committed members of Maharishi's movement identify themselves with mainstream denominations.

Many critics—Christian and secular—have questioned the claim that TM is not religious. These critics often point to the TM initiation ceremony, the *puja*, which contains religious elements such as candles, incense, and a Sanskrit chant that makes reference to Indian deities.

Likewise, critics looking for religious elements in the TM organization find plenty of evidence. Maharishi's adherents refer to him as "His Holiness." They call the lineage of Indian masters who inspired Maharishi the "Holy Tradition."

Over the years, quite a few Christian authors have issued publications exposing the religious nature of TM and warning that TM practice is incompatible with Christian faith. Naturally, there was more motivation to produce this literature during the period when TM was a popular fad, and it appears that the number of these publications has dropped accordingly.

In 1984, Jaime Cardinal Sin (1928–2005), Catholic archbishop of Manila, Philippines, issued a statement in which he examined aspects of TM practice and Maharishi's teaching and found them "in open contradiction to Christian Doctrine" (www.ewtn.com/library/newage/sinmahar.txt).

In the opinion of Cardinal Sin, Maharishi's teachings involve an impersonal God rather than the personal God of Christian doctrine who has a relationship with individual humans. "Maharishi removes the distinction between the Creator and the creature. This directly leads to, or is an equivalent form of, pantheism." Cardinal Sin states that Maharishi ignores or denies other items of Christian doctrine including original sin, the immortality of the soul, and the redemptive power of Christ's suffering.

Many people who question the secular nature of TM point to a 1977 court decision in New Jersey. The case involved a class in TM and the Science of Creative Intelligence (or "SCI," a term that Maharishi used for the underlying theory behind TM) taught in five New Jersey high schools in the mid-1970s. Course materials and TM instruction were provided by the TM organization.

The plaintiffs in *Malnak v. Yogi* included parents of high school students and Americans United for Separation of Church and State. The defendants included Maharishi (who did not testify or appear in court) and several of his organizations and chief supporters.

The trial involved a near-microscopic examination of the TM initiation ceremony (the *puja*), as well as the language in TM movement publications. The court ruled in favor of the plaintiffs, barring the teaching of TM in New Jersey public schools on constitutional grounds: "Defendants have failed to raise the slightest doubt as to the facts or as to the religious nature of the teachings of the Science of Creative Intelligence and the *puja*. The teaching of the SCI/TM course

> **Study Aid #163**
>
> **Current Issues**
>
> Whether or not TM can be taught in public schools
> Rising prices of TM meditation training
> Compatibility with orthodox Christian teachings:
>   Hindu religious backgrounds
>   "Centering Prayer" techniques

in New Jersey public high schools violates the establishment clause of the first amendment, and its teaching must be enjoined."

Although many Christians are reluctant to adopt TM because of its religious overtones, they may be attracted by the practical claims of TM—relaxation, stress relief, lower blood pressure, and so on. They may also desire the sense of inner silence and peace that TM practitioners report.

Certainly, the benefits of meditation are not unique to TM. Christianity has a rich contemplative tradition with much to offer those seeking an agreeable form of meditation. Christians seeking an alternative to TM might consider the Jesus Prayer or, for Catholics, the rosary.

One form of meditation that has become highly successful with Christian individuals and groups is Centering Prayer. Developed in the mid-1970s by three Cistercian monks—William Meninger, Basil Pennington, and Thomas Keating—the instructions for learning and practicing Centering Prayer are remarkably similar to those for TM. The main difference is that the word or sound used as a focus of meditation is chosen by the practitioner and not delivered by a teacher or group. Also, there is no instruction ceremony; the practice can be learned for free from a book or website.

Although TM is nowhere nearly as popular as it was three decades ago, Maharishi's successors continue to promote it. The David Lynch Foundation for Consciousness-Based Education and World Peace, established in 2005 by the noted film director, offers grants to schools for teaching TM to students in grades 6 through 12.

In April of 2008, the foundation staged a benefit concert for its campaign to teach TM to one million "at-risk" students. The concert featured the surviving Beatles and contemporary celebrities like Jerry Seinfeld and Sheryl Crow. Although tame by the standards of the 1960s, the Lynch Foundation has given TM more publicity than it has had in many years. It has also raised some of the old controversy.

In 2006, the foundation withdrew a $175,000 grant offer to Terra Linda High School in San Rafael, California, due to local protests over the religious nature of TM. Christian observers who are interested in the ongoing relationship with TM will undoubtedly be watching the progress of the Lynch Foundation campaign to teach meditation in American schools.

Further Reading

Jack Forem. *TM: The Essential Teachings*. Hay House, 2012.

David Lynch. *Catching the Big Fish*. Tarcher, 2007.

Norman Rosenthal and Mehmet Oz. *Transcendence: Healing and Transformation*. Tarcher, 2012.

Robert Roth. *TM: A New Introduction*. Primus, 1995.

82

Soka Gakkai: History, Beliefs, Practices

Guy McCloskey

History

The Soka Gakkai (Value Creation Society) dates its founding as November 18, 1930, when Tsunesaburo Makiguchi (1871–1944) and Josei Toda (1900–1958), progressive Japanese educators, published Makiguchi's *Soka Kyoiku Taikei* (The theory of value-creating pedagogy), in which Makiguchi argued that the ultimate purpose of education is the happiness of the child. The two men had encountered the Lotus Sutra–based Buddhist teachings of Nichiren (1222–82) two years earlier and aligned themselves with the Nichiren Shoshu head temple, Taiseki-ji. Soon, the focus of the organization became religious rather than educational, and its membership grew to three thousand as it expanded beyond educators to include the general populace.

During World War II, the militarist Japanese government ordered that *kamifuda*, Shinto talismans, be enshrined in every home. The Nichiren Shoshu priesthood accepted the decree and summoned Makiguchi and Toda to the head temple, instructing them and their followers to do the same. When they refused, they were banned from visiting the temple in order to avoid any government suspicion of collusion. The priesthood also deleted phrases from Nichiren's writings that placed buddhas above Shinto deities and modified the format of their worship to accommodate government demands.

In July 1943 Makiguchi and Toda were arrested as "thought criminals" and imprisoned. Makiguchi died in prison on November 18, 1944. Toda was released in 1945, shortly before the end of the war, with his health weakened and his business enterprises in ruins.

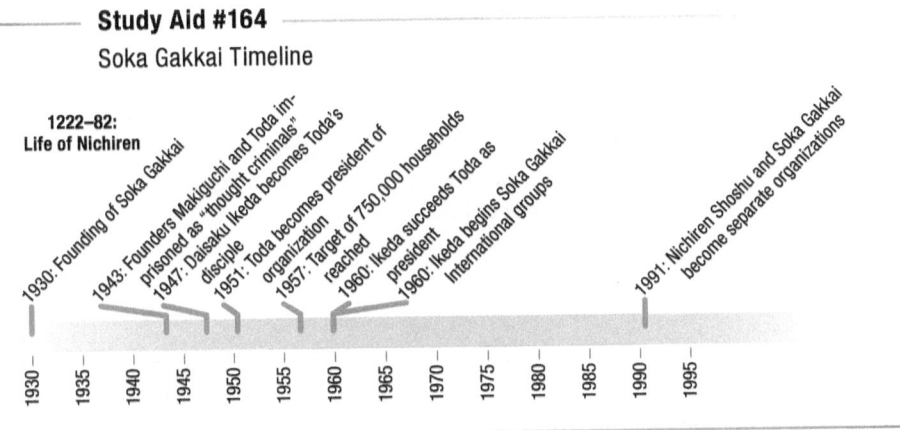

Study Aid #164
Soka Gakkai Timeline

Daisaku Ikeda (1928–) met Toda for the first time at a Soka Gakkai discussion meeting in August 1947. The nineteen-year-old Ikeda was impressed by Toda's answers to his questions about life and Japanese society. He felt that he could trust Toda and adopted him as his mentor. He went to work for one of Toda's publishing companies and began his earnest and lifelong practice of Nichiren Buddhism as Toda's disciple.

Toda became president of the organization on May 3, 1951, and, in his inaugural address, shocked the audience of three thousand members by declaring his intention to realize a membership of 750,000 households before his death. His failure to do so, he said, would mean that there should be no funeral service for him and his remains should be tossed into the sea.

That target of 750,000 households—a 150-fold increase in membership—was achieved in late 1957, several months before Toda's death on April 2, 1958, thanks in great part to Ikeda's efforts in leading the propagation efforts of members throughout Japan.

Ikeda served as Toda's youth chief of staff and was his closest disciple and his chosen successor. He became president of the Soka Gakkai on May 3, 1960, and has led the organization to a global membership of twelve million practitioners in 192 countries and territories. He has traveled widely and engaged in some sixteen hundred dialogues around the world, emphasizing the humanistic Buddhist values of peace, culture, and education.

In 1991, the uneasy relationship with the Nichiren Shoshu priesthood ended when the high priest excommunicated the entire Soka Gakkai membership and proceeded to destroy multiple temple facilities that had been donated by the organization, including the sixty-six-hundred-seat Grand Main Temple. The vast majority of members remained with the Soka Gakkai. Members worldwide consider the excommunication their spiritual independence, allowing them to continue as an exclusively lay movement, free to engage in interfaith dialogue and further expand the modern application of Nichiren's teachings.

Soka Gakkai International-USA (SGI-USA) began with Japanese war brides coming to the United States in the late 1950s and early 1960s with their returning American military husbands. Ikeda made his first overseas trip in October 1960, when he established organizations in Honolulu, San Francisco, Seattle, Chicago, New York, Los Angeles, and Washington, DC. The American affiliate now operates more than one hundred centers, serving some 125,000 members. It is the most diverse Buddhist association in the country.

Beliefs

The Soka Gakkai practices Nichiren Buddhism as taught by the eponymous thirteenth-century founder of the school. It has made his writings widely available, including a two-volume collection in English. Ikeda, as the modern interpreter of the philosophy, takes the lead in expounding the teachings for contemporary followers.

Nichiren studied the Lotus Sutra of the historical Buddha Shakyamuni, or Gautama Siddhartha (circa 580–460 BCE), and determined that the title of the sutra in the Japanese reading, *Myoho-renge-kyo*, preceded by *nam*, or devotion, contains the essence of the entire sutra and the universal law of life that is immanent within all living beings. There is no discrimination in Nichiren Buddhism; the same potential for Buddhahood, or enlightenment, is present in every living being, just as the pure lotus flower blooms in a muddy swamp.

In one of his earliest extant writings, Nichiren (Gosho Translation Committee 1999, 1:3) states:

> If you wish to free yourself from the sufferings of birth and death you have endured since time without beginning and to attain without fail unsurpassed enlightenment in this lifetime, you must perceive the mystic truth that is originally inherent in all living beings. This truth is Myoho-renge-kyo. Chanting Myoho-renge-kyo will therefore enable you to grasp the mystic truth innate in all life.

Chanting *Nam-myoho-renge-kyo* (I devote myself to the Lotus Sutra of the Wonderful Law) places one's life in harmony with the rhythm of the universe and evokes the Buddha wisdom from within, clarifying the course to follow in this existence for the sake of one's own fulfillment while contributing to the welfare of others.

Realizing that cause and effect originate within one's own karmic existence enables one to take responsibility for—and control over—one's circumstances and relationships with people and things in one's environment. The *bodhisattva*—a seeker after enlightenment—manifests the ideals of wisdom and compassion, vowing "to attain enlightenment only after having first saved others from suffering."

Chanting *Nam-myoho-renge-kyo* is not directed to an external power, but is an expression of the determination of the human spirit to harmonize with the ultimate reality of the universe. Through continuing in this practice, one brings forth the highest potential from within one's life, a process referred to as "human revolution." Ikeda states in the preface to his twelve-volume historical novel *The Human Revolution* (2004):

> A great human revolution in just a single person will help achieve a change in the destiny of a nation and, further, will cause a change in the destiny of all humankind.

Practices

The repeated invocation of *Nam-myoho-renge-kyo* is the primary practice of Nichiren Buddhists. Soka Gakkai members, as disciples of Nichiren, in addition to chanting *Nam-myoho-renge-kyo*, follow a daily morning and evening liturgy consisting of the recitation of portions of the second and sixteenth chapters of the twenty-eight-chapter Lotus Sutra based on the translation from Sanskrit into Chinese by the renowned Kumarajiva (344–413).

Nichiren inscribed a mandala, called the Gohonzon, or fundamental object of devotion, for his followers that embodies the eternal and intrinsic law of *Nam-myoho-renge-kyo*. Transcriptions of the Gohonzon are enshrined in members' homes, where it is the focus of their morning and evening chanting of *Nam-myoho-renge-kyo* and recitation of the Lotus Sutra.

There are three basics in applying Nichiren Buddhism to daily life: faith, practice, and study. Faith begins with one's willingness to engage in a consistent, correct practice with the expectation that positive results will follow. Practice is for the sake of oneself and others based on the regular chanting of *Nam-myoho-renge-kyo* and reciting the sutra passages, as well as sharing Buddhist teachings with others so that they, too, can transform the inevitable sufferings of existence in this world. Study focuses on the writings of Nichiren and their modern application as elucidated by Soka Gakkai president Ikeda.

The Soka Gakkai is action-based; its members are determined to show actual proof of the benefits of their practice in their daily lives in response to Nichiren's

---

Study Aid #165
Soka Gakkai Beliefs

Teachings of Nichiren (1222–82) Buddhism
Lotus Sutra primary text
Enlightenment (Buddhahood) within reach of all
Chanting of *Nam-myoho-renge-kyo*
Recitation of portions of Lotus Sutra
Three basics: faith, practice, study

exhortation to realize *kosen-rufu*, the widespread propagation of his teachings for the sake of world peace.

> My wish is that all my disciples make a great vow. (Gosho Translation Committee 1999, 1:1003)

> The "great vow" refers to the propagation of the Lotus Sutra. (Gosho Translation Committee 2004, 82)

Soka Gakkai members gather regularly in small groups for discussion meetings within their local community, at which they share their faith experiences and study Nichiren's teachings. Their daily Buddhist practice, however, is completed before their home altars. In the United States, SGI-USA is the most diverse among all Buddhist associations.

Further Reading

Pat Alright. *Basics of Buddhism*. Taplow, 1999.

Gosho Translation Committee. *The Record of the Orally Transmitted Teachings*. Soka Gakkai, 2004.

———. *The Writings of Nichiren Daishonin*. 2 vols. Soka Gakkai, 1999–2006.

Daisaku Ikeda. *The Human Revolution*. World Tribune, 2004.

Richard Hughes Seager. *Encountering the Dharma: Daisaku Ikeda, Soka Gakkai, and the Globalization of Buddhist Humanism*. University of California Press, 2006.

Burton Watson, trans. *The Lotus Sutra*. Wisdom, 2009.

Shin Yatomi. *Buddhism in a New Light*. 2nd ed. World Tribune, 2012.

83

Soka Gakkai: Theological Exchanges, Current Issues

WILLIAM AIKEN

Perhaps the single word that best characterizes the Soka Gakkai in its relations with other religions is "evolving." In the space of a relatively short span of years, the Nichiren Buddhist lay society has gone from being perceived as an exclusivist Buddhist cult on a mission to refute the teachings of other religions to being understood as a religion committed to interreligious understanding, dialogue, and cooperation. There are perhaps numerous reasons for this transformation, but chief among them are (1) the separation of the lay Buddhist society from the clergy of the more orthodox and fundamentalist Nichiren Shoshu school; and (2) the leadership of the group's third president, Daisaku Ikeda, and his well-articulated vision of the Lotus-Nichiren tradition as a broader, more inclusive movement that intentionally values diversity and dialogue.

In its earlier years as a lay society that was affiliated with and based on the teachings of the Nichiren Shoshu school, the Soka Gakkai carried out intense propagation efforts based on the position of that school that all teachings other than Nichiren's were heretical or lesser and should be abandoned in favor of Nichiren Buddhism. Engagement with other religious communities that was not for the purpose of proselytizing was essentially absent.

As the Soka Gakkai grew and spread to countries outside of Japan, things began to change. In May 1972, Soka Gakkai president Daisaku Ikeda began a series of dialogues with the Oxford historian Arnold Toynbee, exploring a wide range of topics that would later be published under the title *Choose Life*. With Toynbee's encouragement, Ikeda embarked on a process of engagement with hundreds of the

> **Study Aid #166**
> **Soka Gakkai–Christian Contacts**
> Proselytizing phase
>   Nichiren *shakubaku* ("break and destroy")
>   Nichiren Shoshu orthodoxy
> Dialogue phase
>   Ikeda's internationalization
>   Respect, conversation, cooperation
>   1995 SGI Charter

world's foremost thinkers, leaders, and activists, including former Soviet premier Mikhail Gorbachev, economist John Kenneth Galbraith, and civil rights activist Rosa Parks. His pursuit of dialogue would span more than forty years and culminate in over sixty books published in twenty-eight languages.

This impulse toward dialogue and exchange, combined with the international growth of the movement and the growing trend toward religious pluralism, led to tensions between the outgoing lay movement and the more tradition-minded clergy. Things came to a head in late 1990 when the Nichiren Shoshu priesthood took punitive action against Ikeda and other top leaders. Among their complaints were that the Soka Gakkai's chorus had sung Beethoven's "Ode to Joy," which they saw as inappropriately praising God.

This eventually led to the excommunication of the twelve-million-member society, an event that its members now view as their moment of "spiritual independence." The split opened the doors for the group to redefine itself, under Ikeda's leadership, as a global movement of Buddhist "humanism," less bound by the exclusivist dogmatism of Nichiren Shoshu and more rooted in what they perceived to be the original Buddhist spirit of compassionate dialogue.

In 1995, the SGI Charter was adopted, which further defined this change in course, stating, "SGI shall . . . respect other religions, engage in dialogue and work together with them toward the resolution of fundamental issues concerning humanity" (article 7). This point was further highlighted by Daisaku Ikeda both in his writings and in his founding of such institutions as the Boston Research Center (now the Ikeda Center for Peace, Learning, and Dialogue), whose programs include public forums and scholarly seminars that are organized collaboratively and offer a range of perspectives on key issues in global ethics.

While the SGI has remained committed to what they view as the compassionate act of propagation, the encounter model has shifted decisively from one of refutation to respectful dialogue, captured by the phrase "when you bow to the Buddha inside another the Buddha inside of them bows in return." This dialogue is also seen as "planting the seed" of Buddhahood in another's life with the belief that over time that seed may sprout and the person may take faith. It has been said that the SGI now seeks to navigate between being a broad movement promoting universal humanistic values and maintaining its particular religious outlook rooted in the Lotus Sutra and the teachings of Nichiren.

True to the Nichiren tradition, Ikeda has maintained the centrality of the Lotus Sutra and the teachings of Nichiren. But differently from some of the more exclusivist interpretations of Nichiren, he holds up the core principle of Lotus Sutra—the universal potential for Buddhahood and the inherent dignity of the human being—as a standard that he believes can illuminate all of the world's religious traditions. He calls for a humanizing of religion, and a refocusing of its role as being of service to human beings and setting a new standard for evaluating religion.

> "Does religion make people stronger or does it weaken them? Does it encourage what is good or what is evil in them? Are they made better and more wise, or less so by religion?" These are questions we need to ask of all religions including of Buddhism.

When we look at how the SGI is viewed by others, we find the picture mixed and also very much in transition. Since there is not much in the way of published literature on Christian exchanges with the SGI and Nichiren Buddhism, one is left to search the web for windows into these views. There are some internet resources that characterize the SGI as a cult, and there are those who see any expression of Buddhism with its nontheism and human centeredness as problematic. But for the most part it is viewed as a modern Buddhist expression. Indeed, it counts among its sympathizers two well-known Baptist ministers, Dr. Lawrence Edward Carter of the Martin Luther King Jr. International Chapel at Morehouse College in Atlanta, Georgia, and emeritus Harvard theologian Dr. Harvey Cox, who published a dialogue with Ikeda titled *The Persistence of Religion: Comparative Perspectives on Modern Spirituality* (I. B. Tauris, 2009). Cox finds within the Soka Gakkai movement "an example in the Buddhist tradition of this movement from hierarchy to egalitarianism, to ecumenical and interfaith openness, and to commitment to human rights and peacemaking."

Today, Soka Gakkai's missionary impulse is seen not only in its propagation activities but also in its broader community outreach. It is an outreach that has in recent years taken on a more interfaith character. As a socially engaged Buddhist movement active in the areas of peace, cultural exchange, human rights, and education, the group has partnered with numerous faith-based organizations and

---

Study Aid #167

Current Issues

Interreligious dialogue with other religions
Peacemaking activities
Engagement in justice activities
Evaluation of the generic category of religion

others in advocating for nuclear disarmament, environmental stewardship, racial and gender equality, free religious expression, and church-state separation. From this standpoint the exchanges with other faiths tend to be seen more as partnerships based upon shared social goals than on scholarly or doctrinal exchanges.

A couple of recent examples of this type of partnering include the following.

The Three Faiths Project, initiated by the SGI-UK and funded by a grant from the home office, brought together twenty-four young people from Buddhist, Islamic, and black Christian centers in South London. Through a series of meetings and workshops, the program aimed to help young people transcend their differences and pursue an engaged community citizenship.

The 9/11 Unity Walk, an interfaith project centered in Washington, DC, brings together people of all ages, backgrounds, and faiths to learn to respect each other through a framework of experiential education, compassionate leadership, and intentional service. Since 2004, the local SGI community has been working together with ten other religious centers to support this event.

In the fall of 2010, the Soka Gakkai celebrated the eightieth anniversary of its founding in Japan and the fiftieth anniversary of its movement within the United States. As its activities over the past twenty-five years have shown, it sees itself as a religious movement that is maturing in its efforts to broadly apply Buddhist-humanist values on a cooperative basis while maintaining its own identity as a faithful expression of the Lotus-Nichiren stream of Mahayana Buddhism.

Further Reading

Karel Dobbelaere. *Soka Gakkai: From Lay Movement to Religion.* Signature, 2001.

Phillip Hammond and David Machacek. *Soka Gakkai in America.* Oxford University Press, 1999.

Christopher Queen, ed. *Engaged Buddhism in the West.* Wisdom, 2000.

84

Soka Gakkai: Adherent Essay

VIRGINIA BENSON

I am a baby boomer who grew up in a suburb of Boston as the youngest of four children. My family belonged to a local Episcopal congregation, and my mother, an earth scientist, taught us that God is love. In college during the late 1960s, as the Vietnam War raged and my generation rebelled, I turned inward and explored existentialist philosophy, then dropped out of school in a futile attempt to find a purpose in life. By the time I finally graduated, I was agnostic and still had no clue how to heal the world. Throughout my twenties and early thirties, happiness eluded me as I labored away at high-powered jobs and tried to find a life partner. Finally at thirty-five, after a painful divorce and an unexpected layoff, I took time out to reflect. Inevitably, I returned to questions about meaning and purpose that had plagued me in college.

At this juncture, twenty-seven years ago, I encountered the Soka Gakkai International (SGI), a lay organization for practitioners of the Buddhist tradition founded by a thirteenth-century Japanese priest and religious reformer named Nichiren. A writer friend introduced me to a lively, open, and diverse group of SGI members meeting in Greenwich Village. I was surprised and intrigued by their adamant claim that reciting *Nam-myoho-renge-kyo*, the core teaching of Nichiren, could effect concrete, intentional changes in anyone's life. It seemed too simple to be true, so I bought a few books by SGI president Daisaku Ikeda and pored over them for several weeks as I learned to recite the liturgy. From this initial study and practice, I found that Nichiren Buddhism not only restored my hope of finding meaningful work but also, I felt, opened up a solid path to world peace—beginning with my own inner transformation.

Indeed, in a short period of time, my life began to change dramatically. My outlook and mood brightened, and I became more self-directed. I decided to move back to the Boston area. I felt strong enough to address long-standing problems in my relationship with my father. Reentering a field I thought I would never work in again, I helped a businessman in his eighties to establish Pioneer Institute, a state and local public policy institute. We made an unexpected success of it. Then, in 1993, I was appointed as the first executive director of the Ikeda Center for Peace, Learning, and Dialogue (formerly Boston Research Center for the Twenty-first Century). Mr. Ikeda established this institute in Cambridge after he gave a lecture at Harvard University on Mahayana Buddhism and how it can contribute to the evolution of a peaceful world in the twenty-first century.

For sixteen years I directed the center's able staff as we hosted educational seminars and forums on East-West philosophy and developed books for college courses on global ethics and humanistic education. This summer, I graduated to senior research fellow, finally having a chance to study in depth the founder's approach to peace, learning, and dialogue. Along the way, I fully reconciled with my father, cared for an invalid mother, created a happy marriage, and served as a grassroots leader in SGI-USA. Today, I feel a profound sense of gratitude to President Ikeda and SGI for helping me find my way from troubled beginnings to a meaningful, contributive life.

The personal arc of "human revolution" I just described is a core concept in the philosophy of SGI, and, in slightly different words, in the teachings of Nichiren. It is a practical application of the profound Buddhist insight into the essential oneness of self and environment. The idea is that the self-motivated inner change of a single individual radiates outward through the web of life and rejuvenates human society. Thus, changes in the self are reflected in one's environment. Through small neighborhood discussion meetings, informal visits, and youth meetings, SGI members help each other deepen our faith, practice, and study of Nichiren Buddhism. The shared goal is for each unique person to improve the way we live in and influence the world around us, and thereby create ever-expanding cultures of peace.

In its "official" relationship with Christianity, SGI has been guided by its founding president, Mr. Ikeda. Under his leadership, Nichiren Buddhism—after insignificant historical contact with Christianity within Japan—became a global religion. In a message to the Sixth International Conference of the Society for Buddhist-Christian Studies in August of 2000, President Ikeda affirmed his consistent commitment to dialogue between Buddhism and Christianity. He said, "The encounter between these two streams of philosophy which have influenced peoples of South and North as well as East and West is perhaps one of the most important in any attempt to address the complex and tenacious problems afflicting humanity."

In this message and in other writings, Mr. Ikeda has recognized the differences of belief between these two traditions, but he has stressed the need to find as many points of convergence as possible. This way, he believes, we can create a "working partnership" to challenge and resolve the urgent problems facing humanity. When dialogue is pursued with this aim of global problem solving, differences in doctrine contribute to a holistic view of the way forward for all peoples. In numerous published dialogues with thinkers inspired by a Christian worldview, Mr. Ikeda has helped to pool wisdom from both traditions for the sake of peace in its fullest sense.

Several basic commonalities between Christianity and Nichiren Buddhism have emerged from Mr. Ikeda's dialogues. For example, our behavioral ideals are similar. Bodhisattva Never Disparaging, a key figure in the parables of the Lotus Sutra, is an ideal extolled and exemplified by Nichiren. This *bodhisattva* respects all people and honors their potential for Buddhahood no matter how hostile or arrogant they may appear to be on the surface. This compassionate ideal resonates with the life of Jesus and his love for all people. The two religions have shown increasing concern about environmental issues. Moreover, each tradition emphasizes personal morality based on the conviction that how one lives one's life determines what happens after death.

SGI became a completely lay-led organization in 1991 when the Japanese Nichiren Shoshu priesthood with which it was affiliated suddenly excommunicated President Ikeda and all SGI members. Since that time, SGI has revolutionized its understanding of Nichiren, coming more closely into line with the original compassionate spirit of his teachings. In the process, SGI has opened itself to much greater engagement with other religious and secular groups that share our peaceful ideals.

As a Nichiren Buddhist living in the United States, I practice a minority religion in a predominantly Christian civic culture. Since I was raised a Christian, my worldview has been deeply influenced by Christianity. My family and many of my friends are at least nominally Christian. As various Buddhist practices and philosophies have taken hold in this country, I encounter more and more people who either practice another form of Buddhism or are familiar with Buddhist philosophy in general. Within the larger tradition of American Buddhism, Zen, Tibetan, and other meditation-based practices remain better known than Nichiren Buddhism, with its distinctive emphasis on chanting *Nam-myoho-renge-kyo* and challenging the problems of daily living.

My relationship to Christianity has positive and negative aspects. For example, I feel indebted to my mother's understanding of Christianity for having fostered in me a spirit of love and service. Without this attitude, I might have lacked the motivation to find a meaningful mission in life—the impulse that brought me to Buddhism. Among my American heroes is Martin Luther King Jr. I admire the Christian ideals that inspired his courageous leadership. Likewise, I am drawn to Jane Addams, a Christian who stood up for peace and justice in her own time. Deeply committed Christians I have met through my peace and policy work have also inspired me.

On the negative side, I struggle as a former Christian with certain delusions about life itself that conflict with the teachings of Buddhism and probably also with the most profound Christian understandings. For example, a contradictory mix of negative feelings—from guilt, unworthiness, and hopelessness to self-righteousness, alienation, and anger—can threaten to overwhelm me at times. As I chant, study, and take action to break through these tendencies, I often can trace their origins back to internalized, perhaps poorly understood, Christian notions. Other Buddhists who formerly were Christians experience similar internal struggles. A typical external struggle for Nichiren Buddhists occurs in personal relationships with Christians who sometimes harbor prejudices against non-Christians and/or nontheists. More tolerant Christians, on the other hand, may have absorbed negative preconceptions about SGI from the internet and other sources, or may confuse SGI with what they know about Nichiren Shoshu, other schools of Buddhism, or New Age spirituality.

I have found that the antidote to such misunderstandings is simply heart-to-heart dialogue, the hallmark of President Ikeda's lifelong practice of "Buddhist humanism." In his estimation, dialogue among human beings, transcending religious (and any other) distinctions, is the most important way to build the base of shared empathy we need for peace. He has stated, "More than dialogue among religious groups, there is a need for dialogue among people. This dialogue should focus not on religious beliefs but on human life. This is of course not easy, but if people do not communicate on this level, things will only get more difficult."

As an American, I feel that many of the values that implicitly underpin our shared civic culture are fundamentally at odds with core values held individually by Christians and Buddhists. Yet based on insights from the dialogues of Mr. Ikeda with Christian thinkers, I am encouraged by the fact that the behavioral ideals of our traditions are similar—that each of us seeks to manifest the compassion of Jesus or of Nichiren. More frank discussions about how we struggle to live up to these ideals in our relationships with others on a daily basis would help to keep us honest, refreshed, cooperative, and effective in our shared struggles to challenge and change the status quo. By expanding our circle of dialogue partners, we might also uncover similar behavioral ideals upheld by other traditions, with similarly advantageous results across the globe.

Finding common ground in our individual struggles to become fully human is an indispensable step toward addressing such global challenges as abolishing war, eliminating nuclear weapons, democratizing the United Nations, and heading off environmental catastrophe. President Ikeda has written, "It is my firm belief that problems caused by human beings can be solved by human being." I am convinced that no social goal, no matter how lofty and idealistic it may seem, remains out of reach if we approach it through sincere dialogue coupled with a willingness to learn and grow from our encounters.

85

NRM:
Nature Religions
Introduction

TERRY C. MUCK

There has surely never been a time when the forces of nature have not been considered to some extent divine. Premodern peoples were convinced that the awesome powers of the sun and the seas, thunder and lightning, wind and rain were the thinly disguised manifestations of gods working their wills on human beings and the world they lived in.

For moderns, the powers of the world around us impressed no less, but instead of imagining those powers themselves to be gods, they were assigned to the control of a Creator God who could work his (and occasionally her) will on all the world. And as moderns grew more sophisticated in their understandings of how the world worked, the awe became respect and wonder at the intricate balances

---

Study Aid #168

Nature Religions

Paganism and neopaganism: Nature-based spiritualities that have arisen in the Western world in late modernity.

Gnosticism: A collection of ancient religions and worldviews that teach that human beings should shun the material world in favor of the spiritual.

Environmentalism: A philosophy, ideology, social movement religion regarding concern for conservation and improvement of the physical world.

and complex interworkings of a creation so large and beautiful, it had to be a work of supernatural origin.

The religions that resulted from these musings have been varied. We suggest three in this section. Neopaganism was and is largely unreflective worship of nature; Gnosticism is a rejection of the material world in favor of a supposed superior spiritual world; and environmentalism is a seeming attempt at nature worship in a way that would be acceptable in an overly rationalized modernity.

86

Paganism and Neopaganism: History, Beliefs, Practices

JOHN MOREHEAD

History

Paganism is an umbrella term for a variety of nature-based spiritualities that have arisen in the Western world in late modernity. The general scholarly consensus is that the term "paganism" comes from the Latin word *paganus*, literally meaning "rustic," "rural," or "country dweller" and referring to the religion of the people of the countryside. However, this etymology is in some dispute, and alternatives have been suggested with *pagani* or *pagus* as references to the "followers of the old or traditional religion." The term "neo-paganism," or "neopaganism," is often used by scholars when referring to these spiritualities in order to distinguish them from classical paganism. Practitioners of these spiritualities often use the self-referential term "Pagan." It is usually capitalized as a sign of respect and legitimacy afforded other expressions of religion.

Paganism is generally understood with reference to a diverse new religious movement that draws upon a variety of pre-Christian sources. The background of paganism involves a number of historical antecedent roots. These include the Romantic movement of the late eighteenth and early nineteenth centuries, medieval Freemasonry, various reformulations of ancient Greek and Roman classical paganism, and folklore and the "cunning craft" practices of remote rural areas in England.

Two figures were especially significant in the history of the development of paganism: Aleister Crowley and Gerald Gardner. Crowley, who had been involved with the Hermetic Order of the Golden Dawn and Ordo Templi Orientis, developed a system of magic called thelemic magick, which he derived from nineteenth- and

> **Study Aid #169**
>
> Paganism and Neopaganism
>
> | Historical Roots: Romanticism, classical paganism, magic | Aleister Crowley—Magick | Gerald Gardner—Wicca | Druidry, heathenism, goddess spirituality |

early twentieth-century European and American esoteric practices. Crowley's magick in turn had an influence upon Gardner. Another significant influence on Gardner was Margaret Murray, an Egyptologist and folklorist who popularized the now-discredited idea of pre-Christian European fertility religion alleged to have survived into the modern period. Gardner incorporated these ideas into his creation of a Mother Goddess–centered form of Wicca or witchcraft, with rituals and strands of thought that would later be imported from Great Britain into the United States. Gardner's Wicca was modified as it was practiced in the United States and came to broader appeal in the counterculture movement of the 1960s and 1970s. Gardnerian Wicca provided both the inspiration and a general template for various forms of paganism.

Many forms and expressions of paganism exist, with Wicca (Witchcraft, the Witches' Craft, or simply the Craft) as the most prominent and serving as the backbone of contemporary paganism. Other major forms include Druidry, heathenism (including Odinism and Ásatrú), and goddess spirituality.

Practices

Paganism is a religion that emphasizes practice rather than belief. Although there are common beliefs associated with paganism, the emphasis is placed upon the experience of the divine through a variety of rituals. These may include drumming, music, dancing, chanting, and meditation.

The basic format for worship in paganism involves the creation of a circle, grove, or coven (for witches). This involves the practice of the creation of a sacred space in the form of casting a circle, most often outside, or at times in a home. Various forces or deities are then invoked and invited into the circle. This invocation may involve the embodiment of the deity in the priestess/priest, which enables those present to participate in the presence of the forces and deities called upon. As a result of this process, magical energy is evoked, and the participant is able to tap into these energies as a means of transforming the self. At the conclusion of the ritual the circle is opened once again.

Most pagans follow a sacred calendar that is cyclical. It is known as the Wheel of the Year and involves eight annual seasonal festivals. These include Samhain, Midwinter (Yule, or Winter Solstice), Imbolc (or Candalmas), Spring Equinox, Beltain, Summer Solstice, Lughnasad (or Lammas), and the Autumn Equinox.

Pagans gather for the Esbats of new and full moon cycles, as well as the major seasonal festivals of Sabbats. Other pagans follow a different calendar that is informed by their cultural perspective and tradition.

Magic is also a common practice, defined by Crowley as "the art or science of causing change in conformity to will." This involves ritually induced trance experiences designed to change the self and in turn influence surroundings. Magical practices within paganism draw from Crowley's thelemic magick as well as Gardner's Witchcraft.

Pagans usually practice their religion individually as solitaries, but they may also come together for public rituals and festivals, as well as conferences. The internet also provides an important venue in bringing the diversity of pagans together in order to share information and experiences, and to form community.

Beliefs

Paganism is not a dogmatic or creedal religion. It is also pluralistic in its understanding of truth and nonauthoritarian in structure. In keeping with these facets, there is great diversity in pagan beliefs. As stated above, paganism is a nature religion. Nature is viewed as a manifestation of the divine and as such is sacred. Concepts of the divine are various and may involve polytheism, pantheism, animism, and even atheism wherein the deities are interpreted as archetypes or aspects of the individual rather than as entities that exist beyond the practitioner. Within paganism, emphasis is placed upon the feminine, particularly the Great Goddess, who also has a consort in the form of the god. Pagans also have an ethical system drawn from their various traditions wherein individuals seek to practice what they will so long as it does not harm another person. The best known of these is the Wiccan Rede, "An Ye Harm None, Do What Ye Will," and the Rule of Three, or Threefold Law, where it is held that whatever energies are released into the world, whether positive or negative, will return to the individual in threefold fashion.

A number of stereotypes circulate concerning paganism, many of which are passed along by Christians. One of the most frequent is the association of paganism with Satanism. In reality pagans do not acknowledge the existence of the

---

Study Aid #170

Paganism and Neopaganism Beliefs

Nature is manifestation of the divine
The circle as the sacred space for worship
Seasonal festivals: Winter and summer solstices, spring and autumn equinoxes
Esbat or Sabbat
Wiccan Rede: An ye harm none, do what ye will.
Rule of Three: Whatever energies you do, good or bad, will return threefold.

Christian devil, and they do not worship this being. Paganism is also a different form of spirituality from the New Spirituality (or "New Age"). It is also worth noting that there is no conversion to paganism. It is commonly reported by pagans that they experience "discovering" that they have affinities with paganism through their reading or discussion with pagans, but pagans do not proselytize and have no evangelistic or missionary component to their spiritual pathway.

Estimating the number of pagans in the West is difficult because most practitioners are solitary and do not necessarily identify with any institutional or larger community expression of their spirituality. Beyond this, while demographic studies have improved in taking paganism into account, nevertheless pagans still tend to be lumped into the broader segment of new religious movements. In spite of these challenges, recent survey data from American Religious Identification Survey puts the number of pagans at 614,000, with 800,000 once children are included. Surveys in England and Wales put the numbers at 42,336, the Canadian Census lists 21,085, the New Zealand census lists 5,862, and the Australian census puts that country's adherents at 23,460. In addition, paganism appears to be going through a demographic shift, with teens being the source for the greatest growth. The internet is a significant factor in this development.

Further Reading

Chas Clifton and Graham Harvey, eds. *The Paganism Reader*. Routledge, 2004.

Graham Harvey. *Contemporary Paganism: Listening People, Speaking Earth*. New York University Press, 1997.

Ronald Hutton. *The Triumph of the Moon*. Oxford University Press, 1999.

Sarah Pike. *New Age and Neopagan Religions in America*. Columbia University Press, 2004.

Starhawk. *The Spiral Dance: A Rebirth of the Ancient Religion of the Great Goddess*. 20th Anniversary ed. Harper, 1999.

Michael York. *Pagan Theology*. New York University Press, 2003.

87

Paganism and Neopaganism: Theological Exchanges, Current Issues

JOHN MOREHEAD

Christian interactions with various expressions of paganism over the years have run the gamut from tragic to problematic. Some of the most tragic encounters have been labeled the "Burning Times," a reference to various instances of persecution and execution of peoples in Europe and North America by Roman Catholics and Protestants during the late medieval, Renaissance, and post-Reformation periods. Added to these events are the infamous witch trials and executions of Salem, Massachusetts. Several aspects of these events are debated, such as the exact numbers of those killed, and whether or not there is a direct religious connection between these unfortunate people and contemporary pagans; nevertheless, these acts of persecution taint Christian history and contemporary perceptions of Christians and Christianity in the minds of many pagans. Therefore, they represent a negative legacy to be overcome in Christian contacts with paganism.

Toward the modern expression of paganism, Christians have tended to engage in two major forms of response. The first is to ignore pagans, as well as the broader tradition of Western esotericism in which paganism is situated, as a minority religious faith that is not to be taken seriously, certainly not as seriously as the major world religions encountered in the history of Christian mission. As paganism has gained greater public visibility and credibility in popular culture, Christians have shifted in their engagement with paganism to the second form of response—that of negative critique.

Several elements of the popular Christian critique of paganism are problematic. The first element serves as the background from which the Christian critique

> **Study Aid #171**
>
> **Christian Responses to Paganism and Neopaganism**
>
> Persecutions in medieval era, Renaissance, and Reformation
> "Witch" trials in colonial America
> Two modern responses: ignore, critique
> Use as "scapegoats" for all that is evil
> Incorrect identification with Satanism
> Misconception of paganism as belief system rather than set of rituals

springs, although this no doubt takes place unconsciously. An analysis of the Christian critique of paganism and witches, whether historic or contemporary, indicates the symbolic function of paganism as a boogeyman of opposition for Christianity. Pagans have come to represent "inverted beings" inhabiting a subversive subculture that are believed to embody heresy, evil, and the greatest fears of Christians. In this way pagans have become a social construction of the evil "other" that is to be opposed. This conception of pagans as the embodiment of religious and social inversion serves as the foundation out of which Christian descriptions and critiques of paganism emerge.

Other elements complicate the Christian encounter with paganism. One of these is a particular misunderstanding of paganism that has dogged it over time. This is the idea that pagans worship the Christian devil, a claim that has found its way into many Christian conceptions and depictions of their spiritual pathway. Pagans are quick to point out that they do not believe that Satan exists, and that this is a Christian belief that finds no place in their religious system. Thus, they do not worship Satan. This denial of the worship of Satan in paganism has been repeated frequently by pagans in print and on the internet, and it appears to be gaining greater recognition in general, perhaps also in the Christian population. Even so, the Christian stereotype of Satan worship continues, but the claim is softened as portrayed in several recent popular books by Christians who have argued that by virtue of pagans' worship of pagan deities there is an implicit worship of Satan.

Another problem in the Christian encounter with paganism arises from Christian depictions of it for other Christians. Many treatments of paganism, and new religions in general, from a Christian perspective approach the topic from the starting point of various core beliefs that are then presented in summary form in relation to the categories of Christian doctrinal concerns. This gives Christian readers the impression that paganism is primarily a system of beliefs, whereas in reality it is focused on ritual—to which diverse beliefs are connected. In addition, the beliefs in question do not have a direct connection to Christian doctrinal concerns. In order to provide a more accurate understanding of paganism, Christian authors would do well to describe it in ways that represent the terminology and priorities of praxis for practitioners, even as they also strive to communicate the essence of paganism.

A further hurdle in the analysis of and description of paganism by Christians takes place in light of the dominant interpretive paradigm for understanding this spirituality. An analysis of the Christian literature on new religions or "cults" reveals a dominant approach that involves a consideration of the teachings of a given new religion as heresy in contrast with the orthodoxy of biblical teachings in areas central to the concerns of Christianity. This analysis and critique is also connected at times to a rational critique of perceived shortcomings in the worldview of the new religions. This approach has been labeled the heresy-rationalist paradigm by Christian researchers, and its emphasis on heresy detection, doctrinal contrast, and worldview refutation of perceived religious competitors in Western culture colors the understanding of new religions in general, and paganism in particular. While the doctrinal and apologetic elements are important, a broader framework is needed that allows for a more objective and empathetic consideration of paganism before entering into disagreement and critique.

Another stumbling block in Christian interactions with pagans surfaces in the culture wars that take place in popular culture as Christians oppose elements of entertainment believed to be influenced by or to include aspects of paganism. This surfaces in concerns raised by fantasy and horror in literature, film, and television programs. One of the chief concerns is alleged witchcraft and occult-related spiritual themes and elements. Unfortunately, this concern involves a hermeneutical error that results in a misinterpretation of aspects of popular culture. The creators of fantasy worlds in popular culture draw upon diverse sources in the nonfictional world in order to create these fantasy worlds. These sources may include folklore, myth, legend, and even religious elements. However, these elements take their meaning from within the story in the context of the fantasy world as defined by the author, not with reference to their external sources. With this interpretive principle in mind, contemporary fantasy stories involving a myth of witchcraft are properly understood as contemporary versions of earlier fairy-tale depictions of the witch from times past, an archetypal figure with no connection to real Wiccans or pagans. Christians should be aware that their misinterpretation and negative critique of these aspects of pop culture are interpreted by pagans as a

---

Study Aid #172

Paganism and Neopaganism Current Issues with Christianity

From cult to sect
From heresy-rationalist paradigm to dialogue
From conflict to personal engagement
Pagan conception of truth as pluralistic
Differing stances regarding proselytizing

form of attack. Friction in popular culture then complicates personal encounters between Christians and pagans.

When Christians and pagans move beyond conflict in popular culture to personal engagement, a few specific issues pose challenges. The first is the pagan conception of truth as pluralistic. This plays itself out in various ways. For example, polytheistic paganism makes room for the monotheism of Christianity, but the monotheism of Christianity takes issue with polytheism. Another challenge arises in differing stances related to proselytizing. Christianity, like many world religions, encourages its adherents to share their faith with others in the hopes of conversion. Paganism is a nonproselytizing spiritual pathway. As mentioned above, pagans, reflecting on their spiritual quest prior to embracing paganism, frequently report discovering their personal affinities with paganism while reading, surfing the internet, or talking to other pagans. Thus, they do not understand themselves as converting to paganism, and pagans do not make efforts at trying to proselytize others to their spiritual pathway. As a result, pagans take issue with Christians for their proselytizing efforts, particularly when directed at pagans, many of whom have had negative experiences with Christianity and the church. Even when Christians make an effort at more sympathetic understandings of paganism, and attempt more dialogical forms of engagement, such Christians are still viewed with suspicion due to their stance on proselytizing. In the pagan view, "missional Christians" are an improvement over more confrontational Christians of the past, but their stance on proselytizing is believed to be in conflict with some aspects of missional Christians and their engagement with pagans.

Over the last several years pagans have made a concerted effort at engaging the broader religious world, as evidenced by their participation in the 1993 Parliament of the World's Religions. A small group of Christians have sought to join them in this endeavor, yet several challenges need to be overcome within Christian concepts and practices related to paganism in order to make this engagement successful.

88

Paganism and Neopaganism: Adherent Essay

GUS DIZEREGA

Neopagans constitute one of America's most rapidly growing religious communities, according to many studies of religion in the United States. Yet neopagans are nearly invisible in the larger public eye. Most groups are quite small, and many more are what we term "solitaries," people who may come together during major celebrations, but otherwise practice on their own. There are few neopagan temples. Because of the fear of many in the general public, usually Christians, many neopagans prefer to remain secret, the better to safeguard their jobs. Neopagans become widely visible only when a legal victory is achieved, as when we won the right to have a pentacle put on the headstones of dead Wiccan soldiers, or when a newspaper reports on a local Samhain (Sow-win) or Beltane Sabbat. In this essay I shall describe who we are in general and, again in general, our relationship with Christianity.

The first and very important point to make is that we are a varied lot. Wiccans constitute the largest formal group, but Druids, Celtic Reconstructionists, Ásatrú, and many others also fall within this broad category as I use it. Not all even like the name "neopagan." Some prefer "heathen" as their descriptive term. Any generalization I make will not quite fit someone whom I would regard as a fellow neopagan. Our identifying characteristics are like the strands in a rope: any two points along a rope will share most strands, but not necessarily all of them.

To put our complexity into perspective, it is difficult to generalize about every Christian denomination, from evangelicals to Catholics to the United Churches of Christ to the Greek Orthodox, and many more. While these diverse groups all recognize the Bible as spiritually authoritative, we have no equivalent text. Many Wiccans have a *Book of Shadows*, but these are not comparable to sacred scripture. For example, they provide common scripts for ritual observances within a given tradition of practice. But I have never encountered a Wiccan who would regard them as infallible guides to spiritual issues.

What nearly all of us do share is a common spiritual focus on the Sacred as it is immanent in the world, rather than transcendent to it. Many neopagans, I among them, recognize there is a spiritually transcendent dimension to reality, and even a common ultimate Source, but this Source is regarded as Monist, as the "Godhead" in Christian mystical terminology. Some neopagans are "radical polytheists," recognizing no such Source. We rarely argue with one another because our focus is elsewhere, on the Sacredness of the world.

Obviously we do not believe in original sin. Not all Christians do either—for example, the Greek Orthodox. But in America most Christian denominations do, and here is one of the key places where we neopagans differ from most of our Christian neighbors.

From this difference emerge many other differences. We do not have a concept of sin or radical evil, although we most definitely believe individuals and societies can fall out of harmony with spiritual reality. We see the world as a source of Sacred knowledge, and see in its basic patterns and wonderful multiplicity insights into Sacred truths. Consequently, we are polytheistic and organize our practices around natural cycles and patterns. In some cases we also focus on our ancestors as spiritual guides and teachers. I will elaborate a little on these issues.

I will use Wicca as my example, because Wiccans are the largest group of neopagans and because I myself am Wiccan. However, and this point is crucial, I do not imply that Wicca is superior to other forms of neopaganism.

Harmony

Wiccan rituals and celebrations focus on bringing us into a deeper harmony with and greater appreciation of Spirit as it is immanent in our world. Our sacred celebrations are either Sabbats or Esbats. Sabbats are celebrated eight times a year, on the solstices, equinoxes, and four seasonally focused times of planting, growth, harvest, and death. Often Sabbats are held publicly as well as privately. If you ever attend a neopagan event, it will likely be a Sabbat.

Esbats are held based on phases of the moon. Most Esbats are held on full moons, when the moon is at its brightest and most complete. Esbats are where a working group, among Wiccans called a "coven," not only honors its deities but also does "work," such as helping a member find a job or performing a healing on someone present or absent. Depending on the kind of work to be done, an Esbat may be held at any of the other major phases of the moon, such as when it is new, or during the waxing or waning quarters. Esbats are private.

Death

Our focus on harmony with Spirit as immanent within the world leads to another distinction with Christianity. We see in the basic patterns of birth, youth, maturity, decline, and death aspects of existence we honor as Sacred. Consequently we do not consider death a spiritual problem, evidence of a "fall," or a sign of imperfection. Many neopagans believe death is followed by some kind of reincarnation, but the issue is not one that engages our attention.

Perhaps a good image that gives you a feel for how many of us see death is to think of a sunset. As the sun sinks toward the horizon, the clouds and sky turn many wonderful colors. The sunset's particular beauty arises in part from its changing patterns and hues, and in part from its temporality. It will end. When the sun finally sets below the horizon, and night prevails, a different kind of beauty emerges: the starry sky.

And so one of our two most central Sabbats is Samhain, that time of year when the forces of death and decay prevail over the forces of life and growth. (Beltane, six months later, is our second principal Sabbat and honors life at its fullest and most vigorous.) We do not worship death, whatever that means, but we honor its place in the Sacred pattern of existence.

Polytheism

Probably nothing sets neopagans apart from Christians so much as our polytheism. We believe there are a multiplicity of deities, male and female, all sacred and all worthy of honor. At our most basic we honor a Goddess and a God, the divine female and the divine male. In practice we often honor them in their many aspects, as a particular goddess, such as Brigit or Hecate, or a particular god, such as Cernnunos or Thor. To say these are aspects is no more to deny their reality than our own. Those of us who are monists see all things as aspects of the Sacred. Radical polytheists simply see endless individuality.

The basic distinction into female and male deities fits both the character of human life and our experiences when encountering such beings. We regard a complete honoring of deities as requiring equal regard to both female and male qualities. If pressed, some of us would award pride of place to the female aspect. We would do so because if the Sacred is immanent within the world, the image of giving birth captures that insight better than that of the Divine Craftsman.

Many of us have also had personal encounters with these deities. Questions such as "Does God exist?" do not interest us. At a panel with other neopagan authors, where we came together to discuss the nature of our deities, a great many of us agreed that when we encountered the Gods, we experienced them as more real than we were. Having no doubt that we existed, we had no problem acknowledging the same for them.

Our focus on Sacred immanence means we are not much bothered by the diversity within our community, or even among pagans more inclusively described to include traditions with unbroken contact with premodern traditions, such as Native American and African Diasporic spirituality. Spirit offers many means for relating more inclusively with it. For many of us this also includes Christianity, so long as Christians are willing to tolerate our own practices as well as those of others different from them.

Pagans and Christians

Recognizing as we do that the Sacred manifests everywhere and can be approached in many ways, we do not seek to convert or proselytize. We welcome interested people and are happy to share what is closest to our hearts, but if you choose another spiritual practice, most all of us will simply wish you sincere blessings along your way. What antagonism to Christianity exists has two roots. Most often it is a reaction to the common Christian view that all other paths are inferior and that some are actively evil. We are often included in that latter category.

The other antagonism to Christianity found among some pagans grows from unpleasant experiences individuals had while growing up within a Christian tradition, before they became neopagans. This was once my own experience. Again speaking for myself, as I came better to understand my neopagan path, I gradually outgrew these early experiences and began to regard Christianity as one valid path among many.

Stretching back into classical times, many pagans have regarded Jesus's teachings as important spiritual insights from a teacher of inspired wisdom. Some today even define themselves as "Christo-Pagans," seeking to integrate Jesus's teachings within a pagan framework.

Further Reading

> Margot Adler. *Drawing Down the Moon: Witches, Druids, Goddess-Worshippers, and Other Pagans in America Today.* Beacon, 1986.
> Gus diZerega. *Pagans and Christians: The Personal Spiritual Experience.* Llewellyn, 2000.
> Joyce Higgenbotham and River Higgenbotham. *ChristoPaganism: An Inclusive Path.* Llewellyn, 2009.
> Philip Johnson and Gus diZerega. *Beyond the Burning Times: A Pagan and Christian in Dialogue.* Edited by John Morehead. Lion Hudson, 2008.
> Sarah Pike. *New Age and Neopagan Religions in America.* Columbia University Press, 2004.
> Starhawk. *The Spiral Dance: A Rebirth of the Ancient Religion of the Goddess.* HarperSanFrancisco, 1999.

89

Gnosticism: History, Beliefs, Practices

CARL RASCHKE

History

The history of Gnosticism during the past two millennia or more is incredibly knotted and complex. Although the Greek word *gnōstikoi* (i.e., "those who possess secret knowledge," or *gnōsis*) occurs in the writings of Plato, the use of the word "Gnosticism" as the designation of a particular religious phenomenon is modern. So-called Gnostics, as actual historical figures, were first identified by the early church fathers as heretics and enemies of what they considered at the time to be the accepted criteria for the emerging Christian orthodoxy—sometimes referred to as "proto-orthodoxy."

The earliest mention of the Gnostics is found in the *First Apology* of Justin Martyr, midway through the second century, when the movement within Christianity was at its height of power and influence. Justin Martyr specifically condemned the teachings of Marcion of Pontus, a wealthy second-century Roman bishop who sought to develop a stream of counterorthodoxy within the fledgling church of the period with his own canon of scripture and a form of radical anti-Judaism that considered the God of the Old Testament an inferior deity separate from the New Testament one. Other church fathers such as Irenaeus, Tertullian, Clement of Alexandria, Origen, and Cyprian wrote extensive tracts and polemics refuting Gnostic teachings throughout the second and third centuries.

Because the orthodox church eventually destroyed the extant writings of the early Gnostics circulating publicly at the time, little was known of them outside the writings of the fathers themselves, who were certainly not unbiased observers, until the twentieth century. It was the discovery of the Nag Hammadi scrolls, the

> **Study Aid #173**
> Gnosticism Timeline
>
>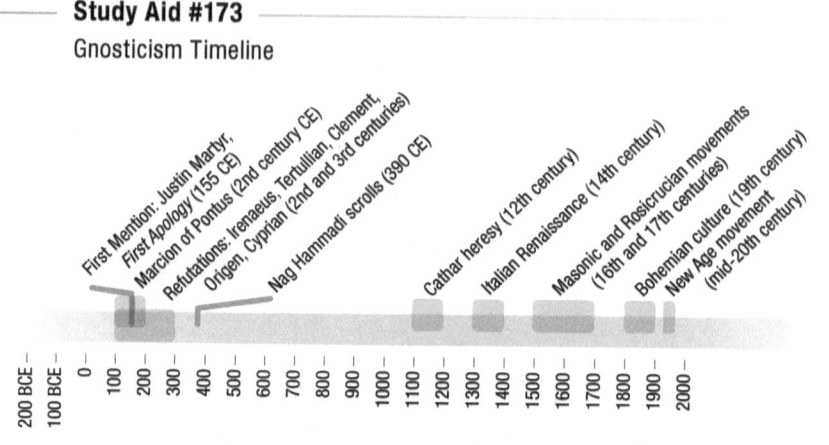

remains of an ancient Christian Gnostic library in Upper Egypt, in the year 1945 that radically changed scholars' perspectives on the movement. Having been most likely buried at some time in the fourth century, the library comprised codices containing not only texts already familiar to researchers but also others that had been previously unknown, as well as a few non-Christian writings. While the unfamiliar documents vastly expanded the scholarly knowledge of the actual Gnostic body of works, the non-Christian literature, particularly the selections from the old Egyptian *Corpus hermeticum*, suggested that Gnosticism itself might predate Christianity, a suspicion voiced by some scholars as early as the nineteenth century.

The search for Gnosticism's pre-Christian origins, however, has been clouded by pure speculation posing as plausible theory, as well as numerous dead ends, following in certain ways the odyssey of scholarship concerning the Dead Sea Scrolls after their discovery around the same time as the Nag Hammadi Library. The more cogent arguments have focused on the various patterns of syncretism, recognized by researchers in the history of religions, that developed with the evolution of the great empires spanning both the Middle East and the Mediterranean following the conquests of Alexander the Great in the fourth century BCE.

One thread of argument has emphasized how the mingling and fusion of myriad pagan practices and beliefs with Platonism during the Alexandrian and early Roman eras gradually found its way into early Christianity to produce the intricate and often strange types of Gnostic cultism, which the early Christian heresiologists condemned. A second line of interpretation has stressed the origins of Gnosticism in Jewish apocalypticism following the Maccabean revolt around 164 BCE and the Roman conquest of Judea a century later. In this view, Gnosticism, which often uses language from apocalyptic sources, grew out of the political failures of the post-Maccabean era and the disillusionment among the Jewish elites of the time with the ideal of national salvation. A third position underscores the well-known and somewhat puzzling pervasiveness of ceremonial magic and occult names in Gnostic cosmology and rituals, while surmising that Gnosticism itself may have been a sophisticated end product in the evolution of the religious esotericism of ancient Egypt and Babylonia after it encountered Hebrew and Greek forms of thought.

The problem of tracing Gnosticism's non-Christian origins has been further confused by the explosion in recent years of popular New Age beliefs and literature, especially the writings of author Dan Brown, which suggest an actual Gnostic origin perhaps for Christianity itself. Today there are numerous ad hoc "churches" and groups that claim descent from the ancient Gnostics themselves and offer their own special take on the history of Gnosticism, published on the internet.

The other difficulty facing scholars and theologians has been the realization that the Gnostic heresy and similar ideas have persisted in Western culture well beyond the Roman world, usually as an underground movement. Historians by now have generally concluded that the Cathar heresy in Languedoc in southern France during the twelfth century, which was bloodily and savagely suppressed over several decades by Pope Innocent III, can be traced back through various intermediaries to the ancient world.

Gnostic themes recur prominently in the Italian Renaissance, in the Masonic and Rosicrucian movements of the seventeenth and eighteenth centuries, in nineteenth-century Bohemian culture, and of course in the contemporary New Age movement itself. While early Gnosticism saw itself as a full-blown Christian competitor and rival to the beginnings of the orthodox church, modern Gnosticism has by and large styled itself as decidedly anti-Christian and self-consciously "pagan" in comparison.

Gnosticism as a topic in the study of religion can no longer be defined simply in the fashion in which the church fathers characterized it. On the other hand, there are certain common features of all Gnostic notions and types of praxis down through the ages. They can be summarized as follows.

Beliefs

Plato used the word *gnōsis* to refer to a kind of intuitive knowledge of the universe that philosophical training, as opposed to commonsense reasoning, might produce. *Gnōsis* in its original Greek meaning signified an inner illumination that could be achieved only by intellectual adepts, and it was often associated with insight into the given relationship between numbers and geometric figures. Gnosis was contrasted with *epistēmē*, or knowledge derived from logical demonstration or dialectical understanding. This kind of "presuppositionless" knowledge, to which philosophers today still give credence, was at the same time transformed in later antiquity into a claim to mystical, mainly "religious," nondemonstrable sorts of cosmic insight in the Hellenistic world, which had little to do with the

> **Study Aid #174**
> Gnostic Beliefs
>
> Inner illumination/intuitive knowledge
> Secret method of salvation
> Illuminati over the common populace
> Inferior material world versus cosmic perfection

teachings of the Platonic academy. Even famous Neoplatonists, such as Plotinus of Alexandria, railed against such claims.

Generally speaking, Gnostics contended that *gnōsis* was far more than a set of privileged insights; it was a method of salvation. Only "those in the know"—today we would call them *illuminati*, or "illumined ones"—could be expected to attain ultimate bliss as well as freedom from the world of human ignorance and suffering. The ancient Gnostics despised common folk, who were considered to be congenitally incapable of rising above their wretched state through such cognitive disciplines. Because they viewed themselves as a secret spiritual aristocracy serving as guardians of true knowledge from the unfit and undeserving, they were regarded by the public at large as arrogant "elitists," which goes a long way to explain why everyday Christians in the first several centuries—in their conviction that Christ died for all sinners—regarded the Gnostics with both loathing and suspicion.

Gnostic cosmology dwelled on the theme that creation itself is the disastrous handiwork of a lesser divinity. While Plato in his dialogue *Timaeus* had introduced the myth of a "craftsman," or *demiourgos*, who shaped the refractory material of the primordial universe into an intelligent order of things, the Gnostics distorted this tradition to imply that the "Demiurge" himself had royally mucked things up. Those Gnostics influenced by Judaism identified this agency with the God of the Old Testament. Other Gnostics developed a baroque and incredibly obscure "creation story" that involved the emanation of the female principle Sophia ("wisdom"), who accidentally fell from the *plērōma*, or divine fullness, and in her confusion produced materiality as the realm of anguish and ignorance. In the Gnostic-Christian version, enshrined in the long and rambling text known as the *Pistis Sophia*, Jesus himself is the *sōtēr*, or "savior," whose sojourn on earth was intended to liberate wisdom from the prison house of matter and show the way back to the *plērōma*.

Practices

Gnostics believed that the soul was a fragment or "spark" of the pleromic substance, which had become fatefully, yet not irredeemably, trapped within matter. Only the person acquiring *gnōsis*, or a secret illumination of the mind through remembrance of this original, divine state, could be rescued from the thick darkness in which the soul found itself. Liberation was possible for those who gave no thought to bodily needs or desires, and it could only be attained by mortifying the flesh and practicing extreme forms of asceticism. Early Christian critics at the same time accused the Gnostics of hypocritically reverting to the practice of extreme licentiousness and orgiastic indulgence, since their contempt for physical existence supposedly justified in the latter's mind an "anything-goes" attitude. Many scholars nowadays, even Christian ones, are skeptical of such charges.

The currently fashionable notion that the early Gnostics represented the "real" church, which scheming orthodox patriarchs wrested from them in an authoritarian coup de grâce, is a pure fantasy reflecting present-day anticlerical prejudices. Gnosticism was always a marginal, albeit highly consequential, stratum within the multilayered history of Christianity, and it still exerts influence—especially through New Age beliefs and attitudes—even to this day.

Sources

Giovanni Filoramo. *A History of Gnosticism*. Blackwell, 1990.

Hans Jonas. *The Gnostic Religion*. Beacon, 2004.

Bentley Layton. *Gnostic Scriptures*. Doubleday, 1987.

Pheme Perkins. *Gnosticism and the New Testament*. Fortress, 1993.

Carl Raschke. *The Interruption of Eternity: Modern Gnosticism and the Origins of the New Religious Consciousness*. Nelson-Hall, 1980.

James Robinson. *The Nag Hammadi Library in English*. Harper & Row, 1979.

Carl Smith. *No Longer Jews: The Search for Gnostic Origins*. Hendrickson, 2004.

90

Gnosticism: Theological Exchanges, Current Issues

CARL RASCHKE

The interplay between Gnosticism and early forms of what nowadays we term Christian "orthodoxy" is not as obvious as was once assumed. Because of the long-standing influence of anti-Gnostic polemics in the writings of the early church fathers, the common scholarly assumption until quite recently was that Gnosticism was by and large an alien "gospel" that first infiltrated, then sought ascendancy in, the Christian communities of the second and third centuries. The famous nineteenth-century German theologian and historian Adolf von Harnack epitomized this point of view when he depicted Gnosticism as the "acute Hellenization" of Christianity.

Harnack maintained that the "essence" of Christianity, encapsulated in Jesus's preaching of the kingdom of God, resisted all attempts to meld it with cultural and historical particularities, and that neither the "Judaizers," whom Paul had fought against, nor the "Hellenizers" (i.e., the Gnostics, particularly Valentinius and Basildes) had succeeded in altering its timeless character.

Current Issues

Late twentieth-century and early twenty-first-century researchers, however, have proposed other, revisionist models. In her best-selling book *The Gnostic Gospels* (1989), Princeton University religion professor Elaine Pagels argued that Gnosticism was but one of several competing strands of early Christianity, one ultimately

> **Study Aid #175**
>
> **Gnostic-Christian Contacts**
>
> Gnosticism as an alien gospel
>   Adolf von Harnack
> Gnosticism as one strand of Christianity
>   Elaine Pagels
> Gnosticism as a Christianized form of a heterodox Judaism
>   Birger Pearson
> Gnosticism as New Age precursor
>   Dan Brown

suppressed and eventually branded as "heretical" by the faction that won out. We now regard the political victor in this early doctrinal catfight as "Christian orthodoxy."

Pagels's arguments have had significant popular as well as academic appeal in recent years, chiefly because they offer a plausible interpretation of why Gnosticism, whose alleged Hellenistic origins outside the early church itself to this day remain obscure, could emerge so suddenly and with such strength about the time they became the object of patristic scorn. Furthermore, Pagels's claim that early Gnostic teachings were radically egalitarian, appealing especially to women who had been marginalized in the dominant social hierarchies of the period, has proved an attractive proposition to contemporary readers.

At the same time, many of Pagels's conclusions remain highly speculative and counterintuitive with regard to what can actually be inferred from the consensus of classical historians and the ancient Gnostic texts themselves. While these texts often do indeed give a certain preeminence to the feminine side of divinity and to the importance of early Christian figures such as Mary (Jesus's mother) and Mary Magdalene, they do not necessarily provide any serious indication that women were regarded that much differently socially in Gnostic groups than in the rest of Roman society as a whole.

This phenomenon can be located in the history of religions, where an asymmetrical relationship between the religious importance of feminine deities and the subordinate social status of women is not at all uncommon. Classical Hinduism is one example. Preclassical Greece is another illustration. Even the growth of Mariolatry during the High Middle Ages bears this trend out.

The modern New Age movement has rekindled a widespread, popular interest in ancient Gnosticism, largely because of the intimate affinity between the two outlooks. Both movements have expressed a preference for esoteric forms of spirituality over publicly revealed truth, for private and ineffable insights over commonly accepted doctrine, for idiosyncratic methods of symbolic formulation over plain communication, for a promiscuous or "Orientalist" kind of religious eclecticism over adherence to any sense of Judeo-Christian, or even an Abrahamic, legacy.

The prevalence of the New Age sensibility in contemporary culture has even led to the founding of various contemporary "Gnostic" cults and churches, which usually claim to have preserved the heritage and essentials of Gnosticism's ancient counterparts. At an empirical level, all the current interest in the "Gnostic" way as an alternative to orthodox teachings has yielded scant progress in understanding exactly who the ancient Gnostics actually were or why they commanded such influence in their day.

The discovery during the 1940s of the Nag Hammadi library in Egypt, a vast repository of previously unknown Gnostic writings, has often been compared to the unearthing of the Dead Sea Scrolls in about the same period.

But while the Dead Sea Scrolls and the ongoing archaeology of the Qumran community that sheltered them have indeed furnished significant knowledge of Judaism at the time of Jesus and altered certain previously held conceptions about the origins of Christianity, the Nag Hammadi scrolls have not resulted in a comparable reappraisal of the early Gnostics, especially their social or organizational structure.

Far less is known about the persons who squirreled away the Nag Hammadi papyri than about the Essenes, the proprietors of the Dead Sea Scrolls. Such a "library" may have been little more than a historical preservation project on the part of Egyptian Coptic monks, who once lived on the site where the scrolls were found.

Much of the current "revisionism" surrounding the significance of early Christian Gnosticism is more a kind of wish fulfillment aimed at satisfying the skeptical predilections of those with an ax to grind against orthodoxy itself than it is the outgrowth of any major material discoveries. As we can see with the staggering popularity of books like *The Da Vinci Code*, which claims to offer a semifictional account of who the Gnostics of old really were, a credulous public primed over a generation with New Age sympathies is likely to believe anything, even if there is scant factual evidence to back it up.

Theological Exchanges

One plausible theory for the appearance of Gnosticism in the second century and its virtual disappearance by the fourth can be traced ironically to Harnack himself, whom much of the present revisionism has sought to discredit. Harnack's description of Gnosticism as "acute Hellenization" makes far more sense if we consider carefully what we do know historically about trends in religious history in the first two centuries after Jesus.

The theory appears even more cogent than the revisionist approach, which, like so many intellectual fashions in Christian history, is nothing more than an attempt to read present-day preferences back into the past. Such a theory builds

> **Study Aid #176**
> Current Issues with Gnosticism
> Popular culture, à la *The Da Vinci Code*
> Feminism in Gnosticism
> Reading present-day preferences into the past
> A form of heterodox Judaism

on the often overlooked and relatively recent scholarship of Birger Pearson, Henry Green, and Kurt Rudolf, who view Gnosticism as a distinctive type of heterodox Judaism that emerged in Egypt and diffused into Christianity.

Thus, such "acute Hellenization"—contra Harnack—took place not in a Christian but in the primary Jewish context. During the first two centuries Christianity was still closely intertwined with its Jewish parents. It was only the growth of systemic Roman persecution of Christians in tandem with the two Jewish revolts in 66–70 and 132–35 CE that ultimately resulted in the separation of the early church from its Judaic parentage.

According to this analysis, the significant Jewish population that had lived in Egypt had already established itself as intellectual pacesetters in comparison with their Palestinian brethren, as can be seen in the outsize influence of a thinker like Philo of Alexandria. When Roman persecution reduced the social standing of many prominent and wealthy Jews in the latter part of the first century, the pessimistic Gnostic outlook became quite attractive and sank deep roots. Since the Roman magistrates rarely distinguished early Christians themselves from Jews (and many in fact were not so easily distinguishable), it was only natural that the Gnostic "heresy" would find fertile soil as well.

These scholars have often emphasized the tie-in between Jewish apocalyptic literature, which in itself was a reaction to gentile oppression, and the central motifs of the Gnostics. The focus of Gnostic documents on such well-known biblical figures as Seth, Enoch, Cain, and Judas betrays this Jewish orientation or worldview. Accordingly, Pearson himself in his *Judaism, Gnosticism, and Egyptian Christianity* (1990) demonstrates how many of the well-known themes of Gnostic cosmology can be derived straightaway from Jewish rabbinic midrash, or textual exegesis, of sections of the Old Testament.

Gnosticism, therefore, can be seen not so much as an indigenous heresy within the church (as conventional scholarship for so long treated it) as a kind of final, radical push and last hurrah for the "Judaizing" faction within Christianity that persisted from the beginning, as the writings of Paul and the Acts of the Apostles underscore.

What research into ancient Gnosticism has clearly impressed upon us is that the familiar, facile sort of division between orthodoxy and heresy has little meaning when it comes to the first several centuries of Christian history. The problem of

Gnostic origins resists any simple and obvious solution not only because of the lack of any centralized apparatus for enforcing "orthodox" opinion among ordinary believers, but also on account of the inherent tension between Hebraism and Hellenism that confounded Jews as well as Christians during the early Roman era.

What we do know is that a certain rendering of the life and teachings of Jesus gradually won over the majority of its early adherents, but whether this outcome was largely the result of historical accidents, ecclesiastic suppression of dissent, or a certain hermeneutical bias coupled with the authority of key scriptures remains difficult to determine.

Sources

Dan Brown. *The Da Vinci Code*. Anchor, 2009.

Henry Green. *The Social and Economic Origins of Gnosticism*. Scholars Press, 1985.

Adolf von Harnack. *What Is Christianity?* Forgotten Books, 2009.

Elaine Pagels. *The Gnostic Gospels*. Vintage, 1989.

Birger Pearson. *Judaism, Gnosticism, and Egyptian Christianity*. Fortress, 1990.

Kurt Rudolf. *Gnosis: The Nature and History of Gnosticism*. Harper & Row, 1983.

Michael Williams. *Rethinking Gnosticism: An Argument for Dismantling a Dubious Category*. Princeton University Press, 1996.

91

Environmentalism: History, Beliefs, Practices

CALVIN DeWITT

There is wide agreement that what is known as "environmentalism" in America begins with a book published in 1864, *Man and Nature*, and in its second edition ten years later, *The Earth as Modified by Human Action: Man and Nature*. Its author, from Woodstock, Vermont, was a US Ambassador to Italy—a position that allowed him to observe the consequences of human action over some geographic range. There also is wide agreement that another four "environmentalists" are among environmentalism's key figures. They begin with Scottish-born John Muir (1838–1914), whose writings and work in Yosemite and the American West proved to be powerful in bringing the wonders of creation to the attention of the US Congress, President Roosevelt, and the wider public. Theodore Roosevelt (1858–1919), sickly as a child but subsequently a robust field biologist and hunter, came to be known as "the first environmental president," whose work in office protected some 230 million acres of public land, including his creating fifty-one bird reservations, four wild game preserves, 150 national forests, five national parks, and eighteen national monuments, including the Grand Canyon as a national monument. Conservationist Aldo Leopold (1887–1948) followed with his famous and widely influential essay "The Land Ethic," and his book *A Sand County Almanac* continues to serve as a major influential environmental source up to the present day. Marine biologist Rachel Carson (1907–64) brought environmentalism fully into American culture with her book *Silent Spring* (1962), which brought about a decade of environmental legislation in the 1970s. During this "environmental decade" nearly every legislator and every American seemed to have become an environmentalist, illustrated most dramatically by the Endangered

> **Study Aid #177**
>
> Environmentalism Timeline
>
>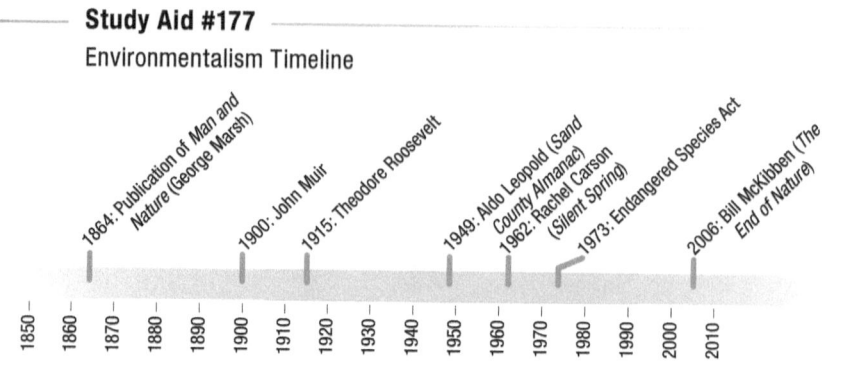

Species Act that passed both houses of the US Congress with but one dissenting vote and was signed into law by President Richard Nixon in 1973. At the heart of these environmental people and endeavors is a widely held dedication to protect and sustain the earth.

Care of the earth is our most ancient, most worthy, and most pleasing responsibility. This is the conclusion of Wendell Berry—essayist and practicing earth-keeper who is among the most widely read and respected environmental writers. The leading scholar on nature and culture, geographer Clarence Glacken, concludes that the root of this perceived responsibility is, from antiquity, the realization by people around the world of a highly ordered created world, coupled with a corresponding desire to live in accord with it. In his comprehensive treatise *Traces on the Rhodian Shore* (1967), he documents how this desire develops from antiquity as people interact with the earth in ways that teach them how to care for it, improve it for habitation, and act to correct adverse effects.

From antiquity, and through the subsequent centuries of the biblical-stewardship tradition, this manifest order was creation's "economy"—the dynamic system of systems that declares God's glory—an economy to be conserved in behalf of its Creator. John Calvin, working from the original text, as was the practice in sixteenth-century French legal "exegesis," wrote about this economy in his commentary on Genesis 2:15 in 1554: "Let him who possesses a field, so partake of its yearly fruits, that he may not suffer the ground to be injured. . . . Let him so feed on its fruits, that he neither dissipates it by luxury, nor permits it to be marred or ruined by neglect. Moreover, that this economy, and this diligence . . . may flourish among us; let everyone regard himself as the steward of God in all things which he possesses." Christianity blossomed, in Glacken's words, as "a philosophy and theology of creation." And the theme of people imaging God's care for creation "has been one of the key ideas in the religious and philosophical thought of Western civilization." Biblical teaching from Genesis, the Psalms, Job, and other scripture teaches about "the workings of an ordered world," including many unsuspected relationships, and about what is necessary for the preservation of it and its immense variety of life. In his speech to Job, God tells Job that nature serves but also limits people, that it is not for people alone but also serves the needs of the other creatures. Yet people are given the unique responsibility of caring for creation and the unique capacity for articulating praise to God.

Toward the end of the eighteenth century, with the coming of the Industrial Revolution, the classical and biblical ideas of a habitable earth cared for by responsible stewardship were seriously shaken, and the seeds of environmentalism were sown. People's confidence as stewards plummeted, as it seemed as if "the lord of creation was failing in his appointed task." People seemed to be going their own way, "capriciously and selfishly defiant of the will of God and of Nature's plan." Seemingly releasing the human economy from the limits of creation's economy, the Industrial Revolution transformed creation from a great "book" of learning to a vast "storehouse" of "natural resources," with its creatures conceptually reclassified as "raw" materials awaiting "harvesting, extracting, and refining." This revolutionary redefinition removed creation as exemplar of order and proclaimer of God's glory. It reduced "creation" to a term for debates on "origins." It suppressed "creation's economy" into meaningless oblivion. Moreover, the multifaceted and highly diverse creation was reduced to three all-inclusive "species": land, labor, and capital. People were ultimately reclassified from *Homo sapiens* to *Homo economicus* as their roles were redefined; their vocations as responsible stewards and imagers of God became "jobs" that would fit into an economy of taxpayers, producers, consumers, and human resources. Stewardship and its long-standing classical tradition in antiquity and its coming into full flower in Judaism and Christianity withered in the heat of the Industrial Revolution. With it the seeds of environmentalism germinated.

Environmentalism sprouted as a corrective response to this reductionism of creation, of its creatures, and of its people as responsible image-bearers and stewards of God. It is not surprising that the people who came to be called environmentalists largely emerged as students of the Bible and creation—often directly from churches. Objecting to the conceptual reduction of creation into "resources," responding to creation's degradation, and motivated by their deeply ingrained callings and vocations, they responded with passion and conviction. Their beliefs would be called environmentalism. And their designation as environmentalists would be degraded, disparagingly, to "enviros."

Beliefs of environmentalism are familiar to people with biblical roots in the stewardship tradition, for good reason. George Perkins Marsh and John Muir both had memorized the entire New Testament in their youth, the first in the Woodstock Congregational Church in Vermont and the second in the Erskine Memorial Presbyterian Church in Dunbar, Scotland, where each was baptized, respectively. Teddy Roosevelt and Rachel Carson came from Reformed and Presbyterian roots, respectively, and were passionate in pursuing their lives as callings and vocations. Aldo Leopold was an avid reader of the Bible, a practice stemming in part from his participation in a Bible study group at Yale, and expressed in his designation

> **Study Aid #178**
>
> **Environmentalism Beliefs (Creation Care)**
>
> Earth is an ordered whole.
> All life has intrinsic value.
> Human beings have power to destroy or heal.
> Humans should not destroy.
> Truth seeking and truth telling supersede political compromise.

of the prophet Isaiah as "the Roosevelt of the Holy Land" in his 1920 paper "The Forestry of the Prophets." He also saw "the land ethic" as an extension of the biblical Mosaic Decalogue and the Golden Rule. The beliefs of these and other environmentalists can be summarized as follows:

- Earth is an ordered whole whose dynamic interacting living and nonliving components are held together in ways that sustain fit habitation for life on earth.
- The well-being of people and all life vitally depends upon living in accord with this ordered and dynamic earth.
- All life has intrinsic value that makes the survival of the lineages of living things literally priceless and not for sale.
- Human beings have both the power to destroy the earth and its life-sustaining systems and the power to prevent such destruction.
- Human beings ought not to destroy the earth, its integrity, or the systems that provide for its continuance and fruitfulness.
- Destroyers of the earth must be countered by efforts and actions that stop degradation of the earth and its creatures.
- Survival of the earth and its dynamic living systems supersedes survival of the systems that are bringing about earth's degradation.
- Truth seeking and truth telling, rather than finding the midpoint between "both sides," must be the basis for human ethics and action.

These beliefs, of course, are easily discovered to be largely those that stem from antiquity and extend through the biblical stewardship tradition and would be subscribed to by most churches. Not everyone, nor every institution, is willing or able to act on these beliefs, however, and it is here that environmentalists may part ways with the churches of their childhood and youth. Some institutions do not want to put these beliefs into visible practice for a wide variety of reasons, and it is largely because of this dampening of felt call and vocation that many environmentalists have left the congregations within which they were raised. Whether they remain or leave their congregations, however, they are among those who are willing to put their own reputations, jobs, incomes, and lives "on the line" in fulfilling their calling. Of those who stay, some may be pastors and church leaders who "give permission" to their congregations to act upon their environmental and "creation-care" beliefs. Others who remain in their churches or synagogues have found it best to get these beliefs put into action at the denominational level, and have been successful in helping to prepare major denominational statements of belief and action on environmental issues. Environmentalism is now part of many congregations and denominations, sometimes as "Christian environmental stewardship" and most often as "caring for creation" or "creation care."

Further Reading

Wendell Berry. *What Are People For?* Counterpoint, 2010.

Rachael Carson. *Silent Spring.* Houghton Mifflin, 2002 (1962).

Clarence Glacken. *Traces on the Rhodian Shore.* University of California Press, 1976.

Aldo Leopold. *A Sand County Almanac.* Oxford University Press, 1989 (1949).

George Marsh. *The Earth as Modified by Human Action: Man and Nature.* Washington, 2003 (1864).

Bill McKibben. *The End of Nature.* Random House, 2006.

John Muir. *Selected Essays.* Library of America, 2011.

92

Environmentalism: Adherent Essay

Roger S. Gottlieb

The idea of a personal God, in whose image I was made and who held me and other people in some kind of special affection, never made sense to me. It just seemed a fantastic combination of such unlikely and self-serving ideas that by the age of ten I declared myself an atheist, and since that time metaphysics of any kind—religious, philosophical, even spiritual—has always left me cold.

At the same time I have had my share, maybe even more than my share, of spiritual, even transcendent, experiences—some with chemical help and many without. The most profound source of those experiences, and the ones that allow me to say that I am (among other things) a kind of pagan, have come from my relation to the natural world. Around the same time that I rejected the idea of God I used to frequent the woods near my house, letting the birch and maple trees, rock outcroppings and leaf piles shelter a lonely, often hurt child. Sky, earth, water, and life in all its forms seemed to hold my emotional pain in a way no adult could or would. What some people doubtless felt at religious services, I felt outside.

Like many explicitly religious teachings, my experiences of nature—which would expand from local woods to include the Rockies, the Himalayas, beaches of Greek islands, and the Sinai Desert—called on me to move beyond, or at least forget for some time, my conventional social ego. Just as a "normal" person cannot love his or her enemies, so it is not as a "normal," socially defined, middle-class, Jewish American leftist of the second half of the twentieth century that nature speaks to me. The beautiful, soothing, and comforting resonance has to do with the fact that I am alive, a product and part of this enormous, delightfully impersonal network of causes and effects, processes of eating and being eaten, cycles of weather and ecological succession and evolution. Whatever disappointments and failures I experience in my social self can, in my moments of natural exaltation, dwindle into insignificance. If a woman I love doesn't love me back, if my career is going nowhere, if the various activist political movements I am part of suffer setbacks, well—at least I am alive, and so are the numberless trillions of other organisms, all in spectacular settings of ocean, sky, mountains, meadows, and rushing rivers.

Over the last two decades my spiritual connection to nature has become both enriched and darkened by a commitment to environmentalism. At least on the surface of this planet, the nature that I love has become "the environment." From the encompassing threats of climate change to the already completed elimination of tens of thousands of species (approximately six an hour, every hour) to the way infants are born with a hundred toxic chemicals in their bloodstream, the comforting power and scope of nature are bleakly subject to the civilization of which I am a part.

Because of these dark realities environmentalism as a religion involves more than awe-inspiring experiences; it also requires personal changes and an ethical commitment to political activism. On the personal level, in a set of daily actions not totally unlike the kinds of rituals and restrictions that mark Orthodox Judaism or Islam, environmentalists are led to pay close attention to what they eat and wear, how they transport themselves or clean their kitchens. In all such contexts there is today a more and a less nature-respecting, and thus moral, way to live. Since humans themselves, whatever our many distinct features as a species, are clearly part of nature as well, the moral obligations of environmentalism are aimed at people as well as what David Abram felicitously describes as the "more than human." Interestingly, the fact that the moral obligations of environmentalism may involve conflict—even organic, local agriculture displaces other species; wind turbines will injure birds; we may have to choose between killing feral cats and allowing them to decimate endangered bird species—does not distinguish it from more conventional religious morality. After all, how am I to "love my neighbor" if my neighbors are at war with each other—or if both neighbors are so needy that both require my full attention at the same time?

Whether or not individual acts of ecological conscience will have much effect on the environmental crisis is doubtful, but the zealous environmentalist is committed to them nevertheless. As the small acts of individual goodness of traditional believers are performed because they believe there is a mysterious cosmic calculus in which they figure, and because they have decided that, whatever the outcome, these are simply the kind of people they choose to be, so the environmentalist recycles, bicycles, and turns down the air-conditioning.

Finally, environmentalism as religion, not unlike the Christianity of the abolitionist movement or of the civil rights struggles of the 1960s, leads to committed, organized, political action. The cure, if such exists, for our current ecological madness is, like the cause, a collective reality and demands a collective response.

Religious social activism has been a frequent part of political history, and when, as America's preeminent environmental activist David Brower puts it, "For me, nature is God," a commitment to working in a large-scale, institutional, challenging political movement is necessarily forthcoming. Brower's religious language is echoed countless times among environmental activists, from the head of Germany's Green Party to the self-descriptions of environmental organizations to the first principle of Environmental Justice ("We affirm the sacredness of Mother Earth").

Christianity's historical relation to nature, and more recently to environmentalism, is complex and variable. On the one hand, there was (and still is in many contexts) a clearly world-denying aspect to Christianity, in which heaven has a reality lacked by a temporary, often painful, earth. This is somewhat rooted in elements of the Hebrew Bible, though subsequent Christianity ignored the nature-respecting elements of Jewish texts in favor of a pervasive dualism that exalted God, soul, and men at the expense of the world, animals and plants, and (the supposedly more like nature) women. In practical terms this led to doctrinal vilification of and cultural and physical genocide against peoples who found the sacred in, rather than outside of, the natural world.

Yet Christian theologians and mystics also found the grandeur of God within and evidenced by the beauties of the earth. St. Francis called on flowers to join him in prayer and moved worms out of the road to save their lives. For generations Christianity talked of two books—scripture and nature—that provide evidence of God. Aquinas asserted that the loss of any part of the natural world would be a loss in our ability to know God.

It is against this variable background, as well as the crushing reality of the current environmental crisis, that contemporary Christian environmentalism has emerged. And emerge it has, in perhaps the fastest large-scale change in a global religious tradition in human history. Examples abound: Pope John Paul II called on humans to change their environmental practices so that nature could return to being the "sister of humanity"; leaders of the World Council of Churches regularly attend international meetings on climate change and call for drastic action on behalf of the planet and its people; Bartholomew, head of Orthodox Christianity, regularly hosts international meetings of scientists, environmental activists, and theologians focusing on the health of a particular ocean, sea, or river; the Evangelical Environmental Network sponsored the highly publicized "What Would Jesus Drive?" campaign, which challenged Detroit to build fuel-efficient cars and Christians to think of the Golden Rule when they made their transportation choices. In these and literally thousands of other examples, it is clear from theologians, religious leaders, and laypeople that not only can one be a sound, believing Christian and an environmentalist, but that the former now requires the latter.

As to the metaphysics of it? Is God out in the world and (as poetic Protestant theologian Mark Wallace puts it) in the "singing river" as well? Do animals go to heaven? (Interestingly, no one ever asks if they go to hell.) Need Christians be afraid, as some clearly are, that all this talk of Nature signals a return of Wicca and paganism? This is clearly up to each denomination, and each individual Christian, to decide. On the whole, however, I believe that the vast majority of sincere believers will make some kind of common cause with environmentalism. As the God of Christianity came to earth and suffered with us, so are the endangered species and oil-slick-covered beaches suffering now. As Jesus's disciples had to remain true despite his death, holding to their faith on Saturday night and not just on Sunday after the miracle occurred, so we who love the earth, who believe that Life is its own Miracle, will have to cling to our faith that some kind of saving grace will arise and that we will be able to proclaim the good news that humans have finally made peace with the brethren with whom we share, each for our own short eternity, this sacred earth.

93

NRM: A-Religions Introduction

Terry C. Muck

One of the most intriguing and counterintuitive categories of new religious movements are religions we have chosen to call "a-religions." Simply, these are religions that get their energy for existing from being distinctly opposed to another religion, or to the category of religion in general. For example, Satanism is categorically opposed to all things Christian. If Christians believe it, Satanists don't. If Christians eschew it, Satanists embrace it. Similarly, atheists deny the truth of the category "religion" itself. Anything religious they deny. And many of the things religions warn us about, atheists consider staples of life.

Given this resistance to religions and religion, why even call such things religions? Because in their very opposition to another religion or to religion in general, Satanists, atheists, and others take on many of the trappings of religious traditions themselves.

Sometimes the religions we are including in this category are called "cults." We have chosen not to use this term extensively in this handbook because it tends to end up being a term of disparagement to almost anyone who disagrees with "us" religiously. When the term is used so negatively, it has no use in a book trying to communicate scholarly information. That is not to say that the term "cult" cannot sometimes be used in a helpful way—it can, by making it a sociological designation for groups that embrace arbitrary authority and see themselves as categorically countercultural. In this last sense it overlaps somewhat with our term "a-religious."

Because the term "cult" has been such a staple of discussions of new religious movements, both negatively and positively, we lead off this section of the handbook

> **Study Aid #179**
> A-Religions
>
> Characteristics
>   Opposed to a specific religion
>   Opposed to religion generically
>   Have their own orthodoxy, orthopathy, orthopraxy
>   Self-identification primarily negative, in resistance to something
>   Cult: A minority religious group whose beliefs and practices an outside observer deems dangerous or strange.
>   Satanists: Philosophies, groups, and individuals who self-identify as satanic and advocate worshiping Satan.
>   Atheists: Deniers of the existence of God.

with two essays on cults to help us sort out the issues that surround those groups so designated.

We prefer to use our term, a-religions, however, to refer to a special group of religions that in many ways try their best not to be religions—usually unsuccessfully.

94

Cults: History, Beliefs, Practices

Suzanne Newcombe

History of the Term "Cult"

There is no universally agreed definition of the word "cult"; it is only rarely used as a self-description and does not refer to any particular belief system. Since the 1920s, the word "cult" has most commonly been used to designate a minority religious group whose beliefs and practices an outside observer deems dangerous or strange.

Historically, "cult" was first recorded in English as reverence or homage to a deity or saint, for example, the "cult of Mary" in the Roman Catholic Church. From the nineteenth century, the word "cult" began to be associated with any religion "other" than Christianity. Specifically, it was used to describe the diverse beliefs of tribal peoples worldwide as well as the Druid revival in eighteenth-century Britain. In the 1890s, it was used to refer to the theosophical movement and the Church of Christian Science, among other groups. Overlapping with the original theological use of the word, in contemporary parlance cults are typically believed to have a charismatic leader who may be "worshiped." Also originating from this usage, a "cult" can refer to a group of people with an intense interest in a celebrity or nonmainstream band, game, book, or film.

Sociological theory on "cults" began with the work of Ernst Troeltsch (1931), who observed a growing tendency in German religiosity that emphasized a kind of "radical religious individualism" of personal experience while avoiding affiliation with traditional religious institutions. Expanding his theories, sociologists have debated various definitions of "cult" without any firm consensus on the meaning of the term. In sociological literature, "cult" is typically used as a technical term that must be specifically defined by the author at the outset of the work (e.g., Wallis 1976).

Characteristics of Cults/New Religious Movements

Some organizations have issued checklists with "characteristics" of "destructive cults." From a sociological perspective, many of these lists contain value judgments that are arguably a matter of opinion rather than fact; for example, a cult is a group with a manipulative leader who financially exploits the members. By using this description, any group that tithes could be seen as a cult. Such value-laden definitions tend to deflect attention away from specific aspects of beliefs and practices that may be causing problems for an individual or society.

Because of the difficulty in separating technical definitions from popular assumptions, many scholars have advocated avoiding the term "cult" altogether in favor of "emergent religions" or "new religious movements" (Richardson 1993). These alternative labels draw attention to more factual aspects of the new minority religions most frequently termed "cults," as well as highlight some of the tendencies such groups may display. Academic research has also focused on categorizing and understanding the various positions new minority religions take in relationship to society (e.g., Wilson 1970).

It is very difficult to make any generalizations that would apply to all new religious groups. Most new religious movements have quite small followings of committed members, often numbering in the dozens rather than thousands. These groups include a wide spectrum of beliefs and practices, appeal to different social groups, and have diverse ways of interacting with society. Many might be considered departures from Christian doctrine, while others combine beliefs of various world religions. Some groups that may be labeled "cults" do not consider themselves religious at all, perhaps having a basis in humanistic psychology or meditation. Some recruit primarily by face-to-face contacts, while others have their primary presence on the internet.

Sociologists argue that new religions have characteristics that do make them distinct from more established religious groups, for example, charismatic leaders and first-generation membership (Barker 2004). Those who convert to a movement are likely to have more zealous attachment to their faith than those who adopt the religion of their parents. This can lead to strong distinctions between "us" and "them" (often the "saved" and the "damned"), a theological position that can cause tensions with those outside the movement. An important element of charismatic leadership is the likelihood of rapid change of both doctrine and practice. Additionally, most new religious movements have atypical demographics; they usually appeal to one section of society more than others. But over time, members of the new movements that survive will have children, and the groups' membership usually begins to look more like that of the general population.

> **Study Aid #180**
>
> Historical Development of Term "Cult"
>
> The Christian church's worship practices
> Any religion other than Christianity
> Devotion to a particular celebrity figure—for example, the cult of Mary
> Small breakaway religious group showing marked deviance
> Highly authoritarian, separatist religious group

"Cults" in the Postwar Period

The relatively rapid social change that characterized the 1960s as an era was also associated with increased interest in new forms of religiosity. Although alternative religions and occult groups have to some extent been present throughout modern history, during the late 1960s and 1970s noticeable numbers of middle-class youths affiliated themselves with groups very different from the faiths of their parents. Sociologists have also described a culture of "seekership" among young people interested in exploring such groups (Campbell 1972). Many of the groups causing popular concern were reinterpretations of Christian doctrine, for example the Unification Church (popularly known as Moonies) and the Children of God, while others were affiliated with Indian spiritual leaders, for example the Maharishi Mahesh Yogi's Transcendental Meditation, Prem Rawat's Divine Light Mission, the International Society for Krishna Consciousness (ISKCON/Hare Krishnas), and Bhagwan Shree Rajneesh/Osho. Many of those who converted to these movements found that their relationships with their parents and relatives became strained as a result of their new beliefs and shift in priorities.

Concerns about cults became much more widespread after November 1978, when over nine hundred members of a religious group called the Peoples Temple, largely made up of US citizens, were killed and/or committed suicide in a remote area of Guyana. The scale of this tragedy inspired much more intense concern, particularly in the media, about those who have joined small and unfamiliar religious groups. The involvement of minority religious groups with several other highly publicized tragedies, for example the release of toxic gas by Aum Shinrikyo on the Tokyo underground in 1995 and the group suicides of the Californian-based Heaven's Gate in 1997, has continued to emphasize the potential danger of some of these small and new minority religions. However, despite such well-publicized tragic cases, the majority of new religious developments are not violent.

Secular Reactions to Postwar "Cults"

Some relatives believe that their loved one may have been forcibly "brainwashed" into adherence to a cult's strange beliefs and practices. The term "brainwashing" originated from Robert Jay Lifton's work, which was based on reports of American prisoners during the Korean War who came to espouse the beliefs of their captors. Thus, those who joined "cults" were believed to have been coerced into membership rather than to have had a legitimate conversion experience. This explanation was also favored by some members who could not explain to themselves their radical changes in belief. However, Eileen Barker's seminal study argued that while social pressure to join a small new religion might be intense, the idea of irresistible and irreversible "brainwashing" could not be justified with evidence in the case of the Unification Church (Moonies). In her study, Barker found a low percentage of those contacted by the church joined, and among those who did join, there was a high turnover rate (Barker 1984).

During the late 1970s and 1980s, some families hired professional "deprogrammers" to forcibly abduct individuals from "cults." Some of those subjected to deprogramming tactics successfully brought charges against the deprogrammers for kidnapping and abduction. Although forcible deprogramming has become less common, some see a role for voluntary "exit counseling" in helping those who leave minority religions to reintegrate into society.

The growth of these new religious organizations inspired a variety of organized responses by worried friends and relatives. One distinct approach has been referred to as the "anticult" movement. Although anticult groups can be quite diverse in their membership, their primary aim is to identify and warn others of the potential harm "destructive cults" can cause to individuals and society. Perhaps the largest organization in this field is the International Cultic Studies Association (ICSA), which developed out of the American Family Federation (1979–2004).

Others have responded by forming research-oriented organizations that focus on clarifying and comparing the beliefs and practices of new and minority religions. For example, Inform was established in 1988 with funding from the United Kingdom Home Office to provide up-to-date, balanced, and reliable information on new and alternative religious movements to the general public.

Partially in response to the anticult activism, other groups have been established to champion the human rights of religious minorities and the right of individuals to have unpopular and nonmainstream religious beliefs. This approach is exemplified by the Ontario Consultants on Religious Tolerance (OCRT).

Conclusion

"Cults" and new religious movements have been appearing throughout history. Yet in the postwar period these groups have been subject to intense scrutiny from both the media and academic researchers. The rapid social changes of the era—increases in wealth, (arguably) decreasing social influence of institutional Christianity in Western countries, and the increasing accessibility of world beliefs and cultures—have all perhaps contributed to a visible public concern about "cults." In

> **Study Aid #181**
> **Common Characteristics of Cults**
>
> Small
> Heterodox
> Charismatic leadership
>
> First-generation membership
> Deviant/separatist

conclusion, it is worth reiterating that although "cults" cause widespread anxiety, the majority of new religious groups do not have a history of violence and attract relatively little attention within their wider societies. As of early 2009, there were over thirteen hundred active new religious movements in Inform's files.

Further Reading

Eileen Barker. *The Making of a Moonie: Choice or Brainwashing?* Blackwell, 1984.

———. "What Are We Studying? A Sociological Case for Keeping the 'Nova.'" *Nova Religio* 8, no. 1 (2004): 88–102.

C. Campbell. "The Cult, the Cultic Milieu and Secularization." In *A Sociological Yearbook of Religion in Britain 5*. SCM, 1972.

J. T. Richardson. "Definitions of Cult." *Review of Religious Research* 34, no. 4 (1993): 348–56.

E. Troeltsch. *The Social Teaching of the Christian Churches*. Allen & Unwin, 1931.

R. Wallis. *The Road to Total Freedom: A Sociological Analysis of Scientology*. Heinemann, 1976.

B. Wilson. *Religious Sects: A Sociological Study*. McGraw Hill, 1970.

95

Cults: Theological Exchanges, Current Issues

SARAH HARVEY

Writing a summary of "Christian contacts with cults" is problematic on a number of levels. First, it must be noted that Christianity is not a coherent whole but is rather composed of a number of different traditions held together by a few common beliefs; as such, there has been no single Christian response to cults. Second, it must be noted that the term "cult" itself is problematic, meaning different things to different people. Third, the terms "Christianity" and "cult" cannot necessarily be considered as two mutually exclusive categories: not only can it be argued that Christianity itself began life as a cult, with a charismatic leader and a small band of dedicated followers, but throughout history cults have both existed within Christianity (the devotion shown to particular saints within Catholicism, for instance) and grown out of Christianity (as a charismatic leader interprets scripture in innovative ways, for instance).

One form of Christian contact with cults has been the development of "countercult groups." Countercult groups are one of five "ideal types" of "cult-watching groups" identified by Eileen Barker (2002) following earlier distinctions between a secular anticult movement and a religious countercult movement (Introvigne 1995). Barker describes countercult groups as approaching cults from a perspective of theological difference, highlighting the cults' deviation in beliefs, and to a lesser extent, practices unlike the countercult groups' own position. The majority of these countercult groups are of a conservative, traditional, and/or evangelical Christian nature, and many are particularly concerned to point out the theological errors of those cults that place themselves within the wider Christian tradition,

> **Study Aid #182**
> **Christians and Cults**
> Early Christianity as a cult Christian countercult groups
> Cults within Christianity Christian cults

including well-established "nineteenth-century sects" such as the Church of Jesus Christ of Latter-Day Saints (Mormons) and the Jehovah's Witnesses. The majority of countercult groups have a twofold purpose: to warn faithful Christians about the "dangers" of the cults and to rescue, through theological argument, those who have "fallen prey to" the cults (Cowan 2003).

While the term "countercult" originated within academic discourse, some groups have appropriated it as a term of self-designation. More frequently, however, these groups favor such terms as "apologetics" or "discernment ministry"; others feel that the term "evangelism" adequately subsumes their focus. Many countercult groups claim to be nondenominational, while others remain firmly within their traditions, which may be Protestantism, Catholicism, or Orthodoxy.

The Countercult Movement

In some ways, the defense of the Christian faith in the light of competing ideologies has been in existence since the very beginning of Christianity (e.g., Acts 17 and Col. 2). Competing views and interpretations of Christianity have always been aired, and as one dogma became dominant, particularly after the Council of Nicaea in 325 CE, other interpretations were labeled as heretical. During the Inquisition, the Roman Catholic Church became "a Countercult Group par excellence" (Barker 2002).

In the United States, the rise of new sects in the nineteenth century—such as Spiritualism, Christian Science, Adventism, Jehovah's Witnesses, and, in particular, Mormonism (the Church of Jesus Christ of Latter-Day Saints)—was a concern for a number of Christian ministers, and the sects became the target of publications outlining their beliefs as heretical. These sects were also a concern for ministers involved in the newly emergent movement of Christian fundamentalism in the first decades of the twentieth century—a movement that is intrinsically linked to the countercult movement in a number of ways, as is its later development in evangelicalism (Melton 2003). These ministers were the forerunners of today's countercult movement that began in the United States and Western Europe following the rise of a youth-/counterculture in general, and new religious movements in particular, in the second half of the twentieth century.

Arguably the most influential figure in the development of the modern countercult movement has been the Baptist minister Walter Martin (1928–89), author of *The Rise of the Cults* (1955) and *The Kingdom of the Cults* (1965), among other books. In 1960, Martin founded perhaps the first modern countercult ministry in the United States, the Christian Research Institute (CRI). Martin also established a daily live call-in radio program, "The Bible Answer Man," and the publication *Christian Research Journal*, to which numerous prominent "countercultists" have contributed, including William M. Alnor, Robert M. Bowman Jr., Ronald Enroth, Bob and Gretchen Passantino, and Hank Hanegraaff, the majority of whom have gone on to found their own countercult groups and/or ministries.

The Spiritual Counterfeits Project (SCP) was one of the first countercult groups with a focus on cults having a background in Eastern religions, such as Hinduism and Buddhism, as well as on the "New Age" movement. The SCP was founded in California in 1973 by Brooke Alexander and others who had been involved in the counterculture of the 1960s, including involvement in "Eastern mysticism," but who had then converted back to Christianity. It began by campaigning against Transcendental Meditation (TM) and claims success in exposing TM as a "version of Hinduism" (TM defines itself as a practice rather than a religion) and contributing to the teaching of it being prohibited from taxpayer-funded schools in America.

In Europe, the Dialog Center International comprises a number of autonomous centers located in the United Kingdom, Ireland, Denmark, Germany, and the Russian Federation, all of which have a loose connection with the original Dialog Center Denmark, founded by the late Professor Johannes Aagaard. In the United Kingdom, the most prominent countercult groups have been Deo Gloria Trust, an evangelical ministry established in the mid-1960s; and Reachout Trust, which was begun by Doug Harris in 1982, initially as a local ministry to Jehovah's Witnesses, but which expanded its focus over time.

It should be noted that in a number of contemporary postcommunist countries, the reinstated mainstream churches have the support of the state in expounding countercult views that highlight cults not only as theologically incorrect but also as "foreign," and cult members (such as Jehovah's Witnesses in Russia and ISKCON and Unification Church members in Kazakhstan) have experienced legal obstacles and even violence. In the United States and the majority of Western Europe, countercult groups do not have state support, and thus their views, existing in competition with alternative perspectives on cults, do not always have influence outside of their own religious tradition, particularly as many of them combine "educating" about cults with proselytizing for their own religious viewpoint. However, in recent

---

Study Aid #183

The Three Responses to Cults

Study	Challenge	Dialogue
Understanding	Questionable practices	Building relationships
Analysis	Evangelism	Learning from

years some countercult groups have become members of FECRIS (in English, the European Federation of Centres of Research and Information on Sectarianism), a pan-European cult-watching group that gained NGO consultative status with the Council of Europe in 2005.

Alternative Responses

The countercult movement has not been the only Christian response to cults. Many Christian groups have been involved in interfaith work, or at least dialogue with members of other religious traditions, which includes "cults" to varying degrees (from the Inter-Faith Network, which engages only with the nine main faiths in the United Kingdom, to the World Congress of Faiths, which includes members of new religious movements). Other interfaith organizations include the World Council of Churches, the Pontifical Council for Interreligious Dialogue, and the Mission and Public Affairs Division within the Anglican Church. Within this latter organization, the Mission Theological Advisory Group has been created as an ecumenical organization working with Churches Together in Britain and Ireland, which has a particular focus on the relationship between the gospel and the contemporary Western culture in which it is proclaimed. It examines and advises on aspects of contemporary culture (including new religious movements) and developments within Christianity.

In some cases, mainstream churches, while retaining their own apologetic stance, have recognized a need for understanding cults on a more objective level, sometimes in order to pastor effectively to the relatives of cult members. In the United Kingdom, for instance, the mainstream churches, including the Anglican Church and the Methodist Church, have supported the work of Inform, and clergy from across the denominations can approach Inform as a source of reliable information when deciding about their degree of contact with a new religion—whether to allow an unfamiliar religious group to hire their church hall, for instance.

Further along the continuum of contact, there have been Christians and Christian groups that have accommodated some aspects of the new religions' beliefs and practices. One example is the Anglican Church of St. James's Piccadilly in London, which, since the early 1980s, has hosted Alternatives, an organization offering a regular program of New Age events, on Monday evenings and weekends. St. James's has been influential in the rise of what Daren Kemp has termed "the Christaquarians": New Age Christians (2003). In the early 2000s, St. Ethelburga's Church in London reopened (after having been devastated by an IRA bomb in the early 1990s) as a "Centre for Reconciliation and Peace," offering "radical hospitality" toward people of other faiths. Its regular program includes Sufi and Buddhist meditation. In the United States, the Unitarian Universalist Church has also been associated with incorporating a variety of other faiths.

Similarly, many new religions claim that they have Christian members among their practitioners, especially movements that claim to be a practice for strengthening faith, such as Subud; to promote a practice or technique for a particular purpose, such as Transcendental Meditation and Elan Vital; or to be the culmination of all religions' teachings, such as Sahaja Yoga. Obviously, this form of "Christian contacts with cults" is often at the level of the individual and thus difficult to map adequately.

Further Reading

Eileen Barker. "Watching for Violence: A Comparative Analysis of Five Cult-Watching Groups." In *Cults, Religion and Violence*, edited by D. G. Bromley and J. G. Melton, 123–48. Cambridge University Press, 2002.

Douglas Cowan. *Bearing False Witness? An Introduction to the Christian Countercult*. Praeger, 2003.

M. Introvigne. "The Secular Anti-cult and the Religious Counter-Cult Movement: Strange Bedfellows or Future Enemies?" In *New Religions and the New Europe*, edited by R. Towler, 32–54. Aarhus, 1995.

Daren Kemp. *The Christaquarians? A Sociology of Christians in the New Age*. Kempress, 2003.

Walter Martin. *The Kingdom of the Cults*. Zondervan, 1965.

Gordon Melton. "The Countercult Monitoring Movement in Historical Perspective." In *Challenging Religion: Essays in Honour of Eileen Barker*, edited by J. A. Beckford and J. T. Richardson, 102–13. Routledge, 2003.

John A. Saliba. *Understanding New Religious Movements*. AltaMira, 2003.

96

Satanism: History, Beliefs, Practices

KENNET GRANHOLM

Defining Satanism is harder than it might seem at a first glance. A good definition, provided by the Swedish scholar Fredrik Gregorius, is "a collective term for movements and ideologies in which Satan plays an important and, for the adherent, positive role, either as a symbol or a spiritual force." In this article, however, I will also deal with a number of groups and philosophies—collectively termed "the Left-Hand Path"—that bear a resemblance to Satanism but do not attribute particular importance to Satan. The term "Satanism" will be reserved for philosophies, groups, and individuals who self-identify as satanic.

History

Satanism as a religious or philosophical movement is a thoroughly modern phenomenon, having its roots in the late-nineteenth-century occult revival and emerging as a distinct movement in the latter part of the twentieth century. The numerous unorthodox Christian groups accused of heresy, such as the Gnostics in the second century CE, the Bogomils and the Cathars in the twelfth century, and the Knights Templar in the fourteenth century, did not expound satanic philosophies. The same goes for the French cases of Gilles de Rais (1404–40) and la Voisin (Catherine Montvoisin, 1637–80), as well as Brit Sir Francis Dashwood's (1708–81) so-called Hell-Fire Club, which was nothing more than a social club for noblemen who regarded Catholicism with ridicule.

In the popular imagination, works of fiction, such as the account of Léo Taxil (pen name for Marie Joseph Gabriel Antoine Jogand-Pagès, 1854–1907) of the links between devil worship and Freemasonry in the 1880s and 1890s, J. K. Huysman's (1848–1907) novel *La Bas* (1891), the occult fiction of Dennis Wheatley (1897–1977), and Hollywood movies such as *Rosemary's Baby* (1968), have largely formed perceptions of Satanism. While portrayals of this sort have not influenced actual Satanism to any large degree, they can be regarded as important sources for the Satanism in the Norwegian Black Metal scene of the late 1980s and early 1990s.

The true origins of religious Satanism lie in the occultism of the late nineteenth and early twentieth centuries. In the 1860s French occultist Eliphas Lévi (Alphonse Louis Constant, 1810–75) discussed the Baphomet entity mentioned in the Knights Templar trials as a devil figure, and described the inverted pentagram, particularly with a goat's head inserted, as the most important satanic symbol. The account was self-prophetic, as the symbol has later become, due largely to Lévi's treatment, the most important symbol for contemporary Satanists. Helena Petrovna Blavatsky (1831–91), cofounder of the Theosophical Society in 1875 in New York, viewed Lucifer as a positive Promethean figure and published a magazine bearing his name. In Denmark, Ben Kadosh (Carl William Hansen, 1872–1936) was involved in fringe masonry, published the pamphlet *Lucifer-Hiram* in 1906, and described himself as a "Luciferian" in the population census of 1921. While the infamous magician Aleister Crowley (1875–1947) is often described as the forefather of modern Satanism, he did not consider himself anything of the sort, and Satan held no exalted position in his teachings. Crowley is, however, a huge influence on most later magical philosophies, and this includes modern Satanism. The German magic order Fraternitas Saturni, founded in 1926, was perhaps the first occult group that actually appropriated the figure of Satan to any significant degree. In 1926 the order's founder, Gregor A. Gregorius (Eugen Grosche, 1888–1964), also published the book *Satanistische Magie*.

The era of modern Satanism began in San Francisco in 1966 when Anton Szandor LaVey (Howard Stanton Levey, 1930–91) founded the Church of Satan. LaVey's *The Satanic Bible*, published in 1969, is the most influential document

---

Study Aid #184

Satanism: A Modern Movement

Late nineteenth to early twentieth century
   Occult revival—Eliphas Lévi
   Theosophy—Helena Blavatsky
   Luciferian—Ben Kadosh
   Magick—Gregor Gregorian
Late twentieth century
   Church of Satan—Anton LaVey
   Temple of Set—Michael Aquino
   Popular culture—for example, *Rosemary's Baby* (movie)

for the practices and beliefs of modern Satanists. In 1975, restructuring in the church led a number of members, chief among whom was Michael A. Aquino (b. 1946), to leave the church and found the Temple of Set. Because the Temple is focused on the Egyptian deity Set instead of Satan, it cannot be regarded as Satanism per se. Dragon Rouge, a magic order employing antinomian symbolism and vocabulary in ways similar to Satanist discourse, was founded in Stockholm, Sweden, in 1990. Both the Temple of Set and Dragon Rouge are more correctly labeled Left-Hand Path organizations.

While the above-mentioned groups abide strictly by secular law and stress the importance of moral conduct, more radical Satanist groups such as the Order of Nine Angles and the Misanthropic Lucifer Order exist. Satanist groups are generally small, with the biggest ones having less than five hundred members. Radical Satanist groups such as the Order of Nine Angles and the Misanthropic Lucifer Order have never had more than a handful of members.

Beliefs

Because Satanism is in no regard a singular movement, there naturally exists no one set of beliefs that can be attributed to all those who would term themselves Satanists, and even less to those groups and individuals who have a family resemblance to Satanism. General tendencies are, however, radical individualism, the use of antinomian symbols, and goals of personal liberation.

The Church of Satan, and much of contemporary Satanism, expounds an essentially atheist and materialist philosophy. Satan is not worshiped as an objectively existing metaphysical being but rather regarded as a symbol and immanent force of rebellion, freedom, and the animal nature of the human being. The church's view of the human being is highly elitist and individualist. In *The Satanic Bible* nine satanic statements are listed, which engage in a critique of the Ten Commandments of Christianity and promote indulgence, an active and aware approach to life, self-interest, and the view that the human being is in essence an animal.

Left-Hand Path orders such as the Temple of Set and Dragon Rouge are generally less materialistically focused and are more interested in the spiritual evolution of humanity. A common factor in orders such as these is an extreme level of eclecticism, where elements are borrowed from most magical traditions, religions, and mythologies from around the world and history.

The Order of Nine Angles is markedly different from most Satanist groups in that it promotes separation from societal norms and laws, and subsequently criminal conduct, as a necessity for satanic initiation.

Most self-identified Satanists are not members of any group but operate in isolation, perhaps having contacts with other solitary Satanists through various forums on the internet. The true numbers of Satanists are therefore nigh impossible to determine. Anton LaVey's *Satanic Bible* is a common basis of most satanic beliefs.

> **Study Aid #185**
>
> Nine Satanic Statements
>
> 1. Satan represents indulgence instead of abstinence.
> 2. Satan represents vital existence instead of spiritual pipe dreams.
> 3. Satan represents undefiled wisdom instead of hypocritical self-deceit.
> 4. Satan represents kindness to those who deserve it, instead of love wasted on ingrates.
> 5. Satan represents vengeance instead of turning the other cheek.
> 6. Satan represents responsibility to the responsible instead of concern for psychic vampires.
> 7. Satan represents humans as just another kind of animal (sometimes better, more often worse than those that walk on all fours), who, because of their "divine spiritual and intellectual development," have become the most vicious animal of all.
> 8. Satan represents all of the so-called sins, as they all lead to physical, mental, or emotional gratification.
> 9. Satan has been the best friend the Christian church has ever had, as he has kept it in business all these years.

Practices

Satanic religious practices are just as diverse as satanic beliefs. What can be said, however, is that the common practice of most contemporary satanic groups, and the related Left-Hand Path groups, is based on Western ritual magic traditions, in particular those expounded by the Hermetic Order of the Golden Dawn and Aleister Crowley.

The Black Mass is probably the one ritual that is most closely linked to Satanism in peoples' imaginations. The problem is that the Black Mass is essentially an imagined ritual act, thought up not by Satanists but by its detractors. The Black Mass is discussed in LaVey's *Satanic Bible* but acknowledged as a literary invention that Satanists would only use as a psychodrama to facilitate their separation from vestiges of lingering Christian sentiments, sans the sacrifice of babies, naturally. The main ritual practices of the Church of Satan revolve around so-called lesser black magic, manipulative practices where the Satanists attempt to influence events favorably to themselves, and greater black magic, which employs ceremony in order to effect change in the world and the practitioner. Greater black magic is described as an emotional rather than an intellectual act. The basic structure of a satanic ritual, as described in *The Satanic Bible*, involves a nude woman acting as the altar and all other participants wearing black robes. The wall is adorned by the Baphomet-sigil (the picture of a goat's head in an inverse pentagram, surrounded by the Hebrew letters for Leviathan), and the room is lit by black candles along with a single white one (representing "the hypocrisy of Right-Hand Path religions"). At the start of the ritual a bell is rung nine times, an invocation of

Satan is performed, and a drink is taken from the ceremonial chalice. Then the four princes of hell are called forth from the cardinal points, the main ritual text—expressing the Satanist's desire for lust, destruction, or compassion—is read, and the parchment containing a representation of this desire is burned. Group rituals may involve a wand representing the phallus, a sword, and a gong.

The Temple of Set rituals are widely varied but often borrow terminology and elements from Church of Satan rituals, such as division into lesser and greater black magic, the ringing of the bell nine times, and an invocation of Set. However, the Temple does not employ a nude altar.

While the practices of Dragon Rouge are highly eclectic, the core of the order's system is based on Kliphotic Kabbalah, exploration of the dark realms of the Jewish mystical tradition; Old Norse mythology, especially rune magic and mysticism centered on the god Odin; Vamacara Tantra, with a focus on Kundalini meditation and activation of bodily energy points called Chakras; and Typhonian Alchemy, an initiatory path leading to self-deification.

The described, but most likely rarely or never practiced, rituals of groups such as the Order of Nine Angles are more radical, involving elements of criminality and human sacrifice.

Many Satanist and Left-Hand Path organizations have some form of initiatory structure, often modeled on the example set by the Hermetic Order of the Golden Dawn. In the individualist ethos of Satanist and Left-Hand Path philosophies, and in opposition to most other esoteric initiatory systems, the idea that initiation is not conferred by the organization but rather effected by the practitioner and then recognized by the organization, is common. Higher levels of initiation then signify increased self-awareness and development along the path of self-liberation.

Further Reading

Gavin Baddeley. *Lucifer Rising: Sin, Devil Worship and Rock 'n' Roll.* Plexus, 1999.

Joel Best, David Bromley, and James Richardson. *The Satanism Scare.* Walter de Gruyter, 1991.

Kennet Granholm. *Embracing the Dark: The Magic Order of Dragon Rouge—Its Practice in Dark Magic and Meaning Making.* Åbo Akademi, 2005.

James R. Lewis and Jesper Aagaard Petersen, eds. *The Encyclopedic Sourcebook of Satanism.* Prometheus, 2008.

Jesper Aagaard Petersen, ed. *Contemporary Religious Satanism.* Ashgate, 2009.

Joachim Schmidt. *Satanismus: Mythos und Wirklichkeit.* Diagonal-Verlag, 1992.

97

Satanism: Theological Exchanges, Current Issues

KENNET GRANHOLM

Most of the perceived historical contacts between Christianity and Satanism are actually conflicts between Christianity and competing religions such as Judaism, Islam, or European pre-Christian religious traditions, or between orthodox dogmatic Christian institutions, predominantly Catholic ones, and heterodox Christian sects, deemed to be heretical. In the dominant Christian discourse these latter groups were often described as engaging in perverted sexual practices and having close affinities with the devil. One of the earliest groups accused in this manner was the Gnostics, who in the second century CE interpreted the tenets of Christianity through Neoplatonic philosophy and regarded the world as created by an evil Demiurge. The path to the true hidden God lay in achieving spiritual insight, *gnōsis*, and thus escaping the material confinements that the evil Demiurge, identified as the biblical JHVH, had imprisoned. In the following centuries, as the church gained a dominant position in European culture, accusations of heresy and more explicit accounts of dealings with the devil increased. The Cathars, founded in Italy in the 1140s, was deemed a big enough threat to warrant the institution of the First Inquisition.

Probably the most famous of the medieval groups accused of devil worship was the Knights Templar. The order was organized in 1118 to protect pilgrims in the Holy Land, conquered from the Muslims during the First Crusade in 1099, and soon gained considerable wealth and power in Europe. The situation caused much envy, and in 1307 King Philip IV of France arrested the members of the order and put them on trial for devil worship. The last grand master of the Knights Templar, Jacques de Molay, was burned at the stake in 1314.

> **Study Aid #186**
>
> The Eleven Satanic Rules of the Earth
>
> 1. Do not give opinions or advice unless you are asked.
> 2. Do not tell your troubles to others unless you are sure they want to hear them.
> 3. When in another's home, show them respect or else do not go there.
> 4. If a guest in your home annoys you, treat them cruelly and without mercy.
> 5. Do not make sexual advances unless you are given the mating signal.
> 6. Do not take that which does not belong to you, unless it is a burden to the other person and they cry out to be relieved.
> 7. Acknowledge the power of magic if you have employed it successfully to obtain your desires. If you deny the power of magic after having called upon it with success, you will lose all you have obtained.
> 8. Do not complain about anything to which you need not subject yourself.
> 9. Do not harm young children.
> 10. Do not kill nonhuman animals unless you are attacked or for your food.
> 11. When walking in open territory, bother no one. If someone bothers you, ask him to stop. If he does not stop, destroy him.

Even though the above examples deal with internal Christian conflicts and entirely fictive accounts of devil worship, they have influenced the later satanic milieu. In some instances, twentieth-century Satanists have used some of the accounts, particularly those concerning the Knights Templar, as legitimating proof of the deep historical roots of Satanism. For example, the Baphomet entity (the name is probably a bastardization of the name of the Muslim prophet Muhammad), mentioned by some of the Templar in confessions made under torture, has become important for modern Satanists.

The French criminal trials of Gilles de Rais (1404–40) and Catherine Montvoisin (la Voisin, 1637–80) are of note when it comes to Satanism. Having squandered most of his fortune, Rais sought the services of various magicians and alchemists and was rumored to have engaged in child sacrifice in order to gain wealth. He was convicted of heresy, sodomy, sacrilege, and murder, and he was hanged and his body burned at the stake in 1440. La Voisin made her living by selling potions and poisons, as well as performing abortions. She was rumored to have organized Satanic Black Masses in her home and was burned at the stake in 1680. In both cases the accounts of satanic practices are incoherent and obscure, and at least Rais seems to have regarded himself not as a Satanist but as a devout Christian. In both trials, but more so in the case of la Voisin, the purported criminal acts weighed more heavily than the allegations of devil worship.

The so-called Satanic Panic of the 1980s and early 1990s is another example of the contacts between a secularized Christian culture and imagined Satanism. The phenomenon can be termed a moral panic, driven by fears that established societal values and norms were being eroded by a satanic underground movement. The panic was primarily instigated by an unfortunate union of psychotherapy and mass media, but in large part the discourses on the subject were Christian-themed, and both the self-proclaimed and publicly identified experts were often conservative Christians. The accounts of Satanism in the Satanic Panic are very different from anything organized satanic groups believe and practice.

As detailed in the entry on the history, beliefs, and practices of Satanism, religious Satanism is a modern construct, having come into existence in the latter part of the twentieth century. The contacts and conflicts between this modern religious Satanism and Christianity have been surprisingly few. During the Satanic Panic, discussed above, some individuals in the satanic milieu were accused of classic satanic crimes, such as child abuse and child sacrifice. However, most often the Satanism of the Satanic Panic was unseen and nonexistent other than in the imaginations of the accusers.

The Satanism expounded in the form of music and subculture termed Black Metal is more for the sake of rebellion than any kind of reflected religious ideology, but examples of hostilities toward the Christian religion and its sacred symbols do exist. In Norway, where this musical subculture first came into existence in the late 1980s and early 1990s, a small group of individuals was responsible for a number of church burnings in the early 1990s. The instances were isolated, and whether this can be seen as any form of religious sentiment or simply a more extreme version of the rebelliousness of Black Metal is unclear. The church burnings largely stopped after the mid-1990s.

Theological Exchanges

That sustained theological exchanges are difficult to uphold between Satanism and Christianity should come as no surprise. Satanism is, simply by the name of the religious atmosphere it represents, in diametrical opposition to Christianity.

The Church of Satan (founded 1966) does engage in a critique of Christianity in general in much of its ideology. An example of this is the ninth satanic statement as presented in *The Satanic Bible* (1969): "Satan has been the best friend the Christian church has ever had, as he has kept it in business all these years." The rest of the statements are modeled to function as quasi-opposites of the biblical Ten Commandments, although they in essence expound ethics that are not in contradiction with Christianity. The Temple of Set, not a Satanist organization per se but a Left-Hand Path movement that has thematic similarities with Satanism, is less vocal in its critique of Christianity. Based on the organization's view that a magus is a magician who has successfully changed the world due to his or her influence, Jesus Christ is described as a magus by some writers in the Temple. This does not mean, however, that Christian theology or the figure of Jesus would be in any way central to the Temple's teachings. Quite the

> **Study Aid #187**
> Current Issues with Christians
> Transgressive symbols and rhetoric
> Moral differences: Imagined or real?
> Hostilities and fears

opposite: on the quite rare occasions when Christianity is discussed, the tone is usually critical. Dragon Rouge, another Left-Hand Path organization, is also predominantly critical of Christianity, although this critique is peripheral in the organization's teachings. In early 2009, however, Dragon Rouge founder Thomas Karlsson engaged in an online debate in which he put forward the suggestion that the Left-Hand Path magician's methods and goals could, from a certain perspective, be regarded as being in line with Christianity. The magician's goal of self-deification could be seen as an attempt to achieve "existential adulthood," which, again from unorthodox perspectives, could be interpreted as the ultimate aim of God; a situation where his "children" grow up by seeking and achieving separation from him. This, however, was an isolated instance and more an example of the rhetorical eclecticism possible in Dragon Rouge than a form of discourse common to it.

The challenge and critique that Satanist and Left-Hand Path organizations direct at Christianity could possibly, when scaling off the worst excesses, function as an impetus to self-reflection and theological development. In large part Satanist philosophies have developed in response to experienced deficiencies and contradictions in Christian philosophy, practice, and culture. In fact, many North American Satanists have a prior background in some Christian denomination. It is unlikely that forms of Christianity could be developed that would accommodate individuals drawn to Satanist philosophy, but the opportunity for open theological debate and growth nonetheless exists.

Current Issues

Transgressive Symbols, Symbolic Language, and Rhetoric

A major part of the Christian and secular opposition toward Satanism derives from the transgressive symbols and rhetoric used by Satanist and Left-Hand Path organizations. These include the figure of Satan, talk about the Prince of Darkness, and symbols such as the inverted pentagram. These symbols and rhetorical markers are used in the antinomian goal of separation from unreflected norms and values, with the aim of personal liberation and freedom and the construction of more conscious values. In themselves, the symbols and rhetoric are not "anti-Christian."

Imagined Moral Differences

The common view that Satanism expounds a system of morals that is in polar opposition to Christian morality is, generally speaking, not true. While small radical groups such as the Order of Nine Angles expound criminal behavior and violence, more "mainstream" organizations such as the Church of Satan, the Temple of Set, and Dragon Rouge entertain moral values that are largely compatible with Christian ones. This includes obedience to law, responsible behavior, and strong opposition to restricting the freedom of others by violent means (e.g., by rape or murder—the practice of animal and human sacrifice is strongly condemned in most of the "mainstream" satanic groups). The nine satanic statements included in Anton LaVey's *Satanic Bible* appear to be in opposition to the Christian Ten Commandments. On a closer inspection, however, and if they are framed in different words, one sees that in many ways they in fact do echo contemporary Christian views.

Hostilities and Fears

Even in a secularized society the idea of Satanism carries with it much fear. The Satanic Panic of the 1980s and the early 1990s was a clear example of this. At times the fears associated with Satanism have resulted in hostility toward self-professed Satanists and black magicians, often taking the expression of accusations of child abuse in ritual contexts. While it is unlikely that Satanism and Christianity and secularized Christian culture will ever find a common ground, it would be beneficial for all if a situation where Satanism could be assessed more objectively arose.

Further Reading

Gavin Baddeley. *Lucifer Rising: Sin, Devil Worship and Rock 'n' Roll*. Plexus, 1999.

Joel Best, David Bromley, and James Richardson. *The Satanism Scare*. Walter de Gruyter, 1991.

Per Faxneld. *Mörkrets apostlar: Satanism i äldre tid*. Ouroboros produktion, 2006.

Jean La Fontaine. "Satanism and Satanic Mythology." In *Witchcraft and Magic in Europe: The Twentieth Century*, edited by Bengt Ankarloo and Stuart Clark, 81–109. University of Pennsylvania Press, 2002.

Malcolm Lambert. *The Cathars*. Blackwell, 1998.

Jeffrey Burton Russell. *Lucifer: The Devil in the Middle Ages*. Cornell University Press, 1984.

———. *Satan: The Early Christian Tradition*. Cornell University Press, 1981.

98

Satanism: Adherent Essay

Don Webb

I am a member and the former High Priest of the Temple of Set, a theistic satanic religion. We are part of a magical and philosophical tradition of spiritual dissent, which despite crude images from movies and low-grade rock and roll has nothing to do with "evil," cruelty, or tattooing numbers on one's forehead. I would like to tell you about our practice, my choice to be a member, and our relationship to mainstream Christianity.

The Logos, or ruling concept of Christianity, is the Greek noun *Agapē*, "Love." The Setian Logos is the Egyptian verb *Xeper* (pronounced Kheffer), "Become." I would describe the law of *Xepera Xeper Xeperu* as a process that affects both things inside and outside of the self. This phrase from the Bremmer-Rhind Papyrus can be translated as "I came into being and by coming into being the way of coming into being is established." Now this has four important meanings:

1. No god or human made me. They have made things that I have used, from good brains to diabetes, but I supplied the spark, out of seeking self-knowledge.
2. The coming into being of all other things I understand through my own process—I am limited to the lens of myself. I try hard to make that a good lens, but I view things in motion by what I went though.
3. For good and bad, I am the judge of meaning and value in the Universe. All things that I successfully start in the objective universe bear my pattern—which can be both good and bad.
4. I must choose my actions to further my self-creation. As Aristotle said, "Men acquire a particular quality by constantly acting a particular way.

... You become just by performing just actions, temperate by performing temperate actions, brave by performing brave actions."

Now there are certain important ideas beyond these. We are not solipsists; we know that the objective universe is not our creation. We believe that the "stuff" that our psyche is formed of is not a substance that is regulated or constrained by the mechanical laws of the objective universe, but that it represents the Will of the archetype of the rebel against cosmic injustice, the Prince of Darkness, whom we call Set, but for most Christians would be called Satan. We are on the side of the knowledge-giving serpent in the Garden of Eden myth. If our souls are made of something in essence different from the clockwork universe, we should be able to demonstrate this by internal creativity—art, philosophy, even fantasy of things not to be seen or heard: and we should be able to cause changes in the objective universe by will alone. In short, the ability to work magic is not only a philosophical notion of Satanism but also a requirement for membership in most organized groups. Ability to pass to the second grade of the Temple of Set requires proof of magical efficacy, for example.

But what of the Prince of Darkness? Isn't this just trading the idea of an all-powerful Creator God for just a guy in red tights? We don't see Set as a god requiring worship or obedience. Gods are human creations, projections of parts of the psyches. It doesn't matter if the projection is Daddy (YHWH), Mom (Wiccan goddesses), or Brother (Jesus). A being that needed our adulation would be a little too insecure. Set, like us, chooses not to be one with the universe but accepts the pains and pleasures of existence and pursues Its own power, pleasure, and knowledge. Its Gift to us enriches the possibilities of Its perception. Free beings with a mix of carnal desires and philosophical inclinations will create an interesting world by ever-shifting mixes of conflict and cooperation, dreaming and going. We do not sacrifice to Set, because that would widen the gap between the human and divine realms; instead, we do as It does: we provide knowledge and choice to those who seek them.

In 1987 Geraldo Rivera had a sensational Halloween special wherein he introduced the myth of satanic ritual abuse. I had been working on an essay about the Salem witch trials. As I watched Mr. Rivera bring forth his "experts" with flimsier evidence than UFO cultists, I was saddened by the lack of critical thinking in America. One gentleman, Dr. Michael Aquino, said what most reasonable people were thinking, "If you know about these heinous crimes, why are you not making arrests?" Quickly they cut to a commercial as the cold water of reason threatened the fires of TV demagoguery. I found out that Aquino was an ex-Green Beret PSYOP (psychological warfare officer) that had founded the Temple of Set, Inc., in 1975, and I found out that one of my best friends, Dr. Stephen E. Flowers, a gifted linguist, not only knew him but was also on the not-for-profit's board. I decided to research the modern satanic movement from its origin with Howard Levey (aka Anton S. LaVey), who crafted a mix of Ayn Rand, monster-movie aesthetics, and practical occultism into the Church of Satan through Michael Aquino's Neoplatonic Temple of Set. I researched the FBI's report on the non-existence of satanic ritual abuse, and finally I wrote Aquino himself—to tell him why I would not join a group but admired his stand against TV superstition. He wrote back telling me in essence that he didn't know why groups worked, but the Temple had a lot of fun trying. Seven years later I was the High Priest and had written my first two books on spiritual dissent, *The Seven Faces of Darkness* and *Uncle Setnakt's Essential Guide to the Left Hand Path*. Now while some of you are hastening to Amazon to get these excellent Yule gifts, I'll talk about our relationship with mainstream Christianity.

Teenagers revolt against their parents. In the Judeo-Christian world this often means a period of inversion of the symbols of faith—this can manifest itself as spray-painted inverse crosses, black fingernails, and unsavory shock-rock. Many Christians make the logical but incorrect assumption that this juvenile rebellion is a sign or gateway to our practice. This fuels hysteria that some "experts" are more than willing to cash in on. These flash points of profitable hatred have led to harassment of our homes, loss of jobs, and strains on families. Fortunately, however, a growing number of Christians understand that we are not after them or their lifestyle and often deplore some of the same stupidity, hatred, and hypersexuality of the society of the spectacle that they do. The notion of a satanic conspiracy doesn't hold up well when we drive average cars, worry about making an honest buck, and complain about taxes just like all other Americans. Christians may find us philosophically repellent—after all, we have a very different view of the nature and purpose of life—but for the most part they don't want to burn us alive atop our books.

Our view of Christianity varies with the individual. For the most part we realize that humans are not able to keep ethical choices without the fear of hellfire, and so we are glad of the "sacred lies" that keep people in line. We are just as human as you, and we understand the idea of a loving God or Goddess could well be a comfort, and that in a universe of hazard and uncertainty it would not be kind of us to ruin another's comfort. As long as Christians are not spurred to attack us, we have no quarrel with them. We don't seek to recruit. The psyche chooses her own companions—we could not be advocates of free will if we were to manipulate minds to think like we do. Thus we will always be a minority religion. Our spiritual dissent is not a dismissal of Christianity, because Christianity does not rule the popular world. We dissent from the "true gods" of the age—namely, that "money is the form of worth," "false equality," "advertising should determine your sex life," and "irresponsibility and stupidity are cool."

I do not see the desirability or the need of any formal relationship between theistic Satanism and Christianity. Theistic Satanists struggle against the grain of the world, promoting personal freedom, access to knowledge, increase of human potential, and an increasing belief in personal responsibility. Many Christians would promote these values. But our motives are different. Christians seek these things for the love of humankind, but are benefited thereby. Theistic Satanists seek these things for themselves, but the world is benefited thereby. Our disbelief in the myth of altruism and our belief that love is precious and can only be truly given to the few separates us from the Christian. The Christian's belief in a god that needs obedience and worship separates the Christian from us. Let us neither despise one another nor be fooled into thinking there is common ground beyond the need to live together on this spinning blue ball.

> Glory and praise to you, O Satan, in the heights
> Of Heaven where you reigned and in the depths
> Of Hell where vanquished you dream in silence!
> Grant that my soul may someday repose near to you
> Under the Tree of Knowledge, when, over your brow,
> Its branches will spread like a new Temple!
>
> Charles Baudelaire. *Les litanies de Satan.*
> Translated by William Aggeler.
> Academy Library Guild, 1954

99

Atheism: History, Beliefs, Practices

JAMES A. BEVERLEY

History

Atheism is commonly understood as denial of the existence of God, where God is viewed in terms of Jewish, Christian, and Muslim theologies. The earliest forms of atheism, however, emerged in Jain and Buddhist denials of the Hindu gods and in Greek philosophical attacks on the gods of Homer. The Greek atomists and sophists had to exercise caution in their public voice, but an atheist trajectory is implicit. The Olympic gods died slowly, but a pyrrhic victory was noted in the famous lines of Aristophanes: "Whirl is king, having deposed Zeus."

Ironically, the first Christian philosophers had to defend themselves against the charge of atheism. Both Justin Martyr (*The First Apology*) and Athenagoras (*A Plea for the Christians*) decry the term but acknowledge their own unbelief about false gods. Soon after, Greek and Roman religion vanished as Constantine gave his imperial sanction to Christian faith. Likewise, the epistemic doubts of Sextus Empiricus (fl. 200 CE) had little impact in his day and even less as Christian and Muslim empires rose. The thinkers in both religions resisted atheism either through frontal dismissal (thus Tertullian's "What has Athens to do with Jerusalem?") or through elaborate metaphysical arguments for God (Averroes, Aquinas).

Atheism emerged again as Reformation leaders fractured the unity of Christendom. A rediscovery of Sextus coincided with a crisis in religious epistemology. The great historian Richard H. Popkin has shown how "the Reformation controversy had opened up Pandora's box in seeking the foundations of certain knowledge." Eventually both Catholic and Protestant dogmatism gave way to

> **Study Aid #188**
> **The Humanist Manifesto**
>
> Knowledge of the world is derived by observation, experimentation, and rational analysis.
> Humans are an integral part of nature, the result of evolutionary change, an unguided process.
> Ethical values are derived from human need and interest as tested by experience.
> Life's fulfillment emerges from individual participation in the service of humane ideals.
> Humans are social by nature and find meaning in relationships.
> Working to benefit society maximizes individual happiness.
> Respect for differing yet humane views in an open, secular, democratic, environmentally sustainable society.

fideism, advanced most powerfully by Michel de Montaigne (1533–92). Even Descartes had to work out his certainties ("I think, therefore I am") under the new cloud of doubt.

In the seventeenth century, skeptics began their assault on the Bible. This opened the door for further questioning in the eighteenth-century age of Enlightenment. Kant raised doubts about our knowledge of God's existence, Hume said we could never be rationally justified in believing that a miracle had occurred, Strauss attacked the integrity of the Gospels, and Voltaire railed against the church. In the next century Darwin promoted evolutionary naturalism, Marx denounced religion, and Nietzsche declared that God was dead. While some of these thinkers might better be called agnostics (I don't know if God exists) than atheists (God does not exist), their intellectual projects were used freely by both groups to justify their beliefs.

In the twentieth century, atheism was expressed in new forms. Freud (1856–1939) argued that religion was illusion, while A. J. Ayer (1910–89) contended that God-talk was meaningless. Atheism also took on institutional forms. Charles Lee Smith founded the American Association for the Advancement of Atheism in 1925. American Atheists, Inc., was started in 1963 and led by Madalyn Murray O'Hair (1919–95). The International Humanist and Ethical Union, founded in 1952, brings together over one hundred organizations that promote atheism. The smaller Atheist Alliance International, founded in 1991, encompasses organizations from thirteen countries.

Atheists developed a new stridency in the first decade of the new century. In terms of impact, Richard Dawkins (b. 1941) led the way with his bestseller *The God Delusion* (2006). Dawkins has become a celebrity in the international atheist community. He is joined by the famous journalist Christopher Hitchens (1949–2011) with his *God Is Not Great* (2007), author Sam Harris (b. 1967), and the distinguished philosopher Daniel Dennett (b. 1942), author of *Breaking the Spell*. They are often referred to as the four horsemen of the atheist apocalypse.

The American atheist community experienced a minor schism in 2009–10 with the removal of Paul Kurtz from leadership at his Center for Inquiry and its related organizations, including the Council for Secular Humanism. Kurtz, a prolific author, came into conflict with his own board and Ronald Lindsay, the new president. The ouster had to do both with personality conflicts and underlying division over how atheism should advance. Kurtz has been highly critical of the vitriolic tone in the new atheism and wants a return to more moderate humanism. He founded the Institute for Science and Human Values in 2010.

Beliefs

As with other worldviews, there is no total uniformity in atheism. Even the common objection to God's existence is expressed in various ways and in different modulation. While Richard Dawkins has become a hero to most skeptics, others object to his polemical style and complain of his sloppy argumentation. The most stinging rebuke came from H. Allen Orr in the *New York Review of Books*.

Differences in style aside, atheists share many common grounds for objection to belief in God. First, atheism asserts that the reality of evil presents an insurmountable barrier to theism. This is famously argued in J. L. Mackie's work *The Miracle of Theism*, but noting the problem of evil as grounds for unbelief has a long history in Western thought. Voltaire made great fun of theodicy in his famous satire *Candide* (1759), set just after the Lisbon earthquake of 1755. Two centuries later, Jewish abandonment of God followed the horrors of the Nazi Holocaust.

Atheists also claim common commitment to rationality. The power of reason is one of the chief motifs in the Humanist Manifesto II (1973). Rationality is connected to an appreciation for science. Thus, the Manifesto states: "Reason and intelligence are the most effective instruments that humankind possesses. There is no substitute: neither faith nor passion suffices in itself. The controlled use of scientific methods, which have transformed the natural and social sciences since the Renaissance, must be extended further in the solution of human problems." The love for reason is coupled with appreciation for science. This has led many atheists to fulminate against pseudoscience and the bogus claims that dominate pop culture. As well, atheists have loved to point out the foibles of church history in resistance to science, most notably in the persecution of Galileo.

Atheists have also shared common contempt for sacred texts, particularly the Bible and more recently the Qur'an. The earliest atheists expressed critique of the Bible in muted fashion because of the threat of persecution and death. However, by the nineteenth century atheists could openly scoff at various biblical texts and teachings. Robert Ingersoll (1833–99) was particularly adept in this regard. He wrote: "I attack this book because it is the enemy of human liberty—the greatest obstruction across the highway of human progress. Let me ask the ministers one question: How can you be wicked enough to defend this book?" A similar

> **Study Aid #189**
>
> **A Secular Humanist Declaration**
>
> | | | |
> |---|---|---|
> | Free inquiry | Ethics based on critical | Reason |
> | Separation of church and | intelligence | Science and technology |
> | state | Moral education | Evolution |
> | The ideal of freedom | Religious skepticism | Education |

spirit dominates current atheist responses to the Muslim scripture. In fact, this contempt extends to Muhammad, the prophet of Islam. Some atheists reprinted the infamous Danish cartoons that enflamed the Muslim world in 2005.

Contrary to theistic claims, atheists assert that their unbelief is the proper ground for morality. All three Humanist Manifestos (1933, 1973, and 2003) have a strong ethical component. The second document reads: "Ethics is autonomous and situational needing no theological or ideological sanction. Ethics stems from human need and interest. To deny this distorts the whole basis of life. Human life has meaning because we create and develop our futures. Happiness and the creative realization of human needs and desires, individually and in shared enjoyment, are continuous themes of humanism."

Contrary to the Manifesto ethos, there are atheists who revel in nihilism, denigrate rationalism, or resist common moral standards. Atheism sometimes comes in a postmodern style, as in Derrida (1930–2004). As well, some skeptics attack the popular devotion to science that permeates atheist ideology. The most significant work here was done by the famous philosopher Paul Feyerabend (1924–94).

Practices

The writers of the first Humanist Manifesto clearly saw their form of humanism as a religious option. Today most atheists object strenuously to any interpretation of atheism as a religion. The stridency of the new atheism, however, makes it easier to draw parallels to standard religious practice. Thus, Richard Dawkins has become the new archbishop, and his work *The God Delusion* serves as sacred text. Skeptics like Orr who question Dawkins are subject to censor, though, thankfully, without any physical threat. Atheist association meetings serve as the worship settings, with the luminaries of atheism (Dawkins and company) functioning as star evangelists. Some atheist gatherings take on the flavor of a worship service. Strategies are implemented with the same zeal that has launched Christian mission to foreign lands.

The passion of the new atheists is most clearly seen in the international campaign to advertise their ideology on buses. The campaign began in the United Kingdom and was the brainchild of the comedian Ariane Sherine (b. 1980), with financial help from Dawkins and others. Buses in the United Kingdom were donned with signs that read: "There's probably no God. Now stop worrying and enjoy your life." A similar campaign in the United States used the slogan: "Why believe in a God? Just be good for goodness' sake." The Italian one reads: "The bad news is that God does not exist. The good news is that you don't need him."

The global human family remains largely religious in the traditional sense, but atheism is doing well. Gallup reported almost a doubling of Americans claiming no religion from 1990 to 2008. Over one hundred thousand Britons have signed up for certificates of debaptism. Census statistics show that a larger percentage of Canadians are becoming secular than are joining any religion, Christian or otherwise. Of European countries, Estonia has the highest percentage of atheists, followed closely by the Czech Republic and Sweden.

Further Reading

Richard Dawkins. *The God Delusion*. Houghton Mifflin Harcourt, 2006.

Tom Flynn, ed. *The New Encyclopedia of Unbelief*. Prometheus, 2007.

Peter Gay. *The Enlightenment*. Knopf, 1966.

Sam Harris. *The End of Faith*. Free Press, 2005.

Christopher Hitchens. *God Is Not Great*. Twelve Books, 2007.

Paul Kurtz. *In Defense of Secular Humanism*. Prometheus, 1983.

Richard H. Popkin. *The History of Skepticism from Erasmus to Spinoza*. University of California Press, 1979.

100

Atheism: Theological Exchanges, Current Issues

JAMES A. BEVERLEY

For most of Western history atheists and agnostics learned to fear Christian power, both Catholic and Protestant. From Constantine on, for almost a millennium and a half, the heretic was silenced, literally and otherwise. If Servetus can burn at the stake (October 27, 1553) in Calvin's Geneva for denying the Trinity, what hope has the atheist? If Bruno can be put to death in Catholic Rome in 1600 for promoting Copernican theories, who would dare spout atheist ones?

Even John Locke's influential *Letter on Toleration* (1689) had this to say: "Lastly, those are not at all to be tolerated who deny the being of a God. Promises, covenants, and oaths, which are the bonds of human society, can have no hold upon an atheist." The poet Percy Bysshe Shelley was ousted from Oxford in 1811 for his atheist views. Likewise, atheism cost Charles Bradlough (1833–91) his actual sitting in England's Parliament until the law was changed in 1886, six years after his election. It is almost as if the apostle had stated: "If God and government be for us, who can be against us?"

Christian philosophers engaged atheism as an intellectual possibility long before there was any practical necessity to do so. After all, the earliest Christians had to worry about Jewish and Roman ideas, not atheist ones. Via Muhammad (ca. 570–632 CE), Islam became the next competing ideology, not atheism. Given this, what explains the space given to proving God in, say, Anselm or Aquinas? The answer lies in the long-standing interest in Greek philosophy that goes back to the early church fathers. Even those Christian thinkers who disliked philosophical speculation (Tertullian and later Bernard of Clairvaux) understood philosophy.

> **Study Aid #190**
> **Key Theological Issues with Atheists**
>
> The crisis of epistemology
> Reason or revelation
> Reason and revelation
>
> Theodicy
> God exists
> God is good
> God is all-powerful

At a practical level, Christians first seriously engaged atheists in the late sixteenth and early seventeenth century. The revival of Sextus Empiricus (fl. 200) and skepticism led to a crisis in epistemology, most notably through Montaigne's *Apologie de Raymond Sebond* (1576). Both Montaigne and his disciple Pierre Charron (1541–1603) argued that Christian fideism is the only secure response to doubt. Montaigne wrote: "The things that come to us from heaven have alone the right and authority for persuasion, alone the stamp of truth."

Christian fideism has been adopted since Charron, notably by Blaise Pascal (1623–62), Søren Kierkegaard (1813–55), Orthodox theologian Lev Shestov (1866–1938), and Karl Barth (1886–1968). Pascal carried a note with him everywhere that read: "Fire. God of Abraham, God of Isaac, God of Jacob, not of the philosophers and the scholars." Shestov wrote: "To find God one must tear oneself away from the seductions of reason, with all its physical and moral constraints, and go to another source of truth. In scripture this source bears the enigmatic name 'faith,' which is that dimension of thought where truth abandons itself fearlessly and joyously to the entire disposition of the Creator." Barth famously wrote: "Belief cannot argue with unbelief, it can only preach to it."

Since post-Reformation times, other Christian thinkers chose a path critical of both fideism and atheism. René Descartes (1596–1650) used a skeptical method to forge a certain starting point (the existence of self) and from there gave rational arguments for God. The "rational" motif was picked up by others, including Samuel Clarke (1675–1729), William Paley (1743–1805), and Richard Whately (1787–1863), author of a great satire on David Hume. A strong use of reason has continued in the twentieth century, most notably with Etienne Gilson, Frederick C. Copleston, C. S. Lewis, William Lane Craig, Richard Swinburne, and Alvin Plantinga, the famous Reformed philosopher.

The role of debate has been significant in Christian reaction to atheism. Copleston (1907–94), the great Catholic philosopher, had a famous BBC radio debate with atheist Bertrand Russell in 1948. Neither one convinced the other, but it was civil. This in itself is significant, given past treatment of atheists by Christian powers. Copleston debated A. J. Ayer the next year and later became Ayer's close friend. In more recent decades, William Lane Craig has had many debates with atheists, including Victor Stenger, Richard Carrier, and Christopher Hitchens.

Atheists who have become Christians do so for a variety of reasons. Some are impressed by the cogency of one or more of the famous proofs for God. Others, like philosophers J. P. Moreland and J. Budziszewski, claim intense religious experiences as part of their conversion. Peter Hitchens (brother of the famous atheist) credits "proper fear" of God as he contemplated a medieval painting in an old hospital in Burgundy (see his *The Rage against God*). Eleonore Stump claims that looking at evil played its part in her journey to God. For many atheists the love of a Christian community is what works, not intellectual reasons. Even more are captured by the singular beauty of Jesus and the sheer power of the gospel story. This was a major element in the conversion of C. S. Lewis.

The multiplicity of factors is significant in the turn of Antony Flew (1923–2010) away from atheism. Raised in a Methodist home, he abandoned theism in his teenage years. After study at Oxford, he published one of the most famous attacks on belief in God. He continued his atheist stance until 2004. His change came in large part because of arguments for intelligent design (see William Dembski, Michael Behe, Phillip E. Johnson, and Stephen Mayer, for example), a reformulation of Aristotle's metaphysics, and some developments in big-bang cosmology.

Flew was also influenced personally by Christian scholar-friends, particularly Gary Habermas (a historian) and Roy Abraham Varghese (a cosmologist). Though Flew never moved beyond deism, he was deeply respectful of Jesus and even open to the possibility of his resurrection. The details are in his book (coauthored with Varghese) *There Is a God*. Mark Oppenheimer's assault on that book in the *New York Times Magazine* is careless and malicious. I recognized this immediately because I knew Flew well as a former student and confidant in his journey to God.

Christian faith is sometimes overturned by the arsenal of the atheist. The damage often relates to a crisis in epistemology, especially given the sweep of postmodernism. It can also be due to admiration for science as the source of proper knowledge. For example, Donald Wiebe, a celebrated Canadian scholar of religion, gave up Christian theism for reasons related to its alleged mythic and unscientific nature. John Hick left orthodox Christianity because of doubts about biblical authority, the incarnation of Jesus, and traditional exclusivist claims. The intellectual problem of evil contributed to John Loftus's unbelief (see his *Why I Became an Atheist*). There is also the emotional power of evil in cases of torture, murder, rape, and so on, especially if such acts are carried out in the name of God. Here, for example, one can read on the sex abuse scandal in the Catholic Church (Jason Berry, *Lead Us Not into Temptation*, and Leon Podles, *Sacrilege*).

Christians who seek to engage atheism face crucial issues, whether academically or personally. First, the influence of the new atheism is overwhelming, both in terms of its success and the ways in which it is changing the style of the atheist polemic. Apologetics has become more important even as its immediate effectiveness is minimized by atheism's new dogmatism. Christians must keep to the high paths of tolerance, wisdom, and love as some atheists do the opposite. As

> **Study Aid #191**
>
> **Engaging Atheists: Three Recommendations**
>
> Keep to the path of tolerance, wisdom, love
> Learn about and relate to postmodernism
> Do not give up on Christian commitments

a tangent, their internal nasty squabbles will at least give clear indication of the truth of the Christian view of humanity's sin.

Second, Christians have to do a better job relating to postmodernists and people of other faiths. Christians usually sound oblivious to the doubts of the former and the certainties of the latter. The postmodernist hears the gospel the way a fundamentalist would hear the views of some cult group. In either case there would be an instant judgment of negativity. Logic would not be the issue. It is about what Carl Becker called "the climate of opinion," and today that is largely a postmodern one.

This is not about changing the substance of Christian faith. Rather, it is about a way of speaking and listening. It is about lack of arrogance. As well, it is about having the ability to be honest about the really tough issues in scripture, church history, and theology. There is harm in not admitting to the power of Darwin's model, as if figuring out the details of creation is so straightforward. Darwin might be wrong, but he is not wrong the way flat-earth theorists are wrong.

In reacting to other faiths, the Christian must not abandon the uniqueness of Christ. However, his greatness and beauty is shown better by pointing positively to him than in denigrating the faith of others, especially if the latter is based on simplistic, uninformed, and nasty interpretations. Hans Küng has rightly asserted the importance of Christians being tough in internal self-critique and gentle in diplomacy with those of other faiths. Diplomacy sets the stage for ongoing conversation and witness and is the necessary preamble to moments when critique is proper and necessary.

Becker describes the rise of atheism this way: "It has taken eight centuries to replace the conception of existence as divinely composed and purposeful drama by the conception of existence as a blindly running flux of disintegrating energy." While the atheist may celebrate this change, even in today's climate of opinion it reads like a distressing course, streaked with darkness and decay. The Christian is under obligation to bring some light and life. It is a wonderful opportunity."

Further Reading

Antony Flew and Roy Abraham Varghese. *There Is a God*. HarperOne, 2007.
Peter Hitchens. *The Rage against God*. Zondervan, 2010.

Hans Küng. *Does God Exist?* Doubleday, 1980.
Thomas V. Morris, ed. *God and the Philosophers.* Oxford University Press, 1994.
Alvin Plantinga. *Warranted Christian Belief.* Oxford University Press, 2000.
Barry Stroud. *The Significance of Philosophical Skepticism.* Clarendon, 1984.
Richard Swinburne. *The Existence of God.* Oxford University Press, 2004.

101

Atheism: Adherent Essay

Ed Buckner

As my good friend the late Clark Adams often noted, "If atheism is a religion, then health is a disease." As Clark's wording and other, similar formulations ("If atheism is a religion, baldness is a hair color" or "If atheism is a religion, not collecting stamps is a hobby") make clear, we atheists do not accept the frequent assertions by some theists that we, too, follow a religion—or that it takes faith to be an atheist. Quotes like these also hint at the sometimes tendentious and antagonistic relationship between Christianity and atheism, with all sides often refusing to accept assumptions deemed crucial by the others. A key starting point that atheists usually make but that Christians seem usually to reject relates to requiring evidence in proportion to beliefs, as David Hume (1748) suggested.

I agree with the analysis offered by philosopher Keith Parsons: "Generations of Christian apologists have assumed that fruitful communication is possible. They have assumed that enough common ground exists for reasonable debate between belief and nonbelief. I share that assumption. That is, I think that believers and nonbelievers share enough background beliefs, values, and standards to engage in fruitful debate about the reasonableness of Christian claims (though some of the wilder effusions of creationists and fundamentalists tempt me into doubt)" (Parsons 2000, 1).

Given that atheism, defined essentially as an absence of supernatural beliefs, is not a religion, nor even according to most atheists a coherent philosophy, this essay will necessarily be unlike others in this handbook. I can quite literally write only of my own personal viewpoint, despite being the leader of a national group of like-minded people, because we are so far from being politically or philosophically monolithic. What I write about here can fairly be said to be a roughly typical set of experiences and ideas, but it cannot be said to be definitive.

Demographics (culture, geography, etc.) predict religious belief far better than theology, and this suggests that most people's religious beliefs are not their carefully considered opinions—they just inherit them. I was born into Christianity (my father was a low-church Episcopal clergyman; my mother was in some ways more committed to Christianity than my father) and left it only gradually, not in a sudden burst of not-seeing-the-light and not out of childish rebelliousness against my parents or against a god in whom I disbelieve. I do not see my lack of faith over the last forty-plus years as a loss, but rather as a valuable gain. That gain was the result of numerous conversations, some casual, some intense, with believers and atheists; of an anthropology course in comparative religion; and of much reading, from C. S. Lewis to Bertrand Russell. I have been active in many different local, regional, and national free thought, secular humanist, and atheist groups, and I have debated dozens of theists, most of them Christians (and all but one of the Christians a Protestant of one variety or another). I personally enjoy debate and think it has at least modest potential for education.

Atheism and Christianity are, with those rare exceptions based on unusual definitions, quite incompatible. When Richard Dawkins wrote a book titled *The God Delusion* (2006), it is almost certain that most (not all?) Christians not only disagreed with Dawkins but also found the book and its title offensive, while most (not all) atheists were exhilarated by the title and pleased by the arguments. Atheists are not persuaded by Christian (or other theistic) arguments and apologetics for many reasons, but the main reason for most of us is that the declared connections between the alleged divine and the actual universe simply do not match. The inadequacies of theodicies—elaborate philosophical justifications that purport to explain away the "problem of suffering" (or "of evil") in a universe designed and controlled by an all-knowing, all-loving, and all-powerful being—are a big part of the problem, but not all of it. For those Christians who suggest that faith is the answer, it must be asked, "Why?" as well as, "Faith in what?" The answer most often reduces to having faith in what another human claims is what a god wants.

Atheism matters to me because I am convinced that only by being realistic and reasonable about human problems and needs can we hope to make human progress. And believing that there is a power above and beyond human beings that designed or cares about human affairs undermines human social development (or worse), as both human history and basic logic demonstrate. I do not think my life or humanity in general ultimately matters—I find no reason to believe there is any externally created purpose or meaning available. Yet I find considerable joy and satisfaction in life, treasure my friends and family, enjoy contemplating beauty, stand in awe of the natural universe, and share pretty much the whole range of human emotions with my fellow human beings. The myth of atheists as cold, unhappy, rationally calculating Mr. Spocks is, so far as my experience demonstrates, only a stereotype. The same can be said, emphatically, for the big lie that atheists lack moral standards or integrity. Like most atheists I know—and I know thousands, many of them reasonably well—I think that value, morality, beauty, and meaning are all human developments but are not less important for that.

What does an atheist value? It is not nearly as simple for us in some ways as for those who belong to a dogmatic Christian organization. I can assert no right to speak for, much less to direct, all atheists; the moral code and political philosophy of every atheist is his or hers, not any organization's. No atheist worthy of the name would ever allow some pompous authority figure to make important moral or political decisions on our behalf, and we proudly disagree with one another on the death penalty, gun control, abortion, tax policies, and virtually every other issue of the day (a strict separation of government and religion comes the closest to achieving unanimity among us). But, powerless as I am to issue decrees, I can comment nevertheless on key values or goals that I think most atheists are resolved to follow, based on principles that all atheists I know consider worthy.

Honor commitments, be honorable—it is not always easy to do what you promise to do, and there are times when commitments must be changed. But those should be rare and, when they do occur, such changes should be made openly and with justification. Atheists want to be taken seriously, and we will be if we do what we say we will. Contracts matter in the eyes of the law, but contracts and other commitments matter even more in the court of public opinion.

Enjoy life—because atheists have an undeserved reputation for being unhappy or bitter, we should be eager to relish the joys that come our way openly. We have learned, sometimes the hard way, that life without an imaginary supreme being ordering us around, forgiving our sins, and supposedly dictating our morality is rich and fulfilling. We must cope with death and illness and great pain at times, and with stress and difficulty always, but we must not forget to recognize the joys of life as well.

Be gracious—one of the steadiest pleasures of life, unrelated to religiosity or the lack of it, is to attend to the feelings and personalities of our fellow human beings.

Be a good friend, parent, spouse, lover, boss, assistant, and so on. Loyalty and support for those we love or work with must have some limits sometimes, but we have richer lives if we err on the side of acceptance, supporting one another even with insufficient grounds.

Have an ethical code, be open about it, follow it, and return to it when you slip.

The biggest lie ever told about atheists, the one most flagrantly and even viciously repeated about us, is that atheists are not, cannot be, moral, ethical people. This is a grave insult not merely to atheists but also to human beings of all sorts: to claim that decency is impossible without fear of divine punishment is as absurd as to claim that human beings will always treat each other well whether anyone pays attention to ethical standards or not. We are highly developed animals, but we are capable of immense cruelty as well as astonishing sacrifice and kindness.

Atheists and Christians can certainly live in the same society and can respect and tolerate each other, can even fight for the religious liberty of the other. But many of us—many atheists and probably an even higher proportion of Christians—are so fully identified with our position on theism that trusting or being at ease with our opposite numbers is difficult. It is, as I discovered when trying to calmly discuss the evidence and arguments with my mother many years ago, not a mere rational or intellectual disagreement. Emotions and self-perceptions are heavily involved. I am not especially optimistic about the relations between atheists and Christians, but I know of some Christians who allow me to think that my pessimism may be misplaced.

Sources

Richard Dawkins. *The God Delusion.* New York: Bantam, 2006.
David Hume. *An Enquiry concerning Human Understanding.* 1748.
Keith Parsons. *Why I Am Not a Christian.* Roswell, GA: Freethought, 2000.

102

NRM: Psychological Religions Introduction

TERRY C. MUCK

Many new religious movements seem geared especially toward that largely Western phenomenon called "individualism." And Western "individualism" has manifested itself in a form of religion that can best be called psychological. One of these new religious movements, Scientology, was founded by a man, L. Ron Hubbard, who originally saw his teachings as an improvement on American psychology, before realizing that what he really had created was a religion. Another can be categorized under an umbrella term, transpersonal psychology. The third religion we deal with in this section, the New Age, is really a very broad movement consisting of diverse spiritual technologies, many of which use psychological techniques to connect the mundane practitioner with the transcendent divine.

> **Study Aid #192**
> Psychological Religions
>
> Scientology: Scientology is the study and handling of the spirit in relationship to itself, others, and all of life. Founded by L. Ron Hubbard.
> Transpersonal psychology: A collection of ideas that converged in the mid-twentieth century originating in ancient religions, evolutionary theory, and Western psychology. Abraham Maslow is an important figure.
> New Age: Beginning in the West in the 1960s, a culturally specific confluence of an Eastern religious metaphysic combined with Western self-help psychology.

These three new religious movements, and others like them, focus their attention on individual salvation, which they often define in terms usually more common in the social sciences than in religious teachings. Needless to say, all of the religions in this book—world, indigenous, and new religious movements—are interested in individual salvation to some extent. But none focus on it so relentlessly, facing fully in the direction of the human actor, usually to the detriment of focus either on the divine or the social grouping. Indeed, the divine, if acknowledged at all, is placed in the service of the individual, the center of the universe.

103

Scientology: History, Beliefs, Practices

Douglas Cowan

Operating in more than 150 countries and claiming as many as ten million members worldwide, the Church of Scientology regularly presents itself as "the fastest growing religious movement on Earth" and "the only great religion to emerge in the twentieth century." In North America, although it is known for the entertainment celebrities it counts among the faithful—Tom Cruise, John Travolta, Kelly Preston, Kirstie Alley, and Isaac Hayes, to name just a few—it has also been the target of trenchant popular satire, most notably on the adult cartoon programs *The Simpsons* and *South Park*. In Europe, on the other hand, principally in France, Germany, and Greece, the Church of Scientology has fought a bitter, continual battle for social legitimacy and legal acceptance. In other parts of the world, the experience of the church varies between these two extremes.

History

Now over fifty years old, the Church of Scientology began with a pulp science fiction writer from Tilden, Nebraska, named L. Ron Hubbard (1911–86). In 1950 Hubbard published *Dianetics: The Modern Science of Mental Health*, the seminal text of what became Scientology. The text appeared both in much abbreviated form in the pulp magazine *Astounding Science Fiction* and as a full-length book. The church claims that within a few years more than 750 groups were practicing Hubbard's method of Dianetics counseling. In 1954, Hubbard formed the Church of Scientology and devoted the rest of his life to expanding and systematizing what he called the religion of Scientology.

The church is represented by a vast and complicated bureaucratic structure, each unit of which is responsible for reaching particular performance targets and each of which is guided in its operation down to the smallest detail. Called "orgs," these units range from the Church of Scientology International, the "Mother Church," to the Flag Service Organization in Clearwater, Florida, and from the MV "Freewinds," where elite Scientologists practice upper-level auditing (see below), to local storefront missions in cities and towns around the world. Wherever they are, each org is dedicated to one of three principal goals: Scientology practice and training; application of the "tech," as Hubbard's educational methods are known; or social reform and betterment.

Beliefs

Although he is not worshiped as a divine figure, Hubbard is the author of Scientology's voluminous scriptures, the touchstone of belief and practice, and the guarantor of authority and salvation for practitioners. For those unacquainted with Scientology, the church appears as an often confusing welter of categories, organizations, neologisms, acronyms, and terms (many of which are defined differently than in common discourse). Hubbard was a prodigious writer, and the church has preserved even the minutiae of his output, turning it into the equivalent of sacred writ. To grasp a basic understanding of Scientological beliefs, however, one must be familiar with relatively few key concepts: thetan, MEST, mind, time track, engram, Clear, and Operating Thetan.

Like many other religious traditions, Scientology regards the human person as the product of three distinct but interdependent constituents: the body, the mind, and the spirit, which is known among Scientologists as the thetan, the basic energetic force animating all life. Rather than simply having thetans, though, Scientologists believe that human beings *are* thetans. That is, we are incarnate spiritual beings, not physical beings equipped with some form of spiritual adjunct. Moreover, since the thetan exists outside the normal frames of spatial and temporal reference, it is not a thing per se. According to Hubbard, "it is the creator of things." Among the thetans' most basic creations is the material universe, which Scientologists know as MEST—matter, energy, space, and time.

Hubbard trifurcates the mind into somatic, analytic, and reactive components or modalities. Governing involuntary bodily functions and autonomic responses to stimuli, the somatic mind receives comparatively little discussion in Hubbard's works, most of which are concerned with the analytic and reactive modalities. The analytic mind is the thinking mind, the individual's rational command-and-control center that is responsible for observation, interpretation, analysis, and behavior. Hubbard taught that, unencumbered, the analytic mind functions efficiently and infallibly in the service of the principal goal of all life, which is to survive. Unfortunately, over the course of millions of years spent in the MEST

> **Study Aid #193**
>
> The Creed of the Church of Scientology
>
> The Creed of the Church of Scientology was written by L. Ron Hubbard shortly after the church was formed in Los Angeles on February 18, 1954.
>
> We of the Church believe:
> That all men of whatever race, color or creed were created with equal rights.
> That all men have inalienable rights to their own religious practices and their performance.
> That all men have inalienable rights to their own lives.
> That all men have inalienable rights to their sanity.
> That all men have inalienable rights to their own defense.
> That all men have inalienable rights to conceive, choose, assist or support their own organizations, churches and governments.
> That all men have inalienable rights to think freely, to talk freely, to write freely their own opinions and to counter or utter or write upon the opinions of others.
> That all men have inalienable rights to the creation of their own kind.
> That the souls of men have the rights of men.
> That the study of the Mind and the healing of mentally caused ills should not be alienated from religion or condoned in nonreligious fields.
> And that no agency less than God has the power to suspend or set aside these rights, overtly or covertly.
> And we of the Church believe:
> That Man is basically good.
> That he is seeking to Survive.
> That his survival depends upon himself and upon his fellows and his attainment of brotherhood with the Universe.
> And we of the Church believe that the laws of God forbid Man
> To destroy his own kind.
> To destroy the sanity of another.
> To destroy or enslave another's soul.
> To destroy or reduce the survival of one's companions or one's group.
> And we of the Church believe
> That the spirit can be saved.
> And that the spirit alone may save or heal the body.

universe, untold numbers of negative experiences—which are neither recorded nor processed by the analytic mind—accumulate in the thetan and dissociate it from both the facility and the skills to survive.

Down to the smallest sensory detail, these negative experiences are stored in the reactive mind, "a stimulus-response mechanism" that records each experience as a separate mental image, called an engram. Gathered together from a thetan's multitude of lives—the time track—and housed in the reactive mind, the totality of one's negative experiences constitutes a person's engram bank, which, according to Scientology, is "the source of all travail, unwanted fears, emotions, pains, and psychosomatic illnesses." Whenever we encounter a situation similar to a trauma experienced in any of our lifetimes, the engram associated with that experience is reactivated. We feel the same fear, anger, guilt, pain, sorrow, or whatever emotion was imprinted during the initial experience, and we are prevented from moving forward until the blockage created by the engram is cleared.

Resolving the internal conflict and external manifestations of one's accumulated engram bank is the first order of business for a beginning Scientologist, who is known as a "preclear." After a number of initial courses of auditing offered by the Church of Scientology (see below), practitioners are declared "Clear" of these amassed engrams and are free to continue their journey up what Hubbard called "the Bridge to Total Freedom." In addition to various adjunct courses and "rundowns," the Bridge beyond Clear consists of numerous courses of auditing designed to take practitioners through the fifteen levels of Operating Thetan. For Scientologists, salvation is progressive and is achieved as individual practitioners make their way up the Bridge and successfully complete a series of increasingly complex (and expensive) courses of auditing—the principal practice of Scientology.

Not unlike Abraham Maslow's well-known hierarchy of needs, Scientologists believe that the will to survival exists by degrees or levels, and our ability to participate in successive degrees is reflected in our progress up the Bridge. Called the Eight Dynamics, these levels involve the survival of (1) the individual, (2) the family unit, (3) social groups, (4) the human species, (5) all life-forms, (6) the physical universe (MEST), (7) the individual as a spiritual entity, and (8) survival through infinity. In the service of these dynamics, one of Scientology's stated goals is to "Clear the Planet"—that is, to bring every person on Earth to at least the state of Clear, and hopefully beyond.

Practices

Many Scientology orgs offer Sunday services, which follow a liturgy similar to that found in mainline Protestant churches (see entry on Christian interaction with Scientology): hymns; prayers; a recitation of the Scientology creed; an inspirational message drawn from Hubbard's writings and read verbatim by the presiding minister from *The Background, Ministry, Ceremonies and Sermons of the Scientology Religion*; and some form of group process activity. Relatively few Scientologists, however, attend these services. The vast majority of their practice is dedicated to the various courses of auditing and training offered by the church. Unlike many other religious traditions, which appeal to faith as the touchstone of belief and practice, Scientology presents itself as supremely rational, the product of

> **Study Aid #194**
>
> **Scientology Beliefs**
>
> Thetan: Spirit, the basic animating force of life. Human beings are thetans.
> MEST: Matter, Energy, Space, Time. The material world created by thetans.
> Mind: The mind has three parts: somatic, analytic, reactive. Living in MEST inevitably causes negative experiences that result in the reactive mind.
> Time track: Many, many lives create a time track, a record of human experiences.
> Engram: Each negative experience creates a record in the reactive mind, an engram.
> Clear: The conflict created by engrams must be removed. A preclear has not removed all engrams, a Clear has.
> Operating Thetan: A Clear who has chosen to go beyond clear on the Bridge to Total Freedom.

rigorous scientific investigation and refinement. In *What Is Scientology?* the church states that Hubbard's method "works 100 percent of the time when it is properly applied to a person who sincerely desires to improve his life." The effectiveness of the auditing system and sacrality of Hubbard's writings that enshrine it are irrevocably connected, and no deviation from his teachings, however minor, is permitted.

In an auditing session, the practitioner meets his or her auditor around a small machine, the Hubbard Electropsychometer, more commonly known as the E-Meter, and which Scientologists regard as a "religious artifact." The E-Meter is essentially a Wheatstone Bridge, a low-voltage skin galvanometer that measures changes in electrical resistance across two electrodes (or "cans") that are held by the practitioner. Registering in a variety of ways on the meter's dial, these changes in resistance are considered proof of the existence of engrammatic blockages in the practitioner. Needle movements are interpreted by the auditor in the context of the questions or exercises engaged by the practitioner. If a particular questions provokes a strong response on the meter, for example, the auditor could conclude that she has encountered a buried engram and will continue to explore that question or experience with the practitioner. Only when the meter's needle no longer moves—when they have together achieved a "floating needle"—is the issue considered resolved, the engram cleared, and the practitioner free to move on in the session. In addition to auditing, several different Training Routines, Objective Processing, and Rundowns are available to Scientologists, all of which are intended to help practitioners apply the principles of Scientology in all areas of daily life.

Organization

The Church of Scientology is one of the most bureaucratically complex new religions in existence. The Church of Scientology International—the "Mother

Church"—is the corporate head of the ecclesial structure, while the Religious Technology Center maintains the copyrights for all Dianetics and Scientology trademarks. All matters related to the publication, translation, and copyright of Hubbard's literary estate rest with Author Services, Inc. The Office of Special Affairs, on the other hand, which was known formerly as the Guardian Office, is responsible for coordinating public relations and the legal affairs of the church. The Flag Service Organization, which is located in the restored Fort Harrison Hotel in Clearwater, Florida, provides the highest-level auditing for Scientology's most elite practitioners. Those who wish to dedicate themselves wholly to the church can join the Sea Organization (known as the Sea Org), a high-commitment, quasi-monastic group that requires, among other things, a billion-year contract with its members. One of Scientology's most controversial organizations, which handles the internal discipline of errant Scientologists, is the Rehabilitation Project Force.

The Church of Scientology also operates a number of social service organizations, including Narconon, its network of drug rehabilitation facilities; Criminon, a prison reform and anti-recidivism program; the Volunteer Minister Program, the members of which wear distinctive yellow T-shirts and are often prominent at the site of different social upheavals. The Citizens Commission on Human Rights prosecutes the Church of Scientology's ongoing battle against the psychiatric profession. In the mid-1990s, Scientology was able to purchase the assets of the bankrupt anticult group the Cult Awareness Network, and now operates it as an organization dedicated to the promotion of religious freedom.

Controversy

Controversy has dogged both *Dianetics* and the Church of Scientology almost from their inception. When Hubbard submitted a draft of *Dianetics* to the American Psychiatric Association, his claims were summarily dismissed—something that could account for the virulent antipathy with which Scientology has regarded both psychology and psychiatry ever since. In 1958, the US Food and Drug Administration seized a quantity of E-Meters on the grounds that the church was representing them as a viable treatment for disease. They were eventually returned, but the church was required to use them only in religious practice. In the early 1970s, the Internal Revenue Service revoked the church's 501(c)3 tax exemption, sparking a two-decade-long battle to win it back—which the church did in 1993. In 1995, the death of Scientologist Lisa McPherson while in church care sparked outrage against Scientology, especially when a wrongful death suit brought against the church by her estate was settled for a still-undisclosed amount. In Europe, both France and Germany have included the Church of Scientology in lists of suspect religious groups and subjected the organization to a variety of surveillance and punitive measures.

Further Reading

Church of Scientology International. *Scientology: Theology and Practice of a Contemporary Religion*. Bridge, 2002.

———. *What Is Scientology?* Bridge, 1998.

Douglas E. Cowan and David G. Bromley. *Cults and New Religions: A Brief History*. Blackwell, 2008.

L. Ron Hubbard. *Dianetics: The Modern Science of Mental Health*. Bridge, 1990.

———. *Scientology: The Fundamentals of Thought*. Bridge, 1988.

James R. Lewis, ed. *Scientology*. Oxford University Press, 2009.

J. Gordon Melton. *The Church of Scientology*. Signature, 2000.

Russell Miller. *Bare-Faced Messiah: The True Story of L. Ron Hubbard*. Key Porter, 1987.

Roy Wallis. *The Road to Total Freedom: A Sociological Analysis of Scientology*. Heinemann, 1976.

104

Scientology: Theological Exchanges, Current Issues

DOUGLAS COWAN

Often labeled a cult by its many opponents, the Church of Scientology is a new religious movement that has done all it can both to present and to legitimate itself as a bona fide religion in the late modern world. Besides its application for official recognition in all countries where it operates, in the 1980s and 1990s the church requested a number of well-known sociologists of religion, religious studies scholars, and theologians to address the issue of whether Scientology should be considered a legitimate religion. In 1980, for example, Dean Kelley, the counselor on religious liberty of the National Council of Churches of Christ in the United States, was commissioned to answer precisely this question. Although he pointed out that Scientology could not possibly have answers to all of life's eventualities and he made no judgment on the group's truth claims, Kelley concluded that "Scientology is a religion and functionally a very effective one." Fifteen years later, Harry Heino, professor of theology at the University of Tampere in Helsinki, wrote that "Scientology in its present form is a religion, offering crucial religious services, a distinctive belief and a tightly organized religious denomination." "As a theologian and philosopher," wrote Urbano Galan of the Gregorian University in Rome, "I can strongly affirm that Scientology is a religion, in the very fullest sense." These essays, and nearly twenty others, have been reprinted and distributed by the Church of Scientology in many different forms.

It is probably safe to say that the majority of Christians have little to do with the Church of Scientology, encountering it only occasionally through the media or the storefront or online offering of its patented "Oxford Capacity Analysis

---
Study Aid #195

The Code of a Scientologist

The "Code of a Scientologist" was first issued in 1954 by L. Ron Hubbard. The code was revised in 1973 and is given here in its final version.

As a Scientologist, I pledge myself to the Code of Scientology for the good of all.

1. To keep Scientologists, the public and the press accurately informed concerning Scientology, the world of mental health and society.
2. To use the best I know of Scientology to the best of my ability to help my family, friends, groups and the world.
3. To refuse to accept for processing and to refuse to accept money from any preclear or group I feel I cannot honestly help.
4. To decry and do all I can to abolish any and all abuses against life and Mankind.
5. To expose and help abolish any and all physically damaging practices in the field of mental health.
6. To help clean up and keep clean the field of mental health.
7. To bring about an atmosphere of safety and security in the field of mental health by eradicating its abuses and brutality.
8. To support true humanitarian endeavors in the fields of human rights.
9. To embrace the policy of equal justice for all.
10. To work for freedom of speech in the world.
11. To actively decry the suppression of knowledge, wisdom, philosophy or data which would help Mankind.
12. To support the freedom of religion.
13. To help Scientology orgs and groups ally themselves with public groups.
14. To teach Scientology at a level it can be understood and used by the recipients.
15. To stress the freedom to use Scientology as a philosophy in all its applications and variations in the humanities.
16. To insist upon standard and unvaried Scientology as an applied activity in ethics, processing and administration in Scientology organizations.
17. To take my share of responsibility for the impact of Scientology upon the world.
18. To increase the numbers and strength of Scientology over the world.
19. To set an example of the effectiveness and wisdom of Scientology.
20. To make this world a saner, better place.

Test," one of the principal entrées into Scientology and the practice of auditing. And there are undoubtedly some Christians who take advantage either of auditing services or educational material produced by the Church of Scientology. In 2007, for example, CNN reported on two American evangelical pastors, both of whom serve low-income, urban congregations, who have used what Scientologists call their "study tech" and Hubbard's program for social betterment, "The Way to Happiness," in their congregations. Both report that these benefited their congregations, indicating that they regarded these programs as tools to augment their own ministries rather than as competitors for it. Beyond these occasional contacts, though, when it happens, intentional interaction between the two religions is more often confrontative. First, though, consider some of the ways in which Scientology both differentiates itself from and incorporates aspects of Christianity.

Scientology and Christianity

The Church of Scientology makes no secret of its differences from Christianity. Contrary to the doctrine of original sin, it teaches that humankind is essentially good, but that this goodness has been blocked throughout a person's time track by the accumulation of engrams. The time track also highlights Scientological belief in reincarnation, something that sets it further apart from Christianity. For Scientologists, salvation is progressive, and the further a practitioner moves along the Bridge to Total Freedom, the closer he or she moves toward perfection, the godlike potential Hubbard taught was the original state of the thetan. The first major stage on that journey—achieving the state of Clear—Scientologists consider comparable to the Buddhist experience of enlightenment, though the church is emphatic that "Clear is a permanent level of spiritual awareness never attainable prior to *Dianetics* and Scientology." Rather than faith, Scientologists rely on the empirical experience of auditing and processing, both to facilitate their spiritual development and to guide their everyday behavior. Indeed, the church teaches that Scientologists "possess a practical system of ethics and justice, based solely on reason. No such system has ever existed before." "Anything religious teachers said or Buddha promised," the church claims, "even the visions of Christianity, are attained in Scientology as result." Clearly, this is incompatible with Christian tradition and teaching.

Although it clearly differentiates itself from Christianity, in its quest for social legitimation the Church of Scientology has appropriated a number of the trappings—especially some of the more recognizable material culture and terminology—of the Christian church. It refers to the E-Meter, for example, as a "religious artifact," which is used by the practitioner and the religious counselor within the confines of a "confessional." Auditing is "a precise form of spiritual counseling between a Scientology minister and a parishioner." While this example has some overtones of Roman Catholicism, most of these borrowings reflect the social dominance of Protestantism. Sunday services follow a liturgy that would be familiar to many Protestant Christians and are conducted by an org's chaplain or some other designated minister. Rather than baptisms or christenings, Scientologists celebrate naming ceremonies for newborns, while very traditional-looking weddings and funerals are available for the other important life stages. L. Ron Hubbard's oeuvre—in both written and spoken form—is the holy scripture of the religion

> **Study Aid #196**
>
> Scientology and Christianity
>
> Theological differences
>   Human nature: Sinful or good
>   Single birth or reincarnation
>   Faith vs. reason
> Similarities
>   Role of confession
>   Some liturgical practices
> Confrontations
>   Competition for adherents
>   Name-calling, on both sides

of Scientology. The large and imposing *Background, Ministry, Ceremonies and Sermons of the Scientology Religion*, bound in burgundy and embossed with the Scientology cross, has the look, feel, and gravitas of a pulpit Bible—and serves the same purpose in a Church of Scientology service. In many Scientology publications ministers or chaplains are depicted dressed in clerical blacks, complete with the "dog collar" familiar to Christians worldwide. Rather than call their clerics "imams" or "rabbis" or adopt the saffron robes of a Tibetan Buddhist or the *khalsa* of a Sikh, Scientologists have assumed the dress and deportment of the dominant religious culture in Scientology's country of origin—the United States.

Christianity versus Scientology

By far the most direct interaction between Christianity and Scientology has been either implicitly or explicitly confrontational, and derives at least in part from the competing exclusivities of each religion's truth claims. Put simply, for each group, if they are right, the other cannot be. While much of the Christian antipathy toward the Church of Scientology is rooted in theological difference, it is also driven by many of the controversial aspects of the church. At the forefront of this contest are members of the evangelical Christian countercult movement, a loose association of pastors, apologists, and interested Christians whose mission is to confront what they regard as the spiritual and social danger of new religious movements. One prominent internet apologist regularly refers to the Church of Scientology as a "hate group," declaring that the group "is a commercial enterprise that masquerades as a religion." Comments like these are ubiquitous among evangelical opponents of new religions such as Scientology.

Responding both to the growth of the Church of Scientology and its appropriation of a mainline Christian "look," many of these critics produce resources designed to highlight simply and obviously the difference between Christianity and Scientology. Groups such as the Watchman Fellowship and the Christian Research Institute have published extensive articles detailing what they consider the signal errors of Scientology in relation to Christianity. Many of these resources, however, are clearly intended less for Scientologists—or as a means to convert Scientologists—than they are for the support of Christians who interact with Scientologists. Put differently, the principal purpose of this material is to reinforce the spiritual and religious superiority of Christianity at the expense of Scientology.

Although both sides claim often dramatic conversions (or defections, depending on one's perspective), no reliable data exists to indicate how successful either group has been in its attempts to evangelize the other. In 2000, *Christianity Today* published a lengthy article on the growth of the Church of Scientology in Clearwater, Florida, home of the church's elite Flag Service Organization. There, the author points out that despite the Church of Scientology's attempts to improve its image in the community through its social betterment work, the overall impression is that it represents less a potential partner in interfaith activity than a very problematic competitor in the religious marketplace. Indeed, the antipathetic language often used by evangelical apologists to describe Scientology—a "cult" or a "hate group" that offers nothing but "quackery" to its deluded participants—and their delight in highlighting every foible and faux pas, every controversy, real or imagined, in which the Church of Scientology is either involved or implicated, reveals more than anything else a deeply rooted contempt for the group. For its part, the Church of Scientology has developed a reputation as a pugnacious religious competitor, quite willing to condemn in very harsh terms those groups or individuals it considers a threat. In terms of this shared antipathy, then, it seems that very little real opportunity for dialogue exists. Rather, there are only competing monologues, with neither side really willing to listen to the other.

Further Reading

Church of Scientology International. *The Background, Ministry, Ceremonies and Sermons of the Scientology Religion*. Bridge, 1999.

———. *Scientology: Theology and Practice of a Contemporary Religion*. Bridge, 2002.

———. *What Is Scientology?* Bridge, 1998.

Douglas E. Cowan. *Bearing False Witness: An Introduction to the Christian Countercult*. Praeger, 2003.

Urbano Alonso Galan. "Scientology: A True Religion." *Freedom magazine*, n.d.

Harry Heino. *Scientology: Its True Nature*. Freedom, 1995.

L. Ron Hubbard. *Dianetics: The Modern Science of Mental Health*. Bridge, 1990.

Dean M. Kelley. *Is Scientology a Religion?* Freedom, 1980.

James R. Lewis, ed. *Scientology*. Oxford University Press, 2009.

105

Transpersonal Psychology: History, Beliefs, Practices

Frances S. Adeney

The ideas that converged in the mid-twentieth century to form transpersonal psychology originated in ancient religions, evolutionary theory, and Western humanistic psychology. As Eastern ideas and practices influenced American society during the late twentieth century, transpersonal psychology integrated some of those ideas with humanistic psychology.

History

Hinduism provided a view of the physical world as illusion—a crudification of divine spirit into matter. Differentiations perceived by humans are actually illusory. Although arrayed in a number of forms, all matter is one. Buddhism contributed the idea that one can transcend suffering and merge into the divine oneness through meditation—a process that reduces awareness of self and leads to enlightenment. The ancient idea that the self mirrors the universe, since all matter is a manifestation of the divine, also fit into transpersonal psychology.

As the post-Enlightenment climate in Europe fostered the rise of science, evolutionary theory postulated that the physical world gradually developed from simple to more complex forms. Transpersonal psychology used that notion to explain how the physical world can be transformed through human elevation to states of higher consciousness. The Eastern religious ideas here met Western scientific theory.

Psychology modeled itself after the physical sciences in the late nineteenth and early twentieth centuries, embracing evolutionary theory. Sigmund Freud taught

> **Study Aid #197**
> Ken Wilber's Spectrum of Consciousness
>
> Prepersonal, Levels 1–3
>   Subconscious motivations
>   Freud's drives, Jungian archetypes
> Personal, Levels 4–6
>   Empirical and rational processes
>   William James, Carol Gilligan
> Transpersonal, Levels 7–9
>   Integrative and mystical structures
>   Emerson's Oversoul, Plato's Forms

that individuals live through stages of earlier human development as part of their psychological growth. Much of human behavior springs from an unconscious part of the personality. Carl Jung's notion of the collective unconscious further links the human psyche to cultures of the past and to all of humankind. Individuals act out of the collective history embedded in their unconscious. Those ideas fit well into transpersonal psychology's use of Eastern thought—that, despite human perceptions of difference, all matter is the same, and higher levels of consciousness can connect humans to that divine oneness.

As the human potential movement grew in the mid-twentieth century, humanistic psychology rebelled against the negative emphasis of psychoanalysis. Attempts to explain the activity of the unconscious in Freudian terms led to a focus on unstable individuals rather than healthy people. In the 1950s Abraham Maslow developed a hierarchy of human needs that stressed human capability to rise to noble thoughts and actions. He postulated the goodness of humans and believed that in the right conditions, psychological growth was natural.

Humanistic, or "Third Force," psychology went on to suggest that humans use only 10 percent of their potential. Humans are capable of growth and good choices, and can determine their own growth in ways unimaginable in traditional psychology. Obstacles to growth include societal structures and learned behavior that blocks human potential for growth.

As those streams of thought converged, transpersonal psychology was born. Although humanistic psychology focused on the individual's ability to develop, it lacked a spiritual dimension and a goal for that growth. Transpersonal psychology provided the spiritual dimension with its belief in a divinely filled universe. God is not distant but imbues all of life. It provided the goal for growth in the belief that as individuals evolve spiritually, the cosmos will eventually return to a fully spiritual state. Cosmic unity will be achieved. Human potential is directed toward the search for a higher level of consciousness.

Beliefs

Although the transpersonal movement is diverse, including several forms of eclectic psychology, New Age manifestations, and educational techniques, general beliefs can be outlined. The beliefs of transpersonal psychology include *monism*, the idea that all is one. Despite appearances of difference—good and evil, poverty and wealth, health and sickness—all is one. Furthermore, that oneness is divine. As persons let go of their confused perceptions and become enlightened, that unity will manifest itself to them. Ken Wilber, an early exponent of transpersonal psychology, describes that belief and the path to discovering the unified nature of all things in his book *The Atman Project*. He currently defines those beliefs as "integral psychology" ("Waves, Streams, and the Self").

Wilber argues that the individual reflects the world and the divine in direct ways because consciousness is all-pervading. The human body is connected to all matter. The mind is in touch with psychic realities. The soul reflects the divine, and the spirit is connected to the infinite. As the divine pervades all things, humans can become enlightened as they touch that higher consciousness. The experience of higher consciousness allows humans to realize their own godlikeness and participation in the divinity of all things.

In this pantheistic view, everything is God. Consciousness is God, humanity is God, the world is God. The goal of human life becomes realizing that unity and participating in it fully. The evolutionary understanding of transpersonal psychology is that as more and more individuals live in the reality of the godlike unity of all things, the world will be transformed back into its original spirit-like reality.

A seemingly contradictory belief of transpersonal psychology is that of the power of the *individual*. That value, derived from Christianity and Western Enlightenment thinking, became a central tenet of humanistic and transpersonal psychologies. In transpersonal psychology, although everything is one and differences are illusory, persons are presumed to be good, creative, and able to fulfill their own growth potential. Choosing to perceive the universe as unfractured and divine leads to higher levels of consciousness. The power of individuals can transform the universe back into its original spiritual state.

Individual *goodness* is a corollary in this belief system. Without goodness, the direction of one's search for higher consciousness might be suspect. But the goodness of the human person ensures that the direction of growth will be a positive

---

Study Aid #198

Transpersonal Psychology's Practices

| Study | Mutual counseling |
| Meditation | Seminars (e.g., Mandala Conference) |

one. Third Force psychologist Carl Rogers's nondirective counseling shows a high level of trust in the person's desire and ability to choose the good. Transpersonal psychology builds on that belief, postulating that spiritually astute people will gear their lives toward enhancing the spiritual quality of life for all.

Those views lead to an *optimistic view of the world*. Since everything, in essence, is divine, all will be well. Persons seeking higher consciousness will succeed in connecting with the divine nature of all things. They will eventually return to *atman*, realizing the illusory nature of what is perceived as evil and all that is wrong in the universe.

Practices

Although the goal of transpersonal psychology is the salvation of the world in its return to spirit, practices are very individual. There is no "church" of transpersonal psychology. Rather, it has the character of a mystic religion. Meditation and study form a crucial part of this New Age movement. Counseling others with transpersonal psychology beliefs and methods is another practice. The John F. Kennedy School of Psychology in Orinda, California, offers a master's degree in transpersonal counseling.

Group activities include individual participation in seminars at New Age conferences, including the annual Mandala Conference in San Diego, California. The Esalen Institute in California includes seminars and experiential sessions on transpersonal psychology. The Association of Transpersonal Psychology fosters communication among scholars and practitioners.

Transpersonal psychology forms a religious synthesis, utilizing practices and beliefs that flow freely among New Age circles. Anthony Sutich, founder of the Association for Humanistic Psychology, also began the Association for Transpersonal Psychology. Transpersonal topics are freely aired at the Association of Humanistic Psychology's annual conventions, which include seminars on phases of the inner journey, archetypal dreams, T'ai Chi and gestalt connections, aikido, the values of ritualization, evolving personal myths, and other New Age topics.

Although it fashions itself as a Fourth Force in psychology, transpersonal psychology remains a subgroup of Third Force humanistic psychology. It still seeks respect in a field that generally disavows religion. The interdisciplinary quality of transpersonal psychology proves problematic in a community of scholars who deem themselves to be scientific. However, transpersonal psychology has brought spiritual dimensions of psychological issues to the attention of the guild. The synthetic nature of transpersonal psychology is remarkable: a monistic worldview merged with humanistic psychology, and an evolutionary theory was infused with a religious hope that humans, by their own choice, can save the world.

Further Reading

Frances S. Adeney. "Empowering the Self: A Look at the Human Potential Movement." *SCP Journal* 5, no. 1 (1981).

———. "Transpersonal Psychology: Psychology and Salvation Meet." In *The New Age Rage*, edited by Karen Hoyt and J. Isamu Yamamoto, 107–27. Fleming H. Revell, 1987.

Abraham Maslow. *A Theory of Human Motivation*. CreateSpace, 2013 (1943).

Ken Wilber. *The Atman Project*. Quest, 1980.

106

Transpersonal Psychology: Theological Exchanges, Current Issues

FRANCES S. ADENEY

Christian contact with the Hindu concepts explored in transpersonal psychology began long before transpersonal psychology emerged from humanistic psychology. According to Christopher Wynter and Fiona Tulk, "Transpersonal is the meeting point of all healing modalities, religions, spiritualities, and philosophies of East and West, ancient and modern. . . . The essence of transpersonal is as old as records of civilization."

Interest in Christian ideas by Hindu scholars and practitioners and interest in Hindu concepts by Christian theologians have flourished during the past two hundred years. Some Indian/Hindu scholars have been fascinated with the person of Jesus Christ. Indian Christian theologians became intrigued with ideas of spirit and the creative energy of the universe, common in the deep traditions of spirituality in India (Kim 2003, 1).

In a nondualistic (*advaitic*) tradition of Hinduism, eighth-century philosopher Sankara regarded God, who is Spirit, and the human spirit (*atman*) as one (ibid., 2). Indian philosophers Swami Vivekananda and Sarvelpalli Radhakrishman reinterpreted this idea in the late nineteenth century. Similarities between the Holy Spirit and the Hindu concept of *atman* (spirit, soul, self) and related ideas also led Indian Christian theologians to regard God (who is Spirit) and the human spirit (*atman*) as one.

Christian theologian Brahmabandhab Upadhyaya (1861–1907), considered the pioneer of Indian Christian theology, developed the notion of the Hindu-Catholic. He believed that one could be born a Hindu and reborn a Catholic. Integrating

> **Study Aid #199**
>
> Religious Influences in Transpersonal Psychology
>
> Hindu understandings of *Brahman* and *atman*
> Christian idea of human ability to know God
> Christian influences on humanistic psychology
> Buddhist meditation techniques

aspects of classical Vedantic into a Thomistic framework, he argued that Hindu forms could be utilized in Christian theology rather than Greek forms, as Western theologies have used (ibid.). *Atman*, the human spirit, and *Brahman*, the Spirit that pervades the physical world, could be united. A series of Hindu-Christian dialogues in 1963 explored the meeting point of Hindu and Christian religions that takes place "in the cave of the heart" (ibid., 3).

Some transpersonal psychologies interact with Christianity by attempting to dispel perceived negative effects of Christian religious teaching. Recent efforts to dispel psychoses thought to arise from Catholic Christianity are documented, for example: "Transcendence and the transpersonal goes against any Christian or Catholic memories that may be in the body and the implications of heresy and blasphemy that can lead to psychoses" ("Dead Heroines").

Points of contact between transpersonal psychology and Christianity also appear through the Christian values incorporated into humanistic and later transpersonal psychology. As the field of psychology developed, it patterned itself after the natural sciences. Freud's assumption that humans were biologically determined creatures with much of the human psyche unavailable to consciousness left little to human freedom. His negative assessment of human behavior resulted from studying people with neuroses and psychoses. Behaviorism followed this First Force trend in psychology by attempting to control human behavior. The deterministic emphasis in Second Force psychology frustrated psychologists Abraham Maslow and Carl Rogers, who believed that persons could choose their behavior on the basis of human goodness and human dignity. Rather than study persons with mental illnesses, they studied healthy individuals, developing a Third Force in psychology. Humanistic psychology, then, emphasized human goodness, the ability to choose, and the human potential to develop.

Many of the values that undergird humanistic psychology are borrowed from Christianity. Christianity teaches that God created the world and humans good, but humans subsequently marred that goodness by falling into sin. Humanistic psychology borrows the idea of human goodness from Christianity but ignores the Christian idea of a sinful part of human nature. Christian belief stresses the limitedness of humans and their difference from God, who is not part of creation but outside of it. Humans can choose their behavior, but their choice is limited by their humanness. Persons are not God and do not have unlimited freedom or ability to choose the good. That contrasts with humanistic psychology's belief in unlimited human potential and the ability of persons to create their own value without reference to God.

Transpersonal psychology, deemed by some a Fourth Force in psychology, expands the notion of human potential into a belief in the godlike qualities of persons and their oneness with the spiritual force of the universe. "The unity of the physical world as an expression of God is the source of transpersonal psychology's spiritual dimension. Stretching toward full human potential becomes a search for the God within, a oneness with the universe, a knowledge of the transcendent power in oneself" (Adeney 1981, 16).

The idea of a spirit that inhabits persons brought the religious idea of *atman* into transpersonal psychology. The "cave of the heart," Augustine's vacuum that only God could fill, became the locus of a link between the individual and the cosmic. *Brahman* and *atman* unite in the *advaitic* experience described in the Upanishads, the experience of the oneness of all things. The personal now "mirrors the universe," and God and the individual are understood to be one substance.

Three streams of ideas now operate together in transpersonal psychology: the Hindu notions of *atman* and *Brahman* as Spirit, the Christian idea of human ability to know God as Spirit, and the value of the individual perpetuated through Christianity and humanistic psychology in the West. Through linking God with *Brahman*, the Spirit that is manifested in the cosmos, and with *atman*, the human spirit, transpersonal psychology becomes a new religion. Even as Indian Christian theologians used Eastern forms of thought to develop their ideas, so transpersonal psychology utilizes Western cultural forms to express Eastern religious ideas.

However, transpersonal psychology does not present itself as a religion. Seeking acceptance as a social science, transpersonal psychology stresses its "objectivity" and links to humanistic psychology. Evolutionary ideas also veil the religious aspects of transpersonal psychology. Christian critiques of transpersonal psychology, however, identify it as religious.

A religion identifies a basic problem in the universe and outlines a way to solve that problem. Theologies that explain the problem of the universe are developed. Theories and practices that lead to the solution of that cosmic problem are developed. Transpersonal psychology outlines the problem of the universe as a separation from spirit and recommends practices that will unite all things into a universal oneness, a spiritual oneness. That understanding of the world has

---

Study Aid #200

Transpersonal Psychology's Issues with Christianity

Nature of God: Personal vs. pantheistic
Human nature: Sinful vs. good
The world: God's creation or devolution of consciousness

called out critical responses from Christian theologians. That critique stresses the religious aspects of transpersonal psychology, stating that those aspects should be recognized as religious and not styled as scientific.

Contrasting transpersonal psychology with Christianity reveals very different views of God, humans, and the world. Christianity affirms a personal God that stands outside of the world, a Creator God who made humans in God's image, giving them limited freedom to choose the good. The "God" of transpersonal psychology is universal Spirit that calls the material world back into oneness with it. Humans are perceived to be part of that Spirit but separated from it. To realize one's godlikeness is to return to Spirit, understanding the unity and oneness of all things. The world in Christian theology is made of matter that is real and tangible, separate and distinct from the God who made it. In transpersonal psychology, the world is a devolution of consciousness into matter. As such, it is basically an illusion. Through meditation, an individual can attain a higher consciousness that understands the self to be Spirit, part of a God that is all things.

Stark differences between those two religious paths are apparent. Transpersonal psychology, as a Third Force, has departed from the social sciences to become a religion. Using Western forms, it purports a pantheistic religion in which God, the world, and humans are of one essence.

Further Reading

Frances S. Adeney. "Empowering the Self: A Look at the Human Potential Movement." *SCP Journal 5*, no. 1 (1981–82).

———. "Transpersonal Psychology: Psychology and Salvation Meet." In *The New Age Rage*, edited by Karen Hoyt and J. Isamu Yamamoto, 107–27. Fleming H. Revell, 1987.

Kirsteen Kim. *Mission in the Spirit: The Holy Spirit in Indian Christian Theologies*. Indian Society for Promoting Christian Knowledge, 2003.

107

New Age: History, Beliefs, Practices

J. Gordon Melton

In common parlance, the term "New Age movement" has two distinct but related uses. In a more narrow sense, it refers to a millennial movement that swept through and revitalized the traditional Western esoteric religious community of Europe and North America in the 1980s with hope of a coming New Age of wisdom and love. More broadly, however, it refers to the whole of that Western esoteric religious tradition that has been a persistent presence in the West at least since the first century CE. While the tradition occasionally faced extinction, it finally found space in the wake of the Protestant Reformation to grow and develop into what is now the third-largest religious tradition currently operating in the West.

History

What emerged a generation ago as the New Age can be traced to ancient Gnosticism. By the second century CE, Gnosticism existed as a set of variant movements throughout the Roman Empire, each offering an alternative way to interpret the Christian revelation. They looked upon Jesus as a manifestation of a transcendent God who came to lead humans, seen as sparks of God trapped in a material world, out of the darkness in which they were engulfed. Jesus brought the knowledge (or *gnōsis*) to gain release and rise through the various levels of the spiritual world back to God. Though Jesus appeared to be human, he was purely spiritual and merely appeared to have a human body.

Gnostic tendencies appeared in the first century, and a variety of leaders adhering to a Gnostic worldview gained a following within the Christian community

> **Study Aid #201**
> Five Key Precursors of the New Age
>
> Emanuel Swedenborg (1688–1772): A Christian mysticism of spirit travel and communication.
> Franz Mesmer (1734–1815): A force known as "animal magnetism" that affected humans.
> Helena Blavatsky (1831–91): One of the founders of the Theosophical Society.
> George Gurdjieff (ca. 1872–1949): The philosophy of the Fourth Way.
> Swami Vivekananda (1863–1902): First brought Hinduism to the West in the late nineteenth century.

in the second century. The champions of what emerged as the orthodox tradition in the church rejected the Gnostics, and by the fourth century, it seems to have survived primarily in Egypt. Its major tendencies, however, would be revived by the Persian prophet Mani (ca. 216–76 CE), whose more dualistic version of Gnosticism would spread across the Roman Empire and eastward all the way to China. Though persecuted, the movement thrived for centuries in India and China, and even survived the rise of Islam.

Esotericism (a designation referring to the practice of keeping some teachings exclusively for the most dedicated members) would reappear century after century either as mystical movements that emphasized either the search for God through the exploration of the inner consciousness or as magical movements espousing skills to manipulate the material world with spiritual energies. Late in the first millennium of the Christian era, the Bogomils established themselves in the southern Balkans and thrived until overrun by the Muslims. The Cathars or Albigensians emerged in southeastern France in the eleventh century, only to be destroyed in the thirteenth century by a combination of Catholic forces.

By the time of the rise of the Cathars, both Islamic and Jewish forms of esotericism had emerged, the former as the devotional movement known as Sufism and the latter as Hasidism, with its map of the spiritual world known as the Kabbalah. When the Inquisition turned on the Jewish community in Spain and Portugal, the resultant scattering of the Iberian Jewish community provided the opportunity for the Christian appropriation of the Kabbalah, which became an integral part of the esoteric world.

The Protestant Reformation of the sixteenth century provided space in which esoteric faith could survive and, since the nineteenth century, actually thrive. An unbroken lineage of esoteric groups emerge with Rosicrucianism in the seventeenth century, from which emerged Freemasonry, Swedenborgianism, Mesmerism, modern ceremonial magic, Spiritualism, theosophy, Christian Science, New Thought, modern neopaganism, and the New Age. Through the twentieth century, theosophy gave birth to a variety of movements from the Arcane School of Alice Bailey and Rudolf Steiner's Anthroposophy to the "I AM" religious movement and the Liberal Catholic Church, each of which produced their own variations and led to the development of an alternative religious milieu throughout the urban communities of the Western world.

The New Age movement emerged in Great Britain among several theosophical groups. Using insights gained from messages received by channeling (mediumship) from what were believed to be highly evolved spiritual beings, groups of teachers began to offer a vision of an era of wisdom and love that would arrive with the next generation as it channeled the wave of cosmic energy released by what astrologers were describing as a move from the Piscean to the Aquarian Age. That energy would awaken all of humanity and lead to a universal uplift of society. Individuals could participate in the coming new age by channeling the energies, engaging in self-transformative efforts, and getting the message of the New Age out to all.

Esotericism survived as a broken tradition through the Middle Ages, as different groups were persecuted to the margins of society. The history of attempted suppression accounts for the set of strategies esotericists developed to survive in a hostile world where governments privileged Christianity and used its power to attack unapproved religious teachings. Some groups emphasized secrecy and kept their real views concealed from all but trusted adherents. Some groups, most notably the Freemasons, denied themselves any religious status while presenting themselves as a mere fraternity discussing interesting new ideas. Many groups adopted Christian symbols and language while presenting themselves as merely a "metaphysical" or "mystical" variation of traditional Christianity and attempted to blend into the edge of the Christian community as another denomination. The significant growth of Western esotericism since the late nineteenth century has paralleled the growth of religious liberty following the French and American Revolutions.

Beliefs

In the absence of a single sacred text analogous to the Bible, esotericism's main teachings must be found in the writings of the many authors who have expounded their own variation of the basic perspective. Amid the diversity, however, the tradition offers an amazing consensus on basic issues. For example, in esoteric thought, God is pictured as utterly transcendent and impersonal, rather than as the personal fatherly figure of Christian faith. For Christians, God created the world, life, and human beings as a distinct act of creation. God (the Creator) and humans (the creatures) are very different. Esotericists generally see the world as having evolved in stages, as God (the original Unity) differentiated into the many and emanated various spiritual realms. Humans, spiritual beings from the highest realms, have fallen into the lowest material realm. Humans suffer from the forgetfulness of their true identity and must rediscover their spiritual nature. Esoteric/New Age teachings provide the knowledge allowing them to awaken and escape.

Christianity (like Judaism and Islam) entered the world as revelation. Christians present the faith openly to all that they may know and receive salvation and its blessings. Esotericism operates on a quite different model. Truth comes as the result of spiritual striving and ultimately is available only to the worthy, those who have taken the effort to understand the nature of the cosmos and who have confronted spiritual reality directly. For some esoteric groups such activity is relatively simple and quick, but for most it involves years of work and the gaining of access to the whole of the truth in multiple stages. These stages are often pictured as levels of initiation, and the inner and complete teachings of such an esoteric group are opened only to the elite members who have mastered each level step by step.

While Christianity poses salvation as the ultimate goal, esotericism generally posits enlightenment as the aim of the religious life. Christians see salvation as a gift by God that confers upon them a new status. Esotericism suggests that enlightenment is attained by pursuing one or more different spiritual disciplines through which one encounters and masters the spiritual realms. As Christians respond to God through prayer, devotion, and attendance at worship services in a communal setting, esotericists seek the divine as they practice various spiritual exercises in what amounts to a school-like setting.

Taking its cue from modern psychotherapy, the New Age movement largely recasts Western esotericism in therapeutic language. Traditional spiritual disciplines (from meditation to divination) have been redefined as tools of transformation, and the search for enlightenment is seen as beginning with an initial experience of awakening followed by a lifetime of healing and transformation toward wholeness and enlightenment.

Practices

The Western esoteric tradition invites people into a variety of spiritual practices awakening them to their essential divinity and providing knowledge of the means to escape from this world back to their true spiritual home. Different esoteric communities are often distinguished by their advocacy (and/or denunciation) of particular approaches to awakening and enlightenment. Esoteric teachers have seen themselves as more or less essential to the awakening process of their students.

Some esoteric groups emphasize magic. The magician explores the spiritual world in an attempt to master the forces and entities one finds there. Traditionally, magic included the invocation of a spectrum of noncorporeal beings over which

---

Study Aid #202

New Age and Esoteric Practices

Channeling	Astrology	Crystals
Clairvoyance	Tarot card reading	Pyramids

the magician asserted dominance through the knowledge of and proficiency in magical ritual. Magical teachings were significantly transformed in the nineteenth century following the destructive critique by both Protestantism and the Enlightenment of their somewhat naive supernaturalism. Contemporary magicians now see themselves as working with a universal cosmic energy that they master by a variety of disciplines that improve concentration and agility.

More popular than magic is the approach that uses meditation as a basic tool to explore and attune the inner self with what is seen as a vast spiritual world. This approach, hallowed by the medieval mystics, resonates with contemplative practices both East and West and has been popularized by a variety of traditions from theosophy to New Thought. It has grown as a practice that can be done by anyone sitting alone in their home and rarely provokes negative reactions from neighbors.

The esoteric devotee may also access various adepts who offer immediate contact with spiritual realities. Practitioners of channeling, clairvoyance, astrology, or tarot cards mediate immediate contact with the spiritual world. While such practices were in centuries past used to seek knowledge of the future, the New Age movement transformed them into opportunities for self-exploration. Simultaneously, the traditional divinatory practices associated with various healing disciplines, which practitioners believed capable of channeling spiritual energy, are called upon in times of mental, spiritual, or physical illness.

Present Status

The New Age movement in the more narrow sense faded away in the 1990s, and today almost no one claims that label. The modern Western esoteric tradition, however, is alive and quite well. It manifests itself both in the many esoteric groups and among individuals who publicly identify with the movement apart from any formal organizational membership. Its core constitutes 2 to 3 percent of the population in North America (six to ten million) and possibly twice that in parts of Europe. At the same time, the permeation of the modern world by esoteric and New Age ideas through the twentieth century has been significant. More than 20 percent of the population in North America follow their horoscope or believe in reincarnation (not exclusive to the esoteric community), again with higher percentages manifesting in Europe.

Esotericism has existed as the major alternative to Christianity since the fourth century and currently exists as the second-largest religious community in the West.

Further Reading

>Catherine Albanese. *A Republic of Mind and Spirit: A Cultural History of American Metaphysical Religion*. Yale University Press, 2007.
>
>Joscelyn Godwin. *The Theosophical Enlightenment*. SUNY Press, 1994.

Nicholas Goodrick-Clarke. *The Western Esoteric Traditions: A Historical Introduction.* Oxford University Press, 2008.

Paul Heelas. *The New Age Movement: The Celebration of the Self and the Sacralization of Modernity.* Blackwell, 1996.

J. Gordon Melton, Jerome Clark, and Aidan A. Kelly. *New Age Encyclopedia.* Gale Research, 2000.

Arthur Versluis. *Magic and Mysticism: An Introduction to Western Esotericism.* Rowman & Littlefield, 2007.

108

New Age: Theological Exchanges, Current Issues

J. Gordon Melton

The modern New Age movement—which arose in the 1970s, thrived in the 1980s, only to die out in the 1990s—represented a phase of development of what is now termed the Western esoteric tradition. In the form of Gnosticism, Western esotericism emerged side by side with orthodox Christianity in the first century in the Mediterranean basin, and its representative communities have been intimately connected with Christianity century by century to the present. Early evidence of the emergence of esoteric thinking can be found in the assertions of Jesus coming in the flesh, as emphasized for example in the first chapter of the Gospel of John and the fourth chapter of the First Epistle of John, designed in part to refute early Gnostic tendencies that became visible in the early church.

Theological Exchanges

Beginnings

By the second century, Gnosticism was offering a challenge to what was emerging as the orthodox Christian teachings. Church leaders such as Marcion and Valentinus offered different options that the church could have adopted. Bishop Irenaeus's second-century text *Against Heresies* became a major force leading to Gnosticism's being pushed to the margins. Gnosticism's last stand would be in the fourth century in the Christian monasteries of southern Egypt.

Manichaeism

The tradition would then find a new champion in the Persian prophet Mani (ca. 216–76 CE), who posed a more dualistic form of Gnosticism that became quite popular by the fifth century. Persecution by the Zoroastrians pushed it into the Mediterranean world, as well as eastward to India and China. Long after it disappeared in the West, it would survive in the East, though eventually it would be reduced to the small community of Mandeans now residing in modern Iraq.

Bogomilism

While orthodox Christianity dominated the post-Constantinian Roman/Byzantine world, just beyond the border other teachings such as Arian Christianity flourished, and new teachings continually arose or were injected by invading armies. Various esoteric groups, usually labeled heretical by the orthodox Christian leadership, emerged only to be suppressed and have their literature destroyed.

Among the most important of the Gnostic-like faiths was Bogomilism, which emerged at the end of the first millennium of the Christian era in what is now Bulgaria. As the Bulgarian Empire expanded in the eleventh century, Bogomilism became the dominant faith. It would remain a potent force in the region, from which it spread south and west, until the fourteenth century, when Bulgaria was overrun by the Ottoman Turks. Largely tolerant of both Eastern Orthodox and Roman Catholic Christianity, Islam proved most intolerant of Bogomilism. It appears that many who constitute the modern Muslim community of the Balkan region are the descendants of the Bogomils.

Albigensians/Cathara

The Bogomils appear to have seeded the Cathar movement in southern France, centered on the town of Albi (hence their alternate name, Albigensians). The emergence of the Cathars in strength in the twelfth century went unnoticed at first,

---

Study Aid #203

New Age and Christianity

Beginnings
  Manichaeism
  Bogomilism
  Albigensians and Cathara
  Reformation
  Rosicrucianism
  Freemasonry

Western esotericism
  New Age proper, 1970–90
  Post–New Age esotericism

lost amid a proliferation of a spectrum of alternative movements like the Spiritual Franciscans, but their radical critique of the church, especially its wealth and corruption, eventually called attention to its esoteric teachings and its establishment of a competing church organization. By the time the pope and the French monarchy took notice of them, the Cathars had become well entrenched. Alarmed, church authorities made a variety of unsubstantiated charges, not the least being that the Cathars practiced devil worship and conducted sexual orgies. In 1184 the pope requested the local bishops to organize inquisitions to seek out and suppress the heretics. These did not become effective until Dominic de Guzmán (1170–1221) was given freedom to found a new evangelistic order in the heart of Cathar territory, whose members were subsequently placed in charge of the Inquisition's courts. The tide turned against the Cathars after their stronghold at Montségur was captured in 1244, their leaders executed, and the surviving members driven into the remote mountains.

The Reformation Era

The Crusade against the Albigensians and the strong Inquisition that emerged from it would set the tone for future interactions between Christianity and any defined as heretics, including those with esoteric beliefs, which would include mystics like Meister Eckhart (ca. 1260–ca. 1327) and groups such as the Jewish Kabbalists, who were targeted by the Spanish Inquisition in the fifteenth century.

Christian interaction with Jews in the generation before the Reformation would lead directly to the recovery of the study of Hebrew as a biblical language and the production of a Hebrew Bible, the latter becoming the basis for translations of the Old Testament in the vernacular languages. However, in the process of encountering Jewish scholars, knowledge of the Kabbalah, which offered an impressive map of the spiritual world of esotericism, was made available across Europe. With Hebrew scholar Johannes Reuchlin (1455–1522) taking the lead, a Christianized "Cabalistic" teaching emerged and was integrated into Western esotericism, even as Jewish Kabbalism would reestablish itself in Eastern Europe in the Hasidic movement.

Rosicrucianism

The disruption of Christendom in the sixteenth century opened space for a variety of new religious movements, including small groups of esotericists. A few esoteric teachers such as the magician John Dee even attained some degree of prominence. Then at the beginning of the seventeenth century, a Lutheran pastor in Germany, Johann Valentin Andreae (1586–1654), anonymously issued a set of publications purporting to reveal the existence of a secret esoteric order, the Rosicrucians. Unable to contact the books' author, people were left free to found their own Rosicrucian orders.

Freemasonry

The initial Rosicrucian groups would provide the context for a set of informal groups formed for the exploration of esoteric ideas. These groups found a way to exist, in spite of their unorthodox interests, by attaching themselves to the stoneworkers' guilds as speculative lodges. As the number of lodges proliferated, national organizations emerged. And just as the stonemasons had jealously guarded their trade secrets, the new Freemasons protected their esoteric teachings. They developed an initiatory system to gradually introduce members to the esoteric worldview, but only after each had sworn an oath of confidentiality concerning what would be revealed.

Freemasonry would spread through the eighteenth century and become notable for its support of both the American and French Revolutions at a time when the idea of revolution remained anathema in Christian thought. As its association with democratic revolutions was noted, many Christian leaders found reasons to denounce Freemasonry, none more than the pope, who attributed to it the loss of the Papal States and the emergence of a unified, secular Italian government. Protestant leaders denounced it as a secret organization, and American churches intensely debated the propriety of members and clergy joining Masonic lodges. In spite of the controversy surrounding it, Masonry would provide a basic set of esoteric teachings and an initiatory organization upon which esoteric groups could build.

Modern Esotericism

Modern esotericism cannot be understood without reference to two prominent teachers that emerged in the eighteenth century. The first was Emanuel Swedenborg (1688–1772). He was the son of a Lutheran bishop and was also a prominent scholar who at the height of his career began to receive messages from what he believed to be angels, who offered him a spiritual interpretation of the Bible. To protect himself from church authorities, he wrote in Latin but eventually moved to England, where he died and where his followers organized the Church of the New Jerusalem, built around his writings. Meanwhile, in France, physician Franz Anton Mesmer (1734–1815) advocated the existence of a universal cosmic energy that he manipulated to treat the sick. Though denounced by the French Academy of Science, his teachings become the basis of a popular healing movement, while magical practitioners found in Mesmer's energy the agent to which they could attribute the efficacy of their practice.

As a new wave of popular esoteric, or occult (as they were then termed), movements arose decade by decade through the nineteenth and early twentieth century, Christian leaders generally denounced them either as revived ancient heresy in new guises or as Satanist movements that communicated with demonic powers.

At the same time, some esoteric groups approached Christians, offering answers to the post-Enlightenment attack upon all things supernatural. Spiritualists, for example, claimed to demonstrate the truth of traditional religious teachings such

> **Study Aid #204**
>
> **New Age Beliefs**
>
> God: Impersonal life force. God is all, and all is God.
> Reincarnation: Endless rebirths until salvation occurs.
> Evil: No original sin, no Satan, no evil. Mistakes, ignorance, *karma*.
> Suffering: The result of greed, hatred, delusion.
> Salvation: Realization of oneness with impersonal life force.

as the reality of miracles and the survival of bodily death. In the late nineteenth century, a group of scientists, many with ministerial training or the children of ministers, became enthused with spiritualist phenomena and set up organizations to investigate esoteric claims. The efforts of a century of psychical research led to the destruction of many claims, such as those involving materialization and teleportation, while offering mixed evidence of telepathy and psychic healing and largely abandoning the issue that began it all—human survival of bodily death.

These two views—the esoteric as satanic occultism and the esoteric realm as a possible source for recovering some lost Christian affirmations—would dominate Christian approaches to Western esotericism through the first half of the twentieth century. The former view would be integrated into the larger Christian concern with cult movements. The more positive approach would lead to the development of Christian-based organizations such as the Churches Fellowship for Spiritual and Psychical Research in Great Britain, to explore the issues raised by psychical research and parapsychology. Both approaches would be pursued with only marginal support from churches, who saw interest in the occult as a relatively minor matter amid all that was before them.

As a whole, Christianity missed the growth of the esoteric tradition and ignored both those who tried to warn of its emergence and those who pointed appreciatively to its potential. Thus, many were surprised when the New Age movement suddenly appeared in the 1970s and showed all the signs of rapid growth. As it grew, pastors often discovered church members attracted to it. While many moved to denounce it, others tried to engage it, prompting new efforts to draw attention to more traditional Christian devotion and spiritual disciplines.

The New Age movement had the effect of largely revising the image of the esoteric community. Old images of satanic occultism were discarded, and a more respectful if misunderstood image of the New Age took its place. At the same time, efforts of Christian leaders to understand and possibly dialogue with esoteric leaders continually floundered. While some Christians had been trained in Buddhist, Hindu, and Islamic thought, none knew the esoteric tradition, nor were there colleges where it could be learned. At the same time, esoteric communities valued experience and phenomena over academic learning and systematic thought. While it possessed many trained leaders, they were not knowledgeable in the traditional language of religion. Finding a foundation for dialogue remained difficult.

Only in the twenty-first century has that situation changed. In the 1970s, Antoine Faivre became the first person appointed to a chair in esoteric studies, at the Sorbonne. Several of his students subsequently moved to found the first department of esoteric studies at the University of Amsterdam, while others have spread out to take positions in religious studies departments throughout the Western world. They not only have begun to master the tradition theologically and historically but also have initiated the process of dialoging with their colleagues in other traditions.

Current Issues

Western esotericism in its post–New Age stage stands in a most unique relationship to the larger Christian community. It traces its existence back to a movement that offered an alternative approach to Christian realities, a movement that essentially lost the battle to survive. It has continued through a variety of movements that emerged at different times and places, but always in competition with Christianity. Christians have persistently seen its emergence as heretical and have persecuted its adherents, often with deadly force. Only with the development of a more pluralistic society and an atmosphere of religious freedom as a positive value has Western esotericism reemerged as a stable religious community.

The New Age movement of the later twentieth century represented a coming-out movement by people in the esoteric tradition. Not only did the movement mobilize many who harbored esoteric leanings, but it also redefined the older movement around a more positive image. With that image change also came a certain refusal to be relegated to the margins of either secular or religious society.

Sources

Antoine Faivre. *Theosophy, Imagination, Tradition: Studies in Western Esotericism*. SUNY Press, 2000.

Wouter J. Hanegraaff. *New Age Religion and Western Culture: Esotericism in the Mirror of Secular Thought*. Brill, 1996.

J. Stillson Judah. *The History and Philosophy of the Metaphysical Movements in America*. Westminster, 1967.

James R. Lewis and J. Gordon Melton, eds. *Perspectives on the New Age*. SUNY Press, 1992.

J. Gordon Melton, Jerome Clark, and Aidan A. Kelly. *New Age Encyclopedia*. Gale Research, 1990.

John A. Saliba. *Christian Responses to the New Age Movement: A Critical Assessment*. Chapman, 1999.

Kocku von Stuckard. *Western Esotericism: A Brief History of Secret Knowledge*. Equinox, 2005.

109

NRM:
Political and Economic Religions
Introduction

TERRY C. MUCK

As we mentioned in the introduction to this handbook, religion in the twenty-first century is in the process of radical differentiation. It is no longer a seamless part of holistic, tribal cultures as it was for premodern societies. But neither is it just a single part of complex, differentiated modern cultures, occupying, according to many scholars, an important part of the cultural sphere (as over against the political, economic, and social spheres). Religion in our postmodern, virtual age is engaged in a process of invading not just our cultural spheres but also our political, economic, and social spheres. That is, there are new religious movements that are primarily political in nature—genuine religions but with expressly political aims. There are also new religious movements that are primarily

---

Study Aid #205

Political and Economic Religions

Civil religion: A set of beliefs, symbols, and rituals that reconnect citizens with their shared history and offer ethical principles for social structure.

Christian Identity: The often misunderstood sect that, during the 1970s and '80s, was the dominant religious tendency among American white supremacists, providing a theological foundation for right-wing extremism.

Marxism: The belief that history, through dialectical tensions expressed in economic class conflict, is moving toward an ideal completion, best understood as anarchic utility.

economic in nature—genuine religions but with expressly economic analyses and aims. We call this radical differentiation.

In this part of our new religious movements section of the handbook, we will look at two new religious movements that have engaged the political sphere—civil religion and Christian Identity. We will then look at a religion (at least as we define religion) that is based on economic rationales—Marxism.

110

Civil Religion: History, Beliefs, Practices

ARTHUR REMILLARD

History

French Enlightenment philosopher Jean Jacques Rousseau first coined the term "civil religion" in his *Social Contract* (1762). Rousseau criticized traditional religion for advancing dogmas that he believed led to ignorance, intolerance, and arbitrary limits on personal liberty. He did not advocate abandoning religion, though. Instead, Rousseau proposed that a civil religion—grounded in a minimal set of "positive dogmas," such as freedom and liberty—could unify society and provide it with a moral grounding.

Rousseau's phrase reappeared in sociologist Robert Bellah's 1967 essay "Civil Religion in America." He theorized that in America, "there actually exists alongside of and rather clearly differentiated from the churches an elaborate and well-institutionalized civil religion" (p. 1). This civil religion, Bellah elaborated, has developed a set of beliefs, symbols, and rituals that reconnect citizens with their shared history and offer ethical principles for social structure. A flood of literature followed Bellah's article. And while many quibbled with the specifics, civil religion remains a useful category for investigating religious dimensions of American society.

America's civil religion originated from both Puritan and Enlightenment sources. In "A Model of Christian Charity" (1630), John Winthrop, the first governor of the Massachusetts Bay Colony, imagined that Puritans shared a special covenant with God. He pledged to protect this covenant by enforcing biblical codes of belief and behavior, making the community a "city upon a hill" for the entire world to emulate. In coming generations, American civil religion would absorb

> **Study Aid #206**
>
> **A History of the Concept of Civil Religion**
>
> "A minimal set of positive dogmas, such as freedom and liberty, that unify a society and provide it with moral grounding."
>
> <div align="right">Jean Jacques Rousseau, <i>Social Contract</i> (1672)</div>
>
> Rousseau's minimal elements of a civil religion:
>
> Deity
> Life to come
> Reward of virtue
> Punishment of vice
> Religious tolerance
>
> "There . . . exists alongside of and rather clearly differentiated from the churches an elaborate and well-institutionalized civil religion."
>
> Robert Bellah, "Civil Religion in America" (1967)
>
> American advocates of civil religion:
>
> John Winthrop: Puritans share a special covenant with God
> Thomas Jefferson: Religious references in Declaration of Independence
> Abraham Lincoln: Political decisions subject to universal moral dictates
> Martin Luther King Jr.: A civil religion that advocates racial equality and nonviolent resistance

Winthrop's sentiments of national destiny and divine purpose. Winthrop's words themselves have often been recited. In 1989, President Ronald Reagan referenced the "shining city upon a hill" during his farewell address to the nation.

The European Enlightenment also influenced America's civil religious structure. Thomas Jefferson's Declaration of Independence (1776) evolved out of an Enlightenment belief that the laws of human nature, as dictated by the divine Creator, demanded that a legitimate government respects the rights of individuals and protects human liberties from the whims of tyrants. Also similar to Enlightenment thinkers, American Revolutionaries drew from the intellectual resources of Greco-Roman culture. Specifically, the Roman Empire became a useful memory, since its leaders too invented a civic theology aimed toward unifying a complex population. Thus, in 1795, the Latin phrase *e pluribus unum* ("out of many, one") first appeared on American coinage.

Just as a civil religion can unify people, it can also become an ideological wedge. Debates between Abraham Lincoln and Stephen A. Douglas in 1858 foreshadowed the civil religious differences that fueled the American Civil War. Douglas favored local decision making even on matters such as slavery, while Lincoln believed that any decision was subject to universal moral dictates. Both asserted that their moral vision for America was objectively true and righteous, and that the other's position would lead to social disorder. When the war ended, the violence ceased but sectional tension remained. In the South, a civil religion of the Lost Cause emerged, where middle-to-upper-class whites began venerating their Confederate past, and using it to advance political agendas such as segregation. During the civil rights movement, however, Martin Luther King Jr. articulated a competing civil religious discourse, one that emphasized racial equality and nonviolent resistance. King's civil religion drew upon a black history in America, born from slavery and inspired by biblical liberation narratives.

Disputes over race, as well as gender, class, ethnicity, sexuality, and science, continue to divide America, making it difficult to imagine the possibility of a common national ethic. But certain themes, such as King's appeal to freedom—a freedom that he believed was a necessary American promise—demonstrate that civil religious language can both integrate people into a national culture and sound a prophetic tone, awakening a sense of moral duty.

Beliefs

Freedom, equality, justice, democracy, sacrifice, free enterprise, and the like are key beliefs in America's civil religious world. Hovering above them, though, is a broader belief in a transcendent power who has prescribed a special intention for the nation. Dating back to the Puritans, this sense of divine purpose would inform such influential policies as "Manifest Destiny," a term used frequently in the 1840s to describe America's westward expansion. The policy assumed that existing populations in these territories—most notably Native Americans—were inferior and in need of America's moral, religious, and political authority. For many antebellum Americans, westward expansion needed a Protestant presence, not simply for the spiritual well-being of Native Americans but also to prevent the spread of Catholicism within the continent. Presbyterian clergyman Lyman Beecher's *Plea for the West* (1835) warned of a papal conspiracy to dominate the West, and he called upon fellow Protestants to lead missions to the region in defense of America.

Study Aid #207

American Civil Religion Practices

Sacred days: Fourth of July
Sacred festivals: Presidential inaugurations
Sacred places: Gettysburg
Sacred texts: The Constitution
Sacred music: The national anthem
Sacred persons: The president

The anti-Catholic quality of American civil religion faded by the mid-twentieth century. John F. Kennedy's 1960 election to the US presidency helped to ease this transition. Kennedy believed in a God, which satisfied many non-Catholics. The abundance of Judeo-Christian language in American public life, however, has become a source of contention for nonbelievers. Adopted in 1791, the First Amendment both prohibits state sponsorship of religion and protects the free expression of religion. The duty of the courts has been to apply these parameters to specific situations—an inherently messy task. In 2000, *Santa Fe Independent School District v. Doe* came before the United States Supreme Court. The plaintiff objected to a Texas high school's practice of reciting a prayer over an intercom before football games. The court narrowly sided with the plaintiff. Justice John Paul Stevens wrote for the majority, who found the practice unduly coercive. Speaking for the minority, however, Chief Justice William Rehnquist criticized the majority's decision, labeling it hostile toward religion. Indeed, the proper place of religious language and images in public life remains an unsettled issue. But even for nonbelievers, there exists a sense that certain beliefs—such as the separation of church and state—rise above individual interests and serve the common good.

Practices

Religious practices reconnect participants to the central elements of their faith. America has no shortage of civil religious practices, with sacred days (the Fourth of July), sacred festivals (presidential inaugurations), sacred places (Gettysburg), sacred texts (the Constitution), and sacred music (the national anthem). There are also sacred rituals, such as reciting the Pledge of Allegiance. In 1892, Francis Bellamy, a Baptist minister and Christian socialist, composed the pledge, hoping that public school children would recite it at the beginning of each school day. The original version read, "I pledge allegiance to my flag and the republic for which it stands: one nation, indivisible, with liberty and justice for all." The pledge's various rewordings have reflected the nation's evolving civil religious perspectives. For example, Bellamy had intended to include the word "equality," but worried that some schools would not use the pledge, since it would imply equality for women and blacks. In 1924, "my flag" was replaced with "the flag of the United States of America" as a way of emphasizing to immigrants their duties to America, not to their homelands. And in 1954, "under God" was included as a symbolic prod at "godless communism." In 2002, the Ninth Circuit Court in San Francisco sided with atheist Michael Newdow, whose lawsuit argued that the phrase "under God" had violated his daughter's First Amendment rights. From Bellamy to Newdow, the pledge's development shows that, just as with civil religious language and beliefs, civil religious practices can both unify and divide.

These practices can also reveal America's improved understanding of itself. Washington, DC, is a civil religious pilgrimage center, with the National Mall displaying America's saints—Washington, Jefferson, and Lincoln. Also, the Smithsonian museums enshrine the images and information that have come to define America's history and culture. In 2004, the National Museum of American Indians opened. And presently plans are in place to open similar museums for women and African Americans. These places signify a growing awareness that many different people have helped to create America.

America's civil religion is a flowing river of meaning, developing along with the nation's complicated and diverse populations. It is perhaps America's allowance of many voices that unites it, with the hope that ideological competition will result in a better nation for everyone.

Further Reading

Robert N. Bellah. "Civil Religion in America." *Daedalus: Journal of the American Academy of Arts and Sciences* 96 (1967): 1–21.

Conrad Cherry, ed. *God's New Israel: Religious Interpretations of American Destiny.* University of North Carolina Press, 1998 (1971).

Marcella Cristi. *From Civil Religion to Political Religion: The Intersection of Culture, Religion and Politics.* Wilfrid Laurier University Press, 2001.

Andrew M. Manis. *Southern Civil Religions in Conflict: Black and White Baptists and Civil Rights, 1947–1957.* University of Georgia Press, 2002 (1987).

Jeffrey F. Meyer. *Myths in Stone: Religious Dimensions of Washington, D.C.* University of California Press, 2001.

Harry S. Stout. *Upon the Altar of the Nation: A Moral History of the American Civil War.* Viking, 2006.

Charles Reagan Wilson. *Baptized in Blood: The Religion of the Lost Cause, 1865–1920.* University of Georgia Press, 1980.

111

Civil Religion: Theological Exchanges, Current Issues

ARTHUR REMILLARD

American civil religion, sociologist Robert Bellah has explained, is a collection of beliefs, symbols, and rituals that serve to unify a diverse population. As a prominent voice in American history, Protestants have been instrumental in shaping this civil religion. However, interactions with different Christian groups and non-Christians have compelled Protestants to define and redefine their civil religious worldview. What follows briefly examines Protestant interactions with Indians, enslaved Africans, Catholics, and Jews. Starting in the colonial era and continuing through the early twentieth century, these contacts established patterns in civil religious exchange that have persisted into the present.

American Indians

Puritans operated on a belief that they were called to do God's work, to build a "city upon a hill" for the world to emulate. For the Puritan minister John Eliot, this meant converting Indians. By 1674, he organized fourteen "praying towns," or segregated Indian villages governed by converts. Along with changing their religion, Eliot coerced Indians to abandon their culture and adopt English clothing, customs, and work habits. The King Philip's War (1675–76) resulted in the near destruction of praying towns, and most surviving Indians returned to their tribes unimpressed with European Christianity. Still, Eliot embodied a mind-set that saw Indian life as profoundly "ungodly" and unsuited for colonial soil. By the

> **Study Aid #208**
> **American Pinch-Points with Civil Religion**
>
> Native Americans   Jews
> African Americans   Gays and lesbians
> Roman Catholics

nineteenth century, this intolerance of Indian religion and culture intensified and was institutionalized. The Indian Removal Act (1830) authorized the transfer of eastern tribes to western territories. William Apes of Massachusetts, a Methodist minister and Pequot Indian, was one of many Indians who voiced opposition. Apes identified with Jesus as a fellow outcast and called Indian removal one of many unjust laws that defied God's law. Apes helped to develop a civil religious discourse for Indians that criticized the dominant culture by announcing Christian and American themes of equality, justice, and freedom.

Enslaved Africans

Christianizing enslaved Africans would also become a priority for the South's white Protestant majority—but this took time. In the early stages of American slavery, slave owners were reluctant to introduce Christianity to slaves. White supremacy had become a bedrock civil religious value among planters, essential for maintaining their social order. If blacks and whites shared the faith, slave owners worried, slaves might feel a sense of equality. By the early eighteenth century, however, missionaries began convincing slave owners that Christianity would improve slave work habits and make them more subservient. So slave owners wanted slaves to hear "Be obedient to those who are your masters" (Eph. 6:5 NASB). But slaves were more influenced by biblical liberation narratives—"Let my people go" (Exod. 8:21). In 1822, Denmark Vesey, an ex-slave and African Methodist, developed a plan to overrun Charleston, South Carolina, that used as a model the story of Joshua and the battle of Jericho. City officials exposed the plan and executed Vesey. They then imposed restrictions on slave religious activity. But Vesey's memory lived on in the slave's imagination, which produced a moral tradition that informed the civil rights movement. As with Indians, African Americans developed their own civil religious discourse, which sought fulfillment of the nation's promises of equality, justice, and freedom.

Catholics and Jews

One product of the Second Great Awakening—a series of revivals in the early nineteenth century—was a strong ideological binding of Protestantism and

> **Study Aid #209**
>
> Examples of Elements of a Civil Religion
>
> Invocation of God in political speeches and on monuments
> Quotation of religious texts on public occasions by political leaders
> Veneration of past political leaders
> Use of political exemplars to teach moral ideals
> Veneration of veterans and casualties of the nation's wars
> Use of religious symbols on public buildings
> Use of public buildings for worship

Americanism. By the mid-nineteenth century, however, scores of Catholics and Jews had arrived at America's shores. In response, a nativist movement began developing among American Protestants. Nativists believed that immigrants could never be "true Americans" unless they converted and abandoned their Old World customs, culture, and language. Ironically, nativism left a lasting mark on one of America's most cherished civil religious temples, the Washington Monument. In 1835, monument planners envisioned its interior walls adorned with "memorial stones" from American states and foreign nations. They wanted to show how Washington was admired both domestically and abroad. In 1851, Pope Pius IX donated a stone taken from the ruins of the Temple of Peace. This outraged leaders of the American Party, a nativist political organization, who urged that the stone be returned to Rome. But monument planners intended on using it. In 1854, under the cover of darkness, a group of men stole the "Pope's Stone" and destroyed it. This event, combined with the Civil War, halted construction. When building resumed in 1880, the quarry previously used was unavailable. Builders had to use marble from another quarry, which had a slightly different shade. The result was a discernable line two-thirds up the monument, a symbol of civil religious discord that visitors can still witness today.

Like Catholics, Jews struggled against prejudice, bigotry, and alienation. Growing up in the New York City ghettos, Benny Leonard saw this firsthand. He decided to fight back—literally. Leonard became a boxer, and from 1917 to 1925 he held the lightweight title while wearing the Star of David on his trunks. He was not alone. From 1901 to 1938, twenty-seven boxing world champions were Jewish. Over time, Jewish athletes like Leonard helped make Judaism seem more familiar to the Protestant majority. American Catholicism also benefited from athletic exposure. In 1918, Knute Rockne became the head coach of Notre Dame University's football team. Under his direction, the Catholic university had tremendous success against the nation's finest Protestant and secular universities. In the ring and on the field of play, Jews and Catholics displayed a unique combination of athletics and piety, which helped to widen the boundaries of America's civil religious landscape.

Theological Exchanges

Civil religious exchanges between Protestants and others have often resulted in broader inclusiveness and a fuller awareness of what religious freedom means. As this was the case with Catholics and Jews, it is now with American Muslims. In 2006, Keith Ellison became the first Muslim elected to Congress. An African American convert, for his swearing-in ceremony Ellison placed his hand on a Qur'an that was once owned by Thomas Jefferson. Critics objected, protesting that he should have used a Bible. Representative Virgil H. Goode of Virginia echoed this sentiment while warning his constituents that lax immigration policies would eventuate in more Muslims winning office and America's inevitable destruction. (Ellison's family line in America extended to the mid-eighteenth century.) Rather than respond with vitriol, on his first day, Ellison located Goode on the Congress floor. The two shook hands and agreed to talk later. Ellison later explained that he did not expect immediate acceptance from Goode but instead wanted to begin building bridges. Goode also received a visit from a delegation of Christians and Muslims from the National Council of Churches. The delegation expressed disappointment with the congressman's words, but Goode stood by his statements. Still, the Ellison affair represents a positive model for civil religious dialogue. Both sides asserted their vision of what America ought to be and, in doing so, planted seeds for further consideration.

Current Issues

In recent decades, evolution, abortion, homosexuality, religious tolerance, and party politics have shaped the Protestant vision of American civil religion. The realities of globalization have complicated these issues and raised new ones. In a globalized America, being a "city upon a hill" has meant for some Christians advocating for federal funding to combat AIDS in Africa. For others, immigration reform has become a priority. In 2006, the National Association of Evangelicals cited biblical passages such as Exodus 22:21 ("You shall not wrong a stranger or oppress him, for you were strangers in the land of Egypt," NASB) to argue that reform should both protect the borders and extend compassion toward undocumented workers. But there was a gulf between the pulpit and the pew. That same year, the Pew Forum on Religion and Public Life found that a majority of white evangelical Protestants, white mainline Protestants, and white non-Hispanic Catholics viewed illegal immigrants as a threat to "traditional" American culture and values. And a Family Research Council poll reported that 90 percent of self-identified "values voters" believed that deportation is biblically justified.

This debate and others like it will assume new dimensions as the boundaries separating America from the world become less distinct. To be sure, American Protestants will remain a prominent voice in these discussions, putting forth their varied visions for how the nation ought to proceed.

Further Reading

Robert N. Bellah. "Civil Religion in America." *Daedalus: Journal of the American Academy of Arts and Sciences* 96 (1967): 1–21.

Edward E. Curtis IV. *Muslims in America: A Short History.* Oxford University Press, 2009.

Joel W. Martin. *The Land Looks after Us: A History of Native American Religion.* Oxford University Press, 1999.

Martin E. Marty. *Righteous Empire: The Protestant Experience in America.* 2nd ed. Harper & Row, 1977.

Mark S. Massa. *Catholics and American Culture: Fulton Sheen, Dorothy Day, and the Notre Dame Football Team.* Crossroad, 1999.

R. Laurence Moore. *Religious Outsiders and the Making of Americans.* Oxford University Press, 1986.

Albert J. Rabateau. *Slave Religion: "The Invisible Institution" in the Antebellum South.* Oxford University Press, 1978.

Steven A. Riess, ed. *Sports and the American Jew.* Syracuse University Press, 1998.

112

Christian Identity: History, Beliefs, Practices

MICHAEL BARKUN

Christian Identity is the often-misunderstood sect that, during the 1970s and '80s, was the dominant religious tendency among American white supremacists. It has also had an influence out of all proportion to its small size. By formulating religious justifications for anti-Semitism and racial inequality, Christian Identity provided a theological foundation for right-wing extremism. Although most Identity believers limited their social and political views to rhetorical expressions, a number were involved in the planning or execution of acts of violence. Significant federal and state law-enforcement efforts and prosecutions, beginning in the mid-1980s, led to the movement's gradual decline.

History

Christian Identity grew out of British-Israelism, or, as it was sometimes called, Anglo-Israelism. British-Israelism was a religious tendency that developed among some British Protestants in the nineteenth century, built around the belief that the so-called Ten Lost Tribes of Israel had migrated westward from Middle Eastern exile and had populated the British Isles. British-Israelites concluded from this revisionist history that the British peoples, whom they now believed to be the literal biological descendants of Israelites, were destined to fulfill biblical prophecy. In some versions, Israelites were also said to be the ancestors of Anglo-Saxon-Celtic peoples; in some, of Germanic peoples; and in some, of all the peoples of northwestern Europe.

> **Study Aid #210**
> **History of Christian Identity**
> British-Israelism: 19th century
> Anglo-Saxon Federation of America: 1930s
>   Howard Rand, William Cameron, Henry Ford
> Christian Identity: 1940s, 1950s
>   Bertrand Comparet, William Potter Gale, Wesley Swift
> Aryan Nations: 1970s, 1980s
>   Richard Girnt Butler
> Decline
>   Southern Poverty Law Center

By the late 1800s, British-Israelism had spread to the United States and Canada. It did not, however, grow significantly in America until the 1930s, when the combination of the anxieties of the Great Depression and the organizational skills of a Massachusetts lawyer, Howard Rand, resulted in a national organization, the Anglo-Saxon Federation of America. Rand's organization differed somewhat from British-Israelism in England through its more explicitly anti-Semitic coloration, partly the product of Rand's collaborator, William J. Cameron, who was a close associate of Henry Ford and the editor of Ford's notorious anti-Semitic newspaper, the *Dearborn Independent*. British-Israelism, in its original, more philo-Semitic form, had foreseen a future of collaboration between Anglo-Saxon peoples and Jews, a prospect anathema to Rand and Cameron (although by the 1940s, even the British-Israelites in Canada and the United Kingdom itself jettisoned the movement's early philo-Semitism). The areas proselytized by Rand before World War II, such as California, became the seedbed for Christian Identity.

Identity itself emerged in Southern California in the 1940s and '50s, the product of three independent but interconnected preachers: Bertrand Comparet, William Potter Gale, and—most importantly—Wesley Swift. Comparet and Swift were both linked to Gerald L. K. Smith, the most important anti-Semitic organizer in the United States at the time. Swift, Gale, and Comparet were also involved in right-wing paramilitary organizations. The addition of Rand's version of British-Israelism present in the area provided all that was necessary for the creation of a theology that incorporated a particularly virulent strain of anti-Semitism, as well as doctrines of racial difference. Since British-Israelism itself was a loose-knit movement with no authority capable of enforcing doctrinal orthodoxy, there was no barrier to the creation of Identity.

Christian Identity reached its high point of influence in the 1970s and '80s. Richard Girnt Butler, a former Lockheed engineer, appointed himself Wesley Swift's successor and transferred Swift's Church of Jesus Christ Christian from California to Hayden Lake, Idaho, in 1973. In association with it, he set up a neo-Nazi political arm, Aryan Nations, which quickly earned national notoriety. Butler's was one of numerous efforts to link Identity with a political agenda. An armed insurgent group in the early 1980s called "The Order," seeking to foment an antigovernment racist insurrection in the West, was about half made up of Identity believers. While few Identity figures have had much formal theological training, after the deaths of Comparet, Gale, and Swift, intellectual leadership fell to Dan Gayman in Missouri and Pete Peters in Colorado. At its height, the movement had perhaps forty thousand adherents, although given its diffuse character, any numerical assessment is bound to be in the nature of an educated guess.

As Christian Identity began to decline in the late 1980s, antigovernment extremists on the far right began to gravitate to forms of neopaganism, such as Odinism, with its explicit rejection of Christianity in favor of a pre-Christian Nordic pantheon. Dan Gayman's Church of Israel in Schell City, Missouri, underwent a bitter split. Of the Identity organizations prominent in the faith's growth period, only Pete Peters's Scriptures for America, headquartered in LaPorte, Colorado, seems to have thrived.

Beliefs

Christian Identity believes that whites are descendants of the tribes of Israel. While there is consensus that all those who can trace their ancestry to northwestern Europeans count as whites, there are occasional disagreements about those at the geographical margins. The major questionable cases involve the Iberian and Italian peninsulas and Slavic Europe. This was to some extent an issue even in British-Israelism, and it has become more consequential in Christian Identity with its more overtly racist philosophy. Part of that racism involves a conception of human creation different from that in the conventional Genesis narrative. According to Identity, God created each race separately, endowing whites with superior talents. Thus only whites may trace their ancestry to Adam, and the Genesis story therefore is for Identity the story only of the creation of the white race. The others were created later, and the flood was God's punishment for miscegenation.

The most distinctive and frequently noted aspect of Identity theology is its so-called two-seed theory. According to it, Adam fathered only two sons: Abel, who of course was slain, and Seth. He did not father Cain. Instead, Cain was the result of copulation between Eve and the devil in the form of a humanoid "serpent," so that sex with Satan was the primal sin in the garden. As Identity traces biblical genealogy, Cain's offspring are the Jews, with two implications: First, they become, quite literally, the "seed of Satan," the descendants of the devil. Second, they have no claim to any biblical or Israelite inheritance. Instead, that belongs to European, Christian whites, who are destined to fulfill prophecy. As a result, for Identity all of human history becomes the story of the warfare between the two seed lines, the seed of Adam and the seed of Cain/Satan, a struggle that will not be resolved until the battle in the last days.

> **Study Aid #211**
>
> **Christian Identity Beliefs**
>
> Israelism: White race descended from ten tribes
> Creation: Each race created separately (whites first)
> Flood: God's punishment for miscegenation
> Two-seed theory:
>   Adam seed line: Abel, Seth, white race
>   Eve/serpent seed line: Cain, Jewish race
> Millenarianism: Tribulation (race war), then victory

Those associated with Christian Identity are consequently end-time believers. However, their millenarianism is quite different from that of most Protestant evangelicals. They reject the dispensational premillennialism so common among conservative Protestants. They do not believe the faithful will be raptured. Instead, they believe they will need to live through the conflicts and chaos of the tribulation, which they often conceptualize in terms of race war. For them, the millennium is a time of white triumphalism, when Jews and colored races will have been either destroyed or subjugated.

While the decline of Identity is surely due in large part to governmental pressure, some of the reason is doubtless the difference between its doctrines and those of most American Protestants. The two-seed theory, with its story of a serpent who looks like a man and who can have intercourse with a woman, while it has exegetical roots that antedate Identity, departs dramatically from the familiar biblical tale of original sin. Similarly, conservative Protestants raised on dispensational premillennialism may find it difficult to accept an end-time vision that rejects the rapture and insists on the necessity of suffering through the tribulation.

Practices

Because Christian Identity believers think of themselves as Israelites, they believe that many of the ordinances found in the Hebrew Bible apply to them. Therefore, practices usually found among Jews can also be found among Christian Identity, albeit in modified form. Thus, they often observe such biblically sanctioned festivals as Passover and may observe biblical dietary restrictions. However, like British-Israelism, Christian Identity has no authority structure. Therefore, a laissez-faire atmosphere exists so far as ritual requirements are concerned, with wide variation among groups and individuals.

There is also a lifestyle overlap between Christian Identity and what is commonly termed "survivalism"; that is, a lifestyle built around complete self-sufficiency, often in the expectation that conventional institutions may suffer a catastrophic breakdown in the near future. Since Christian Identity believers are often suspicious of and/or alienated from government and do not wish to live near Jews and nonwhites, they gravitate toward sparsely populated areas. The propensity to adopt survivalism also depends on how imminent one believes the tribulation to be. This tendency to go "off the grid" has led to clusters of Identity followers in commune-like settings in such areas as the Ozarks and the Pacific Northwest, where they can live with little interaction with others.

As the term "Christian Identity" has become associated with violence and antigovernment activities, believers have ceased using it. They prefer a variety of other, nonpejorative terms, referring to themselves, for example, as "covenant people," "kingdom people," "kingdom covenant," and so on. When asked whether they are Christian Identity, many deny it.

Further Reading

Michael Barkun. *Religion and the Racist Right*. University of North Carolina Press, 1996.

Protocols of the Learned Elders of Zion. RiverCrest, 2004.

Chester Quarles. *Christian Identity: The Aryan American Bloodline Religion*. McFarland, 2004.

Charles Roberts. *Race over Grace: The Racialist Religion of the Christian Identity Movement*. iUniverse, 2003.

113

Christian Identity: Theological Exchanges, Current Issues

MICHAEL BARKUN

Christian Identity has had a confusing and complex relationship with what might be termed orthodox or mainstream Christianity. In the first place, because it is so small, many otherwise well-informed Christians either have never heard of it or know only in some vague and general way that it is connected to the extreme right. Second, the organizational structure of Christian Identity makes it difficult for the movement to relate in a systematic way with other faith groups even if it should wish to. Third, it is occasionally and very misleadingly grouped with the so-called new Christian right, even though, as will be demonstrated below, the two are poles apart on critical issues. Finally, some regular contacts with mainstream Christian clergy have been forced on Identity believers who have been incarcerated and have asserted religious rights within institutional settings.

The Size of Christian Identity

No systematic and reliable attempt has ever been made to determine the number of Identity believers. As is true of other very small religious groups, they tend to slip through even those religious surveys that employ very large samples. Sampling problems apart, Identity believers tend to be unusually suspicious and secretive, since many hold antigovernment views and/or fear of government surveillance. Estimates of Identity's size have ranged from a few thousand to as many as one hundred thousand. Circumstantial and anecdotal evidence suggests that the estimates at the extremes are almost certainly incorrect, and that at the peak of its

> **Study Aid #212**
> **Christian Identity Facts**
> Demographics: 40,000 (estimate)
> Institutionally autonomous
> Influenced other separatist groups
>   KKK, neo-Nazis
> Means of influence
>   Publications, Bible study groups, internet
> Different from Christian Right
>   Detest Jerry Falwell, Pat Robertson
>   Reject dispensational premillennialism
>   Do not support state of Israel

influence in the 1970s and early 1980s, the movement had perhaps forty thousand active believers, a very small number when one considers the impact Identity had on the extreme right.

The Structure of Christian Identity

Whatever the number of Christian Identity adherents, Identity has never assumed the character of a religious denomination. It might best be termed a sect. It has been made up of completely autonomous churches, publications, Bible study groups, and electronic and print "ministries," as well as organizations that straddle the line between religion and politics. Thus Identity beliefs have penetrated and sometimes dominated some Klan and neo-Nazi circles. An unknown (and unknowable) number of individuals have also doubtless maintained Identity beliefs without affiliating with any Identity organization.

Despite occasional attempts to create coordinating mechanisms, the jealousies of individual preachers and religious entrepreneurs have always prevailed. As a result, there has never been any means by which the greater Identity community could speak to or interact collectively with other faith groups. Even British-Israelism, out of which Identity sprang, had greater cohesiveness, since the British-Israel World Federation in London has acted as clearinghouse for the independent Anglo-Israel groups. Thus the extraordinarily fragmented character of Christian Identity has militated against anything resembling dialogue with other Christians.

Christian Identity and the "New Christian Right"

The appearance of politically mobilized conservative Protestants, beginning in the late 1970s, gave rise to the term "new Christian right." Unfortunately, in some hands this became a residual category for any politically conservative Protestant political expression, regardless of doctrinal or other considerations. As a result, Christian Identity was sometimes grouped with it as one of its manifestations. In fact, nothing could be further from the truth. While Christian Identity believers disagree about many things, they are united in their detestation of such figures as Pat Robertson and the late Jerry Falwell.

From a doctrinal standpoint, Christian Identity stands apart from most conservative Protestants in its rejection of dispensational premillennialism. Identity does not believe the saved will be raptured prior to the tribulation. Rather, they will have to endure the tribulation. For that reason, many Christian Identity believers have adopted a survivalist lifestyle. The Identity doctrine of the separate creation of races, according to which Adam was the progenitor only of the white race, flies in the face of generations of mainstream Christian teaching.

In addition to doctrinal issues, however, there are also significant political issues that separate Identity from politically active conservative Protestants. The latter as a general rule are strong supporters of the State of Israel, sometimes in the belief that that serves American strategic interests but often because they believe that a strong, indeed expanding, Israel is essential for the fulfillment of biblical prophecy. For many Christian Zionists, wedded to John Nelson Darby's concept of "rightly dividing" the words of scripture, Christ's return is impossible before prophecies concerning the Jews are fulfilled, and these, in turn, require a Jewish state whose boundaries approximate those of the Davidic kingdom.

For Identity, these beliefs are tantamount to racial and religious treason. They therefore regard most evangelicals, and the new Christian right in particular, as having "sold out" to Jewish interests. Since Identity believers consider Christians of northwestern European descent to be the true Israelites, for them Jews are "counterfeit" Israelites, whether in the United States or in the State of Israel, and their allies among Christians are said to be doing the devil's work. Hence dialogue is impossible.

Even if some channels for dialogue were opened, Identity leaders have been ill equipped to engage in it, since few have had much formal theological training. One need only look at the backgrounds of the three founders of Christian Identity: Bertrand Comparet was a lawyer; William Potter Gale was a career military officer; and Wesley Swift, the only one with any formal religious training, may have gone to a small Bible college. The same spotty education is true in the second

---

Study Aid #213

Christian Identity Websites

America's Promise Ministries
God's Order Affirmed in Love (GOAL)
Gospel Broadcasting Association

Kingdom Identity Ministries
Orange Street Congregational Church
Posse Comitatus

generation: Swift's successor, Richard Girnt Butler, was an engineer. The most theologically sophisticated Identity thinker, Dan Gayman, began as a schismatic Mormon. Pete Peters, originally a rancher, also attended a small Bible college. Many Identity figures have been autodidacts, in part because there has never been an Identity seminary.

Identity Believers in Institutional Settings

The most sustained and structured relationships between Identity believers and mainstream Protestant clergy have taken place in prisons. Under conditions of incarceration, Protestant chaplains have had to deal with the religious needs and requests of those who have self-identified as Christian Identity. Their situation has been made considerably more complex by the fluid state of First Amendment free exercise law in recent years, an outgrowth of the so-called peyote case in 1990 (*Employment Division of Oregon v. Smith and Black*). The immediate effect of that decision was to increase the power of states to regulate behavior, even if an ancillary effect of the regulation was to burden religious practice. Congress in effect reversed the Supreme Court's action by passing the Religious Freedom Restoration Act (RFRA) in 1993, but the court declared the act unconstitutional as applied to the states in 1997. Finally, in 2000, Congress passed the Religious Land Use and Institutionalized Persons Act (RLUIPA) to prevent any government from substantially burdening religious exercise related to either land use or persons in institutionalized settings. This legislation passed constitutional muster in 2005 in a case with a number of prisoner plaintiffs, including at least one Identity believer (*Cutter et al. v. Wilkinson*).

The results have been threefold: First, there has been a period of considerable uncertainty concerning the reach of the free-exercise clause since 1990, raising questions for prison chaplains dealing with religions unfamiliar to them, and in fact Protestant chaplains have generally known little about Christian Identity. Second, during the period between the passage of RFRA and the decision to declare it unconstitutional with respect to the states in 1997, there was significant litigation begun by prisoners in state institutions to increase the scope of religious practices available to them. Finally, RFRA remains valid for inmates in federal prisons, and protections have now been extended to state prisoners through RLUIPA. Consequently, at both federal and state facilities, Protestant chaplains must deal with the accommodation of Identity prisoners.

The dilemma faced by chaplains has been exacerbated by several factors: First, as already noted, few mainstream Protestants know very much about Christian Identity. Yet they have had to mediate issues dealing with Identity literature, religious articles, and rituals. Second, the fragmented character of Identity means that the faith has no central organization capable of ministering to the needs of incarcerated believers, so that those needs must by default be dealt with by clergy of mainstream denominations. While some Identity groups do maintain what they term prison ministries, those are often more for purposes of recruitment than for dealing with daily religious needs. Finally, many prisons are racially polarized, with inmates divided between white and black gangs. The racist views espoused by Christian Identity consequently may increase levels of potential violence in such closed and volatile institutional settings. The rights granted by RLUIPA may, by the language of the statute, be suspended if the good order of the prison requires it. Consequently, clergy dealing with Identity religious requests—for example, requests for Identity literature—are often torn between what believers claim they are entitled to and require for religious reasons, and restrictions that prison administrations believe are necessary to prevent outbreaks of violence.

Further Reading

Henry Ford. *The International Jew*. Qontro Classics, 2009.

Andrew Macdonald. *The Turner Diaries: A Novel*. Barricade, 1996.

Chester Quarles. *The Ku Klux Klan and Related American Racialist and Antisemitic Organizations*. McFarland, 2008.

Binjamin Segal and Richard Levy. *A Lie and a Libel*. University of Nebraska Press, 1996.

114

Marxism: History, Beliefs, Practices

James Thobaben

Marxism is an economic philosophy—with a wide variety of social, economic, political, and philosophical expressions—based on the works of Karl Marx and his associates, especially Friedrich Engels. The central claim is that history, through dialectical tensions expressed in economic class conflict, is moving toward an ideal completion, best understood as anarchic utility. In true communism all persons choose what to do with their lives, which, in turn, results in cooperative and completely functional social conditions.

Marxism is, at its core, an epigenic social developmental theory; historical change moves in a predictable direction, though manifest in varying class-based behaviors conditioned by the particularities of the actual socioeconomic environment. Classes and societies (and perhaps the particular rules that finally govern them) arise out of conflicts that develop as material (technological and organizational) forces generate incompatibilities within existing productive relations (class-based social roles).

Marxist theorists, as with many using developmental theories, are not always clear as to whether causation pushes change toward an inevitable end given human conditions, or the telos is actually drawing the dialectical process toward itself. Regardless, until the telos of communism is reached, class conflict will continue, moving through dialectical stages that resolve in a synthesis generated by class assertion and material advancement, followed by the generation of new classes (or newly assertive classes), in turn followed by more conflict until finally the threshold is crossed for a classless society. The basic stages of development are as follows:

Primitive communalism: hunter-gatherer culture with no classes

Slave society: two classes, owner and slave

Feudalism: aristocracy and serfs in rigid class structure, with some new classes emerging with the rise of the nation-state

Capitalism: rising capitalist class owns production and, while not owning individuals, does own their labor through wage-purchase of the labor of the working class (proletariat), which developed out of peasantry with the rise of industrialization; the workers are, thus, "alienated" from their own labor and its produce (in this stage, money is the encapsulation of social power and is held disproportionately by the capitalists and the bourgeois through appropriation of worker labor)

Socialism (first-phase communism): workers become conscious of their class and obtain control of the means of production, generally through revolution

True communism: classless society directed by communalistic anarchist cooperation

The Four Roots of Marxist Thought

The philosophy of Marx and Engels derives from four streams of thought. This is not to deny important personal factors, such as Marx's familial heritage, Engels's operation of family mills in England, and the experiences both had in actual efforts to effect social change. Still, their ideas, while original in many ways, are also the product of various antecedent intellectual movements, primarily

German idealist philosophy (especially Hegel and the Young Hegelians)

Scottish economic philosophy (primarily Adam Smith and David Ricardo)

Christianity (especially the concept of linear time, with a telos of the "kingdom of God," and Christian communalist examples)

French socialist philosophy and political activism

German Idealist Philosophy

Marx and Engels, his ofttime collaborator, were part of a movement called the Young Hegelians in the 1840s. After the death of Hegel in 1831, various intellectual disciples sought to lay claim to his legacy, usually by placing an emphasis on one or the other theme in his writings. The more sociopolitically conservative were also more conservative with the Hegelian corpus, asserting that *The Phenomenology of Spirit* and what eventually became the Bismarckian welfare state marked a conclusion to a society's dialectical tension. The so-called Young Hegelians, more to the left, did not agree, choosing instead to use master-slave language in attacking the accepted cultural claims of Germany and, in particular, its Christianity. While initially sympathetic with the Young Hegelians, Marx and Engels finally distanced themselves, concluding that the problem with society was not spiritual, neither as particular expressions of a specific religion nor in the broad Hegelian sense. Further, to even claim such was a reflection of the deeper error. Critiquing the Young Hegelian movement in *The German Ideology* (1845–46), they declared that what drove the historical dialectic was economic, specifically conflict between oppressing and oppressed classes associated with material development (technological and organizational). The spiritual generally, and the religious specifically, is just an opiate to dull the pain of oppression and alienation. When in the form of organized religion, this opiate can be and often is used manipulatively by economic power holders.

Scottish Economic Philosophy

Economic theory was blossoming with the rise of capitalism in the late eighteenth century. Adam Smith's understanding of the "invisible hand" (cooperative outcome generated through individual choice) was not functioning under capitalism, according to Marx (though the invisible hand is not entirely unlike what he envisioned would operate when the classless society emerged). Rather, the mercantile-like appropriation of the capital-owning classes alienated workers from their own products. According to Marx's labor theory of value, a theory based to a greater or lesser extent on Adam Smith's and David Ricardo's work, the value of any object is vested through the power of labor needed to alter resources and produce the product. Marginal theories, to the contrary, are developed on the idea of scarcity—that is, that a product must be useful and that its value is primarily determined by its rarity to those demanding to use it. Smith, when describing his labor theory, states that "the real price of every thing, what every thing really costs to the man who wants to acquire it, is the toil and trouble of acquiring it" (2003, 1:5). And likewise, its ongoing value to its holder depends on the labor required to replace it. According to Marx, this labor value is, essentially, stolen by the owners of machinery who can increase their own profit by selling below the actual cost, while depriving the workers of their just deserts. The work of workers, to the capitalists, is a virtually unlimited commodity, like an unregulated commons, from which they take the resources of labor without accountability.

Study Aid #214

Marxist Stages of Development

Primitive communalism / Slave society / Feudalism / Capitalism / Socialism / True communism

Christianity

The Christian influences on Marxism come primarily through the unintended adoption of cultural understandings (especially linear time and the idea of a sociopolitical telos) and examples of socialism drawn from Christian experimental communities. The Marxist understanding of time, which is filtered through Hegelian dialectical philosophy, assumes a definite beginning and definite end. The idea of linear time was a cultural assumption in nineteenth-century Europe, deeply rooted in the monotheistic tradition of Christendom. The final end of time, for Marxism, is the achievement of the delayable, but still inevitable, "telos" (a sort of godless kingdom of God, an anarchy of irrepressible cooperation). As far back as the prophets (a favorite source for those Marxists who were more tolerant of religion), the individual is told that the day is coming when each person shall recline under his or her own fig tree, free from oppressors. In the New Testament, the Gospels and Revelation include references to rulers being cast aside and yokes of domination thrown off. Early Marxism, probably unintentionally, drew on these images of the eschaton. It even adopted one of the dominant interpretive structures when implying (and sometimes claiming outright) that the final communist stage harkened back to primitive communism, but now improved through the struggle, thus echoing the Christian claim about the eschatological reemergence of the prelapsarian paradise, though finally improved by Christ's sacrificial grace.

To some Marxists, Christian efforts at utopias foreshadowed this ideal, though Christianity at the "capital" stage of history was deemed an impediment. The positive examples for Marxists included their near contemporaries the Shakers and Icarians (heterodox communalists) and violent reformers of the sixteenth century such as Thomas Müntzer and the radical Anabaptists of Münster, as well as the then three-century-old Hutterite Brethren (orthodox communalists). Generally, these are viewed by Marxists as rightly intended, but confused, efforts that should have included the rejection of spiritual transcendence; indeed, Marx mocked efforts to develop a society-wide Christian socialism. Negatively, religious examples finally demonstrated that religion is "an opiate for the masses" that dulls the pain of their suffering and thereby impedes the process of revolution, or even that religion is itself the intentional instrument of the oppressing classes.

French Socialism and Activism

Marx and Engels were deeply influenced by French socialism. One of the predecessor organizations to the Communist League and First Internationale, the League of the Just, was based in part on utopian socialist values espoused by French Revolutionary Gracchus Babeuf. Henri de Saint-Simon argued for the elimination of the aristocracy and the ruling of society by skilled technocrats according to a completely revised understanding of Christianity that eliminated all orthodox dogma; his "scientific socialism" assumed societal evolutionary epochs, a concept

> **Study Aid #215**
>
> **The Four Roots of Marxist Thought**
>
> German idealist philosophy (especially Hegel and the Young Hegelians)
> Scottish economic philosophy (primarily Adam Smith and David Ricardo)
> Christianity (especially the concept of linear time, with a telos of the "kingdom of God," and Christian communalist examples)
> French socialist philosophy and political activism

accepted with modification into Marxist thought (though without mystical undertones). Charles Fourier's experiments in meritocratic communalism, while certainly not always favorably described by early Marxists, nonetheless showed that socialism could be implemented. In addition, Fourier's (and, perhaps, English socialist R. Owen's) dismissal of traditional family and favoring of the social rearing of children was generally adopted into Marxist theory. In the mid-nineteenth century, Étienne Cabet, a strong leveler (anticlerical) and primitivist Christian, led the Icarians in their utopian efforts, which Marx found a compelling example. August Blanqui, a significant philosophical hero of the nineteenth-century French secular socialists, apparently brought into common usage the term "dictatorship of the proletariat," which fit well the concepts of Marx and Engels. Sometimes Marx and Engels supported the theories being espoused by these various thinkers, and sometimes they sought to purge them as false alternatives to true socialist thinking; either way, the French socialists were very influential on their thought. The acme of Marx and Engels's engagement with French socialist thought was their active support of the 1871 Paris Commune.

Influences of Marxism

As a philosophy, Marxism was not dramatically influential in the nineteenth century, though not through lack of effort on Marx's or Engels's part. Indeed, their political activism served to elevate their philosophy among later revolutionaries. Marx was deemed a moral exemplar, as was Engels to a lesser extent. Particularly important was their activity in Germany in 1848 and their support of the French socialists in the 1870s.

In the twentieth century, Marxism gained in its position among radicals, displacing competing versions of socialism and anarchism. Advocates disdained labor organizations that would compromise with capitalists. In Russia, and contrary to the development pattern described by Marx, the Marxist-Leninists took over an agrarian society. Similarly, versions of Marxism (sometimes Stalinist and sometimes Maoist, often with strong nationalism) came to dominance in areas of Latin American, Africa, China, and Southeast Asia. Throughout the first half of the twentieth century, versions of Marxism competed with social contract democracy. Now, in the Global South, some Marxist governments remain in power, though most have made significant compromises for the sake of participation in world markets. Marxism is gladly dismissed by some in the former Soviet Bloc and for others elicits nostalgia. In the West, Marxism is less an activist cry and more an academician's philosophical tool. The argument that class and economics significantly shape social order remains intact, but not the assertion that such is exclusively so nor that a communist telos will be achieved. Instead, Marxist economic theory functions primarily as a check on the more dominant capitalist, mixed-economy, nationalist, and social contract political theories prevalent today.

Further Reading

Karl Marx. *The Communist Manifesto*. Penguin Classics, 2002.
Karl Marx and Friedrich Engels. *The Marx-Engels Reader*. Norton, 1978.
David McLellan. *Karl Marx: A Biography*. Palgrave-Macmillan, 2006.
Peter Singer. *Marx: A Very Short Introduction*. Oxford University Press, 2001.
Adam Smith. *The Wealth of Nations*. Bantam Classics, 2003.

115

Marxism: Theological Exchanges, Current Issues

JAMES THOBABEN

Marxist political philosophy is based on at least two central assumptions: (1) human reality is materially defined, and (2) through dialectical tension and resolution, human society develops toward true communism (either directed by the nature of society's structure or drawn by its telos, an issue of open debate among Marxists). As a competing eschatological worldview, Marxism comes into direct competition with Christianity. As a contrary philosophy, based on the materiality of humans, it is completely opposed to Christianity. Yet the economic analysis of Marxism and the compassionate behavior endorsed by Christianity have sometimes been appealing to those situated in opposite camps.

Christian communalist efforts long predate Marxism, beginning with the Jerusalem community described in Acts. Through the first and well into the second Christian millenniums, monastic communities flourished, almost always including a vow of poverty coupled with an obligation of all to work as able and to receive according to need—the latter being a concept adopted from Acts 2 (similar language was later used by nineteenth-century French socialists and then, in time, picked up by Marx). The monastic communities were generally incorporated into the broader organization of the church in both the East and the West. This was not the case with the communalistic expressions arising out of the Reformation, which almost always asserted the spiritual, ecclesial, and sometimes political superiority of their communities, with some of these manifesting as violent and strongly apocalyptic theocracies, and others as strong pacifistic, separatist gathered bodies. The Münster polygamist communalists (1534–35) exemplify the former (and were often favorably cited by later twentieth-century Marxists); the Hutterian Brethren (Jakob Hutter martyred in 1536), who remain vibrant, exemplify the latter.

In the eighteenth and nineteenth centuries, with the rise of religious freedom and before the publication of *The Communist Manifesto* in 1848, Protestant communalist experiments proliferated. Some of these were temporary for given religious groups, in times of expediency; others were fundamental to community structure. Some US and European examples include the strict pietistic Woman in the Wilderness community and Ephrata; the heterodox Shakers, Mormons, and Perfectionists (Oneida); and the orthodox Harmonists, Zoarites, and the Community of True Inspiration (Amana). All were communalist for a significant period, largely separatist, and in some cases modified family structure. These served as examples of practical communism to Marx and Engels and the broader secular socialist movement, even while they were deemed misguided, too separatist, and too weakly committed to societal change. The socialists, though, did find allies for social change among some in the nineteenth-century evangelical movement in the United States and sometimes in more traditional churches in Europe. In Britain, this included the Chartists and those associated with F. D. Maurice, who wanted subtle but continual change in the government, and later C. Kingsley. The intersection of the intellectual Christian socialists and utopian communalism was most clearly evidenced by the effort of T. Hardy in establishing Rugby in Tennessee. Even so, all these were considered too reformist (even if sometimes violent) rather than revolutionary by Marx and Engels, who far preferred the 1871 Paris Commune as a model to any Christian example.

Initially, Marxism grew out of an overtly anti-Christian, or at least antichurch, philosophical school generally called the Young Hegelians. These were primarily leftist disciples of Hegel, who favored an interpretation of his work that deemed the problems of Europe, and especially Germany, as "spiritual." Though soon rejecting this movement, Marx and Engels clearly agreed with their disdain for any established religious order, that is, state-sponsored Christianity. Contrary to most of the Young Hegelians, Marx and Engels considered religion not so much a false spirituality as a narcotic to dull the pain of oppression. While religious structures were used to oppress the working class, especially through landholding and identification with the upper classes in Europe and with the bourgeois in the United States, the primary problem with Christianity was the enabling toleration of class-based suffering as oppressed persons looked forward to a nonexistent

---

Study Aid #216

Marxism and Christianity

Differences	Similarities
Materialism	Economic analysis
Eschatology	Compassionate behavior/communalism

future and, thereby, lost the will and opportunity to fight against their alienation now. Even the best efforts by the religious are placations. "Christian Socialism is but the holy water with which the priest consecrates the heart-burnings of the aristocrat" (*Communist Manifesto*, 1848, chapter 3).

At the end of the nineteenth and beginning of the twentieth century, given urbanization and immigration, as well as the end of slavery, Christian social justice focused primarily on women's rights and alcohol prohibition, and secondarily on urban poverty and labor concerns. Edward Bellamy published *Looking Backward* (1888), in which he describes a Christian socialist utopia; the work was quite popular with other radicals of the day, including Marxists. His cousin, Francis Bellamy, was a Baptist preacher and socialist who wrote the Pledge of Allegiance. In Britain, Christian socialism became identified with a formal political party. In Germany, while radical efforts (including Marxist) continued, immediate felt-urgency diminished with the rise of the Bismarckian welfare state. The Bellamys, in turn, influenced Walter Rauschenbusch, Harry Ward, and the urban-defined, social justice–oriented interpretation of the ministry of Jesus called "the Social Gospel" (in the specific sense of the term) of the early twentieth century. They were also influenced by the Fabians, a strongly leftist British intellectual group ultimately shaping the nascent Labour Party, but deemed woefully inadequate by Marxist Trotsky as being too much like Owenites and "church socialists."

By the beginning of the twentieth century, Marxism had found a place among competing radical movements, which, in turn, had found a place among organizing workers, especially immigrants and those without craft skills. In the United States this was evidenced in the Industrial Workers of the World (IWW or Wobblies), the most radical of the large unions, which had a Catholic priest, Thomas Haggerty, as a cofounder. Relatively early, most of the leadership of the IWW disavowed religion. In the burgeoning urban areas the pro-Marxist organizers found themselves in direct competition with Protestant evangelistic efforts, most notably the Salvation Army. While sometimes using violence and intimidation to silence the Salvationists, more often the IWW used mockery and satire, typified by Joe Hill's popular song "The Preacher and the Slave" (popularly know as "Pie in the Sky"). Using the melody of "In the Sweet Bye and Bye," the Wobblies declared the Salvationists to be "the starvation army," promising hungry workers they would "eat, bye and bye . . . you'll get pie in the sky when you die." The competing understandings of the role of religion in the radical labor movement, Christianity in particular, are described in Upton Sinclair's *The Jungle*, which includes characters who are atheistic, generally Marxist, socialists, and those who are Christian socialists. J. Stitt Wilson, Methodist minister, eventual mayor of Berkeley, California, and publisher of *The Christian Socialist* (1907), may have been a prototype for Sinclair's character Mr. Lucas.

The strongest political moment for socialism in the United States came with the presidential efforts of Eugene Debs, both before and after World War I. Debs used strongly Christian imagery, though he doubted the sincerity and the usefulness of organized Christianity in the drive for social justice, thus displacing the Christian rural populism of W. J. Bryan on the left end of the American political spectrum. In the 1920s Christian socialists attempted to develop their own formal international movement, which eventually became the International League of Religious Socialists, generally favoring some degree of Marxist analysis, but not revolutionary pragmatics. The best-known spokesman was Norman Thomas, a minister strongly influenced by the Social Gospel and the efforts of Debs, who was affiliated with the Fellowship of Reconciliation. Thomas left the doctrinally orthodox church and eventually became (six times) candidate for president of the Socialist Party of America. He claimed not to be a Marxist in the full sense and requested a Christian funeral, though he remained leader of a movement that did and does claim a Marxist philosophical foundation. By the time of Thomas's last run for the presidency, in 1948, the Christian-socialist component of radical leftist politics in the United States was clearly in decline, and the movement virtually died out by the 1950s, due to the end of the New Deal, the Red Scare McCarthy hearings, dismay at the revelations about Stalinist Marxism, and disdain among strict Marxists for any religiosity. Among some black leaders—such as African American organizer A. Philip Randolph, although, as with most mid-twentieth-century civil rights leaders, he disavowed any affiliation with Marxism—a mixture of Christianity and socialism suited well their concerns about racism.

Among early feminists, various versions of socialism were popular. For instance, Frances Willard, long-serving president of the Woman's Christian Temperance Union (WCTU), labeled herself a gospel socialist, proclaiming that "in every Christian there exists a socialist, and in every socialist a Christian" (1893). Similarly, Ida Wells, the antilynching advocate, seems to have identified with socialism, though not Marxism. From a distinctly Catholic perspective, similar arguments were later adopted by Dorothy Day, who advocated for communalism (or at least strict simplicity and strong charitable giving) among believers and a sort of anarcho-syndicalism, developed from her faith and earlier affiliation with the Marxists and anarchists of the IWW and her reading of Tolstoy. The case can be made that the social efforts of the WCTU and the leadership in the Salvation Army were a stronger voice for women's rights than the Marxists, especially in the latter nineteenth and twentieth century.

The claim of incompatibility between Christianity and socialism was raised by the most orthodox Marxists. It was also raised by some important religious figures. In 1878, Pope Leo XIII denied the compatibility of "the main tenet" of socialism and Catholicism, which was reiterated in 1891 and by Pope Pius XI in 1931 on the grounds that the consequence of socialism was social disorder. Even so, *Rerum Novarum* (1891), by Pope Leo XIII, while again challenging Christian identification with true socialist movements, did call for engagement in efforts to achieve social justice. This would be magnified with the 1963 publication of *Pacem in Terris* by Pope John XXIII.

> **Study Aid #217**
> **Marxist Concepts**
> Dialectical materialism
> Economic determinism
> Historical materialism
> Marxian socialism
> Overdetermination
>
> Scientific socialism
> Technological determinism
> Class: proletariat-bourgeoisie
> Worker alienation

A vehement opposition to socialism, communism, and Marxism was loudly declared on the radio beginning in the period between the two world wars. Some of the best and most vocal examples were radio preachers, who used the new technology overwhelmingly more effectively than any Christian leftists. Among those in the evangelical movement (broadly defined), the most notable figure was Pentecostal preacher Aimee Semple McPherson. She defined Marxism broadly, using the label against Upton Sinclair when he ran against Frank Merriam (1928) for governor of California, perhaps helping to defeat the author who had two decades earlier described the politically leftist Christian preacher. The lead anti-communist Catholic voice was that of Father Charles Coughlin, who, as did McPherson, used the developing technology of radio to broadcast a strongly anti-Marxist message. Coughlin, though, cannot be readily describe as "left" or "right" in a simplistic manner since his broadcasting career arose to counter the Ku Klux Klan and in strong support for Roosevelt as a friend of the working class, even while eventually that career was marked by anti-Semitism and at least tentative support for forms of European fascism as the best antidote for the threat of European Marxism. Senator Joseph McCarthy, a Catholic, seems to have been sympathetic with some of the anti-Marxist arguments, though not the tendency toward nationalist socialism. Radio-preacher and evangelist opposition to Marxist communism continued well into the 1950s, as typified by Carl McIntyre, Billy James Hargis, and the young Billy Graham.

During the early 1960s a Christian-Marxist dialogue developed, especially driven by the policies of Pope John XXIII and various declarations by the World Council of Churches. Central concerns were a divided Europe, the threat of nuclear annihilation, and the proxy wars being fought in Africa, Southeast Asia, and Latin America. Key figures were drawn from Protestant churches (e.g., Lehman, West, Ogletree, Moltmann, Ricoeur), the Roman Catholic Church (e.g., Girardi, Metz, Rahner, Sölle), and Western and Soviet Bloc Marxists (e.g., Machovec, Bloch, Schaff). Though the arms race was in full swing and proxy wars were being fought across the globe, Cold War lines were being challenged inside the West and the Soviet Bloc. An informal dialogue in Europe and in the United States began among academics, especially opening up after the Prague Spring and student uprisings of 1968. Later versions sporadically appeared, such as Daniel Berrigan and Howard

Zinn traveling to Hanoi, marking a transition toward a radicalized hybridization in the West and South. In the Soviet Bloc, a clampdown limited participants. Liberation theology displaced dialogue in favor of an authoritative pedagogy (e.g., Gutiérrez, Boff, Sobrino) reportedly arising from oppressed peoples, especially in Latin America and to some extent sub-Saharan Africa. Paradoxically, at the same time, house churches were developing in the People's Republic of China in response to the perceived failures of Maoism as a worldview and Marxist materialism (though not necessarily in opposition to the government on nonreligious matters). The value of the Marxist-Christian dialogues and, later, liberation theology were questioned in the West by Paul Ramsey, followers of Reinhold Niebuhr, and eventually Pope John Paul II on the grounds that the general assumption that humans were intrinsically good or morally neutral could not be accepted by Christians. The political implications of this religious challenge to Marxism turned out to be sociopolitically significant when coupled with the diplomatic positions of Ronald Reagan, Margaret Thatcher, and Mikhail Gorbachev and, importantly, the political and religious advocacy of Lech Walesa.

Marxism remains a significant analytical tool for some Christian scholars, notably Terry Eagleton. Versions of Marxist class critique are used, albeit in very mediated versions, by some who self-identify as the religious Left. In the Global South, liberationist versions are evident (e.g., Nicaragua, Venezuela).

Further Reading

Paul D'Amato. *The Meaning of Marxism.* Haymarket, 2006.
Terry Eagleton. *Why Marx Was Right.* Yale University Press, 2012.
Denis Janz. *World Christianity and Marxism.* Oxford University Press, 1998.
Alasdair MacIntyre. *Marxism and Christianity.* Duckworth, 1995.
David McClellan. *Marxism and Religion.* HarperCollins, 1987.

116

Marxism: Adherent Essay

ROGER S. GOTTLIEB

"Don't tell them you're a Marxist," my wife frequently cautions me. "It's like saying you're a dinosaur." On the other hand, there is Jean-Paul Sartre's famous claim that Marxism will be relevant as long as capitalism exists. And finally, there is my self-description: when I was on a panel at a New Age spiritual center and asked what kind of Marxist I was, I told them I was a "nice Marxist."

But, a religion? Of course historians, usually antagonistic, have often compared dogmatic attachment to Marx's analytical categories and predictions to that with which people of faith cling to their ideas. More precisely, there is the way in which Marx's image of a perfected social state—communism—resembles the visions of a messianic age offered by Judaism and Christianity. And there is also the conceptual structure of Marxism, which offers a kind of totalizing theory to understand human history, contemporary social relationships (particular the way different dimensions of social life relate to each other), what the future holds, and what is ethically required of us.

Yet the dogmatic version of Marxism was never mine, nor could it have ever been. For one thing, I came of age knowing what self-described "Marxists" (or "Marxist-Leninists") had done in the Soviet Union and throughout the world. For another, my initial exposure to Marxist ideas came not through *Capital*'s (1867) attempt to find the "laws of motion of society" but through the more philosophical, morally oriented ideas of the 1844 *Manuscripts*. And finally, during the same period of my life in which I was embracing a particular form of Marxism, I had already had considerable experience of hallucinogenic states of non-normal consciousness and was engaged in fairly rigorous spiritual practices of meditation and yoga.

So theoretically it has always been necessary for me to see Marxism through the lens of its failures as well as its successes, as a tradition that is constituted greatly by frequent reinterpretations, reassessments, and innovations, and at best a partial truth, inadequate to its own totalizing pretensions.

All that said, for nearly forty years it has been one of the pillars of my intellectual, political, and moral personality. I still believe that Marxism's account of class structure, the social and historical primacy of the power vested in the control of the forces of production, descriptions of the dynamic of capitalist development, and model of an ideal society in which technological forces are used rationally for the common good remains central to any coherent account of social life. So also is Marx's original idea of ideology (later much more highly developed in the writings of Western Marxists and Marxist feminists): that what we believe, and indeed even our personality structures, are shaped by historical forces out of our personal control, forces that benefit powerful social groups.

The fact that Marxism does what it does through a kind of analytic rigor does not exclude it from the realm of religion. Buddhism, after all, offers a highly rigorous account of human psychology; and Jewish writings from the Talmud to the more recent Musar movement contain quite intellectualized versions of the understanding of personal change. Similarly, awareness of errors, the need for reform, and innovation make Marxism quite similar to religious traditions. What was the Reformation, after all, but an innovation (albeit one claiming to go back to some original truth)? Or the development of Mahayana Buddhism or Reform Judaism? Such religious developments claim a fundamental misunderstanding of an original teaching, and/or a need to change in the light of new historical realities (as in, for example, Vatican II).

But if there is a central ground on which Marxism and religion can meet, it is ultimately that of faith. For Marxists must believe that something profoundly better than the present social order is possible, that people can learn from their errors, that it is not impossible for human beings, confronted with Trotsky's fateful alternative of "socialism or barbarism," to choose the former. The negation of this Marxist faith is the social future depressingly envisioned by Jürgen Habermas, where we are divided into the "social engineers and the inmates of closed institutions," a social future in which no learning is possible, because a combination of violent repression and in some ways more lethal "colonization" of our cultural and moral consciousness prevents us from learning, changing, or organizing into a collective revolutionary force.

Just as any religious person must look at the overwhelming dimensions of unjust suffering in human history and make a commitment to faith in God or spiritual truth despite that reality, so the Marxist must look at all the failures of working-class politics—from the Second and Third Internationals to the frequent self-interested moral bankruptcy of trade unions—and retain a sense of possibility. The Italian Marxist Antonio Gramsci captured this Marxist faith eloquently when he called for a "pessimism of the intellect and an optimism of the will," knowing, I suspect, that an optimistic will required an intellect slanted toward a kind of ultimately unjustified social hope. Along with the clear moral imperative to serve the interests of the working class, conceived as the vast majority of non-owners of forces of production, it is this social hope that constitutes the religious element of Marxism.

For most of its history, of course, Marxism has been the declared enemy of Christianity. What was religion to Marx but a drug-like attempt to use illusions to sooth socially caused pain? What were Marxists to the Christian establishment but hooligans who denied the sanctity of the church, laughed at its central metaphysical claims, and condemned it as the witting or unwitting servant of the rich and powerful? It is hardly surprising that the two were, when possible, at each other's throats. The Christian establishment, to its shame, often supported fascism simply because it was not communism. When communists took power, they often subjected Christianity (and other religions) to brutal repression.

Yet there is a good deal more to the story, for, in alliances that doubtless would have shocked both Marx and any nineteenth-century pope, we can find many examples of what might loosely be termed "Christian socialists." These include Latin America's liberation theologians, Americans such as Dorothy Day, and—in the form of the Christian Socialism movement—dozens of members of Britain's parliament. And even in the early days of Marx's writings, there were attempts to combine socialist political activism with theological reflection.

Morally, it is not hard to see what Catholics have called the "preferential option for the poor" as morally kin to the Marxian socialist concern with the working class. A Christian orientation surrounds history with the presence and intentions of God; a Marxist view informs Christian attempts to "love thy neighbor" and care for "the least of these" with the understanding that no such love and care can have more than a palliative effect in a capitalist society. As long as economic and political life are dominated by a small, self-interested group, traditional Marxism teaches, we will have unnecessary poverty and aggressive wars. To this, twentieth-century Marxism adds that we will also have a destructive culture, imperialist expansionism, and a distorted culture of consumerism, passivity, and conformism. As well, while some will claim an "absolute truth" for their religious teachings, others will willingly acknowledge that their own traditions, as human interpretations of divine will, have made some terrible mistakes. As anyone who claims the term "Marxism" today must begin, I believe, with an account of how the crimes of Stalin or Mao came about, so any Christian must account for, among other things, centuries of anti-Semitism, misogyny, and genocide against native peoples. With a virtue that each claims but that has historically not been practiced very widely, both Christianity and Marxism share the obligation to develop a profound humility about their own moral record.

This common obligation is all the more interesting because both claim to be universalizing structures that tell individuals where and how they should fit into overall historical (Marxism) and cosmic (Christianity) realities.

As for my own "nice" Marxism? It grows out of my study of Marx's original writings, as well as that of dozens of theoreticians and political activists from the Frankfurt school (Horkheimer, Adorno, Marcuse) to socialist feminists (Sheila Rowbotham, Ann Ferguson) to Green Marxists (James O'Connor, Joel Kovel). It jettisons any sense of certainty of ultimate working-class victory, but tries (these days with some difficulty) to keep hope alive that such a victory—informed by feminism and environmentalism and ethnic/racial equality—is still possible. And it remains certain that any more conventionally religious understanding of reality will be morally thin to the point of emaciation if it does not take as its own what is still relevant and true in Marxism's understanding of history and society.

117

NRM:
Social Religions
Introduction

TERRY C. MUCK

Finally we will look at four new religious movements that have taken firm root in the social life of Western cultures: the Unification Church; Freemasonry; the Family International, formerly known as the Children of God; and Baha'i. In many ways one could not find more different new religious movements, one based on an Eastern metaphysic, two on Christian stories, one on Middle Eastern Islam. Yet in their appeal, they have all attempted to satisfy urges on the part of adherents that are not just religious but also social in their concern.

It is worth noting again that especially in this sector of the new religious movement marketplace, some of the movements we identify as having distinct religious elements do not themselves identify as religions. Freemasons strongly reject the

---

Study Aid #218

Social Religions

Unification Church: Sun Myung Moon is/was the apex of God's work in history in his mission to complete the work of Jesus.

Freemasonry: A fraternal order and a way of life that makes good men better.

Children of God: In many ways David Berg, the founder of The Family International, was a fundamentalist Christian interested in missions.

Baha'i: Originally an offshoot of Islam in Iran, Baha'i appeals to many of the universal social concerns for peace and justice in the world.

religion label that many outside the movement hang on it. Since one of our goals in this handbook has been to honor the movements we include by letting them self-identify, we would normally not include such groups. Freemasonry, however, has become such a cause célèbre among conservative Christians on precisely this point that we felt we had to include it—with the important recognition of this disclaimer on their part of not being a religion.

118

Unification Church: History, Beliefs, Practices

JAMES A. BEVERLEY

History

The Unification Church is one of the most famous and controversial new religious movements. It was founded in 1954 in Korea by Sun Myung Moon. Moon was born in 1920 in what is now North Korea and was influenced by traditional Protestantism, several native Korean movements, and larger Asian moral and spiritual values. The Unification Church proclaims that Moon is the apex of God's work in history in his mission to complete the work of Jesus.

According to Moon, he received a visitation by Jesus on April 17, 1935. Moon pursued a spiritual path as he studied in Seoul, South Korea (1938–41) and Japan (1941–43). He was married in November 1943. His first son was born in April 1946, and two months later Moon left for North Korea without wife or child. He did not return to his family for six years and was arrested twice during the interim. He was freed by UN forces on October 14, 1950.

Moon's marriage ended in 1953, and he launched his Holy Spirit Association for the Unification of World Christianity the next May. Missions to other countries began later in the decade. In 1960 Moon married a young disciple named Hak Ja Han, and their marriage forms one of the most important dates in Unification history. Moon and his wife visited the United States in 1965 and settled there in 1971.

The church first gained notoriety for its support of Richard Nixon and for its giant rallies at Madison Square Garden (September 18, 1974), Yankee Stadium (June 1, 1976), and the Washington Monument (September 18, 1976). Moon became one of the most visible targets of the growing anticult movement, particularly after

> **Study Aid #219**
> **Unification Church Beliefs**
> Authority: The Bible plus *Divine Principle*
> The fall: Adam and Eve transgress
> Christology: Jesus fails as restorer of family
> Soteriology: Restoration of the family through Sun Myung Moon
> Indemnity: Living lives as acts of contrition for sin

the Jonestown suicides in November 1978. Moon's followers became the objects of kidnapping and deprogramming.

Moon was charged with income tax evasion by the American government on October 15, 1981. He was found guilty and went to prison in Danbury, Connecticut, in the summer of 1984, six months after his son Heung Jin died in a car accident. Moon was released from a Brooklyn halfway house in the summer of 1985 and continued to lead the church in its various educational, cultural, and political programs. On the latter, he held strategic meetings with Mikhail Gorbachev on April 11, 1990, and with North Korean leader Kim Il Sung in November 1991. His followers view these meetings as symbolic of Moon's supremacy over communism.

In 1998 Nansook Hong, Moon's former daughter-in-law, published a devastating memoir, *In the Shadow of the Moons*. In it, Hong accused her ex-husband, Hyo Jin Moon, of adultery, drug addiction, and physical and emotional abuse. As well, she gave a startling report that Sun Myung Moon had an illegitimate child after his 1960 marriage. She claimed that Mrs. Moon told her this in the context of Nansook's complaints about her own husband.

In 2008 Moon transferred leadership of the international movement to his youngest son, Hyung Jin. He also appointed In Jin, a daughter, to head the American church. The oldest surviving son, Hyun Jin, had been on course for the top position but lost to his younger brother. The movement experienced a serious schism in 2010, when Hyun rebelled against his parents and gained control of some Unification enterprises. In June 2010 Sun Myung Moon issued a proclamation in support of the youngest son. Sun Myung Moon died on September 3, 2012, at the age of ninety-two.

Beliefs

Unification Church theology is largely framed by the Christian tradition, though Moon offers significant alterations to classical orthodoxy. Moon retains a Christian monotheism, but trinitarian formulations are lacking. Jesus is not viewed as coequal with the Father, as in the Nicene Creed. The Bible is not the sole source of authority but is supplemented with the main Unification text, *Divine Principle*, by Reverend Moon, as well as his sermons and edicts.

Moon interprets the fall of Adam and Eve as sexual transgression. According to him, Satan seduced Eve and then Eve engaged Adam sexually before the proper time. This brought ruination to the human family. Tragically, Jesus failed to find the Second Eve and Reverend Moon was chosen to be the third Adam. Moon is known as True Father, his wife as True Mother, and together they are True Parents. Their children are born without original sin, though like Adam and Eve they can choose a path of rebellion.

Unificationists are taught that Jesus was not sent to die at Calvary but that his death was a secondary option after Jesus failed to get married. Moon teaches that Jesus was the illegitimate child of Zechariah and Mary. This dynamic created conflict between Joseph and Mary but also between Jesus and his stepbrother John the Baptist. Moon teaches that John's missteps in his relationship to Jesus hurt the will of Jesus to carry out God's ideal plans. According to Moon, he was able to find a bride for Jesus (a woman named Chang Sung Chong) and performed a marriage ceremony for them. The church claims to have a letter to Reverend Moon from Jesus thanking him for his new wife.

Unification soteriology focuses on the restoration of the family. This forms the context for the large wedding ceremonies that have contributed to public awareness of Moon. Moon also has instructions for married members to perform several sex rites (in private) that reverse the effects of the fall. All members (married or otherwise) are grafted into Moon's family as Blessed Children. Since 1999 members are also encouraged to liberate their own ancestors through rituals and financial payments. Most often these rituals are under the guidance of Hyo Nam Kim at Cheongpyeong Heaven and Earth Training Center in South Korea.

Moon placed increasing emphasis on the role of the spirit realm in his own mission. He encouraged focus on heavenly revelations from Heung Jin after the latter's death in early 1984. He even gave his blessing in 1987 to a follower from Zimbabwe who claimed to channel Heung Jin's spirit. The ministry of this black Heung Jin ended in 1988 because of aberrant teaching and his physical assaults on other Unificationists, including Bo Hi Pak, a top aide to Reverend Moon.

Study Aid #220
The Blessing Ceremony

Marriage, the creation of a new family, is a central ritual for the Unification Church. The ceremony, presided over by Sun Myung Moon as long as he was alive, has five steps.

1. The Chastening: Repentance and forgiveness
2. Holy Wine: Bestowal of grace
3. Holy Blessing: The wedding ceremony
4. The Separation: Forty days of sexual abstinence
5. Consummation: A three-day ceremony of beginning

The spirit emphasis returned in 1995 with the work of Mrs. Hyo Nam Kim. She gives messages from Heung Jin and Soon-Ae Hong (1914–89), the mother of Hak Ja Han (wife of Sun Myung Moon). Mrs. Kim and Soon-Ae Hong are both given the honorific title Dae Mo Nim. Mrs. Kim has become a major figure in Unification life because of her role as medium and as the principal figure in ancestral liberation. Unificationists also follow messages from Dr. Sang Hun Lee, a Unification scholar who died in 1997. He has relayed input by and about figures like Buddha, Jesus, Muhammad, Marx, Stalin, Hitler, and deceased US presidents.

Practices

As in the larger Christian tradition, Unificationists gather for worship every Sunday. This is preceded by a Pledge Service at 5:00 a.m. in the individual families. Sundays schools are often held for children. Reverend Moon encouraged followers to have midweek and Friday evening meetings. As well, all members are to spend time every morning reading from Reverend Moon's sermons, a new tradition known as Hoon Dok Hae. There are also major church holy days for members worldwide. These include Parents' Day, Children's Day, Day of All Things, God's Day, Day of the Victory of Love, and True Parents' birthday.

Holy days are set by the lunar calendar. Members dress in holy robes or their finest clothing. They are instructed in proper bowing to True Parents or to their pictures. There are always offerings of food and some teaching instruction. The holy days and general worship services often end with dramatic shouts of victory. Members are also encouraged to have social time together after worship, especially on the holy days of the church cycle.

The Unification Church generally offers a conservative ethic. Reverend Moon placed great stress on sexual purity and opposed homosexuality. Moon was no advocate of feminist ideology, but women can sometimes have significant power. The church opposes abortion and cremation but has a moderate position on euthanasia. Given emphasis on the family, divorce is discouraged. Members are instructed to signify their separation from evil through the use of Holy Salt, created by Moon on his wedding day in 1960. Sprinkling of the salt in one's home or office creates a barrier against Satan.

There is no radical distinction between a clergy class and laity. The highest status is given to True Parents. The True Children are also idolized unless they have abandoned the family. Early pioneers are richly honored, but leadership positions depend on Moon's changing plans and orders. Given Moon's wide-ranging religious, social, and political vision, members find themselves working as missionaries, educators, dance instructors, reporters, business leaders, and so on. Members are also instructed to respect other faiths, and Moon implemented major programs to work with leaders of all traditions.

Further Reading

Eileen Barker. *The Making of a Moonie*. Blackwell, 1984.

James A. Beverley. "Spirit Revelation and the Unification Church." In *Controversial New Religions*, edited by James R. Lewis and Jesper Aagaard Petersen. Oxford University Press, 2005.

Robert E. Buswell Jr. *Religions of Korea in Practice*. Princeton University Press, 2007.

George Chryssides. *The Advent of Sun Myung Moon*. St. Martin's Press, 1991.

Nansook Hong. *In the Shadow of the Moons*. Beacon, 1998.

Michael Inglis, ed. *Forty Years in America*. Holy Spirit Association, 2000.

119

Unification Church: Theological Exchanges, Current Issues

JAMES A. BEVERLEY

The Unification Church was incorporated in 1954 as the Holy Spirit Association for the Unification of World Christianity. Its founder, Sun Myung Moon, traces the movement's earliest beginning to his encounter with Jesus on April 17, 1935, and the call for Moon to complete the mission of Jesus. After connections with several new Korean religions, Moon attracted his own followers in the mid-1940s, but membership remained small for a decade.

Traditional Korean Christians opposed the Unification Church from the beginning. Moon and his followers were accused of heresy, especially around alleged teaching that Moon was a messiah figure. Moon had been influenced by local theories that the second coming would occur in Korea. Conservative Christians also attacked him for charismatic excesses in worship. By all accounts Moon was a dynamic and powerful personality. This did not stop criticism.

In addition to ongoing doctrinal concerns, Moon was charged with unfaithfulness to his first wife, bigamy, and engaging in sex rituals with his female disciples. Here is the context for the allegations. Moon was married in 1943, but his wife (Choi Sun-Kil) left him in 1953. She was annoyed at his religious pursuits and enraged at the attention he gave female devotees. The failed marriage, a relationship with a Korean woman (Myung Hee Kim) that led to pregnancy, and a zealous group of female disciples presented a ripe environment for rumors.

In spite of persecution in Korea, Moon and his followers maintained their zeal. Missionaries were sent to various countries, most notably Japan and the United States. Both Miss Young Oon Kim (1914–89) and David Kim (1914–) arrived in Oregon in 1959. Colonel Bo Hi Pak began his mission work in 1961 while he

> **Study Aid #221**
> **Life of Sun Myung Moon**
> Born: February 25, 1920
> Died: September 3, 2012
> Spouses: Choi Sun-Kil (1943–53), Hak Ja Han (1960–2012)
> Children: 16
> Occupations: Religious leader, businessman
> Founder: Unification Church
> Notable book: *Divine Principle*
> Conviction: US tax evasion

served as military attaché at the Korean embassy in Washington. In the 1960s the American media and religious establishments paid little attention to the Unification Church. This changed dramatically in the next decade.

Moon and his family moved to the United States in 1971. Large national tours and giant rallies created media awareness. Unification support for the embattled Richard Nixon led to further notoriety. The Christian Student Coalition at UC Berkeley went public against Moon. Later, a group of "Concerned Christians" from the southern United States wrote an indictment under the title *The Satanic Beliefs of Rev. Moon*. A *Washington Post* article in 1974 quoted the general secretary of the Korean National Council of Churches calling the Unification Church "a cult . . . a new sect which has been undermining the established church." Three years later even the more liberal US National Council of Churches wrote a damning critique of the theology of *Divine Principle*, the main sacred text of the Unification Church.

There were some positive developments with evangelical Christians in the late 1970s and early 1980s. First, some evangelical leaders met twice in 1978 with Unification scholars and students at the Unification Seminary in Barrytown, New York. The dialogue was candid yet respectful. Participants acknowledged differences but also said stereotypes had been broken. Unificationists were also pleased when evangelical leaders (most notably Jerry Falwell) defended Reverend Moon's religious liberties and protested US government attacks on him.

Witness to Unificationists has been for the most part up to individual Christians in their private contacts. There are no mission groups targeting Unificationists, and no countercult groups specialize in the Unification Church. Generally, relations between Unificationists and evangelical Christians are framed by the opposing theological paradigms and the larger social and cultural attacks on the movement as a cult. On the latter, evangelical Christians should protect the religious liberties of Unificationists, particularly in Japan, where recently members have been subject to forcible confinement.

At the theological level various evangelicals wrote about Unification doctrine and life in the early days of controversy in America. Though aiming at a popular

> **Study Aid #222**
>
> **Current Unification Church Issues**
>
> Death of founder (Moon died September 3, 2012)
> Failed prophecies (e.g., January 13, 2013, Foundation Day)
> Leadership succession (Hyung Jin or Hyun Jin)
> Pressures of a works soteriology

market, both James Bjornstad (*The Moon Is Not the Son*) and Jerry Yamamoto (*The Puppet Master*) based their analysis on primary Unification material. In *Heavenly Deception* (1980) Chris Elkins wrote a memoir of his life in the movement and his return to Christian faith. Later, the Unification Church was analyzed by, among others, Walter Martin (*Kingdom of the Cults*), Ruth Tucker (*Another Gospel*), and by this writer in Ronald Enroth's edited volume *Evangelizing the Cults*.

Traditional Christians who joined Moon in the earliest days in Korea were attracted by his zeal and charisma and by his sacrifice. Likewise, in the 1970s the dedication of Unificationists made an impact on American college students. The national crusades and mass rallies were potent signals of a dedicated movement. Converts today join more because of the appeal of the basic Unification message about joining together all races and all religions. Here it helps that Moon had visible success in uniting religious leaders for various causes and matching couples from different races and nationalities. Moon was also adept at bringing high-profile academics, politicians, media figures, artists, and sports stars into his orbit.

Today four crucial issues influence Christian understanding of and witness to members of the Unification Church. First, Sun Myung Moon died on September 3, 2012. As with all new religious movements, the death of the founder creates a crisis of the highest order. How the Unification Church navigates the crisis is of crucial importance.

Second, before he died, Moon created an enormous prophetic dilemma for the movement. He predicted the emergence of heaven on earth and connected it to the date of January 13, 2013. Some critics have skewed the date to refer to mass suicide, but this is grossly unfair to Moon's optimistic social and political agendas. Nevertheless, the tenor of his instructions would lead any reasonable interpreter to imagine a radical transformation connected to that day. Moon has coined the phrase Cheon Il Guk in reference to the new apocalyptic. The day came and went without significant, observable changes.

Of course, earlier failed prophecies created no major dissonance in Moon or among followers. Moon maintained for years that a new heavenly kingdom would arise by 1981. His predictions were often and specific. He stated in one sermon: "The third seven-year course will be over in 1981. By then all negativity and opposition will be wiped out." It is rather ironic that the year 1981 brought an indictment from a grand jury against Moon for income tax evasion.

The prophetic failure related to 1981 got little attention within the movement, and Moon moved on to other goals. John Lofland documented an even earlier failed eschatology in his study (*Doomsday Cult*) of the first American disciples. Young Oon Kim, one of the first missionaries to America, taught repeatedly about 1967 as a major eschatological turning point. That did not materialize, and 1981 became the new milestone. Most recently it was 2013.

Third, Unification followers have been dramatically upset by the division in Moon's family over succession of leadership. Moon chose his youngest son (Hyung Jin) over his oldest (Hyun Jin) to head the international movement. Hyun chose to rebel against his father's choice, and this has led to internal chaos. In the spring of 2010 there were even physical altercations at a Unification worship service in Brazil. Hyun Jin verbally and physically attacked a local Unification leader who was in favor of the younger brother. The bitter disputes extend to senior leadership worldwide and have created havoc, emotionally, financially, legally, and spiritually.

The whole debacle has created a psychic opening for disciples to question the integrity of the Moon ideology itself. For the first time in Unification history, dissent and doubt have manifested themselves publicly in major ways. This is mainly courtesy of the internet and its blogs and social networking sites. Video of the Brazil assault was posted online, as were videos of later visits by Hyung Jin Moon (the international president) and his sister In Jin (head of the American Unification Church) to the Brazilian Unification community.

Lastly, Unificationists are under enormous burdens in terms of works salvation. On the one hand, salvation is explained as an act of grace through the unmerited mercy of Sun Myung Moon. For the most part, however, salvation is based on doing the works of Father Moon and obeying his every edict. As of 1999 this even demands payment to liberate one's ancestors on both sides of the family, going back every generation to Adam and Eve. Liberation at the price of coinage has caused some Unification thinkers to recall Luther's critique of indulgences in sixteenth-century Germany.

Further Reading

George Chryssides. *The Advent of Sun Myung Moon*. St. Martin's Press, 1991.

Nansook Hong. *In the Shadow of the Moons*. Beacon, 1998.

Michael Inglis, ed. *Forty Years in America*. Holy Spirit Association, 2000.

Massimo Introvigne. *The Unification Church*. Signature, 2000.

Richard Quebedeaux and Rodney Sawatsky, eds. *Evangelical-Unification Dialogue*. Rose of Sharon, 1979.

Herbert Richardson, ed. *Ten Theologians Respond to the Unification Church*. Rose of Sharon, 1982.

J. Isamu Yamamoto. *The Unification Church*. Zondervan, 1995.

120

Freemasonry: History, Beliefs, Practices

Steven Tsoukalas

History

Masonic historians and scholars are uncertain about the historical antecedents of Freemasonry (Masonry, Masonic Lodge, the Lodge, the Craft). The only general consensus reached is that Freemasonry formed officially when the Grand Lodge of London arose in 1717 at the Goose and Gridiron Ale House. There are several theories concerning the antecedent origins of Freemasonry. Most popular is that it formed from medieval stonemasons' professional guilds (operative masons), members of which desired moral teaching that corresponded to the tools (see below) of these professional stonecutters. Another popular theory finds the Knights Templar, a crusading order, forced underground by persecution stemming from Pope Clement V. The Knights were excommunicated in the fourteenth century and as a result of persecution invented secret recognition signs. Other theories propose origins at the time of Adam, the building of King Solomon's temple, and in institutional connections with the ancient mystery religions of Greece, Rome, and Egypt. Evidence for these theories is either nonexistent or quite sparse.

By 1730 scores of "lodges" (local assemblies of Masons formed under the auspices of a Grand Lodge) arose in England. From there, other countries (including the United States) saw formation of Grand Lodges. Shortly after its formation in London, ritualistic degrees were created, and subsequently other Masonic Grand Lodges worldwide (Blue Lodge, Symbolic Lodge) possessed at least the three basic, foundational degrees of Freemasonry.

With the passing of time other degrees were added, and two popular rites were formed in order to provide furtherance in Masonic education: the Scottish Rite (nothing to do, formation-wise, with Scotland) consisting of degrees 4–32 with an honorary 33rd degree, and the York Rite, consisting of degrees 4–13. Other allied groups later formed: Shriners, Eastern Star (for women), Rainbow (for girls), and De Molay (for boys). Until recently a man who completed foundational degrees and at least one rite could join the Shriners. Now a Mason can join the Shriners after completing only foundational Freemasonry.

It was not too long before disagreements arose, birthing non-"recognized" (by England) lodges. For example, in 1773 the Grand Lodge of England severed ties with the Grand Orient of France. French Freemasonry today is atheistic and therefore (among other reasons) not recognized as "regular" Freemasonry. Thus, the Grand Orient, along with scores of other nonregular Masonic groups, is considered clandestine.

United States Freemasonry (under English authority) started in Massachusetts (some say Pennsylvania) in the 1730s. Generally one can picture growth and expansion into other areas of the country during westward expansion.

Beliefs

Most Masonic Grand Lodges describe Freemasonry as a fraternal order and "a way of life" that "makes good men better." A man-affirming belief in the existence of God (it matters not what God this is) may petition a local lodge for membership, usually under the sponsorship or vouching of another Mason. No atheists can join. After time and further procedures, vote is taken by the local lodge. Upon unanimous decision, the candidate moves through the first three degrees of Freemasonry. The three basic degrees correspond to the working guilds of Freemasons, or stonecutters: Entered Apprentice, Fellow Craft (Journeyman), and Master. These contain both moral and religious teachings, in part by taking the working tools of operative masonry and investing them with moral and/or religious content.

An example of moral teaching is the symbolism of the square and compass (which, overlapping with the letter "G" in the center, is a Masonic symbol found on cars, rings, and lapel pins). Here the candidate learns to perform actions squarely (fairly) with all people, never straying morally beyond the circumference drawn by the (moral) compass.

Examples of religious teachings (which imply morality) include belief in God. Individually a man may believe in his personal deity, but corporately Freemasonry affirms the existence of "The Great/Grand Architect of the Universe." When prayers are offered during ritual to the Great Architect, in practice Masons see their personal deities represented by or coming under the canopy of the Great Architect, or they acknowledge the Great Architect as a name for their deities. The White Lambskin Apron reminds the candidate "of that purity of life and conduct so essentially necessary to gain admission into that Grand Lodge above, where the Supreme Architect of the Universe presides." The Common Gavel, though "used

> **Study Aid #223**
>
> **Freemasonry Beliefs**
>
> Freemasonry not a religion but a fraternity
> Members must affirm belief in God
> Three basic Masonic degrees
>   Entered Apprentice
>   Fellow Craft
>   Master Mason

by operative masons to break off the rough and superfluous parts of stones," is utilized by Freemasons "for the more noble and glorious purpose of divesting our hearts and consciences of all the vices and superfluities of life, thereby fitting our minds, as living stones, for that spiritual building, that house not made with hands, eternal in the heavens."

Practices

The ritual (largely in code in the United States and Canada) makes a man a Mason. Each of the degrees is ritualistic, with the local lodge guiding candidates through lessons like those mentioned above and teaching them secret handgrips and obligations. Important is the Masonic Obligation, wherein the candidate promises "in the presence of God" never to reveal the secrets of Freemasonry. Up until the mid-1980s many if not all lodges contained oaths and obligations with stated penalties such as having the tongue torn out, the heart plucked out, and the bowels severed if the candidate ever knowingly violated his obligations. Today many Grand Lodges have removed these penalties.

Prayer used to invoke the blessings of the Great Architect of the Universe is vitally important in Masonic ritual. With this practice one Mason prays to the Great Architect of the Universe on behalf of all Masons assembled. All bow reverently before the Great Architect of the Universe.

Teachings of Masonic symbolism occur throughout ritual. The institution expects that the candidate will "practice" Freemasonry, living the lessons of the degrees.

Perhaps no Masonic teaching has captured more attention than the Legend of Hiram Abif, the great legend of the third (Master Mason) degree. The Bible mentions Hiram in 1 Kings and 2 Samuel. He, as a skilled bronze-worker, aided King Solomon in building the temple of Israel. Freemasonry adds Masonic legend to this historic account. Hiram was a Master Mason in possession of certain Masonic secrets. He was accosted by three ruffians who wanted from him the secrets of a Master Mason. Hiram, in an act of Masonic heroism and fidelity to the Craft, refused to disclose the secrets. He was subsequently murdered by the ruffians and buried, with a sprig of evergreen placed atop the grave. King Solomon, upset at the death of the master builder, sent a search party to recover Hiram's corpse. The body was found and brought to Solomon, who attempted to "raise" it with the (secret) grips of Entered Apprentice Mason and Fellow Craft Mason. Both grips failed to raise the corpse due to the rotting flesh. However, Solomon successfully raised Hiram with the "strong grip of a Master Mason."

Throughout the world, lodges enact the death, burial, and raising of Hiram. The candidate for the degree plays Hiram, the master of the lodge plays King Solomon, three Masons the ruffians. The play begins. The candidate, blindfolded (hoodwinked), is accosted by the three ruffians, each in turn. The ruffians ask him to disclose the secrets of a Master Mason. The candidate's conductor answers for the candidate, "I will not." At this answer the third ruffian states, "Then die!" The candidate is then struck on the head with a soft instrument and pushed onto a sheet held by several Masons. The sheet is lowered to the floor. This ritual ends with the master of the lodge praying, "Have compassion on the children of Thy creation . . . and save them with an everlasting salvation." The master then "raises" the candidate/Hiram with the strong grip of a Master Mason. Some Masonic rituals instruct candidates to "imitate our Grand Master Hiram Abif . . . that we may welcome the grim tyrant Death, and receive him as a kind messenger sent from our Supreme Grand Master [Great Architect], to translate us from this imperfect to that all-perfect, glorious and celestial Lodge above, where the Supreme Architect of the Universe presides." Gleaned from this symbolism are doctrines of the immortality of the soul or resurrection from the dead.

As a result of the beliefs and practices of Freemasonry, and especially because of the candidates' identification with Hiram, it is not uncommon when attending Masonic funeral services to hear official statements that a deceased Mason (who has a Masonic Apron upon his corpse or upon his casket) has indeed entered the celestial Lodge above, where the Great Architect of the Universe presides.

Further Reading

Carl Claudy. *Foreign Countries*. Macoy Publishing and Masonic Supply Company, 1971.

Henry Wilson Coil. *Coil's Masonic Encyclopedia*. Macoy Publishing and Masonic Supply Company, 1961.

Albert G. Mackey. *Mackey's Revised Encyclopedia of Freemasonry*. Macoy Publishing and Masonic Supply Company, 1966.

Allen E. Roberts. *The Craft and Its Symbols*. Macoy Publishing and Masonic Supply Company. 1974.

Steven Tsoukalas. *Masonic Rites and Wrongs*. P&R, 1995.

121

Freemasonry: Theological Exchanges, Current Issues

STEVEN TSOUKALAS

Beginnings: John T. Desaguliers and James Anderson

Though uncertain as to the historical antecedents leading to the rise of Freemasonry as we know it today, Masonic historians generally agree that John Theophilus Desaguliers, a well-educated scientist, philosopher, and Protestant cleric, had much to do with the development of modern Freemasonry, which began in London in 1717.

Desaguliers's connection with Freemasonry, however, surfaces for the first time in 1719. Nonetheless, it is plausible that the development of Masonic ritual and symbolism arose by his hand or direction. We know for certain that under the direction of Desaguliers, the *Charges of a Freemason* and certain other Masonic regulations came to print in Reverend James Anderson's *Book of Constitutions* in 1723, and it is most likely that Desaguliers directed Anderson in writing the *Book of Constitutions*. To this day both Desaguliers and Anderson are acknowledged by Freemasons for their tireless work in the development of Freemasonry's ritual and other forms of Masonic teaching, and it is likely that biblical themes in older and modern Masonic rituals appear because of the influence of these two men.

Denominations and Freemasonry

As early as 1738 there was intense Roman Catholic reaction to the teachings and principles of Freemasonry. Well known are the early papal bulls issued by Pope

> **Study Aid #224**
>
> **Some Christian Views of Freemasonry**
>
> Scores of denominations have official statements regarding Freemasonry.
> The Roman Catholic Church has opposed Freemasonry.
> Some Roman Catholics are Masons and defend Masonry.
> Some Christians see Freemasons as a competing religion.

Clement XII in 1738 and Pope Benedict XIV in 1751. Clement and Benedict's bulls of condemnation focused upon Masonic swearing of oaths of silence, with penalties of grievous punishment, which held authority in the Roman Catholic's life, the naturalism of Freemasonry, and Freemasonry's religiously universal character. From that time until now, the Roman Catholic Church has been opposed to Freemasonry. In 1983, under the official direction of Pope John Paul II, the Roman Catholic Church once again affirmed its ban of members becoming Masons. Yet one still finds Roman Catholics who are Freemasons, which evidences loose enforcement (if any at all) of the bans and condemnations. As a result, Catholics who are Masons have posted defenses of Freemasonry and their involvement with Freemasonry.

Scores of books, essays, and official denominational studies or statements exist on the parts of other denominations. Those that reportedly have formal written documents or statements against Freemasonry include the Russian Orthodox Church, Church of Scotland, Free Church of Scotland, Orthodox Presbyterian Church, Lutheran Church–Missouri Synod, Wisconsin Evangelical Lutheran Synod, Evangelical Lutheran Synod, Baptist Unions of Scotland and Great Britain and Ireland, British Methodist Church, Free Methodist Church, Eastern Orthodox Church, Reformed Presbyterian Church, Assemblies of God, Evangelical Mennonite Church, Grace Brethren, Christian Reformed Church in North America, Synod Anglican Church of England, General Association of Regular Baptist Churches, Independent Fundamentalist Churches of America, and Presbyterian Church in America.

Theological Issues

In reaction to this opposition, Masonic writers offer several counterresponses. Though Freemasonry insists that all candidates affirm belief in a supreme being, Freemasons claim that (1) it matters not to Freemasonry who this supreme being is, (2) Freemasonry is not a religion but a fraternal organization intended to make good men better, (3) it possesses no theology, (4) it offers no way of salvation, (5) no discussion of sectarian religion is allowed in official lodge meetings, (6) there are scores of denominations with no position against Freemasonry, and (7) there are

> **Study Aid #225**
>
> **Freemason Positions Regarding Christianity**
>
> Freemasons may define God however they wish.
> Freemasonry is not a religion but a fraternal organization.
> Freemasonry possesses no theology.
> Freemasonry offers no way of salvation.
> No discussion of sectarian religion is allowed in official lodge meetings.
> Scores of denominations have no position against Freemasonry.
> Thousands of Christian clergy are Freemasons.

hundreds if not thousands of Christian clergy in the ranks of Freemasonry, and these clergymen have no theological problems with it.

Though Freemasonry as a worldwide institution does not claim to be sectarian (Christian, Muslim, Buddhist, Hindu, or any other sect), Christians state that it is in part its exclusive (e.g., no atheists) yet religiously modified (belief in one God) universal claims that afford its candidates—who represent many religions other than Christianity—the opportunity to join. Further, Freemasonry's harnessing of several religions' teachings is in part responsible for opposition from Christian churches. Christian churches and Christian authors writing about Freemasonry assert that Freemasonry does indeed have a particular-to-the-institution supreme being, is indeed a religion possessing a theology and a way of salvation for all members (including those who belong to religions other than Christianity), and that therefore, despite its nonsectarian claims, Freemasonry ends up being a sectarian religion, specifically the Freemasonic religion.

Masonic jurisprudence surely affirms that it does not matter to the institution who or what the individual deity of each candidate is. But Christians and certain Christian denominations are concerned that Freemasonry indeed offers a theology to its initiates. They cite an example of theological teaching in Masonic ritual found in the first degree (Entered Apprentice), wherein a corporate prayer is offered to the "Almighty Father of the universe" to endue the candidate with his divine wisdom in order that the candidate may "the better be enabled to unfold the beauties of true godliness, to the honor and glory of Thy Holy Name." Christians also call attention to the Masonic appellation "Great/Supreme Architect of the Universe," noting how certain Masonic authors have written that each candidate is to find his personal deity under that appellation.

As for a way of salvation, Christians have asserted that certain symbolic Masonic teachings either allude to an afterlife in the presence of the Great Architect of the Universe or are specific concerning this afterlife. Quoted often are the Masonic symbolisms of the White Lambskin Apron and the Common Gavel. In wearing the apron, the candidate is "reminded of that purity of life and conduct so essentially necessary to gaining admission into the celestial Lodge above, where the supreme Architect of the Universe presides." With the symbolism of the Common Gavel, candidates are "taught to make use of it for the more noble and glorious purpose of divesting our hearts and consciences of all the vices and superfluities of life; thereby fitting our minds as living stones, for that spiritual building, that house not made with hands, eternal in the heavens." Some Christian apologists claim that the "thereby" in the just-quoted symbolism evidences a way of salvation, and that this is buttressed by open-to-the-public Masonic funeral statements that the deceased Mason is in the celestial Lodge above.

Masons and Masonic writers respond to such charges by reiterating that Masonry is not a religion, has no theology, and that the above-quoted symbolism is just that, "only symbolic." This raises central questions: What is the definition of a religion? and What does "symbolic" mean? In the past when prolific and well-known Masonic scholars and writers such as Albert Mackey and Allen Roberts were quoted by Christians seeking to demonstrate that Freemasonry is incompatible with Christianity, Masons at times responded with "That's Mackey's [or Roberts's] opinion." In one Masonic sense this is true, and Masons are correct in pointing this out.

Two Christian reactions, however, concerning this point have arisen. First, though indeed various statements by Masonic authors are the opinions of those authors, what type of opinions are they? Christians point out that Mackey, Roberts, and others are well learned in Masonic ritual teachings and are merely echoing conclusions founded upon proper interpretation of Masonic ritual in the context of Masonic jurisprudence. Second, and in my estimation more importantly, Christians have begun to make this Masonic response less of an issue by first going to official Masonic rituals and other documents published by the Grand Lodges of various states, provinces, or geographic areas, noting that it is the ritual and its obligations that make a man a Mason, and that therefore ritual may be considered the "canon" of Freemasonry.

Finally, Masons call attention to two examples of direct contact with Christianity: (1) many Christian clergy fill the ranks of Freemasonry's membership roles, and (2) several presidents of the United States were Freemasons. Masons argue that it is obviously unlikely that the men in these two groups have witnessed any incompatible elements between Freemasonry and Christianity. Christians have responded that it is logically possible that these clergymen and presidents either were ignorant of Masonic teaching or, if they were not, that they should have renounced the institution. Such a response then invites an examination of Freemasonry and its teachings that are specifically gleaned from Masonic rituals.

The debate still lingers: Is Freemasonry compatible with Christianity? To Masons it is compatible, for Freemasonry contains nothing offensive to Christianity. To many Christians it is incompatible, given Freemasonry's stark religious character and its teachings that oppose core Christian doctrines.

Further Reading

John Quincy Adams. *Letters on the Masonic Institution*. Tentmaker, 2001.

Carl Claudy. *Foreign Countries*. Macoy Publishing and Masonic Supply Company, 1971.

Henry Wilson Coil. *Coil's Masonic Encyclopedia*. Macoy Publishing and Masonic Supply Company, 1961.

Forrest D. Haggard. *The Clergy and the Craft*. Macoy Publishing and Masonic Supply Company, 1970.

Albert G. Mackey. *Mackey's Revised Encyclopedia of Freemasonry*. Macoy Publishing and Masonic Supply Company, 1966.

Allen E. Roberts. *The Craft and Its Symbols*. Macoy Publishing and Masonic Supply Company, 1974.

Steven Tsoukalas. *Masonic Rites and Wrongs*. P&R, 1995.

122

The Family International: History, Beliefs, Practices

JAMES CHANCELLOR

From their beginning on the beaches of Southern California in the late 1960s, the Children of God (COG)/The Family International (TFI) has developed into one of the most successful and most controversial faith communities to grow out of the Jesus People movement. The authoritarian nature of the founding prophet, the radical "forsake all" approach to discipleship, the total rejection of conventional Christianity and American values, and the development of an extraordinary sexual ethos marked the COG as one of the more radical Christian "cults" and a prime target of the modern anticult movement. For over forty years TFI has not only endured but also prospered.

TFI has gone through any number of "revolutions" and significant ideological, theological, and lifestyle shifts that pushed them to the very extreme margins of the broader Christian community and, in the minds of most, well beyond. Recently, TFI has entered a new era—"The Offensive" and "The Change Journey"—which involve subtle shifts in theology and a radical revisioning of Family culture.

History

The COG/TFI began with David Brandt Berg (1919–94), an itinerant evangelist loosely associated with the Christian and Missionary Alliance denomination. He established the movement in 1968. The COG soon developed into a highly structured communal organization noted for an aggressive style of evangelism, high levels of tension with the outside world, strong internal discipline, and sustained antiestablishment rhetoric.

> **Study Aid #226**
>
> **Core Values of The Family International**
>
> *Passion for God.* We love God with our hearts, souls, minds, and strength. We seek a close personal relationship with Jesus, and to grow in emulating His attributes and living His love.
>
> *Pursuing God's Spirit.* We desire to know and understand the truth of God's Word, the essence of His divine nature. We value the foundational principles of the written Word, hearing from God, and following His guidance.
>
> *Discipleship.* We aim to create an atmosphere in which members can follow Jesus according to the personal call He gives them, and enact their commitment to God's will for their lives.
>
> *Love for humankind.* God's unconditional love for humanity that knows no boundaries of race, creed, or status, motivates and guides us to help meet the needs of those we come in contact with, whether spiritually or practically.
>
> *The power of one.* We value each individual and his or her unique talents, skills, and strengths. We believe that every person can contribute to changing the world by changing one heart at a time.
>
> *A sense of community.* We cultivate brotherhood and camaraderie. We seek to develop a spirit of unity, love, and a sense of belonging that provides practical and spiritual support to our members. Together we can do more.
>
> *Spiritual solutions.* We apply spiritual principles to everyday challenges to overcome obstacles, resolve conflict, maximize potential, and heal hearts. We seek to share our spiritual wealth and knowledge with others.
>
> *Diversity and innovation.* In ministry and mission service, creativity and personal initiative are highly valued. When God guides, and we take action to follow Him, anything is possible.
>
> *Living "as unto Him."* We put our faith into action and reach out to weary and troubled hearts, the disadvantaged, downtrodden, and needy, as unto Jesus.

In 1972, Berg ordered his disciples out of North America to begin the missionary task of reaching the entire world with the message of Jesus. Colonies were established throughout the world. Berg withdrew from personal contact with the disciples but continued to maintain control through the leadership structure and his correspondence, known as MO Letters (after Berg's pseudonym, Moses David).

In 1978, due to serious internal conflicts, Berg fired almost all leaders and disbanded the organization. Individual communities continued on, maintaining ties to Berg. Other disciples formed smaller units or traveled nomadically. In 1980 the communities were called together again and the movement was renamed "The Family."

In 1976, Berg introduced a revolutionary new sexual ethic, "Flirty Fishing," the use of sexual allure and sexual intercourse as a means of witnessing and establishing supportive friends. The new sexual ethos also included open sexual relationships among disciples, termed "sharing." Disciples were encouraged to establish sexual fellowship with other members. Nudity and open sexuality became common features of most Family homes through the mid-1980s.

Berg authorized sexual contact between children, and between minors and adults. Sexual contact between adults and young teens was common during the late 1970s and early 1980s. By the time of Berg's death, Family leadership had discontinued Flirty Fishing and banned adult sexual activities with minors.

A significant change came in 1991, when Berg issued a New Year's message, "Consider the Poor." Disciples were to begin helping the poor and helpless "just like Jesus did." Disciples now conduct extensive ministries to prisons, street gangs, illegal aliens, refugees, unwed mothers, drug addicts, and abused children all over the world.

In October of 1994, David Brandt Berg died. Maria and Peter Amsterdam now lead TFI together. In 1994, Peter and Maria issued the "Love Charter," which spelled out the rights and responsibilities of Family members. Final authority remained at the top; however, disciple life became far more democratic and less controlled. The newly revised Charter has again substantially reduced the regulations and limitations on disciple life.

In 1989, TFI drew a distinction between members who were willing and able to carry the full burden of disciple life and those unwilling or unable to bear the yoke. By 2004 membership was subdivided into five categories: Family Disciples, Missionary Members, Fellow Members, Activated Members, and General Members. The last two constitute "Outside Members." In the year 2000 TFI moved to place greater emphasis on the growth, care, and spiritual development of Outside Members.

Beliefs

Family theology has generally reflected its evangelical holiness roots. Their core beliefs center on Jesus and salvation, Father David as "God's Prophet," the "End Times," revelation and the "Spirit World," and the "Law of Love."

From the very beginning, the disciples have understood themselves as "Jesus people." Personal salvation through faith in Jesus Christ is the linchpin of Family theology. Witnessing for Jesus and attempting to have others pray to receive Jesus as Savior is the essential task of disciple life.

David Berg's role as God's Prophet for the End Times is an essential aspect of Family theology. The disciples have a high view of the Bible. In time, some of Berg's writings achieved equivalent, if not superior, status to God's Word. TFI continues to produce current revelation; the core teaching comes from direct revelations from Jesus, Berg, and other persons resident in the Spirit World. Individual disciples are also strongly encouraged to pursue the gift of prophecy and stay connected to the Spirit World.

Family disciples are End Time people. Their End Time beliefs are similar to those held widely in the evangelical Protestant world. What marks off Family theology is the special role the disciples will play in this grand drama and the intensity of their conviction that the end is near.

Total commitment is another significant aspect of the belief system. Disciples are to "forsake all" for the cause of Jesus and Father David. Total commitment is still the ideal, and until very recently communal living was the requirement for the highest level of membership.

The Law of Love is without question the most distinctive and controversial aspect of Family theology. The Law stipulates that all activity and relationships are to be guided by love for one another. In the early 1970s, Berg began to teach that sex was a basic human need, like eating or sleeping, and if a brother or sister was in need, that need should be met in love. The Law of Love stands above all other laws. The three critical aspects of the Law of Love were sexual relationships among adult members, the Flirty Fishing ministry, and sexual activity between adults and minors.

Transformations

The trajectory of TFI is away from its "radical and revolutionary" roots and toward a more accommodating and normative relationship with the outside world. We will consider four locations for accommodating responses: authority, membership, End Time theology, and the sexual ethos under the Law of Love.

Authority

From the beginning, the COG was a highly authoritarian movement. Berg was God's End Time Prophet, Commander and Chief of God's End Time Army, and King of God's New Nation. Absolute obedience was required. The Family remains under strong leadership. But much has changed in both the style and substance of authority. Since 1994 authority has continually been directed downward to local communities, authority structures have been reduced or eliminated, and disciples are encouraged to make their own decisions based on their own level of faith. Their rights are now guaranteed under the "Love Charter."

Membership

In the COG, membership was all or nothing. Over the past fifteen years, the whole concept of membership in TFI has radically changed. Until recently there were five categories of membership, ranging from fully committed Family Disciples "down" to Activated Members, who simply took spiritual direction from TFI. In a radical departure, as of June 2010 all distinctions in membership levels are abolished, and all are considered equal members who operate at the level of their own faith. The Activated Program is now the major emphasis of Family ministry. Each home is expected to develop an ever-growing "congregation" of Activated members who will be spiritually mentored, expected to tithe to their sponsoring home, and engaged in evangelism.

Eschatology

There has been no change in the formal End Time theology. However, TFI now speaks of thirty or perhaps fifty years until the return of Christ, and end-time expectations appear to be far less central to their living faith.

The Law of Love

The sexual ethos under the Law of Love is the dimension that marks them in the minds of many as a "pernicious and dangerous cult." Once started down the path toward complete sexual freedom, it proved very difficult to find a stopping place. By the beginning of the 1980s, Flirty Fishing was ubiquitous. Sexual sharing among adult members was so common and so open that some homes posted weekly "sharing schedules." Full nudity and group showers were commonplace.

The first indication that something might be wrong came in 1983. Flirty Fishing and sexual sharing not only created a plague of STDs but also placed an enormous strain on marriage relationships. Families began to disintegrate. Then the AIDS epidemic broke out, and in 1987 Flirty Fishing was quickly discontinued. However, the principles behind Flirty Fishing were never repudiated.

At roughly the same time, the serious negative consequences of the sexual abuse of the children began to surface. By the end of the 1980s, it was quite clear to Maria and other leaders that the whole sexual experiment with children had been a terrible mistake. In 1986 strict guidelines were put in place to "protect our children and teens from premature sexual experiences." In the early 1990s, TFI published an open letter in which they confessed their error, apologized for the harm done to the children, and placed the blame squarely on the shoulders of Berg. Serious sexual, physical, and emotional abuse of children was clearly an aspect of Family life from the mid 1970s through the 1980s. In the seventeen years I have studied TFI, I have never seen evidence of new abuse of the children. TFI has turned the corner on this issue, and today Family children are as safe, if not safer, than children in the wider society.

While sexual sharing among adults still constitutes an important aspect of the Family ethos, the wild years have passed. Sharing continues, but on a much more limited scale and with far more discretion. The second generation is far more conservative on this issue than their parents. At one level, it might appear that TFI is moving steadily toward a more normative Christian understanding of sexual morality. But such an assumption would clearly underestimate the depth and strength of the Law of Love in Family culture. The unique sexual ethos virtually defines this religious community. I see no evidence that this is likely to change in the future.

The Change Journey

"The Offensive" has been under way in TFI since 2008 and is in process. The foundational publication is "The Change Journey! New Thinking. Redirection. Our Future." In this letter, Jesus speaks directly that TFI "needs to change in a variety of ways to be successful in the future" and to become "a more inclusive culture." To that end, a number of significant new initiatives have been adopted. Secular employment and business ventures that facilitate the mission are now allowed. Parents may send their children to public schools, and young people may attend university while still members of a Family home. Those who choose "to pursue a different career or lifestyle" are to be supported and loved, with every effort made to maintain positive relationships with them. Perhaps most significantly, minors who wish to leave may continue to live in Family homes with their parents as nonmembers until they complete their education and are prepared to live on their own.

For religious communities with a living prophet, almost anything is possible. TFI appears to be in a state of transition toward a more accommodating relationship with the outside world. The transition of authority to Maria and Peter is now complete, aided by the continuous flow of guidance and affirmation from Father David and Jesus. The level of overt persecution and state hostility has diminished considerably. The current organizational structure is well suited for substantial growth while at the same time maintaining a core of elites to guide the expanding community and ensure that the core theological and ideological commitments are retained. Many of these commitments will remain profoundly at odds with the mainstream of the Christian faith, no matter how wide you imagine that stream may be.

Further Reading

William Sims Bainbridge. *The Endtime Family: Children of God*. SUNY Press, 2002.
David Berg (Moses David). *The Mo Letters*. World Services, 1979.
James Chancellor. *Life in the Family*. Syracuse University Press, 2000.
J. Gordon Melton. *The Children of God: The Family*. Signature, 2004.

123

The Family International: Theological Exchanges, Current Issues

JAMES CHANCELLOR

The Children of God (COG)/The Family International (TFI) began as a radical revolution against "the System"—the political, educational, social, and religious institutions of modern society. The System included conventional churches of all stripes. David Berg, in his first MO Letter, made clear that the conventional churches, in rejecting his prophetic office, had ceased to be the church.

> [God speaking] They claim to be mine—My Wife—My Church—but the relationship is in name only.... Therefore is this hypocrisy and not a marriage.... Their temples are temples of men and of devils.... She has harmed Mine anointed. Therefore shall I beat and harm her with great wrath. (MO Letter A, "The Old Church and the New Church," 1969)

For the first decades of TFI, Berg consistently referred to the wider church as "god damned Churchianity," "a damnable deception and an accused counterfeit." Disciples were generally required to keep as much distance as possible from conventional Christians, who were understood to be weak, worldly, and uncommitted at best, and unwitting agents of the Evil One at worst. Disciples were fully cognizant that there were other Christians in the System, but disciples' profound sense of spiritual superiority as "God's End Time Army" prevented any sense of identity with other Christian communities. Over my years of research on TFI, I have encountered over twenty disciples who left the movement, spent considerable time in the System, then returned to the fold. None reported attending any

> **Study Aid #227**
>
> Mission Statement of The Family International
>
> The Family International (TFI) is an international Christian community committed to sharing the message of God's love with people around the globe. We seek to bring hope and spiritual renewal through the unconditional love of Jesus Christ that knows no borders or boundaries of race, creed, or social status. We strive to make a difference in our world by offering spiritual solutions for the challenges of life and translating God's love into actions that manifest kindness and compassion and improve the lives of others. We endeavor to follow the example of Jesus, whose ministry was "to preach the Gospel, . . . to heal the brokenhearted, to proclaim liberty to the captives and recovery of sight to the blind" (The Bible, Luke 4:18 NKJV).
>
> We are committed to:
>
> *Making the World a Better Place: Sharing the message of God's love for humankind.*
>
> Our passion is to change the world through empowering people to develop a personal relationship with God, and in turn, to change their part of the world. We seek to provide a supportive and energizing environment for personal spiritual growth, for sharing the good news of God's love and salvation, and for the application of Christian ethics and values to everyday life.
>
> *Spiritual Development: Providing spiritual and emotional support for managing the challenges of modern life.*
>
> TFI members provide opportunities for people's spiritual development through means such as personal counseling and coaching, support groups, seminars, retreats, and personal comfort and encouragement in times of distress or hardship. Members also engage in a variety of educational and character-building programs for children, as well as faith-based instruction for parents and educators.
>
> *Humanitarian Assistance: Enhancing the quality of life of the disadvantaged, displaced, and those without hope.*
>
> TFI members strive to meet the needs of others through a wide range of humanitarian efforts, including emergency relief efforts, volunteer training, capacity building for the underprivileged, education initiatives and schools for the disadvantaged, sustainable development programs, benefit performances, computer literacy programs, medical relief, food and aid distribution, HIV and drug awareness, support, and prevention. Members also provide emotional and spiritual support for relief workers, and engage in visitation programs in hospitals, orphanages, refugee camps, and homeless shelters.

church or developing any relationship with non-Family Christians during these periods of separation.

The open antagonism and hostility of TFI toward the conventional church has been mutual. While attending a professional conference in the mid-1990s I was in conversation with a number of evangelical seminary professors. We spoke of our work, and when I indicated I was researching the Family, there was shocked silence, then the comment, "Why, that is the most evil pernicious cult on earth;

how could you be interested in that bunch?" From its earliest days, TFI has been the target of Christian countercult organizations. It is featured prominently and very negatively in virtually every Christian resource work on cults or new religions. Over the past seventeen years, I have interviewed several hundred Family disciples. Almost all recounted stories of "persecution" at the hands of church officials, ministers, and particularly Protestant missionaries. They consistently spoke of harassment, attempts to publicly expose the more unusual dimensions of Family life, attempts to undermine their supporters, and efforts to have government officials prosecute or drive them out. A number spoke of serious privations and periods of imprisonment as a result of this "persecution" from "church Christians."

David Berg went into essential retirement in 1989 and passed away in 1994. Leadership of TFI passed to his consorts Maria and Peter Amsterdam. It was around this time that a shift in approach to the churches began to take hold. In 1991 the MO Letter "Go to the Churches" came down to the disciples. This letter encouraged the disciples to visit and perhaps even fellowship with open-minded congregations. Not a great deal came of this; the "open-minded" churches had little interest in TFI's enthusiastic evangelism and spirited worship, and those congregations that did resonate with the Family mission were more than uncomfortable with some peculiarities of Family theology and practice. More significantly, this letter encouraged the disciples to direct their converts toward local churches for spiritual care and training in the Christian life. One group of young disciples spent a two-week road trip in a small town in middle America. As they prepared to move on, they directed their converts to a local church. They were soon contacted and invited back, with assurance of food and lodging if they would just direct future converts to this church. In about a week, the pastor discovered their identity as the Family and sent them on their way.

In 1992, the MO Letter "Consider the Poor" authorized the disciples to begin social ministries. This initiative created a minor revolution, with disciples increasingly pouring their energies into a wide range of social ministries, including work in prisons and refugee camps all over the world. These activities have brought the disciples into an ever-widening range of contact and mutual work with Christians and Christian organizations that were previously outside their normal day-to-day contacts.

In the current climate, TFI has made a substantial, if not drastic, shift in their appreciation of "church Christians." It is probably best to hear it in their own words.

> Due to the majority of David's comments about the churches being disparaging and strident, we've developed a tendency to pass judgment on other churches and Christians across the board, labeling them in negative terms, or making overgeneralizations about church Christians, or unfavorable—and sometimes erroneous—comparisons between the Family and other Christians. Maria and I do not feel that the diametric contrast of "the churches are in the wrong, and we are in the right" is accurate. We have not updated our perspective toward the churches as we should have. There are

numerous churches, parachurches, study groups, and religious and missionary organizations that are progressive, faithful in witnessing, and broadening their horizons to find new ways to bring the Gospel to others. There are Christians the world over who actively live their faith. We should admire and respect their beliefs and faithful efforts to serve the Lord. . . . For the record, we want to state that we need to let go of any negative comparisons, generalizations, or judgments of other Christians. We are not anti-church or anti-church Christians. We don't have to agree with them on every point; we may have some doctrinal differences, or varying applications of doctrine, but a) there's probably a lot more that we agree with them on now than we might have 20 or 40 years ago, and b) we should respect them and be open to working with them to win the world. It's not that we think that everyone in the Christian world will embrace us, arms open wide—nor is that our goal. But the reality is that we are all part of God's family. They have their problems and we have ours. They have their strengths and we have ours. We can give and take, learning from them, sharing our knowledge with them. We are all a part of the body of Christ. (Peter Amsterdam, *Backtracking through TFI History*, May 2010)

In my initial interview with Peter Amsterdam, he asked me about the possibilities of the Family being more accepted within the broader community of evangelical Christianity. I offered little hope without major revisions in Family theology and culture. There have been major revisions, but some issues still stand as barriers. TFI has to some extent revised their understanding of David Berg, seeing some of his writings as appropriate for the time but no longer valid and in some cases as simply wrong. However, they still hold that he was God's Prophet and hold some of his writings to be inspired, "God's Word." In addition, TFI continues to receive direct revelations from Jesus, Berg, and other entities resident in the Spirit World. There is no question that Family leadership is in the process of reclaiming the Bible as their core scripture. The official position now is that Berg's writings "do not supersede the Bible" and that "the Word of God, as revealed in the Bible, is the yardstick by which to judge all revelation and messages received."

Perhaps the most significant barrier is the Family construct of human sexuality reflected in the Law of Love. Two quotes from the TFI Statement of Faith stand out. "It is our belief that heterosexual relations, when practiced as God ordained and intended between consenting adults, are a pure and natural wonder of God's creation, and permissible according to Scripture." While this sounds innocuous, it is the Family understanding that these sexual relations are not restricted to the bonds of marriage. In addition, "We believe that the marital metaphor used in the Bible to describe the intimate spiritual relationship between Jesus and His Church is meant to represent the passionate union of heart, mind, and spirit that Jesus seeks with each of His followers." The subtext here is that auto- or heterosexual acts are to be incorporated into the disciple's prayer life and worship of Jesus.

The Family International is on a clear trajectory toward a future that is far more aligned with mainstream Christianity. It remains to be seen how this renewed emphasis on the central place of the Bible will be reflected in future changes in Family theology and culture.

Further Reading

> Deborah Davis and Bill Davis. *The Children of God: The Inside Story*. Zondervan, 1984.
>
> Kristina Jones, Celeste Jones, and Juliana Buhring. *Not without My Sister*. HarperCollins, 2007.
>
> James Lewis and Gordon Melton. *Sex, Slander, and Salvation*. Center for Academic Publication, Stanford University, 1994.
>
> Miriam Williams. *Heaven's Harlots*. Harper Perennial, 1999.

124

The Family International: Adherent Essay

CLAIRE BOROWIK

Over thirty years ago, I began a personal quest to discover purpose and a way to live my faith, untainted by materialism or the status quo. Although I was not from a Christian background, I had been brought to faith in Christ as a small child while attending a daily vacation Bible school with neighbors. I experienced a genuine conversion, and despite a lack of any formal religious instruction, my faith became a shaping influence in my childhood and adolescent years. In the quest to find others who shared my faith, I joined a local Anglican church as a young teenager. The experience proved to be disillusioning, as the ideals I held regarding commitment to God and a higher purpose did not seem to play a role in the institution. Later in my teen years I participated in charismatic Catholic meetings and mission work in Brazil and found a greater depth and sincerity; nevertheless, I found the formality of the institution to be at odds with my understanding of God's love.

My first encounter with members of The Family International occurred while I was living in Brazil as a young adult in 1978. Besides expressing countercultural views that I found appealing, they radiated a compelling sincerity and passion to share God's love with all people that was unlike anything I had experienced before. Not only did they believe in the Bible, but they also believed that it was possible to live as the early Christians had, forsaking worldly possessions and pursuits, and living and working communally for the purpose of bringing salvation through faith in Jesus to as many as they could.

Integral to this fervor to reach the world was the understanding that the end of times prophesied throughout the Bible was imminent, and as the prophet Ezekiel exhorted, each of us was responsible to lead people to Christ while there was still time (Ezek. 3:17–21). This conviction led to a worldwide campaign to witness and reach the world, resulting in over thirty-three million people praying to receive Jesus as their Savior, and the distribution of 1.2 billion Gospel publications in nearly 150 countries in The Family International's forty-year history.

In the youthful verve and dedication of the members, who were from a number of nations, I found a sincere desire to make the world a better place and to help people to find faith-based answers to the many problems they faced. There was no question in my mind that I had found what I had been searching for—a way to serve God and humanity, without the boundaries imposed by formal institutions.

The people who had left their lives behind to serve God without reservation were extraordinary individuals. Although they had few possessions, they willingly shared what they had. In them I found people who genuinely cared for others in a deep and selfless way. What I had sought in a number of churches, I found in a group of counterculture youth who had abandoned their secular lives to serve God, much like the original Saint Francis of Assisi movement.

Shortly after joining the movement in Brazil, I proceeded to Argentina, where I served with the organization for the next fifteen years. Argentina in the early 1980s was a repressed society, seeking to overcome the draconian measures of a military dictatorship that had left scars on its people and parents mourning their lost sons and daughters from the Dirty War. As the military government crumbled and democracy began to take root, some freedoms were permitted, and we slowly began to witness more openly and distribute Christian literature.

Our efforts to reach the Argentine people were hindered by the authorities, and members were periodically incarcerated or had their homes searched in the middle of the night under flimsy pretenses. In the early 1990s, I and twenty fellow missionaries were imprisoned for over three months on a pretrial basis, while our children were taken into state care. Ultimately, all charges were dropped, and the higher court reviewing the case deemed the proceedings and the mistreatment we endured to be "an anachronistic continuation of the most severe inquisitive system" (Federal Court of San Isidro, Case No. 34.269, Buenos Aires, Argentina, January 11, 1990).

In addition to participating actively in mission and humanitarian work, I have served as a public affairs director for the organization for twenty years, first in Argentina, and later in the United States and Canada. I am currently codirector of international public affairs for the organization.

The Family International, as a progressive new religious movement, has experienced substantive change throughout its forty-year history, both structurally and theologically. The organization is currently undergoing what portends to represent the most monumental change to date. Core tenets of Family theology and practice are under examination to determine whether they are relevant or current, and a significant change in culture is underway. Therefore, in elaborating on the Family's relationship with mainstream Christianity, it is important to differentiate between three key factors: (1) the historic relationship developed in the writings of the founder, David Brandt Berg (1919–94), (2) the relationship at the grassroots level, and (3) the current philosophy.

(1) Historically, David Berg leveled harsh criticisms at mainstream Christianity in his writings. He took mainstream Christianity, particularly American churches, to task for their lack of commitment to the Great Commission and to their faith, and for their accommodation to the forces of secularization. He posited that Christ's call to his followers to forsake all that they had, as per Luke 14:33, and to "go into all the world and preach the gospel" (Mark 16:15) was just as valid today as when Christ first issued the call. Berg contended that modern Christianity had deviated from these core principles, and he sought a revival of the early church paradigm.

Contextually, Father David's early message was congruent with the radicalism of the 1960s. He perceived the Family (then known as the Children of God) as a definitive departure from mainstream Christianity and its accommodation to the greater society and the forces of secularization that he considered to be at variance with the core values of Christianity.

(2) Despite his criticisms of mainstream Christianity, on occasion Father David encouraged members to cooperate with other churches. Members have frequently collaborated with other churches and assisted them in their mission work over the years, as is reflected in this excerpt of a book dedicated to the life of the Italian priest Father Ildebrando Antonino Santangelo.

> They [the Children of God] were travelling around the world, in groups, coming from America. They manifested much religious fervor, and they prayed and sang wherever they happened to be. They were living [at the monastery in Brucolli]; they attended the monastery courses and animated some of the meetings. I remember that their presence was edifying. (Nicolò Scuderi, *Il servo di Dio*, Elledici, 2008)

(3) In recent times, Karen Zerby and Steve Kelly, current spiritual and administrative directors of The Family International, have instituted a conceptual shift toward a more welcoming stance of mainstream Christianity, and a view of The Family as playing a role, albeit unique, in the totality of Christianity and its commission on earth.

> There are over a billion Christians in the world today, all of whom share equally in the responsibility to do their best to witness to others about Jesus and His love, and to offer them salvation. There are many, many sincere, faithful Christians throughout the world who have dedicated their lives to witnessing and missionary service, or who do their best to witness in their workplace or to their acquaintances, family, and friends. In this, we are few among many—and we are privileged to be numbered with those who have the courage and self-sacrifice to give their lives for the purpose of helping others to find Jesus, to know Him and His love and truth. (Steve Kelly, "Offensive Briefing #7," The Family International, 2009)

In summary, while The Family International does not have an official relationship with mainstream Christianity, the movement has historically perceived itself as divergent from the mainstream, due to the high level of commitment to the cause of Christ expected of its members, as well as its unconventional beliefs. (See The Family International's statement of faith at http://www.tficharter.com/en/statement-faith.) "The Family pushes the envelope of Christianity. Besides pushing the spiritual envelope, we also go beyond traditional boundaries as far as our commitment to our mission, our lifestyle, and our interpretation and application of Christian doctrine" (Karen Zerby, "Pushing the Envelope—Our Brand of Christianity," The Family International, 2009).

The Family does not perceive its role as providing competition to mainstream Christian denominations in the religious marketplace; nor has it sought to become a mainstream denomination. It strives to offer a unique gospel message that will appeal to the unchurched or to those who don't find traditional Christianity attractive, and to nominal Christians who lack an understanding of their faith; members do not seek to persuade Christians to leave their denominations. The unsaved and the unchurched are unquestionably the primary focus of members' witnessing initiatives.

The movement's ability to invest its labor and resources in missionary work, rather than in creating a mainstream denomination, has enabled members to focus primarily on the Great Commission. Despite having limited financial resources and a small membership that hasn't exceeded seven thousand adult members, the movement has circled the globe with the gospel message in literature, song, and multimedia productions.

On a personal note, I consider it vital to The Family's future that it maintains its uniqueness in the Christian marketplace, which is core to its success in reaching the world with the gospel message. It is also crucial that the Family's message and practice are current, relatable, and appealing to the public, to enable us to better reach people with the gospel message. I believe that the process of change currently underway will enable members and the organization as a whole to better achieve that goal.

I also consider it important that, as an organization, we are able to learn from the experience and successes of other Christian organizations. We have much to learn from mainstream denominations and churches in regard to planting churches and establishing perdurable results in recruiting new members and expanding our membership base, which are crucial to the Family's future. It is my hope and prayer that we can build good relations and collaborate with other Christian organizations when possible, while maintaining our core ideology and commitment to the Great Commission.

125

Baha'i:
History, Beliefs, Practices

CHRISTOPHER BUCK

History

The Baha'i faith was founded by two men: the Bab (the "Gate," 1819–50) and Baha'u'llah (the "Glory of God," 1817–92). Baha'i history begins on May 22, 1844, when a young merchant, Sayyid 'Ali-Muhammad Shirazi (the Bab), proclaimed himself to be a Messenger of God and Herald of a greater One to follow. The Bab's religious claims outraged the clerics of Shi'a Islam, the predominant religion in Persia, who pronounced the death sentence on the Bab. He was executed before a firing squad of 750 soldiers in Tabriz on July 9, 1850.

The Bab's primary purpose was to prepare the way for the advent of a messianic figure greater than himself. Baha'is believe that this was none other than Mirza Husayn-'Ali Nuri Mazandarani, known by his spiritual title, Baha'u'llah. In 1852, Baha'u'llah was arrested because he was a Babi leader and thrown into jail in the capital of Persia, Tehran. During four months of imprisonment Baha'u'llah experienced prophetic visions that bade him arise for the uplift of humanity and the unification of the world in a federation of nations.

After his release in 1853, Baha'u'llah was exiled, first to Baghdad, then to Constantinople, later to Adrianople in 1863, and finally, in 1868, to a penal colony at 'Akko in Palestine (now Israel). After several years, he was released to live in the house of Udi Khammar, where Baha'u'llah revealed the Kitab-i-Aqdas ("The Most Holy Book") as his laws for the new faith.

Throughout his nearly forty-year prophetic career, Baha'u'llah revealed a prodigious corpus of writings that constitute the heart of Baha'i scripture—the equivalent of a hundred books. Baha'u'llah passed away on May 29, 1892.

Study Aid #228
Baha'i Timeline

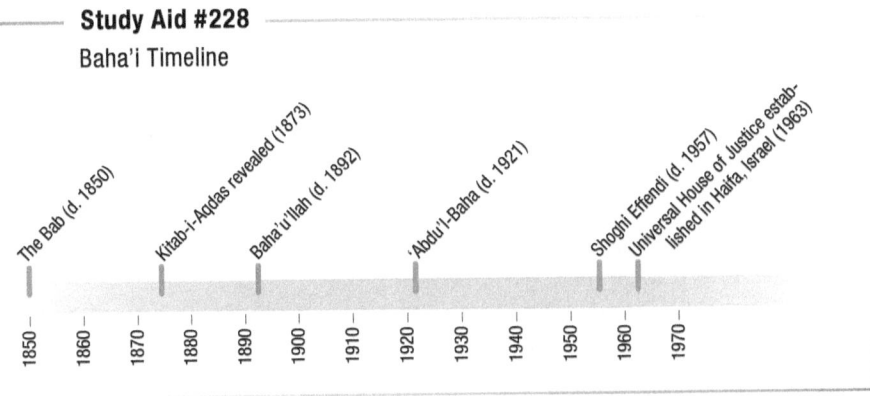

In his will and testament, Baha'u'llah designated his son 'Abdu'l-Baha—who had long emerged as the natural and obvious leader—as his successor. 'Abdu'l-Baha had traveled throughout North Africa, Europe, the United States, and Canada in 1910–13, promoting Baha'u'llah's gospel of social salvation—justice, virtue, and unity.

'Abdu'l-Baha led the Baha'i world until his passing in 1921. His grandson, Shoghi Effendi, who was studying at Oxford University at the time of 'Abdu'l-Baha's "ascension" (as Baha'is honorifically refer to his death), assumed the leadership of the Baha'i community, as explicitly provided for in 'Abdu'l-Baha's own will and testament. Shoghi Effendi orchestrated the worldwide development and expansion of the Baha'i religion through a series of global initiatives, or "Plans," that proved highly successful in the systematic growth of the new religious community. As a result, the Baha'i faith now comes close to being the most widespread religious community in the world today—exceeded only by Christianity.

Five years after Shoghi Effendi's passing in 1957, Baha'i representatives from the various worldwide National Spiritual Assemblies (democratically elected Baha'i councils) met in 1963 in Haifa, Israel, to elect the first Universal House of Justice, a nine-member international council (elected every five years) that now directs the affairs of the Baha'i world, with its seat on Mount Carmel in Haifa, Israel. This is considered a divine institution, as Baha'u'llah had explicitly ordained the Universal House of Justice.

Not all places in the world are open to the Baha'i tradition. Ever since the Islamic Revolution of 1979, the Islamic Republic of Iran has systematically oppressed the Baha'i community. Through draconian measures that exclude the Baha'is from the protections of Iran's constitution, the regime bars Baha'is from the constitutional rights enjoyed, at least in theory, by other religious minorities.

Beliefs

Baha'i belief acknowledges one true God as an "unknowable Essence," far beyond the reach and ken of humans. In other words, God may not be *comprehended* but only *apprehended*. God is a profound mystery, yet with clues everywhere, pervading creation. Since God cannot be known by essence, only the nature and will of God can be appreciated.

"Progressive Revelation" is the Baha'i belief that Messengers of God successively appear throughout history to establish world religions that renew and amplify spiritual teachings and declare new social laws suited for that day and age. These Messengers of God reveal, from age to age, God's will and purpose. Baha'is consider such religious figures as Abraham, Moses, Zoroaster, Buddha, Christ, and Muhammad to be such Messengers of God.

Many world religions look forward to a time when the world will be saved by a world-messiah. Baha'is see these messianic expectations as convergent. In 1863 in Baghdad, Baha'u'llah proclaimed himself to be the "Promised One" of all religions, and as the one who Christ foretold would come in the spirit and power of Christ himself—not as a reincarnation, nor as the incarnation, but as the "Manifestation" of God.

Baha'is believe that Baha'u'llah symbolically fulfills the prophecies of the major world religions. For example, Baha'is regard Baha'u'llah as the return of the spirit and power of Christ. Baha'is also believe that Baha'u'llah has come, in fulfillment of Jewish prophecies, as the Lord of Hosts and "Everlasting Father" (even though these were not traditionally believed to be prophetic titles). Baha'u'llah, moreover, is seen by Baha'is as the return of Jesus in Sunni Islam; as the return of Husayn in Shi'a Islam; as Shah Bahram Varjavand for the Zoroastrians; as Maitreya, or the Fifth Buddha, in Buddhist millennial belief; as Kalki Viṣṇuyaśas in Hindu (Vaisnavaite) chiliasm. Many Native American Baha'is also believe in Baha'u'llah as the return of White Buffalo Calf Woman for the Lakota, the return of Deganawidah among the Iroquois, and the return of Viracocha among the Quechua Indians. In a word, they believe that Baha'u'llah is the world-messiah.

A Baha'i accepts the teachings of Baha'u'llah and the interpretive authority of 'Abdu'l-Baha and Shoghi Effendi, as well as the ongoing governing authority of the Universal House of Justice. Baha'is live according to the laws and precepts revealed by Baha'u'llah in the Most Holy Book, as further interpreted by 'Abdu'l-Baha and Shoghi Effendi, and as adapted by the Universal House of Justice, to new situations in which Baha'i principles may be wisely applied.

Study Aid #229

Baha'i Beliefs

One God	Equality of women and men
Oneness of humanity	Elimination of prejudice
Common foundations of all religions	Universal education
Harmony of science and religion	

> **Study Aid #230**
> Baha'i Demographics
> Number of Baha'is in the world: 7,447,000
> Percentage of world population: 0.1 percent
> Countries where Baha'is make up more than 50 percent of population: None
>
> Baha'is have promoted their message of unity in more countries than any other smaller religion. The Baha'i religious tradition is the only religion to have grown faster in every United Nations region over the past one hundred years than the population. Hence it is the fastest-growing religion over that period. Baha'is have viable communities in every country of the world except North Korea and the Vatican.

Baha'is often talk about the "Three Onenesses": that there is but one, almighty God; that world religions, in their pure form, impart divine truths; and that humanity—metaphorically, biologically, and spiritually—is "one family." The purpose of the Baha'i faith is to unify the world by establishing a common foundation for harmonious and prosperous individual and social life. Some of the more prominent Baha'i beliefs include the equality of men and women; the harmony of science and religion; the elimination of prejudices of all kinds; the need for a universal language; peace among nations, races, and religions; disarmament; and world self-governance through international law, where the purpose of justice is understood to be a precondition for the appearance of true unity and prosperity.

On each continent, Baha'is have built magnificent temples that are open to everyone who wishes to experience their architectural beauty and soulful atmosphere. Perhaps the most celebrated Baha'i house of worship is the Lotus Temple in New Delhi, India, which attracts more visitors annually than the Taj Mahal. In 2008, UNESCO designated the Shrine of the Bab (and surrounding Baha'i terraces and gardens at the Baha'i World Centre on Mount Carmel in Haifa, Israel) and the Shrine of Baha'u'llah in 'Akko as "World Heritage sites"—the first modern religious edifices to be so designated.

Practices

The purpose of life in the Baha'i view is to know and worship God, to acquire virtues, and to carry forward an ever-advancing civilization. Individually, Baha'is pray, fast, meditate, and work. Baha'u'llah teaches that when done in the spirit of service to humanity, work is a sacred undertaking and thus is a form of worship. Baha'is promote unity through nonpolitical means.

Baha'is have a spiritual, solar calendar of nineteen months of nineteen days each, with four or five intercalary days to round out each solar year. Each day, month, year, and cycle of years is given a name that reflects one of the attributes

> **Study Aid #231**
> Baha'is by World Region
>
> | | |
> |---|---|
> | Asia | 3,551,000 |
> | Africa | 2,176,000 |
> | Latin America | 941,000 |
> | North America | 527,000 |
> | Europe | 144,000 |
> | Oceania | 108,000 |

of God, as manifested in such human perfections as Honor, Justice, Mercy, Generosity, Grandeur, and the like. By keeping these sterling qualities of character in mind, Baha'is learn, over time, what it means to be honorable, just, merciful, generous, and noble.

The Baha'i year begins on the first day of Spring (March 21), following a nineteen-day period of fasting, from sunrise to sunset, lasting March 2–20. At the beginning of every Baha'i month, each Baha'i community gathers for a nineteen-day feast, consisting of spiritual, consultative, and social portions. Baha'is observe nine holy days, on which work is suspended.

Baha'is participate in a series of open "study circles," each of which is a guided group self-study in a dynamic sequence of brief courses. Each course equips participants not only with fundamental *knowledge* about the Baha'i religion, but also with basic *skills* necessary to effectively teach the Baha'i faith to others, and to organize children's classes, lead activities among junior youth and youth, hold inspirational devotional gatherings open to all, and facilitate the learning process among believers and those interested in the faith.

The world, Baha'is believe, evolves not only physically, but also spiritually and socially. Baha'is understand that, in this day and age, the will of God for humanity is to bring about global unity through diversity as the next logical stage in the world's social evolution. Baha'i principles and social teachings are for the world at large. Baha'is believe that, if carried out in socially and scientifically enlightened ways, these divinely revealed precepts and practices will have a leavening influence and will eventually transform the world.

Sources

'Abdu'l-Baha. *The Works of 'Abdu'l-Baha*. Baha'i Reference Library (BRL). http://reference.bahai.org/en/t/ab/.

Baha'u'llah. *The Works of Baha'u'llah*. BRL. http://reference.bahai.org/en/t/b/.

Christopher Buck. *Paradise and Paradigm: Key Symbols in Persian Christianity and the Baha'i Faith*. State University of New York Press, 1999.

———. *Symbol and Secret: Qur'an Commentary in Bahá'u'lláh's Kitáb-i Íqán*. Kalimat Press, 2004.

Shoghi Effendi. *The Works of Shoghi Effendi*. BRL. http://reference.bahai.org/en/t/se/.

Brian Lepard. *In the Glory of the Father: The Baha'i Faith and Christianity*. Baha'i Publishing, 2008.

Peter Smith. *An Introduction to the Baha'i Faith*. Cambridge University Press, 2008.

Michael Sours. *Preparing for a Baha'i/Christian Dialogue*. 3 vols. Oneworld, 1990–94.

Universal House of Justice. *The Works of the Universal House of Justice/Baha'i International Community Documents and Statements*. BRL. http://reference.bahai.org/en/t/uhj/.

126

Baha'i: Theological Exchanges, Current Issues

CHRISTOPHER BUCK

Issues that arise in the course of Baha'i-Christian interfaith encounters, beginning with issues arising from Baha'i-Christian religious dialogue, may be briefly summarized as follows.

Individual Salvation and Social Salvation

The Baha'i faith has a simultaneous emphasis on both personal and social transformation. Shoghi Effendi, great-grandson of Baha'u'llah and "Guardian" of the Baha'i faith from 1921 to 1957, has written that the Baha'i faith's mission is "the salvation, through unification, of the entire planet" (Effendi 1980, 116).

Baha'u'llah came for the salvation of entire societies as well as souls. From the Baha'i perspective, salvation history is a process that has progressively unfolded throughout the course of prophetic history, and which has reached its most advanced stage in the advent of Baha'u'llah.

> The declared purpose of history's series of prophetic revelations, therefore, has been not only to guide the individual seeker on the path of personal salvation, but to prepare the whole of the human family for the great eschatological Event lying ahead, through whose moral and social principles the life of the world will itself be entirely transformed. (Baha'i World Centre 2005, 54)

> **Study Aid #232**
> Typology of Baha'i-Christian Contacts
> Witness   Disinterest   Dialogue
> Interest   Polemics

The Baha'i statement issued by the Baha'i World Centre *One Common Faith* (2005) begins with the observation that, in the early twentieth century, the "dominant world faith" was not Christianity, but "a materialistic interpretation of reality" (ibid., 3). Yet, as the twentieth century approached its close, "a sudden resurgence of religion as a subject of consuming global importance" emerged as a worldwide phenomenon (ibid., 5). The concomitant "search for justice and the promotion of the cause of international peace" had the effect of "arousing new perceptions of the individual's role in society" (ibid., 6–7) insofar as the "rational soul does not merely occupy a private sphere, but is an active participant in a social order" (ibid., 15).

The Baha'i Faith and Christianity

The most important recent Baha'i outreach to Christian leaders is the letter addressed to the world's religious leaders in April 2002 by the Universal House of Justice. The nine members of the Universal House of Justice are elected—by plurality vote, with no nominations or campaigning allowed—by members of Baha'i national councils (each known as a "National Spiritual Assembly"), who convene once every five years in Haifa, Israel, site of the Baha'i World Centre. In "To the World's Religious Leaders," interfaith dialogue is highly regarded: "In the context of the transformation taking place in the human race's conception of itself, the most promising new religious development seemed to be the interfaith movement." In the same letter, the Universal House of Justice addresses the primary role of religion, Christianity included, as follows:

> Religion, as we are all aware, reaches to the roots of motivation. When it has been faithful to the spirit and example of the transcendent Figures who gave the world its great belief systems, it has awakened in whole populations capacities to love, to forgive, to create, to dare greatly, to overcome prejudice, to sacrifice for the common good and to discipline the impulses of animal instinct. Unquestionably, the seminal force in the civilizing of human nature has been the influence of the succession of these Manifestations of the Divine that extends back to the dawn of recorded history.

The Universal House of Justice, "as the governing council of one of the world religions," urges religious leaders, in a "spirit of goodwill," to act concertedly to address the greatest problems that face the world today: "Vast numbers of people

> **Study Aid #233**
>
> **Baha'i-Christian Theological Exchanges**
>
> Baha'i is fulfillment of Christianity   All religions are one
> Baha'u'llah is successor to Jesus   Reject original sin, the Trinity, Satan

continue to endure the effects of ingrained prejudices of ethnicity, gender, nation, caste and class." "Tragically, organized religion," the Universal House of Justice goes on to say, "has long lent its credibility to fanaticism." The problem is that "the greater part of organized religion stands paralyzed at the threshold of the future, gripped in those very dogmas and claims of privileged access to truth that have been responsible for creating some of the most bitter conflicts dividing the earth's inhabitants."

Acknowledging that there are "certainly wide differences among the world's major religious traditions with respect to social ordinances and forms of worship," the Universal House of Justice maintains that religion, ideally, has "the unique power" to better the world.

The Universal House of Justice's letter extends an open invitation to the world's religious leaders—leaders of Christianity included—to work collaboratively through interfaith endeavors: "Inspired by this perspective, the Baha'i community has been a vigorous promoter of interfaith activities from the time of their inception."

Current Social Issues of Deep Concern to Baha'is

Before "social justice" served as the secular philosophy of modern democracies in the twentieth century, the Baha'i Faith had already established ethical principles and social laws for the ennobling of individuals and the ordering of societies. Social justice can only be universal if predicated on the unity of the human race. Justice and unity are thus the hallmarks of Baha'i precept and praxis, as Baha'u'llah declared: "The well-being of mankind, its peace and security, are unattainable unless and until its unity is firmly established" (Baha'u'llah 1978, 167). As a collective ethical orientation, the Baha'i concept of social justice is dynamically linked with the principle of unity. "The purpose of justice," Baha'u'llah declared, "is the appearance of unity among men" (ibid., 67). A Baha'i theory of social justice can be articulated from the Baha'i sacred writings themselves and amplified by policy statements made by the Baha'i International Community, a religious nongovernmental organization (NGO) with consultative status at the United Nations (UN).

Formed in 1948 as an NGO at the United Nations, the Baha'i International Community (BIC) represents an association of democratically elected national and regional (as in the case of Alaska and Hawaii) Baha'i governing bodies known as National Spiritual Assemblies. In 1970, the BIC was granted consultative status (now called "special" consultative status) with the UN Economic and Social

Council (ECOSOC), followed by consultative status with the United Nations Children's Fund (UNICEF) in 1976 and with the UN Development Fund for Women (UNIFEM) in 1989, when working relations with the World Health Organization (WHO) were also established. In close association with the UN Environment Program (UNEP); the Office of the High Commissioner for Human Rights; the UN Educational, Scientific and Cultural Organization (UNESCO); and the UN Development Program (UNDP), the BIC has served as the primary channel for promoting Baha'i universal values for the common good at the international level. Social issues of deep concern to Baha'is, as represented by statements of the BIC, include, inter alia, the following:

1. Racism, racial discrimination, xenophobia, and related intolerance
2. Human rights reform
3. Right to freedom of religion or belief
4. Advancement of women
5. Freedom of conscience
6. Social development
7. Minority issues
8. Religious persecution
9. Climate change
10. Eradication of violence against women and girls
11. Eradication of poverty
12. Full employment and decent work
13. Mobilizing institutional, legal, and cultural resources to achieve gender equality
14. Situation of the Baha'is in the Islamic Republic of Iran
15. Situation of the Baha'is in Egypt
16. A new framework for global prosperity
17. Search for values in an age of transition
18. Sustainable development
19. Overcoming corruption and safeguarding integrity in public institutions
20. The right to education
21. Protection of minorities
22. Women and health

Study Aid #234

Baha'i Social Issues

Abolishing racism	Advancement of women	Eradicating poverty
Human rights	Sustainable development	Full employment
Freedom of religion	Climate change	Right to education

> **Study Aid #235**
> **Current Baha'i and Baha'i-Christian Issues**
> Persecution in Iran and Egypt
> One common faith
> Christ and Baha'u'llah
> Individual salvation/social salvation
> Baha'i outreach to Christians

Baha'is believe these current issues transcend religious and national boundaries. Since they are problems without borders, their solutions must likewise cross religious boundaries.

Baha'i Social Action and Public Discourse

Baha'is are currently engaged in "three broad areas of action": (1) "expansion and consolidation of the Baha'i community itself," (2) participation in "social action," and (3) engagement in "the discourses of society" on such issues as "governance, the environment, climate change, the equality of men and women, human rights, to mention a few" (Universal House of Justice, letter dated January 4, 2009, to the National Spiritual Assembly of the Baha'is of Australia).

Sources

Baha'i International Community (BIC). Statements and Reports. http://www.bic.org/statements-and-reports/statements.

Baha'i World Centre. "The Kitab-i-Aqdas: Its Place in Baha'i Literature." In *The Baha'i World*. Baha'i World Centre, 1993.

———. *One Common Faith*. BRL, 2005. http://reference.bahai.org/en/t/bic/OCF/.

———. "To the World's Religious Leaders." April 2002. http://www.bahai.org/selected-writings/message-worlds-religious-leaders/.

Baha'u'llah. *Tablets of Baha'u'llah Revealed after the Kitab-i-Aqdas*. Baha'i Publishing Trust, 1978.

Christopher Buck. "Baha'i Faith and Social Action." *Encyclopedia of Activism and Social Justice*, edited by Gary L. Anderson and Kathryn G. Herr, 1:208–13. Sage, 2007.

Shoghi Effendi. *The Promised Day Is Come*. Rev. ed. BRL, 1980. http://reference.bahai.org/en/t/se/PDC/.

———. *The World Order of Baha'u'llah*. BRL, 1991. http://reference.bahai.org/en/t/se/WOB/.

Paul Lample. *Revelation and Social Reality: Learning to Translate What Is Written into Reality*. Palabra, 2009.

Michael L. Penn and Aditi Malik. "The Protection and Development of the Human Spirit: An Expanded Focus for Human Rights Discourse." *Human Rights Quarterly* 32, no. 3 (2010): 665–88.

Part 5

Essays

127

Essays Introduction

Terry C. Muck

The essays in this section explore several of the ways religion is affecting the world today. Religion affects every aspect of our everyday lives. Religion influences politics, economics, social life, and cultural patterns. It is still an important element of identity formation among individuals. Some scholars are even suggesting that there is a genetic basis to religion, an "altruism gene" that accounts for the selfless behavior most religions advocate.

That these essays are necessary today in order to understand modern religion is a sign of our differentiated cultural context. Religion has always been something of a coping mechanism humans use to explain suffering, evil, and death. When indigenous religions held sway across the land, such coping was a part of one's total life pattern. But when religion became differentiated from the rest of life, it became necessary to see it function over against the various sectors of life. And its influence could vary from sector to sector, positive in the cultural sector, nonexistent in public life, negative in political life, neutral in economic life. From one cultured system to another, of course, the relative impact of religion could vary dramatically.

Thus, we need an essay on the good, the bad, and the ugly of religion and human rights in the world today, as well as on religion and violence/peace, religion and gender, and so on. Further, religion makes a unique contribution to each of these sectors. Religion represents transcendence in a world system that has tried to eliminate transcendence as an operating feature of daily life. We might put it this way: whereas once upon a time the transcendent was an essential feature of all of life, it has now been shuttered in a private room labeled "religion." As a result religion must justify its right to influence every area of life from which it has been separated.

Authors of the following essays were asked to give us a status report on how human religious traditions in general are comporting themselves in the world today. Are the religions contributing to peace in the world today? Or are they being used as mandates and rationales for violence? What message are the religions sending around the world in regard to family life? With regard to economic life? Are the religions helping solve the environmental crisis or exacerbating it?

We need to be informed about these issues. We need to know whether our tradition is contributing to the solutions of the world's problems or whether those acting in our religion's name are using it to make problems worse.

128

Religion and Science

S. Mark Heim

Religion is what cultures throughout human history have put forward as the most encompassing descriptions of the nature and purpose of our world and our place in it. Prior to the rise of modern science, religious traditions addressed many topics now treated in the sciences: disease and healing, astronomy and cosmology, the biological processes of nature. Learned people in any of these areas were likely the same people who were most highly trained in their religious sources. No clear line separated a religious worldview and a scientific one. The practical roots of many scientific disciplines, such as medicine or chemistry, are found in such settings. What we call science is a web of methods for the investigation of nature and a rolling inventory of correlated results from those investigations. Just as "religion" only slowly came to be distinguished as a distinct feature of culture alongside others, so "science" only slowly attained the character of a unified account of such scope that it could be considered on the same plane as religion as an encompassing account of humans and our world—as an expansion, a replacement, or a complement.

At different times, different religious cultures have been at the forefront of developments in knowledge of the natural world and technological innovation. China (Confucian, Taoist, Buddhist), India (Hindu), Islamic culture (spread across many geographical areas), and Europe (Christian) have each in some fields and periods been leaders. Modern science arose in late medieval and Renaissance Europe, and this history gives rise to continuing arguments about the religious conditions for scientific thought. Was Christianity obstacle or midwife to early modern science? To what extent were other religious sources (notably, Islam) significant? One secular historical narrative sees science as the product of Enlightenment rationality's rejection of religious tutelage, a revolution against medieval Christian superstition. It points to instances of conflict between church authorities and early scientists (Galileo). Critics of this narrative note that the great early modern scientists were Christians, often of decided theological interests (Kepler, Newton), who saw no conflict in these commitments. There is continuity as well as rupture between late medieval natural philosophy (already deeply reliant on Greek and Islamic sources) and the new views of nature. Some maintain that only certain theological perspectives provide the combination of contingency and order necessary for the emergence of empirical science. Monotheistic creation meets this need in supposing the world is the purposeful creation of a rational being who yet acts in freedom. This implies that the world has an integral order, but that order cannot be known deductively but only by investigation. What God has done will be orderly and consistent (supporting the expectation that law can be found in nature), yet it is also contingent (requiring an empirical exploration). This combination is crucial, in contrast with the expectation that the world is subject to capricious deities or powers or that it is governed by a metaphysical order that could not be otherwise, so that with the right religious philosophy, all specifics can be deduced from first principles.

Prior to the modern period, scientific endeavors often required a religious rationale, to deflect fears of destructive magic or charges of impiety. In the contemporary world the situation is frequently reversed, as religious apologists commend their tradition with claims about its affinity with science. This was often the case with the modern Christian missionary movement. And it is true today as Islamic scholars advocate for the underappreciated extent of Islamic contributions to the rise of science, or as Buddhist scholars emphasize commonalities between Buddhist philosophy and modern physics. The prestige of science has suffered somewhat in light of concerns about negative effects of technological society on the environment, the development of new classes of weapons of mass destruction, and the scientific rationales claimed as justification for various oppressions (racial theory, eugenics, Marxist "science of history"). Thus Christianity's supposed nurture of modern science has led some to condemn it as especially responsible for ecological degradation.

There are several different models that describe or prescribe the nature of the relation between science and religion, some of which have been more to the fore in particular periods or settings. Francis Bacon's view that God had written two books for humanity, a book of God's word (scripture) and a book of God's works (nature), was very popular among early scientists. This was a model of consistency and complementarity, not unlike Aquinas's view of the relation between revelation and reason. Today there are those who have some affinity with this approach. They would seek an integration, in which the two are ultimately facets of a single metaphysical or philosophical system. For many this is a horizon point of aspiration, to be reached only after much purification of the methods of both parties, not a possibility that can be extensively realized now.

In the nineteenth century many characterized the relation as one of conflict or warfare. This is most commonly a model deployed on behalf of science, assuming

> **Study Aid #236**
> Religion and Science Exercise
>
> 1. Make the best argument you can for each of the following two statements:
>   Religion provides the most encompassing description of the world in which we live and its meaning.
>   Science provides the most encompassing description of the world in which we live and its meaning.
>   In your argument for each, make the case as if you believed it, even though they are contradictory. For each statement, indicate which authorities, both ancient and modern, you would cite to defend your argument.
> 2. Write your own statement of how you think religion and science relate to one another and to the world in our day and age.
> 3. How might a Christian statement of the relationship between religion and science compare and contrast with some other religion's statement(s)?

that religion simply offers alternative answers to the same questions science addresses, answers that are progressively falsified or rendered superfluous by science. Thus the war is a series of relentless advances by science and rearguard actions by religion. This model was particularly supported by those who sought to emancipate education from religious connections, and it is revived today by the so-called new atheists, who generally claim science as a central ground for their attack on religion. But the model can also be propagated by zealous religious devotees who see science as undermining specific necessary beliefs or expressing a spiritual hubris.

Other models characterize the relation as much more tangential. Science and religion may be said to deal with incommensurate subjects, for instance a physical world and its causes and effects on one hand and a moral work of ethical convictions on the other. This was the argument of Stephen Jay Gould, summarized in his description of "nonoverlapping magisteria." Religion and science cannot conflict because, though appearances may sometimes be to the contrary, they refer to different things. As Galileo is said to have remarked, "The Bible shows the way to go to heaven, not the way the heavens go." Some view the relation as a dialogical one. While the two may be different enough that their views can never be entirely contained in the same plane, still they are intertwined to the extent that specific elements of one can be relevant for particular concerns in the other. Rather than the careful fencing of each other's turf (the incommensurability model), or opposition (the conflict model), or unity (the complementarity model), the dialogical model sees a looser resonance between the two perspectives where each is informed by the other but need not be conformed to it.

All of the models we have reviewed treat science and religion as two fixed parties. This is at best highly schematic. The variety of religions is obvious. The singular noun for "science" suggests a fixed reference point. But when we think of science, there are three different kinds of thing we may have in mind. The first is the sum content of current scientific knowledge and theory in all relevant disciplines: science as information. The relation of religion and science has to do with the relation between religious convictions and the current results of scientific study. Efforts of monotheistic traditions to relate their beliefs in creation with the biological theory of evolution would be an example. So would be the efforts of biogenetic researchers to explain and justify their work with stem cells and human embryos to a wider public in a way that can connect scientific procedures with religiously grounded cultural views of human integrity and creation.

The second way of thinking of science is the history of science (in which the data set of current scientific knowledge stands as only the latest momentary cross-section): science as movement. There have been many sciences (Ptolemaic, Newtonian, Einsteinian). On this count, the relation of religion and science is an ongoing story, with the interaction varying from one faith tradition to another and from one period to another within the same tradition. The broad argument we have just noted over the religious role in scientific development (or in reference to a specific incident like the trial of Galileo) would be an example, as would be Thomas Kuhn's work on the social conditions for scientific revolutions. Even in the relatively short history of modern science, the content of the assured scientific knowledge that religion addressed has changed, often in quite dramatic ways. The dialogue has changed accordingly. Prior to Charles Darwin, biology was commonly regarded as the scientific discipline most congenial to the incorporation of religious interpretation or to use for religious apologetic. William Paley's *Natural Theology* was a textbook that spanned both perspectives. It was Newtonian physics, with its explanations of terrestrial and cosmic motions under a single set of laws, that seemed to challenge the need for divine action. By the twentieth century, this situation changed radically, and cosmological physics became in many ways a more favored site for dialogue, by virtue of acceptance of the big bang theory of the origin of the universe and the "fine-tuning" of various constants that allow a complex universe. Biology, on the other hand, became the ground for intense debate regarding evolution.

The third meaning of science is the philosophy of science, reflection on the distinctively scientific way of knowing: science as method. The unity of science rests upon the claim that there is a common methodology across all the relevant disciplines and upon the presumption that the results of the various disciplines are ultimately consistent and mutually translatable. That is, physiological processes described in biological terms could in principle be translated into a compatible description in terms of molecular chemistry, and that description into one in terms of basic physics. In addition, it is sometimes urged that mathematics is the common language of the sciences. Scientific disciplines exhibit extraordinary capacities to generate agreement about proper conclusions across practitioners of varied cultural and religious backgrounds, and they regularly demonstrate the ability to confirm those conclusions with accurate predictions and technological achievements. These qualities are truly remarkable—to the extent that they come to constitute a paradigm of what counts as true knowledge in our contemporary cultures—and they require religious recognition and understanding.

The philosophy of science does not focus on the specific results of scientific investigation but on the practices that (theoretically) distinguish it from other human endeavors. In this perspective, the relation of religion and science is analytical. It depends on how one chooses to characterize the ways of knowing in each field. Are these separate and opposed: faith versus reason, tradition versus experiment, mystical versus mathematical? Or are they overlapping and complementary? Examples in this connection would be the contentions of most philosophers of science that common textbook presentations of scientific method do not adequately describe actual scientific practice and minimize intuitive and evaluative factors, particularly in regard to scientific discovery. Science is in fact a wide spread of distinct and specialized disciplines. No one is a "scientist" in general, any more than someone is religious in general. Philosophy of science indicates that the idea of a single universal scientific method is highly problematic, and many scientists contend that there are emergent properties treated in one discipline (such as chemistry) that are not in principle reducible to descriptions given in another (such as physics). From the religious side, examples would be arguments over whether Christian theology ought to aspire to share a method with science, or over whether Buddhist catalogs of meditative practices and outcomes are to be regarded as the same as experimental data.

In the United States the legal and political issues of the relation of religion and science are mainly dealt with in this arena. In court cases bearing on teaching about creationism or intelligent design in public schools, the focus falls on methodology. Without going to the point of which view is true, the courts feel competent to define what is science and what is not, and hence what belongs in a science classroom. A similar discussion surrounds the place of religious studies in university curricula, and the extent to which such study can involve teaching or study from a religious viewpoint.

If we focus on the informational content of science, there are three main arenas in which religion and science engage. The first we may call analytical, in which science describes what is the case about the composition of the world and its replicable functions. So, for instance, over time science has refined its understanding of nature as composed of different types of matter with varying properties, which are formed by combinations of a set number of elements (enumerated in the periodic table), each element having certain chemical properties determined by variations in their atomic structure. Those variations in atomic structure have to do with subatomic constituents (such as electrons) whose nature and activities are understood through the mysterious properties of quantum phenomena that underlie them. This analytical exploration has taken science into realms of the unimaginably large (galaxies and the scope of the entire universe) and the unimaginably small (the subatomic).

The second arena of relation is a narrative one. It is important to note that this dimension was not a premise of most earlier science, which understood timeless analytical understanding, verified by experimental repetition, as the necessary standard for any scientific discipline. If many theories make replication of results a hallmark of scientific method, certain branches of science press this limit. Evolutionary biology and cosmological physics are two prominent examples. In the first case, analytical exploration of the nature of living things suggested a time component to explanatory understanding. To comprehend how organisms were composed and functioned appeared to require attention to their history as a species. For example, the protein structure of DNA in organisms is crucial to understanding how processes within the organism work. But that structure's particular role in the reproductive process, as genes are passed on, also suggested an explanation for changes in the function of one organism as opposed to another (why one person is a hemophiliac and another is not, for instance). In the second case, scientific investigation into the very small (the quantum world) and the very large (the universe) produced a very unexpected convergence. Looking out into space, it was discovered, was actually looking back in time. This was not only true because light from distant objects takes time to reach us and thus what we see was the case long ago. It was also true because the various parts of the universe were receding from each other, part of a directional motion picture of a kind of explosion that could by inference be run backward toward an earlier time when all the receding components of the universe were located at a common point. The closer that one approached that time and place, the more the behavior of the universe corresponded to the behavior that we otherwise find only in the strange quantum world of extremely small subatomic phenomena that underlie everyday matter. In these ways, time became a central category of science. Einstein's incorporation of time into physics with the integration of space and time was reflective of this. Within the narrative stream, four points stand out as of special religious interest, points where science and religion frequently engage. These would be the origin of the universe itself, the origin of life, the origin of biological species, and the origin of humanity.

The third arena we may call the human. It is not cleanly distinct from the first two, since the human must be treated within the scope of matter and biological development. But it stands out because it focuses, on the one hand, on the central focus of religious concern and, on the other hand, reflexively on the scientist as the subject of science. Cognitive science, neurological research, and evolutionary psychology are all attempts to understand the function and limit of the very mental equipment that performs religious response and scientific investigation themselves. What is at issue are human capabilities such as free will, altruism, love, objectivity. Questions that once belonged exclusively to philosophy or religion—What is the nature of consciousness? Does mind exercise causative power on the body, or are its contents entirely determined by prior physical events?—can increasingly be discussed only with attention to scientific studies as well, or even regarded as issues entirely within the purview of science.

The pluralism of religions means that the points of particular reinforcement or friction in relation with science will vary somewhat by tradition. Biblical traditions hold a belief in creation that requires some integration of scriptural accounts of divine creativity with scientific explanations of the origin of the universe and the origin of humanity. A purely materialist science is incompatible with fundamental Christian, Muslim, or Jewish convictions. By contrast, questions of the origin of the universe or humanity are minimally important for Buddhism. But analytical understanding of human brain function is of crucial relevance to Buddhist understandings of mind and the mind's relation to phenomena. Materialistic naturalism is unacceptable to Buddhists not because of its threat to the existence of God or a soul (neither of which Buddhism affirms) but because of its rejection of the mutual conditioning of mind and body—particularly the power of mind—that lies at the heart of the Buddhist solution to suffering. In keeping with these divergent emphases, evolutionary biology and cosmological physics receive a great deal of attention from many Christian (and anti-Christian) writers, while neuroscience and cognitive science are areas of special emphasis for Buddhists.

The rapid pace of scientific development indicates that the relation of religion and science will continue to be an issue of great importance, both theoretically and practically. The history of that relation suggests that though major themes we have identified will remain crucial, the interaction will be shaped in the future as it has been in the past by unexpected scientific advancements that realign the forms of the arguments.

Further Reading

Aristotle. *Metaphysics*. Penguin, 1999.
Ian Barbour. *Religion in an Age of Science*. HarperCollins, 1990.
Charles Darwin. *On the Origin of the Species*. Dover, 2006.
Richard Dawkins. *The Blind Watchmaker*. Norton, 1996.
René Descartes. *Meditations*. Penguin, 1999.
Stephen Hawking. *A Brief History of Time*. Bantam, 1998.
Phillip Johnson. *Darwin on Trial*. InterVarsity, 1991.
Thomas Kuhn. *The Structure of Scientific Revolutions*. Chicago, 1962.
C. S. Lewis. *Miracles*. HarperSanFrancisco, 2001.
Lucretius. *On the Nature of Things*. Penguin, 2007.
Nancey Murphy, ed. *Whatever Happened to the Soul?* Fortress, 1998.
John Polkinghorne. *Theology in the Context of Science*. Yale University Press, 2010.

129

Religion and Gender

Ursula King

Religion and gender are highly complex areas of human experience, and the precise meaning of "gender" is much debated. "Gender" is often used as a synonym for women, but this is misleading since gender concerns men as well as women and relates to their respective identities, subjectivities, and social relations, as well as to the unequal power structures that exist between the two genders.

Gender is so often connected with women especially for two reasons: (1) Gender studies originally developed out of women's and feminist studies, and they draw extensively on critical feminist scholarship. (2) Gender studies remain at present still more concerned with women than men because of the urgent need to overcome the deeply entrenched marginalization and oppression of women in history, society, and culture, including their roles and images in different religions.

Inspired by the development of women's and feminist studies, a growing movement of men's studies, including men's studies in religion, has also come into existence in recent years. This still possesses less momentum and urgency than women's studies regarding the need for fundamental social, political, and religious changes, given the almost universal dominance of males in different world religions and cultures. Men's studies in religion have already produced considerable research on religion and masculinities, on male sexuality and spirituality, on male identities, and on gender-sensitive understandings of God and divinities, but there is still a long way to go before developments in this field will catch up with women's and gender studies in religion.

Gender-critical thinking does not occur "naturally" or spontaneously; it involves a decisive effort in developing perceptive discernment and critical thought. Whereas sex is usually understood in binary terms as two mutually exclusive categories of male and female closely aligned with biological differences, the idea of gender is used in association with difference and diversity, in terms of multiple, rather than single, versions of femininities and masculinities that call into question general claims about women and men.

Gender thinking therefore requires what has been described as "making the gender-critical turn," which has to be acquired and learned by intentionally developing a new analytical and critical awareness. This involves a profound transformation of consciousness, but also of all knowledge, scholarship, and social and religious practices. The consciousness of individuals and society must arrive at this gender-critical turn before the perspectives and dynamic of gender relations can be fully perceived and evaluated for what they are.

The complex controversies around the meaning of both religion and gender prove that these are not only academic matters but also issues that involve personal commitment and fundamental choices about the nature of one's life and one's religion. Applying a critical gender perspective to everything one does requires a profound transformation of one's worldview and a radical paradigm shift in one's thinking and action.

Religion and gender are not simply two parallel categories that function independently; they are mutually embedded within each other in all religions. It is because of this deep hidden embeddedness that gender is sometimes so difficult to identify and separate out from other aspects of religion until one has been consciously trained to do so. Making a gender-critical turn involves the recognition that religions have created, enforced, and legitimated gender, but sometimes also transformed and liberated it. It is because of this complex mutual interrelationship that the topic of religion and gender provides such a fascinating object of study.

I will first discuss some gender perspectives that can be applied to all religions, and then provide some examples to illustrate the new insights gained from applying gender thinking to different religions.

General Issues

Many religious teachings and practices—especially scriptural statements, religious rites, beliefs, theological doctrines, institutional offices, and authority structures—are closely intertwined with and patterned by gender differences, even when gender remains officially unacknowledged and is deemed invisible, at least for untrained eyes. The existing social and religious arrangements are considered "natural" or normatively prescribed by sacred scriptures or other religious teachings, handed down from the ancestors or "God-given," and thus unalterable. It is only since the Enlightenment that such attitudes have been generally called into question and that intellectual and social changes, greatly facilitated through new means of communication, have been immensely accelerated and have taken on an increasingly collective and now global character.

Critical gender studies in religion have conclusively demonstrated that there are no gender-neutral phenomena. Everything is subtly, and often invisibly, patterned by a gender dynamic operating in language, thought, experience, and institutions. Traditional, religiously defined, and socially prescribed gender roles, if rigidly enforced, can become dehumanizing prisons, even though anthropological, historical, and comparative studies provide overwhelming evidence that gender roles are also remarkably fluid across different religions and cultures.

The impact of gender analysis, coupled with an ethical commitment to gender justice, will lead to a deconstruction as well as a reconstruction of religious traditions and practices. At present this process has barely begun, and setbacks are unavoidable. More inclusive, critical "gender thinking" will dislocate individual and social identities, including those relating to religion. It will create the possibility for new social arrangements and new religious developments across the globe.

Religious beliefs, thoughts, and practices are not only profoundly patriarchal but often also thoroughly "androcentric" (male-centered) through being predominantly shaped by male perspectives and experiences. These have been one-sidedly equated with all human experience and were accepted as universal norm by men and women alike, without giving full and equal recognition to women's knowledge and experience.

A critical analysis of religious phenomena, histories, and texts in terms of their specific "lenses of gender" provides some intriguing perspectives. These relate to external and internal aspects of religion; they reveal the interstructured dynamics of power, both institutional and personal, of authority and gendered hierarchies that have shaped religious life throughout human history. Without claiming to be exhaustive, I suggest three major perspectives that can help us to discern the gendered patterns of religion.

The first perspective inquires, What are the status and roles of women in specific religions in comparison with those of men? What access do women have to equal participation in religious life, to religious authority and leadership? Have women formed their own religious communities and created rites of their own? Do they have the authority to teach and interpret foundational texts and central practices of their tradition? What religious roles have women taken on as healers, priestesses, saints, mystics, founders, and leaders of religious groups, for example?

Comparative historical studies have shown that women generally hold higher positions in archaic, tribal, and noninstitutionalized religions than in highly differentiated religious traditions with complex structures and hierarchical organizations that have evolved over a long time. Women magicians, shamans, visionaries, prophetesses, and priestesses are found in primal and ancient religions, in tribal and folk religions, and in some new religious movements today. During the early, formative period of a religion, women often play a leading role; they may be closely associated with the work of a religious founder or even found a new religious group themselves. Subsequently they are often relegated to the background, lose much of their independent agency, or their work is taken over by men. This can be seen among the women in early Buddhism, in the Jesus movement and early Christianity, among the women associated with Muhammad's work, or with nineteenth-century Christian missionary movements.

The second perspective moves to the more difficult area of religious language and thought by asking, What are the images and symbols associated with women in religious writings, sacred scriptures, and religious thought? How are female images connected with teachings on creation and salvation, or with the understanding of sin and evil? Do religious traditions project images of women that are as strong and powerful as those of men? Or does their language remain exclusive and androcentric, disempowering women and emphasizing their dependence and subordination? Do particular religions possess the symbolic resources to support the full equality and partnership of women and men in our twenty-first-century society? What are the gendered symbols of the sacred? What metaphors are drawn upon in speaking about ultimate reality or the disclosure of the spirit?

The gendered language of religion is equally inscribed in religious attitudes to body, sexuality, and spirituality. The sacralization of virginity and the development of asceticism and monasticism have produced profoundly misogynist views in different religions, but the history of their influence still remains to be written. The narrow prison of traditional gender symbols reflects historically and socially located human perceptions of immanence and transcendence. Androcentric images of the divine have been recognized as symbols of power and oppression for many women. The desire for a feminine divine is strong, and many women and men are attracted to ancient figures of the Goddess and other female expressions of the divine.

The third perspective focuses on religious experience and thus relates more to the internal, personal aspects of religion than to its external manifestations. How far are religious experiences differently engendered? What is women's spiritual experience? How far do women's spiritual autobiographies or the writings left by female saints and the mystics of different religions testify to women's spiritual agency, autonomy, and authority? How far are their language and images different from those used by men? How far do women mystics express a mysticism of love rather than a mysticism of being? What is women's spiritual heritage, and to what extent does it reflect their spiritual equality?

How far have women's religious and mystical experiences been differently articulated, with distinct metaphors, concepts, and genres of their own, without their accounts being part of the official historiographies of religious institutions or of the systematic articulations of faith found in theological and philosophical traditions of learning? There is the additional question of how far most religions validate mainly the ordinary lives of women with their domestic and family duties focused on immediacy and immanence. How far have they encouraged women to have a spiritual space of their own and seek nonordinary paths of spiritual devotion and freedom, a religious quest that reaches for transcendence? The comparative study of female and male mystics from a perspective of gender differences is only in its infancy, but it raises some fundamental questions, not least for contemporary religious practice and for the understanding of spirituality by both genders.

Spirituality is often discussed in such general terms that no attention is given to either women or gender differences. As in most other areas of life, men have usually defined what counts as spirituality, who can practice and teach it, who holds spiritual authority, and what the spiritual life is all about. And this has had a deep impact on the spiritual lives of women.

Although ultimately gender-transcendent, spiritual ideals are far from gender-neutral. They are shaped by deeply embedded patriarchal structures and androcentric thought that has affected all traditional spiritual practices and teachings. On first encounter, spiritual advice appears to be quite neutral and seems to refer to apparently asexual beings of no specific gender. But on closer examination such advice frequently turns out to be antibody, antiwoman, and antiworld.

Our understanding of God, of ultimate reality in whatever form, and of ourselves as persons is deeply interconnected. Since we are always embodied selves patterned by different genders, male and female approaches to spirituality have been profoundly influenced by their respective human embodiments.

Many traditional stereotypes continue to influence people's attitudes when thinking about spirituality. Most pervasive are the customary associations with masculinity and femininity that are still deeply rooted in Western culture. Masculinity is often perceived to be linked to reason, transcendence, and divinity, whereas femininity is associated with body, immanence, and humanity. Such stereotypical associations provide some, though not all, explanations for why women were often deemed unable to reach the exalted, transcendent heights of the spirit. This is true not only true in Christianity and Judaism but also in other religions such as Buddhism and Jainism. The widespread perception that women are inferior to men, characteristic of so many religious teachings, has meant for a long time that women were excluded from the realms of spiritual authority and from the spiritual hierarchies of established religious institutions.

Christian feminists have strongly critiqued traditional Christian spirituality because of its institutional control by the church, its hierarchical and dualistic models of spirituality, and the hiddenness and repression of women's spirituality. Feminist spiritualities, by contrast, seek a recovery of the body, of eros and the material realm, a strong emphasis on relationality and interconnectedness, an orientation toward justice, and deep reverence for the sacredness of life.

Feminist spirituality is rooted in women's experience and oriented toward bonding among women; it creates an ever-larger web of relations that connects with others, the cosmos, and the divine. It believes in the inherent goodness of matter, body, and the world, thrives on ecological sensitivity, and reimages God and divine-human relations. It has created new rituals and liturgies, drawn from Wicca and folk traditions celebrating especially life and nature cycles, but it is also based on the imaginative reinterpretation of traditional religious rites and texts.

Religions have frequently assigned women to a position of inferiority and subjugation. Within Christianity it is only in the modern period that the biblical teaching about both man and woman being created in the image of God, each representing the *imago Dei*, has been interpreted in a truly egalitarian sense that affirms equality and partnership. This important teaching, linked to the recognition of the full humanity of women, had a considerable influence on the first wave of the women's movement in the mid-nineteenth century, and on some feminist thinking ever since.

A close study of the interpretation of the Bible reveals a profound ambivalence regarding the relationship of men and women, due to texts that express on one hand the subordination of women and on the other their equality with men. Male interpreters have given more emphasis to the subordination texts than to those proclaiming the equality of both sexes, so that Christian biblical interpretation has been rightly characterized as "a masculinizing exegesis." But this tendency is found in many religious traditions, as is evident from the texts gathered in Serinity Young's *Anthology of Sacred Texts by and about Women* (1994), as also from many articles in her two-volume *Encyclopedia of Women and World Religion* (1999).

Gendering the Spirit: Global Transformations

Contemporary women's involvement with spirituality has truly prophetic and radical features. The whole modern women's movement has sometimes been described as a spiritual revolution. The development of women's spirituality took off in a big way in the last decades of the twentieth century, but women's interest in spirituality goes back to the first phase of the modern women's movement in the nineteenth century. At that time women not only worked to change their social, legal, and political position but also strove to take a more active part in the religions to which they belonged. Religious motivation and spiritual aims played an important part in the lives of many early women campaigners for social and legal reforms. This is evident from the biographies of such well-known figures as Mary Wollstonecraft, Florence Nightingale, Elizabeth Cady Stanton, and Matilda Jocelyn Gage. Historians of the modern women's movement have only recently begun to pay closer attention to the many religious elements and spiritual ideals drawn from Christianity that helped to shape the thinking and actions of these and other women reformers.

An interesting example is provided by the first-ever interfaith event, the celebrated 1893 World's Parliament of Religions, held in Chicago. Often mentioned in interfaith dialogue circles today, the considerable presence of women participants and their contribution to this event is far less often acknowledged. It was mainly Jewish and Christian women from the liberal Protestant traditions (but not from among Catholics) who took part in this first ecumenical assembly of faiths in world history. Significant women leaders were involved in the organization of the

> **Study Aid #237**
>
> Religion and Gender Exercise
>
> 1. Using gender-critical thinking (that is, thinking that sees through the lens of men's and women's descriptions and roles), describe what you believe to be the gendered pattern of Christianity. Divide your gender analysis into four sections.
>   Compare ideal women's roles described in Christianity with the ideal men's roles.
>   What images, symbols, and language are commonly used for women?
>   What images, symbols, and language are commonly used for men?
>   Compare and contrast women's spiritual experiences with men's spiritual experiences.
> 2. Using gender-critical thinking, describe what you believe to be the gendered pattern of a religion other than Christianity. Divide your gender analysis into four sections.
>   Compare ideal women's roles described in this religion with the ideal men's roles.
>   What images, symbols, and language are commonly used for women?
>   What images, symbols, and language are commonly used for men?
>   Compare and contrast women's spiritual experiences with men's spiritual experiences.

parliament and spoke at its opening and closing ceremonies, so that the parliament was rightly claimed as a breakthrough for women in religion. Their hopes were high in forecasting the equal participation of women in religious offices and institutions. Sadly, this remains a goal not yet reached in our own time, over a hundred years later.

The creative tensions that exist in the field of religion, spirituality, and gender, and the new spiritual ideas, rituals, and practices that are emerging out of the women's and men's movement in religion, bear witness to much zest, energy, and fresh religious creativity. This process of transformation is happening not only in the West but also globally. Instead of being defined and confined by traditional religious teachings, women are now taking more and more part in helping to redefine religion and spirituality everywhere. This is true of Christian, Jewish, or secular women not only from Europe and North America but also from around the whole world. The Pakistani scholar Durre S. Ahmed has forged the brilliant expression "gendering the Spirit" for this transformation. Her book of this title brings together a collection of essays on women's alternative approaches to Buddhism, Hinduism, Islam, and Catholicism in South Asia. It provides plenty of evidence that there is a "silent revolution" going on among women of faith around the world, so far little noticed among outsiders.

For women's full participation in all aspects of religion and spirituality, it is essential that women are as fully trained and qualified in their intellectual and spiritual attainments as men. This was already recognized at the 1893 Chicago World's Parliament of Religions, whose speakers stressed not only the new opportunities for women in religion, but also the need to study the sacred languages and scriptures for themselves. Since that remarkable event over a century ago, an ever-growing number of highly educated Jewish women rabbis, Christian women ministers, and female theology and religion scholars are playing their part in shaping contemporary religious practice and scholarship in the West.

Similar developments can now be observed in Hinduism, Buddhism, Islam, Sikhism, and other religions in Asia, Africa, and elsewhere in the world. Women around the globe are fast acquiring both scholarly and spiritual competencies; they are gaining new knowledge, agency, authority, and public visibility, sometimes only reluctantly acknowledged or even strongly resisted within their own communities. Contemporary Muslim, Buddhist, Hindu, and many other women who have acquired a critical gender awareness often also possess an activist inclination to work for change in their own communities and in wider society. This transformative process can only happen when women gain full access to literacy and education at all levels. With regard to the religious heritage, this means the ability not only to read and write but also to understand and interpret religious thought; to offer spiritual advice with discernment, authority, and wisdom; and to acquire full "spiritual literacy."

A surprising cross-cultural development is the discovery of the global spiritual heritage of women. So many spiritual "foremothers," female saints, mystics, and women's religious communities and practices are now being discovered that our knowledge about women in world religions has greatly increased in recent years. A comparative historical inquiry provides much evidence, though, that most religions have validated women's lives more in terms of domestic observances and family duties than they have encouraged women's search for religious enlightenment, holiness, or liberation.

In spite of numerous social obstacles and interdictions from families, friends, and religious authorities, many women of different religions have struggled throughout history to pursue a spiritual path of their own. The comparative history of Jain, Buddhist, and Christian nuns, which still remains to be written, provides ample proof of women following extraordinary paths of spiritual devotion and attainment. Women often had the greatest difficulties in rejecting their prescribed social roles as wives and mothers by following a path of renunciation and asceticism, and creating their own religious communities. Since there has been widespread male resistance to female claims to autonomy, independent power, and spiritual authority, women's activities remained in most cases constrained and controlled by male religious hierarchies, and this is still mostly the case today. Nowhere is this struggle more evident than in the richly documented history of Christian nuns and sisters, in whose cloisters and convents appeared countless women scholars, mystics, artists, activists, healers, and teachers over many centuries of Western history.

One of the most striking examples of the innovative process of "gendering the spirit" is Sakyadhita, the global women's movement for Buddhist nuns and laywomen inaugurated in 1987 in Bodhgaya, India. Its aims include the creation of a global network of communication among Buddhist women, the education of women as teachers of Buddhism, research on Buddhist women, and the full ordination of Buddhist nuns. So far, Sakyadhita has organized eight international conferences in different Asian countries. Much effort goes into education and the reinterpretation of texts, but also into reforming unjust, nonegalitarian practices and the development of a socially engaged Buddhism, where the issues for Buddhist women in Asia are different from those of Buddhist women in the West.

The experiences of Buddhist nuns have rarely been recorded in Buddhist texts, nor have they been much investigated by scholars. This is changing now that Buddhist women have organized themselves to study their own history and activities, as can be seen from publications such as *Innovative Buddhist Women: Swimming against the Stream* (Tsomo 2000). The contemporary controversy over the higher ordination of Buddhist nuns in Theravada countries well illustrates how women from one major non-Western religious tradition are pressing for spiritual and practical equality in their religion.

Women's asceticism, based on traditional spiritual practices and the reinterpretation of religious traditions within a modern, postcolonial context, has become a fascinating focus for the investigation of women scholars. In Hinduism, for example, contemporary women's ashrams, ascetics, gurus, and new religious communities provide important examples of female initiative and spiritual agency in appropriating traditional Hindu religious practices while reinterpreting and transforming them in the context of modernity and postmodernity. The profound ambivalence of Indian women's spiritual resources is evident from the contradictory ways in which these are used by Hindu women reformers on one hand and the Indian secular feminist movement or extreme Hindu fundamentalists on the other. The same goddesses, practices, and beliefs can become sources of agency, empowerment, and resistance or, by contrast, can be used to further enforce gender divisions, traditional social roles, and malpractices.

Much has been written on Islam and gender, especially by secular feminists, but the complex attitudes held toward the rereading of classical religious texts and their ambiguities among secular, Muslim, and Islamist feminists in different Islamic countries are probably less well known. All groups seem to agree that women's greatest challenge in Islam is their lack of religious expertise and training. An exceptional counterexample is provided by Indonesia, with the largest Muslim population in the world, where thousands of institutions train both women and men as specialists in Islamic knowledge. Women can move into positions of religious authority by becoming scholars of Islam and judges. By rereading the Qur'an, Indonesian Muslim women leaders are thus "shaping Islam" and utilizing its resources as a significant force for social change.

The impact of gender thinking on women in the Muslim world expresses itself not only in social, legal, and educational developments but also in the area of spirituality. Depending on the sociohistorical context of different countries and cultures, Muslim women are actively involved to different degrees in reinterpreting Islamic thought and practices and thereby claiming more mosque space for themselves. It is little known, however, that separate women's mosques have existed in central China for several hundred years, whereas Muslim women in the United States and in Britain have recently organized prayer meetings led by women and have demonstrated to gain more access to mosque space, although they have met considerable opposition. It is clear, though, that Muslim women, like women of other faiths, will go on working toward achieving greater gender equality in the practice of their religion.

At present, it is still too early to predict what the future impact of a radical rearrangement of gender relations will be on existing religious traditions. It may well be that the space and flexibility for constructive gender renegotiations and for the symbolic reordering of religious beliefs will vary widely between different religions. But there can be no doubt that gender thinking is now a global development that affects religions and spiritualities worldwide, revealing the reciprocal embeddedness of religion, spirituality, and gender.

Further Reading

Durre S. Ahmed, ed. *Gendering the Spirit*. Zed, 2002.

Leila Ahmed. *Women and Gender in Islam*. Yale University Press, 1992.

Stephen B. Boyd, W. Merle Longwood, and Mark W. Muesse, eds. *Redeeming Men: Religion and Masculinities*. Westminster John Knox, 1996.

Paula M. Cooey, William R. Eakin, and Jay B. McDaniel, eds. *After Patriarchy: Feminist Transformations of the World Religions*. Orbis Books, 1991.

Lynn Teskey Denton. *Female Ascetics in Hinduism*. SUNY Press, 2004.

Nancy Falk and Rita Gross, eds. *Unspoken Worlds*. Wadsworth, 2001.

John Stratton Hawley, ed. *Fundamentalism and Gender*. Oxford University Press, 1994.

Ursula King. "Religion and Gender: Embedded Patterns, Interwoven Frameworks." In *A Companion to Gender History*, edited by Teresa A. Meade and Merry E. Wiesner-Hanks, 70–85. Blackwell, 2004.

Ursula King and Tina Beattie, eds. *Gender, Religion and Diversity*. Continuum, 2004.

Asra Nomani. *Standing Alone in Mecca*. HarperSanFrancisco, 2005.

Karma Lekshe Tsomo, ed. *Innovative Buddhist Women*. Curzon, 2000.

Pieternella Van Doorn-Harder. *Women Shaping Islam*. University of Illinois Press, 2006.

Serinity Young, ed. *Anthology of Sacred Texts by and about Women*. Crossroad, 1994.

130

Religion and the Environment

SANDRA L. RICHTER

In its power to shape the value systems and ethical boundaries of human behavior, religion has always played a role in the discussion of environmental ethics. Generations of commentators have linked their sacred texts to particular, mandated actions toward the land, its flora, and its fauna. This is particularly apparent in the history of biblical interpretation. But since the days of Lynn White's epoch-defining article "The Historical Roots of our Ecological Crisis" (White 1967), the verdict regarding the impact of the Judeo-Christian tradition upon Western society's environmental ethic has been less than positive. Rather, White's diagnosis of Christianity as "the most anthropocentric religion the world has seen," and his conclusion that Christianity therefore "bears a huge burden of guilt" for the philosophical and ethical framework that has fueled the modern technological exploitation of nature, has been echoed by many.

But as Robert Gottlieb states in his introduction to an important anthology on the topic, "Religions have been neither simple agents of environmental domination nor unmixed repositories of ecological wisdom. In complex and variable ways, they have been both" (Gottlieb 1996, 9). Moreover, Thomas Sieger Derr's point is well taken that the abuse of this planet is unique to neither Eastern nor Western, preindustrial nor industrial, third- nor first-world societies. Rather, "it is simpler and surely more accurate to say that human self-seeking is a constant in our natures, and that no culture, no matter what its religion, has managed successfully to eliminate it" (Derr et al. 1996, 20–21).

Ecotheology

With the burgeoning awareness of environmental crisis in contemporary society, theological reflection upon humanity's relationship with the earth has expanded significantly. For Christians this has involved the quest for some precedent in the history of Christian commentary that would speak to the current threat. David Kinsley's work is particularly helpful here in that he surveys Christian theologians throughout the ages, identifying their work as either "ecologically harmful" or "ecologically responsible." Irenaeus, Augustine, and most expressly St. Francis of Assisi are named as having laid the foundations for a sound Christian environmental ethic (Kinsley 1994, 103–23). Daniel Swartz offers a similar survey of early Jewish commentary, characterizing the Mishnah and Talmud as unequivocally affirming that "God owns everything in the world; we are but tenants in the garden, meant to till and to tend, to serve and to guard" (Swartz 1994, 90). And although the Middle Ages witnessed the thorough urbanization of the Jewish community, Swartz affirms that the writings of the rabbis continued to celebrate the beauty of nature, humanity's responsibility to protect it, and the virtue of moderate consumption.

In the modern era, Walter C. Lowdermilk (1940, 12–15), Joseph Sittler (1954, 367–74), and Richard Baer Jr. (1966, 1239–41) served as early prophetic voices of the ecotheology movement. Thomas Seiger Derr (*Ecology and Human Need*, 1973 and 1975), Paul Santmire (*The Travail of Nature*, 1985), and Roderick Nash (*The Rights of Nature: A History of Environmental Ethics*, 1989) provide a survey of the proliferation of voices since the environmental movement of the 1960s and '70s. Additional points of entry into the contemporary discussion include *Ecotheology: The Journal of Religion, Nature and the Environment*; the Evangelical Environmental Network and its journal *Creation Care*; Roger S. Gottlieb, *A Greener Faith: Religious Environmentalism and Our Planet's Future* (2006); Matthew Sleeth, *Serve God, Save the Planet* (2006); Jon Isaak, ed., *The Old Testament in the Life of God's People: Essays in Honor of Elmer A. Martens* (2009); and Ellen Davis, *Scripture, Culture, and Agriculture: An Agrarian Reading of the Bible* (2009). The foci of these contemporary, Christian ecotheologians tend toward two broadly defined headings: (1) theologians committed to biotic rights—a morality that affirms nature's membership in God's world and thereby attributes to it ethical rights, and (2) those seeking an answer to the environmental crisis by a reconsideration of humanity's role as steward.

Ecotheology in the Bible: The Old Testament

The message of environmental ethics may be located first in the creation narratives. In Genesis 1, God announces his plan for the cosmos: an interdependent biosphere described in terms of a perfect "week." On the seventh day of this week, God is enthroned over his creation, communicating God's complete satisfaction with all that has gone before, as well as creation's ongoing dependence on the sovereignty of the Creator. The penultimate climax of the piece is the sixth day, on which a steward is enthroned, under the Creator but over the creation.

> Then God said, "Let us make *'ādām* in our image, according to our likeness; and let them rule." (Gen. 1:26)

Here God's design is dependent upon both the sovereignty of the Creator and the participation of the Creator's stewards. These stewards are fashioned in the image of their Creator so that they might facilitate his plan. Their explicit role is specified in Genesis, chapter 2:

> Then Yahweh Elohim took the human [*'ādām*] and put him into the garden of Eden to tend it [*lĕ'obdāh*] and guard it [*lĕšomrāh*]. (Gen. 2:15)

The larger message of these accounts is clear: the garden belongs to Yahweh, but humanity has been given the privilege to rule and the responsibility to care for this garden under the sovereignty of their divine lord.

But with humanity's rebellion, the entire cosmos is cast into chaos. Humanity rebels against God (Gen. 3:6), the land rebels against humanity (Gen. 3:17–18), and the animal kingdom and humanity are transformed into predator and prey (Gen. 9:2–4).

Yet even in this "fallen" state of affairs, we find God's expectation that humanity steward God's property responsibly. Thus, the law codes of ancient Israel are replete with regulations regarding land tenure, agriculture, warfare, wild creatures, and husbandry.

Land Tenure

In the political language of the book of Deuteronomy, the land of Canaan is identified as the land grant that Yahweh promised "to Abraham, Isaac, and Jacob, to them and to their descendants after them" (Deut. 1:8; see also Deut. 4:40). Thus, throughout the books of Joshua and Judges we are told that it is Yahweh who owns the land, and the tribes of Israel are his tenants—each having been appointed to their particular patrimony according to God's good pleasure. As a result, the only legal means of permanent land transfer in Israel is inheritance (Lev. 25:8–17, 23). Moreover, Deuteronomy is expressly clear that Yahweh retains the right to reclaim his land and evict his people (Deut. 28:15–68; 29:24–28). As it was in the garden, so it is in the land of Israel. The land belongs to God, and it is humanity's conditional privilege to live upon it.

In concert with Israel's understanding that it was Yahweh who actually owned the land of Canaan, a number of laws address the longevity of the land's fertility. The core of these is the Sabbath rest—a command to humanity to regularly cease production so that the land might replenish itself.

> You shall sow your land for six years and gather in its yield, but the seventh year you shall let it rest and lie fallow, so that the needy of your people may eat; and whatever they leave the wild animal may eat. You are to do the same with your vineyard and

your olive grove. Six days you shall do your work, but on the seventh you shall rest; in order that your ox and your ass may rest, and the son of your female servant and the immigrant may be refreshed. (Exod. 23:10–12)

The sort of fallowing described here not only aided in the recovery of fertility but also broke the natural cycle of noxious plant pests and diseases. Then as now, such farming practices limited short-term yield. But they helped to ensure long-term fecundity. And then as now, long-term fecundity protected the poor. Important to the contemporary discussion is that Israel's fallow law communicated a critical ideological principle: in Israel, it was not acceptable to take from the land everything that the populace *could*. Rather, God's people were commanded to operate with the long-term well-being of Yawheh's land as their ultimate goal. They were instructed to leave enough so that the land would be able to restore itself for future harvests and future generations, even though such practices cut into short-term profits. The rationale for this perspective? "Because I am Yahweh, says your God" (Lev. 25:17), and "the land is mine" (Lev. 25:23).

Agriculture

As discussed, the Old Testament sees Israel as Yahweh's land steward. This status as a tenant on Yahweh's land is most evident in the laws of the tithe, the firstfruits, and the firstborn. In the ancient Near East a tenant was expected to reserve a portion of his harvest for his landlord, a populace was expected to pay a percentage of their produce to the central government, and a vassal kingdom was expected to pay an annual percentage of the gross national product to its suzerain. In Israel's pastoral and agricultural world this meant a percentage of their crops and flocks belonged to their divine landlord.

You shall surely tithe all the produce of your seed, that which comes forth from the field year by year. And you shall eat in the presence of Yahweh your God, in the place where he chooses to place his name—the tithe of your grain, your new wine, your oil, and the firstborn of your herd and flock—in order that you may learn to fear Yahweh your God all your life. (Deut. 14:22–23 author's translation; cf. Deut. 15:19–20; 18:3–5; Lev. 27:30–31)

One of the specifics of Israel's responsibilities as Yahweh's land steward was that the citizenry not exhaust the produce of the land in their quest for personal or national economic security. Rather, Israel was commanded to share the produce of the land with the marginalized among them. Thus, although the cereal crops of wheat and barley were the mainstays of the community, and olive oil and viticulture were essential to the domestic and commercial venues of the Israelite economy, Yahweh commands that Israel refrain from fully harvesting these dietary anchors. Instead, he requires that the farmer reserve a portion of his harvest for the orphan, the widow, and the refugee.

> When you reap your harvest in your field and have forgotten a sheaf in the field, do not go back to get it; let it be for the immigrant, for the orphan, and for the widow, in order that Yahweh your God may bless you in all the work of your hands. When you beat your olive tree, you shall not go over the boughs again; it shall be for the immigrant, for the orphan, and for the widow. When you gather the grapes of your vineyard, you shall not go over it again; it shall be for the immigrant, for the orphan, and for the widow. And you shall remember that you were a slave in the land of Egypt; therefore I am commanding you to do this thing. (Deut. 24:19–22, author's translation; cf. Lev. 19:9–10; 23:22)

Interestingly, as these gleaning laws required that a portion of the harvest remain in the field, this system also guaranteed what agriculturalists speak of as "crop residue"—the organic material necessary for the maintenance of essential humus in the soil.

Warfare

In the ancient world, the long-term value of food-bearing trees was critical to a settled economy. The reason for this is that these trees, if maintained, would produce calorie-rich, preservable, commercially valuable food for *generations*. Ancient Israel was blessed with an array of indigenous fruit- and nut-bearing trees including the fig, olive, date, apricot, almond, and others. Although highly prized, all of these trees faced the same developmental reality: full maturity preceded production. The all-important olive tree could take five or six years to *begin* to flower, and as many as twenty years to reach full productivity. The treasured female date palm took up to twenty years to begin to produce fruit. As Stager states, "It is commonly said that one plants an olive yard not for one's self but for one's grandchildren" (King and Stager 2001, 96). It is therefore no surprise that a standard aspect of wartime strategy among the Babylonians, Assyrians, Hittites, and especially the Egyptians was the decimation of a besieged enemy's vineyards and orchards. The goal was to cripple the city for decades beyond the actual assault, be that assault successful or not. And as detailed in numerous recent publications, the Assyrians habitually communicated this military objective through text and image in order to intimidate their enemies (Richter 2010, 365–68).

Yet in Deuteronomy 20:19–20 we find an interesting little law:

> When you besiege a city for many days, to make war against it in order to capture it, you shall not destroy its trees by swinging an ax against them. Indeed you may eat from them, but you shall not cut [them] down. For is the tree of the field a man that it should be besieged by you? Only a tree that you know does not produce food may you destroy and cut down, and you may build your siegeworks against the city with which you are at war until it falls. (author's translation)

What is the rationale for Deuteronomy's law? Clearly the sort of environmental terrorism described in this passage was the norm in Israel's cultural context,

> **Study Aid #238**
> Religion and the Environment Exercise
> 1. Define "ecotheology." Then (a) pick a Christian theology, ancient or modern, whose work has been "ecologically harmful" and explain why; and (b) pick a theologian, ancient or modern, whose work has been "ecologically helpful" and explain why.
> 2. Outline the Old Testament teachings and contributions to ecology related to the following three topics:
>   creation/fall
>   land/agriculture
>   animals, wild/domestic
> 3. Explain how the urbanization and post-theocratic political status of the New Testament people of God pushed the issues of creation care to the periphery. Then explain why those same issues have come back to center stage vis-à-vis creation care in this century.

and historically it had proved itself highly effective. Yet Israel is forbidden from the practices of their neighbors. Apparently, although such military strategies might deliver instant results, the long-term detrimental effects on one's own or the enemy's life support systems were ultimately self-destructive. In Israel, even in the midst of the crisis of warfare, human enterprise was not a worthy excuse for wiping out the future productivity of the land.

Wild Creatures

And what of the creatures that inhabited the land with God's people? Throughout the Old Testament we read that even in a fallen world, God rejoices in the beauty and balance of his creation. Moreover, God has designed the created order so that his wild creatures will have the food, water, and habitat they need to survive and prosper. It is Yahweh who "sent out the wild donkey free" and "gave to him the wilderness for a home"; it is by his command that the eagle nests in the high country (Job 39:5–6, 26–27). In the flood narrative, although God judges humanity because of its corruption, he rescues animal-kind along with Noah's family, and his re-creational covenant is with "every living creature" (Gen. 9:10). Psalm 104 states that God is the one "who sends forth the springs into the wadis; between the mountains they flow; giving drink to each of his wild creatures" (vv. 10–11 author's translation). The *politeia* of ancient Israel reinforces this value system.

In concert with Deuteronomy 20:19–20—the sparing of the fruit trees during siege warfare—a common idea is communicated: if Israel were to take both tree and fruit, mother and offspring, the means of life would be exterminated. This law is, once again, in contrast to the practice of Israel's neighbors. For in Assyria seizing the mother *with* her young was apparently a mark of royal prowess, celebrated iconographically alongside the royal slaughter of wild (but caged!) lions

(Richter 2010, 368–71). Hence in contrast to the practice of the larger culture, the citizenry of the kingdom of God is instructed in the wisdom of preserving the creatures with whom they shared the promised land.

Animal Husbandry

Regarding the treatment of domestic animals, the Sabbath ordinance again applies.

> But the seventh day is a sabbath belonging to Yahweh your God; you shall not do any work, not you or your son or your daughter or your male servant or your female servant or your ox or your donkey or any of your domesticated beasts. . . . And remember that you were a slave in the land of Egypt, and that Yahweh your God brought you out of there with a mighty hand and with an outstretched arm. Therefore, Yahweh your God has commanded you to keep the day of the sabbath. (Deut. 5:14–15 author's translation)

As is true today, farm animals were maintained in Israel exclusively to facilitate the well-being of humankind. Yet Israel was commanded to honor their God by allowing their livestock to cease production and rest. Deuteronomy 25:4 further commands that the Israelite not muzzle his ox while he threshes the grain. As discussed above, in the smallholder farms of the central hill country, the cereal crop was absolutely crucial to the survival of the community. And the Iron Age farmer leaned heavily upon the strength of his animal for the labor-intensive task of extracting the grain that would become the primary food supply for human and beast. And as I have discussed elsewhere, in this subsistence economy, every kilo counted. Specifically, it has been demonstrated that the typical Iron I Israelite family experienced a yearly shortfall of *sixty days* of food. Thus, the three to four kilos (5–7 pounds) of grain that an ox might consume over the course of a day of threshing made a difference (Richter 2010, 371–72). The point here is that the Israelite farmer was commanded to treat his animal with kindness and humanity even though such kindness might well cost the farmer a portion of his *essential* food supply. Here we have an ancient law that offers a pointed critique of a current norm—the widespread and profoundly inhumane practice of "factory farming" of livestock in America (ibid., 372–74). In contrast to current practices, the *politeia* of Israel understood that the humane treatment of the domestic animal was a divine ordinance, not an economic option.

Slaughter and sacrifice were also strictly legislated in Israel. Although the citizenry regularly slaughtered and consumed the animals they raised, Levitical law mandated that every domestic animal be taken before the priest first. The rationale was to ensure that the animal's *nepeš* (life) was taken with consideration and mercy (Lev. 17). Hence, the Talmud details a method of slaughter that renders the animal immediately unconscious with a minimum of suffering, and commands that the slaughterer never forget the magnitude of his task—the divine concession that allows him to bring death to living things. In Israel, even the wild gazelle had to be slaughtered with due care (Deut. 12:15, 22; 14:5; 15:22). Again, these ancient Israelite laws cast a very unfavorable light on contemporary practices in America. As Matthew Scully has painfully detailed in *Dominion: The Power of Man, the Suffering of Animals, and the Call to Mercy* (2002), the fact that animals used in agriculture in America have almost no legal protection, in concert with our seemingly insatiable appetite for cheap meat, has resulted in an industry that would prefer that the average citizen remain unaware of its methods. In contrast, at every juncture, Israel was constrained to consider the life of the animal that served them and which they consumed, by covenant law (Richter 2010, 374–75).

In sum, we find that in Israel, the drive for economic security and surplus was always tempered by God's command for charity, long-term stewardship of agricultural land, and the active protection of wild and domestic creatures. Even national security did not justify the abuse of the land or the reckless destruction of its flora. Moreover, Israel's covenant announces that true economic security would come only from the careful stewardship of these divinely disseminated resources.

The New Testament

Whereas there is ample material in the Old Testament for the formation of a Christian ecotheology, this is not true of the New Testament. Rather, the urban audience of the New Testament, the post-theocratic political identity of God's people, and the corpus's singular focus on making plain the character of the new *'ādām* seem to have pushed the issues of creation care, so evident in the Old Testament, to the periphery.

As a result, more than one New Testament theologian has concluded that there is no ecotheology to be found in the new covenant—or that the New Testament is actually opposed to environmental concern. The argument is that as the created order is bound only for destruction in the eschaton, the earth's resources ought to be utilized as aggressively as possible to accomplish eternal results—the conversion of souls. And, logically, if the earth is destined for annihilation, what would be the point of human conservation? Here we find the echo of Lynn White's initial indictment: that Christianity posits a dichotomy between people and nature in which "man and nature are two things, and man is master, and therefore, whereas the exploitation of people would be ethically evil, the exploitation of creation was right and good" (White 1967, 1205).

But a host of New Testament scholars disagree. In his survey of the literature, Douglas Moo identifies 2 Peter 3 and Revelation 21 as the passages most attuned to a perceived destruction (2 Pet. 3:10–12) or passing away (Rev. 21:1) of the earth. Here heaven and earth "flee" from God's presence (Rev. 20:11) and are "dissolved with fire" (2 Pet. 3:12) (Moo 2006, 463–68). But Moo argues convincingly that when this New Testament language is read in the context of standard Old Testament judgment imagery, and informed by the message of the rest of the New Testament, the final message is, as Colin Gunton expresses it, "transformation within continuity" (Gunton 1992, 31). Romans 8:19–21 is perhaps the most indicative of the New Testament passages regarding God's ultimate purposes for the creation.

> For the creation waits with eager longing for the revealing of the sons of God; for the creation was subjected to futility [i.e., "frustrated"], not of its own will, but because of him who subjected it, in hope that the creation itself also will be set free from its bondage to decay into the freedom of the glory of the children of God. (ESV)

Here not only humanity anxiously awaits "the revealing of the sons of God," but all of the created order as well. For with the return of the Last Adam, creation itself is finally freed from the chaos of *'ādām*'s rebellion. The curse is lifted, the cosmos liberated, and the earth healed from the effects of humanity's sin. God's ideal design for creation, as detailed in Genesis 1, is restored. The book of Revelation offers a glimpse of the master plan. Here what Christians name "heaven" is identified as "a new heaven and a new earth," where the cosmic river of Eden is free to flow, and the tree of life has multiplied such that it lines the central street of the city (Rev. 21:1; 22:1–2). The iconography of this description makes it clear that "heaven" is Eden restored, this very earth healed of its scars and washed clean of its diseases (Richter 2008, 119–36). Greg Beale draws the same analogy, seeing the new cosmos as "an identifiable counterpart to the old cosmos and a renewal of it, just as the body will be raised without losing its former identity" (Beale 1997, 40–41). And although, surely, "the continuity between this world and the next one is difficult to determine" (Moo 2006, 464), the fact that Paul dares to associate the final destiny of this planet with the ultimate expression of a believer's identity as the redeemed child of God (i.e., the resurrection of the body) speaks volumes regarding the intrinsic value that God places upon this planet and its creatures.

Hence, although the audience of the New Testament is indeed more urban than that of the Old Testament, with agriculture and pastoralism no longer the dominant industries, and the populace no longer united under a singular political aegis, the New Testament continues to echo the message of the Old. "For by Him all things were created, both in the heavens and on earth, visible and invisible, whether thrones or dominions or rulers or authorities—all things have been created by Him and for Him" (Col. 1:16 NASB). In other words, in the new covenant the garden still belongs to God, and God still intends that its resources be utilized for his purposes. Moreover, according to the New Testament God's most central purpose for the garden is to redeem it.

Conclusions

It would seem then that the Bible as a whole communicates several incontrovertible messages regarding environmental ethics. The primary of these is that creation, with all of its flora and fauna, belongs to God, not to humanity. In concert with this message is the often-repeated theme that humanity lives on this planet as lessees, not lessors, and is therefore expected to behave accordingly. Moreover, we find that the divine Landlord has plans for his creation, plans that extend into the eschaton. Thus, although there are many in the contemporary discussion who, rightly or wrongly, blame the current environmental crisis on the communities of the Judeo-Christian tradition, I argue that the rule of faith and practice that stands behind these traditions actually provides very fertile soil for a robust Christian ecotheology. According to the Bible, the concern for the long-term stewardship of this planet and its creatures is not simply a contemporary ideological fad; rather, it is the mandate of the Almighty.

Further Reading

G. K. Beale. "The Eschatological Concept of New Testament Theology." In *Eschatology in Bible and Theology*, edited by Kent E. Brower and Mark W. Elliot, 11–52. InterVarsity, 1997.

Thomas Sieger Derr, with James A. Nash and Richard John Neuhaus. *Environmental Ethics and Christian Humanism*. Abingdon, 1996.

Robert Gottlieb. *This Sacred Earth: Religion, Nature, Environment*. Routledge, 1996.

Colin Gunton. *Christ and Creation*. Paternoster, 1992.

Philip King and Lawrence Stager. *Life in Biblical Israel*. Westminster John Knox, 2001.

David Kinsley. *Ecology and Religion*. Prentice-Hall, 1994.

Douglas Moo. "Nature in the New Creation: New Testament Eschatology and the Environment." *Journal of the Evangelical Theological Society* 49, no. 3 (2006): 449–88.

James A. Nash. *Loving Nature: Ecological Integrity and Christian Responsibility*. Abingdon, 1991.

Sandra Richter. "Environmental Law in Deuteronomy: One Lens on a Biblical Theology of Creation Care." *Bulletin for Biblical Research* 20 (2010): 355–76.

———. *The Epic of Eden*. IVP Academic, 2008.

Holmes Rolston III. *Environmental Ethics*. Temple University Press, 1988.

Matthew Scully. *Dominion: The Power of Man, the Suffering of Animals, and the Call to Mercy*. St. Martin's Press, 2002.

Daniel Swartz. *To Till and Tend: A Guide to Jewish Environmental Study and Action*. Coalition on the Environment and Jewish Life, 1994.

Lynn White. "The Historical Roots of Our Ecological Crisis." *Science* 155 (1967): 1203–7.

Ben Witherington III. *The Indelible Image*. 2 vols. IVP Academic, 2009–10.

131

Religion and Politics

RICHARD V. PIERARD

Because religions tend to make absolute and ultimate claims on their adherents, separating the religious from the political realm is virtually impossible. This complex situation renders any generalization about religion and politics risky and almost invariably open to qualification. The state, an institution whose authority encompasses a large population and makes demands on all individuals dwelling within its established geographical boundaries; and the nation, a sentiment or feeling among a large body of people that they share certain real or imagined characteristics and that they deserve to live separately from others who seemingly are different from them, are the fundamental concepts of contemporary politics. Nationalism was occasionally an element in revolutionary movements in the past, but in its modern form it originated in the West and over time was transported to other parts of the world. The genius of modern nationalism is linking the physical power of the state with the psychological power of national consciousness, resulting in the creation of (or the intense desire for) that distinctive institution of the contemporary world, the nation-state. In this situation people sense an inner connection with their rulers, willingly support them, and accede to their demands.

Religion and Political Identity under the Abrahamic Religions: Christianity

Since religion is such an integral part of national identity, it is difficult to distinguish between nationalism as a secular and a religious affirmation. In antiquity the Roman authorities allowed religious pluralism to exist as long as the populace rendered primary allegiance to the emperor. The small, apolitical Jewish community was regarded as harmless and allowed a de facto exemption from participating in the state (emperor) cult. The rapidly growing Christian populace was treated differently: those who would not engage in the civic rite of sacrificing to Caesar were severely persecuted. When Christianity was legalized and eventually became the official religion of the empire, its adherents sought state assistance in suppressing deviations (heresy) from the universally acknowledged (or "catholic") faith and even sought support in propagating it among peoples who did not know Christ. The result was the emergence of Christendom, linking the spiritual power of the church with the physical power of the "secular" rulers.

The idea, however, of a "universal" church that claimed the spiritual allegiance of all Christians quickly faded. In the Byzantine East and its Russian successor, the ruler exercised authority over the church and made it an adjunct of state power. The various Eastern Orthodox churches took on the cultural characteristics of the peoples where they ministered, and the triumph of Islam guaranteed that no real unity, whether theological or cultural, would exist among them.

The Christendom ideal persisted in the Western or "Latin" church, which called itself the Roman Catholic Church and whose leaders (popes) through the "two-swords" doctrine asserted authority over the lay rulers of Europe. They claimed that the papacy, founded by the apostle Peter, possessed two swords (Luke 22:38)—the spiritual and the secular. The pope handed one sword to the temporal princes to maintain peace and punish evildoers, while the ultimate power remained with the papacy. As the power of the states grew and papal authority diminished, this teaching became increasingly ineffective. Then two transformative movements in the West brought an end to Latin Christendom—the Reformation and the Enlightenment. The former shattered the unity of the church, opening the way for lay rulers to exercise power apart from spiritual overlordship, and the latter provided the ideological basis for secular nation-states. A corollary idea advanced by the Reformation-era Anabaptists was the detachment of organized religion from the governmental authority (known as the separation of church and state) and the granting of full religious freedom to adherents of minority faiths.

In the modern era Christianity and secular nationalism coexisted in the West. The Roman Catholic Church did not like this situation—for example, Pope Pius IX's *Syllabus of Errors* (1864) and the church-state conflicts in Italy, Germany, and France—but in the twentieth century finally came to terms with it by concluding concordats (treaties) with even dictatorial states and through the extraordinary changes flowing from the Second Vatican Council (1962–65). Theocracy, which appealed to some evangelical Calvinist groups on the political right, especially in the United States, had little influence. After the French Revolution, in the Protestant-dominated areas of the West the idea of divine rule rapidly metamorphosed into a deistic civil religion, whereby the particular denominations and churches functioned undisturbed, with full freedom of expression (e.g., the First Amendment to the United States Constitution), but the influence of even legally established churches upon the determination of public policy gradually waned. The public order itself was religified through rhetorical expression, and chaplains served to give religious sanction to legislative bodies and military activities. Political leaders freely referred to a generic, undefined God—as in "God save the queen" and "God bless America"—and religious language was used in public symbolism—the United States as "one nation under God," whose national motto is "In God We Trust." The idea of church-state separation enhanced this development, although some secularists opposed even innocuous affirmations of civil religion.

In the United States the various competing denominations and ethnic minority churches expressed particular religion. However, religious conflict intensified in the post–World War II years through the campaign for African American civil rights that centered on the black churches and with ministers like Martin Luther King Jr. in the forefront. At the same time, an intense struggle between secularists and people of faith led to the emergence of a religiopolitical right that converted emotional religious issues like abortion and homosexuality into political questions. Alleging that a "God gap" existed in the political realm, this political right predominated in the Republican Party and maligned Democrats for their lack of piety. Democratic leaders countered this perception through such symbolic actions as "faith-based" social programs and publicly affirming their faith. Resulting was the curious spectacle in which the supposedly secular United States now was the most overtly religious of all the modern industrial countries.

Meanwhile, Christianity made enormous strides in sub-Saharan Africa, becoming the majority faith in many areas, and several state leaders declared their faith. Although generally a positive force, unfortunately Christianity did not head off the state-sponsored genocide in Rwanda-Burundi or the antihomosexuality campaign in Uganda.

Religion and Political Identity under the Abrahamic Religions: Judaism and Islam

Because the Jewish community was stateless, it remained largely outside the political pale in areas under Christian and Islamic domination. The millet system in the Ottoman Empire allowed Jews, as well as the Orthodox Christian communities, some limited self-government but clearly as second-class citizens. In the Christian world, Jews had been expelled from many places while those remaining were segregated into urban ghettos. Those who had fled to the East—Poland and Russia—were more numerous and lived in villages and towns, but they possessed few political rights. The Enlightenment fostered Jewish emancipation in Europe, and many Jews entered public and professional life. Some were affected by modern nationalism and advocated Zionism—the idea that Jews should have a separate state of their own in Palestine. The movement blossomed in the twentieth century, with the demise of the Ottoman Empire and substantial immigration of Jews to Palestine. The Holocaust (Nazi Germany's attempt to exterminate Jewry) made the need for a secure homeland all the more obvious, and in 1948 the Jewish state

> **Study Aid #239**
> Religion and Politics Exercise
> 1. Define the words "state" and "nation" and show how they combine to form the modern concept of a "nation-state."
>   What is the relationship between "nationalism" and "religious commitment" from a Christian point of view?
>   Relate all four terms to the concept of "Christendom."
> 2. How does a Christian concept of politics differ from the Jewish and Muslim ones? Pay particular attention to the historic differences between "Christendom" and "Islamization."
> 3. Choose one of the so-called Asian religions—Hinduism, Buddhism, Confucianism, Shinto—and discuss in general terms how the worldview of that religion makes its adherents see the relationship between religion and politics differently from the ways Christians view it.

of Israel was founded. The intense rivalry between the Jewish settlers and the indigenous Arab occupants (with backing from neighboring Muslim states) for control of Palestine has resulted in Israel living under a constant state of siege. Also affecting the country is the political dominance of the Orthodox Jewish establishment, which is striving to implement halakhic religious law, while more secular Jews desire a liberal-democratic state rather than a theocracy.

For most people in the Islamic world, politics and religion are closely related, but just how this should occur runs the gamut from rigid theocracy to liberal-democratic governments. The question of authority in the Muslim community goes back to its founding, where in the public realm the world and the sacred were brought together through the implementation of divine laws (the *shari'a*) that the Prophet Muhammad explicated in the Qur'an and Sunna, and that were expounded upon by later legal scholars. The caliph (successor) was the Prophet's vice-regent on earth, and as the leader of the Muslim community he regulated matters in the here and now. But as Muslim expansion continued over the next two centuries, multiple sources of authority and power developed within the empire, resulting in various independent polities. Religious unity developed locally without necessarily referring to the central power, and these local rulers came to be known as sultans (ones having authority) or emirs (commanders). By the ninth century the caliphs no longer interfered in religious affairs, as that was now the responsibility of the ulama, the teachers of the holy law, who were both jurists and theologians. Islamic rulers tended more to be leaders of armies and peoples than heads of state. The caliphate died out in 1258, but the Ottomans revived the title in 1517. It was abolished in 1924.

Secular nationalism took root in the Muslim world as a way of resisting European imperialism. This was best seen in Kemal Ataturk's modernization (Westernization) of Turkey after World War I, and the subsequent formation of secular national states—Egypt, Syria, Iraq, Iran under the Pahlavi monarchs (shahs), Pakistan, Malaysia, and Indonesia. However, in the later twentieth century a conservative resurgence, radical and militant in nature and often labeled as "fundamentalist," has sought to undo the secularizing reforms by abolishing law codes and social customs imported from the West, Islamizing the schools and universities, and returning to the Holy Law of Islam and an Islamic political order. Examples of this include the Wahabi movement in Saudi Arabia, the Muslim Brotherhood in Egypt, and various jihadist groups, with the Iranian revolution of 1979 being the most spectacular. There the supporters of Ayatollah Ruhollah Khomeini overthrew the shah and established the Islamic Republic of Iran. Western leaders tended to regard these as antidemocratic movements that needed to be suppressed, and in the twenty-first century many Muslim conservatives saw the US-sponsored conflicts in western-central Asia as a war against Islam. Some argued they were a renewal of Western imperialism (to gain oil supplies) and intended to uphold the existence of the United States's Jewish client state Israel. Other radicals portrayed the United States and its allies as mythic, satanic entities, thereby transforming nationalism into a religious force. The actions of Muslim terrorists and holy warriors, culminating in the attack in New York in 2001, were aimed at challenging and eliminating Western influence, either Christian or secular, in the Islamic world. The global jihadist movement associated with al-Qaeda and Osama bin Laden also has a transnational agenda, the creation of a broader Islamic political entity under the rule of *shari'a*.

Religion and Political Identity: Hinduism

The body of religious teachings that prevailed in India (Hinduism itself is a modern construct that originated during the British raj) survived the influx of monotheistic religions that came in during foreign rule—Islam under the Mughals and Christianity under the British—and in the twentieth century was politicized. The secular nationalism evident in the early years of the Indian National Congress (founded 1885) was soon overshadowed by a religious nationalism first promoted by L. Bal Gangadhar Tilak, which tried to consolidate Hindu opinion against the Muslims in India. His contemporary Mahatma K. Gandhi, to the contrary, saw all religions as true and advocated interreligious tolerance. He believed Hindus and Muslims could work together to achieve self-rule and build the new India. Gandhi used mainly Hindu religious concepts into which he instilled political meaning (such as *satyagraha*—"soul force"), but he wanted religion to be the moral force directing individuals. All good politics has its roots in truth and justice, which are the essentials of true religion. All religions are equal because they teach brotherhood and peace and provide freedom. The next generation of leaders, Jawaharlal Nehru and Mohammed Ali Jinnah, could not agree on the nature of the new country: Nehru wanted a secular, democratic, nonreligious state, one not based on any sense of religious communalism, while Jinnah fought for a separate Muslim entity known as Pakistan. Independence in 1947 and the brutal partition left two mutually hostile political entities in the Indian subcontinent—one consciously Muslim and the other officially secular with coexisting religious faiths, including Hinduism, Islam, Sikhism, Christianity, and several small communities. The Indian Constitution guaranteed to all citizens the freedom of conscience and the right to practice and propagate the religious faiths of their choosing.

Hindu fundamentalists rejected the idea of a secular India and advocated establishing and strengthening the cultural traditions of an imagined golden age. They formed societies in the early twentieth century that after independence worked to undermine secularism and promote Hindu nationalism. The most aggressive of the Hindu revitalization groups is the RSS (Rashtriya Swayamsevak Sangh, the National Volunteer Organization). Founded in 1925, it spawned a large number of front organization and demonized Christianity and Islam. (A person connected with it assassinated Gandhi in 1948.) It incorporated religious, cultural, and political fundamentalism and promoted Hindutva (Hinduness), a concept that originated in the 1920s and became the central idea animating the Hindu nationalist movement. The political expression of Hindutva is the BJP (Bharatiya Janata Party, the Indian People's Party), founded in 1980 as the successor to an earlier political party. It soon became the second-largest party in India, participated in a coalition government in 1998–2004, and currently holds power in several states. A cultural organization, the VHP (Vaswa Hindu Parishad, the World Hindu Council), established in 1964, is a pan-Hindu body that strives to bring together all the various Hindu sects under one banner. It was involved in the 1992 mob action that demolished the five-hundred-year-old Babri Mosque in Ayodhya, built on the site of an earlier Hindu temple, which initiated rioting around the country. Adherents of Hindutva have engaged in numerous terrorist acts against Muslims and have sought laws to forbid conversions to Christianity, especially among the oppressed Dalit communities.

From time to time the Sikhs were in conflict with the central government over their desire for more autonomy. In 1984 a group of armed Sikh dissidents ensconced themselves in the Golden Temple at Amritsar, Punjab, the central shrine of Sikhism, and the Indian army stormed the temple. Sikh members of Prime Minister Indira Gandhi's bodyguard sought revenge by assassinating her four months later, and riots broke out across the country, where thousands of Sikhs were massacred. Gradually, reconciliation took place, and in 2004 a noted Sikh economist, Manmohan Singh, became prime minister.

Religion and Political Identity: Other Asian Faiths

Generally regarded as apolitical, Buddhists have tended to be involved in politics in a variety of ways. In Sri Lanka the Sinhalese leadership drew on Buddhist support in the struggle against the Hindu Tamils and offered as an alternative to secular nationalism the promise to uphold the teachings of the Buddha. The government then took action against the militantly Buddhist JVP (People's Liberation Front) and co-opted the opposition. In Thailand, Buddhism provided society with a religious and moral framework and was closely linked to the government, but the growth of secularism weakened its ability to influence political life. In Cambodia it continues to be recognized as the state religion, whereas in Vietnam it is more a cultural force. In Tibet, Lamaistic Buddhism shaped cultural institutions even as Chinese rule ensured that its political influence would be minimal. The major voice of Tibetan Buddhism, the Dalai Lama, has spent his adult life in exile. In Mongolia the faith was closely connected with the Tibetan variety and was heavily regulated during the communist era. It is now enjoying a resurgence since the establishment of democracy, and some Buddhists are involved in politics. Buddhism in Japan is characterized by its numerous sects and linked syncretistically with Shinto, but adherents of the lay reform movement Soka Gakkai, an offshoot of Nichiren Buddhism, are heavily involved in politics.

In East Asia the political influence of religions other than Christianity is unclear. Chinese Confucianism is more a system of values and morals than an organized faith per se. The ancient philosophical system was oriented toward the government and the cosmic order, and it was promoted by the examination system, which produced the scholar-bureaucrat. The concept of the emperor as enjoying (or losing) the mandate of heaven persists in a secularized form in modern-day secular communist China. The Confucian influence remains evident in Korea and Vietnam, particularly the emphasis on filial piety (honoring one's ancestors) and moral values. The Chinese authorities regard a new religion, Falun Gong, as a serious threat and in 1992 suppressed it, causing it to come out in violent opposition to the regime. The rapidly growing Christian movement also is viewed with suspicion.

Shinto (the "way of the gods"), although influenced by Confucian values, is distinctively a Japanese faith. In the Meiji era of the late nineteenth century it came to occupy a central place in political ideology. The *tenno* (emperor) cult fed nationalism and the development of an authoritarian, expansionist state in the years leading up to the Pacific War of 1941–45. Shinto evolved into a distinct civil religion, one that glorified centralized power and militarism. An important symbol is Yasukuni Shrine in Tokyo. Founded in 1869, it houses the souls of the dead of various wars, and their names are inscribed in books there. The American occupiers in 1945 abolished Shinto as a state religion and deprived the emperor of his deity, but allowed tennoism to remain in a secularized form as a symbol of national unity. Although a legal separation of religious cult and state occurred, Yasukuni remains, and even the executed war criminals are included among the honored dead. Because the majority of the Japanese continue to practice Shinto rites, all shrines are maintained through private contributions, but the civil religion component of the faith essentially no longer exists.

Further Reading

J. H. Bavinck. *The Church between Temple and Mosque*. Eerdmans, 1966.

M. T. Cherian. *Hindutva Agenda and Minority Rights: A Christian Response*. Centre for Contemporary Christianity, 2007.

Obery M. Hendricks. *The Politics of Jesus*. Doubleday, 2006.

Mark Laing, ed. *Nationalism and Hindutva: A Christian Response*. ISPCK, 2005.

Kun Sam Lee. *The Christian Confrontation with Shinto Nationalism*. P&R, 1966.

Bernard Lewis. *What Went Wrong? The Clash between Islam and Modernity in the Middle East*. Oxford University Press, 2002.

Charles Marsh. *Wayward Christian Soldiers: Freeing the Gospel from Political Captivity*. Oxford University Press, 2007.

Leo Pfeffer. *Church, State, and Freedom*. Rev. ed. Beacon, 1967.

Richard Pierard and Robert Linder. *Civil Religion and the Presidency*. Zondervan, 1988.

Walter Skya. *Japan's Holy War: The Ideology of Radical Shintō Ultranationalism*. Duke University Press, 2009.

132

Religion and Violence

SALLIE B. KING

A number of false generalizations about religion and violence are widespread. On the one hand, it is believed by many that religion is one of the world's greatest causes of war and violence, or even the greatest cause. This view has recently received a strong boost from the works of the "new atheists" (Richard Dawkins, Sam Harris, Christopher Hitchens, Daniel Dennett), who excoriate religion for causing violence. While no one should deny that religion has historically participated and continues to participate in a horrific amount of violence, it is surely simplistic and reductionistic to blame religion in some unique way for human violence. The truth is clearly far more complex, with human psychology, as well as political and economic forces, playing major roles in causing violence. On the other hand, defenders of religion often say that the very essence of (at least) their religion is peace. This view is also simplistic and flies in the face of the historical fact that every major religion has been and continues to be deeply involved in major violence. Nonetheless, it is true that deeply religious people have made the most significant contributions to nonviolence in history.

Inasmuch as religion is deeply involved in both violence and nonviolence, it is helpful to see the relationship between religion and violence set out along a continuum. Here one end of the continuum represents overt participation in violence by religious bodies and individuals, and the other end of the continuum represents direct engagement in active nonviolence by religious bodies and individuals. In the center of such a continuum one might position the contribution of religions to just-war theory. Where martyrdom belongs in such a continuum depends upon whether that martyrdom is intended to bring only one's own death or the deaths of others as well. Such a continuum might look like the one at the top of p. 765.

> **Study Aid #240**
> Religion and Violence Continuum
>
> | Most violent | | Least violent |
> |---|---|---|
> | State violence | Just-war theory | Principled nonviolence |
> | Religious terrorism | | Martyrdom of oneself |
> | Martyrdom intending others' deaths | | |

Religion and Violence

Participation in violence by religion includes state violence when that state identifies itself with a religion and/or uses religious justifications for violent acts or war, as in the Crusades. It also includes individuals and nonstate groups who commit violent acts with a fundamentally religious motivation—that is, religious terrorism—such as the 1994 massacre of Palestinian Muslims at prayer at a mosque in Hebron by Jewish militant Baruch Goldstein.

Religious violence is by no means a thing of the past, nor are there any major religions that are exempt from it. In the latter half of the twentieth century, Christianity was deeply involved in the "troubles" in Northern Ireland, Judaism and Islam in the struggle over Israel and Palestinian statehood, Hinduism and Islam in communal violence in India, and Buddhism in the Sinhalese-Tamil war in Sri Lanka. In the twentieth century, the concept of "holy war" has been invoked by Christians in the Spanish Civil War, by Muslims in al-Qaeda, by Buddhists in Sri Lanka, by Hindus in Kashmir, and by Jews in the settler movement in Israel/Palestine (Popovski et al. 2009, 312–13). Religious violence is also seen in attacks upon women, both in the form of systematic, institutionalized violence against women, such as was found in Taliban-controlled Afghanistan, and in the form of more random violence, such as the 2009 stoning death of a Somali woman for alleged adultery (she was divorced) by a Somali Islamist group.

The question that is perhaps at the heart of understanding the relationship between religion and violence is this: In situations of violence where religion is present, is religion merely being used by other forces in order to promote a secular cause? Or is there something intrinsic to religion that makes religion itself a root cause of violence? This question is not amenable to a simple answer, as there are multiple examples of both scenarios.

Some violent conflicts are directly about religion. Examples are conflicts in places such as Nigeria and other places where a population is divided between Christians and Muslims, and a part of the Muslim population is agitating for governance according to *shari'a* law, while the Christian population is resisting such governance. Such situations from time to time erupt into vicious rioting. Another example of violence directly caused by religion has been the long history of attacks by Christians on Jews; these attacks were often instigated by religious leaders and justified by religious rationales such as taking revenge on the "killers of Christ." A third example of direct religious violence is attacks on Baha'is in Iran, motivated by the fact that the Baha'i faith is anathema to some Muslims and Muslim states.

In those cases where a conflict is fundamentally about something other than religion, religion still often plays a major role. For example, the contemporary struggle between the Arab world, especially Palestine, and Israel is not about religion; it is about land ownership. However, the question of ownership of the land is deeply charged with religious meaning inasmuch as many religious Jews believe that that land was given to them by God. This belief plays a major role in the Jewish settler movement's ongoing effort to expand the territory of Israel. This movement, in turn, plays a large role in making a resolution of the situation impossible to achieve. Another major difficulty is the fact that Jerusalem is deeply important to all three Abrahamic religions; it will not be possible to resolve the Israel/Palestine issue without satisfying all three religions on access to sites sacred to them. Another example of religion playing a major role in a conflict that is fundamentally nonreligious can be seen in the way in which Confucian, Shinto, and Buddhist ideologies were called up, often blended, interpreted in a nationalistic fashion, and put into the service of Japan's expansionist twentieth-century wars in Asia and the Pacific, promoted by the enthusiastic efforts of the Japanese Shinto and Buddhist leadership. That leadership went about Japan and the war fronts using these ideologies to exhort the faithful, students, workers, and soldiers to give their all for the war effort.

Again, religion is not a fundamental cause of the civilizational struggle now underway between the Muslim world and the Western world; this struggle is about relative power and control, respect, globalization, access to oil, perceived and real historic and recent injustices and injuries, and vast disparities in wealth. However, religion does play a role. Some of those real and perceived injustices and injuries date back to the time of the Crusades, a time when religion and empire marched arm in arm in both the Christian and the Muslim worlds, setting up a conflict that is vividly recalled to this day in the Muslim world. Moreover, recent polling has revealed that one of the most important things that Muslims are looking for from the West is respect for Islam; it seems that such respect is necessary in order for a more harmonious relationship to be possible.

A general principle in the study of religion and violence is this: when religion combines with empire and/or colonialism, violence very frequently results. A related principle is this: in a religiously plural society, when religion combines with governmental rule, violence against religious minorities may well result. This is especially the case when the ruling power perceives members of a different religion as a threat to the body politic, either potentially as a "state within the state"—as the Chinese state from time to time viewed Buddhists in their monasteries, particularly when the wealth and population of those monasteries became vast—or as a kind of traitor to the larger group, as in Muslim attacks upon former Muslims who have converted to a different religion. This danger to religious minorities when religion and government combine is one of the major reasons behind Western countries' embrace of secularism.

Because religious identity often parallels ethnicity, language, geographic location, political identity, and/or nationalist aspiration, these various markers of identity often exist in a complex mix. When such a mix is present, it is common for those in a violent conflict to use religious identity as a marker of the sides of the conflict, and to use religious symbolism and ideology to justify the conflict and to bring those in conflict into a more intense state of enmity. One example of this can be seen in the 1990s wars in the former Yugoslavia, which were fundamentally caused by long-standing political tensions among its constituent regions, many of them with nationalist aspirations, and suppressed anger over massive atrocities committed during World War II, but in which there was also long-standing interreligious hostility. Though these wars are often called ethnic wars, the various groups actually all belong to a single ethnic group, the Slavs. The divisions among them are constituted by distinct regional national identities that are aligned with religion. Since Serbs are almost entirely followers of the Serbian Orthodox Church, Croats are largely Roman Catholic, and Bosnians are largely Muslim, religion is aligned with the nationalist and separatist aspirations of the various groups and plays an important role in defining political lines. Moreover, the Muslim presence in the region stems from the fifteenth-century Ottoman occupation, which led to the conversion of many Bosnians to Islam in a historically Christian region. An ideology developed among Serbs and Croats in which Bosnian Muslims were seen as traitors to Christianity and to the Slavs. When war came in the 1990s, many Orthodox Church leaders voiced hostility toward Muslim groups and maintained staunch support of those engaged in violence against them. The Catholic Church was divided, with some leaders condemning the genocidal violence and others maintaining silence (Palmer-Fernandez 2004, 136).

Mark Juergensmeyer has argued for an inherent connection between religion and violence in his *Terror in the Mind of God*. Factors cited by Juergensmeyer as constituting this inherent connection include the following: (1) A good deal of contemporary religious violence committed by individuals (religious terrorists) is the result of religiously committed people living out in a rigid and fanatical way what they believe is a literal interpretation of their scripture; this includes adhering to a literal reading of religious law. (2) There is a great deal of violence in the scriptures of most of the major religions. God himself is sometimes portrayed as a warrior and occasionally commands war or killing. This scriptural violence is taken as license by some followers to act violently themselves. (3) Many religions extol religious martyrdom and ennoble the martyrs as heroes. (4) Many religions teach a mythic history of cosmic warfare; followers may see themselves as participating, on the side of God, in this cosmic warfare. Such warfare requires an all-out commitment, without reservation. It trains one to think in absolute terms of a struggle between good and evil in which one demonizes one's opponents as cosmically evil. (5) People may do things that they would never do under any other circumstances—such as kill—if they feel that it is sanctioned by God (or by the Buddha, in the case of nontheistic Buddhism).

Martyrdom and Auto-Violence

Martyrdom is the act of consciously chosen and embraced death for the sake of religion. Religiously, martyrdoms are acts of faith and witness to faith; the word "martyr" derives from the Greek word *martys* (witness). Politically, martyrdoms are acts of those with little power who are faced with the aggression of the powerful and refuse to submit. In dying, the martyr defies the hegemony of the powerful; this act may be publicized and glorified by the martyr's cofaithful, sometimes resulting in a significant act of collective defiance and resistance.

Paradigmatically, in Judaism and Christianity, martyrdom is embraced by spiritual heroes who refuse to submit to demands of conversion—Jews who refuse to convert to Christianity, Christians who refuse to worship the Roman gods. That the meaning of martyrs' deaths is entirely dependent upon an interpretive framework supplied by religion can be seen in the case of the Jewish Zealots who died at Masada in 73 CE rather than submit to the power of Rome. In this case, the killing was not done by the Romans; the Masada Zealots accepted death at each other's hands rather than submit to the Romans. These deaths might be seen as murders from a strict legal perspective, but they are never called such; secular authorities sometimes call them suicides, inasmuch as the Zealots apparently submitted willingly to their deaths. The Zealots are nonetheless regarded as martyrs in the Jewish tradition, and Masada is embraced as a holy site in Israel.

The Arabic word for martyr is *shahid*, meaning witness and martyr. Causes of martyrdom in Islam include death on the battlefield when fighting a just war called by a legitimate authority, death while on pilgrimage to the holy city of Mecca, death while in the service of God, and death suffered due to one's Muslim faith. Military martyrdom is urged by the Qur'an in numerous places, where heavenly rewards are promised to those who die on the battlefield. These rewards include for the martyr forgiveness of sins, entrance into paradise, and ability to intercede for his or her relatives. While the Muslim conception of martyrdom is substantially different from that of the Jewish and Christian traditions, it should be noted that the Christian Crusaders were urged to commit themselves to war by Pope Urban II, who promised the Crusaders the remission of their sins, thus removing this obstacle to their enjoying eternal paradise after death. Thus, both the Crusader and the *shahid* were promised paradise.

Clearly, from the perspective of a study of religious violence, there is a great difference between intentional martyrdom that results only in one's own death

> **Study Aid #241**
>
> Religion and Violence Exercise
>
> 1. Make the best argument you can for each of the following statements.
>   Throughout history, religion has provided humans with the most egregious motivation to do violence to fellow human beings.
>   Throughout history, religion has provided human beings with the most powerful motivations to work for peace for all humankind.
>   In your argument for each, make the case as if you believed it, even though they are contradictory and/or you may think they are incomplete as stated. For each statement, indicate which authorities, both ancient and modern, you would cite to defend your argument.
> 2. Write your own statement of how you think religion, violence, and peace interrelate to one another.
> 3. How might a Christian statement of the relationship between religion and peace compare and contrast with some other religion's statement(s)?

and intentional martyrdom that results in the deaths of others as well. Buddhism in East Asia has a tradition of self-sacrifice dating back to medieval China. In this tradition, a monk may sacrifice himself in protest when Buddhism is being attacked or suppressed. This tradition was revived in Vietnam in 1963 by the venerable monk Thich Quang Duc in response to the suppressing of Buddhism by the pro-Catholic regime of Ngo Dinh Diem. Thich Quang Duc went to a busy crossroads in Saigon, assumed a meditation posture, and burned himself to death without the slightest movement, while a crowd watched and photos were taken. Subsequently, throughout the duration of the war years, many Vietnamese monks, nuns, and laypeople burned themselves to death as part of the effort by the Unified Buddhist Church of Vietnam to end the war. The Buddhist leadership explained this to be an effort to reach the hearts of those who were intent on perpetrating the war and to move them such that they would no longer want to see the war continue. It was understood as the holy act of a *bodhisattva*, one who sacrifices oneself for the sake of others, and evoked deep and widespread reverence.

Perhaps the least violent of all cases of self-sacrifice are those in which the future martyr knows that death is approaching and that he or she could easily avoid martyrdom without violating any spiritual or moral commitments, yet remains in place and suffers martyrdom in an intentional, chosen way. An example is found in the deaths of seven Cistercian monks killed by Muslim extremists in 1996 at the monastery of Our Lady of Atlas in Algeria. The monks saw death approaching and determined to follow in the footsteps of their master, Jesus, the ultimate Christian martyr, who asked God to forgive his killers. The letters the monks left behind make it clear that they were determined to die with love for their killers in their hearts and to joyfully accept the grace of martyrdom. Their deaths have an ongoing significance for Christian-Muslim relations, as well as for personal spirituality, that cannot yet be measured.

Religion and Just-War Theory

The intention behind the creation of just-war theories, for the most part, is not to justify war, but to place limits upon what is seen as the regrettable inevitability of war. Martin Luther, for example, saw the Gospels as indicating that the Christian should be a pacifist; he nonetheless recognized that the state requires the use of violence for the good of all. He therefore advocated the "two-kingdom" theory, which urges personal nonviolence for the individual Christian, while permitting limited state violence. Religions have varied considerably in the extent to which they have made an effort to clarify what is and is not acceptable in warfare from their respective religious points of view; Christianity and Islam have made the most extensive efforts. Despite these varying efforts, there is little evidence that polities, even explicitly religious ones, have allowed themselves to be guided by these norms.

The most universally cited justification for going to war (called *jus ad bellum*, justice in going to war, in the Roman Catholic tradition) is the notion that a ruler has a duty to protect his or her citizens—that is, self-defense. This notion is found in all the major religious traditions. Other justifications for going to war affirmed in some religions are fighting in obedience to a commandment of God (Judaism) or fighting to secure justice or to protect the helpless (Islam).

In addition to justifying going to war, just-war theorizing also has attempted to specify what actions are and are not acceptable in the course of war (the Catholic *jus in bello*, just conduct within war). In Islam, for example, the Qur'an stipulates that a war must be conducted on a battlefield, that only soldiers may be attacked—not women, children, the elderly, or clergy. Terrorism (attacks on civilians) is absolutely forbidden. Wounded enemies and prisoners must be humanely treated. Homes and crops may not be destroyed. The use of poisons is forbidden.

Such norms notwithstanding, it is rare indeed to see a state pull back from war for religious reasons. Perhaps the most notable exception is found in the Indian king Asoka the Great. Initially, King Asoka (third century BCE), of the powerful Mauryan dynasty, greatly expanded the empire by use of military force. After conquering the kingdom of Kalinga, Asoka came to deeply regret the heavy toll of death and suffering that resulted from the battle. He converted to Buddhism, publicly expressed his regret for the Kalinga war, and though at the peak of his military power, forswore any future expansionist wars.

The extent of death caused by modern warfare, in which millions of people may be killed, and the existence of nuclear weapons and other weapons of mass destruction have raised new questions for the religions in their efforts to consider the righteousness of warfare in light of religious ethical norms. Some, including Pope John XXIII, have questioned whether war can be justified any longer, given modern conditions. In the last decades of the twentieth century, the United Church of Christ and the United Methodist Church developed a just-peace theory, asserting against the just-war tradition that war is inherently unjust, that peace is possible, and that active peacemaking is an integral mission of the church.

Religion and Nonviolence

Just as every major religion has been deeply involved in major acts of violence, every major religion has its peace heroes as well. Of these, the Hindu Mahatma Gandhi takes pride of place, for while many religions claim that the essence of their religion is peace, it was Gandhi who pioneered a realistic and effective way to put religious nonviolent ideals into practice. Inspired by his Hindu ideal (based upon the Bhagavad Gita) of selfless service to humanity as a path to God, Gandhi introduced the idea of "hating the sin, not the sinner" as a way to oppose harmful actions (such as the British occupying India) without opposing the welfare and true good of one's opponent (here, the British administrators and soldiers) and thus showed the way to be nonviolent without being passive.

In Christianity, the historic peace churches (Church of the Brethren, Mennonites, and Religious Society of Friends, aka Quakers) understand pacifism to be an inherent part of the Christian faith. Christians of these churches take their pacifism from the example and teaching of Jesus Christ and add that the pre-Constantinian church also saw Jesus in this way. Naturally, a good deal of Christian peace leadership has come from these churches from the time of their formation up to the present. Twentieth-century contributions made by historic peace churches include advocacy for a legal exemption from compulsory military service on the basis of religious belief ("conscientious objection"), advocacy for a peace tax fund (as an alternative to taxes supporting the military), work to rebuild Europe after World War II (recognized by a Nobel Peace Prize to British and American Quakers in 1947), and the creation of Christian peacemaker teams.

Individual Christians of other Christian churches sometimes conclude that although their particular church does not understand pacifism to be an inherent part of Christianity, they as individuals do. A prominent example of such a person is the Catholic Dorothy Day, cofounder of the Catholic Workers Movement and an important and outspoken pacifist from 1935 through World War II and until her death in 1980. Another example is the Baptist Martin Luther King Jr., who embraced Gandhi's methods and ensured that the civil rights movement in the United States was nonviolent.

Muslim advocates of nonviolence argue for the compatibility of nonviolence and Islam as long as that nonviolence is a form of action and not passive. A prominent Muslim hero of nonviolence is Abdul Ghaffar Khan, a great nonviolent leader of

Muslims in India under British rule. He led the Khudai Khidmatgar, a nonviolent Muslim movement with one hundred thousand activists, in opposition to British rule, cooperating with Mahatma Gandhi and using many of the same tactics as the latter. He was convinced of the complete compatibility of Islam and nonviolence and viewed his nonviolent struggle with the British as jihad.

In Judaism, Rabbis for Human Rights, an organization of Orthodox, Conservative, Reform, and Reconstruction rabbis and rabbinical students, won the Niwano Peace Prize in 2006. They have stood in the way of bulldozers attempting to raze the homes of Palestinians in Israel, opposed the construction of the Israeli West Bank barrier wherever it divided villages or involved the expropriation of Arab-owned land, and acted as human shields protecting Palestinians from members of the Jewish settler movement during the olive harvest. A contemporary American rabbi, Marc Gopin, has for decades worked as a back-channel diplomat with religious, political, and military figures on both sides of conflicts, but especially the Arab-Israeli conflict. As a researcher on religion and peacemaking, he argues that religion is the missing element in resolving many conflicts insofar as many traditional people will not be brought into a peace process if their religion is not a part of that process. He also demonstrates that religions have traditional resources for overcoming enmity and resolving conflict that could be tapped for peacemaking.

In Buddhism, the Engaged Buddhism movement has emerged in the twentieth and twenty-first centuries as a major new initiative promoting Buddhist engagement with practical issues in the world. Within this pan-Buddhist movement there have been several major national-level movements using nonviolence to work for peace. The Dalai Lama and the Tibetan liberation movement lead a movement of principled nonviolence in the effort to gain autonomy for Tibet from China. In the 1960s Thich Nhat Hanh and the Unified Buddhist Church of Vietnam led the "Third Way" nonviolent "Struggle Movement" that sided neither with the North nor the South but with life and peace. In Burma/Myanmar, Aung San Suu Kyi and the National League for Democracy have led a nonviolent struggle since the 1980s to bring an end to the military regime that heads that country and to institute democracy and human rights.

The interreligious movement in and of itself is regarded by many as an important religious initiative for peace. Insofar as interreligious conflict plays a role in intercommunal violence and war, it follows that the promotion of interreligious understanding and cooperation can be a proactive step in preventing future violence and wars from occurring. The existence of local interfaith organizations with regular meetings of religious leadership and/or the faithful can promote the development of relationships and friendships between communities that can resolve conflicts at an early stage. There are also international interfaith organizations whose raison d'être is explicitly peacemaking, such as the World Conference of Religions for Peace, the Fellowship of Reconciliation, and the World Congress of Imams and Rabbis for Peace.

Further Reading

Peter Ackerman and Jack Duvall. *A Force More Powerful: A Century of Nonviolent Conflict*. Palgrave, 2000.

Roger Fisher, Bruce Patton, and William Ury. *Getting to Yes*. Penguin, 2011.

Mark Juergensmeyer. *Terror in the Mind of God: The Global Rise of Religious Violence*. University of California Press, 2000.

Emmanuel Katongole and Chris Rice. *Reconciling All Things*. InterVarsity, 2008.

Gabriel Palmer-Fernandez, ed. *Encyclopedia of Religion and War*. Routledge, 2004.

Vesselin Popovski, Gregory M. Reichberg, and Nicholas Turner, eds. *World Religions and Norms of War*. United Nations University Press, 2009.

Ken Sande. *The Peacemaker*. Baker Books, 2004.

Glenn Stassen, ed. *Just Peacemaking*. Pilgrim, 2008.

Walter Wink. *The Powers That Be*. Doubleday, 1998.

133

Religion and Human Rights

Frances S. Adeney

Religions have been interacting with incipient ideas of human rights since the beginning of recorded history. Although content differs widely across religious traditions, all religions articulate a vision of a better world and ideals for human behavior. All include a dimension of moral obligation and instruction in how to fulfill the obligations of the religion. Religions have traditionally fulfilled the role of outlining how people should treat one another to ensure a good society. It does not automatically follow, however, that all religions teach human rights as many understand them in contemporary Western societies.

Three main issues divide modern societies on the question of human rights and religion. The first is *human nature* itself. What does it mean to be human? Who is included in the circle of humanity and for what reasons? Are human rights inherent in human nature, or are other sources necessary to ascertain the veracity of human rights?

A related issue is the *role of religion* in defining and advocating human rights. Is God or a divine power needed to adequately define and source human rights? What is the role of human responsibility in relation to human rights, and how do religions address this issue? What role have religions played in the development of international human rights and the global culture of human rights today? How does the diversity of moralities among religions relate to the idea of universal human rights?

A third critical issue is the *content of human rights*. Are religions necessary to define the content of human rights? Are human rights universal, and if so of what do they consist? What is the proper balance between rights that address material needs and those that address human freedoms? Do cultural differences render human rights incommensurable across societies? Do philosophical explorations of human rights yield a different set of human rights than religious explorations?

How should human rights be balanced with human responsibilities to others, individually or in societal groups?

In order to address these issues, we need to clarify the meaning of key terms.

Religion. The human institutions that order behavior through belief in and interaction with a divine dimension of life.

Human. Those creatures that are more than other animals—those sentient beings that reason and create, that speak and write. The parameters of humanness have not been defined as including all people by every religion or societal group. Limited definitions of humanness have caused problems with the concept of rights, as sometimes persons in nonaccepted groups are considered subhuman and therefore not entitled to rights and privileges of the in-group.

Rights. What a person is entitled to by virtue of being human or by position in society. Human rights then become what one is entitled to by virtue of being human. Modern Western values purport that human rights include basic necessities of life, certain basic freedoms, and treatment that is in accord with human worth and dignity.

Human Nature

Traditionally religions have defined human nature in relation to God (Judaism and Christianity), a higher power (deism and some indigenous religions), or a divinity inherent in the material world (pantheism in Eastern religions and some indigenous religions, e.g., Native American religions). Some religions (Confucianism and some sects of Buddhism) define human nature without reference to a God or higher power.

In all of those religions, human nature is considered valuable, and humans are responsible for caring for nonhuman forms of life in the world. That responsibility is directly linked to the value of humans, making human nature, at least in part, a source for rights. The right to be valued and cared for by other human beings because of inherent human value thus becomes a source for human rights as well as responsibilities.

Many religions also posit God or a higher power as a source for human rights. According to Judaism, Christianity, and Islam, God created humans in God's own image, thus rendering their value inestimable. Because of the value of God's human creations, persons are entitled to fair treatment and should be valued for their humanness. Pantheistic religions, Hinduism and Buddhism, Native American religions, and some other indigenous religions consider the material world to be a manifestation of divinity. Thus all creation has worth and should be treated with respect.

Religions have failed to live up to the ideal of God-given rights or rights inherent in human nature through much of human history. The violence religions have perpetuated has, at times, been linked to the parameters of human nature as defined by a religion's adherents in a particular time and place. Persons excluded from the circle of humanity as defined by the religion were oppressed, enslaved, and sometimes annihilated. Culture-bound definitions of human nature have had a huge impact on how well people live out the ideal of human rights lodged in human nature and understandings of the divine.

The Role of Religion in Defining/Advocating Human Rights

Before the twentieth century, when the international discourse around human rights began in earnest, religious traditions contributed to a moral climate that helped set the stage for a worldwide concern for human rights. They did this in three ways: First, religions provide ideals. Religions envision a world without suffering. Second, they show that a sense of moral obligation is inherent in following a religious path. No religion recommends an amoral stance toward others. Third, religious traditions outline the content of those moral obligations in terms of their beliefs about the divine, the world as it is, and ways to change the world for the better.

Hinduism as a family of religions puts forth a vision of all of life as divine. The religious path provides a way of life that affirms that sacredness in every phase of life. Ancient scriptures, especially the Manava Dharma Sutra (Treatise on Human Duties), outlines the ways that persons should act toward others. The Vedas, another ancient Hindu scripture, stresses noninjury to others as both an ideal and a moral obligation. The relationship between the understanding of the divine nature of all things and the duty to avoid injury to any life-form has provided a basis for human rights advocacy from a Hindu perspective.

As *Buddhism* developed out of Hinduism, the stress on noninjury to others expanded to an idea of compassion for suffering—the suffering that is inherent to life itself. Many Buddhist traditions do not focus on an idea of a divine presence in or of the universe. Instead, the centrality of meditation or actively being present in every moment lends itself to the practice of compassion. The Buddhist scripture collection known as the Anguttara-Nikaya describes the relation between suffering and duty. In our own age, the Dalai Lama builds on these ancient ideas, teaching that world problems can be solved only through kindness, love, and respect for all.

Confucianism, like Buddhism, is sometimes considered to be an ethical system rather than a religion because it focuses on moral obligations. According to the *Analytics* of Confucius, to keep society functioning smoothly, parents and children, elder and younger siblings, teachers and students, husbands and wives, and rulers and subjects—all have distinct responsibilities in each relationship. Although responsibility differs according to one's role in the relationship, every person must act respectfully in accordance with the rules of that relationship. The dignity and worth of each individual is prefigured in Confucianism, as moral obligations toward others keep society on course.

> **Study Aid #242**
> Religion and Human Rights Exercise
> 1. Although all religions have a view of human rights, not all religions have the same view. Three issues divide the religions' views of human rights.
>   Human nature
>   Role of religion in society
>   Content of specific human rights
>   For each of these three issues, first write a description of the issue; then compare and contrast two different religious views of each issue.
> 2. Compare the Christian view of human rights with the Confucian view of human rights. How might the contrasts in these views affect the interactions that modern-day China has with the United States, in political, economic, and social interactions? Do you think it is necessary to create a third view of human rights, taking the best and most essential of both the Christian and Confucian, in order to facilitate conversations between the two?

Judaism stresses the idea of justice in relationships from the first book of the Torah, when Cain, who murdered his brother, asks, "Am I my brother's keeper?" (Gen. 4:9). Cain was given shelter in cities of refuge, a tribute to Judaism's respect for humans as persons, regardless of their behavior. In later centuries, the vision of the prophet Isaiah became central—a vision of loosing the bonds of wickedness, undoing the yoke of oppression, and sharing bread with the hungry (Isa. 58:6–7). Widows and orphans were special recipients of goodwill and shared possessions. Rules about usury protected people who were in debt. And the Year of Jubilee, when all debts were to be forgiven, kept a notion of human dignity alive.

Christianity continued Judaism's focus on the moral obligation to love one's neighbor. Jesus expanded the boundaries of whom that included through his parable of the Good Samaritan (Luke 10:25–37). One's neighbor in this story is the one in need, the one who has been hurt and treated unjustly. The moral obligation that Jesus presented went beyond the bounds of one's group or religious affiliates to include all people. The Christian scriptures show how the apostle Paul built on that universality by asserting that, in Christ, distinctions between classes, races, and genders disappear (Gal. 3:28).

When the Prophet Muhammad received his vision of the Qur'an in the seventh century CE, it became clear that one's responsibility for others was rooted in responsibility toward God. A central practice of *Islam* is giving to the poor. Almsgiving is one of five major pillars of the religion, and the obligation is not an insignificant one. The dignity of all persons is also expressed in the Qur'an's injunction to allow toleration of religious choice to govern the behavior of Muslims in power. All people should have the right to practice their religion. That notion of freedom of conscience became central as international human rights developed in the twentieth century.

Indigenous religions in Africa, Asia, and the Americas show a vast diversity of visions and moral obligations. However, the idea that all persons have moral responsibilities toward others appears as a theme in all religions. Native American traditions stress the sacredness of all life and the obligation of adults to care for the sacredness of the earth and its inhabitants. African traditions often focus on the animation of living things, respecting the spirit that lives within animals and persons.

Complexities and Limitations of Religious Contributions to Human Rights

Despite the common themes that preview ideals of human rights in religions, religions have often ignored those ideals in the interests of power and gain for their own groups. At times, the circle of humanness was narrowly drawn. Strangers and those in other tribes were considered subhuman and therefore not included in injunctions to treat others with respect invoked by the religion. For example, Spanish queen Isabella and king Ferdinand's conquests in South and Central America included conquering the Indians as a prelude to Christianization. Some argued that the subhuman Indians could not choose Christian practices but had to be forced into them through conquest and civilizing influence (Muck and Adeney 2009).

Sometimes the rights of certain groups were abrogated because of war, famine, or political power. At such times the ideals of a religion can give way to the pragmatism of survival and propagation of one's own group. For instance, the language of the United States Constitution gave slaves only two-thirds status as humans. Neither slaves nor women were given the right to vote when the Constitution was instituted.

The International Human Rights Movement

During the twentieth century, the modern search for universal values and the devastating effects of two world wars led to an effort to craft a universal declaration of human rights. The United Nations appointed Eleanor Roosevelt to direct that effort. Throughout the proceedings, the issue of the role of religion in defining and advocating human rights was discussed. The religious contributions of world religions found their way into the resulting document, the Universal Declaration of Human Rights, completed in 1948. The document was rendered in secular terms to ensure that it would be acceptable to people of all religions or no religion. Yet the role of world religious leaders in formulating that document is undeniable (Glendon 2002).

Debates about the role of religion in human rights abound among philosophers and religious leaders today. Some argue that an idea of God is needed as a source for human rights; others argue that human nature alone is sufficient. The diversity of moralities among religions influences conceptions of the possibility of a universal idea of human rights. Some argue that values in religious traditions overlap and that an idea of universal human rights is possible. Others argue that an incommensurability of values renders any single notion of human rights obsolete in our postmodern era. The relation of human responsibility to human rights, another important debate, is addressed by the Declaration of Human Rights by the World's Religions.

The Content of Human Rights

Those issues lead directly to the third critical issue—the content of human rights. If human rights are universal, of what do they consist? That question produces ongoing discussion among proponents of the international movement of human rights.

Among those efforts, Christian theologian C. S. Lewis developed a list of twenty universal values, many of which relate to human rights (*Abolition of Man*). Canadian Philosopher Charles Taylor delineates six modern Western values that he believes Western thinkers and societies understand to be universal (*Sources of the Self: The Making of the Modern Identity*). Those values include human rights as described by the United Nations Universal Declaration of Human Rights.

The Declaration of Human Rights by the World's Religions affirms as universal the rights listed in the United Nations Universal Declaration of Human Rights and links responsibilities to those rights agreed upon by world religious leaders. Some religions have developed theologies of human rights that relate both to the universal declaration and to interreligious questions regarding human rights (Adeney and Sharma 2007).

The content of human rights as documented in the United Nations Declaration continues to be developed by "covenants" worked out by that body during the sixty-five years since the declaration was made. Those covenants struggle with the balance between rights that address material needs and those that address human freedoms, rights due to children and women, and rights of religious freedom.

Some would argue that cultural differences render those efforts of the international human rights movement erroneous since all values are culturally located rather than universal. Others argue that universal values may take cultural forms without losing the heart of the value in question. Philosophical explorations of human rights may yield a different set of rights than religious explorations since the divine component is taken out of the equation. Balancing human rights with responsibilities, individually and in societal groups, may yield different opinions depending on the culture and nation delineating that balance. The ongoing discussion of Asian values and human rights, for example, shows that national sovereignty may sometimes trump human rights, producing differing versions of recognized human rights in a society (Ng 2007).

Issues of ideals, moral responsibility, and the content of human rights provide a rich forum for ongoing discussion. Religions have historically been part of that discussion and will continue to offer insights in the future of human rights discourse.

Further Reading

Frances S. Adeney and Arvind Sharma. *Christianity and Human Rights*. SUNY Press, 2007.

Abdullahi An-Na'im, Jerald Gort, Henry Jansen, eds. *Human Rights and Religious Values*. Rodopi, 1995.

Barbara Barnett and Elizabeth Bucar. *Does Human Rights Need God?* Eerdmans, 2005.

Mary Ann Glendon. *A World Made New*. Random House, 2002.

Paul Gordon Lauren. *The Evolution of International Human Rights*. University of Pennsylvania Press, 1998.

Terry C. Muck and Frances S. Adeney. *Christianity Encountering World Religions: The Practice of Mission in the Twenty-First Century*. Baker Academic, 2009.

Kam Weng Ng. "Human Rights and Asian Values." In *Christianity and Human Rights*, edited by Frances S. Adeney and Arvind Sharma, 151–66. SUNY Press, 2007.

134

Religion and the Family

Desiree L. Segura-April

The family is the most basic building block of society, but family structure varies greatly across the world. The form the family takes can range from a relationship between two people (two adults, or one parent and a child) to an intergenerational extended family of multiple people. Every culture, in every time and place in history, has some type of family structure, and religion has often played a key role in determining this structure and the value placed upon the family. The interplay between the family and religion is complex and also varies greatly across cultures, but almost all religions have beliefs and practices that influence the way the family functions and its role in society. The academic study of this interplay, however, has been relatively scarce until recent times, and even today it is difficult to find empirical research from around the world measuring the impact of religion on the family and vice versa. Just as families vary greatly according to their cultural and social context, religions are expressed in uncountable ways as well. Therefore, this essay will attempt to describe a generalized ecological understanding of the family and give illustrations from a variety of contexts, showing ways in which some expressions of a variety of religions affect the family both positively and negatively, and suggesting ways that the family has also affected religion. The essay will draw from studies of the linkage between religiosity and families, where "religiosity" will be explored as a "three-dimensional construct composed of (a) religious beliefs . . . (b) religious practices . . . and (c) religious communities" (Dollahite et al. 2004, 413). The family structure and experience is influenced by religion (and vice versa) in these three dimensions.

The role of the family in society is central because "families are the thread that holds the human race together. Through our families we are connected to the past—the distant times and places of our ancestors—and to the future—the hope of our children's children" (Garbarino 1982, 62). Urie Bronfenbrenner's ecological model for human development helps to explain more clearly the centrality of the family within society (Bronfenbrenner 1979). This model posits that there are microsystems within which each person grows and develops, and the family is the central microsystem. Religious communities form another microsystem, but religion also functions at the level of the macrosystem, influencing beliefs and worldview, including central beliefs about the family. When children are born, they spend the majority of their time initially interacting with the members of their family, and this contributes greatly to the way in which they grow and develop. Families socialize their members, instilling both formal and popular religious beliefs and practices.

Social scientists have identified the following three commonalties in form among the great diversity of families around the world: kinship, marriage, and childbearing. The first of these, kinship, is socially defined and represents "a consensus about the scope and limits of family membership" (Garbarino 1982, 63). Kinship extends from the individual outward through blood and marriage connections. Religion can play a role in determining with whom one can make marriage connections, and in some expressions of some religions, one would not be considered fully part of the group without also demonstrating blood kinship connections. For example, in ancient Judaism, Jews were forbidden to marry foreigners. In practice, however, this was not always followed, which led to non-Jewish people intermarrying with those of Jewish descent. This not only brought together new bloodlines but also created a mixture of religious practices. In all contexts, a clear understanding of how families fit into the kinship structure is necessary in order to fully understand the complexities of religious teachings about intermarriage and other related issues.

Second, in most cultures the family includes some form of contract or enduring relationship between two people, most commonly known as marriage. All major religions include teachings about marriage, and most include rituals surrounding this practice. In the Abrahamic religions, there are many laws and rules pertaining to marriage. Marriage is viewed as a sacred commitment and carries responsibilities for both parties. In some contexts, marriage is a sacrament, and it is the ideal for people within the society. "Of the legal injunctions in the Qur'an, about a third relate to marriage and the family" (Sherif-Trask 2004, 396). All Muslims are expected to marry, and a Muslim family is established by this contractual agreement between a man and a woman. Among Chinese Confucian and Taoist traditions, the family is the main unit for establishing social harmony, order, and unity. "Before any individual and society, there is the family" (Shang 2003, 222). It is believed that if the family is good and happy, then the whole society will have peace and harmony. Alternately, in Thai Buddhism, marriage is not seen as a religious ritual or duty. "It can be seen as the gratification of a couple dealing with cravings for sensual pleasure (*kama tanha*)" (Suwanbubbha 2003, 147). The Thai ideal for family emphasizes a sharing and a bonding between men and women.

> **Study Aid #243**
> Religion and the Family Exercise
>
> 1. Social theorists suggest that the families of the world, no matter what the religion, have three things in common.
>   Kinship
>   Marriage
>   Childbearing
>   Cite a biblical passage that you think illustrates each of these elements of families—perhaps it does not exhaust the meaning but shows an element of each. Then cite a contrasting viewpoint from another religion for each.
> 2. The parent-child relationship is crucial to families. Compare Confucian filial piety with the biblical commandment to "honor one's father and mother."

The third commonality focuses on the family as the place in which childbearing takes place, and this is viewed as a central purpose for the family among many religions. In contemporary times, some married couples are choosing not to bear children. These couples are now often recognized as families, even though they do not have children. Most families, however, will include the bearing of children, and most religions still encourage this as the ideal.

Many religions emphasize that procreation is a central goal of marriage. The Yoruba in Nigeria, Africa, view marriage and childbearing as a religious duty and "regard children as God's gift or blessing from heaven that cannot be refused" (Togonu-Bickersteth 2003, 168). The approval of a potential marriage is linked to the bride's ability to bear children: a new bride is expected to have a child within the first year of marriage, and infertility gives a man the right to seek additional wives. However, in contemporary times, due to a focus on population control, some sub-Saharan African groups are beginning to caution against excessively large families. Among traditional Chinese families, the most important goal of the family is to reproduce in order to pass on the family name and glory. According to Confucian tradition, "as is stated in Mencius [4.1.26], 'There are three things which are unfilial, and to have no posterity is the worst of them.' Many Chinese, if not most, still believe this today" (Shang 2003, 223). This does not, however, mean having as many children as possible. On the contrary, there have been different Chinese theorists who taught that either an increase or decrease in population was necessary, depending on the circumstances. The focus has always been on what is best for the society, rather than for an individual family, in order to maintain harmony and order. Among Hindus, bearing a child, especially a son, was traditionally viewed from the Vedas onward as essential to living a prosperous life, and it was necessary in order to have a good ritual death (Patton 2009). The Vedas "argue for the centrality of sacrifice and offerings to a variety of gods, for the 'goods' of ancient Indian life—cattle, fertility, rains, and offspring, particularly sons" (Patton 2009, 229).

Judaism, Christianity, and Islam all teach that God commanded humans to "be fruitful and multiply." This commandment has traditionally been interpreted to mean that married couples have a responsibility to bear children in order not only to populate the earth but also to reproduce their communities of faith. "Jewish authorities . . . not only understood this command as an order to procreate and to abstain from celibacy but also saw procreation as a fundamental component of the Jewish religion" (Baumgarten 2009, 17). In Islamic ethics this is seen as the main purpose of marriage and is "an obligatory religious mission" (Giladi 2009, 155). "Pronatalist teaching" is also common among the Latter-Day Saints in the United States (Dollahite et al. 2004, 419). Fertility and family planning have historically been a part of the teaching of many Christian groups. Certain groups, such as Roman Catholics, have traditionally been prohibited from using any form of contraception due to an emphasis on procreation. However, in contemporary times, many adherents of Catholicism, especially in the United States, have challenged this viewpoint with their behaviors.

In contrast to this approach, Thai Buddhism has no parallel to the "be fruitful and multiply" commandment, although it does teach that to be born human is good. There are no prohibitions against family planning as long as the methods used do not destroy any life (Suwanbubbha 2003).

The focus on bearing children inevitably implies a responsibility toward raising those children, and much of the interplay between religion and the family has to do with the relationship between children and parents, the roles and responsibilities of each, and the rituals of both daily life and life-cycle rites of passage. According to Jewish traditional sources, parents have a legal and moral obligation to feed, clothe, and educate their children. The education of children has focused primarily on religious education and initiating them into Judaism. However, the interpretations and applications of these obligations have varied over time and as Judaism has been practiced within a wide variety of geographical settings. Islamic ideas of childhood first developed in the medieval Middle East, although small children and women were generally marginalized within patriarchal-patrilineal societies. Nevertheless, documents show an understanding of the unique stage of childhood within the life cycle of humans. Rules and laws were also put in place describing methods of child rearing, proper care of children, the education of offspring, and systems of rites of passage for incorporating children into Muslim societies. The Qur'an emphasizes the vulnerable in society, including children, and Islamic morality and law with regard to children is based upon these teachings. Under traditional Islamic law, fathers have a specific obligation to their children because they have the power of guardianship over them, which means they exercise ownership of the child's property and person. This includes their physical care, their socialization, and their education (Giladi 2009, 159). As well, the law provides specifically for Muslim infants to have *hadana*, which can be understood as providing for their emotional and physical needs, including love, attention, and devotion (Sherif-Trask 2004). In Christianity, biblical texts and theological treatises have focused on parents teaching their children the faith, with education and child rearing also as prominent themes. "Christians across time and denominational lines have emphasized the need for adults to 'train children in the right way' (Prov. 22:6), to bring them up 'in the discipline and instruction of the Lord' (Eph. 6:4), and to 'recite' and 'talk about' the words of the Lord 'when you are at home and when you are away, when you lie down and when you rise' (Deut. 6:7)" (Bunge and Wall 2009, 86).

In contrast to this emphasis on the role of parents, among some Hindu families in India, children are not segregated from adults by such clearly defined separate roles for parents and children as found in Western contexts. "As one Indian scholar working with a Western sociologist put it, 'You bring up your children; we live with ours'" (Patton 2009, 227). Another example of a contrasting religious view of the role of parents can be found in some new religious movements that emphasize alternative kinds of families, "which could relieve children from what was seen as the oppression of the institution of the nuclear family" (Hardman 2002, 399). While certainly this cannot be applied to all of these groups, some groups have relegated the raising of children to other adults within the religious community.

In most contexts, part of the responsibility of parents toward their children is to ensure that certain rites and rituals are fulfilled for their children. Many of these are religious practices that are performed by the family within a religious community. Once again, there is a great deal of variance in the ways in which these practices are expressed, even among adherents of the same religion, depending on the cultural and social context. There are rituals pertaining to the birth and naming of children, when children start school, the initiation of children into the religious community, and when children pass into adulthood. In Judaism, for example, circumcision (for boys) and naming ceremonies (for both boys and girls) remain key elements of the practice of their faith in all contexts. The bar mitzvah is a central rite of passage into adulthood for Jewish boys, and in contemporary times a similar rite has been developed for girls within some strands of Judaism. Within the home, children play a central role in the celebration of the Passover Seder. In Christianity, infant baptism or baby dedication is performed among many groups, and this is an important time for the family to initiate their child into the faith community. Rituals may also take place within the home and are viewed as an important part of the spiritual formation of children. Christian families often read the Bible together, celebrate liturgical seasons such as Advent and Lent, and spend time in prayer together as a family (May et al. 2005). In Roman Catholicism in Latin America, a child's first communion is an important event in the life of the family and the church. According to ethnographic work done in the Muslim Middle East in the twentieth century, ritual events continue to play a role in the life of Muslim children, including circumcision for all boys and some girls, birth and naming ceremonies, and graduation from Qur'anic school, especially for boys (Giladi 2009). Within the home, Muslim children are often expected to participate in the daily prayers alongside adults. In parts of rural India, some Orthodox Hindus continue to follow menstrual observances for a girl or mark the initiation into adulthood with special gifts seen as blessings for the girl, such as a sari or flowers (Patton 2009, 228). In Native American religious traditions, puberty ceremonies are often performed both within the extended family and publicly. Among the Dakota, the Ishna Ti Awica Dowan girls' puberty ceremony was prohibited for one hundred years by the US government, but in 1998 the ritual was revived after "recognizing the relationship between the loss of the Ishna Ti and the erosion of family responsibility" (Churchill 2003, 175). These ceremonies teach girls about sexuality, marriage, and child care. In contemporary times, elder women also encourage girls to become educated and seek ways to contribute to their nations, rather than only emphasizing motherhood as the next stage in the girl's life. They are viewed as an important way of establishing and preserving a girl's identity and value. In some ceremonies, they are also establishing a girl's divinity because during the ceremony the girl actually becomes a sacred female being from her tradition, such as the White-Painted Woman (Apache) or Changing Woman (Diné) (Churchill 2003, 185).

The cycle is complete when families celebrate the ritual of marriage for their children and new families are formed. As mentioned above, in most religions there are special ceremonies and rituals related to marriage. In some cases, religion has condoned child marriages as well, although in contemporary times this is being challenged from a legal and ethical standpoint, especially in light of the United Nations Conventions on the Rights of the Child, which has been ratified in all but two countries in the world. Islamic law, for example, allows minors, predominantly girls, to have marriage contracts made for them even from the time of birth, but consummation of the marriage is not allowed until the girl reaches puberty (Giladi 2009).

Not only do religions discuss the obligations that parents have to children but they also have often focused on the responsibilities that children have toward their parents. Children are seen as important in a variety of Islamic texts because they contribute to making marital ties between their parents stronger, will carry on the father's name and thus the family line, will provide for their parents in old age, and will inherit a portion of their parents' estate (Sherif-Trask 2004, 398). In Jewish textual sources, from the Bible to the Mishna and Talmud to the midrashic texts, Jewish authorities discuss legal obligations of children toward their parents. These obligations are based on the command to honor one's father and mother and, in practice, have led to a variety of responsibilities that children are expected to fulfill for parents, grandparents, and even in-laws (Baumgarten 2009, 18). This same commandment is seen in Christianity, but the interpretation and application of it has varied greatly among different expressions of Christianity. In some more conservative Christian groups, who emphasize the disciplining of children as paramount, the obligation for children to obey their parents is highlighted also.

In some instances, religion can be seen as negatively affecting the family also. For example, some religious teachings about the roles of women have been seen as limiting the full development of girls and women, both in the home and in society. These types of teachings can be found in many religions and are interpreted and applied differently even within the same religion. The family is the place where these roles are first learned and reinforced. Some research has indicated "a relation between religiosity and higher acceptance of spousal abuse, . . . especially in conservative religious communities" (Dollahite et al. 2004, 416). Other studies have challenged this view and argued that religiosity can be a protective factor through its impact on reducing alcohol and drug abuse and thus decreasing domestic violence. Some studies in the United States have shown that Christian orthodoxy has sometimes led to authoritarian attitudes among parents that have had a negative impact on the family environment. Harmful religious rituals—such as the *sati* in India, where widows were burned on their husband's funeral pyre, or female genital mutilation for religious purposes in Africa—have been perpetuated primarily within the family.

Up to this point, the impact of religion on the family has been the primary focus of this essay. However, in recent years, it has been recognized that the family can also influence religion. There still remains much research to be done to fully understand this dynamic, but Thornton (1988) argues that it is important to have a reciprocal understanding of the interrelationships between family and religion. The impact of religion on family structure and behaviors is often more well known, but "at the same time many family changes have evoked debate and controversy within and between churches and have been the catalyst for changes in the doctrines and programs of religious groups" (ibid., 27). Among Western religions, one example of this can be seen in the response to changing behaviors in regard to birth control. In the nineteenth and early twentieth centuries, Protestants, Catholics, and Mormons in the Western world all responded with opposition to these changing behaviors and maintained their traditional stance opposing the use of contraceptives for family planning. "Laws were passed [in the nineteenth century] prohibiting the advertising and distribution of contraceptives in many countries, including the United States" (ibid., 39). These laws were still in force until after World War II, although prosecutions were few. With time, however, many Christian churches changed their official stance, and Jewish groups have also accepted birth control. The Roman Catholic Church has still not accepted artificial methods, but its stance has relaxed in the allowance for "natural family planning." This is one example of how behaviors within the family have actually influenced religion. Other examples include the change in some religious groups in regard to the acceptance of divorce and remarriage, changes in the understanding of women's role within the home and employment outside of the home, sexual practices outside of marriage, abortion, and cohabitation, although these all continue to be debated among many religious groups.

Some social theorists argued in the 1960s that the institutions of the family and religion would be weakened and perhaps even cease to exist as a result of the rapid modernization of societies. "From this perspective, both institutions are viewed as archaic leftovers from the structures of premodern societies, filling needs that have been profoundly modified in the modern era" (Houseknecht and Pankhurst 2000, 1). The reality, however, has been that families and religion have adapted and changed but have remained vitally entrenched within modern and postmodern postindustrial societies. Much study remains to be done to fully understand the complexities of the interrelationships between these two institutions, and the careful study of the link between families and religious beliefs, practices, and communities is still relatively new. Nevertheless, it seems clear that these are two institutions that are malleable and adaptable but enduring. Perhaps this is because all humans are born into some type of family and all religion has some link to the human experience, which at its very basic level is lived out among that family.

Further Reading

Elisheva Baumgarten. "Judaism." In *Children and Childhood in World Religions*, edited by D. S. Browning and M. J. Bunge, 15–82. Rutgers University Press, 2009.

Urie Bronfenbrenner. *The Ecology of Human Development*. Harvard University Press, 1979.

Marcia Bunge and John Wall. "Christianity." In *Children and Childhood in World Religions*, edited by D. S. Browning and M. J. Bunge, 83–150. Rutgers University Press, 2009.

Mary Churchill. "Reproductive Rites and Wrongs." In *Sacred Rights: The Case for Contraception and Abortion in World Religions*, edited by D. C. Maguire, 175–98. Oxford University Press, 2003.

David C. Dollahite, Loren D. Marks, and Michael A. Goodman. "Families and Religious Beliefs, Practices and Communities." In *Handbook of Contemporary Families*, edited by M. Coleman and L. H. Ganong, 411–31. Sage, 2004.

James Garbarino. *Children and Families in the Social Environment*. Aldine, 1982.

Avner Giladi. "Islam." In *Children and Childhood in World Religions*, edited by D. S. Browning and M. J. Bunge, 151–216. Rutgers University Press, 2009.

Charlotte Hardman. "Children in New Religious Movements." In *The Oxford Handbook of New Religious Movements*, edited by J. R. Lewis, 386–418. Oxford University Press, 2002.

Sharon Houseknecht and Jerry G. Pankhurst. *Family, Religion, and Social Change in Diverse Societies*. Oxford University Press, 2000.

Scottie May, Beth Posterski, Catherine Stonehouse, and Linda Cannell. *Children Matter: Celebrating Their Place in the Church, Family, and Community*. Eerdmans, 2005.

Laurie Patton. "Hinduism." In *Children and Childhood in World Religions*, edited by D. S. Browning and M. J. Bunge, 217–76. Rutgers University Press, 2009.

Geling Shang. "Excess, Lack, and Harmony: Some Confucian and Taoist Approaches to Family Planning and Population Management." In *Sacred Rights: The Case for Contraception and Abortion in World Religions*, edited by D. C. Maguire, 217–36. Oxford University Press, 2003.

Bahira Sherif-Trask. "Muslim Families in the United States." In *Handbook of Contemporary Families*, edited by M. Coleman and L. H. Ganong, 394–408. Sage, 2004.

Parichart Suwanbubbha. "The Right to Family Planning, Contraception, and Abortion in Thai Buddhism." In *Sacred Rights: The Case for Contraception and Abortion in World Religions*, edited by D. C. Maguire, 145–66. Oxford University Press, 2003.

Arland Thornton. "Reciprocal Influences of Family and Religion in a Changing World." In *The Religion and Family Connection*, edited by D. L. Thomas, 27–50. Religious Studies Center, Brigham Young University, 1988.

Funmi Togonu-Bickersteth. "Family Planning and Abortion: Cultural Norms versus Actual Practices in Nigeria." In *Sacred Rights: The Case for Contraception and Abortion in World Religions*, edited by D. C. Maguire, 167–74. Oxford University Press, 2003.

Contributors

Editor

Terry C. Muck, executive director, Louisville Institute, Louisville, Kentucky.

Associate Editors

Gerald McDermott, professor of religion, Roanoke (Virginia) College, and senior fellow, Baylor Institute for the Study of Religion.

Harold A. Netland, professor of philosophy of religion and intercultural studies, director of the doctor of philosophy program, Trinity Evangelical Divinity School, Deerfield, Illinois.

Essayists

Frances S. Adeney, professor of evangelism and global missions, Louisville Seminary, Louisville, Kentucky.

William Aiken, director of public affairs, Soka Gakkai International USA, Washington, DC.

Yaakov Ariel, professor of religious studies, University of North Carolina, Chapel Hill, North Carolina.

Michael Barkun, professor of political science, Syracuse University, New York.

Virginia Benson, senior research fellow, Ikeda Center for Peace, Learning, and Dialogue, Cambridge, Massachusetts.

James A. Beverley, professor of Christian thought and ethics, Tyndale Seminary, Toronto, Canada.

Craig Blomberg, professor of New Testament, Denver Seminary, Colorado.

Claire Borowik, codirector of international public affairs, The Family International.

Russell H. Bowers, Christian leadership development, World Vision, Cambodia.

Christopher Buck, attorney, independent scholar, and adjunct professor at Pennsylvania State University.

Ed Buckner, president, American Atheists, Smyrna, Georgia.

James Chancellor, professor of Christian missions and world religions, Southern Baptist Theological Seminary, Louisville, Kentucky.

George Chryssides, research fellow in contemporary religion, University of Birmingham, United Kingdom.

Douglas Cowan, professor of religious studies, Renison University College, Waterloo, Ontario, Canada.

J. Andrew Dearman, professor of Old Testament, director and associate dean, Fuller Texas, Houston, Texas.

Calvin DeWitt, professor of environmental studies, University of Wisconsin, Madison, Wisconsin.

Gus diZerega, independent scholar, Sebastopol, California.

Charles Farhadian, professor of world religion and Christian mission, Westmont College, Santa Barbara, California.

Rolf Furulli, lecturer in Semitic languages, University of Oslo, Norway.

Geoff Gilpin, independent scholar, Madison, Wisconsin.

Roger S. Gottlieb, professor of philosophy, Worcester Polytechnic Institute, Worcester, Massachusetts.

Kennet Granholm, assistant professor of the history of religions, Stockholm University, Sweden.

Rita M. Gross, former professor of comparative studies in religion, University of Wisconsin-Eau Claire, Eau Claire, Wisconsin.

Sarah Harvey, research officer, Inform, London, England.

S. Mark Heim, professor of Christian theology, Andover Newton Theological School, Newton Centre, Massachusetts.

Irving Hexham, professor of religious studies, University of Calgary, Alberta, Canada.

Sebastian Kim, professor in theology and public life, York St. John University, York, England.

Sallie B. King, professor of philosophy and religion, James Madison University, Harrisonburg, Virginia.

Ursula King, professor emerita of theology and religious studies, University of Bristol, Bristol, United Kingdom.

Guy McCloskey, national advisor, Soka Gakkai International USA, Chicago, Illinois.

J. Gordon Melton, distinguished professor of American religious history, Baylor University, Waco, Texas.

Eloise Hiebert Meneses, professor of anthropology, Eastern University, St. David's, Pennsylvania.

Paul Louis Metzger, professor of Christian theology and theology of culture, director of New Wine, New Wineskins, Multnomah University, Portland, Oregon.

Robert L. Millet, professor of ancient Scripture and emeritus dean of religious education, Brigham Young University, Provo, Utah.

John Morehead, executive director, Western Institute of Intercultural Studies, Salt Lake City, Utah.

Suzanne Newcombe, research officer, Inform, London, England.

Shirley Paulson, head of ecumenical affairs, Christian Science Church, Glenview, Illinois.

Richard V. Pierard, professor emeritus of history, Indiana State University, now living in Hendersonville, North Carolina.

Larry Poston, professor of religion, Nyack College, Nyack, New York.

Musa Qutub, professor of geography and environmental studies, Northeastern Illinois University, Chicago, Illinois.

Sarmad Qutub, applications engineer, Knowles Corporation, Itasca, Illinois.

Carl Raschke, professor of religious studies, University of Denver, Colorado.

Arthur Remillard, assistant professor of religious studies, Saint Francis University, Loretto, Pennsylvania.

Sandra L. Richter, professor of Old Testament, Wheaton College, Wheaton, Illinois.

Richard Robinson, senior researcher, Jews for Jesus, San Francisco, California.

Desiree L. Segura-April, professor of children at risk, Fuller Theological Seminary, Pasadena, California.

Jonathan Seitz, assistant professor, Taiwan Theological Seminary, and Presbyterian USA Mission coworker.

Arvind Sharma, professor of comparative religion, McGill University, Montreal, Canada.

Richard Shaw, professor of religion and mission, director of Wayland Mission Center, Wayland Baptist University, Plainview, Texas.

John K. Simmons, professor of philosophy and religious studies, Western Illinois University, Macomb, Illinois.

William Svelmoe, professor of history, Saint Mary's College, Notre Dame, Indiana.

James Thobaben, professor of social ethics, Asbury Theological Seminary, Wilmore, Kentucky.

Steven Tsoukalas, associate professor of apologetics and Christian thought, Wesley Biblical Seminary, and teacher of world religions at Wheaton (Illinois) College.

Christopher Vecsey, professor of the humanities and Native American studies and religion, Colgate University, Hamilton, New York.

Don Webb, high priest of Set (emeritus), and freelance writer and educator, Austin, Texas.

Richard Fox Young, professor of the history of religion, Princeton Theological Seminary, Princeton, New Jersey.

Index

Aagaard, Johannes, 575
Abbasids, 152, 157–58
'Abdu'l-Baha, 715
Aborigines, Australian, 387–88
Abraham, Islam and, 167–68
Abu Bakr, 152
Adam, 154, 178, 466–67, 655
Adha, Eid al-, 155
adivasis, 189, 191, 193
affections, religious, 32–34, 102
Africa, 343–72
African Initiated Churches (AIC), 362–65
African Israel Church, 364
African National Congress (ANC), 357
Afro-Brazilian religions, 427–29, 431, 433, 443
afterlife, the, 66, 430, 445–46
Agamas, 50
agriculture, environment and, 748–51, 752–53
ahl al-dhimma, 157–58, 176
Ahmed, Durre S., 742
Ahn Byeung-Moo, 285
AIC. *See* African Initiated Churches (AIC)
AIRFA. *See* American Indian Religious Freedom Act (AIRFA) of 1978
Akhenaten, Pharaoh, 323
Aladura movement, 364
Al Aksa Mosque, 329
Albigensians, 636–37
Aleaz, K. P., 65
Alexander, Brooke, 575
Alexander the Great, 321
Alfonso, Pedro de, 159
Ali, 152
Ali, Noble Drew, 501

aliyah, 128
Allah, 154, 166–67, 177, 334, 508
Allotment Act of 1887, 412
alms. *See* giving, charitable
Alopen, 90, 222
amaNazarites, the, 364–65
Amazonian religions, 429, 431, 433
American Indian Religious Freedom Act (AIRFA) of 1978, 422–23
American Party, the, 650
Amo, Anton Wilhelm, 343–44
Amsterdam, Maria and Peter, 701
Analects, the, 217–18
analytic mind, the, 609–10
anatta, 83–84, 101–2
ANC. *See* African National Congress (ANC)
ancestor worship, 206, 220, 223–24, 232–33, 348
Anderson, James, 694
Andrae, Johann Valentin, 637
Andrews, Charles, 77–78
angels, Islam and, 154
Angkor Empire, 241
Anglo-Saxon Federation of America, 654
anicca, 83–84, 107–8
animals, treatment of, 751–53
animism
 in the Americas, 403–6, 427–29, 449, 452–53
 in India, 206–7
 in Korea, 272–73
 in Oceania, 375, 378–81
 in Southeast Asia, 240, 243–44
Anjiro, 276
anointed class, Jehovah's Witnesses, 476–77
anthropology, science of, 12, 13, 47

795

anticult movements, 571, 573–76
anti-Semitism, 124–28, 130–31, 146–50, 653–56, 660
Apess, William, 416, 649
Apostasy, Great, 464
Apron, Masonic, 691–92, 696
Aquino, Michael A., 580, 589–90
archaeology, religious studies and, 12
Architect of the Universe, 691–92, 696
a-religions, characteristics of, 566
Arumuka Pillai, 49–50
Aryan Nations, 655
Arya Samaj, the, 60–61, 198
asceticism, 743–44
Asoka, King, 81–82, 88, 770
Assyrian Empire, 321, 323
atheism, 566, 592–605
atman, 54, 625–26, 627
Atonement, Day of, 325
attachment, Buddhism and, 83
audit, religious, 5–6
auditing, Scientologist, 612, 617
Augustine, Saint, 130, 146, 308, 361
Australia, 387–88, 398
authority system, Oceanic, 378–79, 390–91
avatar, Jesus as, 65, 76, 204–5
Axial Age, 43–44
Ayurveda, 513
Azariah, Vedanayagam Samuel, 199
Aztecs, the, 427, 429, 431–33, 434, 436–37

Bab, the, 714
Babeuf, Gracchus, 666
Babylonian Empire, 321
Babylonian Talmud, 116
Bacon, Roger, 159
Baha'i, 679, 714–24
Baha'i International Community (BIC), 722–24
Baha'u'llah, 714–16
Balfour Declaration, 173
Baltics, the, 298
Bantu Prophets in South Africa (Sundkler), 363
Baphomet, 579, 581, 584
baptism, 196–97, 479–80, 482
Barcelona disputation, 132–33
Barker, Eileen, 571, 573–74
bar mitzvah, 121
Barth, Karl, 67–68, 598
base communities, liberation, 450–51
Basri, Ammar al-, 158
Bastide, Roger, 443
Bauman, Zygmunt, 8–9

behavioral system, modern, 457–59
Bellah, Robert, 643–44
Bellamy, Edward, 671
Bellamy, Francis, 646, 671
Beltane, 545
Bengal Renaissance, 54
Berbers, the, 360–61
Berg, David, 679, 699–701, 712
Berry, Wendel, 558
Bhagavad Gita, the, 53, 73
bhakti, 53, 62, 68, 191
Bharatiya Janata Party (BJP), 210, 761
Bhawani Ma, 50
Bible, the
  the environment and, 747–54
  Islam and, 166–67, 168–69
  Jehovah's Witnesses and, 462, 478, 479, 483, 485–86
  Nation of Islam and, 503, 507
  priority of, 20, 22
biblical studies, 13
BIC. *See* Baha'i International Community (BIC)
big-man status, 379, 391
biotic rights, 747, 752–53
Birkat Ha-Minim, 131
birth control, 784, 787
BJMA. *See* British Messianic Jewish Alliance (BJMA)
BJP. *See* Bharatiya Janata Party (BJP)
Black Elk, Nicholas, 412, 416
Black Mass, the, 581–82
Black Metal music, 585
Black Stone, the, 155
Blanqui, August, 667
blasphemy, Islam and, 372
Blavatsky, Helena Pretovna, 579, 630
blessing, gospel of, 284, 291–92
bloodletting, Aztec, 431–32
blood libel, the, 124–25, 133, 147
boarding schools, Native American, 412
bodhisattva ideal, 85
Bodhisattva Never Disparaging, 531
Boff, Leonardo, 451
Bogomilism, 636
Bolivia, 449
bones, oracle, 216
Book of Changes, 216–17
Book of Mormon, 463, 466
Booths, Festival of, 325
Boris, Kynaz, 299
Boxer Rebellion, 224–25
Brahman, 54, 64–65, 187–89, 203–4, 626–27

Brahman-atman, 54, 626, 627
brahmavidaya, 64–65
Brahmo Samaj, 54, 60–61, 198
brainwashing, 570–71
Brazil, 427–29, 449
Bridge, Scientologist, 611, 617
British-Israelism, 653–54
British Messianic Jewish Alliance (BJMA), 316
Bronfenbrenner, Urie, 782
Brotherhood Church, 364
buckskin Bible, 411
Buddha, definition of, 84
Buddhism
  in China, 218–21, 236
  family and, 782, 784
  human rights and, 776
  in India, 189
  in Japan, 270–72, 520–24, 525–27
  in Korea, 273–74
  nationalism and, 761–62
  in Southeast Asia, 240–42, 244, 245–47, 258–60, 265
  Transpersonal Psychology and, 620
  violence and, 769, 772
  women and, 743–44
  as world religion, 81–114
Buddhist Council, Third, 88
Buddhist Jews, 138, 140
Bulgaria, 298–99
burial, 121, 192
Burning Times, 539
Butler, Richard Girnt, 654–55, 661
Byzantine Empire, 322, 328

Cabet, Étienne, 667
Cain, 655
calendars, 430, 536–37, 717–18
caliphs, Islamic, 152, 759
Callaway, Henry, 363
Calmette, Pierre, 64
Calvin, John, 304–5, 558
Cambodia, 240–41, 246, 249, 252, 258
Cameron, William, 654
Candomblé, 429
Cao Dai, 245
capitalism, 664, 665
Cardinal Sin, Jaime, 517
Carey, William, 61, 196–98, 361
cargo cults, 379–80, 386–87
Carson, Rachel, 557, 559
Carvaka, 57

Castaneda, Carlos, 453
caste system, Hindu, 52–53, 67, 187–89, 195–99, 211–12
catalog approach, 12, 13–14
Cathars, 636–37
Catholic Church. *See* Roman Catholic Church
Celts, the, 297, 308
Centering Prayer, 518
ceremony. *See* ritual
cessationism, 468
Cham Muslims, 243
Change Journey, The, 704
charity. *See* giving, charitable
Charron, Pierre, 598
Cheondogyo, 274
child abuse, sexual, 703
childbearing, family and, 783–84
China, 88–91, 216–39, 243, 762
Cho Yonggi, 280, 284
Christian Hebraists, 123, 125–26, 134
Christian Identity, 641, 653–62
Christianity, origins of, 327–28, 332–34
Christian Research Institute (CRI), 575
Christian Science, 489–97
Christology
  Islam and, 157, 166–67, 178
  neo-Hindu, 67
  of new religious movements, 474, 486–87, 490–91, 508, 629
  See also Jesus
Chun Hyun Kyung, 283–84
Church of Christ, Scientist, 489–97
Church of India, 200
Church of Jesus Christ of Latter Day Saints, 378, 463–75, 784
Church of Jesus Christ on Earth, 364
Church of Satan, 579, 580, 581–82, 585
Church of Scientology, 609, 612–13, 615
Church of the East. *See* Nestorian Christians
circle, ritual, 536
circumcision, Judaism and, 121
civil religion, 641–51
cleansing, ritual, 155, 271
Clear, 611, 612, 617
Clotild, 302
Clovis, King, 302
Code of a Scientologist, 616
coercion, conversion and, 35
Colenso, John Henry, 362–63
Collier, John, 421
colonialism, 159–62, 195–99, 224–25, 258–59
Columba, 310

"come and see," 100
Common Gavel, Masonic, 691–92, 696–97
common grace, 23
Common Word, A, 163
communalism, Christian, 666–67, 669–70
communism, 664
comparative studies, religious, 11–12, 13–14
Comparet, Bertrand, 654, 660
compassion theology, 97–99
conflict resolution, 37
Confucianism, 217–18, 274, 762, 776, 783
Congo, Kingdom of, 354–55
Conservative Judaism, 118, 119, 124
Constant, Alphonse Louis, 579
Constantine, Emperor, 130
contextualization, 169–70, 231–32, 255–57
contraceptives, 784, 787
contra Iudaeos literature, 131
conversion
    atheism and, 599
    Buddhism and, 104–5, 259–60
    cults and, 570–71
    Hinduism and, 69–79, 204–5, 213
    Islam and, 159–62, 169–70, 176, 179–80
    Judaism and, 131–34, 136, 137–38, 141–42, 147
    in Kosovo, 314–15
    in Latin America, 448–49
    new religious movements and, 469–70, 538, 542
    in Oceania, 384–85, 392–93, 395–96
    transformation and, 35–37
Copleston, Frederick C., 598
Cortés, Hernán, 434
Cosmic Tree, the, 298
cosmology, 46, 47, 99, 378, 550
Coughlin, Charles, 673
countercult groups, 571, 573–76
counterstory, Jewish, 131–32
covenant, 119, 135
Craig, William Lane, 598
creation
    the environment and, 558–61, 747–48, 754
    new religious movements and, 550, 588–89
    religious studies and, 17, 23
    sacrifice and, 429
Creeks, the, 406
CRI. *See* Christian Research Institute (CRI)
cross, the, 288, 478–79, 482, 495–96
cross-cultural, world religions as, 45–46
Crowley, Aleister, 535–37, 579, 581
Crusades, the, 124–25, 146, 158–59, 178–79

Cuauhtlatoatzin, 436–37
cults, 370, 566–77
cultural Christianity, 235–36
Cultural Revolution, 233
cultural system, modern, 457, 459
culture. *See* contextualization; syncretism, religious
Custer Died for Your Sins (Deloria), 416
custom movements, 393–94
Cyrene, 359
Cyril, 299, 302–3

Dakota, the, 786
Dalai Lama, 108–10, 762, 772
Dalit theology, 65. *See also* caste system, Hindu; untouchables
dana, 98
Dangun myth, 273, 283
Daoism, 218, 221, 244, 247, 282–83
Darby, John Nelson, 660
Darkness, Prince of, 589
Darwin, Charles, 13–14
da'wah, the, 152, 265
Dawkins, Richard, 593, 594, 595–96
Day, Dorothy, 672, 771
Dayananda, Sarasvati, 60–61
death, 121, 192, 545
Debs, Eugene, 671–72
Declaration of Human Rights by the World's Religions, 778–79
Deedat, Ahmed, 162
deicide, charge of, 135, 136, 149
Dejiao, 245
Delawares, the, 411
Deloria, Vine, Jr., 416
Demiurge, the, 550
democracy, Hinduism and, 205–6
De Molay, 691
demonic, the. *See* Satan
Dennett, Daniel, 593
Deo Gloria Trust, 575
dependence, sacrifice and, 429
dependent origination, circle of, 83
deprogrammers, professional, 571
Desaguliers, John T., 694
Descartes, René, 598
desecration of the host, 125, 133
desire, Buddhism and, 83
destiny, 308, 430
dharma, 52–53, 54, 59–60, 82–83
dhimmis, 157–58, 176
dialectics, Marxist, 665

Dialog Center International, 575
dialogue, interreligious, 31–35, 266–68, 317–18
diamond vehicle. *See* Vajrayana Buddhism
Dianetics: The Modern Science of Mental Health (Hubbard), 608, 613
diasporas, religious. *See* migration
Diego, Juan, 436–37
differentiation, 6–8, 46, 457–58, 641–42
discovery, right of, 414–15
disputations, Jewish-Christian, 132–33, 147
divination, 309–10, 633
Divine Principle (Moon), 682
divorce, 175–76
Dobrawa, 300
Docetism, 495–96
Doctrine and Covenants, 466
dogma, Jewish, 118
Dome of the Rock, 329
domesticated animals, 752–53
Dominican order, 132, 159, 167, 249
Donar, 297
Donghak movement, 274
doshas, 513
dowry, marriage, 175
Dragon Rouge, 580, 582, 586
dreams, 308–9, 378, 404–5
Dreyfus affair, 127–28
Druidism, 297
du'a, 155
dual belonging, 105–6, 315–16
dual covenant theology, 135, 341
dualism, 232, 291
dukkha, 83, 84, 107–8
dynasties, Chinese, 219, 222–25

Eastern Star, 691
Ebina, Danjo, 286
ecology. *See* environment, religion and
economics, Scottish, 665–66
economic system, modern, 457–59
ecstatic experience, 405
ecumenism, 263–64, 277–78, 398–99
Eddy, Mary Baker, 489–93
education, Christianity and, 310
Edwards, Jonathan, 16
Egypt, 323
Eight Dynamics, Scientologist, 611
Eightfold Path, Noble, 84
Eleven Satanic Rules of the Earth, 584
Eliot, John, 648–49
Ellison, Keith, 651
E-Meter, Scientologist, 612, 613, 617

emirs, Islamic, 759
emotions, religious, 32–34, 102
emptiness, Buddhism and, 83–84, 99
Endangered Species Act of 1973, 557–58
Endo, Shusako, 101–2
Endovelicus, 299
Engaged Buddhism, 85, 102, 107–8, 236, 772
England, 315–16
engram, 611, 612, 617
enlightenment, Buddhist, 83–84, 99
Enlightenment, the
  Africa and, 343–45
  Judaism and, 118, 126–28, 134–35
  nationalism and, 757
  new religious movements and, 593, 644
environment, religion and, 398, 533, 557–65, 746–55
erudition, 310
Esbats, 544
eschatology
  creation and, 754
  messianic, 155, 479, 487, 716
  millenarian, 656
  teleological, 667
esotericism, 630–40
Estonia. *See* Baltics, the
ethics. *See* morality
Ethiopian movement, 364
Europe, 295–318
evangelism
  in Africa, 356–57, 361–63
  Buddhism and, 87–94, 100
  in Oceania, 375–76
  theology of religion and, 26–30, 35–36
evil, problem of, 107–8, 594
evolution, theory of, 13–14
exclusivism, 21, 166–70, 290–91
exit counseling, 571
extinction pattern, 185
extremism, religious, 367–68

Fabians, the, 671
factory farming, 752
faith, 598, 676–77
Faivre, Antoine, 640
fall, the, 466–67, 683, 748
family, religion and, 265, 781–88
Family International, The, 679, 699–713
family tree, religious studies, 12–13
fanaticism, religious, 367–68
Fard, W. D., 500–503, 506, 508
farming, environment and, 748–51, 752–53

Farrakhan, Louis, 502–3, 507
fasting, Islam and, 154, 155
fate, 308, 430
FECRIS, 576
Felix, Bishop, 301
feminism, 672. *See also* women
feudalism, 664, 665
fideism, 598
First Amendment, the, 420–21, 646, 661
Fitr, Eid al-, 155
Five K's, Khalsa, 191–92
Five Pillars, Islamic, 155–56, 325
Flew, Antony, 599
Flirty Fishing, 700–702, 703
floating needle, Scientologist, 612
flying, yogic, 514
folk religions. *See* indigenous religions
folk Shinto, 271
Ford, Henry, 654
foreknowledge, destiny and, 308
Fourier, Charles, 667
Four Noble Truths, Buddhist, 83–84
Franciscan order, 159, 167, 223
Francis of Assisi, 303–4
Fraternitas Saturni, 579
Frazer, James Gordon, 12
freedom, religious, 420–21, 422–23
Freemasonry, 638, 679–80, 690–97
French socialism, 666–67
Freud, Sigmund, 620–21, 626
fulfillment theology, 232
functionalism, 14–15
fundamentalism, Islamic, 153, 172, 760

Gabriel (angel), 151, 154
Gale, William Potter, 654, 660
Gandhi, Mahatma, 60, 61, 77–78, 760, 771
Gardner, Gerald, 535–37
Garnet, Henry Highland, 500
Garvey, Marcus, 501
Gautama, Siddartha, 81
Gavel, Masonic, 692, 696–97
Gayman, Dan, 655, 661
Gemaras, the, 116
gender, religion and, 736–45. *See also* women
general revelation, 23
German idealist philosophy, 664–65, 670
Germany, 297–98, 316–17
Gernet, Jacques, 228, 231–33
ghosts, Chinese, 220
ghusl, 155
giving, charitable, 154, 156, 749–50, 777

Glacken, Clarence, 558
Glagolitic alphabet, 299, 303
globalization, 212–13
Gnosticism, 495–97, 533, 547–56, 583, 629–30
Goa, 69–70
goals, Christian, 18
God
  Baha'i and, 715–16
  Christian Science and, 490, 496
  Freemasonry and, 691–92, 695–96
  image of, 17, 31, 741
  Islamic, 154, 166–67, 177, 334
  Jehovah's Witnesses and, 486
  Jewish, 118, 119, 133
  Mormon, 464, 466
  name of, 229–30, 323
  Nation of Islam and, 503, 508
  the New Age and, 631, 639
  science and, 730
  Transpersonal Psychology and, 627–28
God Is Red (Deloria), 416
gods, Chinese, 220–21, 247
Gohonzon, 523
Golden Age of Spain, 116, 124–25
Golden Bough, 12
Goode, Virgil H., 651
Good Samaritan, the, 32–33
Gopin, Mark, 772
Gospel of Barnabas, 162
Goths, 299
government. *See* politics
grace, 23, 97–99, 391–92
Grand Orient, 691
Gray, Richard, 355
Great Apostasy, the, 464
Great Architect, Masonic, 691–92, 696
Great Britain, 315–16
Great Century, the, 224
Great Commandment, the, 26, 29–30, 163
Great Commission, the, 26, 29–30, 87, 713
great crowd, Jehovah's Witnesses, 477
great vehicle. *See* Mahayana Buddhism
Greece, 296
Gregorius, Gregor A., 579
Grosche, Eugen, 579
group conversion, 384–85, 392–93
Guadalupe, Virgin of, 436–37, 444–45
Guanyin, 247
Gurdjieff, George, 630
Guru Dev, 510
Guru Granth Sahib, 192
Guru Nanak, 189, 191, 192

Gutiérrez, Ramón, 444
Guzmán, Dominic de, 637

hadana, 784–85
Hagelin, John, 514
Haggerty, Thomas, 671
Hajj, the, 155
halakhah, 116, 120
Ham Sok Hon, 101
han, 283
Han, Hak Ja, 681
Handsome Lake, 411
Han Kyung-Chik, 279
Hanullim, 273, 274
harmony, Wiccan, 544
Harnack, Adolf von, 552, 554–55
Harris, Doug, 575
Harris, Sam, 593
Hasidic Judaism, 117
Haskalah, the, 118, 126–28
Hatsumode, 271
healing, spiritual, 412–13, 492–93, 494–95
heaven, 66. *See also* afterlife, the
Hebraists, Christian, 123, 125–26, 134
Hebrew Bible, 321, 333
Heeb, 140
Hegelians, Young, 665, 670
Hellenism, 322, 323, 327
heresy, 59–60, 131, 469–71, 495–97, 547–56
Hick, John, 599
hidden Christians, 277, 287
hierarchy, social, 52–53, 67, 187–89, 195–99, 211–12
High God, African, 349–50
Hijra, the, 151
Hilda of Whitby, 302
Hinduism
  family and, 783–84, 785
  human rights and, 776
  in India, 187–91, 195–99, 203–6, 209–13
  nationalism and, 760–61
  scriptures and, 346–47
  in Southeast Asia, 241, 242
  Transpersonal Psychology and, 620, 625–26, 627
  as world religion, 49–79
Hindutva, 61, 209–11, 761
Hiram Abif, 692–93
Hislop, Alexander, 482
historical religions, characteristics of, 44–47
Hitchens, Christopher, 593
Hitchens, Peter, 599

Hizzuk Emunah (Troki), 133
holidays, 120–21, 131–32, 155
holiness, Buddhism and, 101–2
Holocaust, the, 128, 135
Holy Salt, 684
homosexuality, Judaism and, 140
Hong, Nansook, 682
Hong Xiuquan, 224
Horseman, Thracian, 298–99
host, desecration of the, 125, 133
Hubbard, L. Ron, 606, 608–9, 613
human, definition of, 775
humanistic psychology, 621, 623, 626–27
Humanist Manifesto, The, 593, 594, 595
human rights, 176, 211, 317–18, 571, 774–79
humiliation, century of, 224
humility, Buddhism and, 101–2
huppah, the, 121
husbandry, animal, 752–53
Hutchinsonians, 126

Iberian Peninsula, 299
Iblis. *See* Satan
I-Ching, 216–17
ICSA. *See* International Cultic Studies Association (ICSA)
idealism, German, 665, 670
identity, religious, 8–9
idolatry, 229
iftar, 155
Ignatius of Loyola, 159
Ikeda, Daisaku, 521–22, 525–27, 530–32
illuminati, 550
image, God's, 17, 31, 741
imagery, religious, 229
impermanence, Buddhism and, 83–84, 107–8
Inca, the, 427, 435
incarnation, 20, 31, 65, 204–5
inclusivism, 21, 67, 165–70
inculturation theology, 417
India, 187–215, 760–61
Indian Ecumenical Conference, 418
Indian Removal Act of 1830, 649
Indian Shaker Church, 411
indigenization, religious. *See* contextualization; syncretism, religious
indigenous religions
  in Africa, 345–50, 367–70, 778
  in the Americas, 401–25, 426–33, 448–49, 452–53, 778
  characteristics of, 183–86

in China, 216–18, 762, 783
of Europe, 295–300
in India, 189, 191, 193, 206–8, 213–14
in North Asia, 269–74
in Oceania, 375–81
in Southeast Asia, 240–47
See also individual religions
individualism, 396–97, 457–59, 606–7, 622–23
Indonesia, 744
Industrial Revolution, the, 559
Inform, 571
Ingersoll, Robert, 594
Inquisition, the, 69–70, 125, 133, 147, 637
insight meditation, 85, 99
integral psychology, 622
integration, religious, 459–60
intermarriage, Hindu, 212
intermarriage, Jewish, 129, 140–41
International Association for the History of Religions (Paris, 1900), 12
International Cultic Studies Association (ICSA), 571
International Workers of the World (IWW), 671
intolerance, conversion and, 35, 36–37
invitation, Islamic, 152, 265
Iroquois, the, 406, 411
Isaac of Troki, 133
Islam
  in Africa, 353–54, 355–56, 371–72
  in Europe, 303–4, 311–12, 314–15, 316–18
  family and, 784–86
  human rights and, 777
  in India, 189
  in the Middle East, 329–30, 334, 339–40
  nationalism and, 759–60
  in North America, 651
  origins of, 320–22, 324–25
  in Southeast Asia, 243, 244–45, 265, 266–68
  violence and, 768, 770, 771–72
  women and, 744–45
  as world religion, 151–80
Israel
  Christian Identity and, 660
  Islam and, 173–74, 317–18
  Judaism and, 118, 128–29, 135, 138–41, 340–42
  origins of, 320–22, 323, 330–31, 339–40, 758–59
IWW. *See* International Workers of the World (IWW)

Jainism, 189, 190, 191–92
Japan
  Buddhism and, 91–92, 101–2, 270–72
  Christianity in, 276–78, 285–88, 292–94
  Shinto and, 269–72, 762
jati. *See* caste system, Hindu
Jefferson, Thomas, 644
Jehovah's Witnesses, 476–88
Jerusalem Talmud, 116
Jesuit order, 64, 90–91, 249
Jesus
  Islam and, 155, 157, 163, 166–67, 178, 334–36
  Judaism and, 120, 132, 134–35, 141, 333–34
  life of, 295
  neo-Hinduism and, 67
  new religious movements and, 474, 486–87, 490–91, 508, 629, 683
Jesus-believing Jews, 142
Jibril (angel), 151, 154
jihad, 371
jinn, 154
Jinnah, Ali, 760–61
Jodo-kyo Buddhism, 271
John Frum cult, 380, 387
John of Montecrovino, 223
John of Plano Carpini, 223
Judah *haNasi*, 116
Judaism
  in Africa, 354, 555
  Christianity and, 311, 315–16, 327–28, 332–34, 340–42
  family and, 784, 786
  human rights and, 777
  nationalism and, 758–59
  in North America, 650
  origins of, 320–21, 323–25
  Roman Empire and, 146, 295–96, 328
  violence and, 768, 770, 772
  as world religion, 115–50
Judson, Adoniram and Ann, 257
Juergensmeyer, Mark, 767–68
Jung, Carl Gustav, 621
Jungle, The (Sinclair), 671
Jun Tai-ill, 285
justice, retributive, 386, 391–92
Justin Martyr, 130–31, 547, 592
just war theory, 770–71
Jyotish, 513

Ka'ba, the, 151–52, 155
Kabbalah, the, 117, 125–26, 134, 630, 637
kachera, 193

Index 803

Kadosh, Ben, 579
kami, Shinto, 271, 520
Kanapati, 63
kangha, 192
kara, 193
Karen tribes, 252
Karlsson, Thomas, 586
karma, 52, 54, 82–84, 98, 107–8
kashrut, 120
Katayama, Tetsu, 278
Kennedy, John F., 646
Kerala, 194–95
kesh, 191–92
Khalsa, the, 191–92
Khan, Abdul Ghaffar, 771–72
Khudai, Khidmatgar, 772
kibock sinang, 284, 291–92
Kim, Hyo Nam, 684
Kimbangu, Simon, 364
Kim Chi Ha, 280
King, Karen, 497
King, Martin Luther, Jr., 644–45, 771
King Follett Discourse, 464
kinship, 403–4, 782
Kinsley, David, 747
kirpan, 193
Kitamori, Kazoh, 287
kitchen god, Chinese, 247
Knights Templar, 583–84
Knorr, Nathan H., 477–78
koans. *See* Zen Buddhism
Kongzi, 217
Kony, Joseph, 370
Koran, the. *See* Qur'an, the
Korea
 Buddhism and, 92, 101, 273–74
 Christianity in, 278–85, 289–92
 Confucianism and, 274
 shamanism and, 272–73
kosher laws, 120
Kosovo, 314–15
Koyama, Kosuke, 288
Kumamoto group, 286–87
Kurtz, Paul, 594
kut, 273
Kwakiutls, the, 406
Kyi, Aung San Suu, 772

Lakota, the, 406, 417
Lakwena, Alice, 370
Lamanites, 463
land, promise of. *See* Zionism

Landa, Diego de, 435
land-tenure, 748–49
Laos, 246, 249, 251, 253
Las Casas, Bartolomé de, 435
Latter Day Saints. *See* Church of Jesus Christ of Latter Day Saints
Latvia. *See* Baltics, the
LaVey, Anton Szandor, 579–81, 589–90
law, Jewish, 116, 118, 120, 131
Law of Love, TFI, 702, 703–4, 708
LDS. *See* Church of Jesus Christ of Latter Day Saints
leadership, church, 264
Lebanon, 338–39
Lee, Sang Hun, 684
Left-Hand Path, 580, 582, 585–86, 588–91
Lekganyane, Ignatious, 364
Leonard, Benny, 650
Leopold, Aldo, 557, 559–60
Lévi, Eliphas, 579
liberation theology, 65, 280, 285, 450–51
life, sources of, 403–6
life-cycle events, 121, 406, 785–86
Life Tree, the, 298
Lincoln, Abraham, 644–45
liquid modernity, 8–9
Lithuania. *See* Baltics, the
little traditions, religious, 347
localization, religious. *See* contextualization; syncretism, religious
Loftus, John, 599
loloma, 391
Lord's Resistance Army (LRA), 370
Lotus Sutra, 522–23, 527
love, 163, 179, 204, 591
Love Charter, TFI, 701, 702
Loy Krathong, 247
LRA. *See* Lord's Resistance Army (LRA)
Lubavitcher Hasidim, 117
Lull, Ramon, 159, 167
Lumen Gentium, 162
Lutheranism, 59, 61, 63, 418–19
Lynch, David, 514, 518

MacCormack, Sabine, 443–44
magic
 indigenous religions and, 206–7, 348–49, 368, 381
 new religious movements and, 535–37, 581–82, 632–33
Mahabharata, the, 53
Maharishi Effect, 512

Maharishi Mahesh Yogi, 510–12, 515–16
Mahavira, 189, 190, 192
Mahayana Buddhism, 84–85, 99, 220, 241, 270–71
Maimonides, 116, 118, 133
Majeke, Nosipho, 362
major-minor pattern, 185
Makiguchi, Tsunesaburo, 520
making authority, Oceanic, 378–79, 390–91
Malacca, 248–49, 250, 251
Malaysia, 245, 250, 253, 265, 266–67
Malcolm X, 502–3, 507
Malnak v. Yogi, 517–18
Mamai movement, 384
mana, 206, 375, 379, 392
Man and Nature (Marsh), 557
mandalas, 523
Manichaeism, 636
Manifest Destiny, 412, 645
Manila Declaration, the, 23–24
Manual of the Mother Church, 491–92
Ma'ohi, the, 385
Maori, the, 390–91, 398
Maramatanga movement, 390–91
Marching Rule movement, 393–94
Marcion of Pontus, 547
marranos, 133
marriage
 family and, 782, 786
 Hinduism and, 212
 Islam and, 174–76
 Judaism and, 129, 140–41
 Unification Church and, 683
Marsh, George Perkins, 557, 559
Mar Thomas. *See* Thomas Christians
Martin, Walter, 574–75
Martini, Raymundus, 133
Martin of Tours, 301–2
martyrdom, 301, 768–70
Marxism, 641, 663–78
Mary, 436–37, 444–45
Masada, 768
Maslow, Abraham, 621
Masons, 638, 679–80, 690–97
mass conversion, 384–85, 392–93
Materialist (Carvaka), 57
material world, 46, 47
Mau Mau movement, 368
maya, life as, 203
Maya, the, 426–27, 435
McCarthy, Joseph, 673
McPherson, Aimee Semple, 673

McPherson, Lisa, 613
Mecca, 151–52, 155
Medellin, 450–51
Medicine Men and Clergy Meetings, 417
Medina, 151
meditation, 85, 99–100, 102, 510–18, 633
mediums, spirit, 368–69
meekness theology, 102
Mejuhon, Nantachai and Ubolwon, 102
Melanesia, 386–87
membership, TFI, 702–3
Mendicant order, 147
merit, 52, 54, 82–84, 98
Mesmer, Franz, 630, 638
Meso-America, 426–53
Messiah, the
 Islam and, 155, 163
 Judaism and, 119, 120, 132, 135
 See also Jesus
Messianic Jews, 142, 315–16, 330–31
MEST, 609, 612
Methodius, 299, 302–3
Micronesia, 385–86
Middle East, 320–42
Mieszka, Duke, 300
migration, 73–74, 185–86, 395–96
Mill, William Hodge, 62
Millennium Dawn (Russell), 476
mind, the, 609–10, 612
Ming dynasty, 223
minim, 131
ministry, the. *See* leadership, church
minjung theologians, 280, 285
minority rights, 176, 211, 317–18, 571
Mirandola, Pico della, 125
Misanthropic Lucifer Order, 580
Mishnah, the, 116
mission, Christian, 26. *See also* evangelism
missionary movement, modern, 356–57, 361–63, 375–76. *See also* evangelism
missions, Spanish, 408–10
Mission Theological Advisory Group, 576
mitzvot, the, 117, 118
modernism
 indigenous religions and, 185
 Islam and, 153, 172
 Japan and, 278
 new religious movements and, 457–60, 641–42
 religious studies and, 8, 12–13
moksha, 51, 52, 54, 66–67
Mongolia, 91
monism, 622

monolatry, 53, 54, 323
monotheism
  Christianity and, 334
  Islam and, 154–55, 157, 166–67, 177–80, 372
  Judaism and, 118, 119, 133, 325
  science and, 730
Montaigne, Michel de, 598
Montezuma, 427
Montvoisin, Catherine, 584
Moo, Douglas, 753–54
Moon, Sun Myung, 681–82, 686–89
Mooneyham, Stan, 258
Moonies. *See* Unification Church
morality
  in the Americas, 432–33, 446
  new religious movements and, 587, 595, 604, 684, 691–92
  world religions and, 204, 291
Mormonism. *See* Church of Jesus Christ of Latter Day Saints
Moroni (angel), 463
Morrison, Robert, 224
mot, 283
Mountain Meadows massacre, 469
Mu'awiya, 152
Muck, Terry, 32
Mudang, 273
Mughal Empire, 189
Muhammad, Elijah, 500–503, 506–7
Muhammad, Prophet, 151–52, 154, 155, 178, 335
Muir, John, 557, 559
Muism, 273
Muller, Max, 11–12
murder, ritual, 368
Myanmar, 240, 249, 251, 252, 257
Myote Mondo, 286

Naga Church, 200
Nag Hammadi scrolls, 547–48, 554
NAGPRA. *See* Native American Graves Protection and Repatriation Act (NAGPRA) of 1990
name, God's, 154, 166–67, 177, 229–30, 323, 334
Nam-myoho-renge-kyo, 522–23
Nanak, Guru, 189, 191, 192
narrative, Judaism and, 131–32
nationalism
  African, 356–57
  Hinduism and, 61, 209–11
  Islam and, 153, 173, 316–17

  in Oceania, 397–98
  religion and, 756–62
Nation of Islam, 500–508
Native American Church, 411, 421
Native American Graves Protection and Repatriation Act (NAGPRA) of 1990, 423
Native Americans, 401–25, 648–49, 786
Native Theological Association, 418
nativist movement, American, 650
natural religion, Islam as, 151
nature, human, 775
Nauvoo, Illinois, 464–65
Nazareth Baptist Church, 364–65
needle, floating, 612
Nehru, Jawaharlal, 760–61
neighbor, the, 31–35, 163, 179
Neo-Assyrian Empire, 321, 323
Neo-Babylonian Empire, 321
neo-Hinduism, 52, 54, 60, 67, 197–98
Neolin, 411
neopaganism, 533–46
Nephites, 463
Nestorian Christians, 88–90, 157–58, 222, 255, 259
New Age movement, 553–54, 606, 629–40
New Christian Right, 659–61
Newdow, Michael, 646
New Guinea, 391
New Year festival, Japanese, 271
New Zealand, 390–91, 398
Nichiren Buddhism, 271, 520–24, 525–27
Niebuhr, Reinhold, 149
Nilakantha Goreh, 49, 59–60, 66–67
Nimrod, 482
9/11 Unity Walk, 528
Nine Angles, Order of, 580, 582
nirvana, 83–84, 99
Noah, Seven Laws of, 118
Nobili, Roberto de, 57, 61, 64, 195–96
Noble Eightfold Path, 84
Noble Society. *See* Arya Samaj, the
Noble Truths, Buddhist, 83–84
Nogqawusa, 368
Nonchurch Movement, 287–88
nonviolence, religion and, 771–72
North America, 93–94, 105–6, 401–25
North Asia, 269–94
North Korea, 279, 292
no-self, Buddhism and, 83–84, 101–2
Nostra Aetate, 135, 136, 149, 162–63
nuns, Buddhist, 743–44
nurture, sacrifice and, 429

objectivity, scholarly, 4, 14, 15–16
Obligation, Masonic, 692
Obon, 271
Occom, Samson, 411, 416
Oceania, 374–99
OCRT. *See* Ontario Consultants on Religious Tolerance (OCRT)
Odin, 297–98
Offensive, The, 704
O'Hair, Madalyn Murray, 593
Okoro, Pedro, 306
Olga, Princess, 300
Onenesses, Three, 717
Ontario Consultants on Religious Tolerance (OCRT), 571
Operating Thetan, 611, 612
oracles, Chinese bone, 216
Oral Law, Jewish, 116, 131
orchards, 750–51
Order, The, 655
Order of Nine Angles, 580, 582
orgs, Scientologist, 609, 612–13
orixás, 431, 433
Orthodox Judaism, 118, 119, 124
Otto, Rudolf, 13, 14, 97–98
Ottoman Empire, 152–53, 162, 322, 329–30, 339–40
Oxford Capacity Analysis Test, 615–16

pacifism, 771–72
padroado system, 249
paganism, 533–46
Pagels, Elaine, 552–53
Palestinian Talmud, 116
pantheism, 622
parenting, family and, 784–86
Parents, True, 684
Parliament of World Religions (Chicago, 1893), 12, 61, 742–43
Parsi, 189, 190–91, 192
Parsons, Talcott, 6–8, 458
particularism, 14, 20–23
partisanship, scholarly, 4
Pascal, Blaise, 598
Passover, the, 131–32, 325
pastors. *See* leadership, church
paterfamilias pattern, 297
paticca samuppada, 83–84
Patrick, Saint, 308
patron deity. *See* monolatry
Paul, the apostle, 28–29, 145, 295, 299
Pax Romana, 27–29

payback system, Melanesian, 386, 391–92
Pchum Ben, 246
peace child, 394
peace churches, 771
Peace Policy, US, 412
Pearl of Great Price, 466
Pentecostalism, 439, 451–53
People's Republic of China (PRC), 225–26, 233, 235–36
People's Temple, the, 570
Persian Empire, 321
personality system, modern. *See* individualism
Peters, Pete, 655, 661
Peter the Venerable, 159
peyote, 421, 423, 661
phenomenology, 14, 22
philo-Semitism, 123, 133–34
philosophy, 13, 133, 204–5, 664–67, 732–33
Pie in the Sky, 671
pietism, German, 59, 61, 63
pilgrimage, Islamic, 154, 155
Pipe and Christ, The (Stolzman), 417
Pledge of Allegiance, 646
pleroma, the, 550–51
pluralism, religious, 21, 29
pogroms, 126
Poland, 300
politics
  in Africa, 368–69, 370–71
  in the Americas, 412, 450–51
  Buddhism and, 81–82, 85, 88
  Jehovah's Witnesses and, 479, 486
  in Korea, 280, 285
  religion and, 47, 458, 756–62
  in Southeast Asia, 266
polygamy, 174–76, 362–63, 464, 466
Polynesia, 384–85
polytheism, 322–23, 324–25, 446, 545–46
poor, the
  Buddhism and, 98, 102, 107
  Christianity and, 212–13, 266, 280, 284–85, 449–51
  the environment and, 749–50
  The Family International and, 701, 707
  Islam and, 156
  Marxism and, 676
Pope's Stone, the, 650
popular culture, 541–42
popular Hinduism, 190, 191, 242
Portugal, 299
postmodern period, 13, 138
prayer, Islam and, 154, 155

Praying Indian Towns, 409, 648–49
PRC. *See* People's Republic of China (PRC)
preclear, 611, 612
premillennialism, Islamic, 155
premodern religious studies, 12
presence, second, 479
Prester John (Buchan), 363
primal experiences, 346, 348
primitive communalism, 664, 665
Prince of Darkness, 589
prison, Christian Identity and, 661–62
proclamation, 27–30, 87, 100
procreation, family and, 783–84
Progressive Revelation, Baha'i, 716
prophets, Islam and, 151–52, 154, 155
prosperity cults, 379–80, 386–87
protection, people of, 157–58, 176
Protestantism
   in the Americas, 409, 437–39, 648–51
   in China, 224–26
   in India, 196–97
   Islam and, 159–62
   Judaism and, 134, 148–49, 650
   nationalism and, 757–58
   in North Asia, 277–78, 279, 281, 286, 289–91
   in Southeast Asia, 250–51, 257–58
Protestantization, 73–74
psychology, 12, 458. *See also* individualism
Pueblos, the, 406, 409–10, 420–21, 444
Pugio Fidei (Martini), 133
puja, 191, 513, 517
pungnyu theology, 283
Pure Land Buddhism, 271
purification, ritual, 271
Puritanism, 643–44
purity. *See* morality

Qing dynasty, 223–25, 226
Qur'an, the, 151, 154, 166–69, 178, 335–36
Qurra, Theodore Abu, 157–58

rabbis, 119
Rabbis for Human Rights, 772
racism, 139, 500–508, 641, 653–57, 662
radical differentiation, 6–8, 641–42
radio preachers, 672–73
Rainbow, 691
Rais, Gilles de, 584
Ra'ita, Habib Abu, 158
Ramabai, Pandita, 199
Ramacandra, 62
Ramadan, 155

Rand, Howard, 654
ransom, atonement as, 478, 486–87
Rashidun, the, 152
Rashtriya Swayamsevak Sangh (RSS), 761
Reachout Trust, 484, 575
reactive mind, the, 610–11
reason, atheism and, 594, 598
rebbe, 117
rebellions, Chinese, 224–25
recitations, Islamic, 151
Rede, Wiccan, 537
Redfield, Robert, 347
Reformation, the, 637, 757
reform Hinduisms, 52, 60–61, 197–98
Reform Judaism, 118, 119, 124
refrigerium, rite of, 361
Regensburg Address, the, 163
reincarnation
   Buddhism and, 82–84, 98, 99
   Hinduism and, 52, 54, 66–67
   Scientology and, 611, 612, 617
relationship, the neighbor and, 31
relativism, cultural, 14
religion, parameters of, xiii, 774
religious freedom, 420–21, 422–23
Religious Freedom Restoration Act (RFRA) of 1993, 661
Religious Land Use and Institutionalized Persons Act (RLUIPA) of 2000, 661–62
religious studies approach, 3–4, 11–18
replacement theology. *See* supersessionism
Requirement, the, 415, 435
resurrection, the, 166–67, 508
retributive justice, 386, 391–92
Reuchlin, Johannes, 125, 637
revelation
   general, 23
   progressive, 466, 468, 716
   specific, 20, 67–68, 154
revivals, Korean, 279, 280, 284, 291–92
RFRA. *See* Religious Freedom Restoration Act (RFRA) of 1993
Rhodes, Alexander de, 249, 256
Ricard, Robert, 442
Ricci, Matteo, 90–91, 223
rice myths, Thai, 241–42
Ricoldo de Monte-Crucis, 167
Riel, Louis, 412
right of discovery, 414–15
rights, definition of, 775
rights, human. *See* human rights
Rinzai Buddhism, 270–71

rites controversy, 91, 223–24
ritual, 368, 393–94, 405–6, 785–86
RLUIPA. *See* Religious Land Use and Institutionalized Persons Act (RLUIPA) of 2000
Rocket Festival, 247
Rockne, Knute, 650
Role of Missionaries in Conquest, The (Majeke), 362
Roman Catholic Church
　in China, 222–26
　family and, 784, 787
　Freemasonry and, 694–95
　Hinduism and, 57, 61, 64, 69–71
　in India, 195–96
　Islam and, 159, 162–63, 167
　Judaism and, 135, 136, 149
　in Latin America, 434–37, 441–46, 448–51
　nationalism and, 757–58
　in North America, 408–10, 414–17, 418, 650
　in North Asia, 276–77, 278–79, 281, 285–86
　in Southeast Asia, 249–50, 256–57
Roman Empire
　in Africa, 353, 359–60
　Christianity and, 27–29, 295–97, 301, 322, 756–57
　in Iberia, 299
　Judaism and, 146, 328
Romero, Óscar, 451
Roosevelt, Theodore, 557, 559
Rosicrucianism, 637
Rousseau, Jean-Jacques, 643–44
Roy, Ram Mohun, 54, 60–61, 197–98
Royal Plowing Ceremony, 247
RSS. *See* Rashtriya Swayamsevak Sangh (RSS)
Ruism. *See* Confucianism
Rule of Three, 537
Rusalkas, 300
Russell, Charles Taze, 476–77, 481
Russia, 299–300
Rutherford, Joseph Franklin, 477, 481–82
Ryu Dong-Shik, 282–83

Sabbats, Wiccan, 544
sacrifice, 380–81, 429, 431–32, 752–53
Saint-Simon, Henri de, 666
Sakyadhita, 743–44
Salat, 155
Salem witch trials, 539
Salt, Holy, 684
salvation
　Baha'i and, 720–21
　Christianity and, 332, 334

Christian Science and, 495–96
Freemasonry and, 691–92, 696–97
Hinduism and, 66–67
Islam and, 154
Jehovah's Witnesses and, 478, 486–87
Judaism and, 118, 133
in Latin American religion, 445–46
Mormonism and, 466–67
in Oceania, 393–94
Scientology and, 611, 617
theology of religion and, 20, 24–25
Unification Church and, 683, 689
world religions and, 47
Salvation Army, the, 671
sam, 283
Samaritan, Good, 32–33
Samaritans, 332
Samhain, 545
samsara, 52, 54, 66–67, 82–84, 98–99
sangha, 258
San Remo Peace Conference, 173
Sanskritization, 70, 190
Santa Fe Independent School District v. Doe, 646
santhara, 192
Sarasvati, Madhasudana, 63–64
Saraswati, Swami Brahmanandra, 510
Satan, 23, 154, 452, 589, 655
Satanic Bible, The (LaVey), 579–81, 585
Satanic Panic, 584–85
Satanism, 537–38, 540, 566, 578–91
sati, rite of, 197–98
Savarkar, V. D., 61, 210
Sawi, the, 394
Sawn, 155
Scandinavia, 297–98, 308–9
Schultz, Paul, 418
SCI. *See* Science of Creative Intelligence (SCI)
science, religion and, 13, 594, 729–35
Science of Creative Intelligence (SCI), 517–18
Scientology, 606, 608–19
Scottish economic philosophy, 665
Scottish Rite, Masonic, 690–91
SCP. *See* Spiritual Counterfeits Project (SCP)
scriptures
　atheism and, 594–95
　Christian. *see* Bible, the
　the environment and, 747–54
　Hindu, 52–53, 73, 346–47
　Islamic, 151, 154, 166–69, 178, 335–36
　Jehovah's Witnesses and, 478, 479, 483, 485–86
　Jewish, 321, 333

Index 809

Mormonism and, 461–62, 463, 466
Nation of Islam and, 503, 507
Satanism and, 579–81, 585
Scientology and, 608–9, 613, 617–18
Sikh, 192
tribal religions and, 346–47
Unification Church and, 682
women and, 741
seasons, the, 406
Second Book, Religions of the, 461–62
second coming, Christ's, 479. *See also* eschatology
sectarianism, China and, 236
sect Shinto, 271
secular, definition of, 8
secularization, 185
secular Judaism, 118
Seeyam, 155
sefirot, 117
self, the, 83–84, 101–2, 392–93, 396–97, 606–7
separatist churches, 363
services, social, 257–58, 266. *See also* poor, the
Set, Temple of, 580, 582, 585–86, 588–91
Seven Laws of Noah, 118
sex, 700–702, 703–4, 708
Sextus Empiricus, 592, 598
shahada, 155
Shaiva, 52, 53
Shaktism, 50, 52, 53
shamanism, 272–73, 283–84, 405, 431
shari'a law, 154, 372
sharing, sexual, 701, 703–4
Shema, the, 118
Shembe, Isaiah, 364–65
Shestov, Lev, 598
Shi'ite Islam, 152
Shinto, 269–72, 520, 762
shirk, sin of, 154
Shoghi Effendi, 715
Shriners, 691
shrines, Shinto, 271, 762
Siddartha Gautama, 81
side-by-side pattern, 185
sidhas, 514
Sikhism, 189, 191, 192–93, 761
Silence, Towers of, 192
Silent Spring (Carson), 557
sin
  Islam and, 154
  Native Americans and, 410, 417
  new religious movements and, 466–67, 478, 495, 617
  theology of religion and, 23

sincerity, theology of, 283
Sinclair, Upton, 671, 673
Singapore, 247, 250–51, 253, 257, 262–63
Singh, Sadhu Sundar, 199
Sinism, 273
Skagits, the, 406
skillful means, Buddhism and, 100
slavery, African, 355–56, 427–29, 649
slave society, 664–65
Smith, Adam, 665–66
Smith, Charles Lee, 593
Smith, Gerald L. K., 654
Smith, Joseph, 463–65, 468–69, 473–75
Social Gospel, the, 671–72
social hierarchy. *See* hierarchy, social
socialism, 664, 665, 666–67, 671–72
social justice, Baha'i and, 722–24
social sciences, 13
social services. *See* services, social
social system, modern, 457–59
Society of Brahman. *See* Brahmo Samaj
Society of Jesus. *See* Dominican order
sociocentric, Oceania as, 393, 396–97
sociology, 13
Soga, Tiyo, 356–57
Soka Gakkai, 271, 520–32
Solomon, 692–93
Solomon Islands, 393–94
somatic mind, the, 609
son of God, 334
Sophia, wisdom as, 550
sorcerers, 348–49
soteriology. *See* salvation
Soto Buddhism, 271
sources of life, 403–6
South Africa, 357
South America, 426–53
Southeast Asia, 92–93, 102, 104–5, 107–8, 240–68
Spain
  in the Americas, 408–10, 414–15, 434–37, 441–45
  Judaism in, 116, 124–25, 147
  Roman Empire and, 299
spiritism. *See* animism
spirits, animistic, 380–81, 431
Spiritual Counterfeits Project (SCP), 575
spiritualism, 638–39, 683–84
spiritual world, 46, 47
square and compass, Masonic, 691
Sri Lanka, 104–5, 761–62
Stark, Rodney, 461
starvation, suicide by, 192

steam, 405–6
stewardship, Christian, 558–61, 747, 749–50
Stoicism, 307
Stolzman, William F., 417
structuralism, 15
St. Thomas Christians. *See* Thomas Christians
Studies in the Scriptures (Russell), 476
study circles, Baha'i, 718
Stump, Eleonore, 599
successors, Islamic. *See* caliphs, Islamic
suffering, Buddhism and, 83, 107–8
Sufi Islam, 152, 244
Suh Nam Dong, 280, 285
Suh Sang-Yun, 279
suicide, 192
sultans, Islamic, 759
summer festival, Japanese, 271
Sunni Islam, 152
supersessionism, 130–31, 135, 137–38, 341
survival, Jewish, 119–20, 139, 141
survivalism, 656–57
Sutra of Jesus the Messiah, 90
svarga, 66
Swami Brahmanandra Saraswati, 510
Swartz, Daniel, 747
Swedenborg, Emanuel, 630, 638
Swift, Wesley, 654, 660
synagogues, Orthodox, 121
syncretism, religious, 231–32, 436–37, 442, 448–49
Syrian Christianity. *See* Nestorian Christians
Syro-Malabar Christianity, 56, 61, 65

tabu, 375
Tahiti, 384
Taiping Rebellion, 224
Talmud, the, 116
Tang dynasty, 222
tanha, 83
tantric Buddhism. *See* Vajrayana Buddhism
Taoism. *See* Daoism
tattoos, Judaism and, 140
Taylor, Charles, 8
Taylor, Doris, 362
Taylor, J. Hudson, 225
Tekakwitha, Kateri, 411, 418
telos, Marxist, 666
Templars, 583–84
Temple, Jerusalem, 325
Temple of Set, 580, 582, 585–86, 588–91
temples, Baha'i, 717
temples, Reform Jewish, 121

tennoism, 762
tenure, land, 748–49
terrorism, 172, 770
Tertullian, 360–61
TFI. *See* Family International, The
Thailand
 Buddhism and, 102, 241–42, 246–47, 762
 Christianity and, 249–50, 251, 256
theistic Satanism, 588–91
thelemic magick, 535–36
theodicy, 107–8, 594
theological approach, 4, 16–26
theosophy, 630–31
Theravada Buddhism, 84–85, 99, 241, 245–46, 258
thetan, 609, 612, 617
Thich Nhat Hanh, 107, 772
Third Buddhist Council, 88
Third Force psychology, 621, 623, 626–27
Thirteen Articles of Faith, Jewish, 116, 118
Thirteen Articles of Faith, Mormon, 464
Thomas, Apostle, 194–95
Thomas, Norman, 672
Thomas Aquinas, 159
Thomas Christians, 56, 61, 65, 195–96
Thor, 297
Thracians, 298–99
Three Faiths Project, 528
Threefold Law, 537
Three Onenesses, Baha'i, 717
Three-Self movements, 226, 279, 290
three teachings, Chinese, 216–20
Tibet, 108–10, 220, 762
Tile, Nehemiah, 364
time track, the, 611, 612, 617
Tinker, George, 418–19
tithing. *See* giving, charitable
Tiw, 297
Tlacaélel, 427
TM. *See* Transcendental Meditation (TM)
tobacco, 405–6, 417
Toda, Josei, 520–21
Toledot Yeshu, 132
tolerance, conversion and, 35, 36–37
Tonga, 384
Tonkin, 249
Torah, the, 119, 131
totemism, 375
tourist industry, the, 397
Towers of Silence, 192
traditionalist religions. *See* indigenous religions
trances, ecstatic, 405

Transcendental Meditation (TM), 510–18
transformation, 35–37, 46, 47
transitional period, religious studies, 12
translation, indigenous religions and, 229–30
Transpersonal Psychology, 606, 620–28
Trebaruna, 299
tribal religions. *See* indigenous religions
Trinity, the
    doctrine of, 24, 31, 360
    Islam and, 166–67
    Judaism and, 118, 133
    new religious movements and, 464, 474, 508
Troeltsch, Ernst, 568–69
Troki, Isaac of, 133
Trompf, Garry, 386–87
true communism, 664, 665
True Parents, 684
Turkey, 316–17, 329–30
two kingdoms theory, 770
two-seed theory, 655–56
Ty, 297
Tyler, E. B., 375
tzaddik, 117

Uchimura Kanzo, 287–88
Uemura, Masahisa, 286
Uganda, 370
ulamas, Islamic, 759
ultra-Orthodox Judaism, 117
Umar, 152
Umbanda, 429
Uncle Tom, 500
underground churches, 236
Unification Church, 679, 681–89
United Nations, 778–79
United States, 93–94, 105–6, 171. *See also* Native Americans
unity, church, 263–64, 277–78, 398–99
universal church, the, 263
Universal Declaration of Human Rights, 778–79
Universal House of Justice, Baha'i, 715, 721–22
universalism, 13–14, 21, 22–23, 46
untouchables, 53, 189, 195, 211
Upadhyaya, Brahmabandhab, 625–26
Upanishads, the, 189
upaya, 100
Urban II, 303
Usuman, 152–53
Uthman, 152

Vaishnava, 52, 53
Vajrayana Buddhism, 84–85, 99, 220

Value Creation Society. *See* Soka Gakkai
Vanuatu, 380, 387
Vaswa Hindu Parishad (VHP), 761
Veda, the, 52–53, 67, 189
Vesey, Denmark, 649
VHP. *See* Vaswa Hindu Parishad (VHP)
Vietnam, 245, 246, 249, 252, 256–57
violence, religion and, 750–51, 764–72
vipassana meditation, 85, 99
Virgin of Guadalupe, 436–37, 444–45
Visaka Bucha, 246–47
Visigoths, 299
visualization meditation, 85, 99
Vivekananda, 60, 61, 630
Vladimir, 300
Voisin, Catherine de, 584
voodoo, 369

Walker, David, 500
war, 309–10, 750–51, 764–68, 770–71
washing, ceremonial, 155, 271
Washington Monument, 650
Watch Tower Bible and Tract Society of Pennsylvania. *See* Jehovah's Witnesses
Water Buffalo Theology (Koyama), 288
WCC. *See* World Council of Churches (WCC)
weddings, Jewish, 121
Weeks, Festival of, 325
Wells, Ida, 672
Wesley, John, 305
West, the. *See* Europe; North America
Wheatstone Bridge, 612
White, Lynn, 746, 753
White Lambskin Apron, Masonic, 691–92, 696
Wicca, 536–37, 544–46
wider hope perspective, 25
Wiebe, Donald, 599
Wilber, Ken, 621, 622
Wilbur, Ken, 621
wildlife, 751–52
Willard, Frances, 672
William of Rubruck, 223
William of Tripoli, 167
Willibrord, 310
Wilson, J. Stitt, 671
Winthrop, John, 643–44
witchcraft, 206–7, 348–49, 368. *See also* magic
Wobblies, 671
Woden, 297–98
women
    gender and, 736–45
    Hinduism and, 197–99

Islam and, 174–76, 315
Korean Christianity and, 280–81
Marxism and, 672
in Native American religion, 404, 786
world-affirming, 183–84, 206–7
World Council of Churches (WCC), 317–18, 469, 483
World Missionary Conference (Edinburgh, 1910), 12
world religions, characteristics of, 44–47
World Tree, the, 298
worship
  indigenous religions and, 184, 192, 452–53
  Jewish, 325
  new religious movements and, 467, 536, 611, 617–18, 684
  popular Hinduism and, 191
worth, sacrifice and, 429
wudu, 155

Xavier, Francis, 57, 61, 64, 195, 276
xeper, 588–89
Xhosa, the, 368

yahid, God as, 133
yahrzeit candle, 121
Yahweh, 323

Yasukuni Shrine, 762
Yavneh, Council of, 115–16
Yeshu, 132
Yiey Maw, 244
Yijing, 216–17
yin-yang, 220, 229, 280–81
Yi Seung-Hun, 278–79
yogic flying, 514
Yonggi Cho. *See* Cho Yonggi
Yoon Sung-Bum, 283
York Rite, Masonic, 691
Yoruba, 783
Young, Brigham, 466, 469
Young, Robert Alexander, 500
Young Hegelians, 665, 670
Yuan dynasty, 222–23

Zakat, 156
Zao Wang, 247
Zen Buddhism, 85, 99, 270–71
Zhuxi, 218
Ziegenbalg, Bartholomäus, 59, 61, 63–64
Zion Christian Church, 364
Zionism, 128–29, 135, 138–39, 660, 758–59
Zohar, the, 117
Zoroaster, 190–91
Zulu, the, 349–50

www.ingramcontent.com/pod-product-compliance
Lightning Source LLC
Chambersburg PA
CBHW032125010526
44111CB00033B/80